Health Care in America

Health Care in America

Can Our Ailing System Be Healed?

John P. Geyman, M.D.
Professor Emeritus of Family Medicine, University of Washington
School of Medicine, Seattle

BUTTERWORTH
HEINEMANN

Boston • Oxford • Aukland • Johannesburg • Melbourne • New Delhi

Every effort has been made to ensure that the drug dosage schedules within this text are accurate and conform to standards accepted at time of publication. However, as treatment recommendations vary in the light of continuing research and clinical experience, the reader is advised to verify drug dosage schedules herein with information found on product information sheets. This is especially true in cases of new or infrequently used drugs.

Recognizing the importance of preserving what has been written, Butterworth–Heinemann prints its books on acid-free paper whenever possible.

Library of Congress Cataloging-in-Publication Data
Geyman, John P., 1931–
    Health care in America : can our ailing system be healed? / John P. Geyman
      p. cm.
    Includes bibliographical references and index.
    ISBN 0-7506-7322-2 (pbk. : alk. paper)
    1. Medical care—United States. 2. Medical policy—United States. 3. Public health—United States. 4. Health care reform—United States. I. Title.

RA399.A3 G49 2001
362.1′0973—dc21

                                   2001035920

British Library Cataloguing-in-Publication Data
A catalogue record for this book is available from the British Library.

To practicing physicians and other health professionals in the clinical trenches of an ailing health care system. You are our best hope for reshaping medicine and health care in the public interest.

*   *   *

And to Gene,
my wife, partner, and best friend over these 45 years, without whose support this task could not have been conceived and completed.

Contents

Preface   ix
Acknowledgments   xiii

Part One   Major Trends Affecting Health Care

1   Cottage Industry to Mergers and Managed Care   3

2   Increased Technology and Complexity of Health Care Services   15

3   Incremental Medicalization of Health Care   29

4   Specialization and Subspecialization   43

5   Increased Public Expectations and Patients' Rights   61

6   An Aging Population and the Shifting Content of Health Care   73

7   Increasing Costs of Health Care   89

8   Decreasing Access to Health Care   101

9   Change of Locus of Control of Health Care   113

10   Conflicting Paradigms of Health Care   129

11   New Roles for Hospitals   145

12   Increased Impact of Litigation   161

Part Two   Where Are We Now?

13   Primary Care as a Battleground   187

14   Private versus Public Sectors and Public Health   205

15   Information Technology and Health Care   221

16 Attempts to Control the Costs of Health Care | 245

17 Attempts to Improve Access to Health Care | 265

18 The Quality of Health Care: Myths, Reality, and Approaches to Improvement | 281

19 Previous Attempts to Reform the System | 309

Part Three   Where Can We Go from Here?

20 Current Politics and Health Care Reform | 327

21 Rationing in a "Free Market" Society: Myths and Reality | 347

22 Organizational Options for a Failing Health Care "System" | 363

23 Lessons from Other Countries | 385

24 Principles and Some Basic Pathways for Health Care Reform | 407

Author Index | 425
Subject Index | 429

Preface

> It is perfectly true, as philosophers say, that life must be understood backward, but they forget the other proposition, that it must be lived forward.
>
> —Sören Kierkegaard

That widespread turmoil exists in the organization, financing, and delivery of health care in the United States as we enter the 21st Century is beyond any doubt. Health care issues have received increasing media coverage and taken center stage in the politics of our time. Health care in America now represents one seventh of the world's largest economy, up from one twenty-fifth just 40 years ago. There is growing awareness, however, that size does not connote strength. Many are increasingly frustrated and unhappy with U.S. health care, whether they are patients, providers, payers, or legislators. The present system is unsustainable in the long run because of its three main problems: escalating costs, limitations of access, and wide variations in quality. An intense national debate is taking place as to how to reform or revise our health care system in the public interest in a fair and sustainable way.

Health Care in America: Can Our Ailing System Be Healed? is intended to make some sense out of the current disarray in our health care system. While the word *system* is subject to many definitions, it generally implies some degree of order as an assemblage of parts into a unitary whole. Health care in America is closer to a nonsystem, or at best a patchwork assemblage of many subsystems that evolved over the years with no strong coherent structure.

Four major approaches have been advanced over the years as the most basic ways by which the health care system can be reformed: (1) incrementalism, the recent and current policy choice; (2) building further on the employer-based health insurance system, with public sector coverage of the unemployed; (3) expanding coverage options within a consumer-choice model without involvement of employers; and (4) developing a single-payer system as a vehicle for universal coverage. All four options retain a mix between the public and private sectors, but the roles and responsibilities of each sector would vary considerably from one approach to another.

My purpose in writing this book is to better understand the rapid and confusing changes that have already transformed health care into an entirely new landscape. Beyond that, my goal is to assess the evidence in favor of or against the likelihood that any of these four basic approaches could effectively remedy the health care system's chronic problems. Health care has been reshaped in recent years as a commodity in a private sector marketplace. The fragility of both the employer-based insurance system and the public sector safety net have been exposed by these changes. A theme throughout the book is to assess the degree to which each sector can contribute to lasting system reform.

My view at the outset was that our health care "system" is in serious trouble and not sustainable over the long term without fundamental structural changes. I came to this project with no preconceived idea on how to reform the system. Over the course of researching a wide range of material for this book, I have concluded that powerful stakeholders within today's flawed system will resist needed reforms if at all possible and that the single-payer option is the most likely alternative to effectively reform the system. However, I have endeavored to give voice throughout the book to leading proponents of other views to help the reader better assess the alternatives along the way.

As the national debate proceeds over how to reform the health care system, it has become clear to me that this is not simply a matter of fine-tuning. We need to reassess the overall "system" through a wide-angle lens to see just how sick it is. Too close a look through a high-powered lens easily can miss the larger picture.

Forty years after graduation from medical school at the University of California, San Francisco, my perspective is that of a physician in the broadest of primary care specialties, family practice, with 13 years in rural practice, 30 years in academic family medicine (including 14 years as a departmental chairman in an academic medical center with strengths in both tertiary and regionalized primary care), editor of national family practice journals over 28 years, and most recently as a member of a Hospital District Board of Commissioners for a local rural health care system on San Juan Island in Washington state. By nature a generalist, I have tried to avoid personal bias while bringing to bear the perspectives of many other disciplines to the task at hand.

Why another book on this subject? Recent years have seen a number of excellent books and other reports examining the increasing problems of our health care "system." Most are written by health care economists and policy analysts with a particular focus on organizational and financing aspects of health care. Others are written for the lay public without enough clinical relevance for clinicians. The clinician's perspective often is missing in these works, and clinicians may find their world described in terms they neither understand nor appreciate. My goal is to bridge the world of health economists, health analysts, and policy makers with that of clinicians in an intelligible way. This book differs from most others in this field by its breadth of coverage and its multidisciplinary synthesis, while retaining the direction and coordination of a single author.

This is not an encyclopedic work. A pragmatic approach to complex issues is taken in as objective a way as possible. Basic issues are addressed, evidence drawn from credible sources, and wherever possible, examples sought from the real world of everyday clinical practice. The three fundamental and interdependent parameters of health care—cost, access, and quality—are tracked throughout the book, since a change in one inevitably affects the others. For example, when the rising costs of health care make it unaffordable for many people, as they now are for tens of millions, access predictably declines, and there can be no quality of care for those with no access.

The intended audience for this book includes physicians (including those in training and medical students), other health care professionals, policy makers, legislators, and others involved in planning, delivery, or evaluation of health care services. This book also ought to be of interest to lay readers concerned about the current problems of health care and the need for reform of an imperfect health care system. I hope that the distillation and synthesis of these various aspects of the health care "system" will lead to broader understanding among clinicians and others in the trenches of everyday health care and enable their larger role in helping to shape an improved, more coherent health care system that is affordable and accessible to the entire population.

This book is organized in three parts, each subsequent part builds on the previous part, and chapters are intended to be read sequentially. In Part One, I have chosen 12 major trends that have shaped our existing health care "system." Some might have framed these issues differently, but I have no doubt that collectively they portray a reasonable profile of how health care has evolved to its present state.

Part Two examines seven facets of the health care "system," representing different views of the elephant. In each case, emphasis is focused on where we are now, together with a targeted review of what major policy initiatives have been tried and to what extent they have been successful.

Finally, Part Three focuses on where we might go from here in improving American health care in the context of our history, culture, economics, and politics. Evidence is reviewed for and against the effectiveness of any of the four basic alternatives to remedy the ills of the ailing health care system. Lessons from other industrialized Western countries are drawn on to the extent that they may be relevant to the American experience. Some principles and values then are proposed that could usefully underpin whatever direction reform takes through what is certain to be a challenging political process in an era of real limits.

The rate of change has become so rapid in American society that it is difficult to understand where we are without pausing to assess the extent of change. This book provides a snapshot of our changed and changing health care "system" that ideally sheds light on the urgency and potential directions of health care reform.

John P. Geyman, M.D.

Acknowledgments

This book has been made possible by the support and help of many. I am indebted to these colleagues who critically reviewed selected chapters and offered helpful suggestions: Drs. Alfred Berg, John Coombs, Eric Larsen, Thomas Norris, Scott Ramsey, William Robertson, Roger Rosenblatt, and Sean Sullivan at the University of Washington; Drs. Tom Bruce (professor emeritus and former dean, University of Arkansas), Paul Brucker (president, Thomas Jefferson University), Jack Colwill (University of Missouri), Paul Fischer (Center for Primary Care, Evans, Georgia), Larry Green (Robert Graham Center for Policy Studies in Family Practice and Primary Care, Washington, D.C.), Gary Hankins (University of Texas at Galveston), Ian McWhinney (Professor Emeritus, University of Western Ontario), Fitzhugh Mullan (Georgetown University), William C. Richardson (president and CEO, William Kellogg Foundation, Battle Creek, Michigan), James Rourke (The University of Western Ontario), John Saultz (Oregon Health Sciences University), Joseph Scherger (Founding Dean, Florida State University Medical School, Tallahassee), Stephen Schroeder (president, Robert Wood Johnson Foundation), Stephen Shortell (University of California, Berkeley), and Eric Wall (regional medical director, Lifewise, a Premera Health Plan, Inc.). Other constructive suggestions were made by Arthur Roeca (health care and medical malpractice attorney, Honolulu), Dr. Paul Young (former executive director of the American Board of Family Practice), and Claire Zimmerman (assistant editor of the *Journal of the American Board of Family Practice*).

Since my goal was to take an evidence-based approach to the issues and problems confronting our health care system, extensive resources were required. This task was greatly facilitated by the efforts of Sarah Safranek and her colleagues at the University of Washington Health Sciences Library, who helped me to become an efficient user of PUBMED and able to retrieve many additional materials from a wide range of sources. Judie Tucker of *Health Affairs* provided many back issues of that publication. Dr. Ida Hellander (executive director of Physicians for a National Health Program) contributed extensive resources developed over the years through the research efforts of PNHP and critiqued a number of chapters. Thanks also are due to the journals and publishers who generously granted permission to reprint or adapt material originally published by them, as cited throughout the book.

This book was written the old-fashioned way—alone in my study with pen, writing pad, and many stacks of reference materials. Not being facile with a word processor, the book would not have come to life without the diligent and meticulous efforts of Virginia Gessner, who prepared the entire manuscript.

Finally, I would especially like to thank Susan Pioli, Director of Medical Publishing at Butterworth–Heinemann, and her colleagues Jennifer Rhuda and Jodie Allen for their encouragement and help all along the way in bringing this book to fruition. And as has always been the case with any of my projects, it could not have been accomplished without the ongoing support of my wife, Gene, who graciously tolerated my immersion throughout the gestation of this book.

PART ONE

MAJOR TRENDS
AFFECTING HEALTH CARE

1
Cottage Industry to Mergers and Managed Care

In 1900, no one in his or her wildest imagination could have envisioned how medical care would be transformed in America over the next 100 years. This chapter charts some highlights of this journey with seven milestones along the way.

DAWN OF THE 20TH CENTURY

Medical care in America at best was rudimentary in 1900, and whatever system there was lacked standards of quality. Physicians in the United States were being trained by the preceptorship system, as was the case in Europe at the time. There were 151 medical schools in the United States in 1900.[1] Many of these were diploma mills conducted by five or six local physicians with the support of student fees. Most schools lacked access to hospitals and many medical students graduated with no hospital training. Teaching standards and licensing laws were lax.[2]

Medical students usually spent two to three years with their preceptor, but most preceptors were too busy to do much teaching. Students were expected to read what few texts were available, and the typical medical school presented two four-month terms of lectures over a two-year period. Students were expected to see patients once a month and attend an autopsy once a year. They then were required to pass a qualifying examination, but medical societies were ineffectual in assuring any quality control of practice and many states didn't even have licensing laws in place.[3-5] There were not yet any specialty boards, and physicians necessarily were generalists.

Most physicians were in solo office practice at the turn of the century. Infectious diseases were rampant. There were no vaccines or antibiotics yet available. Surgical skills were important, even in office practice, and anesthesia was basic—open-drop ether when general anesthesia was required. Blood transfusions were not yet available. Six of nine women died of pregnancy-

3

related complications,[6] and average longevity at birth was 48 years for males and 51 years for females.[7]

The scientific revolution brought major changes that led to reorganization of U.S. medical schools, with the shift of many to universities. Two institutions that led the way in this transition were Harvard and Johns Hopkins. A legendary figure towering over the medical landscape of the time was Sir William Osler, who had been appointed in 1889 as professor of Medicine and physician-in-chief of the new Johns Hopkins Hospital. He set three priorities in organizing the Department of Medicine there: patient welfare, teaching of medical students and residents, and contributing to the advancement of internal medicine.[8] He was tireless and productive in all three areas as a classic generalist clinician-teacher-scholar, to the point that the Oslerian tradition survives to this day as a venerable tradition (but often not followed!). He was a leader willing to question tradition in medical practice and eliminate useless procedures.[9] For example, he championed this view about excessive prescribing of drugs:

> Upon us whose work lay in the last quarter of the nineteenth century fell the great struggle with that many-headed monster Polypharmacy—not the true polypharmacy which is the skillful combination of remedies, but the giving of many—the practice of at once discharging a heavily-loaded prescription at every malady, or at every symptom of it.[10]

The American Medical Association (AMA) formed its Council on Medical Education in 1904 and established the first standards for medical education. A four-year course of medical studies was to be required, followed by a one-year internship. The AMA then approached the Carnegie Foundation to conduct a rigorous evaluation of U.S. medical schools. Dr. Abraham Flexner had completed a critical expose of U.S. higher education and was selected for this task.[11]

THE FLEXNER REPORT

After two years of work on this project, the Flexner Report was published in 1910, with the following main conclusions:[12,13]

1. There had been a tremendous overproduction of poorly trained physicians.
2. The proliferation of proprietary medical schools was responsible for this overproduction.
3. Medical school expenses had, and would continue to, increase dramatically due to the need for laboratories.
4. Less expensive medical schools were not justified solely because they allowed access to medical education for the poor.
5. Hospitals under educational control were necessary for medical schools to perform their mission.

As a result of the Flexner Report, medical education became standardized, with a three or four year curriculum for medical students that contained more systematic clinical teaching and increased hospital training. Flexner believed that all medical schools should be tied more closely to the academic standards of universities. His report carried great weight, many medical schools were forced to close; only 80 such schools were still open by 1927.[11]

Hospitals grew in size after World War I, and soon became the central base of the health care system with active involvement in medical education. Solo practice still was the dominant form of medical practice, but the idea of group practice was slowly starting to take root in a limited way.

The post-Flexner years in the United States witnessed broad advancements in health care throughout the country. Many well-trained physicians entered practice (three fourths as general practitioners in 1930), bringing modern medicine, pediatrics, obstetrics, anesthesia, and surgery to people in both urban and rural settings.

THE GREAT DEPRESSION AND THE RISE OF INSURANCE PLANS

The Great Depression, starting in 1929 but extending through the 1930s, had a severe impact on medical care throughout the country. People lacked the means to pay for care or insurance, so revenue to hospitals and professionals dropped sharply. Two major changes were wrought during the stark times of the 1930s—the beginning of direct federal involvement in health care and the emergence of a nonprofit health insurance industry.

As an integral part of President Franklin D. Roosevelt's New Deal, the Social Security Act was passed in 1935. Federal funds were thereby made available to local health departments for maternal and child health services.[13]

Lest we think that the idea of universal health coverage and prepayment did not arise until the latter part of the 20th century, the seeds were sown (in rocky ground) in 1932 by the Committee on the Costs of Medical Care (CCMC). Three recommendations made by that group are still relevant, almost 70 years later:[14]

1. Medical service should be furnished largely by organized groups.
2. Basic public health services should be extended so they will be available to the entire population according to its needs.
3. The costs of medical care should be placed on a group payment basis through the use of insurance or taxation or both.[14]

Blue Cross and Blue Shield established the first private health insurance plans on a nonprofit basis, providing coverage at discounted rates for hospitals and physicians, whereby more people could afford care and hospital beds could be kept open. Insured patients could then have access to medical care with minimal out-of-pocket payments.[15]

The practices of physicians were strikingly different in the 1930s compared to today, with an emphasis on the treatment of infectious diseases and surgical procedures. As an individual example of the times, Table 1-1 presents the most common diagnoses in a rural general practice in Minnesota in 1935.

Table 1-1 Most Common Diagnoses in a Rural Minnesota Practice between June 1934 and September 1935

Diagnosis or Procedure	No. (%)
Abscess, incision and drainage, follow-up	26 (10.7)
Immunization, diphtheria	24 (9.8)
Mastoiditis, drainage, follow-up	17 (7.0)
Epididymitis, scrotal tap	14 (5.7)
Otitis media, myringotomy, follow-up	14 (5.7)
Tonsillectomy and adenoidectomy	14 (5.7)
Arthritis, follow-up	11 (4.5)
Fracture, major bone, follow-up	7 (2.9)
Pneumonia, follow-up	6 (2.5)
Pertussis, follow-up	5 (2.1)
Uterine prolapse, pessary placement, follow-up	5 (2.1)
Abortion, threatened, follow-up	4 (1.6)
Office counseling, unspecified	4 (1.6)
Measles, hemorrhagic, with pneumonia, follow-up	4 (1.6)
History and physical examination, infant	4 (1.6)
Renal colic, follow-up	4 (1.6)

Source: Reprinted with permission from Haddy RI, Hill JM, Costarella BR, Gordon RE, Adegbile GS, et al. A comparison of rural practice in the 1930s and today. *J Fam Pract.* 1993;36:65–69.

WORLD WAR II

The years during and after World War II saw a remarkable growth in scientific and medical knowledge, as well as acceleration of the trends toward specialization in the medical profession and centralization in the hospital industry. The university medical centers and large teaching hospitals were at the hub of these trends. By 1950, 19 specialty boards fractionated the medical procession into specialties with increasingly narrow concerns. Maldistribution of health professionals represented a growing problem, especially in rural America, and regionalization of hospital facilities became the norm. Physician visits shifted from the home to office or institutional settings, together with continued growth in group practice.[16] Meanwhile, a major shift was taking place in nursing practice from private duty to hospital nursing.[13]

General practice probably reached its zenith in the 1930s and early 1940s, then entered a long decline as specialization took over. The nation faced a growing shortage of primary care physicians, and access to health care became a national concern. Four reports were issued in a span of 100 days in 1966, each calling for a concerted effort to train generalist physicians to meet this need.[17–20]

Another major development in the years following World War II was the emergence of voluntary health insurance, especially for the employed and their dependents.[21] The growth of employer-based health insurance was fueled in part by its tax exempt status to employers. It was more available in larger, urban-located companies, however, leading to urban-rural inequities in health insurance coverage.[22]

THE GREAT SOCIETY: PASSAGE OF
MEDICARE AND MEDICAID

In response to widespread concerns over access to health care, the Medicare and Medicaid laws were passed in 1965 as part of President Lyndon Johnson's Great Society program. Medicare and Medicaid provided some access to care, although not comprehensive, for the disadvantaged and elderly. The effect of cost reimbursement and fee schedules for physicians helped to reverse shortages of hospital beds and physicians, as well as deficits in medical education and research.[15]

In response to a perceived shortage of physicians in the 1950s and 1960s, enrollment in U.S. allopathic and naturopathic schools rapidly expanded. Together with the influx of foreign medical graduates, the total number of physicians was felt to be in increasing oversupply by the 1980s. However, the real problems of physician supply involved geographic and specialty maldistribution.

Organized medicine did not stand tall as a constructive change agent during the 1950s and 1960s as the population's access to health care eroded. The AMA opposed expansion of the physician supply as well as the passage of Medicare and Medicaid. At that time the AMA was thought by many to be the most powerful lobby in the capitol.[23,24]

There were both positive and negative effects to the passage of Medicare and Medicaid. On the plus side, of course, many millions of elderly and disadvantaged Americans gained access to health care. On the negative side, however, a long period of health care inflation was ushered in, which shifted the nation's overriding health priority from access in the 1960s to cost containment in the 1980s. The extent of error in budgetary projections is interesting. Federal actuaries projected a $10 billion outlay for Medicare in 1990, only about 10 percent of what it turned out to be.[25]

The 1970s and 1980s were halcyon days for providers of health care. Physicians and hospitals had most of their services paid for by open-ended cost reimbursement and professional fee schedules. The health care marketplace was relatively unrestrained and the ranks of people without access to care again grew. The poor and working near-poor fared no better in many cases, since there were many inequities between states in eligibility for Medicaid. By the mid-1980s, effective cost containment measures were required.

INTEGRATION, CONSOLIDATION, MANAGED CARE,
AND COMPETITION

By the 1980s, it was clear that the country had a surplus of physicians, especially in the non-primary care specialties, as well as hospital beds. Health care costs were out of control and the major payers—the federal government and larger employers—were forced to take action. Both horizontal and vertical integration started to link health care systems. Physicians became more involved in group activity, including formation of independent practice associations (IPAs). Increasing aggregation also took place among carriers and health main-

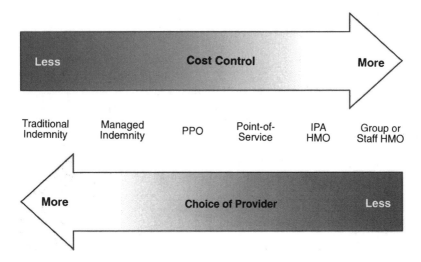

Figure 1-1   Spectrum of health care plans. (Reprinted with permission from Dowling WL. The future of managed care. Presented at 28th Annual Advances in Family Practice and Primary Care course. Seattle, WA: University of Washington, September 14, 2000.)

tenance organizations (HMOs).[15] Even the indemnity insurance carriers recognized the need to control costs by dealing more directly with providers than exchanging money with subscribers. Blue Cross and Blue Shield announced in the early 1990s that 90 percent of benefits would be provided through managed care contracts by the year 2000.[15]

Figure 1-1 illustrates the wide spectrum between traditional indemnity insurance (e.g., Blue Cross, Blue Shield) and group or staff HMOs in terms of rigor of cost controls and degree of choice of provider.

Meanwhile, similar trends were occurring throughout the health care industry. Hospitals were forming physician-hospital organizations (PHOs) and buying primary care practices. Larger employers took favor with managed care and began to offer managed care options to their employees. Pharmaceutical manufacturers began to develop systems for more efficient drug distribution. Increasing consolidation was underway among hospitals, physicians, other health professionals, purchasers, and suppliers.

The term *managed care* has come to mean everything and nothing in common usage. An accurate current description, as used by William Dowling, professor and chairman of the Department of Health Services at the University of Washington, is as follows:[26]

Organizational involvement in the delivery and/or financing of care aimed at influencing the provision of services.

No longer synonymous with HMO.

Encompasses a broad spectrum of organizations that vary in mission, ownership. Public health perspective, financial incentives, clinical interest or competence, etc.

Table 1-2   Typical Features of Managed Reimbursement

Philosophy	Follow the "80/20" rule
	• Hospitals and specialists account for 80% of total health care costs
	• 80% of costs are generated by only 20% of patients
	• The 20% paid for primary care "gatekeepers" can control the other 80%
Method of payment	Capitation or prospective payment
Impact on physicians	Increasing discounts
	Managed care intrusions, more paperwork and telephone calls
	Increasing workload
	More denial of services
	Saying "no" to patients
	Less choice and autonomy
	Unrelenting regulatory pressure

Source: Adapted from materials developed by Integrated Health Systems, Inc., Arthur Anderson & Company, SC, 1993.

Assumed by the media to mean for-profit, micromanaging company with no concern for quality.

The essential elements of a typical managed care program are listed in Table 1-2. (Actually "managed care" often is more managed *reimbursement* than care.) It is obvious that the many effects on the physician have caused frustration on the part of physicians and patients alike.

The impact on medical practice of these changes was pronounced. As president of the Kaiser Family Foundation and chairman of the Council on Graduate Medical Education (COGME), Alvin Tarlov observed:[27]

The intersection in the 1980s and 1990s of a plentiful supply of physicians, the introduction of underwriting systems based on prepayment and shared risk, and the development of large corporations for health care is bringing about a fundamental restructuring of the health services system and a transformation of the practice of medicine. Actions of this order that restructure a system, taken for the greater good, always have some unintended, unanticipated, and undesirable effects. But the actions are forceful and rarely reversed, at least in the near term. We should understand the roots of these changes, be outwardly directed, and assist society in achieving its goals within the context of the social purposes, for which the health care system exists.

By the late 1990s, employer-based coverage had made a major shift to one or another form of managed care. Figure 1-2 shows the nearly complete shift from conventional indemnity plans to some type of managed care or managed competition from 1988 to 2000.

Managed care has passed (and is passing) through several recognizable stages in its evolution. Jeff Goldsmith, president of Health Futures, Inc., conceptualized these stages as shown in Table 1-3.[28] Of particular interest is the change

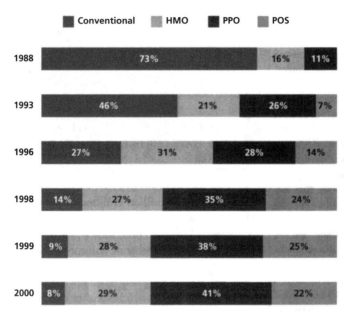

Figure 1-2   Health plan enrollment for covered workers, by plan type, 1988–2000. (Reprinted from *Employer Health Benefits: 2000 Annual Survey*, Kaiser Family Foundation and Health Research and Educational Trust [9/7/00]. Text of this report is available on the Internet. Website: www.kff.org/content/2000/20000907a.)

Table 1-3   Evolution of Managed Care

	Stage I	*Stage II*	*Stage III*
Objective function	Price	Value/consumer satisfaction	Health status improvement
Cost targets	Inpatient days	Resource intensity	Health risks
Locus of control	External	Peer driven	"Contract" with family
Focal point	Inpatient hospital	Physician network	Home/neighborhood

Source: Reprinted with permission from Goldsmith J. Risk and responsibility. The evolution of health care payment. In: Institute of Medicine. *2020 Vision: Health in the 21st Century: Institute of Medicine 25th Anniversary Symposium, Institute of Medicine.* Washington, DC: National Academy Press, 1996:56.

of focal point from hospital and inpatient care in Stage I, to physician network in Stage II, and to the home or neighborhood in Stage III. A case can be made that the Oregon Health Plan (to be discussed further in Chapters 16 and 21) represents Stage IV, with its focus on the covered population.

Some form of managed care had virtually replaced the previous cost-based reimbursement and fee-for-service medicine by the 1990s, both for people covered by employer-based insurance as well as those on federally funded pro-

Table 1-4 Transition from Hospital to Health Care Systems

Hospital	Health Care System
Acute patient care →	Continuum of care
Treating illness →	Maintaining/promoting wellness
Caring for individual patients →	Accountable for the health status of defined populations
Commodity product →	Value added services—emphasis on primary care, health promotion, ongoing health management of chronic illness
Market share of admissions →	Covered lives
Fill beds →	Care provided at appropriate level
Manage an organization →	Manage a network of services
Manage a department →	Manage a market
Coordinate services →	Actively manage and improve quality

Source: Reprinted from Shortell SM, Gillies RR, Devers KJ. Reinventing the American hospital. *Milbank Q.* 1995;73(2):131–160.

grams. Even for the Medicaid population, 40 percent were enrolled in managed care in 1996.[28] The landscape was changed, with intense competition among HMOs, PPOs, and point-of-service (POS) programs. (POS programs permit enrollees to choose, at the point of service, whether to see providers within the plan or outside the plan's panel or network.) What appeared to be intractable health care inflation was brought under control, as was the growth rate of health insurance premiums. Purchasers now were requiring documentation of quality of services as measured by performance information.[29] Table 1-4 represents the overall change in priorities that evolved in the health care system by the 1990s.

Although managed care can be credited with significant success in cost containment so far, a major backlash had developed by the mid-1990s. HMOs and insurance carriers were being singled out as the culprit, based on such inflammatory issues as "gag rules" for HMO physicians, denial of services, and "drive-through deliveries."[29] Since the outcry over short hospital stays for obstetric deliveries, 46 states and the District of Columbia have enacted various kinds of consumer-protection measures, including prohibitions against "gag clauses" for physicians, holding health plans liable for malpractice as a result of their clinical decisions, and mandates for independent appeals processes.[30] One study of 766 physicians practicing in the largest urban counties in California in 1996 revealed many of these physicians felt that quality of care was being compromised by pressure from managed care organizations (Figure 1-3).[31]

HMOs have been placed on the defensive by gathering political forces. Legislation at the federal level for a Patient's Bill of Rights is receiving bipartisan support as it works its way through Congress. The main issue of controversy concerns the right to sue HMOs. Such legislation, aimed at correcting abuses of the HMOs and empowering recipients of their services, is being supported by broad segments of the society, including many consumer groups, the legal community, and organized medicine. In reaction to this backlash, some

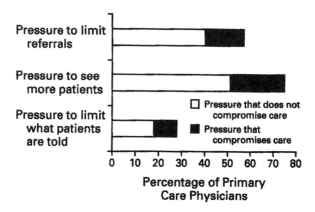

Figure 1-3 Percentage of physicians who reported pressure in their practices, according to type of pressure. Results have been weighted in such a way as to represent the total population of primary care physicians in the areas studied. (Reprinted with permission from Grumbach K, Osmond D, Vranizan K, Jaffe D, Bindman AB. Primary care physicians' experience of financial incentives in managed-care systems. *N Engl J Med.* 1998;339:1516–1521.)

HMOs have made some policy changes, such as the recent decision by United Healthcare to forego preauthorization review. Even that change came under immediate suspicion, however, as many still called for federal legislation to assure accountability by HMOs for responsible provision of access and quality of care.[32]

END OF THE CENTURY

The environment of health care in the United States at the end of the 20th century was at the least confused, if not chaotic. Some form of managed care covered three quarters of the population. Sixty-five million Americans were enrolled in HMOs,[33] and almost 80 percent of physicians had at least one managed care contract.[28] About half of primary care physicians and 20 percent of specialists received part of their reimbursement through capitation,[28] while about 45 percent of primary care physicians and 40 percent of specialists were employees of health care organizations.[34] HMOs had undergone consolidation through many mergers, with the five largest national HMOs controlling a 50 percent market share by 1997 (the largest single HMO resulted from the merger of Aetna and Prudential Healthcare units to cover over 22 million enrollees).[35] As a result of these changes, health care had been transformed into a commodity. In reaction to the negative impact of marketplace ethics on the distribution of health care services, Edmund Pellegrino had this to say from his base at the Center for Clinical Bioethics at Georgetown University.[36]

> the role of the government is both to protect the personal liberty and attend to those common goods that liberty destroys when it becomes license. How

this balance is to be achieved is a constant struggle of democratic societies and institutions. What is crucial in health care is that any policy must take cognizance of the common social good, the shared moral claim on medical knowledge, and the special nature of health care as a human activity.

Size or market share held no protection for the managed care industry, now under fire. Partly in reaction to federal cutbacks of $115 billion through the Balanced Budget Act of 1997 (BBA97), an estimated 400,000 beneficiaries of Medicare HMOs were involuntarily disenrolled and forced to choose another managed care or fee-for-service plan. These beneficiaries represented 7 percent of the 6 million Medicare HMO enrollees. Public confidence in HMOs was not helped by the fact that most of these disenrollments took place in for-profit HMOs.[37] Patient satisfaction was dropping in many managed care plans. One large national study, for example, revealed satisfaction with HMO quality of care and medical outcomes little over 50 percent in 1996.[38] Meanwhile, physicians and other providers were showing increasing frustration and disenchantment with the bureaucratic "hassle factor" of daily practice. In California's wild medical marketplace, most physicians experienced sharp income drops, many opted out of managed care programs, and an estimated 2,000 physicians left the state.[39]

CONCLUDING COMMENTS

Looking back, it is interesting to note how quickly the U.S. health care marketplace has transformed itself, and not for the better. As the rate of change continues rapidly, the question remains, what next? That question becomes the focus for the rest of this book. First, we need to consider other major trends influencing the health care system, then what is being done to correct the major problems, and finally what organizational options are available that bear on future scenarios.

REFERENCES

1. *Medical Schools of the United States 1906.* Chicago: AMA Council on Medical Education, 1906:46.
2. Kaufman M. American medical education. In: Numbers RL (ed). *The Education of American Physicians: Historical Essays.* Berkeley: University of California Press, January 1980:7–28.
3. King LS. Medical education: The AMA surveys the problems. *JAMA.* 1982;248:3017–3021.
4. King LS. Medical education: The decade of massive change. *JAMA.* 1984;251:219–224.
5. Starr P. *The Social Transformation of American Medicine.* New York: Basic Books, 1982.
6. Healthier mothers and babies. *Morb Mortal Wkly Rep.* 1999;48:849–858.
7. United States Bureau of the Census. *Historical Statistics of the United States, Colonial Times to 1970. Part 1.* Washington, DC: U.S. Dept. of Commerce, Bureau of the Census, Government Printing Office, 1975:56.
8. Harvey AM. William Osler and medicine in America: With special reference to the Baltimore period. *Md State Med J.* 1976;25:34–42.
9. Geyman JP. The Oslerian tradition and changing medical education: A reappraisal. *West J Med.* 1983;138(6):884–888.

10. Osler W. The treatment of disease. In: McGovern JP, Roland CG (eds). *William Osler: The Continuing Education*. Springfield, Ill: Charles C Thomas, 1969:240–241.
11. King LS. The Flexner report of 1910. *JAMA*. 1984;251:1079–1086.
12. Flexner A. Medical education in the United States and Canada; a report to the Carnegie Foundation for the Advancement of Teaching. New York, 1910.
13. Rosenblatt RA, Moscovice IS. *Rural Health Care*. New York: John Wiley, 1982:33.
14. Falk IS. Some lessons from the fifty years since the COMC Final Report, 1932. *J Public Health Policy*. 1983;4(2):139.
15. McNerney W. C Rufus Rorem award lecture. Big question for the Blues: Where to go from here? *Inquiry*. 1996 (Summer);33:110–117.
16. Rosenberg C. The therapeutic revolution: Medicine, meaning, and social change in nineteenth century America. *Perspect Biol Med*. 1977;20:485–506.
17. National Commission on Community Health Services. *Health Is a Community Affair; Report*. Bethesda, MD: National Commission on Community Health Services, 1966.
18. *The Graduate Education of Physicians: The Report of the Citizens Commission of Graduate Medical Education*. Chicago: American Medical Association, 1966:40.
19. American Medical Association, Ad Hoc Committee on Education for Family Practice. *Meeting the Challenge of Family Practice; Report*. Chicago: American Medical Association, 1966:1.
20. Witten CL, Johnson AN, Michaelson J, Lotterhos W. The core content of family medicine. A report of the Committee on Requirements for Certification. *GP*. 1966;34(5):225–246.
21. Somers AR, Somers HM. *Health and Health Care: Policies in Perspective*. Germantown, MD: Aspen Systems Corp., 1977.
22. Roemer MI. *Rural Health Care*. St. Louis: Mosby, 1976.
23. Radovsky SS. U.S. medical practice before Medicare and now—differences and consequences. *N Engl J Med*. 1990;332:263–267.
24. Campion FD. *The AMA and U.S. Health Policy since 1940*. Chicago: Chicago Review Press, 1984.
25. Ginsberg E. Ten encounters with the U.S. health sector, 1930–1999. *JAMA*. 1999;282:1665–1668.
26. Dowling WL. The future of managed care. Presented at 28th Annual Advances in Family Practice and Primary Care course. Seattle: University of Washington, September 14, 2000.
27. Tarlov AR. Shattuck lecture—The increasing supply of physicians, the changing structure of the health-services system, and the future practice of medicine. *N Engl J Med*. 1983;308:1235–1244.
28. Jensen GA, Morrisey MA, Gaffney S, Liston DK. The new dominance of managed care: Insurance trends in the 1990s. *Health Aff (Millwood)*. 1997;16(1):125–136.
29. Bailit MH. Ominous signs and portents: A purchaser's view of health care market trends. *Health Aff (Millwood)*. 1997;16(6):85–88.
30. Kuttner R. Must good HMOs go bad? Second of two parts. The search for checks and balances. *N Engl J Med*. 1998;338:1635–1639.
31. Grumbach K, Osmond D, Vranizan K, Jaffe D, Bindman AB. Primary care physicians' experience of financial incentives in managed-care systems. *N Engl J Med*. 1998;339:1516–1521.
32. Rose JR. Utilization review: Skeptical reaction to United Healthcare's "we trust doctors" gambit. *Medical Economics*. January 24, 2000:30.
33. Hillman AL. Financial incentives for physicians in HMOs. Is there a conflict of interest? *N Engl J Med*. 1987;317:1743–1748.
34. Simon C, Emmons DW. Physician earnings at risk: An examination of capitated contracts. *Health Aff (Millwood)*. 1997;16(3):120–126.
35. Feldman RD, Wholey DR, Christianson JB. HMO consolidations: How national mergers affect local markets. *Health Aff (Millwood)*. 1999;18(4):96–104.
36. Pellegrino ED. The commodification of medical and health care: The moral consequences of a paradigm shift from a professional to a market ethic. *J Med Philos*. 1999;24(3):243–266.
37. Laschober MA, Neuman P, Kitchman MS, Meyer L, Langwell KM. Medicare HMO withdrawals: what happens to beneficiaries? *Health Aff (Millwood)*. 1999;18(6):150–142.
38. Jensen J. HMO satisfaction slipping: Consumers. *Mod Healthc*. 1996;26(41):86, 88.
39. The California nightmare: Is this where managed care is taking us? *Med Economics*. January 24, 2000;48–64.

2
Increased Technology and Complexity of Health Care Services

The last 80 years, and particularly the last 45 years since the end of World War II, completely transformed health care in the United States as a result of accelerating technological innovation and change. Almost all of today's approaches and techniques of diagnosis and treatment of disease were unknown in 1950.[1] Among prescription drugs, 75 percent of the 200 top-selling drugs in 1972 were no longer in that group in 1987, and 10 percent of the 200 top-selling drugs each year are new.[2] New, noninvasive diagnostic procedures have burgeoned since 1975, including computed tomography (CT) scanning, magnetic resonance imaging (MRI), and ultrasound. Minimally invasive techniques also have flourished, including arthroscopy, laparoscopic abdominal surgery, and more recently, minimally invasive cardiac surgery. Table 2-1 presents a timeline for some of the noteworthy technological advances since 1920.

The speed with which new procedures or techniques have been assimilated in this country's health care system often is breathtaking. One of many examples is the increase in liver transplants from 26 in 1981 to 1,182 only 6 years later.[1] By 1996, about 60,000 heart valve replacements were performed each year, as well as 150,000 knee prostheses.[3]

Despite the remarkable progress, these advances have raised at least as many problems as they solved. We are now deluged with technology-related issues, including economic, legal, ethical, and social questions as to how best to incorporate the best of it into changing health care while avoiding its negative impacts. This chapter presents a brief overview of these technological advances, how they are driven, their benefits and harms, and what steps are being taken to manage technological change.

MEDICAL TECHNOLOGY DEFINED

The term *medical technology* covers a broader spectrum than one might consider on first thought. The New Technology Committee of Kaiser Permanente,

Table 2-1   Chronology of Some Technological Advances in Medical Care

1920
First use of x-rays in diagnosis
  1930
  Discovery of electron microscopes
  Sulfa drugs developed
  Start of blood bank
  Early use of insulin for diabetes mellitus
    1940
    Penicillin a breakthrough for many infectious diseases
    Modern anesthesia emerged with muscle relaxants
    Genetics linked to biochemistry
    DNA molecule described
    Nitrogen mustard—the first chemotherapy agent for cancer (lymphoma)
      1950
      Start of fiberoptic endoscopy
      First hearing aids with transistors
      Early use of computers
      First use of tricyclic antidepressants
      Advances in prosthetic limbs
      Increased use of radiation therapy for cancer
      Increasing use of cortisone and derivatives
      Increasing recognition of genetic basis of disease
      First randomized clinical trials
        1960
        Kidney transplants in growing use
        Immunology established as active clinical field
        First use of ultrasound
        First laser surgery
        Biological psychiatry and emergence of psychoactive drugs
        Start of coronary bypass surgery
        First hip replacements
        First cardiac pacemaker
        Oral contraceptives in common use
        Renal dialysis for chronic renal failure
          1970
          First CT scanner
          First use of angioplasty for coronary artery disease
          Emergence of genetic engineering
            1980
            MRIs become widely used
            Smallpox eradicated
            Growing use of recombinant vaccines and drugs
            Liver transplantation
               1990
              Peptic ulcer tied to *Helicobacter pylori*
              Progress with antiretroviral drugs
              Introduction of laser refractive eye surgery
              Other organ transplantation
              Genotypes identified for some breast and colon cancer
                2000
                FDA approval of robotic device for computer assisted surgery

for example, divides new procedures and technology into the following four categories:[4]

1. New procedures that involve new and expensive equipment (e.g., lithotripsy).
2. New procedures that do not involve new equipment or drugs (e.g., in vitro fertilization).
3. New drugs (e.g., genetically engineered drugs, very expensive drugs, such as Ceredase).
4. New technologies developed for life-threatening diseases (e.g., liver or heart transplantation).

Lewis Thomas, one of the country's best known and discerning analysts of medical progress, described three levels of technologies:[5]

1. *Nontechnology*—noncurative care for patients with advanced diseases whose natural history cannot be changed (e.g., intractable cancer, advanced cirrhosis).
2. *Halfway technology*—also care that is noncurative but may delay death (e.g., liver or heart transplants).
3. *High technology*—curative treatment or effective prevention techniques (e.g., polio vaccination).

Unfortunately, most of our technological advances are of the halfway type. Since these tend to be overused with no curative results, they are the most expensive and present the most challenging task for society to manage their adoption in a cost-effective way.

DRIVERS OF TECHNOLOGIC CHANGE

Scientific advances following World War II were pushed ahead in the medical technology arena by a large federal investment in biomedical research. New technologies found a fertile environment for rapid adoption and dissemination. During the 1960s to 1980s, most of the population was covered by private insurance, Medicare, or Medicaid. Physicians were flowing in large numbers into more narrow specialties, many of which were based largely on application of the new technologies. Hospitals had grown to excess capacity and, in the preprospective payment era, thrived on a cost-based reimbursement system. In a fee-for-service system, an increasing volume of diagnostic and therapeutic procedures brought financial rewards to hospitals, physicians, suppliers, manufacturers, and investors. New technologies first found their way into larger urban hospitals, but soon many smaller hospitals in outlying and rural areas also acquired their CT scanners and many of the newer technologies.

Aggressive marketing practices by manufacturers of pharmaceuticals and medical devices have played an enormous role in the rapid dissemination of new medical technologies into U.S. health care. For example, direct-to-consumer (DTC) drug advertising has become big business and is expected to quadruple to a total annual expenditure as high as $7.5 billion by 2005.[6] Public acceptance and demand for new technology are fueled by the glamour of science, which is further hyped by the media, in many instances even before a potential future advance reaches the world of clinical practice. Increasing utilization of new technology is driven by other factors, too, including provider-induced demand and the buffering effect of insurance coverage protecting patients from direct payment of such costs.

Until the mid-1980s, there was little cost consciousness within the health care system. What Victor Fuchs, noted health economist at Stanford University, called the "technological imperative" thrived—"the desire of the physician to do everything he has been trained to do, regardless of the benefit-cost ratio."[7] The impact of the technological imperative can be enormous, particularly with a growing supply of procedure-oriented specialists imprinted during their training with the importance of their procedures as the latest in medical practice. Walter McNerney, for many years a leader of Blue Cross/Blue Shield, was one of the first to document that the more hospital beds or surgeons in a community, the higher is the rate of hospital admissions and surgical procedures.[8] Further, as the saying goes, "if all you have is a hammer, all your problems will be nails."

Throughout this surge of technology in medicine, there were minimal barriers to quick adoption of new procedures, devices, drugs, and techniques. Even in the cost-containment years since the mid 1980s, with prospective reimbursement to hospitals by diagnosis-related groups (DRGs) and a shift to managed care and competition, there is still no effective requirement or process at the national level to prove cost-effective outcomes before a new technologic advance is put into broad use. The debate over high-dose chemotherapy–autologous bone marrow transplantation (HDC-ABMT) provides an interesting case in point. At a cost of at least $200,000 for each individual procedure, its use has been established for acute leukemia, Hodgkin's disease, non-Hodgkin's lymphoma, and stage III and IV neuroblastoma. It also is being used, or proposed, for many other cancers, at earlier stages in disease.[9] Although probably halfway technology, without demonstrated positive long-term outcomes, the potential demand for this expensive procedure is great. David Eddy, a well-known expert in clinical decision making and proponent of cost effective health care, reported an in-depth analysis of all published studies up to 1992 of the benefits and harms of HDC-ABMT compared with conventional chemotherapy for metastatic breast cancer. He concluded that median disease-free survival, median overall survival, and actual survival is not superior with HDC-ABMT versus conventional chemotherapy.[10] Based on his experience as vice president of Clinical Evaluation and Research for Aetna Health Plans, William McGivney observes:[9]

One would expect that with such a large attendant cost, the cancer care community would proceed cautiously with the use of this technology for investigational indications on a limited basis until scientific data convincingly demonstrated the safety and effectiveness of HDC-ABMT for these indications. Actually, just the opposite seems to be occurring; that is, the use of HDC-ABMT seems to be growing almost exponentially, far outpacing the ability of clinical research to generate data to support such use.

MEDICAL TECHNOLOGY AS A DOUBLE-EDGED SWORD

The cumulative growth of health care services clearly has been driven by technological advances. In interventional cardiology, for example, rates of coronary angiography increased from 154.4 to 405.6 per 100,000 population between 1980 and 1992, while rates for coronary bypass surgery increased from 60.2 to 121.9 per 100,000 in the same time period.[11] Other industrialized nations had access to this same medical knowledge but have been much slower to adopt such procedures on such a wide scale. Great Britain, for example, performs only one third as many cardiac catheterizations as the United States.[12]

While nobody can question the value of the Sabin polio vaccine or the use of hip joint replacement to alleviate many years of hip pain in a patient with advanced osteoarthritis of the hip, many thoughtful observers have increasingly questioned the value of so much more medical care. The downside of more medical care, of course, may include negative impacts on both costs and the quality or outcomes of care.

In an excellent paper, Elliott Fisher and Gilbert Welch (based at the Center for the Evaluative Clinical Sciences at Dartmouth Medical School) addressed the issue of unintended consequences in the growth of medical care. They called attention to the law of diminishing returns with the growth of medical care (Figure 2-1).[13]

Several studies have demonstrated the downside of more medical care from different points of view. Two examples make the point. One study compared routine follow-up after hospitalization with structured discharge procedures requiring more frequent follow-up visits; although intended to reduce the rate of readmission, there was a 36 percent increase in hospital readmission rates and a trend toward increased mortality.[14] Another study showed higher mor-

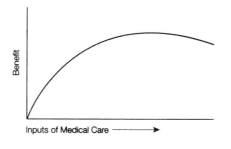

The first unit of input provides substantial benefits (imagine the first physician in a community), while additional units provide declining additional benefits (imagine the thousandth physician). Eventually, increasing inputs lead to no additional benefit (the "flat of the curve"). At some point, in theory, additional inputs lead to harm.

Figure 2-1 The law of diminishing returns. (Reprinted with permission from Fisher ES, Welch HG. Avoiding the unintended consequences of growth in medical care: How might more be worse? *JAMA*. 1999;281:446–453.)

bidity and mortality with more medical care among risk-adjusted Medicare beneficiaries with acute myocardial infarction in New York and Texas. Texans with mild left main or three-vessel coronary disease were much more likely to receive angiography and revascularization but ended up with lower exercise tolerance, more angina, and higher overall mortality two years later.[15]

TECHNOLOGY AND COSTS

As will be seen in more detail in Chapter 7, expenditures for health care services in the United States have increased markedly, due in considerable part to the boom in medical technology. Table 2-2 shows doubling of spending for physician and hospital services between 1975 and 1995, together with a 13-fold increase for home health care.[13]

New technology can be cost effective or inflationary, depending on whether it is substitutive or additive to other interventions. Thus, CT scanning was found in the late 1970s to decrease the cost of diagnostic evaluations of patients with suspected brain tumor (by eliminating the need for some hospital admissions) whereas the use of CT scanning increased the costs of care for patients with suspected stroke (no other studies or interventions were replaced).[16,17] Some technologies are cost effective for individual patients but inflationary overall. Such is the case with laparoscopic cholecystectomy, which has been found to reduce hospital stays by one third yet lead to an overall increase in total costs due to a lowered threshold for performing the procedure.[18,19]

Many factors in addition to advancing technology contribute to escalating costs of health care, including inflation, population growth, aging of the popu-

Table 2-2   Intensity of U.S. Health Care: Growth over Time and Variation across Regions

| | *Growth in Capacity over Time* | | | |
	1975	*1995*	*Ratio 1995/1975*	*Variation across Regions, Ratio 90th/10th Percentile*[a]
Health spending per capita[b]				
Hospital services	$667	$1,331	2	2.2
Physician services	$304	$767	2.5	2
Home health care	$8	$109	13.1	10.9
All personal health care	$1,454	$3,344	2.3	2.1
Physician workforce per 100,000				
All physicians	158	238	1.5	1.8
Cardiologists	2.3	5	2.2	5.2
Radiologists	0.9	4.6	5.3	3.0

[a] Data used to determine geographic variation in spending were for the Medicare population older than 65 years only. Variation across regions was quantified as the ratio of the 90th percentile to the 10th percentile of per capita spending or physician supply in U.S. Hospital Service Areas.

[b] Spending data for 1995 are for entire U.S. population. Data for 1975 are expressed in terms of 1995 dollars based on the consumer price index, excluding health care.

Reprinted with permission from Fisher ES, Welch HG. Avoiding the unintended consequences of growth in medical care: How might more be worse? *JAMA.* 1999;281:446–453.

lation, patient and physician preferences, and the potential threat of malpractice claims. However, it has been estimated that physicians influence or directly control at least 70 percent of health care expenditures.[20]

With regard to the potential impact of physician-induced demand, it has been demonstrated without question that the higher the level of professional uncertainty or disagreement about a particular diagnostic or therapeutic intervention, the higher the variation from one physician to another. Wennberg has shown, for example, less than a twofold variation in the treatment of hip fractures (i.e., not much debate or uncertainty among physicians as to how to manage them) versus an almost sixfold variation in the use of carotid duplex diagnostic procedures (i.e., lack of consensus among physicians about which patients to screen by this technique).[21]

Weisbrod pointed out another important factor associated with the skyrocketing cost of new technologies—the demand for health insurance. He observed that costly new procedures, such as organ transplants, increase the demand for insurance (i.e., inflationary overall) while lost-cost vaccines decrease such demand.[1]

TECHNOLOGY, OUTCOMES, AND QUALITY OF CARE

As the drive toward cost containment proceeded, health care purchasers, employers, government, and the public have raised serious questions as to whether recipients of health care are getting their money's worth. Unfortunately, there are many examples where newer technologies cannot be demonstrated to be cost effective or, even worse, prove to be dangerous. Until the development in recent years of outcomes research that focuses on outcomes that matter to patients (e.g., mortality, morbidity, quality of life), many new technologies were based on *surrogate outcomes* (i.e., physiologic or anatomic endpoints often not correlated with outcomes important to patients). Rick Deyo, internist educator and clinical investigator at the University of Washington, offered some sobering examples of failed technologies, initially widely used, that were based on surrogate outcomes (Table 2-3).[22] In the first example, encainide (flecainide) successfully suppressed ventricular arrhythmias, its intended purpose, but killed patients in the process.

As part of their study of the benefits and harms of medical care, Fisher and Welch have given us a useful way to think about the potential harms of diagnostic and therapeutic interventions. Figure 2-2 presents their conceptual framework of pathways, whereby too many clinical interventions can be harmful. On the diagnostic side, they note that a lowered threshold for diagnosis (through more sophisticated diagnostic procedures) may readily lead to worry, disability, unnecessary treatment, and adverse events.[13] One example is that spiral CT now can detect hepatic lesions only 2 mm in diameter,[23] one tenth the size of lesions detectable by imaging studies in 1982.[24] Table 2-4 shows the effect of four diagnostic tests in finding more disease.[13]

On the treatment side, harmful outcomes can result from more treatment induced by lowered treatment thresholds in four situations (Table 2-5). The risks of harm from treatment may outweigh potential benefits when the patient's disease is either advanced or inconsequential. The same negative equation may

Table 2-3 Examples of Dissociations Between Surrogate Outcomes and End Results

Treatment	Surrogate Outcomes	End Results
Encainide, flecainide for ventricular arrhythmia after myocardial infarction	90% Suppression of complex ventricular ectopy	Mortality twice as high as placebo
Clofibrate for hypercholesterolemia	Lower cholesterol levels, fewer ischemic heart disease events	Mortality 25% greater than with placebo
Plasmapheresis for rheumatoid arthritis	Lower erythrocyte sedimentation rate, complement levels	No improvement in pain relief, function, or number of inflamed joints
Finasteride for benign prostatic hyperplasia	Shrinkage of prostate size	No improvement in urinary frequency or urgency
Biofeedback for low back pain	Reduced electromyographic activity in paraspinous muscles	No significant reduction in pain

Source: Reprinted from Deyo RA. Using outcomes to improve quality of research and quality of care. *J Am Board Fam Pract.* 1998;11:465–473, Table 7-1.

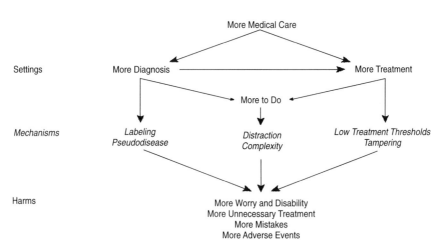

Figure 2-2 Pathways by which more medical care may lead to harm. (Reprinted with permission from Fisher ES, Welch HG. Avoiding the unintended consequences of growth in medical care: How might more be worse? *JAMA.* 1999;281:446–453.)

Table 2-4   Influence of Diagnostic Testing on Disease Prevalence

	Prevalence of Disease (%) Based on		
Disease Setting	*Traditional Test (Clinical Examination)*	*Advanced Tests (New Technology)*	*Increase (Ratio)*
Abdominal aortic aneurysm: 201 men with hypertension or coronary artery disease	2.5	9.0 (Ultrasound)	3.6
Thyroid nodule: 100 unselected patients	21.0	67.0 (Ultrasound)	3.2
Deep venous thrombosis: 349 trauma patients	0.9	57.6 (Duplex ultrasound)	64
Pulmonary embolus: 44 deep venous thrombosis patients	15.9	52.3 (Ventilation-perfusion scan)	3.3

Source: Reprinted with permission from Fisher ES, Welch HG. Avoiding the unintended consequences of growth in medical care: How might more be worse? *JAMA*. 1999;281:449.

Table 2-5   Situations in Which a Lower Treatment Threshold May Lead to Harm

Domain	*Treatment Threshold Lowered So Treatment Is Provided*
Spectrum of disease	To patients whose prognosis is good, regardless of treatment
	To patients whose prognosis is poor, regardless of treatment
Competing risks	When death is likely from other causes, even if treatment of the primary disease is successful
Patient values	To a patient who is not bothered by current symptoms
Risk of treatment	By providers whose outcomes are unknown or where higher risks may overwhelm the benefits

Source: Reprinted with permission from Fisher ES, Welch HG. Avoiding the unintended consequences of growth in medical care: How might more be worse? *JAMA*. 1999;281:450.

apply when the patient has other significant disease risks, is not sufficiently symptomatic to desire treatment, or when treatment outcomes are unknown and likely to be higher than expected.[13] All these situations occur frequently in everyday clinical practice. For example, a 1997 study estimated that operative risk for carotid endarterectomy outweighed the benefits in over one half of patients.[13,25]

MANAGING MEDICAL TECHNOLOGY

Advances in medical technology in fact are a double-edged sword. In an environment where a constant stream of new technology is being developed, how can the beneficial be separated from the harmful, the cost effective from the cost ineffective? As we have seen, historically, this has not yet been done well. Consideration of the process of assessment and adoption of medical technologies is of interest.

The Adoption Process

Although payments to physicians represent about 20 percent of total health care expenditures in the United States, physicians generate about 70 percent of all health care services delivered.[26] They therefore are key players in the rate of acceptance and dissemination of new technology. About one in three physicians adopts a new technology in any given year.[27] "Early adopters" share several characteristics in common—they tend to be younger, more often are subspecialists than generalists, more likely to be in urban group practice, more likely to have academic or national affiliations, and seek being "on the cutting edge" of change.[27] In highly competitive markets, market forces also may accelerate the adoption process.[28,29]

In view of the central role that physicians play in the adoption of new diagnostic and therapeutic interventions, they are under intense pressure from manufacturers, suppliers, and often the public to adopt a new technique before its efficacy, safety, and outcome have been well demonstrated. History is full of failures in this regard—a recent one is the withdrawal from the market of appetite suppressant drugs associated with cardiac valve defects. There is wisdom in the common advice to avoid being the first, or last, to adopt a new technique.

Technology Assessment

Health technology assessment (HTA) has been defined as the "careful evaluation of a medical technology for evidence of its safety, cost, cost-effectiveness and its ethical and legal implications both in absolute terms and in comparison with other competing technologies."[30]

The United States took an early lead among industrialized nations by establishing the first HTA program at the national level as part of the congressional Office of Technology Assessment (OTA, 1975) and the National Center for Health Care Technology (NCHCT, 1978).[31] Ironically, both organizations were later abolished (the NCHCT in 1982 and the OTA in 1995), and there is no longer a national HTA agency in either the public or private sector.[31] Political pressures by vested interests largely were responsible for these closures. In the case of NCHCT, for example, intense political pressure was brought to bear by the medical device industry and several medical professional societies.[32-34] So, the United States reverted back to a fragmented, largely ineffective system for health technology assessment while many other industrialized nations found it essential to establish strong national HTA agencies (including Canada, Australia, Sweden, and France).[31]

This is not so say that active technology assessment is not being done in the United States. Recent years have seen a growth spurt of other HTA activities, especially in the private sector, including medical professional organizations, academic medical centers, networks of hospitals and health care plans, health insurers, and the drug and device industry.[35] There are many problems, however, with these efforts, often subtle and inapparent, as pointed out by Perry and Thamer in their excellent 1999 article on the subject.[31] These include variations in the quality of evidence used, the extent of peer review, the effect of self-interest, and the biases of sponsoring organizations. One's confidence in such assessments is not increased on recognizing that many for-profit and not-for-profit research organizations are funded by the private sector, such as pharmaceutical, biotechnology, and medical device manufacturers. Even such agencies as the National Institutes of Health (with their priorities to advance medical knowledge, not to resolve major issues in health care) do not serve the need for effective HTA. The same is true for the Food and Drug Administration (with its focus on individual products, not comparative evaluations of competing technologies and without a requirement for evidence of long-term outcomes).[36]

In short, despite repeated calls over the last 20 years for a national system for HTA, there is still no coordinated system in place that can address major issues affecting medical practice and the health care system overall. In its recommendation for such a system, the Physician Payment Review Commission in 1994 expressed concerns that coverage decisions of health plans and government programs should not depend "on the happenstance of which particular plan, employer, judge or jury is empowered to make the judgment."[37] In response to these problems, Perry and Thamer[35] proposed the establishment of a national entity to ensure that

1. Issues raised by technologies with national implications are addressed promptly after they are identified.
2. Assessments are performed by an organization in which the vested interest is minimized or absent.
3. Adequate support is provided for HTA-related research, at least for studies of technologies deemed to be of high priority and with national implications.
4. Coverage and reimbursement decision makers in federal and state government health programs as well as in the private sector have access to sound scientific knowledge.
5. Information about health care technologies is exchanged and collaboration promoted.

Technology Management

Whatever system of health technology assessment evolves in this country, such assessments, if they are to be effective, must be directly linked to management decisions concerning coverage and payment for services.[31,38,39]

Returning to the recent proposals made by Fisher and Welch to reduce the adverse outcomes of medical care, Table 2-6 displays four dimensions of the problem, together with some constructive approaches.

Table 2-6   Reducing the Risk of Harm from More Medical Care

Underlying Causes	*Suggested Approaches*
1. Constrained model of disease	*Account for disease spectrum*
Harms of labeling and pseudodisease are exacerbated when disease spectrum is ignored	Provide data on the natural history of the increasingly mild disease detected by advanced diagnostic technology
Risks of treatment are misspecified when disease is treated as a dichotomous variable	Evaluate the benefits and harms of treatment of mild disease
2. Excessive extrapolation	*Draw inferences with care*
From results in one group of patients (those eligible for trials) to others	Were results for patients of similar illness severity reported in the trials?
From results for one intervention (e.g., treatment for hypertension with thiazides) to another (treatment with calcium channel agents)	Has benefit been proven for this specific intervention?
From results in centers that participated in clinical trials to the results in practice	Are the risks of treatment at your center known?
3. A missing level of analysis	*Evaluate the impact of the system*
The impact of system resources on treatment and outcomes are rarely examined	Study the impact of changes in capacity (technical capabilities, capital resources, workforce)
Quality improvement initiatives and other system changes are usually unevaluated	Hold quality improvement efforts and system change to rigorous standards of proof
4. We look for more to be better	*Acknowledge that it might not be*
Evidence of harm from more medical care may be discounted or interpreted as absence of benefit	Consider seriously the possibility that harm may occur from more medical care
Research focuses on identifying benefits of new technology	Pursue research on the potential harms of medical care and provide guidance on what not to do

Source: Reprinted with permission from Fisher ES, Welch HG. Avoiding the unintended consequences of growth in medical care: How might more be worse? *JAMA.* 1999;281:451.

CONCLUDING COMMENT

In this chapter, we have seen the inexorable wave of technological change wash over medicine and health care, together with some of the positive and negative impacts of this change. There is no question but that many advances of biotechnology improved the diagnosis and treatment of disease. In some instances, technological breakthroughs have been sufficiently curative or preventive as to decrease the cost while increasing the quality of care, as illustrated by polio vaccination. On the other hand, many technological advances, although widely applied, increased the cost and potential harm of care with no demonstrable benefits.

The challenge is to adopt and apply technology in an appropriate and cost effective way, based on evidence of improved patient outcomes. Despite the concerted efforts by many, however, an effective national system of technology assessment and management still is not in place to counter the negative effects of medical technology. This increases the stakes of efforts to assure a high quality of care and at the same time separate necessary and appropriate care from ineffective and harmful care, to be discussed in Chapters 18 and 21.

REFERENCES

1. Weisbrod BA. The nature of technological change: Incentives matter! In: Committee on Technological Innovation in Medicine, Institute of Medicine, Gelijns AC, Dawkins HV (eds). *Adopting new medical technology. Medical innovation at the crossroads*, vol. 4. Washington, DC: National Academy Press, 1994:10.
2. Cleeton D, Goepfrich VT, Weisbrod BA. The consumer price index for prescription drugs; dealing with technological change. Working paper, University of Wisconsin, Madison, Center for Health Economics and Law, 1998.
3. Gorman C, Siler C. Transplants. *Time.* 1996(Fall):73.
4. Lairson PD. Kaiser Permanente's new technology committee: Coverage decision making in a group model. Health maintenance organization. In: Committee on Technological Innovation in Medicine, Institute of Medicine, Gelijns AC, Dawkins HV (eds). *Adopting new medical technology. Medical innovation at the crossroads*, vol. 4. Washington, DC: National Academy Press, 1994:103–104.
5. Thomas L. *The lives of a cell: Notes of a biology watcher.* New York: Bantam Books, 1975.
6. Growth seen in ads for direct-to-consumer drugs. *AMA News.* April 27, 1998:16.
7. Fuchs VR. *Who shall live? Health, economics, and social choice.* New York: Basic Books, 1974:6.
8. McNerney WJ. Why does medical care cost so much? *N Engl J Med.* 1970;282:1458–1465.
9. McGivney WT. Autologous bone marrow transplantation: A microcosm of the U.S. health care system. In: Coverage decision making in a group model. Health maintenance organization. In: Committee on Technological Innovation in Medicine, Institute of Medicine, Gelijns AC, Dawkins HV (eds). *Adopting new medical technology. Medical innovation at the crossroads*, vol. 4. Washington, DC: National Academy Press, 1994:109–116.
10. Eddy DM. High-dose chemotherapy with autologous bone marrow transplantation for the treatment of metastatic breast cancer. *J Clin Oncol.* 1992;10(4):657–670.
11. National Center for Health Statistics, Gillum BS, Graves EJ, Kozak LJ. Trends in hospital utilization: United States, 1988–92. Vital and health statistics. Series 13. No. 124. Washington, DC: Government Printing Office, 1996; DHHS publication no. (PHS) 96-1785.
12. Tu JV, Pashos CL, Naylor CD, et al. Use of cardiac procedures and outcomes in elderly patients with myocardial infarction in the United States and Canada. *N Engl J Med.* 1997;336:1500–1505.
13. Fisher ES, Welch HG. Avoiding the unintended consequences of growth in medical care: How might more be worse? *JAMA.* 1999;281:446–453.
14. Weinberger M, Oddone EZ, Henderson WG. Does increased access to primary care reduce hospital readmissions? *N Engl J Med.* 1996;334:1441–1447.
15. Guadagnoli E, Hauptman PJ, Ayanian JZ, Pashos CL, McNeil BJ, Cleary PD. Variation in the use of cardiac procedures after acute myocardial infarction. *N Engl J Med.* 1995;333:573–578.
16. Larson EB, Omenn GS. The impact of computed tomography on the care of patients with suspected brain tumor. *Med Care.* 1977;5(7):543–551.
17. Larson EB, Omenn GS, Loop JW. Computed tomography in patients with cerebrovascular disease: impact of a new technology on patient care. *Am J Roentgenol.* 1978;131(1):35–40.
18. Escarce JJ, Chen W, Schwartz JS. Falling cholecystectomy thresholds since the introduction of laparoscopic cholecystectomy. *JAMA.* 1995;273:1581–1585.
19. Steiner CA, Bass EB, Talamini MA, Pitt HA, Steinberg EP. Surgical rates and operative mortality for open and laparoscopic cholecystectomy in Maryland. *N Engl J Med.* 1994;330:403–408.
20. Relman AS. The location of medical resources by physicians. *J Med Educ.* 1980;55:99.

21. Wennberg JE. *The Dartmouth Atlas of Health Care 1999.* Chicago: AHA Press, 1999.
22. Deyo RA. Using outcomes to improve quality of research and quality of care. *J Am Board Fam Pract.* 1998;11:465–473.
23. Urban BA, Fishman EK, Kuhlman JE, Kawashima A, Hennessey JG, Siegelman SS. Detection of focal hepatic lesions with spiral CT: Comparison of 4- and 8-mm interscan spacing. *Am J Roentgenol.* 1993;160:783–785.
24. Tanasecu DE, Waxman AD, Drickman MV, et al. Liver scintigraphy in colon carcinoma: Correlation with modified Duke pathological classification. *Radiology.* 1982;145:453–455.
25. Matchar DB, Oddone EZ, McCrory DC, et al. Influence of projected complication rates on estimated appropriate use rates for carotid endarterectomy. *Health Serve Res.* 1997;32:325–342.
26. Eisenberg JM. *Doctors' Decisions and the Cost of Medical Care: The Reasons for Doctors' Practice Patterns and Ways to Change Them.* Ann Arbor, MI: Health Administration Press Perspectives, 1986.
27. Freeman MP. The rate of adoption of new procedures among physicians. The impact of specialty and practice characteristics. *Med Care.* 1985;23(8):939–945.
28. Hillman AL, Pauly MV, Kerstein JJ. How do financial incentives affect physicians' clinical decisions and the financial performance of health maintenance organizations? *N Engl J Med.* 1989;321:86–92.
29. McCarthy TR. The competitive nature of the primary-care physician services market. *J Health Econo.* 1985;4(2):93–117.
30. Perry S, Eliastan M. The National Cancer Center for Health Care Technology. *JAMA.* 1981;245: 2510–2511.
31. Perry S, Thamer M. Medical innovation and the critical role of health technology assessment. *JAMA.* 1999;282:1869–1872.
32. Perry S. The brief life of the National Center for Health Care Technology. *N Engl J Med.* 1982;307:1095–1100.
33. Mervis J. Technology assessment faces ax. *Science.* 1994;266:1636.
34. Leary WE. Congress's science agency prepares to close its doors. *New York Times.* September 24, 1995;sect A:26.
35. Perry S, Thamer M. Health technology assessment, decentralized and fragmented in the U.S. compared to other countries. *Health Policy.* 1997;42:269–290.
36. *Directory of Health Technology Assessment Organizations Worldwide.* Washington, DC: Medical Technology and Practice Patterns Institute, 1998.
37. United States Physician Payment Review Commission. *Annual Report to the Congress.* Washington, DC: United States Physician Payment Review Commission, 1994.
38. Eisenberg JM. Ten lessons for evidence-based technology assessment. *JAMA.* 1999;282: 1865–1869.
39. Summit meeting on Conditional Coverage of New Medical Technology, Medical Technology Leadership Forum; July 26, 1999, Bethesda, MD.

3
Incremental Medicalization of Health Care

Little did George Orwell imagine when he first formulated the great truisms of Doublethink that the realm in which such paradoxes would first take hold as surrogates of common-sense would not be that of war and peace, freedom and slavery or even truth and falsehood but that of health. It was ecology that sought to make a battle cry of the minimalist aesthetic "Less is more." And it was in 1978, not 1984, that leaders from 134 governments and 67 United Nations' bodies, WHO and UNICEF affiliates, responsible to the world's peoples for the public health, meeting at Alma-Ata in Soviet Kazakhstan, declared as their common goal the provision of Health For All by the year 2000, and described that health not ultimately in terms of freedom from disease, but in terms of access to primary health care.[1]

Madeleine Goodman and Lenn Goodman, 1987[2]

INTRODUCTION

The process of boundary expansion of health care itself contributes to the growing influence of medical technology on U.S. health care. The term *medicalization* was coined by two medical sociologists, Irving Zola and Ivan Illich, to describe "the historical" conditions under which the iatrogenic causation of ill health is mediated through environmental and cultural transformations, rather than pharmacological, surgical, radiological, or psychotherapeutic treatment.[3] Indeed, there is an extensive literature on medicalization as a powerful boundary expander, much of it written by medical sociologists, anthropologists, historians, and even philosophers. This chapter draws on some of that literature to explore the dimensions and impact of medicalization on health care services.

The domain and goals of "health care" are easily subject to global definitions that have been redefined on many occasions in recent decades. Consider, for example, the epidemiological transitions shown in Table 3-1. As pointed out by Lincoln Chen, professor of International Health at Harvard University School

29

Table 3-1   The Epidemiological Transition of Disease

First Generation of Diseases
Common childhood infections
Malnutrition
Reproductive risks

Second Generation of Diseases
Cardiovascular
Oncotic
Degenerative

Third Generation of Diseases
Environmental threats
   Air, water, chemical
   Ozone depletion, global warming
New/emerging infections
   HIV/AIDS, Ebola virus, plague
   Tuberculosis, dengue, cholera
Sociobehavioral pathologies
   Violence
   Drug abuse
   Mental and psychosocial illness

Source: Reprinted with permission from the National Academy Press. Chen LC. World population and health. In: Institute of Medicine. *2020 Vision: Health in the 21st Century.* Washington, DC: National Academy Press, 1969:19.

of Public Health, many countries around the world now must deal with a third generation of diseases quite different from those of 75 or even 30 years ago. These pose new threats in terms of environmental problems, new kinds of infection, and various sociobehavioral pathologies.[4]

A useful way to conceptualize the interactive domains of health care, individual behavior, and environmental influences is displayed in Figure 3-1. This concept gives free rein to very broad definitions of health care.

The following exchange in a medical journal several years ago illustrates the kind of debate around the clinical boundaries of health care, in this instance concerning violence.

One physician's view:

The medicalization of social problems may be *de rigueur*, but violence isn't a medical problem and doesn't have a medical solution. I decline to accept the role of a guilt-laden social engineer. In fact, I refuse to be a social engineer at all, except when my own family is concerned. I gladly bear that responsibility.[5]

Another view:

To say violence is only a public health problem is unduly narrow. To label violence as a social problem does not excuse physicians from helping to find

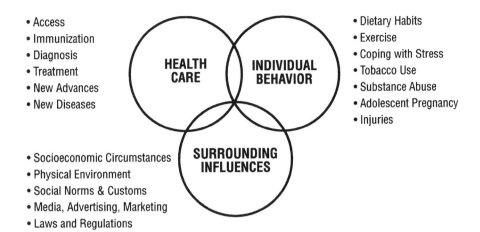

- Access
- Immunization
- Diagnosis
- Treatment
- New Advances
- New Diseases

HEALTH CARE

INDIVIDUAL BEHAVIOR

- Dietary Habits
- Exercise
- Coping with Stress
- Tobacco Use
- Substance Abuse
- Adolescent Pregnancy
- Injuries

- Socioeconomic Circumstances
- Physical Environment
- Social Norms & Customs
- Media, Advertising, Marketing
- Laws and Regulations

SURROUNDING INFLUENCES

Figure 3-1   Determinants of health. (Reprinted with permission from Tarlov AR. The rising supply of physicians and the pursuit of better health. *J Med Ed.* 1988;63:94–107.)

solutions. Any effort involves the entire community, including the school systems, law enforcement agencies, the criminal justice system, legislatures, churches, and families as well as the medical community. As I stated in my essay, physicians do not have to "do it all," but there are many things physicians can do.

In looking at the issue from a perspective of medical intervention, patients refuse advice, fail to comply and even die despite a doctor's best efforts, but doctors continue to urge patients to quit smoking, reduce alcohol consumption, form good nutritional habits, get a mammogram, wear a seat belt, practice safe sex, etc. No less is expected when it comes to violence.[6]

There are many other practical examples of issues that raise controversy among physicians as to whether they are, or should be, part of their everyday clinical responsibilities (e.g., counseling concerning gun control, legalization of heroin requiring physician prescription control).

GENESIS OF BOUNDARY EXPANSION

The genesis of medicalization in any given area is multifactorial, yet varies from one content area to another. Some of the important factors include scientific and biomedical advances; professional and hospital industry interests; market forces; advertising and educational campaigns by manufacturers, health care agencies, and others; increased public expectations and demand; and favorable reimbursement policies by payers. Arnold Relman, as editor of *The New England Journal of Medicine*, in 1980 called attention to the emergence of a large medical industrial complex.[7] Arthur Barsky described the dynamics of such factors in these terms.[8]

Health is industrialized and commercialized in a fashion that enhances many people's dissatisfaction with their health. Advertisers, manufacturers, advocacy groups, and proprietary health care corporations promote the myth that good health can be purchased; they market products and services that purport to deliver the consumer into the promised land of wellness. A giant medical-industrial complex has arisen, composed initially of for-profit health care corporations such as free-standing ambulatory-surgery centers, free-standing diagnostic laboratories, home health care services, and of course proprietary hospitals. But the market is so lucrative that the products of the medical-industrial complex now range all the way from do-it-yourself diagnostic kits to "lite" foods, from tooth polish to eye drops, from health magazines to Medic-Alert bracelets, from exercise machines to fat farms.

Two examples provide some perspective of how these variables can influence a boundary expansion movement in any particular area. The first is the expansion of pediatrics as a field since the 1950s, into the "new pediatrics," otherwise heralded as ambulatory pediatrics, psychosocial pediatrics, and behavioral pediatrics. This change has come under considerable study, with some difference of opinion as to the main factors generating this expansion. One explanation for this change was put forward by Pawluch, who held that declining numbers of children with serious illnesses by the mid-20th century led to a more-routine, less-challenging pediatric practice. She postulated that the survival of pediatric practice required the specialty to take on the management of children's "troublesome behavior."[9] Although pediatric practice in large part, after World War II, did shift to the ambulatory care of acute, self-limiting, or chronic diseases, others have argued that market conditions played a minor role in this boundary expansion and in fact failed if it were a market strategy, since most pediatricians refer most children with behavioral problems to other nonphysician professionals.[10,11] In a comprehensive historical review, Sydney Halpern made a strong case that other factors played the major role in this expansion of pediatrics, especially the leadership of academic pediatrics, the advent of Medicaid and other Great Society programs, and the funding by federal agencies and private foundations of pediatric research and training in psychosocial problems of children.[11] Still others have called attention to the fact that the management of these problems is time consuming and poorly compensated by payers, prompting referral to other nonphysician professionals.[12,13]

A second example shows the powerful influence that legislatures in state governments can have on medicalizing a particular area. Scoliosis screening in children became a popular idea in recent years, even before any evidence was available for its effectiveness. In fact, 26 states have come to mandate school scoliosis screening.[14] In 1996, the U.S. Preventive Services Task Force assessed all available data on the outcomes of scoliosis screening, concluding that "there is insufficient evidence to recommend for or against routine screening of asymptomatic adolescents for idiopathic scoliosis"; routine visits to clinicians for screening examinations at specific ages also were not recommended.[15] We are left with many ineffectual state programs in place for a controversial screening procedure, with many calling for repeal of these programs on the basis of low positive predictive value of the screening examinations and high numbers of children requiring further evaluation.[16] A recent population-based study in Rochester, Minnesota, for example, showed that 94 (4.1 percent) of 2,242 children screened were referred for further evaluation; of these only 5 children were found to have scoliosis needing treatment.[16]

SPECTRUM AND TYPES OF MEDICALIZATION

It is interesting to note some of the various tracks taken by some of the procedures or areas of knowledge that expanded the boundaries of medical practice. Five tracks, which in some instances overlap, illustrate the almost unlimited potential for boundary expansion of health care and medical practice.

Sociomedical-Cultural

Without trying to tease out the various factors responsible for these changes, it is clear that obstetric delivery shifted from the home, perceived as a largely normal experience, to the hospital, a much higher technological setting, over the course of the 20th century. On many hospital obstetric services, the proportion of "normal deliveries" is outweighed by others involving one or another actual or potential complication. Until more recent years, women had relatively little choice of options for anesthesia or options for management of labor, instead being asked to fit into one or another protocol of the obstetric service. At Los Angeles County General Hospital in 1960, for example, all primigravida received saddle block (low spinal) anesthesia, while general anesthesia was common practice for deliveries in Denver; in each case, hospital protocols were in place and defended as best practice without supportive outcome data.

As hospital deliveries became the expected norm, infant bottle feeding soon followed. The hospital stay inhibited breast feeding, and nursery protocols implied to many mothers that breast feeding was insufficient and that bottle feeding was at least as good. The "naturalizing" of bottle feeding was supported by attending physicians and nursing staff, to the point that breast feeding became the less common choice made by women.[17]

Meanwhile, at the other end of the life cycle, the aging process has become increasingly medicalized. Foucault coined the term, the *clinical gaze*, whereby problems, phenomena, and people are viewed as clinical problems.[18] In a thoughtful paper on the medicalization of aging, Carroll Estes and Elizabeth Binney described the effects of this "clinical gaze" on medical practice. The development of geriatrics (and gerontology as its growing knowledge base) is a good illustration of the process of medicalization with its targeted focus on illness, chronic disease, disability, and physiological/psychological decline, as well as its call for increased funding for research in aging. Nevertheless, there are pitfalls of an overly aggressive application of the biomedical model to aging, whereby an increasing segment of the population with declining quality of life takes up more medical resources than can be afforded by the society.[19] John

McKinlay warned against the futility of devoting a continuously increasing amount of energy and resources to the task of pulling a near-endless parade of people out of a rushing stream without finding out how they are being pushed in upstream.[19,20]

Binney and her colleagues sum up their concerns about the progressive medicalization of aging in these terms:[21]

Medicalization is not a new process, nor is its conceptualization as a social problem. It could be argued that the medical community and the medical-industrial complex have been engaged in a process of medicalization of aging, certainly from the inception of Medicare and Medicaid in the 1960s. However, the continued growth and current evolution of the process raise serious questions and cause for concern. In many ways, the medicalization of aging in the post-PPS/DRG era represents a "medicalization of the home," a final frontier in the total medicalization of life. Alterations in the site and provision of health care, and in the spatial and temporal relations between care, caregivers, and care recipients have potentially major effects not only on the outcome of care, but on the experience and meaning of aging in modern societies. While research may assess aspects of the former, the effects on the latter may not be known for quite some time, particularly as the effects differ cross-nationally. The deinstitutionalization created by PPS may have the unintended consequence of creating a "total institution" of the family and home in which the labor previously performed in the hospital is transformed and transferred into the home, further medicalizing old age.

James Goodwin, a geriatrician based at the Center on Aging at the University of Texas Medical Branch in Galveston, agrees that care for the elderly has become over-medicalized and lost sight of the important goal of relief of suffering. He observes that the hospice model has these advantages over the white-coat-scientist model in everyday use:[22]

Although this model evolved for the compassionate care of the terminally ill, many values of hospices are appropriate for the care of older patients who are not dying, including an understanding that each person is unique, a realization that everyone dies, a recognition that comfort and happiness are very important, an appreciation of the many unmeasurable adverse consequences of medical evaluations and treatments, a willingness to make compromises in carrying out plans, depending on changing circumstances, and an ability to treat without diagnosing.

And, of course, there is no question that the process of dying itself has been medicalized well beyond what was a more natural and expected event years ago. Death has become medicine's enemy, representing a failure of biomedicine, often the endpoint of disease beyond the reach of medical treatment.[23,24] Although hospital deaths are trending down in recent years, most people still die in hospitals or long-term care facilities, not in the home, as was the case many years ago. Attending physicians in hospitals commonly pursue more diagnostic tests and therapeutic interventions even into the last 24 to 48 hours of life in the face of incurable disease. McCue, a physician, noted (like many others) that medicalization of dying often has deprived dying patients of their autonomy and dignity.[25]

Application of New Technology

The advent of fetal monitoring provides a good example of a new technology that transformed and further medicalized, obstetric care. Quickly adopted into mainstream obstetric care during the 1970s, without the benefit of positive outcome studies of its use, it rapidly moved the management of labor to a higher technology setting. Laboring women were monitored continuously on most obstetric services, often with invasive internal monitors. A new science developed around the interpretation of fetal monitor tracings, which in a growing number of cases led to earlier and more aggressive intervention. Although other factors probably are involved, it seems certain that this technological "advance" played a large part in escalating the rate of cesarean section from 5 percent of births in the 1960s to about 25 percent by century's end. On the positive side, however, the infant mortality rate dropped by two thirds, from 20 per 1,000 live births in 1970 to 7.2 in 1998.[26]

Refinement of Diagnostic Tools

We saw in the last chapter how more refined diagnostic procedures inevitably identify more disease, often in an early and asymptomatic stage. As one approaches "normal," one needs to increasingly ask where "disease" starts and the normal range leaves off. Table 2-4 in Chapter 2 quantified the increased prevalence expected as a result of these diagnostic advances for abdominal aortic aneurism, thyroid nodule, deep venous thrombosis, and pulmonary embolism.[27-31]

Of course, there are many other examples whereby modern diagnostic tests identify conditions as "abnormalities," which frequently leads to further diagnostic or treatment intervention as well as the need to monitor the conditions. In each instance, the patient is "labeled" with the problem, with one more thing to worry about. Two further examples make the point. One study showed that one half of young adults have lumbar disk bulge without back pain,[32] while another demonstrated knee abnormalities in one quarter of asymptomatic young adults.[33]

Changing Definitions of Existing Diseases

In an effort to make available earlier treatment to patients with early disease, several professional groups have recommended lowering the threshold for diagnosis of four common diseases: diabetes mellitus, hypertension, hypercholesterolemia, and obesity. Table 3-2 lists the old and proposed new definitions for these diseases, and Table 3-3 shows the impact on disease prevalence if these recommendations are widely adopted.

What might appear to be a modest definitional change can have enormous impact on disease prevalence. Thus, 42 million new cases of hypercholesterolemia would be so labeled if a cholesterol level above 200 mg/dl is accepted as "abnormal," whereas the four new definitions together would label 140 million adults in the United States (75 percent of the adult population) with at

Table 3-2   Source and Description of Old and New Disease Definitions

Disease	Source	Old Definition	New Definition
Diabetes	Expert Committee on the Diagnosis and Classification of Diabetes Mellitus	Fasting glucose level >140 mg/dl	Fasting glucose level >126 mg/dl
Hypertension (requiring treatment)	Joint National Committee on Detection, Evaluation, and Treatment of High Blood Pressure	Systolic BP* >160 mmHg or diastolic BP >100 mmHg	Systolic BP >140 mmHg or diastolic BP >90 mmHg
Hypercholesterolemia	Air Force/Texas Coronary Atherosclerosis Prevention Study	Total cholesterol level >240 mg/dl	Total cholesterol level >200 mg/dl
Being overweight	National Heart, Lung, and Blood Institute	Body mass index >27 kg/m^2	Body mass index >25 kg/m^2

* BP = blood pressure.

Source: Reprinted with permission from Schwartz LM, Woloshin S. Changing disease definitions: Implications for disease prevalence. Analysis of the Third National Health and Nutrition Examination Survey. *Eff Clin Pract.* 1999;2(2):77.

Table 3-3   Changes in Prevalence of Four Common Conditions under Newly Recommended Definitions

Condition	Disease Prevalence		New Cases	Increase
	Old Definition	New Definition		
Diabetes	11,697,000	13,378,000	1,681,000	14%
Hypertension	38,690,000	52,180,000	13,490,000	35%
Hypercholesterolemia	49,480,000	92,127,000	42,647,000	86%
Being overweight	70,608,000	100,100,000	29,492,000	42%
Any condition	108,750,000	140,630,000	31,880,000	29%

Note: Numbers have been rounded to the nearest thousand. The U.S. adult population was 18,500,000 at the time of these measurements.

Source: Reprinted with permission from Schwartz LM, Woloshin S. Changing disease definitions: Implications for disease prevalence. Analysis of the Third National Health and Nutrition Examination Survey. *Eff Clin Pract.* 1999;2(2):80.

least one of these four diseases.[34] Imagine the implications of these new definitions for cascading health care services, laboratory studies, use of prescription drugs, and inflationary overall costs, quite aside from potential adverse effects. In their excellent and provocative paper analyzing these implications, Schwartz and Woloshin question the assumptions behind these recommendations, advising caution on three counts:[34]

1. The supporting evidence is incomplete. Outcome data are inconclusive for hypertension and diabetes, and the definitional changes for obesity and diabetes are not based on trials but instead entirely on extrapolations from the experience of patients with overt diabetes and morbid obesity.
2. There are competing priorities for health care services, and all patients with these conditions still are not being managed optimally, even under the "old" definitions.
3. Diagnosis and treatment carry their own harmful effects, which could outweigh unknown potential benefits.

Definition of New Disease

Striking as the foregoing examples are of medicalization beyond the bounds of supporting evidence, definition of previously normal conditions into diseases also contributes to boundary expansion of medical practice. Quill, Lipkin, and Greenland described the evolution of four examples of anatomico-physiologic phenomena as "overlap syndromes." The four are poorly defined problems commonly encountered in primary care: mild mitral valve prolapse, hypoglycemia, irritable colon, and premenstrual syndrome.[35] In each instance, the clinician must decide the extent to which these conditions are diseases or normal variants.

Quill and his colleagues have this to say as to how readily physicians can start dealing with the problems as diseases:[35]

It is easiest for us as physicians to conceptualize them as diseases, and to emphasize their potential for adverse effects. In this way we have the satisfaction and safety of actively "protecting" the patient and ourselves if things go wrong. This tendency is supported by most clinical studies, which are based on patients referred to tertiary medical centers, often leading to overestimation of the risk of complications and associated adverse phenomena. Medicine has less insight and understanding about the risks and implications of labeling normal variants as disease, a process sometimes called "medicalization."

They carry out an in-depth analysis of mitral valve prolapse as an example of inappropriate medicalization of a common, usually benign condition, which inevitably leads to overreaction by clinicians, overtreatment, and unnecessary worry and disability. Table 3-4 summarizes the potential risks and benefits accruing to patients, physicians, and society from the diagnosis of mitral valve prolapse.

Another huge area of troublesome medicalization lies in the broad area of somatizing complaints. In six studies of patients in various primary care settings, 38 to 60 percent were found to have symptoms with no serious medical basis, and psychosocial factors have been found to be the major factor triggering a visit to physicians in 25 to 50 percent of all primary care visits.[36] Such common symptoms as fatigue, headaches, and dizziness seldom are caused by

Table 3-4   Potential Risks and Benefits of Diagnosing the Mitral Valve Prolapse

	Risks	Benefits
Patient	Somatization	Explanation for puzzling symptoms
	Unnecessary testing, treatment, and disability	Recognition of real preventable risk
		Sick role
	Inaccurate attribution of symptoms	Feel reassured and normal
	Alienation from one's body	Increased physician attention
Physician	Inaccurate diagnosis	Easy explanation for complex symptoms
	Iatrogenic harm	Feel and appear competent
	Scientific error	Tight bonding with patient
	Pressure to treat by "informed" patient	Intellectual challenge and income from tests and visits
	Reinforce unhealthy illness behavior	Recognition and minimization of real risk
Society	Medicalization	Detection of real risk and disease prevention
	Disability	Make normal feel more normal
	Unnecessary cost	
	Inappropriate stratification and assessment of risk	

Source: Reprinted with permission from Quill TE, Lipkin M, Greenland P. The medicalization of normal variants: The case of mitral valve prolapse. *J Gen Intern Med.* 1988;3(3):267–276, Table 3.

serious disease, and the typical adult has at least one somatic symptom every four to six days.[37]

In addition, somatizing patients are much higher utilizers of health services and have high rates of iatrogenic illness.[38] In view of these well-documented circumstances and the fact that many of these patients are time intensive as "difficult patients," Barsky and Borus make a compelling case that this situation will be even more of a problem in the era of managed care, since visit times will be compressed, patients may express their "disease" in more urgent ways, while at the same time feeling little financial disincentive as prepaid subscribers to capitation plans.[36]

IMPACT OF MEDICALIZATION ON THE HEALTH CARE SYSTEM

The cumulative effects of incremental medicalization have inevitably led to increased utilization of health care services as well as increased costs of care. Moreover, the numbers and types of providers continue to escalate. Americans consult physicians at about twice the rate as 70 years ago (average of 5 visits today compared to 2.5 visits per year in 1930)[39] and seek out the services of a growing array of nonphysician providers as well. Although nonphysician providers charge less for their services than physicians, their services still add up to major amounts. A lactation consultant, for example, may take up to 90 minutes for a first visit with a patient seeking help with breast feeding, with follow-up visits typically of 30 minutes duration.[40]

BACKLASH TO MEDICALIZATION

A number of trends within the last 15 to 20 years represent some degree of backlash against overmedicalization and overapplication of technology in health care. Consider the following: the emergence of birthing rooms as a low-technology option for low-risk pregnant women on some hospital obstetric floors; the resurgence of breast feeding as a "natural" choice for postpartum women; some shift toward hospices for terminal care in out-of-hospital settings; the growing number of self-help groups available to patients and families confronting a variety of chronic diseases; and the turning away by many people from allopathic medicine to a host of alternative health care providers. The last example has shown remarkable growth—large national surveys of the use of alternative medicine in the United States showed an increase from 33.8 percent in 1991 to 42.1 percent in 1997. The largest growth in visits were for herbal medicine, massage, megavitamins, self-help groups, folk remedies, energy healing, and homeopathy. Extrapolation to the U.S. population suggested Americans made about 629 million visits to alternative medicine providers in 1997 (more than the total visits to all U.S. primary care physicians), with total out-of-pocket expenditures of about $27 billion in that year (exceeding the total 1997 out-of-pocket expenditures for all U.S. hospitalizations).[41] Many payers, hoping for less expensive alternatives to allopathic care, began to cover alternative or complementary medicine services. Today Medicaid pays for chiropractic services in 33 states, biofeedback in 10 states, acupuncture in 6 states, and naturopathy in 5 states.[42] A recent survey of 18 major managed care organizations and insurance providers revealed that 14 of them offered at least 11 of 34 complementary and alternative therapies. A public and political groundswell in this direction even resulted in the upgrading by Congress of the Office of Alternative Medicine to a full-fledged National Center for Complementary and Alternative Medicine within the National Institutes of Health, with a $50 million budget for fiscal 1999.[43]

CONCLUDING COMMENTS

Medicalization of health care has had a profound effect on the shape and problems of the current health care system. Multifactorial in its genesis, on the one hand, it is a powerful sociologic and cultural force and, on the other, propelled by many other forces. Most of these are subtle and difficult to measure. It is easy to make the case that the self-interest of suppliers and providers of health care products and services (e.g., direct-to-consumer drug advertising) play a predominant role in furthering the medicalization process. Less obvious are the many well-intentioned efforts in the not-for-profit sector that produce the same result (e.g., group advocacy for more research support for the care of specific diseases).

Regardless of its causes, medicalization of health care has played an enormous role in increasing the utilization and costs of health care services in the United States, while at the same time exposing many people to unnecessary anxiety and harms of treatment. When disease is defined too broadly, too much of the population becomes defined as "sick," often on an arbitrary basis, with no therapeutic value. We saw good examples of this in the last chapter.

Despite some degree of demedicalization in the form of a backlash toward lower-tech, alternative therapies, the cumulative effect of both continue in the same direction—more demand by an increasingly informed and empowered consumer. Despite the backlash, most of the changes through medicalization appear to be firmly in place and irreversible. We consider the impact of these changes more fully in later chapters, particularly in Chapter 7, which deals with the intractable problem of inflation of health care costs.

REFERENCES

1. Alma-Ata 1978 Primary Health Care. *Health for All*, Series No. 1. Geneva, Switzerland: World Health Organization, 1978.
2. Goodman MJ, Goodman LE. Medicalization and its discontents. *Soc Sci Med.* 1987; 25(6): 733–740.
3. Illich I. Medicalization and primary care. *J R Coll Gen Pract.* 1982;32:463–470.
4. Chen LC. World population and health. In: Institute of Medicine. *2020 vision: Health in the 21st Century. Institute of Medicine 25th Anniversary Symposium.* Washington, DC: National Academy Press, 1996:19.
5. Fletcher JL Jr. "Medicalization" of America: Physician heal thy society? Letter. *Am Fam Physician.* 1994;49(7):1595.
6. Hamberger LK. "Medicalization" of America: Physician heal thy society? Reply. *Am Fam Physician.* 1994;49(7):1598.
7. Relman AS. The new medical-industrial complex. *N Engl J Med.* 1980;303:963–970.
8. Barsky AJ. The paradox of health. *N Engl J Med.* 1988;318:414–418.
9. Pawluch D. Transitions in pediatrics: A segmented analysis. *Soc Problems.* 1983;30(4):449–465.
10. Costello EJ. Primary care pediatrics and child psychopathology: A review of diagnostic, treatment, and referral practices. *Pediatrics.* 1986;78(6):1044–1051.
11. Halpern SA. Medicalization as professional process: Postwar trends in pediatrics. *J Health Soc Behav.* 1990;31(1):28–42.
12. Haggerty RJ. Behavioral pediatrics: Can it be taught? Can it be practiced?" *Pediatr Clin North Am.* 1982;29(2):391–398.
13. Butler JA. "Financial aspects of practice." *J Dev Behav Pediatr.* 1985;6(4):194–195.
14. Higginson G. Political considerations for changing medical screening programs. *JAMA.* 1999;282:1472–1474.
15. DiGuiseppi C, Atkins D, Woolf SH, eds. *US Preventive Services Task Force Guide to Clinical Preventive Services* (2nd ed). Alexandria, VA: International Medical Publishing, 1996:525.
16. Yawn BP, Yawn RA, Hodge D, et al. A population-based study of school scoliosis screening. *JAMA.* 1999;282:1427–1432.
17. Apple RD. The medicalization of infant feeding in the United States and New Zealand: Two countries, one experience. *J Hum Lact.* 1994;10(1):31–37.
18. Foucault M. *Birth of the clinic: An archeology of medical perception.* New York: Pantheon-Books, July 1973.
19. Estes CL, Binney EA. The biomedicalization of aging: Dangers and dilemmas. *Gerontologist.* 1989;29(5):587–596.

20. McKinlay JB. A case for refocusing upstream. The political economy of illness. In: Conrad P, Kern R (eds). *The Sociology of Health and Illness: Critical Perspectives.* New York: St. Martin's Press, 1989.
21. Binney EA, Estes CL, Ingman SR. Medicalization, public policy and the elderly. Social services in jeopardy? *Soc Sci Med.* 1990;30(7):761–771.
22. Goodwin JS. Geriatrics and the limits of modern medicine. *N Engl J Med.* 1999;340:1284.
23. Callahan D. *The Troubled Dream of Life: Living with Mortality.* New York: Simon and Schuster, 1993:198.
24. Mendez OE. Death in America: A clinician's perspective. *Crit Care Clin.* 1993;9(3):613.
25. McCue JD. The naturalness of dying. *JAMA.* 1995;273:1039–1043.
26. National Center for Health Statistics. *Health, United States, 2000.* Hyattsville, MD: National Center for Health Statistics, 2000:152.
27. Fisher ES, Welch HG. Avoiding the unintended consequences of growth of medical care: How might more be worse? *JAMA.* 1999;281:446–453.
28. Lederle FA, Walker JM, Reinke DB. Selective screening for abdominal aortic aneurysms with physical examination and ultrasound. *Arch Intern Med.* 1988;148:1753–1756.
29. Ezzat S, Sarti DA, Cain DR, Braunstein GD. Thyroid incidentalomas: Prevalence by palpation and ultrasonography. *Arch Intern Med.* 1994;154:1838–1840.
30. Geerts WH, Code KI, Jay RM, Chen E, Szalai JP. A prospective study of venous thromboembolism after major trauma. *N Engl J Med.* 1994;331:1601–1606.
31. Moser KM, Fedullo PF, LitteJohn JK, Crawford R. Frequent asymptomatic pulmonary embolism in patients with deep venous thrombosis. *JAMA.* 1994;271:223–225.
32. Jensen MC, Brant-Zawadzki MN, Obuchowski N, Modic MT, Malkasian D, Ross JS. Magnetic resonance imaging of the lumbar spine in people without back pain. *N Engl J Med.* 1994; 331:69–73.
33. Kornick J, Trefelner E, McCarthy S, Lange R, Lynch K, Jokl P. Meniscal abnormalities in the asymptomatic population at MR imaging. *Radiology.* 1990;177:463–465.
34. Schwartz LM, Woloshin S. Changing disease definitions: Implications for disease prevalence. Analysis of the Third National Health and Nutrition Examination Survey, *Eff Clin Pract.* 1999;2(2):76–85.
35. Quill TE, Lipkin M, Greenland P. The medicalization of normal variants: The case of mitral valve prolapse. *J Gen Intern Med.* 1988;3(3):267–276.
36. Barsky AJ, Borus JF. Somatization and medicalization in the era of managed care. *JAMA.* 1995;274:1931–1934.
37. Egan KJ, Beston R. Response to symptoms in healthy low utilizers of the health care system. *J Psychosom Res.* 1987;31(1):11–21.
38. Fink P. Surgery and medical treatment in persistent somatizing patients. *J Psychosom Res.* 1992;36:439–447.
39. Stoeckle JD, White GA. *Plain Pictures of Plain Doctoring.* Boston: MIT Press, 1985.
40. Auerbach KG. The medicalization of breast feeding. *J Hum Lact.* 1995;11(4):259–260.
41. Eisenberg DM, Davis RB, Ettner SL, et al. Trends in alternative medicine use in the United States 1990–1997: Results of a follow-up National survey. *JAMA.* 1998;280:1569–1575.
42. Brunk D. Some alternative treatments covered by Medicaid plans. *Fam Pract News.* 2000;(Jan 1):44.
43. Jancin B. Rocky marriage: Payers and alternative medicine. Fam Pract News 2000;(January 1, 2000):38.

4
Specialization and Subspecialization

Specialization, which has been stimulated by shifts toward hospital care and uncontrolled because of a lack of adequate planning, has also been accompanied by an increased fragmentation of medical care. Furthermore, specialization as a general phenomenon appears to have been associated with observable inefficiencies in the delivery of services. Underutilization, overtraining, duplication, and varying levels of compensation for the performance of similar tasks have all been cited as factors in rising health care costs, the forces of inflation aside . . . this should not be interpreted as an argument for despecialization, it is, instead, a plea for achieving a balance between generalism and specialism, for improved efficiency in the delivery of services, and for a move away from fragmentation.

Robert Knouss, 1976[1]

The statement by Robert Knouss was made in 1976 while he was serving as director of the Division of Medicine of the Bureau of Health Manpower. It captures some of the consequences of specialization within the health care system and the need for an appropriate balance between generalism and specialism. There has been an ongoing tension between generalism and specialism in medical care from time immemorial. Unfortunately, however, this is not merely an abstract issue or one affecting only the physicians involved. A healthy, affordable health care system depends on an appropriate balance between the two.

This chapter explores the impact of specialization on the evolving U.S. health system with a fivefold purpose: (1) to give some historical perspective to this issue, (2) to summarize efforts in the United States to shape an appropriate generalist/specialist mix, (3) to describe the impact and current debate concerning overspecialization on our health care system, (4) to outline the influence of managed care on specialization, and (5) to briefly examine some of the forces that increasingly are taking all the present structures of specialization under siege.

HISTORICAL PERSPECTIVE

To think that the process of specialization is a product of "modern" times is to miss the mark widely. Consider the observation by Herodotus, describing medical practice in the Nile valley of Egypt before 2000 BC:

> The art of medicine is thus divided; each physician applies himself to one disease only and not more. All places abound in physicians; some are for the eyes, others for the head, others for the teeth, others for the intestines, and others for internal disorders.[2]

As noted in Chapter 1, medical education in the United States at the start of the 20th century lacked both quality and content. Emphasis was on experiential training through preceptorships or apprenticeships, formal education was deficient, and the sale of fake medical licenses and diplomas was by no means rare.[3]

The Flexner Report of 1910 was instrumental in the reform of medical education in the United States. New standards were applied and improvements made in medical schools throughout the country, and many schools were forced to close. Postgraduate training by way of internship became a requirement.[4] Increased emphasis was directed in medical schools to the biomedical sciences as a foundation for medical practice. As an inevitable result of these changes, biomedical research gained impetus, accompanied by the development of boards, organizations, and residency programs in a growing number of specialties.

Among the first specialty organizations were the American College of Surgeons (1913) and the American College of Physicians (1915). The first specialty to be defined with its own board was ophthalmology in 1917. The next specialty to be proposed, curiously enough, was general practice, at the opposite end of the spectrum as the ultimate generalist field. But that proposal was defeated at a 1919 meeting of the AMA.[5] Instead, general practice was not to be accepted as a specialty in its own right until 50 years later, in 1969, when family practice became the nation's 20th specialty.

The growth of specialization has been the dominant feature of American medicine over the last 75 years, particularly since World War II. Table 4-1 lists all of today's specialty boards in terms of the sequence of their appearance. It is interesting to note the different kinds of definitions for these specialties. For example, some were defined by anatomy (e.g., ophthalmology and dermatology); one by gender (obstetrics-gynecology); two by age (pediatrics and internal medicine); and many by basic approach to management (most surgical specialties).

Especially after the 1940s, the university medical centers and large teaching hospitals were at the hub of increasing specialization and subspecialization. Advances in medical technology first were offered in tertiary care centers, which distanced themselves from everyday community-based medical practice. Simultaneously, teaching in medical schools placed major emphasis on the study of disease and technical competence, and more humanistic aspects of care were relatively devalued.[6]

The growth of specialization led to a decline of generalism in U.S. medical practice. In 1900, there was one general practitioner for every 600 people;[7] by

Table 4-1   Year of Organization of Specialty Boards

Board	Year	Board	Year
Ophthalmology	1917	Surgery	1937
Otolaryngology	1924	Anesthesiology	1938
Obstetrics-gynecology	1930	Plastic surgery	1939
Dermatology	1932	Neurologic surgery	1940
Pediatrics	1933	Physical medicine and rehabilitation	1947
Orthopedic surgery	1934	Preventive medicine	1948
Psychiatry-neurology	1934	Thoracic surgery	1950
Radiology	1934	Family practice	1969
Colon-rectal surgery	1935	Allergy and immunology	1971
Urology	1935	Nuclear medicine	1971
Internal medicine	1936	Emergency medicine	1979
Pathology	1936	Medical genetics	1991

the late 1960s, that ratio dropped to one for every 3,000 people. Over the 40-year period from 1930 to 1970, the ratio of general practitioners to specialists reversed from 80 percent general practitioners to 20 percent specialists to about 20:80 percent. The shortage of general practitioners was all the more acute since almost one half of them were over 55 years old in 1969 and no more than 10 percent of medical school graduates planned careers in general practice.[8]

The mid-1960s to mid-1970s saw a growing concern over the shortage of generalist physicians, culminating in four major national reports in 1966 which called for a strong national effort to train a larger number of generalists.[9–12] These reports were instrumental in the approval of family practice as a specialty in 1969. In the early 1970s, the federal government initiated grant programs for the training of increased numbers of primary care physicians under the definition of family practice, general internal medicine, and general pediatrics.

The widely perceived physician shortage of the 1960s led to the expansion of existing medical schools and the opening of others. Many espoused a mission to train more primary care physicians; and although their rhetoric often attracted training grants, their performance was mixed, at best. The biggest change over the last three decades of the 20th century was accelerated growth in the total number of physicians, with overproduction of specialists in most fields. The proportion of generalists (family practice, general internal medicine, and pediatrics) dropped from 37.3 percent of active physicians in 1970 to 32.3 percent in 1994.[13]

Specialization within medicine has clearly brought great benefits to the public, but the net effects of this process cut both ways. In a thoughtful paper discussing the division of labor within medicine, Menke in 1970 had this to say about specialization (equally true today):[14]

> Specialization is both a product of and a contributor to the scientific information explosion in medicine. It subdivides both doctor and patient, increases the difficulty of attaining a clear sense of medical identity for students and young physicians, and places additional strain on the traditional doctor-patient relationship. Specialization emphasizes the science of medicine and

[handwritten note:] ✱ "I am not resp. for the patient - I am responsible for his heart, lungs, ears, etc."

its rational processes in the treatment of disease and contributes to deper-
sonalization, aggravates patient anxieties, and implicitly encourages quack-
ery. It is probably the major factor disturbing traditional ethical and economic
patterns in medicine, and it dominates medical education and research and
medical practice, promotes jurisdictional disputes within the profession, and
weakens organizational strength and professional power.

GENERALIST-SPECIALIST MIX: THE ELUSIVE 50:50 GOAL

As we have seen, the late 1960s and early 1970s witnessed some major federal
initiatives to increase the number and geographic distribution of generalist clinicians, as increased demand for health services coincided with the passage of
Medicare and Medicaid and a perceived shortage of physicians. These initiatives included new training grant programs for family medicine, general internal medicine, and general pediatrics; sponsorship of nurse practitioner and
physician assistant training programs; creation of the National Health Service
Corps (NHSC); and an array of service-linked programs, including community
health centers and area health education centers.[15] However, no explicit policy
goal was set for the optimal generalist-specialist balance. The 50:50 goal finally
was established by the Council on Graduate Medical Education (COGME) in
its 1992 report, when it was obvious that the overproduction of physicians and
specialists had become a serious problem. In addition to setting the 50:50 goal,
COGME, in 1992, called for limitation of the number of federally funded first-
year residency positions to 110 percent of the number of U.S. medical graduates (to limit the influx of foreign medical graduates), doubling the number of
minority group medical students, and eliminating shortages of physicians in
underserved areas.[16]

In their excellent 1996 article, Marc Rivo and David Kindig reported the
results of the nation's efforts to increase the numbers of generalist physicians.
The results are discouraging:[16]

> From 1965 to 1992, the numbers of family physicians, general internists, and
> general pediatricians grew by only 13 percent (to 88 per 100,000 population),
> while the number of specialists increased by 121 percent (to 124 per 100,000)
> Over that same 27 year period, the proportion of generalists among all active
> physicians dropped from 51 percent to 35 percent. Of the 1990 graduates of
> U.S. medical schools, no more than 28 percent entered residency training
> and practice in generalist fields, far short of a 50 percent goal. Despite
> the addition of 125,000 new physicians entering the work force in the
> previous 10 years, the number of people without access to primary care
> physicians in urban and rural underserved areas continued to increase (even
> by a measure of 50 generalists per 100,000 population, only 1 generalist per
> 3,500 people).

The current and projected shortage of generalist physicians is especially acute
in underserved urban and rural areas. There are wide variations in the supply
of practicing physicians by specialty in rural and metropolitan areas. For
example, there now are only about 50 practicing generalist physicians in rural
(non-MSA) America (31 family practice, 13 general internal medicine, and 6

general pediatrics).[17] Among all specialties, family practice consistently has been demonstrated as the main specialty to locate and maintain practice in these underserved areas, which matches well with the need for generalists trained and prepared to provide primary care for patients of all ages.[18]

As part of the Balanced Budget Act of 1997 (BBA97), the U.S. Congress enacted various provisions intended to restrain the growth of residency positions and create new incentives for the training of generalist physicians. These provisions included a cap on the total number of residents partially funded through Medicare direct (DME) and indirect (IME) payments, a voluntary reduction program whereby hospitals could receive transition funding to hire replacement staff or redesign services as they reduced house staff positions, and new formulas to help support generalist residents in ambulatory and other non-hospital sites. Further adjustments were made in the Medicare Balanced Budget Refinement Act of 1999 (BBRA) to further assist primary care practice and rural teaching facilities,[19] but so far they have had little impact on either the generalist/specialist mix or the total number of physicians being trained. A September 2000 report from the AMA's Division of Graduate Medical Education concluded that[20]

> workforce projections and recommendations from COGME, while thorough and thoughtfully developed, have had little effect. Similarly, a consensus statement developed by six major professional organizations in 1996[21] to address the projected physician oversupply has not noticeably affected the size or balance of U.S. GME.

In an accompanying editorial, Jeremiah Barondess makes this important point, which has never yet been accepted as the overriding goal for the restructuring of graduate medical education:[22]

> Alteration of the structure of the health care system, including the physician workforce mix, can only be informed if the education and training system in medicine joins with the training program accreditation and board certification processes to come at these issues primarily through the lens of patient and population need, rather than the needs of the profession.

According to National Resident Matching Program (NRMP) data, the proportion of graduating medical students entering generalist residency positions has been about 30 percent in recent years. In their modeling study to estimate the future impact of today's generalist/specialist imbalance, Kindig and his colleagues made projections to the year 2040 based upon the proportion of U.S. medical graduates entering one of the three generalist specialties. At the 50 percent entry figure (unrealistic), a 50:50 balance is not achieved until 2040; at a 30 percent entry level, little progress is made; while at the 20 percent level, generalists even decline somewhat by 2040.[15] Figure 4-1 displays these hard facts.

What then is the likely impact on the capacity of U.S. generalist physicians to meet the health care needs of the public? Michael Whitcomb, with a long interest in physician supply issues and now senior vice president for medical education at the Association of American Medical Colleges (AAMC), makes a strong case that the number of physicians per 100,000 population is a much better policy guidepost than the 50:50 ratio. He points out that many health

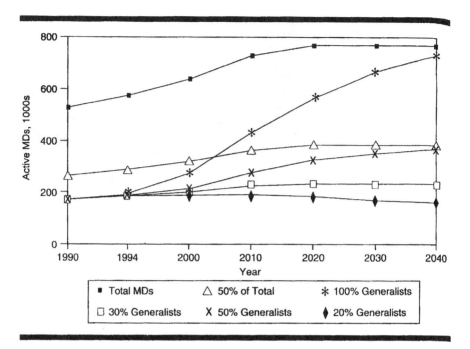

Figure 4-1 Projections of generalist physician supply, 1990–2040. (Reprinted with permission from Kindig DA, Cultice JM, Mullan F. The elusive generalist physician: Can we reach a 50% goal? *JAMA.* 1993;270:1069–1073.)

policy analysts conclude that about 65 generalist physicians for 100,000 population (1 per 1,500 people) is about right. This is the approximate generalist supply in the United Kingdom and most U.S. closed-panel HMOs.[23] By that measure (with the important caveat of geographic maldistribution issues), the present supply of generalists is not far off the mark but declines in future years unless 30 percent generalist production becomes the norm (Table 4-2).

In recent years, COGME has backed away from the 50:50 generalist/specialist goal in favor of projections based upon physician workforce needs measured in numbers per 100,000 population. In its eighth report (1996), COGME called for generalist requirements of 60 to 80 per 100,000 and for specialists between 85 and 105 per 100,000 (which sorts out as an approximate mix of 42:58 percent).[24] Those numbers were projected based in large part on the 1995 analysis of Sandy Gambliel, deputy chief of the Workforce Analysis and Research Branch of the Bureau of Health Professions, and her colleagues. They projected physician requirements for the generalist/specialist mix for the year 2020 based on their best estimates of managed care enrollments, the physician supply, and two scenarios: in Scenario A, 20 percent of medical graduates enter generalist practice; in Scenario B, COGME's proposal is fully implemented, so that 50 percent of U.S. medical graduates enter medical practice as generalists. By either scenario, there is a shortage of generalists (and a surplus of specialists) over the coming 20 years, as shown in Table 4-3.[25]

Table 4-2 Generalist and Specialist Availability per 100,000 Population, 1990–2040, Alternative Scenarios

			Year			
Projection	*1990*	*2000*	*2010*	*2020*	*2030*	*2040*
30% Generalists						
Generalists	69.5	75.0	79.7	79.8	77.5	76.8
Specialists	142.0	163.9	177.8	180.9	178.9	177.8
20% Generalists						
Generalists	69.5	69.9	67.8	62.4	56.0	53.2
Specialists	142.0	168.7	189.3	197.9	200.0	201.1
50% Generalists*						
Generalists	69.5	79.7	97.9	109.5	116.8	123.5
Specialists	142.0	159.7	160.3	151.9	140.3	131.8

* Denotes percentage of graduates after 1993 who are assumed to be practicing as generalists 10 years after graduation.
Source: Reprinted with permission from Kindig DA, Cultice JM, Mullan F. The elusive generalist physician: Can we reach a 50% goal? *JAMA*. 1993;270:1072.

Table 4-3 Projected Physician Requirements with Projected Supply of Generalists and Specialists in 2020

	Requirements		*Supply*		*Supply Minus Requirements*	
	Number	*Ratio per 100,000*	*Number*	*Ratio per 100,000*	*Number*	*Ratio per 100,000*
Scenario A						
Total patient care	563,000	173	674,000	207	111,000	34
Generalists	263,000	81	178,000	55	−85,000	−26
Specialists	300,000	92	496,000	152	196,000	60
Scenario B						
Total patient care	563,000	173	619,000	190	56,000	17
Generalists	263,000	81	264,000	81	1,000	0
Specialists	300,000	92	355,000	109	55,000	17

Source: Bureau of Health Professions' managed care analysis forecast. Adapted with permission from Gambliel S, Politzer RM, Rivo ML, Mullan F. Managed care on the march: Will physicians meet the challenge? *Health Aff (Millwood)*. 1995;14(2):137.

Under the best of circumstances, projections for an optimal mix of generalists and specialists within the physician workforce are fraught with problems. What, for example, will be the long-term impact of women in medicine in terms of productivity? The proportion of women in most medical schools is now approximately 50 percent, and many female physicians opt for part-time or shared practices. Other important variables include changes in retirement ages of physicians, the impact of new technologies, and changing trends in rates of subspecialization in internal medicine and pediatrics (currently estimated to be about 40 percent and 20 percent, respectively).[26]

GENERALISM, SPECIALISM, AND THE HEALTH CARE SYSTEM

What's so bad about having too many specialists? That question has generated intense debate within the medical profession and other quarters for many years. Beyond the intuitively obvious answer (at least to me) that a generalist base is the most logical foundation for a health care system (as reflected by such countries as England and Canada), four major reasons filter out of the smoke of debate: (1) decreased quality of care, (2) increased cost of care, (3) decreased patient satisfaction, and (4) decreased physician satisfaction. Stephen Schroeder, now president of the Robert Wood Johnson Foundation and an internist with an extensive background in practice and teaching as well as long-term interest in health policy, makes a strong case that all four measures are negatively affected by a growing oversupply of specialists.[21]

The terms of this debate pit the three primary care specialties against all the others, each side bringing its own perceptions and biases to the dialogue. Primary care physicians are trained and committed to all elements of primary care as defined by the Institute of Medicine (IOM) during the late 1970s and more recently updated in their book, *Primary Care: America's Health in a New Era* (1996). The current definition put forward by the IOM's Committee on the Future of Primary Care:[13]

> Primary care is the provision of integrated, accessible health care services by clinicians who are accountable for addressing a large majority of personal health care needs, developing a sustained partnership with patients, and practicing in the context of family and community. The critical elements of primary care include:
>
> - integrated and accessible health care services;
> - services provided by primary care clinicians—generally considered to be physicians, nurse practitioners, and physician assistants—but involving a broader array of individuals in a primary care team;
> - accountability of clinicians and systems for quality of care, patient satisfaction, efficient use of resources, and ethical behavior;
> - the majority of personal health care needs, which include physical, mental, emotional, and social concerns;
> - a sustained partnership between patients and clinicians; and
> - primary care in the context of family and community.

As soon as primary care was defined, of course, many specialties rushed forward to claim their share of the primary care role. The most humorous example of that in my experience was an academic pathologist in Minnesota during the 1970s who, tongue in cheek, claimed to be a "family pathologist" (with you from birth to death). The next definition, urged especially by specialist groups, became "principal care," which refers to continuous care of a regular patient whereby that physician provides most of the patient's care. Thus, a nephrologist or oncologist may provide principal care to a patient over years with chronic renal disease or cancer but still fall short of the IOM's definition of the essential elements of primary care—accessibility, comprehensiveness, coordination, continuity, and accountability.

The IOM's 1996 report on primary care pulled together the findings of many studies showing that specialist services are more costly, less comprehensive, and less accessible for a broad range of complaints presented by patients than primary care physicians.[13] Many studies have shown that primary care physicians use fewer resources, fewer technologies, and admit to the hospital less frequently than specialists. There have been fewer comparative studies of quality of care, particularly outcomes, and their findings are somewhat mixed. The largest study to date, the national Medical Outcomes Study, showed that specialist care outcomes for hypertension and diabetes mellitus are no better than care provided by generalists.[27] On the other hand, a recent systematic review of the quality of care literature showed better knowledge and quality of care by specialists when practicing within their own domain, including superior outcomes in some studies for such problems as acute myocardial infarction and asthma.[28] The complexity of the impact of specialism on quality of care is well illustrated by this observation by Schroeder:[29]

> Quality of care suffers when surgeons and other procedure-oriented specialists have insufficient patient volume to hone their skills and judgment. Abundant anecdotal and statistical evidence suggests that many specialists, especially those in large metropolitan areas, have a very low frequency of performing the "bread and butter" procedures in their specialty. Quality is also impaired when specialists are forced to do general care to take up slack time, if their temperament or education is not suited to care outside their specialty. It may not be coincidental that the United States has both the highest ratio of certain specialties per population and the first or second most expensive medical care system in the world. The high rates of operations and procedures in the United States certainly include some that are unnecessary and whose costs contribute to high medical bills. There is essentially no waiting period for surgery (at least for insured patients), except for those awaiting organ transplantation. Thus, to the extent that physicians can induce demand by performing procedures that may not be indicated, reducing the numbers of specialists might both decrease costs and enhance quality of care. In addition, the patient's satisfaction is related to interactions with his physician, and it seems reasonable that these interactions might be more pleasant if the physician providing general care had chosen to do so, rather than being forced to do so for economic reasons. For the same reasons, physicians are probably most satisfied with their work when they are doing what they had chosen to do in the first place.

Considerable interest has focused on the extent to which a "hidden system" of primary care (i.e., principal care by specialists) addresses actual needs for primary care. Very little is known about that, but a 1998 study by Roger Rosenblatt and his colleagues in Washington State sheds some light on the question. They evaluated the extent of primary care services received by 373,505 Medicare beneficiaries in terms of three outcome measures: (1) which special-

ists accounted for the majority of visits by patients over a year's time (a continuity measure), (2) what services were provided outside of their domain (comprehensiveness measure), and (3) was influenza vaccination given. They found
that these patients averaged 7.48 outpatient visits per year, with 14.7 percent
seeing only specialists. About one half of all ambulatory visits to family physicians and general internists represented a majority of outpatient care for those
patients, compared to 21 percent of visits to medical specialists and 11.7 percent
of visits to surgical specialists.[30] Although some specialties provided some services outside of their specialty (especially pulmonologists, general surgeons,
and gynecologists), little evidence was found that most specialists assume a real
primary care generalist role.

There are many reasons to expect that specialists are more effective within
their own domains of knowledge, skill, and experience, as is equally true for
generalist physicians in their domain. Harold Sox, a general internist with a
long interest in clinical decision making, has done some interesting comparative studies of the diagnostic decision-making process of subspecialists and
primary care physicians. He described very different clinical circumstances for
each group, as summarized in Table 4-4.[31] Not only are patient expectations
different for a specialist visit compared to a primary care visit, but the patient
population and clinical experience of the two kinds of physicians are vastly different. In a classic article on sample selection and the natural history of disease,
Ellenberg and Nelson found, for example, that hospital clinic studies (mostly
referral clinics) report much higher rates of recurrent seizures after previous
febrile seizures in children compared with population-based studies.[32] The
primary care physician sees a different patient population than the consulting
specialist, often with a lower probability of disease and at earlier stages of
disease, so it is not surprising that their practice styles are quite different.

Walter Rosser of the Department of Family and Community Medicine at the
University of Toronto added to our understanding of these differences by his
literature review of differences in diagnostic approach taken by primary care
physicians and specialists. He found that available studies reflected the differences shown in Figure 4-2. Each type of physician brings a different level of
knowledge about the patient to a given patient visit, as well as experience with
a different prevalence of disease.[33]

Table 4-4   Characteristics of Physicians That May Affect Decision-Making Style

Primary Care Physician	Referral Physician
Deals with multiple problems and diffuse complaints	Asked to focus on one problem
	Brief relationship
Longitudinal partnerships	Relative stranger
Knows the patient's character	Asked to solve the problem
Knows the psychological setting of illness	Intermediate to high probabilities of disease
Knows pattern of health complaints	
Can tolerate uncertainty	
All probabilities of disease	

Source: Reprinted with permission from Sox HC. Decision-making: A comparison of referral practice and primary care. *J Fam Pract.* 1996;42:156.

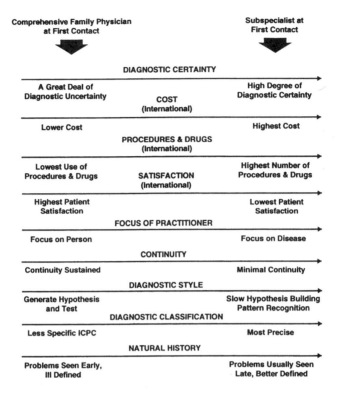

Figure 4-2   The continuum of a first point of contact with the health care system. (Reprinted with permission from Rosser WW. Approach to diagnosis by primary care clinicians and specialists: Is there a difference? *J Fam Pract.* 1996;42:140.)

The process of specialization and subspecialization, in recent years, has progressed way beyond the bounds of existing specialty disciplines and certifying boards. Some new areas of specialist practice may be more market driven (e.g., hospitalists, pain, or sleep disorder specialists), others cut across all disciplinary lines in their focus on molecular biology (e.g., medical genetics and genome mapping). Figure 4-3 shows the rapid growth curve for both AMA- and ACGME-accredited programs and American Board of Medical Specialties certificates, while Table 4-5 lists an additional large number of self-designated practice specialties as reported to the AMA.[34]

SPECIALIZATION AND MANAGED CARE

All health policy analysts agree that managed care requires a higher proportion of generalist physicians and a lower proportion of specialists. Although these needs may vary somewhat from closed-panel HMOs to other managed care arrangements, the rapidly changing marketplace already has confirmed the high-priority need for more generalists and fewer specialists. The 25th anniversary

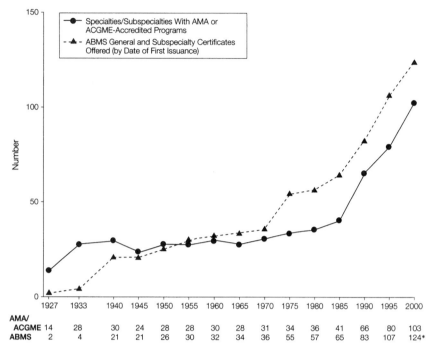

Figure 4-3 Growth of graduate medical education accreditation and certification, 1927–2000. AMA, American Medical Association; ACGME, Accreditation Council for Graduate Medical Education; and ABMS, American Board of Medical Specialties. Asterisk indicates 12 certificates approved but not issued. (Reprinted with permission from Donini-Lenhoff FG, Hedrick HL. Growth of specialization in graduate medical education. *JAMA.* 2000;284:1284–1289.)

of the Institute of Medicine featured a symposium addressing future health care needs, including projections for required changes in the physician workforce likely to emerge between now and the year 2020. Its excellent report, *2020 Vision: Health Care in the 21st Century* (1996), exemplifies the rethinking of the health care system and its workforce which is required. Eugene O'Neil, codirector of the Center for the Health Professions at the University of California, San Francisco, and executive director of the Pew Health Professions Commission, observed that, "we have essentially a set of 19th century work rules operating in a 21st century institution" (which is dominated by supply) and "medicine is overly focused on individual practitioners providing clinical service to individual patients who present with acute care treatment needs."[35] He called for restructuring of the physician workforce by specialty and function to meet a new set of rules and values in the new health care system demanded by the public and purchasers of health services. These values are especially necessary to deliver health care of higher quality and better outcome, at lower cost, and with increased patient satisfaction. Table 4-6 shows a remarkable concordance of the 10 most-important managed care competency areas, based on a recent study of residency directors and managed care medical directors.[36]

Table 4-5   American Medical Association Self-designated Practice Specialties/Areas of Practice Without Identical Counterparts in the Accreditation Council for Graduate Medical Education or American Board of Medical Specialties (ABMS) Populations

Abdominal surgery	Neurology/diagnostic radiology/neuroradiology
Addiction medicine	Nutrition
Allergy	Obstetrics
Clinical pharmacology	Palliative medicine
Dermatologic surgery	Pediatric allergy[a]
Diabetes	Pediatric cardiothoracic surgery
Epidemiology	Pediatric ophthalmology
Facial plastic surgery	Pediatric surgery (neurology)
General practice	Pharmaceutical medicine
Gynecology	Proctology[b]
Head and neck surgery	Psychoanalysis
Hepatology	Sleep medicine
Hospitalist	Sports medicine (physical medicine and rehabilitation)
Immunology	Surgical oncology
Internal medicine/pediatrics	Transplant surgery
Legal medicine	Trauma surgery
Medical management	Vascular medicine

[a] The ABMS issued pediatric allergy and immunology certificates from 1944 to 1971.

[b] The ABMS issued proctology certificates from 1940 to 1956.

Source: Reprinted with permission from Donini-Lenhoff FG, Hedrick HL. Growth of specialization in graduate medical education. *JAMA*. 2000;284:1288.

Table 4-6   Ten Most Important Managed Care Competency Areas

	Rank of Competency Areas	
Competency Areas	Residency Program Directors (n = 140)	Managed Care Medical Directors (n = 147)
Time management	1	4
Case management	2	1
Ethics	3	3
Practice guidelines	4	5
Evidence-based medicine	5	20
Cost-effective clinical decision making	6	8
Clinical epidemiology	7	10
Disease management	8	9
Referral management	9	6
Patient satisfaction	10	7
Practice profiling	12	2

Note: Competency areas shown are those to which the highest-rated managed care tasks belong. There were no significant differences in mean importance among the 10 highest-rated tasks. However, as a group, these 10 tasks were rated significantly more important than the remaining 16 tasks ($p < .001$ by paired t tests with Bonferroni adjustment). Overall $F_{25,247} = 32.37$; $p < .001$ by within-subjects analysis of variance.

Source: Reprinted with permission from Yedidia MJ, Gillespie CC, Moore GT. Specific clinical competencies for managed care. Views of residency directors and managed care medical directors. *JAMA*. 2000;284:1097.

SPECIALTIES UNDER SIEGE

Returning to the IOM symposium looking forward to a restructured health care system in a new century, there is wide agreement that we have too many physicians as well as a mismatch, by type, to the needs of the evolving system. Health care analysts are in general agreement that the medical profession should be downsized (*right sized* is the more acceptable euphemism). Most observers believe that the profession should be reoriented on a primary care paradigm, which already has taken place in the managed care marketplace.

A much larger perspective seems to be needed to envision how the nation's physician workforce needs to be restructured. Rosemary Stevens, widely regarded as the country's leading historian and student of specialization in American medicine, sees the present structure of specialty boards and organizations besieged by jurisdictional issues, on the one hand, and new cross-cutting fields (e.g., nuclear medicine), on the other. Her overview is instructive:[37]

> By the 1990s, the profession was facing the challenge of redefining itself, in relation not only to the growing power of organizations (insurers, employers, regulators) but also to an expanded domain of public interest in what doctors do. This double sense of outside "ownership" of the medical role was reflected in movements as diverse as consumer rights in the health system, the rise of bioethics as a new discipline whose practitioners were often not physicians, the development and use of clinical practice guidelines and limits on care as models for medical decision making (side by side with the acceptance of shared decision making by doctor and patient), and the sheer familiarity of the medical world to the public at large. The great expansion of medical information on the Internet in the 1990s made everyone potentially an instant expert. Today debates in the press range from physician assisted suicide, through limits on time spent in hospital for childbirth or mastectomy, to proposed changes in coverage under Medicare. Research both defines and reflects the changing scene.

O'Neill argued for the creation of new relationships within primary care as well as with specialty care. One of his recommendations is to develop a single pathway to a generalist's career in medicine, which would represent a unification of the existing primary care specialties and still allow for some specialization by age group or even by gender of patients served.[35] In many practice environments, the most commonly demanded generalist would likely be a generalist closer to the family practice model, but there has to be flexibility on that point, if only because of supply and demand issues. For example, even though the growth of family practice as a specialty has been remarkable over the last 30 years, AMA data show that the overall proportion of physicians in general or family practice dropped from about 18 percent to 12 percent of all office-based U.S. physicians between 1970 and 1995. Furthermore, almost one half of today's generalist physicians are general internists, and residency positions in internal medicine account for the largest single specialty by far within the U.S. graduate medical education establishment.

Although some have called for greater collaboration among the primary care disciplines and even working toward a single generalist pathway,[38–40] very little progress has been made along this line. Specialty boards and organizations generally are well entrenched and serve as "tribes" to their constituents. At the start of a new century, although there may be cordial relationships in many institutions, the three generalist specialties (family practice, general internal medicine, and general pediatrics) usually are more competitive than collaborative, conduct parallel but mostly separate training programs, and read parallel but separate literature. It is remarkable how high the fences between specialties can be while their clinical functions and values are so similar. (A visitor from Mars would be surprised and confounded.)

CONCLUDING COMMENTS

The nation's specialty-dominated medical education system has not been effective in addressing a distorted imbalance between generalists and specialists. The medical education establishment never was driven primarily by the needs of the population in a rational health care system. A surplus of specialists has been trained, which developed its own demand for services. With the emergence of managed care in a more competitive marketplace in recent years, however, countervailing forces are starting to move toward redistribution by specialty.

Since we have been so ineffectual within medicine in anticipating and recharting our own course, we have much to learn from our informed outside critics. Consider the view of Walter Benjamin in a hard-hitting 1989 essay in *The New England Journal of Medicine*:[41]

> The American Medical Association was born in the middle of the 19th century, when almost all physicians were general practitioners, virtually indistinguishable from one another. Now with more than 100 specialties and subspecialties, the center of the medical profession is not holding. Aside from the MD degree, what do a psychiatrist and a pathologist have in common? A public health physician and an anesthesiologist? A specialist in nuclear medicine and an ophthalmologist?

Concerning the indefinite and crucial need for a generalist base in medicine, the perspective of Ed Pellegrino, internist and medical philosopher, is on target:[39]

> no matter what happens to technology, politics, economics, and even medicine, the human need for a physician who can "put it all together" will survive. The generalist meets a fundamental unchanging need of sick persons. Indeed, specialization, which so many regard as the nemesis of general medicine, is the most potent reason for its permanence.

An excellent health care system requires a strong specialist sector as well as a solid primary care base, with fluid collegial and cooperative interrelationships between the two and both working in the best interests of individual patients and populations being served. The United States still has a predominant specialist sector with a primary care base insufficient to meet the needs of the entire population for primary care physicians. The restructuring of the nation's physician workforce should be based on the needs of the entire population for health care that is accessible, affordable, and of the best quality that collective resources will permit. Other factors that will play a large part in rationalizing the future physician workforce, to be discussed in later chapters, include barriers to access to care (Chapter 8), changing paradigms of care (Chapter 10), attributes of other health care systems with quality of care outcomes superior to the United States (Chapter 18), and definition of *medical necessity* (Chapter 21).

REFERENCES

1. Knouss RF. Health manpower—The right kind. In: *Health Manpower Issues*. Department of Health, Education and Welfare Publication No. (HRA) 76-40, Government Printing Office, 1976:17–18.
2. Margotta R. *The Story of Medicine*. New York: Golden Press, 1968:25.
3. Canfield PR. Family medicine: An historical perspective. *J Med Educ*. 1976;51:904.
4. Shaw WJ. Evolution of a specialty. *JAMA*. 1963;186:575.
5. Greenwood G, Frederickson RF. *Specialization in the Medical and Legal Professions*. Chicago: Gallaghan Company, 1964:45.
6. Engel G. Care and feeding of the medical student. *JAMA*. 1971;215:1135.
7. Silver GA. Family practice: Resuscitation or reform? *JAMA*. 1963;185:188.
8. What's ahead? *Med Economics*. 1969 (September 2, 1969):16.
9. *Health Is a Community Affair. The Report of the National Commission on Community Health Services*. Cambridge, MA: Harvard University Press, 1966.
10. *The Graduate Education of Physicians: The Report of the Citizens Commission of Graduate Medical Education*. Chicago: American Medical Association, 1966:40.
11. *Meeting the Challenge of Family Practice. The Report of the Ad Hoc Committee on Education for Family Practice of the Council on Medical Education*. Chicago: American Medical Association, 1966:1.
12. Editorial: The core content of family medicine, report of the committee on requirements for certification. *GP*. 1966;34:225.
13. Donaldson MS, Yordy KD, Vanselow NA. *Primary Care: America's Health in a New Era*. Washington DC: National Academy Press, 1996.
14. Menke WG. Divided labor: The doctor as specialist. *Ann Intern Med*. 1970;72:943.
15. Kindig DA, Cultice JM, Mullan F. The elusive generalist physician: Can we reach a 50% goal? *JAMA*. 1993;270:1069–1073.
16. Rivo MC, Kindig DA. A report card on the physician work force in the United States. *N Engl J Med*. 1996;334:892–896.
17. Colwill JM, Cultice J. *Increasing Numbers of Family Physicians—Implications for Rural America. Update on the Physician Workforce*. Washington, DC: Council on Graduate Medical Education, U.S. Department of Health and Human Services, Public Health Service, Health Resources and Services Administration, 2000.
18. Council on Graduate Medical Education. *Physician Distribution and Health Care Challenges in Rural and Inner City Areas*. Washington, DC: U.S. Department of Health and Human Services, Public Health Service, Health Resources and Services Administration, 1998.
19. Council on Graduate Medical Education. *The Effects of the Balanced Budget Act of 1997 on Graduate Medical Education*. Washington, DC: U.S. Department of Health and Human Services, Public Health Service, Health Resources and Services Administration, 2000.
20. Brotherton SE, Simon FA, Tomany SC. U.S. graduate medical education, 1999–2000. *JAMA*. 2000;284:1121–1126.
21. Mitka M. Consensus panel offers response to oversupply. *American Medical News*. February 24, 1997:1.
22. Barondess JA. Specialization and the physician workforce: Drivers and determinants. *JAMA*. 2000;284:1301.
23. Whitcomb M. Family medicine in Canada: Where have all the physicians gone? *Can Fam Physician*. 1999;45:2015–2016.

24. Council on Graduate Medical Education. *Patient Care Physician Supply and Requirements: Testing COGME Recommendations.* Washington, DC: U.S. Department of Health and Human Services, Public Health Service, Health Resources and Services Administration, 1996.

25. Gambliel S, Politzer RM, Rivo ML, Mullan F. Managed care on the march: Will physicians meet the challenge? *Health Aff (Millwood).* 1995;14(2):132–142.

26. Colwill JM. Personal communication. November 2, 2000.

27. Greenfield S, Rogers W, Mangotich M, et al. Outcomes of patients with hypertension and non-insulin dependent diabetes mellitus treated by different systems and specialties. Results from the Medical Outcomes Study. *JAMA.* 1995;274:1436–1444.

28. Harrold LR, Field TS, Gurwitz JH. Knowledge, patterns of care, and outcomes of care for generalists and specialists. *J Gen Intern Med.* 1999;14:499–511.

29. Schroeder SA. The making of a medical generalist. *Health Aff (Millwood).* 1985;4(2):22–46.

30. Rosenblatt RA, Hart LG, Baldwin LM, Chan L, Schneeweiss R. The generalist role of specialty physicians: Is there a hidden system of primary care? *JAMA.* 279:1364–1370.

31. Sox HC. Decision-making: A comparison of referral practice and primary care. *J Fam Pract.* 1996;42:155–160.

32. Ellenberg JH, Nelson KB. Sample selection and the natural history of disease: Studies of febrile seizures. *JAMA.* 1980;243:1337–1340.

33. Rosser WW. Approach to diagnosis by primary care clinicians and specialists: Is there a difference? *J Fam Pract.* 1996;42:139–144.

34. Donini-Lenhoff FG, Hedrick HL. Growth of specialization in graduate medical education. *JAMA.* 2000;284:1284–1289.

35. O'Neill EH. The workforce for health. In: Institute of Medicine. *2020 Vision: Health in the 21st Century.* Washington DC: National Academy Press, 1996:95.

36. Yedidia MJ, Gillespie CC, Moore GT. Specific clinical competencies for managed care. Views of residency directors and managed care medical directors. *JAMA.* 2000;284:1093–1098.

37. Stevens R. *American Medicine and the Public Interest. A History of Specialization.* Berkeley: University of California Press, 1998:xxv.

38. Benson JA Jr. Isn't it time for one family of generalists? *J Am Board Fam Pract.* 1990; (3; suppl):29S–37S.

39. Pellegrino ED. Medical education: Time for change—yes—but—. *J Am Board Fam Pract.* 1990;3(suppl):55S–63S.

40. Geyman JP. Training primary care physicians for the 21st century. *JAMA.* 1986;255:2631–2635.

41. Benjamin WW. Will centrifugal forces destroy the medical profession? *N Engl J Med.* 1989;32:1191–1192.

5
Increased Public Expectations and Patients' Rights

Americans think of illness and disability as a condition that can be fixed by an expert, in this case a physician. Accordingly, they want more medicine, more research, and more physicians—all with a lower cost and equitable distribution. This was the case in 1930 and it is still the case today at century's end. However, the fact that each individual is ultimately responsible for the maintenance of his or her own health is a lesson that most Americans still need to learn.

Eli Ginzberg, 1999[1]

One of the most profound changes in U.S. health care in recent decades is the sea change in public expectations and empowerment of patients, particularly since the advent of the Great Society programs of the 1960s. These changes have transformed the dynamics of the doctor-patient relationship, often leaving patients and physicians buffeted by forces beyond their control.

In his excellent book, *Life Without Disease: The Pursuit of Medical Utopia*, William Schwartz observes that a revolution had taken place by 1970, with about 80 percent of Americans with some kind of health insurance covering about 50 percent of health care costs.[2] In his words:[2]

> This increase in coverage led to a change in the public's attitude toward health services. The newly insured no longer had any incentive to moderate their demands on the health care system but instead demanded the best the system could offer. And physicians, for their part, felt free to err routinely on the side of over-treating, in some instances to enhance their own income and in others to protect themselves against the perceived threat of malpractice suits (practicing so-called "defensive medicine").

Instead of feeling much financial limitations in their choice of health care services, patients increasingly expected someone else to pay for them. They now expected the latest of technology, regardless how small or uncertain the benefit, and resisted any efforts to limit services by their insurance plans or government programs.[3]

61

Two other factors add to the way in which the public views health care today: (1) the public's growing disenchantment with allopathic medicine, as noted in the last chapter, and (2) the advent of the Information Age, whereby patients can feel expert on their medical problems after a few hours on the Internet. Recent years have seen a radical shift in health care consumerism. Yankelovich Partners conducts an annual "credibility" study of major social institutions in America for *Time* magazine. These studies have shown that public confidence in physicians and the health care system dropped precipitously after the October 1987 stock market crash from a confidence level above 50 percent to about 22 percent, where it has remained since then.[4]

Against this background, this chapter will further examine four key areas: (1) the public perception of health care as a right; (2) patient expectations, attitudes, and preferences; (3) patients' satisfaction with their health care; and (4) efforts to codify patients' rights.

HEALTH CARE AS A RIGHT

The right to health care has been an intensely debated topic for over 50 years in industrialized Western nations among policy makers, legislators, economists, ethicists, and others. It has been subject to various interpretations and degrees of implementation from one country to another. A brief overview of some international markers in this debate provides useful perspective to understanding the ongoing debate in the United States.

Health care has been recognized as a right since 1948 by virtue of the Universal Declaration of Human Rights as adopted by the General Assembly of the United Nations. Article 25 of that document provides that[5]

> Everyone has the right to a standard of living adequate for the health and well-being of himself and his family, including food, clothing, housing and *medical care* and necessary social services, and the right to security in the event of unemployment, *sickness*, disability, widowhood, old age or other lack of livelihood in circumstances beyond his control.

This right to health care was later adopted, as well, by the World Health Organization (WHO) in its Declaration on the Rights of Patients.[6] Note that these are very broad definitions of health. The WHO defined *health* as "a state of complete physical, mental, and social well-being and not merely the absence of disease or infirmity"[7] and established a goal for "the attainment by all people of the highest possible level of health."[8]

There has even been an effort to apply the principles of the International Declaration of Human Rights into binding treaty obligations. Therefore, Article 12 of the International Covenant on Economic, Social, and Cultural Rights recognizes "the right of everyone to the enjoyment of the highest available standard of physical and mental health."[8,9]

Despite the lofty language of these international documents, the reality of access to health care varies somewhat from one country to another. The United States, however, is the "odd man out" in being virtually the only developed nation in the world that does not assure universal access to medical care.[10]

As is discussed further in Chapter 20, five unsuccessful attempts were made during the 20th century to establish universal access to health care in the United States: in 1912, the 1930s, the 1960s, the 1970s, and most recently the failed Clinton Health Plan of 1994. In the individualistic American culture, however, there so far has been too much distrust and opposition to enactment of a national health plan assuring universal coverage. Instead, as the debate has gone on, patchwork efforts have been made to provide access to health care for subgroups of the population. Medicare and Medicaid, of course, were the first such examples. Later examples include the right of convicted and confined prison inmates to adequate medical care[11] and the right to psychiatric treatment for involuntarily committed patients with mental disorders.[12] Federal legislation through the Consolidated Omnibus Reconciliation Act of 1985 required all hospitals receiving Medicare reimbursement to provide emergency care, including appropriate transfer if necessary. In addition, over one half of the states have enacted legislation requiring all general hospitals to provide emergency care as a condition of their licensure.[13]

Despite such legislation, these measures often have fallen short of their intent. Many observers noted the common disconnects; Ruth Roemer, for example, noted two such shortfalls: "entitlement without availability (e.g., physicians refusing Medicaid patients) and availability without entitlement (e.g., hospitals turning away the uninsured)."[8] Furthermore, legislative statutes frequently proved difficult or impossible to enforce. In Alabama, for example, a federal court monitor was established to enforce minimal constitutional standards for treatment of the mentally ill. The state legislature, however, never provided appropriate funding for the state hospitals and the monitor's office was closed.[14]

As an ethicist at the University of Notre Dame, Larry Churchill brought useful insights and wisdom to the matter of health care as a right in his book *Rationing Health Care in America: Perceptions and Principles of Justice*. He makes these thoughtful observations:[15]

> There is a moral right to health care, but not of the sort often claimed. It is a right grounded not in purchasing power, merit, or social worth, but in human need. The right to health care finds its rationale in a social concept of the self, in a sense of common humanity, and in a knowledge of common vulnerability to disease and death.
>
> ... A right to health care based on need means a right to equitable access based on need alone to all effective care society can reasonably afford.
>
> ... A right to health care is not a license to demand care. It is not a right to the very best available, or even to all one may need. Some very pressing health needs may have to be neglected because meeting them would be unreasonable in the light of other health needs or social priorities. Health care is unique among needs and should enjoy a high place among our basic requirements for life. This does not mean that it should displace all else. My right to a kidney transplant, say, is circumscribed by a wide variety of factors which are ultimately decisions for society to make about the importance of this procedure: the number of qualified surgeons it trains, the network for histological matching it supports, the decision to have optional or assumptive kidney donor policies, and on and on.

Today, the concept of health care as an entitlement, desired by many in the United States, remains an abstraction. It cannot be legislated without major structural reforms of the health care system. Part of the impasse is due to the lack of clarity of what such a system would look like, what it would cost, and what tradeoffs would be required of individual patients to assure the viability of universal access to care.[16]

PATIENTS' EXPECTATIONS, ATTITUDES, AND PREFERENCES

Driven especially by the growing awareness of public dissatisfaction with managed care and other issues relating to health care, a number of major public opinion polls have been carried out by policy-related research organizations. One recent group of studies sheds considerable light on current American attitudes toward health care, health resources, the uninsured, and the role of government in health care. This group of studies includes five surveys designed by researchers at the Harvard School of Public Health for the Robert Wood Johnson Foundation, each involving telephone interviews during 1999 of random national samples of 1,000 to 1,200 adults. Other studies in this group involved the Roper Center for Public Opinion Research, the Henry J. Kaiser Family Foundation, and the Employee Benefit Research Institute (EBRI) as well as the *National Journal*'s cloakroom polling websites. In each instance, the sampling error for all these studies ranged between 3 and 5 percent.[17]

Table 5-1 displays respondents' changing health care priorities from 1993 to 1999. Cost remains the most important single issue, while concerns about

Table 5-1   American's Health Care Priorities, 1993 and 1999

	1993	1999
Most important issue		
Cost	42	34
People not covered by health insurance	35	31
Quality of care	14	26
All equally important (vol.)	7	8
Among those choosing quality of care		
Doctors and hospitals do a bad job of treating patients	*	13
Health plans and HMOs make it too hard for people to get care	*	74
Neither (vol.)	*	2
Both (vol.)	*	6
Don't know	*	5

Notes: "Vol." means that a response was volunteered. HMO is health maintenance organization.

Sources: *NBC News/Wall Street Journal* poll (March 1993); and Harvard School of Public Health/Robert Wood Johnson Foundation/International Communications Research poll (May 1999). Reprinted with permission from Blendon RJ, Young JT, DesRoches CM. The uninsured, the working uninsured, and the public. *Health Aff (Millwood).* 1999;18(6):205.

quality of care have increased considerably over that six-year period, with some negative views about health plans and HMOs concerning access to care.[17]

When asked about their understanding of the problems of the uninsured (the percentage of nonelderly Americans without health insurance rose from 14.8 percent in 1987 to 18.3 percent in 1997), most respondents were not aware of the extent of this problem. In addition, in 1999, 57 percent of the respondents felt that the uninsured could receive needed care anyway from physicians and hospitals, and about one half expressed opposition to increased taxes and any major governmental solution to the problem.[17]

This same group of studies revealed some interesting findings concerning employer-based health insurance. About two thirds of the respondents in 1996 felt that health benefits were by far the most important employee benefit[17] and 75 percent of the employed respondents reported that they preferred their employers to purchase their health insurance rather than receive additional wages and purchase coverage themselves.[18] When asked their opinions about two possible private-sector responses to the problem of uninsurance, respondents were evenly divided (in 1993 as well as 1999) as to the options of required employer coverage versus individual tax credits. Based on the results of these studies all together, Robert Blendon and his colleagues concluded that there is more public support for strengthening the present system (even if a two-track system) than for dismantling the system, particularly since 64.2 percent of working Americans and their families today have employer-based health insurance coverage.[17] As we shall see in later chapters, this conclusion is open to serious question.

Shifting from attitudes toward health insurance and the health care system to patients' expectations in their choice of physician, it comes as no surprise that a caring attitude and communication skills are the leading factors considered in this choice. This has been true for years, and an opinion poll in 1998 showed this to be a continuing pattern,[19] not unexpected as the process of health care becomes more regulated and impersonal (Figure 5-1).

PATIENT SATISFACTION AND THE EXTENT OF CHOICE

There is an increasing body of evidence that the extent of choice available to individuals in their choice of health plans plays an important role in their satisfaction or dissatisfaction with health care.[20] Unfortunately, however, survey estimates have shown that 44 to 58 percent of U.S. workers have no choice of plans.[21] In an effort to better understand how the matter of choice plays out, a national study was done by Princeton Survey Research Associates with a survey design developed by researchers at the Henry J. Kaiser Family Foundation and Harvard University. This telephone survey involved a random sample of 1,204 employed adults less than 65 years of age, with a response rate of 49 percent and a potential sampling error of 3 percent.[22]

In this survey, the first finding was that 42 percent of respondents had no choice at all of health plans. Especially striking in these results is the correlation with income level, with 65 percent of those with annual incomes less than $10,000 the most vulnerable, lacking any choice (Table 5-2).[22]

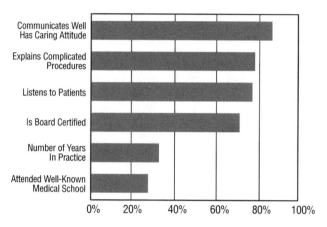

Figure 5-1 Factors influencing choice of physician. Note: N = 800 registered voters surveyed October 17–23, 1998. Source: Public Opinion Strategies. (Reprinted with permission from Factors influencing choice of physician. *Fam Pract News*. 1999;29(2):1.)

Other findings of this survey provide solid evidence that the less choice the respondents had in their choice of health plans, the higher was their dissatisfaction with these plans and their health care. Table 5-3 breaks down their responses in terms of kinds of dissatisfaction by extent of choice of health plans.[22]

Based on this study, the investigators confirmed how important choice is in selection of health plans by individuals but still wondered why those who chose managed care still had negative perceptions about that choice. They speculated that patients may choose managed care for cost reasons but then are unhappy because of restrictions of services.[22] This is consistent with Eddy's view of today's public expectations about health care—wanting the cake but eating it, too.[3]

Two other recent studies provide further insight into patients' perceptions about their choices in managed care plans. In one study of 8,394 patients enrolled in such plans, Kevin Grumbach and his colleagues found that 94 percent of patients valued having a primary care physician who knew their medical problems, but 46 percent felt they should be able to decide on their own whether to see a specialist without the need for a "gatekeeper" decision by the primary care physician.[23] Another study explored respondents' attitudes toward the extent to which they could choose their own providers, whether the choice be a primary care physician from an insurance company list, a specialist by referral only, or a nurse instead of a physician as a primary care provider. The responses were mixed in each case, with about one third of respondents minding a lot, another one third minding little, and the remaining one third minding not at all these restrictions in choice. As expected, those minding a lot were the most vulnerable, including the elderly, patients in poor health, and those with ischemic heart disease.[24]

Table 5-2 Percentage of Americans Reporting That They Had No Choice of Health Plans By Selected Variables, 1997

Variable	Had No Choice[a]
Total sample ($N = 761$)[b]	42%
Dependent status	
Has a dependent child	43
Does not have a dependent child	41
Insurance type	
Heavy managed care	37[c]
Light managed care	41
Traditional insurance	53
Whether employer forced a change in plan in past 5 years	
Forced to change plans	50[c]
Not forced to change plans	38
Employment status	
Self-employed	34
Employed (except self-employed)	43
Not employed	47
Employed full time	40
Employed part time	47
Income	
Less than $10,000	65[c]
$10,000–$19,999	53
$20,000–$29,999	49
$30,000–$49,999	39
$50,000–$74,999	35
$75,000–$99,999	34
$100,000 or more	42

[a] Had no choice of plans at the time respondents chose their current health plan.

[b] Excludes "do not know"/"refuse" responses (17 subjects).

[c] $p < 0.05$.

Sources: Kaiser/Harvard/Princeton Survey Research Associates Care Survey, 1997. Reprinted with permission from Gawande AA, Blendon RI, Brodie M, Benson JM, Levitt L, Hugick L. Does dissatisfaction with health plans stem from having no choices? *Health Aff (Millwood).* 1998;17(5):187.

Again returning to the plight of individual patients with high expectations for their own health care, the stage is set for frustration and dissatisfaction with whatever care is provided. As Barsky has written:[25]

> Medical triumphs intimate a world in which whatever ails us can be treated away. This creates a problem of rising expectations: having come to imagine that somewhere there is a treatment for almost everything that ails us, we experience refractory symptoms and residual impairment as insupportable— as a mistake, an injustice, a failure of medical care. Illness seems all the more disturbing because we think it need not have happened at all. Because we expect so much from medical care and preventive medicine, and because we have invested so much in them, we become frustrated and disappointed by medicine's achievements, substantial though they are.

Table 5-3   Opinions about Managed Care Among Americans with a Choice of Plans, by Variety of Choices, 1997

Respondents with a Choice of Plans Who	Not Enough Variety	Enough Variety
Give their plan a C, D, or F grade	50%	17%
Say managed care plans		
Make it harder to see specialists	68*	52
Decrease the time doctors spend with their patients	68	62
Decrease the quality of health care	58*	46
Make it easier to get preventive services	44	55
Have helped to keep health care costs down	32	37
Make health care more affordable for people like them	52*	68
Trust their health care plan to do the right thing for their care, at least most of the time	62*	89
Trust their primary care doctor to do the right thing for their care, at least most of the time	77	90

* $p < 0.05$ compared with respondents who report that they had enough variety when they chose their current plan.
Source: Reprinted with permission from Gawande AA, Blendon RI, Brodie M, Benson JM, Levitt L, Hugick L. Does dissatisfaction with health plans stem from having no choices? *Health Aff (Millwood)*. 1998;17(5):191.

Despite the known importance of choice in health care coverage, this has proven to be a difficult and divisive issue for employers, policy makers, and others. The original HMO Act of 1973 had provisions for choice between an HMO and a fee-for-service plan, but these provisions later were repealed.[22] As recently as 1997, the President's Advisory Commission on Consumer Protection and Quality in the Health Care Industry could not reach consensus to include such a guarantee in their final recommendations.[22,26]

PATIENTS' RIGHTS

The story of patients' rights in the United States is one of incremental gains over the last 30 years. A series of court opinions established the right to informed consent in 1972.[27] A year later, the U.S. Supreme Court, in its *Roe* v. *Wade* decision, assured the constitutional right of pregnant women to continue or terminate their own pregnancy. Also implied in this decision is the right of privacy in the doctor-patient relationship from interference by the state.[28,29]

Various groups have put forward bills of rights for patients. The American Hospital Association issued a rather general 12-point bill in 1973, including rights to be given complete information about diagnosis and treatment, to refuse treatment, to receive respectful care, and to have privacy and confidentiality in their care.[27] More recently, the American Association of Health Plans (AAHP), partly in response to the managed care backlash in 1997, issued their "Putting Patients First" document (also known as the "Nine Commandments"). These provisions included such assurances that "gag rules" restricting physicians' discussions with patients about treatment options would be removed, patients would have rights to appeal denials, and physicians would be required to participate in quality-improvement programs.[29] Meanwhile 18 "Principles for Consumer Protection" were put forward in 1997 by Kaiser Permanente, Group Health of Puget Sound, the Health Insurance Plan (HIP), the American Association of Retired Persons (AARP), and Families USA. Among others, these principles included guarantees that health plans provide coverage for out-of-area emergency care, 24-hour availability of care, and continuity of care through a primary care physician.[30]

Critics of each of these initiatives have called attention to their limitations. Reacting to the AAHP's document, for example, Jerome Kassirer (then editor of the *New England Journal of Medicine*), described it as a "thinly veiled attempt to ward off state and federal legislative actions to curb the abuses of managed care."[31] In the case of the 18 "Principles for Consumer Protection," even the authors conceded that they were intended primarily as a marketing strategy to encourage health plans to compete on an equal basis.[29]

An Advisory Commission on Consumer Protection and Quality in the Health Care Industry was appointed by President Clinton in 1997. It proposed a national Bill of Patients' Rights, including rights to make medical decisions based on full information, to be treated with respect, to have confidentiality, to receive emergency care, to have an independent appeals mechanism, and other contract-based consumer protections.[26] Before and throughout the presidential election campaign of 2000, some kind of a national Bill of Patients' Rights received broad bipartisan support as politicians on both sides of the aisle fell over themselves in an effort to respond to the public's demands for assured access to quality health care at affordable cost. Such a bill was passed that year by the U.S. House of Representatives with the sponsorship of Charles Norwood, Republican from Georgia, and John Dingell, Democrat from Michigan. However, intense debate surrounded some of its provisions. The most controversial provision would allow patients to sue their HMO or health plan for unlimited damages if they are denied medical care that they expect and need. The bill also would require insurance companies to pay for Emergency Room treatment without prior authorization as well as allow a patient to see an obstetrician-gynecologist without primary care referral.[32] The issue remained a political football after defeat of the House bill 51 to 48 in the Senate, and critics have been buoyed by the June 2000 unanimous decision of the U.S. Supreme Court ruling that HMOs cannot be sued (in federal courts) under federal law for giving physicians financial incentives to hold down costs of health care.[33]

Powerful opposition forces have been mobilizing against a politically popular Bill of Patients' Rights. The health insurance industry points to the progress in cost containment made by managed care with a final denial rate of physician recommendations of only 3 percent overall and 1 percent for hospitalization and surgical requests.[34] The industry also notes that three quarters of health plans offer a point-of-service option;[35] and that most people in employer-sponsored health plans are not constantly switching insurers or planning to switch.[36] The industry further warns of the inevitable renewed inflation of health care costs if tort liability is placed on health plans and employers and if proposed additional benefits are mandated. Charles Kahn, president of the Health Insurance Association of America, points out that some legislative provisions could result in premium increases of more than 30 percent.[37] For example, mandated benefits for mental health, chemical dependency treatment, and dental services have been projected to increase premiums by 9 to 15 percent.[38] Donald Johnson, editor and publisher of *Health Care Strategic Management*, predicts that HMOs might not even deny claims any more, that managed care will be dead, and that HMOs may return to traditional insurance practice of collecting higher premiums and paying higher claims. He also predicts that the health insurance industry will further consolidate as many insurers leave the business, that more employers will stop providing health insurance to their employees, and that the number of uninsured Americans will escalate.[39] Thus, the access to care problem may become even worse than it has been in recent years, when the number of uninsured grew by about 1 million people each year.[40]

John Iglehart, founding editor of *Health Affairs*, sums up the risks of unintended consequences of a Patients' Bill of Rights in these cautionary words:[41]

> politicians of every stripe have seized on the shortcomings of managed care to propose, in a variety of forms, a patients' "bill of rights." This impulse caters to the popular belief that difficult allocation issues can be avoided if politicians simply spell out the rights of patients enrolled in health plans. If only it were that easy in a society as entrepreneurial and litigious as the United States. Unlike other industrialized nations, which compel employers to contribute to if not cover the entire cost of health insurance, the employer-based system here is voluntary. Neither federal nor state laws generally require employers (except Hawaii) to finance health coverage for employees and their families. Under this voluntary approach, nearly two thirds (64 percent in 1996) of all nonelderly Americans receive health benefits through the workplace, but that number has declined from 69.2 percent (1987). Congress, rather than stipulating what employers must purchase, would set down rules for what health plans must sell. This popular approach may be easier politically, but it could lead to unintended consequences. Take the Health Insurance Portability and Accountability Act, which provides people losing group coverage a guarantee to individual coverage regardless of health status. Some carriers, believing that people who exercise this right will be poor medical risks, have lawfully priced their products at rates 140 to 600 percent above the standard premium, making them largely unaffordable. So when government offers up a patients' "bill of rights" within an experience-rated insurance system, there is a possibility of unintended consequences such as lost coverage and higher premiums or both, rather than simply the increased protections politicians are serving up with such bravado.

CONCLUDING COMMENTS

Health care as a right remains controversial in the United States, hanging up particularly on how that right is defined. Many would agree that such a right relates to *basic* health care, but that kind of definition remains contentious and elusive, as we will see in Chapter 21 on rationing and attempts to define medical necessity. Certainly public expectations for health care remain high, and the concept of a global budget for health care has not yet been accepted. The public has been buffered from the real costs and tradeoffs of health care by their insurance coverage (whether private or public) and politicians, who naturally tend to find the enactment of benefits more satisfying than dealing with limits (the dreaded R-word of rationing).

The current impasse in Congress over a Patients' Bill of Rights illustrates political gridlock from countervailing forces. There can be no question, for example, that costs of insurance premiums and health care services will increase dramatically if HMOs become legally liable for setting exclusions. Public demand for the right to sue HMOs is propelled by such special interest groups as the Association of Trial Lawyers of America (ATLA). On the other side, the health insurance industry lobbies hard for legislators to oppose opening the Pandora's box of a new growth industry in health care law.

Beyond the debate about overly broad definitions of health care benefits is the continued unacceptable reality of lack of access to even basic health care for many Americans. The inequities and medical and social costs of our present health care system will be further discussed in later chapters on access (Chapters 8 and 17), costs (Chapters 7 and 16), and quality (Chapter 18).

REFERENCES

1. Ginzberg E. Ten encounters with the U.S. health sector, 1930–1999. *JAMA.* 1999;282:1665–1668.
2. Schwartz WB. *Life Without Disease: The Pursuit of Medical Utopia.* Berkeley, University of California Press, 1998:14.
3. Eddy DM. *Clinical Decision Making: From Theory to Practice.* Boston: Jones and Bartlett, 1996:70.
4. ·Mycek S. We're not in Kansas anymore. *Trustee.* September 1999;52:22.
5. Adopted by the General Assembly on 10 December 1948. Printed in: von Munch I, Buske A (eds). *International Law the Essential Treaties and Other Relevant Documents.* 1985:435ff.
6. Carmi A. On patients' rights. *Med Law.* 1991;10(1):77–82.
7. Hayes JA. Health care as a natural right. *Med Law.* 1991;11(5–6):405–416.
8. Roemer R. The right to health care—Gains and gaps. *Am J Public Health.* 1988;78(3):241–247.
9. Buergenthal T. International human rights law and institutions. In: *Health and Constitutions.* Washington DC: Pan American Health Organization, 1987:Chapter 1.
10. Furrow BR, Johnson SH, Jost TS, Schwarz RL. Health law: Cases, materials and problems. 1991:602.
11. Mariner WK. Medical care for prisoners: The evolution of a civil right. *Medicoleg News.* 1981;9(2):4–8.
12. Curran WJ. The constitutional right to health care. Denial in the court. *N Engl J Med.* 1989; 320:788–789.
13. Giesen D. A right to health care? A comparative perspective. *Health Matrix.* 1994;4(2):277–295.
14. Kaye NS. The right to health care, letter. *N Engl J Med.* 1989;321:693.
15. Churchill LR. *Rationing Health Care in America: Perceptions and Principles of Justice.* Notre Dame, IN: University of Notre Dame, 1987:90, 91, 94–96.
16. Marwick C. Report: Health care reform must affirm "right." *JAMA.* 1993;270:1284–1285.
17. Blendon RJ, Young JT, DesRoches CM. The uninsured, the working uninsured, and the public. *Health Aff (Millwood).* 1999;18(6):203–211.
18. Ostuw P. Health insurance continues to be most important benefit according to recent EBRI Gallup poll. *EBRI Notes.* 17(11). Washington, DC: EBRI, November 1996; and EBRI (Greenwald poll), April 1999.
19. Factors influencing choice of physician. *Fam Pract News.* 1999;29(2):1.
20. Ullman R, Hill JW, Scheye EC, Spoeri RK. Satisfaction and choice: A view from the plans. *Health Aff (Millwood).* 1997;16(3):209–217.

21. McLaughlin C. Health Care Consumers: Choices and Constraints. Paper presented at the Robert Wood Johnson Foundation's meeting, The Power of Choice in the Health Care Marketplace and Its Consequences, Washington, DC, November 19, 1997; Davis K. Testimony before the President's Advisory Commission on Consumer Protection and Quality in the Health Care Industry, hearing and consumer choice of health insurance plans and providers. Washington, DC: June 25, 1997.

22. Gawande AA, Blendon RI, Brodie M, Benson JM, Levitt L, Hugick L. Does dissatisfaction with health plans stem from having no choices? *Health Aff (Millwood).* 1998;17(5):184–194.

23. Grumbach K, Selby JV, Damberg CT, et al. Resolving the gatekeeper conundrum: What patients value in primary care and referrals to specialists. *JAMA.* 1999;282:261–266.

24. Schur CL, Dorosh E. Attitudes toward cost-containment features of managed care: Differences among patient subgroups. *Am J Manag Care.* 1998;4(10):1385–1391.

25. Barsky AJ. The paradox of health. *N Engl J Med.* 1988;318:414–418.

26. Advisory Commission on Consumer Protection and Quality in the Health Care Industry. Consumer bill of rights and responsibilities report to the president of the United States. Available at the website: www.hcqualitycommission.gov/cborr/consbill.htm, November 1997.

27. Annas GJ. *The Rights of Hospital Patients.* New York: Avon, 1975.

28. Annas GJ, Glantz LH, Mariner WK. The right of privacy protects the doctor-patient relationship. *JAMA.* 1990;263:858–861.

29. Annas GJ. A national bill of patients' rights. *N Engl J Med.* 1998;338:695–699.

30. Pear R. Three big health plans join in call for national standards. *New York Times.* September 25, 1997:A1.

31. Kassirer JP. Managing managed care's tarnished image. *N Engl J Med.* 1997;337:338–339.

32. Rooner J. The perils of patients' rights. *Business and Health.* November 1999:18.

33. Greenberger RS. Supreme Court shields HMOs from lawsuits. *Wall Street Journal.* June 13, 2000:A3, A6.

34. Health Care Advisory Board. *The Impact of Managed Care on the Health Care Industry, December 1997.* Washington, DC: Health Care Advisory Board, 1998.

35. American Association of Health Plans. *Dispelling Managed Care Myths.* Washington, DC: American Association of Health Plans, 1998.

36. National Research Corporation. *Satisfaction Report Card, 1998.* Lincoln, NB: National Research Corp., 1998.

37. Kahn CN III. Patients' rights proposals: The insurers' perspective. *JAMA.* 1999;281:858.

38. Jensen CA, Morrisey MA. *Mandated Benefit Laws and Employer-Sponsored Health Insurance, 1999.* Washington, DC: Health Insurance Association of America, 1999.

39. Johnson DEL. Patients' bill of rights will change hospitals. *Health Care Strategic Manage.* October 1999:2.

40. Quinn JB. Fighting for health care: "Patients' rights" can curb unethical plans, but your coverage might still be chopped. *Newsweek.* March 30, 1998:45.

41. Iglehart JK. Politics and patients' rights. *Health Aff (Millwood).* 1998;17(5):6.

6
An Aging Population and the Shifting Content of Health Care

Another major force, which increasingly will affect the organization, process, and financing of the health care delivery system, is the aging of the population. The hospital industry has been designed and built largely for the care of acute illness. And as seen in earlier chapters, the emphasis of the health care system, as a whole, over the last 75 years, has been on the diagnosis and therapy of acute illness. Today, with a dramatic shift underway toward an older population, the health care system must be restructured for the care of an increasing burden of chronic disease.

This chapter examines six dimensions of the impact of an aging population on the health care system: (1) demographic projections for the elderly population, (2) a shift in the content of health care for older Americans, (3) organizational aspects of care of the elderly, (4) aging and the costs of care, (5) palliative and end-of-life care, and (6) some comparisons with other industrialized countries.

DEMOGRAPHICS OF AGING

An enormous "age wave" is building in the United States, and the numbers are striking. The proportion of the population 65 years of age and older is the fastest growing segment of the population, with a projected increase from 34 million in 1995 to 39 million in 2010 and almost 70 million in 2030. Within those projections are continued growth in the numbers of elderly between 75 and 84 years of age, as well as for those over 85 years of age (Figure 6-1).[1] The U.S. Bureau of the Census projects that the population aged 85 and older will double from 3.5 million in 1996 to 7 million in 2020, then redouble to 14 million by 2040 as the large Baby Boom generation born after World War II (up to about 1964) reaches that age group. By that projection, 1 American in 20 would be 85 years or older in 2050 compared to 1 in 100 today.[2] The change already is remarkable, with almost 1 million people over age 90 today as compared to only 5,000 in 1964.[3]

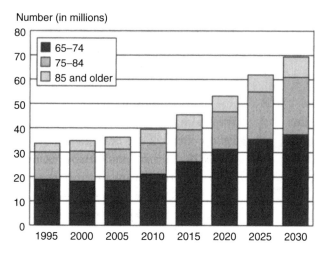

Figure 6-1   The coming surge in the population of age 65 years and older. (Data from the Institute for the Future; U.S. Census Bureau. Reprinted with permission from The Institute for the Future. *Health and Health Care 2010: The Forecast, the Challenge.* San Francisco: Jossey-Bass, 2000:17–24.)

One important factor embedded in these population projections is the continued increase in life expectancy for both males and females. Over the last 75 years, declines in death rates at first were due largely to control of infectious diseases and, since 1960, from a reduction in death rates from cardiovascular disease. The average life expectancy increased by more than 30 years for Americans during the 20th century and still is expected to increase for both men and women until 2040 (Figure 6-2).[1]

The older population in future years will be different in many respects from previous generations. Retirement at age 65 (or earlier) will be less common. Many elders will continue to work, perhaps in a new area, for many more years. The recent lifting of federal income restrictions for older Americans' receiving Social Security benefits can be expected to increase that trend toward continued growth in income-producing work in the older years. Although functional capacity and the quality of life for many elderly people will be better compared to their parents and grandparents, not all of the projections are so positive. Most older people rely on help received from family, especially from their spouse, if married. Women tend to outlive their husbands, and many are left with financial constraints and poverty. Over one half of women aged 75 and older have incomes below $10,000 per year, and very few have incomes over $20,000 per year.[2]

As the older population becomes more diverse, more elderly people will have less family support to draw on. The Hispanic, African-American, Asian, and Native American populations all are growing faster than the rest of the population and will constitute about one third of the U.S. population by 2010.[1] However, only one quarter of black women aged 65 and older are married (42

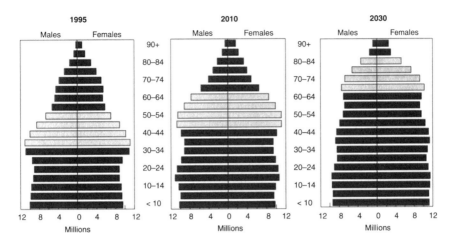

Figure 6-2   Baby boomers are aging. (Data from U.S. Census Bureau. Reprinted with permission from The Institute for the Future. *Health and Health Care 2010: The Forecast, the Challenge*. San Francisco: Jossey-Bass, 2000:17–24.)

percent of whites and 37 percent for Hispanics), while 57 percent of black men are married (77 percent for whites and 67 percent for Hispanics).[2] These unmarried older adults will be considerably more vulnerable to the problems of aging and can be expected to need more health and social services than their married counterparts.

AGING AND THE CONTENT OF CARE

As the population ages with extended lifespans and as medical technology further enables more effective and efficient care of acute illness, the predominant burden of disease shifts to chronic conditions. Chronic illnesses often are multifactorial in etiology, usually coexist with other chronic diseases, and are less effectively treated by the biomedical model than acute illnesses. The Centers for Disease Control and Prevention estimate that 50 percent of an individual's health status is determined by lifestyle behaviors, such as smoking and alcohol abuse.[1] New paradigms of care are needed beyond the biomedical model to address these problems, as pointed out in Chapter 10, such as application of the biopsychosocial model and disease management approaches. The goal of care in many instances becomes alleviation of symptoms and enhancement of function more than cure.

Figure 6-3 shows a continued increase over the next 50 years in the numbers of Americans with activity limitation, with limitation in major activity, and with inability to carry on a major activity at all, as estimated by investigators at the Institute for Health and Aging at the University of California, San Francisco. It is striking that, by each measure, the population with these limitations will not be too far short of doubling over that period.[4] In addition, the prevalence of dementia increases even faster with advancing age, affecting about one third of people over 85 years of age.[5]

The World Health Organization defined the *burden of disease* as a combination of untimely death and disability. It established the WHO Global Burden of Disease Study for the better understanding, monitoring, and projecting of rates of mortality and disability from diseases, injuries, and risk factors. The study compares diseases in terms of "one year of healthy life lost." Already apparent is that the burden of such problems as depression, alcohol dependency, and schizophrenia have been very much underestimated. The Institute of the Future projected that the number of deaths in the United States from noncommunicable disease will increase by 77 percent (to about 50 million) between 1990 and 2020. Heart disease will remain the leading cause of death and disability, but mental illness (especially unipolar major depression) will replace cancer as the second most common cause of death and disability within the next 10 years.[1]

Joanne Lynn and Anne Wilkinson, investigators at the Center to Improve Care of the Dying at Georgetown University, observed that service needs of individuals are quite similar in health, diversify during serious illness, but then converge again as similar toward the end of life (Table 6-1). They further note

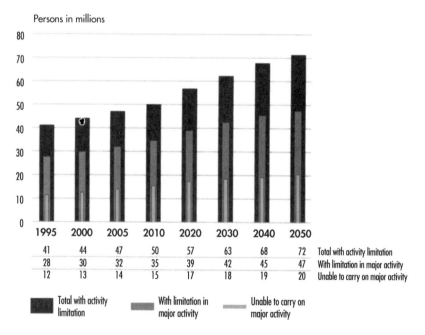

Persons in millions	1995	2000	2005	2010	2020	2030	2040	2050	
	41	44	47	50	57	63	68	72	Total with activity limitation
	28	30	32	35	39	42	45	47	With limitation in major activity
	12	13	14	15	17	18	19	20	Unable to carry on major activity

Total with activity limitation   With limitation in major activity   Unable to carry on major activity

Figure 6-3 Numbers of people limited by chronic conditions. (Estimates by Hoffman C, Rice DP, University of California, San Francisco–Institute for Health and Aging, 1995. *Chronic Care in America: A 21st Century Challenge.* Princeton, NJ: Robert Wood Johnson Foundation, August 1996:18.)

that the most common pattern of dying is to die slowly of chronic diseases, with gradual but relentless decrease of functional capacity (Figure 6-4, as illustrated by congestive heart failure).[6]

The focus of geriatric medicine so far has been directed primarily to the recognition and management of acute and chronic diseases in the frail elderly, with little emphasis on health promotion and disease prevention for all older people. This is starting to change. It is now recognized that many of the health risks of older adults can be reduced by an active preventive program including diet and exercise.[7] Falls can be reduced or prevented by physical training, cardiovascular fitness can be maintained by aerobic exercise, and weight training can limit muscle loss and preserve strength. A healthier lifestyle, even if adopted in later years, can increase life expectancy and decrease both disability[8] and health care costs.[9]

Table 6-1 Service Needs over the Life Course

Health ⇒	*Serious Illness* ⇒	*Last Phase of Life*
Prevention	Rescue, cure	Symptom relief
Lifestyle issues	Rehabilitation	Spiritual issues
Reproduction	Explanation, prediction, planning	Family issues
Growth, maturation	Life-prolongation	Rehabilitation explanation, prediction, planning
(Almost all primary care) ⇒	(Diverse medical and surgical specialty services) ⇒	(Primary care, especially nursing, counseling, etc.)

Source: Reprinted with permission from Lynn J, Wilkerson AM. Quality end of life care: The case for a MediCaring demonstration. In: Lynn J, Harold JK (eds). *A Good Dying: Shaping Health Care for the Last Months of Life.* New York: Haworth Press, 1998:152.

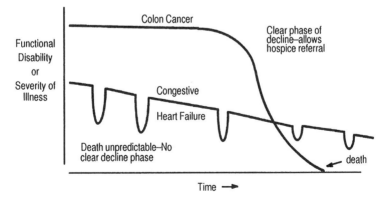

Figure 6-4 Illness impact trajectory. (Reprinted with permission from Lynn J, Wilkerson AM. Quality end of life care: The case for a MediCaring demonstration. In: Lynn J, Harold JK (eds). *A Good Dying: Shaping Health Care for the Last Months of Life.* New York: Haworth Press, 1998.)

AGING AND COSTS OF CARE

Although, to an increasing extent, most older people are relatively healthy, a minority have multiple chronic conditions requiring complex care. It is well known that 5 to 10 percent of people over 65 years of age account for about two thirds of annual health care expenses for this age group.[10–12] By 2040 Medicaid's portion of total spending on long-term care alone could reach $125 billion (in 2000 dollars).[13] Figure 6-5 provides a graphic picture of the relentless growth in the annual direct medical costs for patients with chronic diseases, most of them elderly, over the next 50 years.

A recent analysis of total spending for health care costs of Medicare beneficiaries revealed, as one would anticipate, escalating costs with increasing longevity. Cumulative expenditures from age 65 years to death, in 1996 dollars, were found to be about $157,000 for persons dying at 80, $235,000 at 90, and $407,000 over 101 years of age. Expenditures for long-term care, especially nursing home care, accelerate faster than acute care costs as elderly patients advance in age; about one half of nursing home costs are paid by Medicaid, with one third out of pocket, and the smallest amount by Medicare. Figure 6-6 graphically reflects these increasing expenditures with age, particularly for nursing home care.

Over one quarter of the Medicare budget and 10 to 12 percent of the total health care budget is consumed by end-of-life care (last 12 months).[14] About one half of Medicare costs in the last year of life occur during the last 60 days,

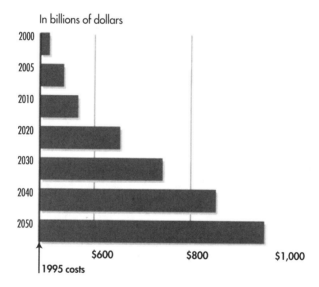

Figure 6-5   Direct medical costs for persons with chronic conditions will nearly double from 1995 levels by 2050. (Estimates based on 1987 National Medical Survey. Reprinted from Hoffman C, Rice DP, University of California, San Francisco–Institute for Health and Aging, 1995.)

with about 40 percent in the last 30 days of life, mostly due to the intensity of hospital-based care.[15]

In view of the high cost of end-of-life care, more attention has been directed in recent years to better understanding what services are provided at the end of life, their quality, and their cost. Two studies shed some light on this issue. Christopher Chambers and his colleagues in the Department of Family Medicine at Jefferson Medical College in Philadelphia examined the relationship in a large university teaching hospital between documentation of a discussion of advance directives and hospital charges during dying patients' last hospitalization. They found that patients without such a discussion incurred more than three times the hospital charges than those with such a discussion.[16] Another large, national, two-part study, involving over 4,000 patients, the Study to Understand Prognoses and Preferences for Outcomes and Risks of Treatment (SUPPORT), was funded by the Robert Wood Johnson Foundation. Phase I of the study revealed many problems with the quality and appropriateness of end-of-life care (e.g., less than half of physicians knew when their patients wanted to avoid cardiopulmonary resuscitation, half of conscious patients had moderate to severe pain at least half the time before dying, and 38 percent of patients spent at least 10 days in an intensive care unit [ICU]).[16] Phase II studied the effects of a controlled clinical trial designed to improve physician-patient communication and the quality of end-of-life care for over 4,800 patients. The results were discouraging, with the intervention failing to improve care or patient outcome.[17]

Cognizant of the likely benefits to Medicare beneficiaries of a more proactive program of health promotion and preventive care, as well as potential cost savings, the Health Care Financing Administration (HCFA) launched its Healthy Aging Project. Medicare's current primary prevention projects are limited to vaccination against influenza, pneumococcal pneumonia, and

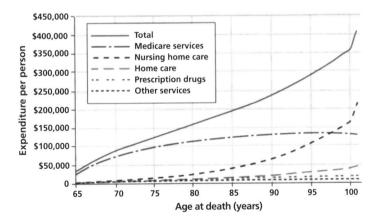

Figure 6-6 Cumulative health care expenditures from the age of 65 years until death, according to the type of health service and the age at death. (Reprinted from Spellman BC, Lubitz J. The effect of longevity on spending for acute and long-term care. *N Engl J Med.* 2000;342:1409–1415 and *Medical Benefits.* 2000;17(10):8.)

hepatitis B; screening mammography; Pap smears; screening for colorectal cancer; and measurement of bone density. While a good start, the Healthy Aging Project is more procedure oriented without strong links to behavioral factors that so often determine improved health outcomes. HCFA is examining ways to increase the effectiveness of these approaches and now lists as its first goal in its new strategic plan "to protect and improve beneficiary health and satisfaction."[18]

ORGANIZATIONAL ASPECTS OF CARE OF THE ELDERLY

The care of chronically ill elderly patients, with their dense concentration of morbidity, is complex and requires coordination with a broad spectrum of public and private resources in many instances. Unfortunately, however, much of this care is fragmented and uncoordinated.

The major specialties involved in care of the elderly are family practice and general internal medicine, which together accounted for almost 60 percent of nonreferred ambulatory visits to office-based U.S. physicians in 1990. Ophthalmology, cardiology, other medical subspecialties, and orthopedic surgery are the other types of physicians most involved in the care of older adults.[19]

Although physicians play an essential and critical role in geriatric care, comprehensive care necessarily requires a multidisciplinary team approach. Many other health professionals are actively involved in care of the elderly, including nurses, social workers, pharmacists, dietitians, psychologists, physical therapists, and occupational therapists. In managed care environments, case management may be provided by a primary care physician or nurse case manager.[20]

Managed care organizations offering capitated coverage to elderly populations have had strong financial incentives to identify high-risk, chronically ill individuals in order to provide them with coordinated care along health promotion and disease management lines. Almost one in five Medicare beneficiaries is now enrolled in a Medicare HMO.[21] Elderly patients are much less likely than younger insured individuals to change health plans (disenrollment from Medicare HMOs in 1996 averaged less than 8 percent).[22] HMOs therefore find it advantageous to invest in health promotion and preventive approaches to reduce the number of future hospitalizations and related costs.[20]

In today's "finance-oriented" system of care, the care of elderly patients is determined more by the uncoordinated policies of various public and private payers, most commonly Medicare, Medicaid, and a diverse group of private supplemental insurers. As a result, there usually is no effective way to efficiently coordinate care across many providers and locations of care, which often include the acute care hospital, emergency room, clinic, convalescent or nursing home, and home care.

Chad Boult and James Pacala, from the University of Minnesota, propose that the "finance-oriented" system be replaced with a "client-oriented" system of care, as a means to better integrate health care services for elderly patients.

In such a system, the primary care clinician or case manager would work directly with the patient in selecting, integrating, and coordinating appropriate services with pooled capitation funding.[20] In recent years, the HCFA has been experimenting with several approaches to integrate acute and long-term care. One such program is PACE (the Program of All-Inclusive Care of the Elderly). This was piloted in San Francisco and later replicated in 19 additional demonstration sites. It has been further expanded as a permanent program funded by HCFA capitation payments (set at Medicare's average adjusted per capita costs multiplied by a factor of 2.39) and state Medicaid funds. By 1999, there were 2,700 frail elderly patients averaging 80 years of age, each with seven to eight medical conditions, all nursing home certifiable, and almost one half with dementia. On enrollment in PACE, these patients agreed to receive all their health care from, or on referral by, an interdisciplinary team including an internist or family physician, a nurse practitioner, nurses, social workers, a physical therapist, an occupational therapist, recreation therapists, and a dietitian. They further agreed to use one hospital, one nursing home, one pharmacy, and one panel of specialists. PACE patients visit an adult day care center two or three days each week for socialization and monitoring of physical, functional, and emotional decline. They see their physicians monthly and are reassessed by their team every three months. They are encouraged to have advance directives and are provided with a seamless system of care whether at home, in the hospital, or at the nursing home.[20]

Cost-effectiveness studies of PACE are underway. Although there has been considerable variation among sites, preliminary quality of care assessments by practicing geriatricians and geriatric nurse practitioners have been encouraging. Reviewers found overall quality of care to be equal to or better than community standards in 92 percent of cases, and 79 percent of enrolled patients were as well or better than baseline predictions 6 to 12 months after entering the PACE program. Annual rates of disenrollment from PACE have been only 4.4 percent.[22] On the other hand, this kind of program runs the risk of fragmentation of the patient's usual care unless the primary care physician remains actively involved in the patient's care.

While various demonstration programs should gain experience with strategies to better integrate health services for the elderly, many have called for more extensive reform of the Medicare program itself. Prescription drug coverage is the current leading issue for Medicare reform.

PALLIATIVE AND END-OF-LIFE CARE

In the earlier 20th century, the life span was considerably shorter and dying was quicker from acute illness or injury. As we have seen, people now live longer and often acquire multiple chronic diseases, from which they die much more slowly. Medical technology has outpaced the social, political, and financial supports within American society for the care of a growing burden of chronic illness, and the health care system still revolves more around acute care than chronic care.[23]

About 2.5 million deaths occur each year in the United States at the dawn of the 21st century. The most common trajectory of dying involves noncancer deaths from chronic diseases after an extended course, the duration of which is difficult to predict. For many patients the "curative" paradigm is applied mostly in an acute care setting, well beyond a time of beneficial results. More than three quarters of all deaths occur in medical institutions, such as hospitals, with only 10 to 14 percent in hospices and 5 to 10 percent in nursing homes or at home.[24] Most noncancer deaths result from acute episodes of chronic illness, especially arrhythmias or infection, disguised as "sudden" deaths.[6]

For many patients, hospitalization prolongs suffering and merely delays imminent death, often with the loss of personal dignity. This situation led Wanzer and his colleagues to observe:[25]

> The intensive care unit should generally be discouraged as a treatment setting for the hospitalized patient who is dying, unless intensive palliative measures are required that cannot be done elsewhere. Too often, life-sustaining measures are instituted in the intensive care unit without sufficient thought to the proper goals of treatment.

George Annas, an attorney and ethicist, goes further:[26]

> If dying patients want to retain some control over their dying process, they must get out of the hospital if they are in and stay out of the hospital if they are out.

Recognizing, however, that the hospital setting cannot be avoided for the care of many patients with terminal illnesses, Miller and Fins make an important proposal—that hospitals establish alternative care units to facilitate palliative terminal care when hospice or other alternative facilities are not available or feasible.[27]

Until recent years, the concept of transitioning from the curative mode to a care mode was not widely appreciated or practiced. As Timothy Quill, an internist and director of the Program for Biopsychosocial Studies at the University of Rochester, observes:[28]

> Physicians and other health care professionals devote their careers to helping people live longer and function better. The single-minded fight for life has yielded enormous successes, yet it has left practitioners without a clear vision of their responsibilities when their patients are dying. Death seems antithetical to modern medicine—no longer a natural and inevitable part of the life cycle, but a medical failure to be fought off, ignored, and minimized. The dark side of this desperate battle has patients spending their last days in the intensive care units of acute hospitals, tubes inserted into every body part, vainly trying to forestall death's inevitability. No one wants to die, but when we really have to, there must be a better way.

And further:

> healing has more to do with caring for the person who is ill than with simply extending biological life. The illnesses of real people include a complex mix of personal history, values, and concepts of self, spirit, and community. Medicine's purpose should include helping persons become more whole and

alleviating their suffering, as well as treating their diseases. This broader conceptualization allows more meaningful possibilities for treating all patients, but particularly those who are dying. Whereas there may not be anything one can do to extend biological life, there is almost always a potential to enhance quality and meaning. Such is the role of a medical healer.

End-of-life care can be improved, and more medical technology is not the answer. A new emphasis within the health care professions, health care organizations, and government agencies is placed on the better provision of palliative care, including a greater use of hospice services.

The transition from cure to care mode often is difficult for many patients, their families, their physicians, and other caregivers to accept. Disease trajectories, especially in noncancer patients, frequently are unpredictable, patients vary widely in how they assess risks and benefits of treatment, and each patient in the last phase of his or her life brings a unique and complex set of history, values, fears, and personal needs to that time. Adding to that complexity is that family members often disagree among themselves or with caregivers as to the best course of action; and caregivers themselves may be uncomfortable, unskilled, or inexperienced with the process of optimal care of patients approaching the end of their lives.

The question of whether or not to use a gastrostomy tube in patients with advanced dementia illustrates some of the difficult clinical, educational, ethical, and religious issues that may be involved in end-of-life care. An estimated 4 million people in the United States have dementia.[29] In advanced stages of dementia, these patients generally cannot feed themselves or walk, are incontinent, may be aphasic, and no longer can relate to other people. Caregivers must work through difficult management issues with family members or other surrogate decision makers concerning such questions as hospitalization and artificial nutrition and hydration.[30,31] Placement of a percutaneous gastrostomy tube is a commonly performed procedure under these circumstances; it was done in 121,000 elderly patients in 1995,[32] about one third of whom had dementia.[33] Despite the frequency of this procedure and the importance of the question, however, much still needs to be done in both public and professional education. There now is compelling scientific evidence that gastrostomy tubes do not prolong life, nor do they prevent suffering. On the contrary, the procedure causes discomfort, requiring upper endoscopy, penetration of the abdominal wall, and intravenous sedation. The rate of long-term complications ranges from 32 to 70 percent,[34,35] and almost three quarters of demented patients end up needing restraints to prevent them from removing the tube.[36] Many caregivers are neither aware of these problems nor the bioethical and legal aspects of this issue.

Geriatricians and ethicists argue that artificial nutrition and hydration are forms of medical therapy (confirmed as well by the U.S. Supreme Court) and reasonably can be withheld if their risks outweigh the benefits.[37] The patient's desires and values need to be part of this decision and may be stated by advance directive, but often they are not known when this decision needs to be made. In addition to the preceding aspects of this issue, religious beliefs often play a role, but even here, neither the Roman Catholic Church nor the Orthodox Jewish tradition requires such an intervention when the patient no longer can eat or drink. The Catholic position approves the use of such a procedure only as long as it "is of sufficient benefit to outweigh the burdens involved to the patient,"[38] while the Jewish position rejects the use of interventions that cause or prolong suffering.[39]

Techniques of palliative care now are sufficiently well developed that most dying patients can have a "good death" if these techniques are applied well by caring health professionals and other caregivers. Concerted efforts are being made at many levels to facilitate such care. There are new initiatives in medical schools to introduce medical students to end-of-life care. The specialty boards in internal medicine and family medicine are giving emphasis to this area. The Institute of Medicine released a report in 1997, *Approaching Death*, which makes recommendations that will help to achieve "a compassionate care system that dying people and those close them can rely on for respectful and effective care."[40]

The Institute for Healthcare Improvement has launched an effort to assist more than 48 participating organizations (home health, hospice, hospitals, VA systems, and a PACE site) to improve end-of-life care. Hospice care (including home hospice) is covered by Medicare and many other insurance plans for periods up to six months.[41] Hospice programs continue to grow around the country; by 1997, there were 3,000 hospices, which served about 450,000 patients and their families, including about one half of patients who died of cancer that year.[42] There are many other examples of health care organizations developing innovative programs along these lines.[43]

SOME INTERNATIONAL COMPARISONS

A recent analysis of patterns of health care for the elderly in eight industrialized countries found remarkable similarities by many measures. In terms of health care expenditures, between one third and one half of total health spending is directed to patients over 65 years of age. The ratio of health spending for persons both older and younger than age 65 is quite similar. The main differences between the United States and the other countries concerning costs is the higher portion of the GDP spent on elderly health care in the United States (at 5.0 percent, double that of New Zealand) and per capita health spending two to three times that of the other countries (Table 6-2).[44]

There also are more similarities than differences among these eight countries in other respects. The proportion of elderly patients cared for in institutions is more similar than one might expect, with respect to total long-term care expenditures and those financed by public funding. All eight countries have explicit or implicit policies promoting deinstitutionalization of care, but they also report an increasing trend toward elderly persons living alone. The exception is Japan, where 50 percent of the elderly live with their adult children; but even there, this number is trending lower as more Japanese women work outside the home and their families become more mobile. Only 10 to 20 percent of the elderly in the other seven countries live with their children. There are three major differences between the United States and these other countries: (1) lesser public coverage of prescription drug costs (65 versus 100 percent), (2) greater reliance on

Table 6-2   Health Spending for the Elderly in Eight Countries, 1993–1995

Country	Percent of Total Health Spending on the Elderly	Ratio of Health Spending for Persons Age 65 and Older to Persons under Age 65	Estimated Percent of GDP Spent on Health for the Elderly	Percent of GDP Spent on Health	Health Spending per Capita, 1997*
Australia (1994)	35%	4	3.0%	8.3%	$5,348
Canada (1994)	40	4.7	3.6	9.3	6,764
France (1993)	35	3	3.4	9.6	4,717
Germany (1994)	34	2.7	3.5	10.4	4,993
Japan (1995)	47	4.8	3.4	7.3	5,258
New Zealand (1994)	34	3.9	2.5	7.6	3,870
United Kingdom (1993)	43	3.9	2.8	6.7	3,612
United States (1995)	38	3.8	5	13.6	12,090

* U.S. dollars in purchasing power parities.

Note: GDP is gross domestic product.

Sources: *OECD Health Data 1999* (Paris Organization for Economic Cooperation and Development, 1999) and authors' calculations. Reprinted with permission from Anderson GF, Hussey PS. Population aging: A comparison among industrialized countries. *Health Aff (Millwood)*. 2000;19(3):191–203.

private funding of retirement, and (3) a higher proportion of private financing of long-term care.[44]

Since considerable interest has developed in recent years in the Canadian model of health care, some studies focused on direct comparisons across the United States–Canadian border. One such study assessed the relative volume and costs of physician services in both countries based on 1992 claims data for elderly patients. Although elderly patients in Canada accounted for 44 percent more evaluation and management services, they had 25 percent fewer procedures. The decreased rate for procedures held for a wide range of inpatient and outpatient procedures, including hysterectomy, coronary artery bypass graft, hip replacement, cataract extraction, endoscopies, and removal of skin lesions.[45] Canada has a considerably lower volume of procedures for which there is low clinical consensus (e.g., the ratio for laminectomy adjusted for age and sex for Canada to the United States was found to be only 0.43).[45]

CONCLUDING COMMENTS

What major conclusions can be drawn from this discussion? Six lead my list, and they all have a direct impact on the need to restructure the U.S. health care system. First, as is the case with other industrialized Western nations, the aging population places new demands upon the health care system, particularly the growing burden for care of chronic illness. Second, as will be discussed further in Chapter 10, a shift in paradigms of care beyond the biomedical model will be required to better care for the needs of an older population. Third, as will become clear in Chapter 11 on the changing role of hospitals, the present health care system has been built around the care of acute illness and is ill suited to the new demands for chronic care. Fourth, health care for older Americans increasingly is fragmented and expensive; moreover, end-of-life care often is impersonal, inappropriate, and lacking in quality, with the harms exceeding the benefits in many instances. Fifth, greater public consensus is needed concerning the many common bioethical issues involved in palliative and futile care, which need to be addressed more directly. And finally, while some promising approaches to constructive change are in process, so far they are too minimal.

The care of an aging population brings to light some fundamental problems of the health care "system." As will be revisited in later chapters, useful approaches to these problems should include de-emphasis on hospital care for end-stage chronic disease, more selective use of medical technology in older patients with multisystem chronic disease, more comfortable transition from curative to palliative care, increased emphasis on team care within a chronic disease paradigm, and closer partnership clinical decision making with patients and their families around the benefits and harms of clinical interventions.

REFERENCES

1. The Institute for the Future. *Health and Health Care 2010: The Forecast, the Challenge*. San Francisco: Jossey-Bass, 2000:17–24.
2. Waite LJ. The demographic face of America's elderly. *Inquiry.* 1996;33:220–224.
3. Mycek S. We're not in Kansas anymore. *Trustee.* September 1999:20–24.
4. *1998 Environmental Assessment: Setting Foundations for the Millennium.* Irving, TX: VHA Inc., 1998.
5. Borson S. Assessment of memory loss. Presented at Advances in Family Practice and Primary Care Continuing Medical Education (CME) Course, Seattle, WA: September 13, 2000.
6. Lynn J, Wilkerson AM. Quality end of life care: The case for a MediCaring demonstration. In: Lynn J, Harold JK (eds). *A Good Dying: Shaping Health Care for the Last Months of Life*. New York: Haworth Press, 1998:137–163.
7. Rowe JW, Kahn RL. Successful aging. *Gerontologist.* 1997;37:433–440.
8. Vita AJ, Terry RB, Hubert HB, Fries JF. Aging, health risks and cumulative disability. *N Engl J Med.* 1998;338:1035–1041.
9. Russell LB. Prevention and Medicare costs. *N Engl J Med.* 1998;339:1158–1160.
10. Freeborn DK, Pope CR, Mullooly JP, McFarland BH. Consistently high users of medical care among the elderly. *Med Care.* 1990;28:527–540.
11. Gruenberg L, Tompkins C, Porell F. The health status and utilization patterns of the elderly: Implications for setting Medicare payments to HMOs. *Adv Health Econ Health Serv Res.* 1989;10:41–73.
12. Gornick M, McMillan A, Lubitz J. A longitudinal perspective on patterns of Medicare payments. *Health Aff (Millwood).* 1993;12(2):140–150.
13. Society, health and aging in the 21st century. President's message. *1999 Annual Report.* The Commonwealth Fund, March 2000.
14. Emanuel EJ. Cost savings at the end of life: What do the data show? *JAMA.* 2000;275:1907–1914.
15. Lubitz JD, Riley FR. Trends in Medicare payments in the last year of life. *N Engl J Med.* 1993;328:1092–1096.

16. Chambers CV, Diamond JJ, Perkel RL, Lasch LA. Relationship of advance directives to hospitals charges in a Medicare population. *Arch Intern Med.* 1994;154:541–547.

17. The SUPPORT Principal Investigators. A controlled trial to improve care for seriously ill hospitalized patients. *JAMA.* 1995;274:1591–1598.

18. Health Care Financing Administration. *Health Care Financing Administration Strategic Plan.* Publication no. HCFA-02135. Baltimore: Health Care Financing Administration, 1998.

19. Rosenblatt R, Hart LG, Gamliel S, Goldstein B, McClendon BJ. Identifying primary care disciplines by analyzing the diagnostic content of ambulatory care. *J Am Board Fam Pract.* 1995; 8:34–45.

20. Boult C, Pacala JT. Integrating health care for older populations. *Am J Manage Care.* 1999; 5(1):45–52.

21. Spellman BC, Lubitz J. The effect of longevity on spending for acute and long-term care. *N Engl J Med.* 2000;342:1409–1415.

22. Nelson L, Gold M, Brown R, et al. *Access to Care in Medicare Managed Care. Results from a 1996 Survey of Enrollees and Disenrollees.* Selected External Research series #7. Washington, DC: Physician Payment Review Commission, 1996.

23. Lynn J. In: Lynn J, Harrold JG (eds). *A Good Dying: Shaping Health Care for the Last Months of Life.* New York: Haworth Press, 1998:xv.

24. National Center for Health Services. *Vital Statistics of the United States 1991*, vol. 2, *Mortality*, Part A, Section I. Publication no. (PHS) 96-1101. Washington, DC: U.S. Government Printing Office, 1996.

25. Wanzer SH, Federman DD, Adelstein SJ, et al. The physician's responsibility toward hopelessly ill patients: A second look. *N Engl J Med.* 1989;32:844–849.

26. Goodman E. Dances of silence. *Washington Post.* December 2, 1995:A21.

27. Miller FG, Fins JJ. A proposal to restructure hospital care for dying patients. *N Engl J Med.* 1996;334:1740–1742.

28. Quill TE. *A Midwife Through the Dying Process: Stories of Healing and Hard Choices at the end of life.* Baltimore: Johns Hopkins University Press, 1996.

29. Costa PT Jr, Williams TF, Albert MS, et al. *Recognition and Initial Assessment of Alzheimer's Disease and Related Dementias.* Clinical Practice Guidelines no. 19. AHCPR publication no. 97-0702. Rockville, MD: Department of Health and Human Services, 1996.

30. Post SG. *The Moral Challenge of Alzheimer Disease.* Baltimore: Johns Hopkins University Press, 1995.

31. Gillick MR. Rethinking the role of tube feeding in patients with advanced dementia. *N Engl J Med.* 2000;342:206–210.

32. Grant MD, Rudberg MA, Brody JA. Gastrostomy placement and mortality among hospitalized Medicare beneficiaries. *JAMA.* 1998;279:1973–1976.

33. Rabeneck L, Wray NP, Petersen NJ. Long-term outcomes of patients receiving percutaneous endoscopic gastrostomy tubes. *J Gen Intern Med.* 1996;11:287–293.

34. Petersen TI, Kruse A. Complications of percutaneous endoscopic gastrostomy. *Eur J Surg.* 1997;163:351–356.

35. Taylor CA, Larson DE, Ballard DJ, et al. Predictors of outcome after percutaneous endoscopic gastrostomy: A community-based study. *Mayo Clin Proc.* 1992;67:1042–1049.

36. Peck A, Cohen CE, Mulvihill MN. Long-term enteral feeding of aged demented nursing home patients. *J Am Geriatr Soc.* 1990;38(11):1195–1198.

37. Lo B, Dornbrand L. Guiding the hand that feeds. Caring for the demented elderly. *N Engl J.* 1984;311:402–404.

38. Catholic Church National Conference of Catholic Bishops. *Ethical and Religious Directions for Catholic Health Care Services.* Washington, DC: United States Catholic Conference, September 1995.

39. Rosin AJ, Sonnenback M. Autonomy and paternalism in geriatric medicine. The Jewish ethical approach to issues of feeding terminally ill patients and to cardiopulmonary resuscitation. *J Med Ethics.* 1998;24:44–48.

40. Committee on Care at the End of Life Institute. *Approaching Death: Improving Care at the End of Life.* Washington, DC: National Academy Press, 1997.

41. Reichel W. End-of-life care and family practice. *Am Fam Physician.* 1999;59(6):1388, 1395–1396, 1399.

42. Mahoney J. An update on efforts by the hospice community and the National Hospice Organization to improve access to quality hospice care. In: Lynn J, Harrold JK (eds). *A Good Dying: Shaping Health Care for the Last Months of Life.* Binghamton, NY: Haworth Press, 1998:139–144.

43. Wilkinson AM, Harrold JK, Kopits I, Ayers E. New endeavors and innovative programs in end-of-life care. In: Lynn J, Harrold JK (eds). *A Good Dying: Shaping Health Care for the Last Months of Life*. Binghamton, NY: Haworth Press, 1998:165–180.
44. Anderson GF, Hussey PS. Population aging: a comparison among industrialized countries. *Health Aff (Millwood)*. 2000;19(3):191–203.
45. Welch WP, Verrilli D, Katz SJ, Latimer EA. A detailed comparison of physician services for the elderly in the United States and Canada. *JAMA*. 1996;275:1410–1416.

7
Increasing Costs of Health Care

The U.S. health care industry continues to be one of the largest, most diverse, and fastest growing industries in the country. It represented one seventh of the U.S. economy in 1998—$1.1 trillion and 13.5 percent of the gross domestic product (GDP)[1,2]—larger than the national economies of all but seven other industrialized nations in the world. National health expenditures have more than quadrupled since 1980. Per capita health expenditures increased from just over $1,000 to $4,000 between 1988 and 1998. Although the growth rate in health care spending slowed during the early and mid-1990s, there is every indication that health care costs will surge upward in coming years.[2]

This chapter reviews and takes a snapshot of five areas related to health care costs: (1) magnitude of overall growth in health care costs, including their major components; (2) who pays for these costs; (3) costs of health insurance; (4) some international comparisons; and (5) projections for health care costs over the next 10 years.

NATIONAL HEALTH CARE EXPENDITURES

Largely as a result of various cost-containment measures to be discussed in Chapter 16, the share of the GDP devoted to health care stabilized at about 13.5 percent from 1993 to 1998. However, as described in an excellent recent review article by economists, research analysts, and health insurance specialists at the Health Care Financing Administration (HCFA), already various signals indicate that the rate of growth of health care costs and expenditures is gaining new momentum. Some factors in this renewed inflationary trend include increasing private health insurance premiums (up from a 3.5 percent increase in 1997 to 8.2 percent in 1998), stabilization of hospital occupancy rates (which had been declining due to over-capacity), rollbacks by Congress of some of the provisions of the Balanced Budget Act of 1997 (BBA97), and the growth in private and public managed care enrollment, which raised demand for increasingly expensive prescription drugs.[2] In addition, as we recall from Chapter 2, the increasing intensity of health care services, together with aggressive marketing of new medical devices and pharmaceutical products, further propel escalating health care costs.

National health expenditures increased rapidly in the United States in aggregate and per capita terms from 1980 to 1998. There was an almost 5-fold increase in personal health care expenditures over that 18-year period, including a 6-fold increase for physician services, 12-fold increase for home health care, and more than a 7-fold increase for prescription drugs.[2]

Personal health care expenditures in 1998 made up 89 percent of overall health spending. Within that large category, recent years have seen some important changes in allocation of expenditures. Although hospital expenditures account for 33 percent of health care spending, they made up only 21 percent of overall health spending increases between 1997 and 1998. On the other hand, the most rapidly growing area of health care expenditures is now prescription drugs; while only 8 percent of overall health spending, they accounted for 20 percent of increased health spending between 1997 and 1998. These and other points are illustrated in Figure 7-1.

Further perspective on the annual change in health care expenditures during the 1990s (not adjusted for inflation) is provided by Table 7-1. Spending increases for physician and hospital services have been constrained since 1994, while drug expenditures have increased sharply. In 1997, for example, they grew by 11.5 percent while the consumer price index (CPI) increased only 2.5 percent.[3]

Physician services account for about 20 percent of annual U.S. expenditures for personal health services. This figure is remarkably constant over the years.[4] Table 7-2 lists median physician compensation by specialty for 1999, reflecting generally higher incomes in the surgical specialties.

Administrative costs represent an increasingly large part of health care expenditures. Figure 7-2 displays the rapidly diverging growth curves for adminis-

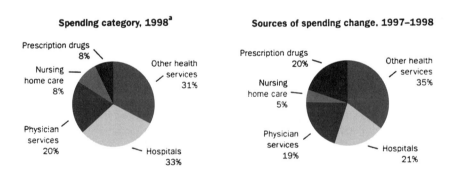

Figure 7-1   Distribution by spending category, 1998, and sources of spending change, 1997–1998. (Note: Other health services include dental services, other professionals, durable medical equipment, over-the-counter medical products, home health services, program administration, and the net cost of insurance, government public health activities, research, and construction. [a]$1,149.1 billion.) (Source: Health Care Financing Administration, Office of the Actuary, data from the National Health Statistics Group. Reprinted with permission from Levit K, Cowan C, Lazenby H, Sensenig A, McDonell P, Stiller J, et al. Healthcare services in the United States during selected years between 1970 and 1998. The Health Accounts Team. *Health Aff (Millwood).* 2000;19(1):127.)

Table 7-1 Annual Change per Capita in Health Care
Expenditures, by Component, 1990–1997

Year	Total Health	Hospital	Physician	Drug
1990	10.1%	9.4%	9.6%	14.7%
1991	7.1	7.1	5.7	12.4
1992	7.3	7.8	5.0	11.7
1993	5.8	6.5	3.7	7.1
1994	3.2	3.0	2.5	4.7
1995	3.8	3.1	3.2	10.9
1996	3.2	2.9	1.4	11.3
1997	3.9	2.4	2.0	11.5

Note: Data presented here are not adjusted for inflation.

Source: Author's calculations using data from Millman and Robertson's
Health Cost Index, expanded to include Medicare. Reprinted with permission
from Ginsburg PB, Gabel JR. Tracking health care costs: What's new in
1998? *Health Aff (Millwood).* 1998;17(5):142.

Table 7-2 Median Direct Physician Compensation, 1999

	1999	1998–1999 Percentage Change
Medical specialties		
Allergy	$181,001	5.71%
Cardiology—general	262,954	3.81
Cardiology—cath. lab	279,710	2.85
Dermatology	186,191	3.1
Endocrinology	158,654	1.25
Family medicine	141,560	3.52
Gastroenterology	222,000	2.14
Hematology and medical oncology	187,000	3.54
Hypertension and nephrology	183,000	1.33
Infectious disease	155,891	1.99
Internal medicine	142,881	2.06
Neurology	174,589	4.42
Pediatrics and adolescent	139,307	5.53
Psychiatry	144,294	2.79
Pulmonary disease	190,781	8.83
Rheumatologic disease	155,000	−0.45
Urgent care	145,139	5.11
Surgical specialties		
Cardiac/thoracic surgery	389,474	1.16
Emergency care	187,200	6.93
General surgery	243,362	0.43
Gynecology and obstetrics	223,584	−0.63
Ophthalmology	230,791	7.34
Orthopedic surgery	293,525	−1.05
Otolaryngology	245,665	0.27
Urology	252,613	3.05

Source: 2000 Medical Group Compensation and Productivity Survey, RSM McGladrey Inc. For the American
Medical Group Association, June 30, 2000. Reprinted with permission from Median direct physician compensation,
1999. *Med Benefits.* 2000;17(15):11.

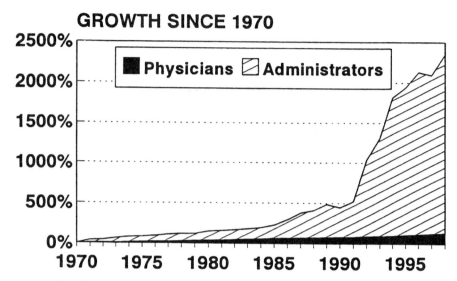

Figure 7-2 Growth in the numbers of physicians and health care administrators from 1970 to 1987. The data are from *Statistical Abstract of the United States* for these years (Table 64-2, 109th ed). Because of a modification in the Bureau of the Census' definition of *health administrators*, the change between 1982 and 1983 is interpolated rather than actual. (Reprinted with permission from Woolhandler S, Himmelstein DU. The deteriorating administrative efficiency of the U.S. health care system. *N Engl J Med.* 1991;324(18):1253–1258.)

 trators and physicians from 1970 to 1987.[5] Administrative costs in hospitals have grown considerably in response to the increasingly complex health care environment, while physicians' billing expenses likewise have grown substantially in an environment with more than 1,200 insurers, each with its own procedures and requirements. Figures 7-3 and 7-4 compare the impact of current administrative costs on per capita expenditures for health care in the United States and Canada. Most of these costs are attributable to overhead within the health insurance industry. The relative simplicity of Canada's single-payer system results in remarkable differences in administrative costs between the two countries.[6]

By contrast, and as an historical curiosity, Figure 7-5 shows the minimum fee schedule for the Siskiyou County Medical Society in northern California as adopted in 1948.[7] Although it is difficult to compare charges across more than 50 years, a rough comparison can be made in terms of the number of hours a typical production worker would need to work to pay for a given service. According to the Bureau of Labor Statistics, the average hourly wage for production workers in 1948 and 1999 was $1.23 (about $8.00 in 1999 dollars) and $13.24, respectively.[8] In 1948, the charge for normal pregnancy (single vaginal delivery, including all prenatal and postpartum care) was $100; the equivalent charge in 1999 was $3,187. It took the typical production worker about 82 hours to earn this fee in 1948, compared to about 240 hours for a worker in 1999.

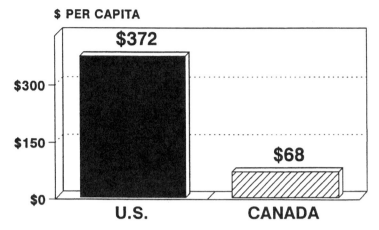

Figure 7-3 Hospital billing and administration, United States and Canada, 2000. (Reprinted with permission from Woolhandler S, Himmelstein DU. *The National Health Program Slideshow Guide.* Cambridge, MA: Physicians for a National Health Program, 2000.)

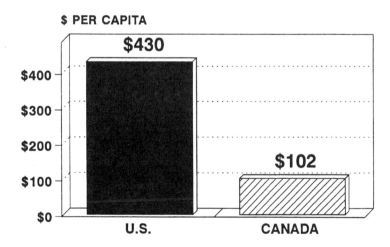

Figure 7-4 Physicians' billing and office expenses, United States and Canada, 2000. (Reprinted with permission from Woolhandler S, Himmelstein DU. *The National Health Program Slideshow Guide.* Cambridge, MA: Physicians for a National Health Program, 2000.)

MINIMUM FEE SCHEDULE
Siskiyou County Medical Society
EFFECTIVE MAY 1, 1948

Procedure or Service:	Minimum Fee:

PATIENT VISITS

Office—first complete $5.00
  routine, follow-up 3.00
Hospital—first complete 5.00
  follow-up 4.00
Home—first complete 5.00
  follow-up 4.80
  night (10 p.m. to 7 a.m.) 7.00
Consultation 10.00
Mileage charge (per mile) one way,
  out of town limits 1.00

PRE- AND POST-NATAL CARE

Pregnancy (complete) $100.00
Caesarian Section 200.00
Curettage 80.00
Circumcision—infant 10.00
  all other ages 35.00
Removal Cervical Polyp 60.00
Perineorrhaphy $150–200.00
Hysterectomy 200.00
            (simple, supracervical)

FRACTURES
(Examples)

Forearm or leg—one bone $30.00
  two bones 52.50
Femur or humerus 75.00
Clavical or scapula 37.50
Ribs 10.00
  Complicating features, casts, splints and after
              care extra.

GENERAL SURGICAL PROCEDURES

Abdominal Laparotomies $150–200.00
Cholecystectomy 200.00
Gastroenterostomy 250.00
Bowel resection 250.00
Thyroidectomy 200.00
Tonsillectomy—children 50.00
  adults 75.00
Herniorraphy—single 150.00
  double 200.00
Hemorrhoidectomy 100.00
  Injection treatment, each 5.00
Hydrocele repair 75.00
Nephrectomy 250.00
Prostatectomy $200–250.00
Vasectomy 50.00
Ligation, Saphenous vein 75.00

MISCELLANEOUS

Assistance to major surgery $25.00
Transfusion 25.00
Wassermann (or other blood test) 5.00
Penicillin (300,000 units) 7.50
Streptomycin—per gram 7.50
Aspiration (any joint or cavity
  including hydrocale) 10.00
Anesthesia—inhalation, spinal or intravenous,
  administered by M. D. for major surgery 25.00
  for minor surgery $5–10.00
  (including tonsillectomy)
Gonorrhea—complete treatment with penicillin . .50.00

These are minimum fees for individual uncomplicated procedures bound on average costs and average time consumption by the physician and also bound on the patient's income up to $3,000.00 per year. Variations from this basis in relation to the above minimum fees are expected to be dealt with fairly at the discretion of the physician who may otherwise jeopardize his ethical standing in the Siskiyou County Medical Society.

Figure 7-5   Minimum fee schedule, Siskiyou County (California) Medical Society, 1948.

Granted that the quality and outcome of obstetric care in 1999 are by no means comparable to 1948, the contrast is quite interesting, at least to this noneconomist, and at the same time reflects a reimbursement pattern favoring procedural over cognitive services in both instances.

WHO PAYS FOR HEALTH CARE?

Although on first glance a busy set of numbers, Table 7-3 tells a fascinating story in terms of who paid for health care services in the United States during selected years between 1970 and 1998. There are many points of interest in these numbers. The share of public funding of total health care payments increased from 37.8 percent in 1970 to 46.2 percent in 1997, then declined slightly to 45.5 percent in 1998, mostly due to cutbacks in Medicare and Medicaid. A majority of health care payments still are made by the private sector, predominantly by private health insurance. The proportion of all insured employees covered by managed care increased from 54 percent in 1993 to 86 percent in 1998.[2] Out-of-pocket expenditures fell from 22.7 percent to 17.4 percent from 1988 to 1997,[2] while the share paid by private health insurance rose in 1998 for the first time since 1990. Medicare remains the largest public payer for health care, accounts for 19 percent of overall health care spending, and covers 38.8 million elderly and disabled beneficiaries.[3] Meanwhile, major changes were taking place in the Medicaid program. By 1998, for the first time, more than one half of Medicaid recipients were in some form of managed care. With a strong economy and low unemployment, together with new welfare-to-work requirements enacted in 1997 under Temporary Assistance for Needy Families (TANF), the number of Medicaid recipients showed a slight decrease in 1997. These are some factors responsible for cost containment of health care services for the population covered by Medicaid since the early 1990s.[2]

As an increasing area for health care expenditures involving an often vulnerable population, the growing costs of nursing home care warrants special comment. More than one half of these costs are paid by public funds (Medicaid and Medicare cover 44 and 14 percent of these outlays, respectively),[6] with almost one third being paid out of pocket by patients and their families. The average daily costs of nursing home care varies widely; a recent report from the Metlife Mature Market Institute found a range from $90 in Hibbing, Minnesota, to $141 in Denver to $278 in Boston.[9] Out-of-pocket expenditures by seniors have doubled since 1977, and now account for one quarter of these payments.[10]

COST OF PRIVATE HEALTH INSURANCE

The average monthly cost borne by employer and employee for insured workers was $341 in 1998 ($4,092 per year), with family coverage costing $461 per month ($5,532 per year). Employee contributions to monthly premiums increased from 20 percent in 1977 to 27 percent in 1998. At the same time, real

Table 7-3 National Health Expenditures, by Source of Funds, Amounts and Average Annual Growth, Selected Calendar Years, 1970–1998

Source of Funds	1970	1980	1990	1994	1995	1996	1997	1998
National health expenditures (billions)	$73.2	$247.3	$699.4	$947.7	$993.3	$1,039.4	$1,088.2	$1,149.1
Private funds	45.5	142.5	416.2	524.7	537.3	559.0	586.0	626.4
Consumer payments	41.2	130.0	384.6	483.5	494.6	513.0	535.7	574.6
Out-of-pocket payments	24.9	60.3	145.0	168.2	170.5	178.1	189.1	199.5
Private health insurance	16.3	69.8	239.6	315.3	324.0	334.9	346.7	375.0
Other private funds	4.4	12.5	31.6	41.2	42.7	46.1	50.3	51.8
Public funds	27.7	104.8	283.2	423.0	456.0	480.4	502.2	522.7
Federal	17.8	72.0	195.2	301.2	326.1	347.3	363.0	376.9
Medicare	7.7	37.5	111.5	166.9	185.3	199.4	211.3	216.6
Medicaid	2.9	14.5	42.7	81.5	86.4	92.3	95.0	100.3
Other federal	7.3	19.9	41.0	52.8	54.5	55.7	56.8	60.0
State and local	9.9	32.8	88.0	121.8	129.8	133.1	139.2	145.8
Medicaid	2.5	11.6	32.7	53.1	59.8	61.8	65.0	70.3
Other state and local	7.4	21.2	55.3	68.7	70.1	71.3	74.2	75.5
Average annual growth in national health expenditures from prior year shown	10.6%[a]	12.9%	11.0%	7.9%	4.8%	4.6%	4.7%	5.6
Private funds	8.5[a]	12.1	11.3	6.0	2.4	4.0	4.8	6.9
Consumer payments	8.1[a]	12.2	11.5	5.9	2.3	3.7	4.4	7.2
Out-of-pocket payments	6.7[a]	9.2	9.2	3.8	1.4	4.4	6.2	5.5
Private health insurance	10.7[a]	15.7	13.1	7.1	2.8	3.3	3.5	8.2
Other private funds	13.2[a]	11.1	9.7	6.9	3.6	7.8	9.1	3.1
Public funds	15.3[a]	14.2	10.5	10.6	7.8	5.4	4.5	4.1
Federal	19.8[a]	15.0	10.5	11.5	8.3	6.5	4.5	3.8
Medicare	[b]	17.2	11.5	10.6	11.0	7.6	6.0	2.5
Medicaid	[b]	17.6	11.4	17.6	6.0	6.8	2.9	5.6
Other federal	9.6[a]	10.6	7.5	6.5	3.1	2.2	2.1	5.6
State and local	10.2[a]	12.7	10.4	8.5	6.6	2.5	4.6	4.7
Medicaid	[b]	16.8	10.9	12.9	12.5	3.4	5.2	8.2
Other state and local	7.1[a]	11.0	10.1	5.6	2.0	1.8	4.0	1.7

Note: Numbers may not add to totals because of rounding.
[a] Average annual growth between 1960 and 1970.
[b] Not applicable.
Source: Health Care Financing Administration, Office of the Actuary, National Health Statistics Group. Reprinted with permission from Levit K, Cowan C, Lazenby H, Sensenig A, McDonell P, Stiller J, et al. Healthcare services in the United States during selected years between 1970 and 1998. The Health Accounts Team. *Health Aff (Millwood)*. 2000;19(1):131.

Percentage increase

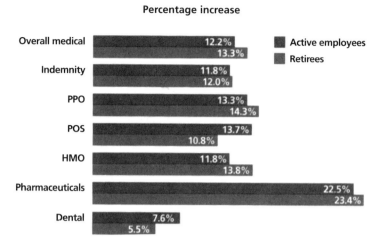

Figure 7-6 Expected premium/equivalent cost increase from 2000 to 2001. (Reprinted with permission from Health care costs 2001. *Med Benefits.* 2000;7(15):1.)

weekly wages for privately employed nonsupervisory workers were 11 percent lower in 1998 than 1977. On the positive side of the ledger, however, insurance coverage for prescription drugs, outpatient mental health, and routine physical examinations showed dramatic increases in coverage between 1977 and 1998.[11]

A July 2000 report by Watson Wyatt Worldwide and the Washington Business Group on Health noted that U.S. health costs have been accelerating for the last four years, with no letup in sight. Overall medical costs are expected to increase by 12.2 percent in 2001 for active employees and 13.3 percent for Medicare retirees. Prescription drug costs represent the single largest portion of these increases, as shown graphically in Figure 7-6.[12]

SOME INTERNATIONAL COMPARISONS

Despite the advent of managed care and intense efforts by government toward containment of health care costs, U.S. health spending per capita grew more rapidly during the 1990s than in the average industrialized country. A recent analysis of comparisons of health financing and delivery systems in the 29 countries of the Organization for Economic Cooperation and Development (OECD) revealed some interesting findings. Per-capita spending for health care in the United States has been consistently much higher than in any other industrialized country. Between 1990 and 1997, per-capita health expenditures increased an average of 4.3 percent per year compared to an OECD median of 3.8 percent per year. Although the United States has the fewest hospital days per capita, it has the highest hospital costs per day and considerably higher physician incomes than the other OECD countries. This comparison becomes even more disturbing when outcomes are considered. The United States remains in the bottom half of most available outcome measures compared to other OECD

Table 7-4   Health Care Spending in Six Countries, 1960, 1990, and 1997

	Per Capita Health Spending*			Percentage of GDP Spent on Health		
	1960	*1990*	*1997*	*1960*	*1990*	*1997*
Australia	$94	$1,320	$1,805	4.9%	8.3%	8.4%
Canada	103	1,696	2,095	5.5	9.2	9.0
Germany	68	1,279	2,339	4.8	8.7	10.4
Sweden	89	1,492	1,728	4.7	8.8	8.6
United Kingdom	74	955	1,347	3.9	6.0	6.7
United States	149	2,799	3,925	5.2	12.6	13.5
OECD median	66	1,286	1,728	3.8	7.2	7.5

Note: GDP is gross domestic product.

* Expenditures were adjusted using purchasing power parities.

Source: *OECD Health Data 98: A Comparative Analysis of Twenty-Nine Countries.* Paris: Organization for Economic Cooperation and Development, 1998. Reprinted with permission from Anderson GF, Poullier JP. Health spending, access, and outcomes: Trends in industrialized countries. *Health Aff (Millwood).* 1999;18(3):179.

countries, and its relative ranking has been falling since 1960.[13] These outcome measures include life expectancy, infant mortality, and years of life lost. While these measures are relatively crude indicators of health status and somewhat insensitive to changes in health care financing and delivery systems, they reflect unfavorably on the world's most expensive health care system.

Table 7-4 displays health care spending for 1960, 1990, and 1997 for six of the OECD countries in terms of both per-capita spending and the percentage of GDP spent on health care services. Our neighbor to the north, Canada, consistently has outperformed the United States on containing health care costs and still has better outcome measures (e.g., concerning care of end stage renal disease, U.S. death rates for dialysis patients are 47 percent higher than in Canada after controlling for age, sex, race, and comorbidities).[14] The percentage of GDP spent on health care increased by 8.3 percentage points in the United States between 1960 and 1997, compared to a 3.7 percentage increase in the median OECD country.[13]

PROJECTED FUTURE HEALTH CARE COSTS

The economists and actuaries of the National Health Expenditures Projection Team recently reported their best estimates for health spending to 2008. Among their projections are continued growth of overall health care spending, to reach $2.2 trillion (16.2 percent of the GDP) by 2008; renewed growth in inpatient hospital costs, since the "easy cuts" already have been made and excess bed capacity somewhat reduced; constrained public spending on health care, particularly as BBA97 provisions take further effect; and private health spending holding between 53 and 55 percent of total national health expenditures. Sharp increases are anticipated for health insurance premiums, and spending on prescription drugs likewise will be inflationary (e.g., an 11.2 percent increase between 1999 and 2001 for prescription drugs).[15]

Soaring prices of prescription drugs fuel an especially inflammatory issue currently being debated between the Congress and the Bush administration concerning a proposed new Medicare drug benefit. There is strong public support, especially among the elderly, for such an added benefit, driven by drug prices that far exceed the rate of inflation. A 1999 report from Families USA in Washington, DC, reveals that the price of the 50 prescription drugs most used by older Americans increased, on average, at twice the rate of inflation in 1998, with Lanoxin, the most commonly used drug, rising about seven times the inflation rate.[16] Critics of adding such a benefit include those concerned about the incremental costs of coverage (estimated by the Congressional Budget Office, to increase Medicare expenditures by $136 billion between 2002 and 2009)[17] as well as concerns by the pharmaceutical industry of government price controls.

CONCLUDING COMMENTS

The relentless growth in health care costs is driven by many powerful forces, including aggressive marketing by suppliers and providers of care, increasing intensity of health care services, the impact of new technologies, and a considerable degree of inappropriate and even unnecessary care. As noted in earlier chapters, a major change in any corner of the "iron triangle" affects one or both of the others. Thus, rising costs, as they become unaffordable for some, lead to decreased access to care, which can lead in turn to negative impacts on quality of care. Concerning access, for example, the higher the rate of cost increases, the more people drop out of insurance coverage and the more out-of-pocket expenditures are required. A report in January 1998 from the Consumers Union in Washington, DC, *Hidden from View: The Growing Burden of Health Care Costs*, examines the impact on access of rising health care costs. This report estimates that the number of Americans spending more than 10 percent of their income on health insurance premiums and out-of-pocket medical costs (i.e., the "underinsured") rose almost 40 percent between 1981 and 1996.[18]

The extent to which escalating costs of health care can be controlled will be addressed in Chapter 16. The unavoidable tradeoffs between cost, access, and quality of health care will be revisited in chapters to follow, particularly those dealing with access, quality, rationing, and organizational options for improving the health care system. First, to explore the impact of rising health care costs on access, we turn to the next chapter.

REFERENCES

1. Igelhart JK. The business of health in a free-wheeling democracy. *Health Aff (Millwood)*. 2000;19(1):6.
2. Levit K, Cowan C, Lazenby H, Sensenig A, McDonell P, Stiller J, et al. Healthcare services in the

United States during selected years between 1970 and 1998. The Health Accounts Team. *Health Aff (Millwood).* 2000;19(1):124–132.

3. Ginsburg PB, Gabel JR. Tracking health care costs: What's new in 1998? *Health Aff (Millwood).* 1998;17(5):142.
4. Median direct physician compensation, 1999. *Med Benefits.* 2000;17(15):11.
5. Woolhandler S, Himmelstein DU. The deteriorating administrative efficiency of the U.S. health care system. *N Engl J Med.* 1991;324(18):1253–1258.
6. Woolhandler S, Himmelstein DU. *The National Health Program Slideshow Guide.* Cambridge, MA: Physicians for a National Health Program, 2000.
7. Personal communication, J.W. Reynolds, MD, Dunsmuir, CA, September 1, 2000.
8. Bureau of Labor Statistics. National employment, hours, and earnings. Available on the website www.bls.gov, September 29, 2000.
9. Nursing home costs vary by state. *Med Econo.* September 18, 2000:22.
10. Senate Select Committee on Aging: American Association for Retired Persons. April 1995 and March 1998.
11. Gabel JR. Job-based health insurance, 1977–1998: The accidental system under scrutiny. *Health Aff (Millwood).* 1999;18(6):62–74.
12. Health care costs 2001. *Med Benefits.* 2000;7(15):1.
13. Anderson GF, Poullier JP. Health spending, access, and outcomes: Trends in industrialized countries. *Health Aff (Millwood).* 1999;18(3):178–192.
14. Hornberger JC, Garber AM, Jeffery JR. Mortality, hospital admissions, and medical costs of end-stage renal disease in the United States and Manitoba, Canada. *Med Care.* 1997;35(7):686–700.
15. Smith S, Heffler S, Freeland M. The next decade of health spending: A new outlook. The National Health Expenditures Projection Team. *Health Aff (Millwood).* 1999;18(4):86–95.
16. Publications and Reports. Prescription drugs. Hard to swallow rising prices for America's seniors. *Health Aff (Millwood).* 2000;19(1):254.
17. Christensen S, Wagner J. The costs of a Medicare prescription drug benefit. *Health Aff (Millwood).* 2000;19(2):212–218.
18. Publications and Reports. Health care costs hidden from view: The growing burden of health care costs. *Health Aff (Millwood).* 1998;17(5):247.

8
Decreasing Access to Health Care

We saw in earlier chapters some landmark initiatives by the government to increase access to health care since the 1960s, particularly the Medicare and Medicaid programs initiated in the mid-1960s and legislation in 1985 mandating hospitals, as a price for licensure, to provide emergency care to all comers regardless of ability to pay. At the dawn of the 21st century, however, one in six Americans is uninsured, and a groundswell of public reaction is gaining strength toward providing access to health care more equitably. The traditional link between employment and health insurance has been attenuated or lost for many Americans, and present trends for the years ahead predict further weakening of the employer-based insurance system.[1]

Health care (especially problems of access and costs of prescription drugs) was one of the main issues throughout the 2000 presidential election campaign. Candidates in both major parties were forced to deal with the problem of the uninsured, and we have seen increased energy by many policy makers and legislators to engage some of the pressing health care issues—access, patients' Bill of Rights, Medicare's future, and HMO liability. Seven physician groups, including even the AMA (recall the AMA's opposition to Medicare and Medicaid during the 1960s), launched a major campaign to establish universal health care coverage as the No. 1 priority in the 2000 presidential election.[2]

This chapter examines four areas to assess the current and projected "access problem": (1) dimensions of access to health care, (2) who are the uninsured, (3) impact of uninsurance on health care, and (4) access and managed care.

DIMENSIONS OF THE "ACCESS PROBLEM"

Almost 43 million Americans now are without health insurance. As noted in the last chapter, the cost of health insurance is rising much faster than either the cost of living or real wages. The National Federation of Independent Business has called the rising cost of health insurance their No. 1 problem, while an additional 675,000 low-income people have become uninsured since losing

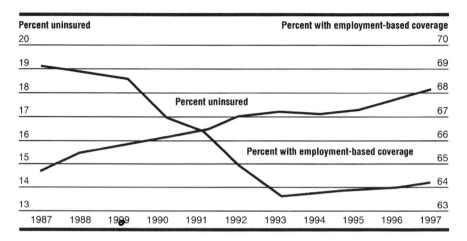

Figure 8-1   Trends in health insurance coverage for persons under age 65, 1987–1997. (Reprinted with permission from Custer WS, Kahn CN III, Wildsmith TF. Why we should keep the employment-based health insurance system. *Health Aff (Millwood)*. 1999;18(6): 115–123.)

their Medicaid coverage as welfare reform provisions were implemented after 1997.[2] The last chapter traced the inexorable increases in health care costs, which have continued despite periodic temporary decreases in the rates of growth. These increasing costs have a direct impact on the number of people without health insurance, both in terms of employers being able to offer health insurance to their employees and the ability of employees to purchase the coverage offered. Figure 8-1 shows the impact of a decrease in health insurance coverage for people under 65 years of age between 1987 and 1997 as the percent of U.S. employers offering health insurance dropped from about 69 percent to 64 percent—over that 10-year period the number of uninsured workers in that age group grew from 14.7 percent to 19 percent.[3] A report by the Center for Studying Health System Change revealed that 20 percent of uninsured Americans in 1996–1997 declined their employers' offers for health care insurance coverage, mostly for cost reasons. This number represented 7.3 million Americans at that time, including 2.2 million children, whose parents declined coverage.[4] It has been estimated that every 1 percent increase in the cost of health care forces another 300,000 people into the uninsured category.[5]

The issue of access to health care is extremely complex. Access to medical or surgical services is one measure of access, but what about prescription drugs, mental health care, eyeglasses, and dental care? Other dimensions that complicate the picture are whether we should consider use of hospital emergency rooms an adequate access measure for health problems with no physician visits? The 1994 National Access to Care Survey conducted by the Robert Wood Johnson Foundation, for example, found that 34.5 million in the United States were uninsured at that time. However, 41.5 million respondents felt that they could not obtain medical or surgical care, dental care, prescription drugs, mental

Table 8-1 Type of "Access" Problems Reported by Low-Income Patients Hospitalized for Preventable or Avoidable Conditions

	Percentage of Low-Income Patients with "Access" Problems Who Reported Type of Reason		
Reason for Problem	*Age 6 Mos–17 Yr*	*Age 18–64 Yr*	*All Ages*
Not up to going	5.1	36.1	29.2
Too nervous or afraid	10.2	33.8	28.6
Unable to find free time to get care	8.1	27.2	22.9
Had to wait too long to get appointment	20.3	20.4	20.4
Problems with child care	32.8	14.3	18.2
Costs too much	13.8	18.1	17.2
Unable to keep medical appointment	7.4	20.2	17.1
Couldn't fill prescription	16.4	16.9	16.8
Transportation difficulties	19.3	15.8	16.5
Didn't know where to get care	8.6	13.8	12.7
Not sure provider would understand needs	22.4	9.1	12.2
Care not available when needed	11.3	12.1	12.0
Denied care	13.4	9.7	10.6
Didn't like place usually got care	17.2	7.9	9.9
Lose pay/trouble getting off work	12.1	6.0	7.3
Language problem	1.8	4.7	4.3

Note: Percentages total more than 100% because some patients indicated multiple reasons.

Source: Hospitalized Patient Interview Survey, United Hospital Fund. Reprinted with permission from Billings J. Access to health care services. In: Kovner AR, Jonas S (eds). *Health Care Delivery in the United States.* New York: Springer Publishing Company, 1999:424.

health care or counseling, and eyeglasses.[6] If that same proportion holds today on a base of almost 43 million uninsured, we now have about 53 million Americans without access to health care, nearly 20 percent of the population.

The United Hospital Fund reported an interesting study in 1997 of low-income patients hospitalized for preventable or avoidable conditions. Patients were interviewed after hospital admission and medical stabilization. It was found that 60.9 percent of low-income patients said they had received no care before admission, and only 17.4 percent had been seen in the emergency room; similar findings for higher income patients were 31.4 and 5.8 percent, respectively.[7] Table 8-1 presents the range of reasons reported on why the respondents did not or could not access the system for care. It is readily apparent that over one quarter of respondents felt they were "not up to going, were too nervous or afraid to go, or were too busy to go."

Another study, the Commonwealth Fund's 1998 International Health Policy Survey, sheds further light on the access problem. In a study involving about 1,000 adults in the United States exploring patient satisfaction with health care, marked differences were found in the responses of study participants to various access barriers or concerns in terms of their insurance coverage status. For example, about two thirds of the uninsured felt they could not afford and could not obtain needed medical care for a serious illness compared to only about 15 percent who had some kind of insurance coverage[8] (Table 8-2).

A further complexity of the access problem is the well-documented fact that insurance coverage by no means assures access to health care. An excellent example of this is provided by a recent national claims-based study of more than 345,000 elderly Medicare beneficiaries. The study found that these beneficiaries received indicated care, as measured by 16 of 40 necessary care markers, less than two thirds of the time. As expected, underuse of indicated care was more prevalent in vulnerable populations, especially among African-Americans and those people living in health professional shortage areas.[9] The same problem has been reported concerning access to dental care, which has been found to be the most prevalent unmet health need among children in America. Only one in five children covered by Medicaid receives preventive oral health care.[10]

If these access figures are unsettling, they are even more so if one projects

Table 8-2   Americans' Reports on Selected Measures, by Insurance Status and Type, 1998

	All Americans	All Uninsured	All Insured	Managed Care	Traditional Insurance
Access/cost: Percent who reported					
Having financial problems paying medical bills	18	42	13	16	9
Inability to get needed medical care in past year	14	37	10	12	7
Not filling prescriptions for financial reasons	17	42	13	14	12
Difficulties (extremely, very, somewhat difficult) seeing specialist and consultants	39	67	34	40	25
Worries/anxieties: percent who said that they are very worried that					
If they become seriously ill, they will not be able to get the most advanced care	21	53	14	16	12
If they become seriously ill, they will not be able to get the medical care they need because they cannot afford it	23	65	15	16	13
They will not be able to pay for (private) care for parents, grandparents, or spouse if they need nursing home care for a long-term illness	36	58	32	37	27
They will wait too long to get nonemergency care	14	35	10	12	8

Source: Commonwealth Fund 1998 International Health Policy Survey. Adapted with permission from Donelan K, Blendon RJ, Schoen C, Davis K, Binns K. The cost of health system change: Public discontent in five nations. *Health Aff (Millwood).* 1999;18(3):214.

the trends ahead over the next few years. The National Coalition on Health Care projects that, by 2009, 61 million Americans will be uninsured if there is an economic downturn with rising cost of living, while some analysts predict that, by 2007, 54 million Americans will be uninsured, even if the current economic boom continues.[2]

WHO ARE THE UNINSURED?

The profile of the uninsured population is complex and sometimes surprising. Table 8-3 presents a demographic snapshot of uninsured Americans, based on 1996 data. Age, ethnicity, and income level make big differences in the odds of being uninsured. One in three or four of young people from 18 to 34 years of age are uninsured, as are one in three Hispanic persons and one in three people with income levels below 150 percent of the federal poverty level (about $33,000 per year for a family of four in 2000).[11] Contrast that with a level of uninsurance of less than 2 percent for elderly Americans eligible for Medicare.[11]

Table 8-3   Nonelderly Population without Health Insurance Coverage by Demographic Characteristics, 1996 Current Population Survey

Characteristics	Percentage of Total Uninsured	Percentage of Uninsured within Categories
Male	53.5	21.0
Female	46.5	17.0
Total	100.0	17.4
Under 18	24.3	13.8
18–20	6.2	23.2
21–24	11.2	32.3
25–34	23.2	23.1
35–44	17.7	16.7
45–54	10.4	13.3
55–64	6.9	13.4
Total	100.0	17.4
White	54.3	13.4
Black	16.9	22.4
Hispanic	23.4	35.0
Other	5.4	20.3
Total	100.0	17.4
<100% poverty level	27.6	33.0
100–149%	16.8	32.8
150–199%	14.9	27.3
200–399%	27.7	14.4
400+	13.0	6.7
Total	100.0	17.4

Source: Employee Benefit Research Institute, 1997; and U.S. Bureau of the Census, 1997. Reprinted with permission from Billings J. Access to health care services. In: Kovner AR, Jonas S (eds). *Health Care Delivery in the United States.* New York: Springer Publishing Company, 1999:424.

Jon Gabel, vice president of health systems studies at the Health Research and Educational Trust in Washington, D.C., pulled together the results of many national household and employer surveys conducted between 1977 and 1998. A portrait emerged of a fragile employer-based health insurance system that fails to insure a growing number of U.S. workers. Over the 21 year period, the cost of job-based insurance increased 2.6-fold while employees' contributions for coverage increased 3.5-fold (all in 1998 dollars). At the same time, the percentage of nonelderly Americans covered by job-based insurance fell from 71 percent to 64 percent. Most of that decline was among lower-income workers with no college education, who are being left behind in an information-based global economy.[12] Real wages for workers who have not completed high school dropped 18 percent since 1973, while college graduates saw a 17 percent increase in hourly wages.[13] An even more recent national telephone survey of more than 5,000 working and nonworking Americans by the Commonwealth Fund found that 60 percent of the uninsured adults worked full time or were married to a full-time worker, and that 19 percent of workers were not offered or were not eligible for an employer-based insurance plan.[14]

 Medicaid coverage is not available for most lower-income workers. Although eligibility for Medicaid varies considerably from one state to another, eligibility generally is limited to one of the following categories: children, elderly, blind or otherwise disabled, pregnant women, single parents, or unemployed parents (in some states). Parents who are employed or adults without children usually are not eligible for Medicaid regardless of income level unless they are blind, disabled, or pregnant.[11] In fact, Medicaid rolls have become even more restricted after welfare reform implemented after the mid-1990s. The 1997 National Survey of America's Families revealed an increasing rate of uninsurance among people who left welfare and joined the workforce. A year after leaving welfare, one half of women and almost one third of children were uninsured.[15]

Employer-based health insurance, the core structure on which the American health care "system" is based, appears to be fraying at the edges and threatening the core. Most uninsured are working in some capacity. A 1997 national study showed that about 85 percent of the uninsured live in households where the head of family has been employed over the previous year.[11] But, for many lower-income workers, the cost of health insurance is beyond their reach. Robert Blendon, of the Harvard School of Public Health and Robert Wood Johnson Foundation, points out that the typical uninsured person is employed and makes between $18,000 and $25,000 per year.[2] How can a worker taking home $1,500 a month pay for coverage costing $400 a month or more? As if the present situation is not alarming enough, future trends are even more disturbing. After an in-depth analysis of our employer-based health system, Gabel summarizes the future in these unsettling words:[12]

Employers are unlikely to ever return to indemnity insurance. PPO coverage represents the new indemnity coverage. As insurers and managed care organizations attempt to restore profitability, premium increases during the next few years will reach the highest levels since 1993. Increases of 5–6 percent may temper the recent movement from lower-price HMOs to POS plans, particularly among employers whose workforce is largely composed of persons lacking a college degree. On the other hand, to attract healthy young workers, employers will offer more preventive benefits. These predictions suggest that the "accidental system," born out of World War II labor shortages, is likely to serve a smaller share of the workforce. A global economy in the information age will produce not only greater wealth but also greater inequalities in income and greater inequalities in health benefits. To ignore this state of affairs constitutes malign neglect.

DECREASED ACCESS AND HEALTH CARE MEASURES

The pressing next question, of course, is what impact does the lack of health insurance have on outcomes of care? Many markers, mostly process measures, indicate the worrisome impact of uninsurance. The 1993 Robert Wood Johnson Foundation Family Health Insurance Survey conducted interviews with more than 27,000 families in 10 states. States with higher percentages of uninsured residents had populations with more access problems and lower health status.[16] Table 8-4, for example, shows that 15.2 percent of adults in three "high-uninsurance" states reported that they are in fair or poor health compared with 8.7 percent of adults in "low-uninsurance" states, with a more than twofold difference by the same measure for children. Table 8-5 shows outcome measures by access to care and age group for emergency care, physician visits, Pap smear, mammography, and immunization status.

A similar study, the Kaiser/Commonwealth 1997 National Survey of Health Insurance, found that almost one in five women between ages 19 and 64 years was uninsured. The effects of uninsurance on their health care is in the same direction, with dramatic differences, such as having a mammogram or being able to obtain needed care in the last year[2] (Figure 8-2).

Another study examined hospitalization rates by access measures for more than 6,000 adults in California hospitals. Not surprisingly, people with poor access to care had much higher rates of "preventable" hospitalization for

Table 8-4   Health Status of Adults and Children, Three High-Uninsured versus Three Low-Uninsured States, 1993

Health Status Measure/Age Group	Three High States[a]	Three Low States[b]
Fair or poor health		
Adults	15.2%	8.7%
Children	4.2	2.0
Limited physical activity		
Adults	28.1	2.0

[a] Florida, New Mexico, and Oklahoma.

[b] Minnesota, North Dakota, and Vermont.

Source: 1993 Robert Wood Johnson Foundation Family Health Insurance Survey. Reprinted with permission from Cantor JC, Long SH, Marquis S. Challenges of state health reform: Variations in ten states. *Health Aff (Millwood).* 1998;17(1):196.

Table 8-5   Access to Care for Adults and Children, Three High-Uninsured versus Three Low-Uninsured States, 1993

Access Measure/Age Group	Three High States[a]	Three Low States[b]
No usual source of care, other than emergency room		
Adults	26.5%	14.6%
Children	12.0	3.6
Did not get emergency care when needed		
Adults	3.6	1.6
Children	1.2	0.5
No physician visits in the past 12 months		
Adults	24.6	20.6
Children	21.4	14.5
No Pap smear		
Adult women, ages 19–64	5.8	4.2
No mammogram		
Adult women, ages 41–64	26.1	17.5
Not fully immunized		
Children, ages 2–4	17.4	14.8

[a] Florida, New Mexico, and Oklahoma.

[b] Minnesota, North Dakota, and Vermont.

Source: 1993 Robert Wood Johnson Foundation Family Health Insurance Survey. Reprinted with permission from Cantor JC, Long SH, Marquis S. Challenges of state health reform: Variations in ten states. *Health Aff (Millwood).* 1998;17(1):197.

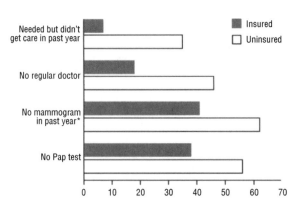

Figure 8-2   Women's access to care and use of health care services, 1997; mammograms were measured for women 50 years of age or over. (Source: Kaiser/Commonwealth 1997 National Study of Health Insurance. Reprinted with permission from Finger AL. Caring for the uninsured: Will the problem ever be solved? *Med Econ.* December 20, 1999:134.)

chronic medical problems, including asthma, hypertension, congestive heart failure, chronic obstructive lung disease, and diabetes.[17] Other reports documented that, when the uninsured are hospitalized, their illnesses and injuries are more acute and advanced than their insured counterparts[18] and that the mortality rate is higher for the uninsured than for people with health insurance.[19,20]

The Robert Wood Johnson Foundation, with a long interest in improving the health and health care of the American people, developed a number of access indicators to monitor access to health care. These indicators are of two types: utilization indicators and outcome indicators. The following examples provide more specific measures of the impact of access barriers based on 1990 national survey results:[21]

- Uninsured preschool children had only 2.8 physician visits in 1990 compared to 3.4 and 6.1 physician visits for those with private insurance or Medicaid, respectively.
- Uninsured children between 5 and 17 years of age made 1.6 physician visits in 1990 compared to 2.5 visits and 3.4 visits if on private insurance or Medicaid, respectively.
- Uninsured children in the same age group had a usual source of care in 1990 in only 73.5 percent of cases compared to 86.9 and 89.3 percent of those with private insurance or Medicaid, respectively.
- Low-income children had a hospitalization rate for asthma more than four-fold greater than for children in high-income families.
- 34 percent of births were unintended at the time of conception among poor women in 1988 compared to 24 percent of non-poor women.
- 20 percent of poor women reported problems obtaining prenatal care in 1990 compared to only 6 percent of non-poor women.
- The infant mortality rate for black infants within the first few weeks of birth is more than double that for white infants.
- Poor adults under age 65 made 4.0 visits to physicians in 1990 compared to 6.2 visits for their counterparts with some form of health care coverage.
- Low-income adults in 1989 had an eight-fold greater hospitalization rate for asthma and a four-fold higher rate for bacterial pneumonia compared to high-income adults.

Furthermore, a study published in November 2000 failed to show improvement in access to care for low-income Americans. Almost one half of uninsured adults with annual incomes below $15,000, for example, reported that they could not see a physician when needed during the past year due to the cost of care. The long-term uninsured in poor health reported they went without needed care about two thirds of the time.[22]

ACCESS AND MANAGED CARE

Since one or another form of managed care has become the dominant structure for American health care over the last 15 years, the next interesting question is, what happens to access to care in HMOs and other forms of managed care?

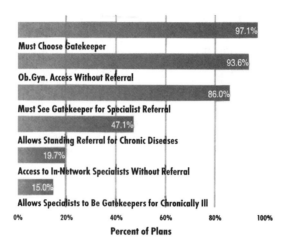

Figure 8-3   HMO rules that apply to all or most enrollees, based on a survey of 314 HMOs in 1998. (Source: InterStudy. Reprinted with permission from Vital signs. HMO rules that apply to all or most enrollees. *Fam Pract News.* September 1, 1999:1.)

HMO enrollees, of course, generally have a primary care physician in a "gate-keeper" role. Ready access to specialists becomes an important issue for many patients, so mechanisms for referral command considerable interest. Figure 8-3 displays HMO rules that apply to all or most HMO enrollees based on a survey by Inter Study of 314 HMOs in 1998.

The National Ambulatory Medical Care Survey provides a large nationally representative survey of the medical practice of office-based physicians. Forrest and Reid analyzed data for six consecutive years (1989 to 1994) comparing referral routes to specialty care for patients in HMOs and in indemnity insurance plans. They found, surprisingly, that primary care patient visits in HMOs were 66 percent more likely to lead to a specialty referral than for such patients with indemnity coverage (referral rates of 6.3 versus 3.8 percent, respectively). Self-referral by the patient directly to a specialist was 37 percent less likely for HMO patients than indemnity patients (31.3 versus 49.5 percent, respectively). Cross-referral from one specialist to another was about the same for each group (2.5 versus 2.8 percent, respectively).[23] Self-referrals were considerably more common in some specialties, especially dermatology, obstetrics-gynecology, ophthalmology, and psychiatry, but less common for HMO patients than indemnity patients for all specialties. Table 8-6 shows self-referral rates for 14 specialties over the 1989 to 1994 period. At the same time, there was suggestive evidence from the analysis by Forest and Reid that primary care physician referrals in HMOs were more appropriate than self-referrals.[23]

Another look at access to care questions is provided by a national study of over 3,000 patients enrolled in Medicare HMOs in 1996. Almost all (96 percent) of these patients reported that they could see the same physician for most scheduled office visits, while only 8 percent had trouble making appointments and 6 percent felt they were not referred to a specialist when desired.[24]

Table 8-6   Self-Referrals, by Payment System and Type of Specialist Physician, 1989–1994

Specialist	Total	HMO	Indemnity	p-*Value*
Allergy/immunology	45.8	29.2	55.4	<.001
Cardiology	37.4	33.0	38.9	.27
Dermatology	66.3	51.1	75.7	<.001
Gastroenterology	24.2	18.2	27.3	.069
General surgery	31.5	20.7	36.3	<.001
Neurology	18.7	7.0	24.3	<.001
OB/GYN	71.5	62.5	76.4	<.001
Ophthalmology	64.9	58.4	67.7	.012
Orthopedics	47.6	27.5	54.9	<.001
Otolaryngology	44.2	26.7	52.6	<.001
Plastic surgery	43.6	20.0	49.0	<.001
Psychiatry	61.9	49.3	64.6	.016
Pulmonary medicine	41.8	39.6	43.1	.58
Urology	33.3	17.3	41.1	<.001

Note: HMO is health maintenance organization. OB/GYN is obstetrics/gynecology.

Source: National Ambulatory Medical Care Surveys, 1989–1994. Reprinted with permission from Forrest CB, Reid RJ. Passing the baton: HMOs influence on referrals to specialty care. *Health Aff (Millwood).* 1997;16(6):160.

CONCLUDING COMMENTS

There "always" have been uninsured people who had difficulty with access to medical care, so why is the access problem so much more acute and worrisome today? Several reasons stand out. First, by latest count almost 43 million Americans are uninsured, a very large number, which is appalling in the most affluent country in the world. Moreover, at least 60 million people will lose their health insurance coverage for at least a month during the current year, so that about one quarter of all nonelderly Americans are uninsured, at least for a time, every year.[25] But perhaps the biggest difference today is the new coalition of forces becoming increasingly mobilized to alleviate an unsustainable problem. Advocacy groups for the uninsured seek the support of legislators, policy makers, and health care organizations in their quest for affordable health insurance coverage. Employers, who are on the line to offer coverage to their employees, balk at the increasing costs of such coverage and pass these costs along to employees with higher premium payments. Employers also are pushing for more cost containment of health care costs and do not feel responsible for the costs for the uninsured, only their own employees. Meanwhile, of course, real limits are being confronted by employers and government at all levels in their effort to find the necessary funds to finance steadily growing demands for health care.

Of particular concern is that the severe access problems described are taking place during the longest economic boom period yet experienced in the United States, together with employment levels exceeding all previous records. Despite these advantages, the fragility of the employment-based insurance system as well as the public safety net have been exposed as overextended in the best of times. It is only a matter of time, not if, an economic downturn magnifies the access problem exponentially. This issue is revisited in later chapters, especially those that deal with attempts to improve access (Chapter 17) and organizational options for reform of the health care system (Chapter 22).

REFERENCES

1. Blendon RJ, Young JT, DesRoches CM. The uninsured, the working uninsured, and the public. *Health Aff (Millwood)*. 1999;18(6):203–211.
2. Finger AL. Caring for the uninsured: Will the problem ever be solved? *Med Econ.* December 20, 1999:132–141.
3. Custer WS, Kahn CN III, Wildsmith TF. Why we should keep the employment-based health insurance system. *Health Aff (Millwood)*. 1999;18(6):115–123.
4. Publications and Reports. "Who declines employer-sponsored health insurance and is uninsured?" *Health Aff (Millwood)*. 2000;19(1):253.
5. Robinson JC. Interview. At the helm of an insurance grant: Aetna's Richard L. Huber. *Health Aff (Millwood)*. 1999;18(6):91.
6. Berk ML, Schur CL. Measuring access to care: Improving information for policy-makers. *Health Aff (Millwood)*. 1998;17(1):182.
7. Billings J, Mijanovich T, Blank A. *Barriers to Care for Patients with Preventable Hospital Admissions.* New York: United Hospital Fund, 1997.
8. Donelan K, Blendon RJ, Schoen C, Davis K, Binns K. The cost of health system change: Public discontent in five nations. *Health Aff (Millwood)*. 1999;18(3):214.
9. Asch SM, Sloss EM, Hogan C, et al. Measuring underuse of medical care among elderly Medicare beneficiaries using inpatient and outpatient claims. *JAMA.* 2000;284:2325–2333.
10. Mouradian WE, Wehr E, Crall JJ. Disparities in children's oral health and access to dental care. *JAMA.* 2000;284:2625–2631.
11. Billings J. Access to health care services. In: Kovner AR, Jonas S (eds). *Health Care Delivery in the United States.* New York: Springer Publishing Company, 1999:424.
12. Gabel JR. Job-based health insurance, 1977–1998: The accidental system under scrutiny. *Health Aff (Millwood)*. 1999;18(6):62–74.
13. Bluestone R. The inequality express. *Am Prospect.* Winter 1995:81–83.
14. Grant Outcomes. Can't afford to get sick: A reality for millions of working Americans. *Health Aff (Millwood)*. 1999;18(6):229.
15. Garrett B, Holahan I. Health coverage after welfare. *Health Aff (Millwood)*. 2000;19(1):175–184.
16. Cantor JC, Long SH, Marquis S. Challenges of state health reform: variations in ten states. *Health Aff (Millwood)*. 1998;17(1):191–200.
17. Bindman AB, Grumbach K, Osmond D, Komaromy M, Vranizan K, Lurie N, et al. Preventable hospitalizations and access to health care. *JAMA.* 1995;274:305–311.
18. Hadley J, Steinberg EP, Feder J. Comparison of uninsured and privately insured hospital patients. *JAMA.* 1993;270:737–741.
19. Franks P, Clancy CM, Gold MR. Health insurance and mortality: Evidence from a national cohort. *JAMA.* 1993;270:737–741.
20. Carrasquillo O, Himmelstein DU, Woolhandler S, Bor DH. Going bare: Trends in health insurance coverage, 1989 through 1996. *Am J Public Health.* 1999;89:36–42.
21. *Access to Health Care: Key Indicators for Policy.* Princeton, NJ: Center for Health Economics Research and the Robert Wood Johnson Foundation, 1993.
22. Ayanian JZ, Weissman JS, Schneider EC, Ginsburg JA, Zaslavsky AM. Unmet health needs of uninsured adults in the United States. *JAMA.* 2000;284:2061–2069.
23. Forrest CB, Reid RJ. Passing the baton: HMOs influence on referrals to specialty care. *Health Aff (Millwood)*. 1997;16(6):157–162.
24. Nelson L, Brown R, Gold M, Ciemnecki A, Docteur E. Access to care in Medicare HMOs, 1996. *Health Aff (Millwood)*. 1997;16(2):148–156.
25. Swartz K. Who owns the problems of the uninsured? *Inquiry.* Summer 1996;33:103–105.

9
Change of Locus of Control
of Health Care

Medical practice is in the middle of a profound transition. Most physicians can remember the day when, armed with a degree, a mission, and confidence, they could set forth to heal the sick. Like Solomon, physicians could receive patients, hear their complaints, and determine the best course of action. While not every patient could be cured, everyone could be confident that whatever was done was the best possible. Most important, each physician was free, trusted, and left alone to determine what was in the best interest of each patient.

All of that is changing. In retrospect, the first changes seem minor—some increased paperwork, "tissue" committees, a few more meetings. These activities were designed to affect the presumably small fraction of physicians who, in fact, deserved to be scrutinized, and the scrutiny was an internal process performed by physicians themselves. But today's activities are aimed at all physicians, are much more anonymous, and seem beyond physician control. Now physicians must deal with second opinions, precertification, skeptical medical directors, variable coverage, outright denials, utilization review, threats of cookbook medicine, and letters out of the blue chiding that Mrs. Smith is on two incompatible drugs. Solomon did not have to call anyone to get permission for his decisions.

David Eddy[1]

This observation by David Eddy, drawn from his landmark book *Clinical Decision Making: From Theory to Practice*, captures the transformation in medicine that, although still a work in progress, has in large part already taken place. After 15 years or more in the new era of managed care, most practicing physicians, regardless of specialty, find themselves beleaguered, frustrated by increasing bureaucracy and "hassle factor," with many taking early retirement. In actual fact, of course, a sea change has taken place in the organizational structure of American medicine. The traditional professional sovereignty of physi-

113

cians over medical practice, which they took for granted, has been replaced by a new system of shared power, authority, and accountability. The medical profession's initial reaction is understandable but still painful.

In an effort to better understand the changing environment of medical practice, this chapter examines four areas: (1) an overview of the major power shifts in health care, (2) increased external controls and regulations of medical practice, (3) the extent of decreased autonomy and professional satisfaction of physicians, and (4) responses of physicians to an increasing regulatory practice environment.

POWER SHIFTS IN HEALTH CARE

As the organizational structure of medical practice undergoes fundamental changes amid a climate with many calling for one or another kind of reform, a less visible but intense power struggle is going on as to who will control the more than $1 trillion system that employs 1 of every 11 working Americans. In an insightful paper presented by Emily Friedman to a National Health Policy Forum in Washington (1994), she observed four major power shifts being attempted through mechanisms of structural, fiscal, and political reform:[2]

1. *Within the health care professions*—an attempt to shift power away from physicians to nursing and other health professions (such as nurse practitioners, physicians' assistants, pharmacists, chiropractors, and others) through "any willing provider" legislation.
2. *Within medicine*—an attempt to shift power from specialist to generalist (e.g., the legislature in Washington State has mandated the graduation of more generalists and less specialists by its state medical school).
3. *Within provider organizations*—an attempt to shift power from physicians to administrators and trustees (e.g., in HMOs and integrated delivery systems).
4. *In the overall health care sector*—an attempt to shift power from provider to payer (largely already true as illustrated by the federal government's control over Medicare policies and procedures since the mid-1960s).

The stakes of this power struggle include money and ownership, control and accountability, the respective roles of for-profit and not-for-profit sectors, and the extent of state and federal governments' role in health care. In their excellent recent paper on the organizational transformation of U.S. medicine, Suchman and his colleagues call attention to the most revolutionary trend now well along—the reorganization of health care delivery into integrated systems. They contrast the health care system before managed care (with a variety of individual and institutional providers caring for an undefined population of individual patients) with an idealized integrated health care system (involving an integrated group of providers caring for a defined population of named individuals, with built-in systems for monitoring process and outcomes of care for individual patients as well as the population being served).[3]

The adjustments of mindset in dealing simultaneously with the population-based concept and the care of the individual patient are difficult for many physicians. Suchman and his colleagues describe nine approaches, by now familiar to most physicians, by which an integrated health care system can develop the infrastructure necessary to achieve a level of function greater than the sum of its parts.[3]

1. *Shared information.* Pooled and shared registration and clinical information, largely computerized, within an integrated system, including problem lists, medication lists, and test results, thereby enabling systemwide monitoring of health status, effectiveness of care, rates of hospitalization and referrals, and other clinical measures as well as provider productivity and performance.
2. *Case management.* This may include health status, screening when patients are first enrolled, identification of high-risk patient groups, and planning of proactive interventions for selected patients; claims data or other systemwide information systems also can identify patients with high utilization of services within the system.
3. *Disease management.* More effective care can be provided within integrated systems, through disease management of certain chronic medical problems, such as congestive heart failure, diabetes, asthma, and depression; interdisciplinary teams can track these patients by evidence-based protocols, which can lead to improved health outcomes for these patients compared to usual care.[4,5]
4. *Practice guidelines.* Although practice guidelines are intended only as guidelines requiring individualization to each patient's desires and needs through informed, shared decision making, they nevertheless can serve as effective means to standardize and synchronize the work of a health care team; many such guidelines, especially in earlier years, have been of questionable scientific value but increasingly are more evidence based and of greater value in guiding clinical care.
5. *Demand management.* Since many, even most, health care decisions are made by patients, demand management programs have been established in a number of integrated systems to provide decision support to patients; this approach may include a call center for questions and telephone advice and other means of patient education and self-help resources.[6]
6. *Evidence-based medicine.* Increasingly, administrators in integrated systems, as well as insurers and other payers, are using evidence-based approaches (described in more detail in the next chapter) as a basis for determining what services will be provided within the system; this can remove the treating physician from the line of fire when a given ineffective and costly service is being requested (or demanded) by a patient or family, but physicians within the system necessarily must be involved in the creation and approval of the spectrum of services to be provided.
7. *Provider contracts and bylaws.* Mutual and reciprocal mechanisms of accountability between an integrated system and its physicians and other providers are established through provider contracts and bylaws covering such areas as responsibilities of both parties, provisions for renewal, modification or termination of contracts, as well as for grievance procedures in the event of disagreements.
8. *Financial integration.* Integrated systems may vary considerably in contract arrangements with providers over the kind and extent of financial risk-

sharing; if the system accepts most or all the financial responsibility, it assumes the right to establish overall management policies and incentives; group practices usually have a system of salaries and bonuses while individual practice associations may withhold a portion of physicians' fees for distribution at the end of the year based on individual and organizational performance.

9. *Physician profiling and incentivization.* Each physician's clinical performance is profiled in an integrated system by collection of information that then is referenced to the local peer group or more general standards;[7] these benchmarks may range from adequacy of preventive services to clinical outcomes, patient satisfaction, patient disenrollment rates, variance from clinical guidelines, use of out-of-network services, and even attendance at educational and committee meetings; this information may be used for feedback to providers as well as for calculation of financial incentives. As Suchman and colleagues point out, however, "Incentives that reward low utilization are more problematic ethically than incentives based on clinical outcomes, quality, satisfaction, and ease of access for patients, particularly if utilization measures are not accompanied by quality indicators."[3] It therefore comes as no surprise that a 1998 study by Kevin Grumbach and his colleagues showed that physicians whose bonuses depended on productivity or referral benchmarks had higher levels of anxiety and concern than those whose bonuses were indexed to quality of care or patient satisfaction measures.[8]

Reflecting on power shifts in health care, Victor Fuchs, professor emeritus of Economics and Health Research and Policy at Stanford University, had this to say in 1998 on changes in medicine:[9]

Professional power is eroding in two ways, at least. One is through intense competition. Another is through the transfer of power and control from the physician to managers. To some extent, that was inevitable because physicians (with some exceptions) were not willing to step up to the plate and try to deal with the problems of exploding costs and managing the delivery of reasonably good quality care. It was almost inevitable that power would shift away from them. But that doesn't mean then I'm happy about the shift. Nor am I happy about intense competition between physicians or between physician groups. Medical care can suffer from too much competition, just as, in the past, it suffered from too little.

The conditions that make the textbook model of competition so appealing are often lacking in medical care. Physicians and patients possess very different information; honesty and trust on both sides are extremely important; and patients often benefit from cooperation among physicians.

In an excellent article exploring the relationships of physicians and organizations under a wide range of "physician organization arrangements" (POAs), Howard Zuckerman and his colleagues identified six essential parameters, which necessarily are involved in any alignment between physicians and health care systems.[10] Figure 9-1 illustrates these factors in a "spider diagram"; in this hypothetical case, the shaded areas show the extent of progress toward each parameter, while the white areas show the gap from the ideal yet to be attained.

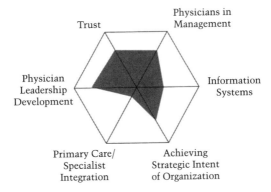

Figure 9-1 Keeping score—physician-system alignment. (Reprinted with permission from Zuckerman HS, Hilberman DW, Andersen RM, et al. Physicians and organizations: Strange bedfellows or a marriage made in heaven? *Front Health Serv Manage.* 1998;14(3):3–34.)

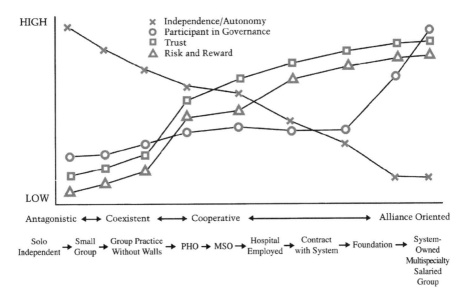

Figure 9-2 Possible physician relationships. (Reprinted with permission from Schultz DV. Physicians and organizations: For whom the bell tolls. *Front Health Serv Manage.* 1998;14(3):46–48; discussion: 49–50.)

As a physician with considerable experience in developing various POAs, Donald Schultz recognizes that the transition from independent physician practice to one or another form of system alignment usually requires radical changes for physicians.[11] Figure 9-2 displays a typical spectrum from independent practice (characterized by autonomous, independent physicians antagonistic to any alignment) to a system-owned, multispecialty salaried group (involving high levels of trust and participation of physicians who accept a less autonomous practice setting).

EXTERNAL CONTROL AND REGULATION OF MEDICAL PRACTICE

To paint a portrait of some of the external controls that permeate and shape today's increasingly regulated clinical environment, examples are chosen from three major categories: the federal government, state governments, and others, including health plans, managed care organizations, and payers. Although limited in scope, this discussion of a few examples illustrates the extent to which medical practice at the point of care now operates under many new constraints.

Federal Government

A little-known (and poorly understood) elephant in the world of medical practice is ERISA (the federal Employee Retirement Income Security Act). Enacted in 1974, this bill was intended mainly to regulate employer-sponsored pension plans but also to establish uniform national standards for health benefits and to protect employees from loss or abuse of these benefits.[12] It is estimated that ERISA applies to about 125 million Americans today.[13] Unfortunately, however, ERISA has had some negative, unintended consequences at the level of patient care. Its provisions have pre-empted state regulation of managed care organizations (MCOs), limiting states' attempts to remedy alleged abuses of MCOs in coverage decisions while providing minimal federal regulation in the resulting vacuum.[14–16] As a consequence, physicians, patients, and state regulators are unable to effectively contest coverage decisions of MCOs, which prevail over physicians' clinical decisions. The struggle therefore is over physicians' autonomy to make clinical decisions against cost containment policies of MCOs, which physicians judge not to be in the best interest of their patients.[12] Courts that, in past years, protested either physicians' autonomy or the physician-patient relationship, under the gun of ERISA, no longer do so.[17]

State Governments

There has been a flurry of activity in state legislatures all across the country in recent years to act on public complaints against policies of MCOs. In 1997, it is estimated that state legislators introduced 1,200 managed care bills and passed 250 of them. Most of these bills were in one of five categories:[18]

1. *Direct access laws* allowing patients direct access to specialists without primary care referral; of 38 such enacted laws, 32 involved obstetrics-gynecologists, 2 for dermatologists, 2 for chiropractors, and 1 for optometrists and ophthalmologists.
2. *Point-of-service laws* requiring insurers to reimburse patients when they go to out-of-network physicians.

3. *Continuity-of-care laws* permitting patients to continue to see providers who have been dropped from the plan or if patients changed plans. By the end of 1999, 23 states have passed legislation assuring patients to continue seeing their physicians, as shown in Table 9-1.[19]
4. *Standing referral laws* allowing the patients with chronic illness to have a one-time referral to a specialist over a long period (e.g., a year); such legislation was passed in four states by 1998, and expected in many more.
5. *Network adequacy laws* requiring health plans to have a network adequate to serve their enrolled patients; these bills deal with such issues as provider/patient ratios, hours of operation, appropriate waiting times, and geographic adequacy; a New Jersey law even stipulated specific criteria for availability (e.g., appointments within two weeks and two primary care physicians within 10 miles or a 30-minute drive).

Concerning the impact of state legislatures on physicians and medical practice, Radovsky observed:[20]

Doctors, ethics, morality, and commitment to public service have largely been legislated or are regulated. Some states require all doctors to take patients with the acquired immunodeficiency syndrome. Some have proposed similar legislation for Medicaid beneficiaries. Many states underpay for services to Medicaid beneficiaries, thereby forcing doctors to include a public service component in their care. Doctors in Massachusetts cannot charge patients covered by Blue Shield or Medicare at levels above those of the reimbursements they receive from these programs, which are based on percentage increments to charging profiles that were often frozen in their relative positions years ago. They are also required, under penalty of law, to report possible missteps by their colleagues and every two years to document 10 hours of training in the avoidance of malpractice. The ability today to control conception, gestation, resuscitation, and life support has made ethics in these areas a subject of state and federal legislation and continuing national debate.

Health Plans, Insurers, and Payers

As basic a decision as a patient's choice of physician has undergone major change in recent years. Under the traditional fee-for-service model, patients were completely free to choose their own physicians. In today's managed care model, the payer has strong influence over choice of physician.

Lawrence Marsh, director of equity research at a large investment bank organization, observed that physicians, in financial terms, are now considered the "means of production" in health care.[21] He notes further that, in the health care industry, "*success* can be defined as the perhaps Utopian ideals of marrying physician satisfaction with patient happiness, with lowered costs and greater delivery efficiency, with appropriate care outcomes."[21] Yet, at least in for-profit health plans, the short-term interests of CEOs and investors may overrule the long-term goals and interests of providers and their patients.

Overemphasis on "the bottom line" by nonphysician administrators may have a deleterious effect on physicians, who may be removed from MCO panels, as well as their patients, who are denied services or may have to change plans (as

Table 9-1   States with Continuity-of-Care Laws on the Books

| | Length of Care | | | Provisions for Pregnant Women | Continuation with Primary Care Providers Only |
	60 Days	90 Days	120 Days		
Arkansas		In all cases			
California		In all cases		Yes	
Colorado	When the doctor leaves the plan				
Delaware			When the doctor leaves the plan	Yes	
Florida	When the doctor leaves the plan			Yes	
Illinois		In all cases		Yes	
Indiana	When the doctor leaves the plan			Yes	Yes
Iowa		In all cases		Yes	
Kansas		When the doctor leaves the plan		Yes	
Maryland		When the doctor leaves the plan			Yes
Minnesota			When the doctor leaves the plan		
Missouri		When the doctor leaves the plan		Yes	
New Jersey			When the doctor leaves the plan	Yes	
New York	When the patient leaves the plan	When the doctor leaves the plan		Yes	
Oklahoma		When the doctor leaves the plan		Yes	
Pennsylvania	In all cases			Yes	

continues

Table 9-1   (continued)

	Length of Care			Provisions for Pregnant Women	Continuation with Primary Care Providers Only
	60 Days	*90 Days*	*120 Days*		
South Carolina		When the doctor leaves the plan			
South Dakota		In all cases		Yes	
Tennessee			When the doctor leaves the plan	Yes	
Texas		When the doctor leaves the plan		Yes	
Vermont	In all cases			Yes	
Virginia		When the doctor leaves the plan		Yes	
Wisconsin		When the doctor leaves the plan		Yes	Yes

Note: These 23 states have guaranteed patients' rights to continue seeing their doctors. In some states, patients are eligible to continue receiving care only in cases where the doctor's contract with the plan was terminated. In other states, patients are covered only if the patient was forced to switch insurers. In this second instance, the new plan must make it possible for the patient to continue seeing his or her former doctor. Some states mandate continuity of care under either circumstance.

Source: Health Policy Tracking Service, National Conference of State Legislatures, September 1999. Reprinted with permission from Coming soon: States with continuity-of-care laws on the books. *Med Econ.* December 20, 1999:51.

they often do) to continue in an established and trusted physician-patient relationship.[22]

DECREASED AUTONOMY AND SATISFACTION OF PHYSICIANS

Almost no physicians are immune from these pressures today. By 1996, one national study of over 1,300 physician recruitments found that two out of three physicians in eight specialties were offered salary as their primary form of com-

Table 9-2 Capitation by Specialty

Specialty	Percentage of Physicians with One or More Capitated Contracts	Only Physicians with Capitated Contracts	
		Percentage of Practice Revenues Capitated	Average Number of Capitated Contracts
Primary care physicians			
General family practice	50.20%	21.5%	3.3
General internal medicine	47.8	19.2	3.3
Pediatrics	63.8	23.7	3.3
Specialists			
Internal medicine: subspecialty	32.7	16.2	3.1
General surgery	18.4	21.6	5.2
Surgical subspecialty	21.7	12.9	2.9
Obstetrics/gynecology	20.6	16.3	2.7
Radiology	30.8	14.4	2.7
Psychiatry	17	31	2.8
Anesthesiology	15.7	18.6	5.8
Pathology	25.5	9.8	2.1
Emergency medicine	24.8	17.1	3
Other specialties	21.2	25.4	5.9
All physicians	32.5	19.2	3.3
p-value for equality means across specialty	$p = .001$	$p = .003$	$p = .116$

Source: American Medical Association Socioeconomic Monitoring Systems survey, 1995. Reprinted with permission from Simon CJ, Emmons DW. Physician earnings at risk: An examination of capitated contracts. *Health Aff (Millwood).* 1997;16:123.

pensation.[23] In 1994, half of all payments in HMOs to primary care physicians was by capitation, with only one quarter by salary or fee-for-service, respectively.[24] An AMA survey in 1995 showed that about one half or more primary care physicians had at least one capitation contract and that specialty physicians also had substantial involvement with capitation in their practices[25] (Table 9-2).

A national study in 1992 focused on the process of utilization review as carried out by 109 firms under contract to purchasers, insurers, and some HMOs. Table 9-3 lists the measures used by these utilization review organizations (UROs). As is only natural, these may be perceived by physicians as challenging or intrusive to their clinical practices. In this study, Mark Schlesinger, B. H. Gary, and K. M. Perreira found wide variation in the procedures used by these UROs, some less threatening and others very intrusive. For example, one third of UROs reported that only 2 percent of initial denials were appealed successfully. Some UROs contacted patients directly, even to provide them with treatment options, a practice that could erode patients' confidence in their physician while the URO has no capacity to provide care itself.[26]

Table 9-3 Impact of Utilization Review on Professional Autonomy

Threat to Professional Autonomy	Specific Measures Used in This Study
Challenges to authority	Influence of medical director and staff on policies and practices at review organization
	Influence of standards developed by medical societies on review criteria used by firm
	Influence of changing patterns of clinical practice on review criteria
	Influence of patient complaints on review criteria
	Influence of employers and other clients on review criteria
Intrusiveness	Extent to which clinicians are required to submit documentation for review process
	Percent of admission requests that are initially denied
	Willingness of URO to adapt review protocols in response to clinician's complaints
	Extent to which nonphysicians are allowed to deny authorization
Standardization	Extent to which review criteria are adjusted for differences in local practice norms
	Extent to which local norms influence exceptions to review criteria
	Extent to which clinician adamancy justifies exceptions to review criteria
	Extent to which physician reviewers are allowed to deviate from formal protocols
Scientific ethos	URO develops its own review criteria
	URO has received research grants from foundations or government
	URO adapts review criteria in response to new findings in medical literature

Note: URO is utilization review organization.

Source: Reprinted with permission from Schlesinger MJ, Gary BH, Perreira KM. Medical professionalism under managed care: The pros and cons of utilization review. *Health Aff (Millwood).* 1997;16(1):110.

Two studies by the Robert Wood Johnson Foundation of comparative levels of physician autonomy and satisfaction are informative in terms of the impact of the managed care environment upon their practices. The first study (1991) surveyed about 500 California physicians less than 45 years old who had been in practice for two to nine years. The second study (1996) examined 111 California physicians under age 50 who were "cohort matched" to the first study, as well as 93 physicians who were "age matched" to the 1991 study. Table 9-4 displays their responses. Over that five-year period physicians felt significant reductions by such measures as the freedom to carefully review histories and test results, their capacity to care for patients requiring extra time and resources, and to care for patients unable to pay for services. When asked whether they would go into medicine again, their negative answers increased

Table 9-4　Perceived Autonomy Among Young Physicians in 1991 and in the 1996 Age-Matched and Cohort-Matched Samples

Physicians Who Say They Have the Freedom To	Sample Size			Response Rate of Age-Matched Sample			Response Rate of Cohort-Matched Sample		
	1991	1996 Age-Matched	1996 Cohort-Matched	1991	1996	1991–96 Change	1991	1996	1991–96 Change
Spend sufficient time with patients	492	92	108	83.5%	69.6%	−13.9%[a]	83.5%	70.4%	−13.1%[a]
Hospitalize patients who, in their opinion, require it[b]	420	79	92	92.6	81.0	−11.6[a]	92.6	83.7	−8.9[a]
Keep patients in the hospital for the length of time they think is appropriate[b]	405	74	87	74.6	71.6	−3.0	74.6	66.7	−7.9
Carefully review patients' medical histories and test results	497	92	110	92.6	70.7	−21.9[a]	92.6	75.5	−17.1[a]
Care for patients even when they are unable to pay the fees and charges	479	87	105	82.9	66.7	−16.2[a]	82.9	70.5	−12.4[a]
Order tests and procedures whenever they want to	493	86	104	80.9	65.1	−15.8[a]	80.9	63.5	−17.4[a]
Control their own work schedule	495	93	111	67.1	57.0	−10.1	67.1	61.3	−5.8
Care for patients who require heavy use of time and resources[b]	419	81	93	83.5	64.2	−19.3[a]	83.5	65.6	−17.9[a]

[a] 1996 significantly different from 1991. $p < .01$, chi-square test.

[b] Question was not asked of radiologists, anesthesiologists, and pathologists.

Source: 1991 Robert Wood Johnson Foundation Survey of Young Physicians and 1996 Survey of California Physicians. Reprinted with permission from Burdi MD, Baker LC. Physicians' perceptions of autonomy and satisfaction in California. *Health Aff (Millwood).* 1999;18(4):139.

from 27.2 percent of the 1991 sample to 33.3 and 37.8 percent of the age-matched and cohort-matched 1996 samples.[27]

A more recent national study of almost 700 practicing internists affiliated with some kind of managed care plan revealed that physicians who are salaried by a staff- or group-model HMO report the highest level of satisfaction with managed care. In addition, physicians with a single contract were more satisfied than those with multiple contracts.[28]

PHYSICIAN RESPONSES TO THE REGULATORY ENVIRONMENT

Physicians have reacted in diverse ways to this sea change in medical practice ushered in by the managed care era. Many sold their practices and joined a hospital-based network, a large multispecialty group, or a physician management organization. Some relocated to states with less penetration of managed care. Others changed to nonclinical work in administration, communication, or education. Still others took early retirement or claimed disability.[29] In fact, disability claims among physicians have increased so much in recent years that some insurance companies have been driven out of that part of the business.[30,31]

The road toward integrated health systems has seen some train wrecks along the way. A recent paper by two California management consultants noted that joining a hospital-based network is no longer a strategy of choice.[32] They pointed out that about three quarters of hospital-owned medical practices are in the red, with one report averaging a loss of $93,000 per year per full-time-equivalent physician.[33] Capitation payments from California HMOs to physicians dropped by 20 to 25 percent between the periods of 1990–1993 and 1997–1999.[34]

Integrated health care organizations are falling apart all over the country, including the bankruptcy of the Allegheny Health System in Pennsylvania, the MedPartners system in California, and many smaller systems in between, contributing to a chaotic medical care marketplace.[35]

Some physicians are breaking free of the restrictions of managed care by refusing to participate in any capitation plans. The experience of one pediatrician in Southern California is instructive as a microcosm of the downside of managed care. He was 1 of 15 physicians in a capitation contract with a hospital-managed independent practice association, representing one third of his practice (about 650 patients). The IPA planned to implement some changes that he refused to accept (i.e., requiring him to perform X rays in his office instead of the hospital unless he paid for the hospital to do them and requiring him to redirect his laboratory work from the hospital across the street to a laboratory 15 miles away). The outcome was positive for his practice—although he lost 150 of his former patients, his practice thrived as he had more time per patient and his practice satisfaction rebounded.[36]

Another response by U.S. physicians to erosion of their autonomy in a new regulatory environment is the recent push toward collective bargaining. With strong support by the AMA and other physician groups, the Quality Health Care Coalition Act (H.R. 1304), sponsored by Rep. Tom Campbell (R-Calif.) was passed by the House of Representatives in June 2000 by a vote of 276–136.[37,38] No similar effort so far has been made in the Senate, but this is a significant effort to rebalance the influence of physicians as they deal with managed care organizations.

Although the movement toward collective bargaining and even unionization has been gathering momentum in some quarters, it generated an intense and divisive debate within the profession. A ruling in November 1999 by the National Labor Relations Board (NLRB) gave further impetus to unionization involvement. That ruling overturned a 23-year-old precedent that resident physicians in training are students and ineligible to bargain collectively, thereby affirming that house staff at Boston Medical Center could do so as employees.[39] Proponents for the right of physicians to unionize point out that employers, whether a hospital or other health care organization, may arbitrarily shut down clinical facilities, lay off staff, or otherwise change the clinical environment without physician involvement or recourse.[40] Critics argue that unionization has no place within the medical profession and carries the risk of eroding the public trust in medicine. As Jordan Cohen of the Association of American Medical Colleges stated,[41]

> the idea of residents joining the ranks of organized labor also has problematic implications for medicine as a whole. If unions succeed in organizing physicians in their formative years of residency, they are sure to see the medical profession in its entirety as fertile ground for expanding their influence and enlarging their dues-paying rolls. At a time when the perceived triumph of cost cutting over quality has raised public suspicion of the health care system to an all-time high, the last thing our profession needs is a stampede of doctors into unions. To be sure, many practitioners (such as those who are self-employed) are currently barred by antitrust laws from joining unions, but many are not so barred. Moreover, who is to know how Congress will view this matter in the future? Indeed, the American Medical Association, in keeping with its lamentable decision to help eligible physicians form "negotiating units," is actively lobbying Congress to permit self-employed[42,43] doctors to organize.[44]

By March, 2000, there were five multistate physician unions, the largest with 15,000 members, including the AMA-sponsored union, Physicians for Responsible Negotiation (PRN). In the wake of the 1999 NLRB ruling, physicians' employers are keeping a close watch on this trend, while the AMA's position is to help physicians form collective bargaining units without their resorting to strike. The AMA considers the withholding of medical care to be a violation of medical ethics, and PRN is the only one of the five unions to rule out strikes.[45] As an attorney with broad experience in health care law, Steven Epstein is seriously concerned about this recent trend toward collective bargaining by physicians:[46]

> Collective bargaining is going to be bad for physicians, bad for patients, and bad for health care costs. Ultimately, it breaks down what doctors are really all about. They're not getting together for patient care. They're getting together because they care more about fees. If physicians want to be treated like employees, they're going to be treated like employees, and they're not

employees. I can't imagine that the government would allow independent physicians to organize, except for political reasons. It clearly violates current antitrust laws. That's not where physicians should be headed. That's not what we need to do now to solve our health care problems.

CONCLUDING COMMENTS

This chapter illustrates the depth and extent of turmoil within U.S. health care, which has been shaken to its foundation and still is amid organizational transformation. Physicians have lost professional autonomy, the process of clinical decision making has been infringed on by third-party regulators, and erosion of the physician-patient relationship has taken place in many instances. These changes are understandably frustrating and bewildering to physicians as they face more "hassle factor" in everyday clinical practice. The problems facing American medicine are even more complex, as is shown in the next chapter, since now conflicting paradigms of health care are in competition, which further divides health professionals. Despite these wrenching changes, however, there are reasons for optimism that a better day can come for physicians and medical practice. Organizational changes, such as a national health program, described in Chapter 22, offer respite from the present morass of bureaucracy in health care. Opportunities for professional renewal and an expanded leadership role of physicians toward system reform are discussed in the last chapter.

REFERENCES

1. Eddy DM. *Clinical Decision Making: From Theory to Practice. A Collection of Essays from JAMA.* Boston: Jones and Bartlett Publishers, 1996;1.
2. Friedman E. The power of physicians: Autonomy and balance in a changing system. Paper delivered at the National Health Policy Forum, George Washington University, Washington, DC, December 2, 1994.
3. Suchman AL, Eiser AR, Goold SD, Stewart KJ. Rationale, principles, and educational approaches of organizational transformation. *J Gen Intern Med.* 1999;14(suppl 1):S51–S57.
4. Hunter DJ, Fairfield G. Disease management. *BMJ.* 1997; 315:50–53.
5. Ellrodt G, Cook DJ, Lee J, Cho M, Hunt D, Weingarten S. Evidence-based disease management. *JAMA.* 1997;278:1687–1692.
6. Vickery DM. Toward appropriate use of medical care. *Healthcare Forum J.* January–February 1996:15–19.
7. Schoenbaum SC. Feedback of clinical performance information. In: Schoenbaum SC (ed). *Measuring Clinical Care: A Guide for Physician Executives.* Tampa, FL: American College of Physician Executives, 1995:105–114.
8. Grumbach K, Osmond D, Vranizan K, Jaffe D, Bindman AB. Primary care physicians' experience of financial incentives in managed care systems. *N Engl J Med.* 1998;339:1516–1521.
9. Iglehart JK. Physicians as agents of social control: The thoughts of Victor Fuchs. *Health Aff (Millwood).* 1998;17(1):91.
10. Zuckerman HS, Hilberman DW, Andersen RM, et al. Physicians and organizations: Strange bedfellows or a marriage made in heaven? *Front Health Serv Manage.* 1998;14(3):3–34.
11. Schultz DV. Physicians and organizations: For whom the bell tolls. *Front Health Serv Manage.* 1998;14(3):46–48;discussion: 49–50.
12. Jacobson PD, Pomfret SD. ERISA litigation and physicians autonomy. *JAMA.* 2000;283:921–926.

13. Hearings Before the Senate Committee on Labor, and Human Resources. 105th Congress, 2nd session (1998) testimony of Meredith Miller, deputy assistant secretary, Pension and Welfare Benefits Administration.

14. Gostin LO. What's wrong with the ERISA vacuum? Employers' freedom to limit health care coverage provided by risk retention plans. *JAMA*. 1993;269:2527–2532.

15. Mariner WK. State regulation of managed care and the Employee Retirement Income Security Act. *N Engl J Med*. 1996;335:1986–1990.

16. Chirba-Martin MA, Brennan TA. The critical role of ERISA in state health reform. *Health Aff (Millwood)*. 1994;13(2):142–156.

17. Hall MA. Institutional control of physician behavior: legal barriers to health care cost containment. *University of Pennsylvania Law Review*. 1998;137:431–536.

18. Frieden J. Practice trends. Access issues to dominate in state legislatures. *Fam Pract News*. March 1, 1998:76.

19. Coming soon: States with continuity-of-care laws on the books. *Med Econ*. 1999(December 20):51.

20. Radovsky SS. U.S. medical practice before Medicare and now—Differences and consequences. *N Engl J Med*. 1990;322:263–267.

21. Marsh LC. The doctor's bottom line. *Health Aff (Millwood)*. 1998;17(4):75–79.

22. Friedman E. Money isn't everything: Nonfinancial barriers to access. *JAMA*. 1994;271:1535–1538.

23. Newsletter. More physicians are accepting salaried positions. *Am Fam Physician*. 1996; 54(8):2349–2350.

24. Gabel J. Ten ways HMOs have changed during the 1990s. *Health Aff (Millwood)*. 1997; 16(3):134–145.

25. Simon CJ, Emmons DW. Physician earnings at risk: An examination of capitated contracts. *Health Aff (Millwood)*. 1997;16:123.

26. Schlesinger MJ, Gary BH, Perreira KM. Medical professionalism under managed care: The pros and cons of utilization review. *Health Aff (Millwood)*. 1997;16(1):106–124.

27. Burdi MD, Baker LC. Physicians' perceptions of autonomy and satisfaction in California. *Health Aff (Millwood)*. 1999;18(4):134–145.

28. Lepore P, Tooker J. The influence of organizational structure on physician satisfaction: Findings from a national survey. *Eff Clin Pract*. 2000;3(2):62–68.

29. Kassirer JP. Doctor discontent. *N Engl J Med*. 1998;339:1543–1545.

30. Tye L. Disability claims by doctors soaring: Physicians leave for big payments. *Boston Globe*. March 29, 1998:A1.

31. Pincus CR. Have doctors lost their work ethic? Physicians' disability claims increase. *Med Econ*. 1995;72(4):24–30.

32. Aymond R, Hariton T. Is disintegration the answer? *Fam Pract Manage*. February 2000:25–28.

33. Rowland RG. MSOs: Getting it right the second time around? *MGM Update*. December 15, 1998:A/53.

34. *Healthcare: An Industry in the ER*. Walnut Creek, CA: PriceWaterhouse-Coopers, September 2, 1999.

35. Aymond R, Hariton T. Regrouping after disintegration. *Fam Pract Manage*. March 2000:37–40.

36. Wiesshar AR. Say goodbye to capitation. *Fam Pract News*. February 15, 2000:9.

37. Is allowing physicians to bargain collectively a good idea? *Fam Pract News*. 2000;30(9):9.

38. MDs fight for antitrust relief. *Fam Pract News*. August 15, 2000:32.

39. Yacht AC. Sounding board. Collective bargaining is the right step. *N Engl J Med*. 2000; 342:429–431.

40. Walbert C. Doctors unionize to counter managed care. *Fam Pract News*. November 15, 1998:49.

41. Cohen JJ. Sounding board. White coats should not have union labels. *N Engl J Med*. 2000; 342:431–434.

42. Klein S. AMA to establish national collective bargaining unit. *American Medical News*. July 5, 1999;1:34.

43. AAMC Executive Council. AAMC statement on negotiating units for physicians. *AAMC Reporter*. 1999;9(2):7.

44. Klein S. Physician antitrust bill pronounced dead for now. *American Medical News*. November 8, 1999:5–6.

45. Preston SH. Doctor unions: Time to join the parade? *Med Econ*. January 24, 2000:76–86.

46. Epstein SB. Knowing the limits of health care law. *Manage Care*. October 2000:42.

10
Conflicting Paradigms of Health Care

A paradigm is a model or framework for how we see the world. The term was used by Thomas Kuhn as it applied to the work of Copernicus, the Polish astronomer, who concluded in the early 16th century that the earth and other planets must revolve around the sun.[1] The system that Copernicus proposed flew in the face of thought patterns in his time and was not accepted until 150 years later. In their 1993 paper calling for a new paradigm in health care, Kent Neff and Dennis Moser, both health care consultants, described paradigms as analogous to filters on a camera (i.e., as long as you're looking through a red filter, the picture will look red regardless of any other adjustments of the camera. And further, only when the filter—or paradigm—is changed, can the red picture be seen).[2] As others also pointed out in recent years, our present paradigm of health care is obsolete and in no way adequate as a conceptual framework to meet current and future needs for the delivery of health care services in America.

Indeed, the word *paradigm* has seen a resurgence of use with respect to health care, especially in the last 10 years. Now we are seeing an active intellectual debate over how to change the existing flawed paradigm for health care overall. Various health care professions are calling for new paradigms, as seen through their own professional "filters," which often include a larger professional role for their own discipline. The fields of nursing, social work, and pharmacy provide examples of those proposals,[3–5] while still other paradigm changes are proposed by those involved in health care management.[6–8]

In view of the relevance and importance of this issue, this chapter has four goals: (1) to examine the current prevailing paradigm for U.S. health care, including its limitations; (2) to describe four major themes within today's flurry of proposed paradigm changes; (3) to briefly describe the landscape of medical practice today in terms of conflicting paradigms; and (4) to consider prospects for future paradigm shifts.

THE CURRENT PARADIGM

The prevailing paradigm in American health care, especially since World War II, has been based on the biomedical model. As Alvin Tarlov observed in an introduction to a conference exploring the Task of Medicine, held in the late 1980s at Wickenburg, Arizona:[9]

> The prevailing paradigm that has shaped medical education, medical practices, and medical research for most of the 20th century envisions disease as the end result of disordered molecular and biochemical processes. Such processes lead to cellular, tissue, organ, and system disturbance or destruction, resulting in disease, a characteristic constellation of specific biochemical, physiological and pathological anomalies. These anomalies are responsible for the specific loss of physical and other functions experienced by the patient and observed by the physician.

> The biomedical model as developed in the United States produced a health care system based on specialist, procedure-oriented providers, medical technology (the higher the better), and a fee-for-service model until the more recent development of capitation and other prospective payment systems. This health care system had all the negative features we already alluded to, including fragmentation, emphasis on the acute care of individual patients, uncontrolled cost increases to the point of reduced access for many Americans, and lack of accountability for beneficial outcomes of care. On the other hand, the biomedical model is seductive, leading to the assumption by many that science can cure all ills.[10]

Now, enter the managed care era. How does this change the prevailing biomedical paradigm? This is a complicated question with both an upside and a downside. On the one hand, the best of managed care programs pay attention to access, quality, affordability, and accountability for the care of whole populations. On the other hand, as Emily Friedman expressed so clearly, there is wide diversity in managed care organizations in terms of mission, values, and quality. She dispels the myth that all managed care is the same in these words:[11]

> Some plans are capitated fully; some use selective capitation; most still use discounted fee-for-service. Most, but not all, plans are investor owned. Some are highly sensitive to their communities; others couldn't care less. Some have employed or exclusively contracted physicians; most do not. Some are regional, some national. Some spend the vast majority of their revenues on patient care; others spend far less. Some are in it for the long haul; others are here today, gone tomorrow. When you've seen one HMO, as the joke goes, you've seen one HMO.

John Golenski, founder and president of the Bioethics Consultation Group in Berkeley, California, has this to say about the impact of managed care and the competitive medical marketplace within our prevailing biomedical paradigm:[10]

> Paradoxically, the hegemony of the market metaphor has simply added consumer behavior to the previous paradigm's inflated expectations of scientific medicine. Americans now believe that there really is a cure for everything and it can be bought. We further seem to hold the belief that the purchase of that cure should be a matter of individual consumer choice. The marriage of the "medicine as a science" metaphor with the image of the competitive free market in health care services may have created a monster which neither individually could have predicted.

Another helpful way to look at where managed care has, or has not, taken us is shown in Table 10-1, which displays a continuum of potential maturation of managed care organizations toward the ideal in terms of goals, policies, values, and procedures. This continuum was conceptualized in 1994 by Jeffrey Kaplan, a physician and corporate medical director for Blue Cross and Blue Shield of western New York. The experience of many managed care organizations to date has fallen way short of the optimal features noted on the left side of Table 10-1 under the "managed health" paradigm.

WHAT'S WRONG WITH THE BIOMEDICAL MODEL?

Fred Gilbert, a physician with the Pacific Health Research Institute in Hawaii, graphically summarized the inadequacies of our present biomedical paradigm in these terms:[12]

American medicine, as practiced at the close of the 20th century, has some major problems that we categorize as being "upside down, inside out and backward." Fortunately, these are all correctable.

By "upside down," he alludes to the health care system's specialist/nongeneralist base. By "inside out," he means that the patient, as the core and entire reason for health care, has become lost in a disconnected system, and patient interests hardly drive that system. And by "backward," he has in mind the many millions of uninsured Americans and the poor comparisons of many U.S. health care outcomes compared to other developed countries.[12]

Another problem with the biomedical model is its neglect of social, environmental, and psychological factors that play such a large role both in the genesis of health problems and their response to treatment. The late George Engel, as professor of Medicine and Psychiatry at the University of Rochester, conceptualized and promulgated the biopsychosocial model as an important response to that omission.[13] Although accepted in some quarters, it has hardly become the prevailing paradigm in medicine. Many diseases can be traced to multifactorial causes that stretch way beyond the boundaries of the biomedical model, such as those involving people who are homeless, poorly educated, unemployed, poor, or mentally dysfunctional. As Gilbert observed, "the most common cause of death in young black men is a 'disease' caused by a gun or knife."[12]

Another major problem with the biomedical model as expressed in today's prevailing paradigm of health care is its emphasis on acute illness. Matthew Menken, a neurologist and medical educator at the Robert Wood Johnson Medical School in New Jersey, recognized this deficit in these words:[14]

In examining the burden of illness in the entire U.S. population to be served in 1990, I have found that there is a preponderance of chronic disorders that collectively reflect behavioral characteristics and societal values and customs, such as coronary artery disease, stroke, headache, lumbosacral pain syndrome, and chronic lung disease. It seems likely that the disorders of the nervous and musculoskeletal systems causally related to violence and trauma,

Table 10-1   The Paradigm Shift

Year Paradigm	2000 Managed Health	1997 Managed Care	1995 Utilization Management	1994 "Sicker Patients"	Prior 1991 Insurance Benefits
Notable methodology to control access, cost, and quality	Informed, responsible consumer Outcomes/efficacy measurement Cost-benefit Cost-utility Episode of care Community rating The feedback loop (to providers) is closed in real-time Informed decision making Constant awareness of "best practices" Case-mixed profiling explains >80% variance	Identify cost-effective practices to rationalize care decisions Accountability increased Proactivity in diagnosis and treatment Cost-sharing, e.g., capitation, in most provider contracts Cost-effectiveness Patient-centric data case mix ($R^2 > 5$) Analytic support for administrative decisions	Conduct outcomes research and analysis Risk reimbursement (moving toward full or partial capitation) Cost shifting (patients have significant out-of-pocket costs, a deterrent to overutilization) Trend analysis/reactivity, e.g., cost-minimization Provider-centric adjustment for age, sex, group experience Provider-specific patient satisfaction surveys Economic credentialing	Casting blame Bad apple management Outlier analysis Variance reporting Provider is targeted Cost and frequency data Global patient satisfaction survey Mixed community and experience rating Homogeneity (average)	Premiums are directly proportional to costs Allow—deny Defined benefit plans Strict and restrictive Redefine benefit contract exclusions Categorical decision making
Defining expectations	Standards Personal accountability for life-style choices	Nonprescriptive guidelines	Benchmarks Algorithms	Retrospective review	Insurance rules
Motivational strategy	Equity in access—the moral imperative Awareness of patient and societal needs	"He who controls utilization must bear its cost" Group practice without walls	Withholds used as incentive Report cards Selective provider networks Urgent care centers	Money withheld as a penalty for costly providers Providers chosen based on geographic need	Claims data reviewed for cost information Consumers choose plan based on cost alone

Information system data input	Electronic medical record Health risk appraisal Point-of-contact data management	Point-of-service management Encounter forms Diagnosis-based review Strict criteria to cull the network	Claims and productivity data-trended Correlation analysis, e.g., specialty analysis, network quality review criteria	Claims data presorted and profiled Procedure review	Financial solvency
Consumer role	Consumer preference	Consumer influence Market-driven Security in access, caring	Consumer awareness Market-sensitive	Consumers underinformed	Consumer passive
Management successes	Disease avoidance and health maintenance Real-time feedback	Advocacy Physician-partner Concurrent review	MSO begins Physicians aware—efficiency Focus in/out Reasonableness Electronic connectivity—MDs (claims, eligibility, alerts)	Electronic connectivity—hospitals	
Quality enhancement	Self-actualization Self-motivation System improvement Employer involvement Confidentiality	TQM/CQI Explicit criteria Common cause variation Informed decision making	Statistical quality control Implicit and explicit criteria Root cause analysis Comprehensive view of quality-offset effect Information system security	Quality assessment Peer review Inspection Chart review	Insurance review Clinical quality assumed by hospital and health department

TQM/CQI = total quality management/continuous quality improvement.

MSO = management services organization.

Source: Reprinted with permission from Kaplan JG. The emerging managed care paradigm: Health care in transition. *Med Interface*. 1994;7(9):58–59.

stress, smoking, diet, sexually transmitted disorders, drug addiction, adolescent pregnancy, environmental pollution, and workplace accidents, among others, cannot be understood and effectively treated with the approach of the cell biologist. For such problems, is there any doubt that a major research effort should focus on personal, family, environmental, and community health, using the methodology of the behavioral and social sciences, including the population sciences? Will the burden of stroke, for example, be reduced more through a greater number of "high-tech" stroke units in tertiary hospitals, or by changes in dietary fat, control of obesity, exercise, less stress, and no smoking?

The influence of managed care on a health care system still dominated by the biomedical model and a surplus of specialists raises still other problems, particularly of an ethical nature. Through the business ethic of the marketplace, health care services have been turned into commodities, and managed care now plays a large role in the pricing, availability, quality, and distribution of these services. The values and goals of the marketplace may, and often do, stand in direct opposition to those of health care—the profit goal versus positive health outcomes for individuals and populations covered by health plans. Two thirds of managed care enrollees are in investor-owned plans, thereby creating a conflict of interest between the interests of investors and plan members and patients. That potential conflict of interest is even more of a problem when physicians' income depends on how much or how little care is provided to patients, whether as a provider or, in the case of physician management organizations, as a stakeholder.[11] In the jungle marketplace of managed care, we already have seen many examples of the pure business ethic at work: Take a short-term approach, make discounted deals to aggregate a large number of "covered lives," build up the stock price, then sell out to a larger plan.

EMERGING THEMES FOR PARADIGM SHIFTS

Among the calls for paradigm shifts, four stand out as particularly important. Each addresses a specific facet of health care, and each has been put forward separately by its proponents. However, there are obvious overlaps between them, and an overall paradigm shift likely will include many of their elements.

Evidence-Based Medicine

The traditional paradigm for many generations of physicians in medical education and medical practice has been based on the global subjective judgment of experts. Professors have put forth their teaching concepts, and procedures have been taught during residency training, based on the experience and judgment of the teachers. This would be fine if all these judgments were based on outcome studies or at least systematic assessment of best evidence available, but that frequently has not been the case. If they were, how would one explain such wide geographic variations in clinical practice from one part of the country to another? Jack Wennberg found, for example, 20-fold differences in carotid endarterectomy rates in 16 large communities in four states, as well as the odds of children undergoing tonsillectomy ranging from 8 percent to 70 percent within the same state (Vermont).[15,16] These differences stretch far beyond any bounds of clinical credibility, which might be expected to result from clinical, demographic, or other geographic differences.

The contrast between the traditional global subjective judgment of experts and the evidence-based approach has been satired in terms of this definition of *eminence*-based medicine:[17]

> The more senior the colleague, the less importance he or she places on the need for anything as mundane as evidence. Experience, it seems, is worth any amount of evidence. These colleagues have a touching faith in clinical experience which has been defined as "making the same mistakes with increasing confidence over an impressive number of years." The eminent physician's white hair and balding pate are called the "halo" effect.

The emergence of evidence-based medicine has been facilitated by the increased emphasis on outcomes research and the growing availability of electronic databases resulting from that research. The movement toward evidence-based medicine has been further fueled by the necessary emphasis on value and cost containment in medical care.

David Sackett and his colleagues defined *evidence-based medicine* as the "conscientious, explicit and judicious use of current best evidence in making decisions about the care of individual patients."[18] Evidence-based practice requires integration of the physicians' clinical expertise and judgment with the best available, relevant, external evidence on a patient-by-patient basis.[19] It also requires incorporation of patient preferences through a process of shared and informed decision making by the physician and patient or family.[20]

In their excellent work on information mastery in medicine, David Slawson, A. F. Shaughnessy, and J. H. Bennett advanced the value of clinical evidence by differentiating between two kinds of evidence: that based on demonstrated positive outcomes that matter to patients (patient-oriented evidence that matters, or POEMs) and disease-oriented evidence (DOE) based on intermediate outcomes without demonstrable beneficial outcomes to patients.[21] Table 10-2 gives examples of both types of evidence. PSA screening remains a DOE until it can be demonstrated to lead to decreased mortality or improved quality of life.

Unfortunately, much of the medical literature, as well as much of traditional medical education, involves disease-oriented evidence. A classic example of the important differences between POEMs and DOEs is illustrated by arrhythmia suppression studies, which initially showed that some arrhythmic drugs effectively suppressed ventricular arrhythmias (DOE); only later was it found that these drugs killed patients (POEM).[22] Another good example of the importance of the evidence-based approach is represented by the recent abandonment of military antishock trousers (MAST) by the American College of Surgeons Committee on Trauma as a recommended procedure in its Advanced Trauma Life Support Program. Although this pneumatic compression garment was known since the 1960s to raise the blood pressure (an intermediate or surrogate outcome), it took numerous studies in recent years documenting its unexpectedly worse outcomes to dispose of this sacred cow. It is now recognized that a

Table 10-2   Example of Hypothetical Disease-Oriented Evidence (DOE) and Patient-Oriented Evidence That Matters (POEM) Studies

DOE ————————————————————————→ POEM
Number of Assumptions Required to Assume Patients Will Benefit
High ————————————————————————→ Low

Drug A lowers cholesterol	Drug A decreases cardiovascular mortality/morbidity	Decreases overall mortality
PSA screening detects prostate cancer most of the time and at an early stage	PSA screening decreases mortality	PSA screening improves quality of life
Corticosteroid use decreases neutrophil chemotaxis in patients with asthma	Corticosteroid use decreases admissions, length of hospital stay, and symptoms of acute asthma	⤍ Corticosteroid use decreases asthma-related mortality
Tight control of type 1 diabetes mellitus can keep fasting blood glucose <140 mg/dl	Tight control of type 1 diabetes can decrease microvascular complications	Tight control of type 1 diabetes can decrease mortality and improve quality of life.

PSA = prostate-specific antigen.

Note: Not all POEM trials have been performed.

Source: Reprinted with permission from Slawson DC, Shaughnessy AF, Bennett JH. Becoming a medical information master: Feeling good about not knowing everything. *J Fam Pract*. 1994;38:505–513.

lower blood pressure buffers against excessive blood loss in many injuries where early surgical treatment is of higher priority than elevation of blood pressure.[23] Kenneth Mattox, Professor of Surgery at Baylor College of Medicine cautions against the unquestioned acceptance of such WAGs (wild assumed guesses) without outcome evidence of effectiveness, and notes further that during the last 25 years, "much medical invention has been technology in search of an indication."[23,24]

Population-Based Care

A second emerging major paradigm shift that has a big impact on the goals and process of health care, as well as the physician-patient relationship itself, is the concept of population-based care. From the time of Hippocrates, traditional medicine has been based on the care of individual patients, preferably within a trusting relationship of sick individuals and healing practitioners. The population-based approach is consistent with the ethic of John Stuart Mill, the greatest good for the greatest number of people.[16] We are seeing a culture clash between these two concepts within the medical marketplace causing confusion, frustration, and turmoil for providers and patients alike.

The idea of population-based medicine is hardly new. It has been established and developed over the last century by the early non-profit HMOs, as exemplified by Kaiser Permanente and Group Health Cooperative of Puget Sound. To many physicians in those early years, health care of that sort was considered not far short of a communist plot. While that perception no longer applies, the clash between these two approaches to health care remains divisive and controversial.

Proponents see population-based health care as the best way to extend the best of evidenced-based care to whole populations covered by managed care organizations, with the potential advantages of improved health outcomes for more people than would result from the care of individual patients by individual providers. Population-based care in HMOs and large group practices may be provided more by multidisciplinary teams than by individual providers, although that is certainly a matter of degree. At Group Health Cooperative, for example, primary care is based on a family practice model, with every enrollee having a personal family physician. Outcome studies at Group Health Cooperative already have demonstrated several noteworthy results of population-based care: a 32 percent decrease in late-stage breast cancer (1989 to 1990), 89 percent of two-year-old children with complete immunizations (1994), and an increase in bicycle safety helmet use by 44 percent together with a 67 percent decrease in bicycle-related head injuries (1987 to 1992).[25]

Although details may vary considerably from one organization to another, population-based care invariably involves a systematic structure for identifying patients at high risk for disease as well as those with established chronic disease, implementing clinical practice guidelines, and tracking health status and measurable outcomes as well as provider performance. Community-oriented primary care (COPC) is such a concept, which merges the care of individual patients with the care of communities.[26] Advocates for the need for population-based approaches point to the all-too-common failures of the current practice model to widely apply available clinical advances to target populations. One compelling example is the recent estimate that only 10 percent of patients with type 1 diabetes in the United States (versus 80 percent in Germany) are using intensified insulin therapy, which, when integrated into specific treatment programs involving patient self-therapy, has been demonstrated to afford improved glycemic control and reduced incidence of visual loss, renal failure, and amputations.[27]

Critics of population-based medicine make several kinds of arguments against its wide application. In one analysis of experience to date with heart failure, researchers noted the lack of positive outcomes from valid research studies and called for controlled studies of this approach.[28] Kassirer has not been persuaded yet that the potential promise of a distributive ethic of population-based care, involving minimal standards of care for populations of patients, is sufficient reason to abandon an individual patient-centered ethic within the current inequitable structure of health care.[29] Although some family physicians advocate that population-based approaches can be applied usefully by primary care physicians in small group or even solo practice,[30] others worry about the erosion of continuity of care and the physician-patient relationship in larger managed care environments, which may assign nonphysician case managers to cohorts of patients. Joseph Scherger, drawing from his experience in community practice as well as academic family medicine, brings this disturbing perspective to this issue:[31]

As health care in America transforms from a cottage industry of private physicians to large organized delivery systems, there is a fundamental question facing family physicians. Are we to continue as personal physicians to a group of families and individuals, or are we to become simply providers of primary care services? The dangerous aspect of this question today is that the transition from personal physician to provider of a limited range of services is occurring subtly and may not be apparent. Just like the frog about to be boiled does not jump out of the water if the heat is turned up slowly, the family physician in a large medical group or delivery system may experience erosion of the personal physician role without realizing the loss until it is gone. Unwittingly, the family physician may welcome some of the changes—less fit-in-appointments disrupting the schedule, giving up hospital work to hospital-based physicians, turning over after hours calls to a nurse connection service. The family physician may then realize that the patient only sees them for a part of their health care, and has little identity with them as their personal physician.

Chronic Disease Management

Disease management is closely allied to population-based practice, as one of the main techniques thereof, reflecting a shift of emphasis from management of acute disease to chronic illness. This shift also connotes stronger emphasis on *care* rather than the predominant emphasis on curing acute illness. Again, it has stirred some of the same controversy within medicine that was just described. Based on their extensive experience with management of chronic illness at Group Health Cooperative, Edward Wagner, B. T. Austin, and M. Von Korff noted that improvements in the process and outcomes of care require redesign of clinical practice to include the elements shown in Figure 10-1.[32]

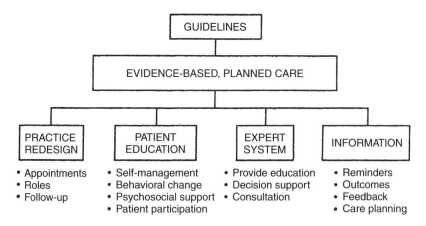

Figure 10-1 Improving outcomes in chronic illness. (Reprinted with permission from Wagner EH, Austin BT, Von Korff M. Organizing care for patients with chronic illness. *Milbank Q.* 1996;74(4):519.)

In his support for increased emphasis on a chronic illness model of care, while by no means abandoning acute care, Gregory Pawlson, in a 1991 address at the annual meeting of the American Public Health Administration, conceptualized the extent of change in terms of education, financing, reimbursement, delivery, and research/quality assessment, as shown in Figures 10-2 and 10-3.[33]

All this is not to disparage the curative model of care but to broaden the goals of health care to unquestionably important areas that are comparatively neglected in our current paradigm of health care—restoring functional capacity; caring for those who cannot be cured; preventing illness, injury, and untimely death; and promoting health.[34]

Although the jury still is out concerning the long-term effectiveness of disease management approaches in many diverse clinical settings, there is some promising evidence in that direction, as shown by Figure 10-4 based upon an HMO Industry Report by Inter Study.[35] Another recent national survey examined 31 programs, nominated as innovative by an expert panel, for chronically

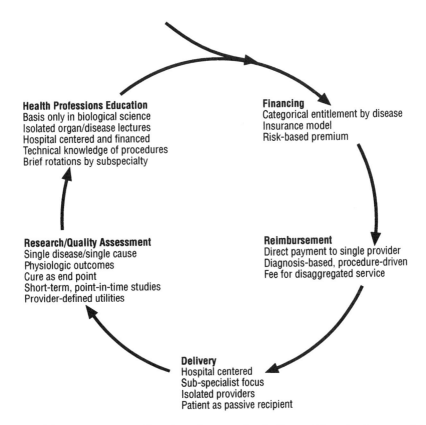

Figure 10-2 Acute care paradigm: how the acute simple disease drives the elements of the health care system. (Reprinted with permission from Pawlson LG. Chronic illness: Implications of a new paradigm for health care. *Jt Comm J Qual Improv.* January 1994; 20(1):33–39.)

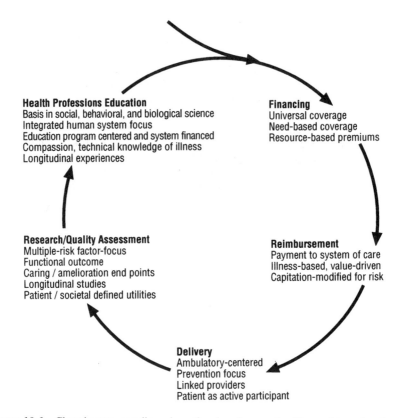

Figure 10-3   Chronic care paradigm: how the chronic complex illness drives the elements of the health care system. (Reprinted with permission from Pawlson LG. Chronic illness: Implications of a new paradigm for health care. *Jt Comm J Qual Improv.* January 1994;20(1):33–39.)

ill older persons. This study demonstrated some evidence of lower cost of services with high patient and physician satisfaction through the case management approach. In one instance, a self-management program at Stanford resulted in improved functional and health status.[36]

Organized Systems of Care

Still another approach, again with some overlap with the preceding models of care, has been emerging among large public and private employers, who are quietly redesigning health care systems for their employees. The Washington Business Group on Health (WBGH) represents the collective interests of such large employers as IBM, FedEx, Hewlett Packard, and the United States Postal Service. Not only have these large employers been concerned about inflationary health care costs but also about what can be done about limiting disability and reducing the incidence of such problems as depression and substance abuse.

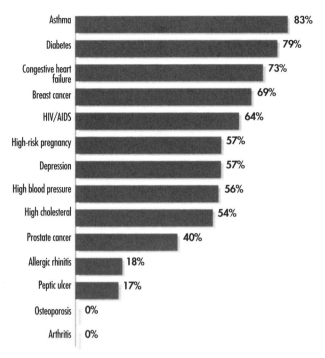

Figure 10-4 Percentage of plans reporting that a disease management program improved patient outcomes. (Reprinted with permission from *The Inter Study Competitive Edge: HMO Industry Report 7.2.* Minneapolis: Inter Study Publications, 1997;70:90.)

As major purchasers, they have become more aggressive in seeking out value in their contracted health plans. To an increasing extent, large employers are committing themselves to enhancing the work environment through health promotion, work life, and disability management.[37]

WBGH members have become major players in the health care marketplace, and their first priority in cost containment has been extended to high-quality outcomes and value over the full spectrum of health care services. Their common denominator is the creation of organized delivery systems (OSCs), which are clinically and fiscally accountable for the health status and outcomes of their enrolled populations. In terms of values, these OSCs are committed to accountability, integration, patient-centered care, and continuous improvement. Their procedures include regular monitoring measurements in three areas:

1. *Care management* (e.g., including such outcome measures as SF-36 results, hospitalization rates for children with asthma, and mammography rates).
2. *Operations management* (requiring health plans to be responsive to employees' needs by such means as 24-hour accessibility, providing appropriate and cost-effective care, and coverage of alternative medicine).
3. *Performance management* (including regular reports on such areas as clinical performance, member satisfaction, and annual changes in health status of enrollees).[37]

These large employers have already demonstrated powerful leverage in the marketplace. As an example, the Digital Equipment Company in Massachusetts, dissatisfied with the health care its employees were receiving from leading health plans around the country, came up with its own performance standards. Revised standards then were developed in partnership with its contracted health plans, and a new collaborative relationship was forged between the company and the health plans. As one result of renegotiation, Digital's employees were assured of mandated health and substance abuse benefits without limit, and they also were guaranteed to have explicit appeal and grievance procedures.[37] Mary Jane England, a physician and president of WBGH, a nonprofit national health policy and research organization, is a strong advocate for the workplace as a natural laboratory for development of integrated and more effective health care systems, with potential applications beyond the workplace of lessons learned from this experience.

THE CONFLICTED ENVIRONMENT OF MEDICAL PRACTICE

The biomedical model, with its strengths and many problems, is being called into question amid the sea changes already being produced by the powerful paradigm shifts just described. To say that the clinical environment in the United States today is chaotic is probably an understatement. Everyone is unhappy with the health care system, even those who like their physician or other providers. Purchasers and payers are interested in cost containment as well as access and quality of care and are demanding more accountability from providers. Hospitals, managed care, and other health care organizations are struggling for survival under circumstances where further downsizing of hospital beds is inevitable as well as the need to become more efficient within the provider workforce. The public remains enthralled with the promise of medical technology and is resistant to the idea of limited resources as long as someone else pays the bills (i.e., their health plan, whether public or private). Physicians are caught in the middle between high patient expectations and the regulatory policies of public and private payers. At the level of the individual physician, the complexity of practice management has become almost impossible for a solo physician as well as an increasing burden in group practice. The conflict between the population-based paradigm and individual patient care is an everyday and thorny issue for a growing number of physicians, especially those employed by large group practices and managed care organizations. Meanwhile, health care issues have become political footballs and health-related litigation continues as a growth industry.

CONCLUDING COMMENTS

It is easier to see the ferment than to project where we are headed as these competing perspectives of health care reshape the marketplace and medical practice. It appears likely, however, that the specialist-driven biomedical model will lose some of its dominance and the overlapping and mutually supportive elements of the four themes for paradigm shifts just described will gain wider application. Golenski's perspective on future paradigm shifts offer much needed wisdom, and I have come to agree with his supportive interest in a public utility paradigm.[10]

> It is probably too soon to propose a specific metaphor for our paradigm. This public utility paradigm may be unacceptable simply on aesthetic grounds, but it does seem to me that many, if not most of the elements emerging from the proposals for reform coalesce to look much like a public utility. Whatever metaphor we find comfortable, I suggest that we look below and behind the specific proposals and reform packages for what social values shift is occurring in our country in relation to the real human need for health care. If my preliminary view bears any resemblance to reality, we are entering a period when the hegemony of professional paternalism, medicine as a science, and the competitive market will be assimilated and transformed into a further metaphor. Hopefully, this time around we will not lose the human, caring qualities of medicine, nor the real constraints of limited resources (both monetary and human), nor the community's legitimate and necessary responsibility to decide what goals and values take precedence.

REFERENCES

1. Kuhn T. *The Copernican Revolution*. Cambridge, MA: Harvard University Press; 1957.
2. Neff KE, Moser DR. Searching for a new paradigm in health care delivery. *Physician Executive.* 1993;19(2):26–29.
3. Harrison E. Nurse caring and the new health care paradigm. *J Nurs Care Qual.* 1995;9(4):14–23.
4. Keigher SM. What role for social work in the new health care practice paradigm? *Health Soc Work.* 1997;22(2):149–155.
5. Webb CE. Prescribing medications: Changing the paradigm for a changing health care system. *Am J Health Syst Pharm.* 1995;52(15):1693–1695.
6. Friedman J. Do less with less. Changes in health care force us to reassess our management paradigm. *Balance.* 1998;2(1):33–35.
7. Ozatalay S, Proenca EJ, Rosko MD. Adoption of a time-based competition paradigm into the health care industry. *J Health Hum Serv Adm.* 1997;20(2):159–181.
8. Westbrook KW. Assessing the strategy-performance paradigm: implications for organizational adaptation in discontinuous environments for home health care providers. *Health Mark Q.* 1997;14(4):27–44.
9. White KL. *The Task of Medicine: Dialogue at Wickenburg*. Menlo Park, CA: The Henry J. Kaiser Foundation, 1988.
10. Golenski JD. Paradigm shift in American health care: Are we ready for a comprehensive system? *Health Matrix.* 1991;1(2):259–265; discussion:267–273.
11. Friedman E. Managed care: Devils, angels, and the truth in between. *Health Prog.* 1999;80(3):22–26.
12. Gilbert FJ. Health care in the United States: The need for a new paradigm. *Hawaii Med J.* 1993;52(1):8–10, 12–13.
13. Engel GL. The biopsychosocial model and medical education. *N Engl J Med.* 1982;306:802–805.
14. Menken M. The changing paradigm of neurologic practice and care. *Arch Neurol.* 1990; 47:334–335.
15. Wennberg J. Dealing with medical practice variations: A proposal for action. *Health Aff (Millwood).* 1984;3:6–32.
16. Eddy DM. *Clinical Decision Making. From Theory to Practice: A Collection of Essays from JAMA.* Boston: Jones and Bartlett Publishers, 1996:5.

17. Isaacs D, Fitzgerald D. Seven alternatives to evidence-based medicine. *BMJ.* 1999;319:1618.
18. Sackett DL, Rosenberg WM, Gray JA, et al. Evidence based medicine: What it is and what it isn't. *BMJ.* 1996;312:71–72.
19. Geyman JP. Evidence-based medicine in primary care: An overview. *J Am Board Fam Pract.* 1998;11:46–56.
20. Haynes , Sackett DL, Gray JA, et al. Transferring evidence from research into practice: 1. The role of clinical care research evidence in clinical decisions. *ACP J Club.* 1996;125:A14–A16.
21. Slawson DC, Shaughnessy AF, Bennett JH. Becoming a medical information master: Feeling good about not knowing everything. *J Fam Pract.* 1994;38:505–513.
22. Echt DS, Liebson PR, Mitchell LB, et al. Mortality and morbidity in patients receiving encainide, flecainide, or placebo. The cardiac arrhythmia suppression trial. *N Engl J Med.* 1991;324:781–788.
23. Mattox KL. Response: The MAST lesson: Contemporary example of society and academic responses to paradigm shifts. *Pharos.* 2000;63(1):26–29.
24. Mattox KL. Editorial comment: What drives the need for new technology? *J Trauma.* 1992;32:768.
25. Thompson RS, Taplin SH, McAfee TA, et al. Primary and secondary prevention services in clinical practice: Twenty years' experience in development, implementation, and evaluation. *JAMA.* 1995;273:1130–1135.
26. Mettee TM, Martin KB, Williams RL. Tools for community-oriented primary care: A process for linking practice and community data. *J Am Board Fam Pract.* 1998;11:28–33.
27. Berger M, Mühlhauser I. Diabetes care and patient-oriented outcomes. *JAMA.* 1999; 281:1676–1678.
28. Rector TS, Venus PA. Judging the value of population-based management. *Inquiry.* Summer 1999;36:122–126.
29. Kassirer JP. Managing care—Should we adopt a new ethic? *N Engl J Med.* 1998;339:397–398.
30. Rivo ML. It's time to start practicing population-based health care. *Fam Pract Manage.* June 1998;37:44.
31. Scherger JE. Does the personal physician continue in managed care? *J Am Board Fam Pract.* 1996;9:67–68.
32. Wagner EH, Austin BT, Von Korff M. Organizing care for patients with chronic illness. *Milbank Q.* 1996;74(4):519.
33. Pawlson LG. Chronic illness: Implications of a new paradigm for health care. *Jt Comm J Qual Improv.* January 1994;20(1):33–39.
34. Institute of the Future. *Health and Health Care 2010.* San Francisco: Jossey-Bass Publishers, 2000:187.
35. *The Inter Study Competitive Edge: HMO Industry Report 7.2.* Minneapolis: Inter Study Publications 1997;70:90.
36. Boult C, Kane RL, Pacala JT, Wagner EH. Innovative health care for chronically ill older persons: Results of a national survey. *Am J Manage Care.* 1999;5(9):1162–1172.
37. England MJ. The evolving health care system: Changing paradigms and the organized system of care. *J Allied Health.* Winter 1997;26(1):7–12.

11
New Roles for Hospitals

> Hospitals in the United States are changing dramatically. Motivated by the high cost of hospital care, payers have worked hard both to keep patients out of the hospital and to discharge them early. Because only the severely ill are now welcome as inpatients, the market has responded with a wide array of creative approaches to provide care outside the hospital: chest pain observation units, outpatient surgery centers, expanded rehabilitation and postacute care settings, and home health care. The future of the U.S. hospital appears certain: fewer beds, sicker patients—essentially an expanded intensive care unit.
>
> Elliott S. Fisher, 1999[1]

This observation by Fisher captures the current scene among U.S. hospitals as they struggle to deal with the forces of the marketplace described in earlier chapters. The acute care hospital has represented the center of the U.S. health care system for over 100 years. Its role in the more-integrated health care delivery system of the future is far from certain but probably will be more peripheral than central.

The purpose of this chapter is to better understand evolving changes in the hospital sector of health care by discussing three topics: (1) a historical perspective on roles of hospitals; (2) seven major trends now reshaping the hospital sector; and (3) the special cases of teaching hospitals, public (safety net) hospitals, and rural hospitals.

HISTORICAL PERSPECTIVE

The history of hospitals is more varied and complex than one might expect, with many sea changes in their role in society over the years. Guenther Risse, an internist and historian, summarized some of these major changes over the last 1,000 years. He noted that "hospital" care during the Middle Ages was based in European monasteries, where monks carried on a practice of diagnosis and healing. Monastic infirmaries provided hospitality, food, and rest to displaced or sick individuals based on the principles of Matthew's six works of mercy in the New Testament.[2]

Monastic healing ended in 1130, with the Council of Clermont's decision that the monks stop practicing medicine. During the Renaissance, many hospitals developed in urban areas where physicians and barber-surgeons offered their treatments of acute ailments. By the late 1800s, hospitals were involved in a broader spectrum of diagnostic and therapeutic procedures, autopsies, drug trials, and medical education.[2]

Early U.S. hospitals were modeled after hospitals in England and Europe. Between 1870 and 1910, in the United States, hospitals grew rapidly and assumed a central role in medical practice and medical education.[3] Advances in medical care rendered the physician's black bag insufficient to accommodate medicine's expanding armamentarium. Hospitals became hubs for special equipment, specialist consultation, surgical anesthesia, and physicians' workshops for medical practice.

After a period of consolidation from 1910 to 1945, hospitals enjoyed a second phase of rapid growth after World War II, from 1945 to 1980. A significant part of that growth was propelled by private philanthropy. Another stimulus was the Hill-Burton Act, enacted by the federal government to support construction of hospitals in underserved rural areas. Since 1980, hospitals have entered a second period of consolidation, associated with exponential increases in hospital services, medical technology, and costs.[4] The major influence forcing change in recent years is the emergence of managed care. As Eli Ginzberg, one of the country's leading health economists, observed in 1990:[5]

> The oft-repeated phrase used to describe the situation of hospitals today—"from cash cow to cost center"—suggests that the hospital sector is about to undergo a catastrophic change, one that will dislodge the acute care hospital from the center of the health care delivery system to a place on the periphery. The most serious challenge to the long-dominant hospital care sector is being mounted by the rapidly growing managed care companies, mostly for-profit, whose strategies and tactics are aimed at restructuring the delivery of health care to the American people with principal emphasis on prevention and primary care services and correspondingly reduced reliance on inpatient treatment. A subtheme of these aggressive efforts is the growing adoption of managed care companies for capitation as the preferred contracting device for purchasing services from physicians and hospitals.

As market forces press for greater efficiencies in the delivery of health care services, and as increasing integration takes place among facilities and providers, managed care organizations and hospitals view each other in new terms. Table 11-1 portrays typical perceptions of each party toward potential partnership with the other in terms of efficiency.

As a result of these changes, hospitals have been called upon to reinvent themselves, extending their focus beyond inpatient care of acute illness toward primary care and management of chronic illness in non-hospital settings.[6]

Table 11-1   An IDS Snapshot: Hospital-HMO Interaction

	In a Way That Enhances Efficiencies Through:	In a Way That Reduces Efficiencies Through:
The hospital affects the HMO	Reputation and branding Referral Pricing Capital	Restricting use of other hospitals Mandating use of more expensive ancillary services from the IDS hospital
The HMO affects the hospital	Referral Better customer and market information Continuum of care Clinical information	Alienation of physicians because of reimbursement decisions Retribution from other HMOs More complex allocation of capital

Source: Reprinted with permission from VHA Inc. *Vertically Integrated Delivery Systems: Evolution and Complexity*, vol. 1. Irving, TX: VHA Inc., 1997.

MAJOR TRENDS AFFECTING HOSPITALS

Cost Containment

Spending for U.S. hospital services per day has increased by an average of about 15 percent per year since 1960, much faster than in other industrialized countries around the world. In 1996, the United States spent more than twice as much per day for hospital services than Canada, over three times as much as the United Kingdom, and over four times as much as the median for OECD (Organization for Economic Cooperation and Development) countries.[7]

Government programs collectively account for almost half the health care dollar (46 percent in 1995), with private health insurance representing almost another third (31 percent). Concerted efforts by public and private purchasers to contain rising health care costs hit U.S. hospitals hard. This is not surprising, since the single largest portion of health care expenditures involves hospital care (36 percent). It therefore is to be expected that hospitals have borne the brunt of cost containment efforts by the major public and private purchasers of hospital services.[8]

A recent study revealed that the average operating margin for both inpatient and outpatient care (i.e., the difference between revenues and expenses) fell from 6.3 percent in 1997, to 4.3 percent in 1998, and to 2.7 percent in 1999. Most of these cuts resulted from reduced payments from managed care organizations and other private payers, together with reductions in Medicare payments.[9] There has been a disproportionate impact on operating margins of smaller hospitals, with hospitals having less than 100 beds falling to average operating margins of less than 1 percent in 2000.[10]

From a policy perspective, the question has been raised as to whether, and how much if at all, total per-capita Medicare spending varies between areas

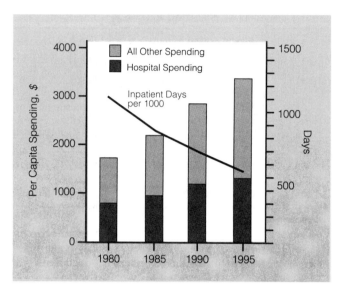

Figure 11-1   U.S. hospital utilization (days per 1,000 patients, line) and per capita health care expenditures (in 1995 U.S. dollars) from 1980 to 1995. Hospital use decreased, while hospital and total spending increased. (Reprinted with permission from Fisher, ES. What is a hospital? *Eff Clin Pract.* 1999;2(3):139.)

served by for-profit versus not-for-profit hospitals. Another recent study examined that question for 1989, 1992, and 1995, finding that such spending was consistently higher in for-profit areas for all three years. The single largest increase in per capita Medicare spending between 1989 and 1995 was for hospital services (a mean increase of $395 and $283 in for-profit and not-for-profit areas, respectively, a difference of about 40 percent).[11]

Decreased Utilization

Utilization of hospital services in the United States has decreased dramatically over the last 20 years. Three measures show the extent of this change. Average length of stay declined from 6 days in 1991 to just 4.7 days five years later.[8] Inpatient days per 1,000 patients dropped by 100 percent between 1980 and 1985, which paradoxically was associated with unabated increases in hospital spending (Figure 11-1). As a result, the average occupancy of U.S. hospitals dropped from nearly 80 percent in 1980 to about 60 percent in 1997.[12]

The percentage of insured people with a hospital admission each year provides another measure of hospital utilization. Here again, the decline is substantial. Over the nine-year period from 1987 to 1996, that percentage fell from 7.4 percent to 5.6 percent, a drop of 25 percent. Patterns of hospital use by patients in managed care organizations have become quite similar to those of patients with other insurance coverage. By 1996, for example, there was no sig-

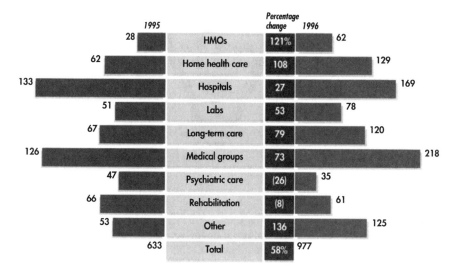

Figure 11-2 Merger and acquisition transactions. (Reprinted from Japsen B. Doc group mergers push dealmaking pace. *Modern Healthcare.* March 10, 1997:3.)

nificant difference in the number of hospital admissions per person or length of stay between the two groups.[13]

Downsizing of Excess Hospital Capacity

Since the advent in 1982 of the prospective payment system by diagnostic-related groups (DRGs) for hospital services for Medicare beneficiaries, reimbursement changes and medical technology have catalyzed a major shift of hospital services from inpatient to outpatient settings. The number of beds in U.S. hospitals dropped by about 15 percent between the early 1980s and 1997.[12]

There is considerable regional variation in the extent of reduction of hospital bed capacity. The national average is now about 3.3 beds per 1,000 population, but many communities in the East have more than 4 beds per 1,000 while some, especially in the West, have decreased hospital capacity to less than 1.7 beds per 1,000.[1]

Although bed capacity has declined somewhat, there is still excess capacity in the system. Only about 10 percent of hospitals closed between 1985 and 1995, when there were still over 5,000 community hospitals in the country.[12]

Mergers, Conversions, Consolidation, and Integration

Mergers became common during the 1990s as hospitals struggled to survive in an environment of declining daily census and reimbursement. Figure 11-2 displays the spectrum of merger and acquisition transactions that took place over just one year, between 1995 and 1996. Especially active were HMOs, with a 121 percent increase in these transactions. As a result, fewer and larger HMOs are serving fewer and larger groups of enrollees.[8]

In terms of ownership, community hospitals fall into three groups of general acute-care hospitals: not for profit (voluntary), public (government), and investor owned (proprietary). In 1995, about 70 percent of beds and 60 percent of these hospitals were in the not-for-profit group, with 18 percent of beds and 26 percent of hospitals in the public (government) group and 12 percent of beds and 14 percent of hospitals in the proprietary, for-profit group.[4] About 9 percent of community hospitals changed ownership between 1980 and 1990 in order to survive, with another 9 percent changing ownership and closing. Public hospitals were the most likely to change ownership status, usually converting to not-for-profit institutions. Conversions to for-profit ownership has also been active since 1980, accounting for almost one third of all hospital conversions between 1990 and 1993.[14] Conversion of hospitals to for-profit status has raised concern among many observers as to the potential negative impact of this change. Molly Coye, as the former senior vice president at Good Samaritan Health System in San Jose, California, made this observation after its sale to Columbia/HCA (the largest hospital company with 342 hospitals in 1996):[15]

> Ultimately the advantages of a more industrialized model of hospital operations—concentrated capital, enormous purchasing leverage, national and regional market strength in contracting, rapid diffusion of technology and best practices in management, and the standardization of processes for quality improvement—have made formidable competitors of Columbia/HCA, Tenet, and other large for-profit systems. These advantages may lead to the demise of independently operated hospitals, whether for-profit or not-for-profit. The reaction of health planners and regulators is often to try to thwart or manage this evolution. But most communities and states do not have the resources to maintain institutions with severely underused capacity, or the legal means to protect selected hospitals by eliminating excess capacity. In these cases, the overriding obligation of community hospital boards and political leaders is to ensure that access to care is preserved and that the financial benefit of these transactions accrues to the community.

As cost containment and managed care pressures mount, hospitals increasingly look to one or another type of affiliation or actual merger with new partners, which in many cases have been their long-term competitors. Table 11-2 shows typical criteria, as developed by Steven Hollis, an experienced consultant to hospitals, by which a board of a not-for-profit hospital may evaluate the feasibility of such a change.

For a term used frequently in recent years, *integration* still often is confusing as it relates to health care services and institutions. VHA, a national network of community-owned health care organizations and physicians, views *integration* as "a continuum, from traditional open systems, in which the financial, institutional, and professional elements are separate, to highly integrated systems, in which all elements are tightly intertwined."[8] Integration can be "vertical" or "horizontal," as shown in Figure 11-3, based on whether the direction is toward assumption of financial risk (vertical) or consolidation of more health care delivery facilities (horizontal).

Table 11-2   Typical Affiliation Criteria Developed by a Not-for-Profit Hospital Board

Criteria	Definition
Mission	The partner must commit to honoring the hospital's mission
Governance	The hospital board must have involvement in the ongoing operation
Regional emphasis	The partner must demonstrate its commitment to the hospital's market
Service continuation	The partner must commit to continuing designated services now offered by the hospital
Regional exclusivity	The hospital must have the exclusive franchise to serve its primary and secondary service areas
Physician integration	The partner must be committed to the rapid development of affiliated physician vehicles for managed care contracts
Access to capitated lives	The partner must demonstrate that the affiliation will improve the hospital's and its affiliated physicians' access to managed care contracts
Risk-taking technology	The partner must demonstrate a willingness to assume risk under managed care contracts and must have the internal systems necessary to manage that risk
Employees	The partner must commit to a continued role for the hospital's employees within the "franchised territory"
Financial strength	The partner must demonstrate the financial strength required to honor commitments
Capitalization of system	The partner must commit to capitalizing the regional network sufficiently to ensure success
Economies of scale	The partner must demonstrate an ability to bring economies of scale to the hospital's operations

Source: Developed by S. R. Hollis with a public hospital client. Reprinted with permission from Hollis SR. Strategic and economic factors in the hospital conversion process. *Health Aff (Millwood)*. 1997;16(2):134.

Hospitals are the initiators of integrated health systems in two thirds of cases, with physicians initiating such systems in only 5 percent of cases and HMO/PPOs in another 4 percent. Although offering the potential advantages of lowered costs, economies of scale, and increased market power, integrated health systems still are the exception more than the rule. By 1996, for example, there were only 570 integrated health systems in the country, with about three quarters as vertical systems and one quarter as horizontal systems.[8]

Shift to Ambulatory and Other Services

Enormous shifts have taken place over the last 20 years, as hospital services have progressively shifted from inpatient to outpatient locations. The ratio of ambulatory care episodes to hospital days of care increased from 4.7 in 1980 to 11 times in 1994, while the number of short-stay hospital days per 1,000 population dropped by a factor of 100 percent. Hospital-based or -sponsored ambulatory facilities include emergency rooms, urgent care walk-in clinics, various

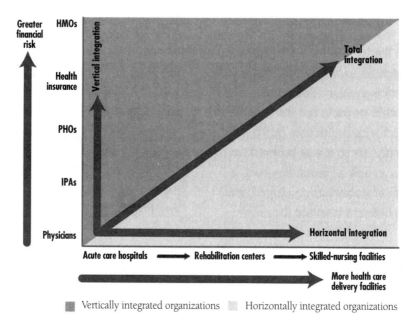

Figure 11-3   Integration defined. (Source: VHA Inc. and Delotte & Touche LLP, 1997. Reprinted with permission from *VHA 1998 Environmental Assessment: Setting Foundations for the Millennium.* Irving, TX: VHA Inc., 1998.)

specialty clinics, surgical centers, health promotion centers, imaging centers, and hospital-sponsored group practices.[4] This sea change has had major impact on the organization, staffing, and financing of ambulatory care services. The magnitude of this change is reflected by the growth of surgical ambulatory care. From 1980 to 1993, the proportion of surgical procedures performed on an out-patient basis increased from 16.4 percent to 54.9 percent with some hospitals reporting over 60 percent of these procedures in outpatients.[16]

The shift by hospitals to outpatient services has not been pain free, however. The Balanced Budget Act of 1997 (BBA97) cut reimbursement for outpatient hospital services. A national accounting firm has projected further shortfalls in Medicare reimbursement, already in the range of −20 percent and dropping.[17]

Increasing Use of Hospitalists

A growing number of hospitals are considering or have already implemented the hospitalist model for care of many of their inpatients. A hospitalist is defined as a physician spending at least 25 percent of his or her time on inpatient care. The major driver for this change is increased efficiency of physicians practicing both in hospital and ambulatory settings. Proponents of this model also point to preliminary data suggesting that care by hospitalists may reduce lengths of stay and lower costs without compromising the quality of care.[18–20]

Twenty years ago, many primary care physicians cared for 10 to 12 patients on any given day in the hospital, whereas that number has dropped to 1 or 2 in many instances today.[21] Conversely, today's hospitalists care for 10 to 15 inpatients at a time.[22] Lurie and Wachter developed a useful approach to estimate hospitalist staffing requirements based on the number of patient admissions per year, length of stay, and workload per hospitalist. For a daily workload of 15 inpatients, three full-time equivalent (FTE) hospitalists would be required in a hospital with 1,500 to 3,000 admissions per year with an average length of stay (LOS) of 3 to 6 days, while 6 FTE hospitalists would be required to cover 5,000 annual admissions with a LOS of 5 or 6 days.[18] It remains unclear how widespread the hospitalist movement will become, but it shows early signs of growing application.

Regionalization

Still another major trend affecting hospitals has been the process of regionalization of some specialized hospital services. Regionalization, as a concept, gained national awareness with the passage of the National Health Planning and Resources Development Act (PL93-641) in 1974.[23] Since then, there has been active development of regionalized approaches in various areas, including perinatal care, neonatal intensive care, trauma care, and certain surgical procedures. Trauma care provides a good example of what can be accomplished through a regionalized approach. Hospitals within a region are classified by three levels:[24]

> Level 1—tertiary, for care of patients with major trauma (as defined by Injury Severity Score (ISS) >12, or Pre-Hospital Index >3, or two or more injuries with Abbreviated Injury Scale scores >2, or hospital stay more than 3 days)
> Level 2—secondary
> Level 3—primary

A regionalized trauma care system also requires other essential components, including improvement of emergency medical services for prehospital care, triage protocols for transport of trauma patients to appropriate hospitals, and centralized coordination and control of prehospital and in-hospital care. Many studies have shown that such regionalized systems can reduce mortality of patients with major trauma.[25–30]

Since Harold Luft, J. P. Bunker, and A. C. Enthoven's classic study of the relationship between surgical volume and mortality in the late 1970s,[31] considerable attention has focused on the implications of that study for regionalized systems of surgical care. They found that many of the more-specialized surgical procedures had a lower mortality outcome if performed in an institution that performed a high volume of such procedures; similar correlations were not found for less-specialized procedures, such as cholecystectomy. A recent modeling study attempted to carry forward this observation by estimating the "volume outcome" effect for 10 surgical procedures. It was projected that as many as 17,000 lives could be saved in the United States each year if these procedures were performed in hospitals that did a high volume of such work.

The largest benefits would be realized for relatively common, intermediate risk procedures (e.g., coronary artery bypass graft and other cardiovascular procedures).[32] Despite this projection, however, there are still wide variations from one state to another in application of volume-based policies for regionalization of surgical procedures. In the case of coronary artery bypass graft (CABG), for example, California has no such restrictions and two thirds of CABG procedures are performed in hospitals that do a low volume of CABGs (less than 200 procedures/year), with one third in hospitals that do a very low volume (less than 100 procedures/year), whereas New York state has rigorous Certificate of Need regulations, with only 20 percent of CABG procedures being done in hospitals that do a low volume of them.[32]

Although volume-related restrictions are appealing, they cannot be applied broadly without consideration of other factors. In the case of surgery for abdominal aneurism, for example, as in many areas of medicine, the unintended consequences could be devastating for patients with ruptured abdominal aneurysms in rural communities, in the event that the local general surgeon has been prevented from performing elective resection of such aneurysms and consequently lost proficiency in that procedure.[32]

SPECIAL CASES

Although the new environment of increased competition and decreasing reimbursement has been difficult for all hospitals, three kinds of institutions—teaching hospitals, public (safety net) hospitals, and rural hospitals—face the most severe threat to their own survival. The dynamics and particulars vary with each case.

Teaching Hospitals

The number of teaching hospitals in the United States depends on the definition used. About 300 nonfederal hospitals are considered "major teaching hospitals," as defined by a ratio of the number of house staff (interns and residents) to the number of beds ≥0.25.[33] About three quarters of the country's resident physicians and virtually all medical students train in these hospitals.[34] If defined by hospitals with at least one medical residency program, about 1,250 hospitals (18 percent of the nation's hospitals) participate in graduate medical education.[34-35] The most highly specialized of these hospitals—the academic health centers (AHCs)—are operated by the country's 125 accredited medical schools, with a mission extending well beyond patient care to include medical education at predoctoral and graduate levels and clinical and basic research.

In contrast to most other industrialized countries, the United States has never had a coherent system for planning or financing medical education. U.S. medical schools and their affiliated hospitals vary widely in terms of ownership, curriculum, and business plan. Before the passage of Medicare in 1965, medical schools and their teaching hospitals depended on diverse revenue sources, including tuition, local and state governments, foundations, and endowments. The enactment of Medicare for the first time provided a predictable base of solid funding for medical education through its provisions for funding of direct and indirect costs of graduate medical education (GME), as well as extra payments to hospitals with a disproportionate share of high-cost cases. As a result of these Medicare subsidies and in concert with the general perception that the country needed more physicians, the medical schools greatly expanded their classes of medical students, numbers of residents (especially in the non-primary care specialties), faculty, and facilities. They became increasingly dependent on Medicare reimbursement. The collective share of the costs of medical education borne by the federal government reached almost 50 percent by 1997.[35]

The heyday of AHCs slowed down with the advent of the prospective payment system by DRGs under Medicare in the 1980s and was brought up short by the budget cuts of the 1997 Balanced Budget Act. The question of how to fund medical education has become especially contentious, with the direct and indirect payments under Medicare coming under closer scrutiny. These funds originally were intended to enable expansion of the physician workforce during the 1960s and 1970s, so that many in Congress and the Bush administration are less sympathetic to their need today as that workforce has become too large, especially in non-primary care specialties.[35]

Teaching hospitals find it increasingly difficult to carry on their teaching mission in the managed care era, which puts a premium on the efficiency of patient care without regard to teaching and research missions. A 1993 study found that costs per case in AHCs were 83 percent higher than those of urban nonteaching hospitals; when adjusted for case mix and area wage levels, AHCs were 63 percent more expensive than nonteaching hospitals, and a 44 percent higher cost remained when direct Medicare GME payments were subtracted out.[36] It is now incumbent on AHCs and major teaching hospitals to defend their increased costs in terms of their larger mission and quality of care. In addition to their missions in teaching and clinical research, teaching hospitals provide about 50 percent of all indigent care in the country.[37] Moreover, considerable evidence demonstrates that major teaching hospitals provide superior quality of care, as shown in Figure 11-4 for comparative adjusted death rates[38,39] and further exemplified by a recent analysis of patient outcomes for over 114,000 Medicare beneficiaries with acute myocardial infarction treated in over 4,600 U.S. hospitals.[40]

As a result of the impact of an increasingly competitive marketplace, managed care, and cutbacks in funding for medical education, academic medicine in the United States now is in very difficult times. Herbert Pardes, dean at Columbia University College of Physicians and Surgeons and former chairman of the Association of American Medical Colleges, brings this perspective:[37]

despite scientific progress and popular support, academic medicine is in serious danger. The problem is that the excitement generated by its success and the recognition of its importance is unmatched with appropriate policy regarding financial support of teaching hospitals and medical schools, which form such a central part of the successful effort in U.S. medical science. Healthcare has been relegated to the marketplace, except for federal support for some older and indigent populations. Health care is treated as a product

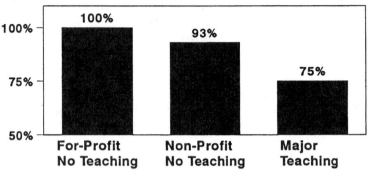

Figure 11-4 Death rates are higher at for-profit hospitals; here, major teaching hospitals are 85.5 percent non-profit, 14.3 percent government, and 0.2 percent for-profit. (Reprinted with permission from Chen J, Radford MJ, Wang Y, Marciniak TA, Krumholz HM. Do "America's best hospitals" perform better for acute myocardial infarction? *N Engl J Med.* 1999;340:286; and Woolhandler S, Himmelstein DU. *The National Health Program Slideshow Guide.* Cambridge, MA: The Center for National Health Program Studies, 2000.)

and its commodification, as described by Senator Daniel Patrick Moynihan (D, NY), involves "health care bought and sold in the market, where the not-for-profit, service orientation of health care providers is threatened."[41]

To stabilize teaching hospitals in their essential missions, former Senator Moynihan called for an all-payer's fund to support medical education and AHCs, but admits that the plight of AHCs still is not on the nation's political agenda.[37] While there is wide recognition that some downsizing of medical education is necessary, the unique roles of teaching hospitals must be preserved.

In an effort to reduce the financial impact of adverse selection (whereby they are hospitals of last resort for sicker patients requiring more intensive resources), AHCs have employed a variety of strategies. Many sought to increase their primary care base through purchase of primary care practices or community hospitals. Others negotiated joint ventures with other providers, insurance companies, or health plans. All increased expectations for clinical productivity of their faculty.[42] The future is unclear for many AHCs. Some probably will close within the next few years, and the issue of financing medical education remains unresolved.

Public Hospitals

The mission of public hospitals is to provide health care services to all persons in the community, which typically includes a high proportion of uninsured and otherwise disadvantaged people who cannot afford to pay for care. Public hos-

pitals are organized in various ways, often under city, county, or state governance, and may be operated under contractual agreement with other institutions,
such as medical schools. As such, they provide a large volume of inpatient,
outpatient, and emergency care in urban communities.[43] In 1990, for example,
public hospitals in the country's largest 100 central cities provided 210,000
outpatient visits and 74,000 emergency room visits compared with 73,000 and
25,000 visits, respectively, by the private hospital sector in those communities.[44]
Public hospitals therefore play a critical safety-net role for a sizable population,
who cannot access the private health care sector. In addition, many public
hospitals are actively involved in medical education and clinical research, and
they often provide specialized services to a much wider geographic area.
For instance, although public general hospitals accounted for only 8 percent of
hospitals in the 100 largest U.S. cities in 1990, they provided 38 percent of burn
care days and 21 percent of neonatal and pediatric intensive care days.[44]

Public hospitals are funded primarily by local subsidy and Medicaid and to
a lesser extent by Medicare. Many operate on the edge of financial disaster. A
recent study found, for example, that two thirds of public hospitals were losing
money in 1997.[45] They therefore have had to undertake various strategies to
compete more effectively in the medical marketplace. In Denver, for example,
Denver Health has been organized as an integrated public health care delivery
system, including a 349-bed acute care hospital, a 911 emergency response
system, 10 federally qualified community health centers, 10 school-based
clinics, the public health department, a regional poison control center, a locked
forensic unit, and a 100-bed nonmedical detoxification unit. Denver Health
initiated a range of coordinated strategies to adapt to the changing marketplace,
including a change in governance, development of a Medicaid managed care
program, linkage with other community-owned or government hospitals elsewhere in the state, and expansion of centers of excellence in trauma care and
prisoner care.[46] Reviewing the essential role and financial fragility of public
hospitals in providing health care to the most vulnerable urban population,
Andrulis and his colleagues called for restructuring of federal and state policies
to assist public hospitals to the competitive marketplace along the kinds of lines
taken by Denver Health.[43]

Rural Hospitals

A third group of hospitals that has been especially vulnerable to the changing
health services environment is the rural hospital. This typically is a hospital
with less than 100 beds in a nonmetropolitan area, but many of these hospitals
are in relatively remote areas with fewer than 30 or 40 beds. These hospitals
face many challenges not shared by their counterparts in metropolitan areas,
including lower reimbursement, high fixed costs, a smaller population to draw
from, a lower census preventing economies of scale, and difficulty recruiting
and retaining physicians, nurses, and other health professionals. Reimbursement
and other regulations related to hospitals tend to be devised for urban hospitals,
including such areas as architectural codes, with little regard for the needs and
circumstances of rural hospitals.

The rural hospital serves a central role within its local health care system and is a source of community identity and pride. Its loss can jeopardize health care for residents in its entire catchment area, which often extends over a wide area around the community itself. In addition to acute short-stay beds, most rural hospitals provide 24-hour emergency care services, and about one half of hospitals with less than 50 beds have facilities for obstetric care. Just less than one quarter of rural hospitals with less than 25 beds have medical/surgical intensive care units. In addition, rural hospitals tend to provide more long-term care for elderly patients than urban hospitals, and many offer outpatient surgery.[47]

A higher proportion of rural hospitals has been forced to close over the last 20 years than hospitals in metropolitan areas. Although many factors usually are involved in the closure of rural hospitals, financial shortfalls due to lower reimbursement and declining census tend to be prominent. The prospective payment system introduced for Medicare beneficiaries during the early 1980s was an important factor in many closures. Ten percent (251) of the nation's rural hospitals closed between 1980 and 1989.[48]

In their efforts to survive and continue to meet the needs of their local populations, rural hospitals have taken various approaches to stabilize their often precarious circumstances, including developing affiliations or partnerships with other hospitals; joining a network for joint purchasing, shared services, physician recruiting, or contracting; forming networks with physicians and other providers; and occasionally joining rural health networks to contract with HMOs or self-insured employers.[47-49] Other promising avenues also are available to some rural hospitals in difficulty. Hospital service districts may provide a base of local tax support to offset financial shortfalls. Conversion to a limited service facility is another important strategy under some circumstances, which can allow retention of appropriate hospital-based services in rural communities threatened by imminent or actual hospital closure. The Montana Medical Assistance Facility demonstrated a successful model of that approach, later replicated in Wyoming, Kentucky, and Florida and recently leading to the Critical Access Hospital Program, established by the federal Balanced Budget Act of 1997.[50]

CONCLUDING COMMENTS

This chapter provides ample evidence that U.S. hospitals are experiencing difficult challenges. The nature of clinical practice has changed dramatically over the last 40 years, with many clinical problems once requiring hospitalization now being managed on an outpatient basis. The magnitude of this change is less apparent in the short term but remarkable in the longer view. During the 1960s, for example, many patients were hospitalized for diagnostic workups including such studies as upper GI series and barium enemas, and the average length of stay for acute myocardial infarction (AMI) was over two weeks. Today, most diagnostic workups are done on outpatients, and the length of stay in the hospital for uncomplicated AMI is only four or five days.

That there still are too many hospitals and hospital beds to meet today's needs is beyond question. Downsizing needs to continue, and specialty-dominated services need to be reined in to appropriate levels based on cost-effective outcomes. However, the special roles of teaching hospitals, public hospitals as safety nets, and rural hospitals in an appropriate form need to be preserved. Many U.S. hospitals already have started to adjust to the new, highly competitive managed care marketplace. Some will succeed, others will not. Hospitals need to keep changing, for the role they enjoyed at the center of the health care system in past years has become more peripheral as managed care organizations and health plans play their increasingly dominant roles in health care.

REFERENCES

1. Fisher ES. What is a hospital? *Eff Clin Pract.* 1999;2(3):138–140.
2. Risse GB. Health care in hospitals: The past 1000 years. *Lancet.* 1999;354(suppl):SIV 25.
3. Iglehart JK. The American health care system. Community hospitals. *N Engl J Med.* 1993; 329:372–376.
4. Kovner AR. Hospitals. In: Kovner AR, Jonas S (eds). *Health Care Delivery in the United States.* New York: Springer Publishing, 1999:158–162.
5. Ginzberg E. Hospitals: From center to periphery. *Inquiry.* Spring 1999;32:11–13.
6. Shortell SM, Gillies RR, Devers JH. Reinventing the American hospital. *Milbank Q.* 1995; 73(2):131–160.
7. Anderson GF, Pierre-Poullier J. Health spending, access, and outcomes: Trends in industrialized countries. *Health Aff (Millwood).* 1999;18(3):184–185.
8. *VHA 1998 Environmental Assessment: Setting Foundations for the Millennium.* Irving, TX: VHA Inc., 1998.
9. McGinley L. Hospitals feel sting of cuts from insurers. *Wall Street Journal* March 16, 2000:B2.
10. The financial state of hospitals: Post-BBA and post-BBRA. *Med Benefits.* 2000;17(11):1.
11. Silverman EM, Skinner JS, Fisher ES. The association between for-profit hospital ownership and increased Medicare spending. *N Engl J Med.* 1999;341:420–426.
12. The Institute for the Future. *Health and Health Care 2010: The Forecast, the Challenge.* San Francisco: Jossey-Bass, 2000.
13. Weinick RM, Cohen JW. Leading the playing field: Managed care enrollment and hospital use, 1987–1996. *Health Aff (Millwood).* 2000;19(3):181–182.
14. Needleman J, Chollet DJ, Lamphere JA. Hospital conversion trends. *Health Aff (Millwood).* 1997;16(2):187–195.
15. Coye MJ. The sale of Good Samaritan: A view from the trenches. *Health Aff (Millwood).* 1997;16(2):107.
16. U.S. Department of Health and Human Services, *Health United States, 1995.* DHHS publication no. PHS 96-1232. Washington, DC: U.S. Government Printing Office, 1995.
17. Armey, Thomas. Deschle shares views on health care legislation. BBA hit private hospitals hardest, congressional leaders say. *Hosp Outlook.* May 1999;2(4):4–5.
18. Lurie JD, Wachter RM. Hospitalist staffing requirements. *Effect Clinic Pract.* 1999;2(3):126–130.
19. Diamond HS, Goldberg E, Janosky JE. The effect of full-time faculty hospitalists on the efficiency of care at a community teaching hospital. *Ann Intern Med.* 1998;129:197–203.
20. Wachter RM, Katz P, Showstack J, Bindman AB, Goldman L. Reorganizing an academic medical service: Impact on cost, quality, patient satisfaction, and education. *JAMA.* 1998;279:1560–1565.
21. Chesanow N. When hospitalists take over—Who wins? Who loses? *Med Econ.* 1998;(December 28):107.
22. Lindenauer PK, Pantilat SZ, Katz PP, Wachter RM. Hospitalists and the practice of inpatient medicine: Results of a survey of the National Association of Inpatient Physicians. *Ann Intern Med.* 1999;130(4, Pt 2):343–349.
23. Katz G. Regionalization among children's hospitals. *Hosp Health Serv Adm.* Fall 1980; 25(4):56–72.
24. Sampalis JS, Denis R, Lavoie A, et al. Trauma care regionalization: A process-outcome evaluation. *J Trauma.* April 1999;46(4):565–579; discussion:579–581.

25. Boyd DR, Cowley RA. Comprehensive regional trauma/emergency medical services (EMS) delivery systems: The United States experience. *World J Surg.* 1983;7:149–157.
26. Cales RH, Anderson PG, Heilig RW Jr. Utilization of medical care in Orange County: The effect of implementation of a regional trauma system. *Ann Emerg Med.* 1985;14:853–858.
27. Mullins RJ, Veum-Stone J, Helfand ME, et al. Outcome of hospitalized injured patients after institution of a trauma system in an urban area. *JAMA.* 1994;271:1919–1924.
28. Hulka F, Mullins RJ, Mann NC, et al. Influence of a statewide trauma system on pediatric hospitalization and outcome. *J Trauma.* 1997;42:514–519.
29. Stewart TC, Lane PL, Stefanits T. An evaluation of patient outcomes before and after trauma center designation using Trauma and Injury Severity Score analysis. *J Trauma.* 1995;39:1036–1040.
30. Mullins RJ, Veun-Stone J, Hedges JR, et al. Influence of a statewide trauma system on location of hospitalization and outcome of injured patients. *J Trauma.* 1996;40:536–545; discussion:545–546.
31. Luft HS, Bunker JP, Enthoven AC. Should operations be regionalized? The empirical relation between surgical volume and mortality. *N Engl J Med.* 1979;301:1364–1369.
32. Birkmeyer JD, Lucas FL, Wennberg DE. Potential benefits of regionalizing major surgery in Medicare patients. *Eff Clin Pract.* 1999;2(6):277–283.
33. Epstein AM. US teaching hospitals in the evolving health care system. *JAMA.* 1995;273:1203–1207.
34. Iglehart JK. The American health care system. Teaching hospitals. *N Engl J Med.* 1993;329:1052–1056.
35. Kuttner R. Managed care and medical education. *N Engl J Med.* 1999;341:1092–1096.
36. Mechanic R, Coleman K, Dobson A. Teaching hospital costs: implications for academic missions in a competitive market. *JAMA.* 1998;280:1015–1019.
37. Pardes H. The perilous state of academic medicine. *JAMA.* 2000;283:2427–2429.
38. Chen J, Radford MJ, Wang Y, Marciniak TA, Krumholz HM. Do "America's Best Hospitals" perform better for acute myocardial infarction? *N Engl J Med.* 1999;340:286–292.
39. Woolhandler S, Himmelstein DU. *The National Health Program Slideshow Guide.* Cambridge, MA: The Center for National Health Program Studies, 2000.
40. Allison JJ, Kiefe CI, Weissman NW, et al. Relationship of hospital teaching status with quality of care and mortality for Medicare patients with acute MI. *JAMA.* 2000;284:1256–1262.
41. Moynihan DP. On the commodification of medicine. *Acad Med.* 1998;73(5):453–459.
42. Goldman L. The academic health care system. Preserving the missions as the paradigm shifts. *JAMA.* 1995;273:1549–1552.
43. Andrulis DP, Acuff KL, Weiss KB, Anderson RJ. Public hospitals and health care reform: Choices and challenges. *Am J Public Health.* 1996;86(2):162–165.
44. Andrulis DP, Shaw-Taylor Y, Ginsberg C, Martin V. *Urban Social Health: Chartbook Profiling the Nation's One Hundred Largest Cities.* Washington, DC: National Public Health and Hospital Institute, 1995.
45. Gray BH, Rowe C. Safety-net health plans: A status report. *Health Aff (Millwood).* 2000;19(1):185–193.
46. Gabow PA. Denver Health: Initiatives for survival. *Health Aff (Millwood).* 1997;16(4):24–26.
47. Nesbitt TS, Kuenneth CA. Rural hospitals, consultation, and referral networks in rural practice. In: Geyman JP, Norris TE, Hart LG (eds). *Textbook of Rural Medicine.* New York: McGraw-Hill, 2000:205.
48. Hart LG, Pirani MJ, Rosenblatt RA. Causes and consequences of rural small hospital closures from the perspectives of mayors. *J Rural Health.* 1991;7(3): 222–245.
49. Moscovice I, Wellever A. Rural health networks: An organizational strategy for collaboration. In: Geyman JP, Norris TE, Hart LG (eds). *Textbook of Rural Medicine.* New York: McGraw-Hill, 2000:261.
50. Geyman JP, Hart LG, Norris TE, Coombs JB, Lishner DM. Physician education and rural location: A critical review. *J Rural Health.* 2001;16(1):74.

12
Increased Impact of Litigation

On March 28, 2000, an article in the *New York Times* reported that a San Francisco jury had just awarded $1.7 million in compensatory damages and $20 million in punitive damages to a 41-year-old woman with metastatic lung cancer who started smoking in 1972 at age 13. The tobacco companies argued that the woman had to know the risks of smoking, since warning labels had been required on cigarette packages since the 1960s. The plaintiff's attorney, however, argued that the tobacco companies had fraudulently misrepresented the risks of smoking and even asked the court for $115 million in punitive damages. The companies had argued for punitive damages of $5 million or less, since they had changed their practices after recent legal settlements between the tobacco industry and the states, whereby the industry agreed to pay $246 billion over the next 20 years to the states that sued them for smoking-related illnesses.[1] Several days after this article appeared, a Miami jury awarded two former smokers $6.9 million in compensatory damages.[2] Three months later, a Miami jury of six jurors deliberated just over four hours before rendering a $145 *billion* verdict in favor of almost half a million state residents in a class action lawsuit. Applauded by the White House and various health care organizations, the Association of Trial Lawyers of America maintained their position that punitive claims are not out of control and that "runaway" juries are a myth.[3]

These cases are just the tip of the iceberg of many health-related legal actions occurring every day, which raise many questions about the fairness of health-related litigation and even the credibility of jury-rendered judgments. There seem to be plenty of villains to go around. In the preceding cases, for example, although the harms of smoking have been well known for many years, until recently there was a long-standing cozy relationship between big tobacco and federal and state governments, with government overlooking these hazards in exchange for large tax revenues. While the marketing practices of cigarette companies cannot be defended, where is the personal responsibility of individual claimants? Aren't we witnessing unconscionable greed on the part of plain-

161

tiff attorneys, who usually take one third of final settlements in the name of justice?

There are many reasons to question whether the current medicolegal system is appropriately designed to adjudicate fairly and effectively health-related disputes. Just as there are serious flaws in the structure of the health care system, so too in the medicolegal system. At the same time, powerful political and legislative forces are resisting structural change of both systems. These forces are fueled by unrealistically high public expectations, as we saw in Chapter 5, for risk-free care with assured positive outcomes. Moreover, a commonly held assumption is that the medicolegal system is intended to improve medical care by protecting patients from clinical incompetence. The medicolegal system clearly fails to meet that goal, instead increasing the cost of health care and, arguably, lowering its quality.

This chapter examines the increasing impact of health care litigation, with a fivefold purpose: (1) to provide an overview of medical malpractice, including its causes, epidemiology, and trends; (2) to briefly describe four other areas of health-related litigation; (3) to illustrate the influence of special interests in health-related disputes; (4) to summarize the impact of health care litigation on costs, defensive medicine, and the physician-patient relationship; and (5) to touch on some of the approaches by government and other organizations in the private sector to redirect the legal process in the public interest.

MEDICAL MALPRACTICE

An increasing number of medical malpractice suits, together with escalating awards, first called attention to "the medical malpractice crisis" in the United States during the mid-1970s.[3] Since that time, litigation of this type has been a growth industry in the legal profession, with a major impact on medical practice, as well as its cost, quality, and the access to care. The last five years have seen an increasing trend for both median jury awards and settlements in this country, including a 46 percent increase in median awards from 1997 to 1998. Table 12-1 shows the proportion of malpractice lawsuits that plaintiffs win. Table 12-2 lists the kinds of injuries most likely to result in a plaintiff verdict in 1998.

The Physician Insurers Association of America (PIAA) was established in 1977 with one goal, to provide information to help reduce the incidence of patient injury and claims. It now represents physician-owned or -directed liability insurance companies, which collectively insure over 60 percent of practicing physicians in the United States. A recent report covers the period from January 1, 1985 to June 30, 1999, and provides a definitive portrait of the medical malpractice terrain.[4] The 10 leading specialties involved in large losses (over $250,000) are listed in Table 12-3. It is readily apparent why obstetrics-gynecology is the most vulnerable to high claims and awards ("bad babies").

The majority of paid claims over the 14-year period spanned by the PIAA database have resulted from health care services delivered in the hospital (63 percent) or physicians' offices (27 percent). It is interesting that house calls,

Table 12-1 The Portion of Malpractice Suits That Plaintiffs Win

	1993	1994	1995	1996	1997	1998
Childbirth negligence	47%	37%	44%	34%	35%	46%
Medical malpractice (overall)	31	34	35	29	37	36
Misdiagnosis	23	38	37	27	36	41
Surgical negligence	28	29	28	29	38	32

Source: Reprinted with permission from Professional liability 1998: A year when malpractice awards mushroomed. *Med Econ.* July 10, 2000:26.

Table 12-2 Outcomes Most Likely to Result in a Plaintiff Verdict in 1998

Outcome	Median Verdict
Brain injury	$4,089,914
Paralysis	$3,000,000
Cancer	$766,500
Spinal nerve injury	$700,000
Death	$678,478
Eye injury	$500,000
Leg injury	$500,000
Intestinal injury	$500,000
Overall injuries	$500,000
Foot injury	$281,682
Genital injury	$200,000
Emotional distress	$130,000

Source: Reprinted with permission from Boxold D. Jury verdict research. *Current Award Trends in Personal Injury.* 1999.

HMO facilities, and birthing centers each accounted for less than 0.2 percent of total paid claims.[4]

Patterns of medical malpractice claims have received considerable analysis over the years and are now quite well understood. The most common triggers of malpractice claims are dissatisfaction with results of treatment, unrealistic patient expectations, patient anger over care or the bill, patients' financial incentives, physician-patient communication problems, physician attitudes, and physician criticism of previous care. It therefore comes as no surprise that physician communication styles correlate well with malpractice liability risk— physicians who are accessible, concerned, and communicative are at low risk, while those who are hurried, appear disinterested, or unwilling to listen or answer questions are at high risk.[5] Also of interest is that the occurrence of an adverse event, even when due to negligence, is not directly predictive of awards to plaintiffs.

Definite patterns also are found concerning types of adverse events by specialty that lead to malpractice liability awards. The most common error in the primary care specialties, not unexpectedly, is error in diagnosis (especially

Table 12-3   Large Loss Indemnity Payments by Specialty, 1985–1999 (Closed Files with Indemnity Paid ≥$250,000; Cumulative Data January 1, 1985–June 30, 1999)

		% of Large			Average Indemnity Per Large Loss Claims
Specialty Group	Paid Claims	Large Loss Claims	Loss to Paid	Large Loss Indemnity Paid	
1. Obstetric and gynecologic surgery	7,783	2,161	27.77	$1,374,121,682	$635,823
2. Internal medicine— nonsurgical	5,453	1,101	20.19	$591,878,593	$537,583
3. General surgery	5,996	1,043	17.39	$552,210,594	$529,444
4. General and family practice—nonsurgical	6,488	957	14.75	$478,932,774	$500,452
5. Orthopedic surgery	4,638	754	16.26	$372,749,314	$494,362
6. Anesthesiology	2,084	462	22.17	$294,480,931	$637,405
7. Pediatrics—nonsurgical	1,3791	366	26.70	$239,183,794	$653,508
8. Radiology—nonsurgical	2,428	396	16.31	$201,053,229	$507,710
9. Neurosurgery	1,022	319	31.21	$192,277,571	$602,751
10. Ophthalmology	1,345	230	17.10	$107,582,176	$467,749

Source: Adapted with permission from Reports of Research Department, Physician Insurers Association of America. *Data Sharing Reports.* Rockville, MD: Physician Insurers Association of America, 1999.

acute myocardial infarction for general or family practice, lung cancer for general internal medicine, and meningitis for general pediatrics); in the surgical specialties, improper performance of a procedure is the most common problem.[4] Also well documented is that lack of knowledge is a much less common problem than system problems in the defendant's practice.[6,7] William Robertson, a physician with long experience in medical education, medical politics, and the medicolegal side of medicine, makes this observation: "systems" errors, not "data deficits," are the real fertilizer for keeping the malpractice arena so nice and green.[8]

The legal process involved in medical malpractice litigation has generated considerable criticism and controversy in recent years. The malpractice liability system was intended to meet two goals:[9]

1. to compensate patients financially in the event of injuries incurred during their medical care; and
2. to prevent physicians and other health care personnel from negligently causing adverse outcomes for patients.

Measured by either goal, the U.S. system is a failure.[10] The Harvard Medical Practice Study, reported in 1991, found that only 2 percent of negligent injuries to patients resulted in malpractice claims,[11] and others have documented that only a minority of such compensable injuries lead to claims.[12,13] At the same time, a large number of claims are brought that involve no medical injury or negligence by the defendant.[11–14] In the Harvard Medical Practice Study, only 28 percent of medical injuries were found to involve negligence.[11]

The accuracy of the medical malpractice litigation system has been called into question by many observers. It presently is based on a standard of medical negligence, and a *tort* is defined as a wrongful act or injury done willfully or negligently. Troyen Brennan, an internist-attorney at the Harvard School of Public Health, together with his colleagues, found that the severity of the patient's disability, *not* demonstrable negligence, is the main factor determining the outcome of a medical malpractice claim. They then logically make this argument for basic reform of the present system:[9]

> If the permanence of a disability, not the fact of negligence, is the reason for compensation, the determination of negligence may be an expensive sideshow.[12] It may pollute the compensation process by creating an adversarial atmosphere and may interfere with quality-improvement efforts.[15]

OTHER FORMS OF HEALTH CARE LITIGATION

Four other areas of litigation provide further perspective of the widening spectrum of litigation related to health care but still represent only the tip of the iceberg.

Managed Care

The cost containment policies of many managed care organizations have brought legal challenges, controversy, and public outrage. Amid the smoke and media attention to a growing number of high-profile cases, it often is unclear where a fair balance lies between legitimate cost containment, the rights of patients, and the public interest. Often the scientific basis of appropriateness and necessity of disputed health care services appears to be lost in the debate.

An especially inflammatory issue has been the use of "gag clauses" by many health plans, restricting communication between physicians and patients. A typical gag clause states: "Physicians shall agree not to take action or make any communication which undermines or could undermine the confidence of enrollees, potential enrollees, their employers, their unions, or the public in . . . the quality of . . . health care coverage."[16] Gag clauses can effectively block fully informed consents and consideration of diagnostic or therapeutic alternatives and are seen by the AMA and many others as unethical intrusions upon the physician-patient relationship.[16]

In many cases, evidence-based outcomes have played little role in litigation proceedings or resulting awards. In the mid-1990s, for example, a jury in southern California awarded $89 million to a patient's estate, when the patient had died of breast cancer after denial of autologous bone marrow transplantation and high-dose chemotherapy ($77 million of this award was for punitive damages; a later settlement reduced this to an undisclosed figure, probably less than $10 million; Fox case).[17] An even more striking example was a jury verdict of $120 million (including $116 million in punitive damages) against Aetna US Healthcare in 1999 in favor of a patient who died of leiomyosarcoma of the stomach after alleged delay of high-dose chemotherapy and bone marrow transplantation (Goodrich case).[17] Some state legislatures have joined the fray by requiring coverage of autologous bone marrow transplants after high-dose chemotherapy for metastatic breast cancer, which have never been shown to be effective and recently have been proven ineffective.[18,19] This led Richard Roberts, family physician-attorney and president of the American Academy of Family Physicians, to observe that "these transplants result from the myth that doing more is doing better—that worse than no hope is false hope."[20]

The issue of punitive damages in litigation against managed care organizations represents a potential time bomb. In their recent analysis of this issue, Studdert and Brennan warn that the Goodrich case could be a prelude to many future awards of this type, which in turn could trigger unfortunate responses by managed care organizations (e.g., relaxation of utilization review standards, reduction of benefits, lower reimbursement to providers and hospitals, increased transfer of risk and control to physicians by way of capitation).[17]

Meanwhile, in Spring 2000, attorneys fresh from class action victories against the tobacco companies, took aim at managed care organizations. Class action lawsuits were filed against five of the country's top HMOs—PacificCare Health Systems Inc., Foundation Health Systems Inc., Cigna Healthcare, Prudential Health Care, and Humana Inc.—collectively representing 32 million enrollees. This led Karen Ignagni, president and CEO of the American Association of Health Plans, to this comment:[21]

> Wealthy personal injury lawyers have a new procedure of first vilifying an industry in the media and then filing lawsuits. Class actions are their weapon. If these lawyers are successful in their litigation game, they may turn back the clock on the health care system, forcing patients to pay more for services and get less results.

Plaintiffs' attorneys are challenging the very principles on which managed care organizations have been created: their responsibility and intent to contain costs by limiting services not considered medically necessary. These legal challenges are being fueled as well by public pressure, trial lawyers, and many legislators. The AMA also supports patients' rights to sue their HMO, even *before* their claims have been reviewed by an independent panel of physicians, and further rejects any cap on damages.[22] The current battleground is in the U.S. Congress over proposed provisions on Patients' Bill of Rights legislation that would enable patients to sue HMOs. While all the momentum in recent years has been in the direction of more litigation against managed care organizations, a June 2000 decision of the U.S. Supreme Court provided some defense of the need of HMOs to pursue cost containment of health care. In a landmark case, *Pegram* v. *Herdrich*, a patient sued her physician and HMO when her plan denied an ultrasound examination. She had presented with abdominal pain, a misdiagnosis was made of ovarian cyst, the ultrasound was delayed for eight days, and she ended up with a ruptured appendix. While not dealing with the clinical merits of the case, the Supreme Court ruled unanimously in favor of the health plan's right to manage costs and deny some services. In effect, the Court held that these decisions should be clinical, administrative, or even legislative but not judicial.[23] This court decision led Steven Epstein, a highly experienced health care attorney, to this observation:[23]

while the court decided that case, plaintiffs' lawyers are still actively attacking managed care in a variety of federal and state cases. They're still intent on destroying managed care and I think that's just very unfortunate. They're getting support from a variety of sources, including the American Medical Association and state medical associations, which makes no sense in terms of what's best for providers. The idea that our litigation system should solve what is in essence a major crisis in health care and that the so-called problems with our health care system, like necessary physician incentives, should be solved by plaintiffs' lawyers who will walk away with millions of dollars if they should win, is an abomination. Our litigation system is a national disgrace, as anybody who has been subject to the system knows. The idea that such a severely broken system will determine our health policy is clearly beyond what I think is appropriate.

As Epstein is quick to add, however, coverage decisions must be distinguished from treatment decisions. Medical malpractice liability more reasonably can be attached to clinical decision making while liability for coverage decisions likely will prove too costly for health plans, purchasers, and ultimately, consumers.

Alternative Medicine

Unconventional therapies, now encompassed under the umbrella of alternative or complementary medicine, have been on an upsurge in U.S. health care, as well as in Canada, Europe, and elsewhere around the world. David Eisenberg's now-classic 1993 report revealed that one or another kind of nontraditional therapy was used by more than 30 percent of Americans in 1990. This care represented 425 million visits and $10.3 billion in out-of-pocket expenses by patients.[24] It has been estimated that demand for these therapies may be growing at a rate of 30 percent annually,[25] and some large managed care organizations (e.g., Oxford Health Plans and Health Net) now offer coverage for alternative therapies. How do these developments affect the potential for malpractice liability?

So far, not too much is known about the liability experience of alternative providers, but a study by Studdert and his colleagues gives us some insight into this area. They examined national claims data for the period 1990 to 1996 for chiropractors, massage therapists, and acupuncturists (who together accounted for two thirds of the 425 million visits in 1990 to alternative medicine practitioners). Their study showed an 81 percent increase in the average severity of claims, as reflected by average indemnity payments, over that six-year period for chiropractors compared to a 47 percent increase for primary care physicians.[26]

The adverse outcomes leading to claims against alternative practitioners are interesting and worrisome. The most common adverse events in each case are as follows:[25]

For chiropractors:
Failure to take X rays or appropriately interpret them.
Continuation of treatment despite adverse effects.

Misleading claims as to qualifications.

Failure to refer, warn, or properly diagnose.

For massage therapists:

Causing soft tissue injuries, or occasionally fractures.

Causing ruptured spinal disks, serious head or CNS damage (though 61 percent of claims are for minor injuries).

Sexual misconduct (14 percent of claims).

For acupuncturists:

Less known, but in one instance, the practitioner infected 35 patients with hepatitis B from non-sterile needles, resulting in a class-action suit by 21 of the patients.

In view of these kinds of liability problems, Studdert and his colleagues advise referring physicians to follow the research on alternative therapies, fully inform patients before referral for these therapies, document this discussion, follow his or her best clinical judgment, and refer carefully to trained, certified, and licensed practitioners. Although chiropractors are licensed in all 50 states, many states do not have licensure provisions for naturopaths, massage therapists, acupuncturists, herbalists, and other "holistic" practitioners.[27]

Electronic Health Information and Services

As computerized health information systems become more widespread in an era of managed care and increasingly integrated delivery systems, new questions arise concerning privacy of identifiable health information, retrievability and quality of health data, and risk of tort-based liability.[28] Although automated information technology can enable faster and more accurate diagnosis,[29] prevention of adverse drug events,[30] rapid literature searches, monitoring of clinical markers and tests for individual patients, and public health surveillance of morbidity and mortality across populations,[31,32] the three potential problem areas mentioned in the first sentence of this paragraph represent problems to be overcome and managed.

E-mail commonly is becoming a communication method between physicians and patients,[33] yet it is vulnerable to being intercepted by anyone with access to a physician's e-mail account, with the additional risk of messages being altered or responded to inappropriately under the false guise of authority.[28] In view of these risks, guidelines have been promulgated by such organizations as the AMA for the use of physician-patient e-mail with such safeguards as these:[28]

1. obtaining informed patient consent before such e-mail use,
2. explaining and using security mechanisms,
3. prohibiting forwarding of these messages without patients' authorization,
4. informing patients as to who will have access to these communications and whether they will become part of their medical records, and
5. avoiding references to third parties.

Telemedicine (now commonly referred to as *telehealth*) likewise carries the risk of invasion of privacy for medical information about individual patients

Table 12-4 Artificial Implants

Device	Number
Artificial eye lens	3,000,000
Breast implants	2,000,000
Artificial joints	1,800,000
Eardrum tube	1,200,000
Dental implants	350,000
Heart pacemaker	500,000
Heart valves	300,000
Implantable defibrillator	10,000
Implantable ventricular assist	1,000
Total artificial heart	100

Source: Reprinted with permission from Hirose TT. The influence of the
Product Liability Act, governmental regulation, and medical economics,
medical devices and their clinical applications. *Artif Organs.* December
1996;20(12):1274–1277.

and breaching physician-patient confidentiality.[34] As a result, similar recommendations for privacy and security have been made by means of cryptography or message authentication.[35] Telemedicine also raises many new questions in terms of liability risk. For example, these services often are provided across state lines, thereby involving different state legal statutes. In addition, the traditional physician-patient relationship is reconfigured between consulting specialists and patients, with yet unclear duties of consultants to patients. Moreover, telemedicine could change the standard of care—on the one hand, potentially by expecting appropriate use and reliability of telemedicine capacity; and on the other hand, resulting in liability for nonuse of available telemedical capacity as evidence of substandard care.[36]

Medical Devices

The liability related to medical devices provides another interesting view of the dynamics and extent of health-related litigation. Medical devices have been regulated by the FDA for the last 25 years under the Medical Devices Improvement Act of 1975, which was intended to assure the effectiveness and safety of these devices. Table 12-4, for example, shows the numbers of implants available on the market as of 1996, representing one of three categories of medical devices.

Product liability legislation, adopted in 1960, led to an exponential increase in the number of lawsuits, and by the mid-1990s, average awards had grown by 400 percent. There were about 200,000 lawsuits for product liability in 1995, with average awards also about $200,000. Figure 12-1 shows the growth pattern of this type of litigation from 1973 to 1991.

Investigators and manufacturers involved in research and development of medical devices have argued that product liability costs threaten future research

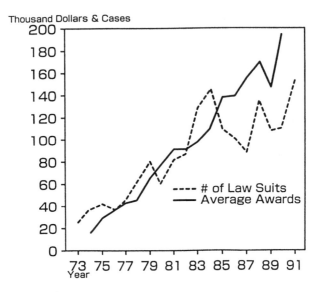

Figure 12-1 Product liability lawsuits and average awards in federal and district courts in the United States are shown. (Source: Administration Office of the U.S. Courts. Reprinted with permission from Hirose TT. The influence of the Product Liability Act, governmental regulation, and medical economics, medical devices and their clinical applications. *Artif Organs.* December 1996;20(12):1274–1277.)

and development of medical devices. A class action suit on behalf of 440,000 breast implant patients, for example, led to a $4.5 billion award in 1993 against five breast implant manufacturers, but that settlement was withdrawn as litigation continued. The Health Industry Manufacturers Association (HIMA) asked for government exemption from the product liability law, claiming that the supply of medical plastics for permanent implants of many kinds will be exhausted within two years without such protection.[37] Willem Kolff, research professor of Bioengineering at the University of Utah, whose work led to development of the artificial heart, predicted that, without government protection, the medical device industry in the United States (which produces one half of the world's output)[37] "will die, and those industries that survive will make prohibitively expensive equipment."[38] Kolff also called for specific limits of liability exposure, including reduction of attorney costs from 33 percent to 10 percent of an award, limiting attorneys' fees to 2 percent of awards from class action suits, and restricting liability of manufacturers to failure due to negligence.[38]

The medical device industry, while recognizing the importance of reasonable government oversight of the safety and effectiveness of its products, has argued that government regulation has been overzealous in some instances, which at times contributed further to its risk of liability. As an example, 80,000 Björk-Shiley heart valves were recalled and removed from the market despite a very low failure rate—only 2 of every 1,000 implants over 10 years.[37]

PROBLEMS OF SPECIAL INTERESTS

It only makes sense that solid science and unbiased outcome studies be the means by which medical advances are incorporated into medical practice or abandoned as ineffective or unsafe. However, in our litigious and media-dominated society, we have many examples where scientific evidence plays little role. This is particularly true when a product, procedure, or concept is held dear to entrenched special interests, which then attack any scientific evidence threatening their self-interest. Consider these illustrative cases.

Case 1

Richard Deyo and colleagues at the University of Washington, with support from a research grant from the Agency for Health Care Policy and Research (AHCPR), had three articles in the early 1990s, published in peer-reviewed scientific journals, disputing the effectiveness of lumbar spinal fusion for patients with low back pain.[39–41] In one national study comparing outcome of Medicare patients undergoing lumbar surgery with and without fusion, they found that outcomes for the fusion patients were much worse—a complication rate 1.9 times higher, blood transfusion rate 5.8 times higher, nursing home placement 2.2 times higher, and mortality six weeks later 2 times higher than patients having surgery without fusion.[40] These findings triggered an immediate backlash by special interests, in this case including some orthopedic surgeons, the North American Spine Society, and a manufacturer of pedicle screws, which was facing litigation by patients alleging poor results from the devices used in spinal fusion. A letter-writing campaign to Congress called for limiting the power of the FDA and elimination of funding for the AHCPR. As a result, the House of Representatives did remove funding for the AHCPR, and in the Senate it was restored only after a contentious debate. One manufacturer even went so far as to call for a court injunction to prevent the AHCPR from producing guidelines for the treatment of low back pain.[41]

Case 2

In 1993, Gregory Simon, a physician-investigator at Group Health Cooperative in Seattle, and his colleagues reported a controlled study of immunological, psychological, and neuropsychological factors in multiple chemical sensitivity (MCS). Their study cast doubt on the value of immunodiagnostic tests used as evidence for disability and liability claims for chemical sensitivity.[42] The backlash, this time, came from advocacy groups for those with MCS, plaintiffs' attorneys, and representatives from immunologic-testing laboratories. The investigators were accused of scientific misconduct, fraud, and conspiracy, and requests were made for revocation of their licenses. Investigations were carried out over the next year at three local institutions, the state medical disciplinary board, and the federal Office of Research Integrity. Although the investigators were completely exonerated, this process was expensive and painful for those involved. A local trial lawyer even sponsored a later workshop promoting the tactic of alleging scientific misconduct as a means of disputing unwelcome research findings.[41]

Case 3

Bruce Psaty, another physician-investigator at the University of Washington, together with his colleagues, reported a case control study in 1995 examining the associations between myocardial infarction and antihypertensive therapy. They found that short-acting calcium-channel blockers were associated with a 60 percent increase in risk of myocardial infarction compared to diuretics and beta-blockers.[43] There was an immediate media blitz over this finding. During the weeks and months to follow, pharmaceutical manufacturers of calcium-channel blockers, together with their paid "hired gun" physician consultants, attempted to distort and denigrate the findings of Psaty's study. While a manuscript describing the study was under editorial review by a journal, pharmaceutical manufacturers tried to find out which journal was reviewing it, pressure was applied through the principal investigator's dean, and it appeared that opponents to the findings were interfering with publication of the study.[41]

Case 4

In December 1991, Paul Fischer, a physician-investigator at the Medical College of Georgia (MCG), and his colleagues wrote an article, published in the *Journal of the American Medical Association*, on cigarette brand recognition by children between 3 and 6 years old. They found that almost all 6-year-olds could recognize the Camel cigarette's logo "Old Joe," about the same level of recognition as for the logo of the Disney Channel.[44] In the same issue of *JAMA*, Joseph DiFranza, a physician-investigator at the University of Massachusetts, had an article showing that Camel cigarettes' share of the youth market increased from 0.5 percent to 32.8 percent after the "Old Joe" advertising campaign.[45] Both physicians were promptly targeted by the manufacturer of Camel cigarettes, the R. J. Reynolds Tobacco Company (RJR), for harassment in an effort to distort and discredit their research. Both received subpoenas to hand over all their research files, including confidential materials relating to the children involved, despite confidentiality agreements signed with the parents. The administration of MCG, which should have backed Fischer, a full professor faculty member, on the basis of academic freedom and human subject confidentiality, instead supported the release of research documents under the Georgia Open Records Act, which even RJR didn't expect to be in effect. The administration of MCG, with support of the State's Attorney General, remained cooperative with the tobacco company against its own faculty member, who resigned to enter private medical practice two years after this published report. Meanwhile, DiFranza was subjected to charges of fraudulent research and scientific misconduct, although he was finally cleared of those trumped-up charges.[46]

Concerning these kinds of cases, William Robertson had this comment about the extent of conflicts of interest:[47]

> Variations on these themes are being played out across our nation in the "tobacco fiasco." The tobacco companies and their leaders persist in denying any causal connection between smoking and bronchogenic carcinoma while many "responsible" parties seek monetary damages on behalf of cancer patients who "didn't know" that cigarettes are dangerous—despite being called "cancer sticks" and "coffin nails" since I was a kid. Both sides have "conflicts of interest" that society seems to tolerate.

IMPACT OF HEALTH CARE LITIGATION

Many impacts of this growing wave of health-related litigation are being felt, most of them negative. Granted that some of these cases are well founded, even the plaintiffs receive only 40 to 45 percent of the total legal system costs, according to the Institute for Civil Justice of the RAND Corporation.[48] The financial costs of this litigation are the most obvious impact. Consider these markers:[48]

- Direct malpractice insurance premiums now exceed $6 billion per year for physicians (versus $1.8 billion in 1982) and $2.1 billion for hospitals.
- Physicians' malpractice insurance premiums go up an average of 6 percent each year.
- The proportion of U.S. physicians being sued for alleged malpractice increased from 1 percent in the 1960s to 3 percent in the 1970s, 7 percent in the 1980s, and 8.2 percent in 1990.
- By 1991, 39 percent of physicians (65.2 percent of those practicing obstetrics and/or gynecology) had encountered at least one claim over their careers.

In addition to the direct costs of litigation, an additional $15 billion is estimated to be spent on defensive medicine, including such specific services as $2.7 billion for preoperative tests ordered by anesthesiologists and $178 million for skull X-ray examinations in emergency rooms.[48] One study in the early 1990s in a large suburban hospital showed that malpractice-related costs (mostly defensive medicine) amounted to an average additional charge of $450 on all inpatient bills.[49]

Beyond the financial costs of health-related litigation are other, less obvious but important impacts. Access to care can suffer when physicians are driven out of areas of practice because of the high cost of malpractice liability insurance, as happened in the case of obstetric care in many parts of the country. There also are powerful impacts on patients, physicians, and the physician-patient relationship. There is good evidence, for example, that malpractice suits can result in isolation, humiliation, depression, and even physical illness for involved physicians.[50,51] William Wehrmacher sums up the effects on the physician-patient relationship in this way:[48]

As an adversarial relationship, malpractice litigation demonstrates a lack of trust, promotes defensive tactics, and is stressful for both patient and physician. Because most unfortunate outcomes are the result of the progress of disease rather than negligence, the tendency to regard less than perfect results as causes for litigation produces dangerous conflicts and interferes with appropriate emotional support for a suffering patient, ultimately leading to poorer response to treatment. Litigation does not improve the patient's care!

APPROACHES TO IMPROVE THE MEDICOLEGAL SYSTEM AND QUALITY OF CARE

Toward Legal Reforms?

Many observers of the medicolegal system have found it inaccurate, inefficient, and not up to its present challenges, much less to an expanding set of new legal challenges certain to accompany whatever health care reform take place, as well as future advances in medical technology and informatics. William White, an experienced medical malpractice defense attorney who specializes in hospital and health care law, summarizes the present system's major problems, as cited by various commentators, as follows:[52]

1. lay juries are not equipped to decide the oft-times complex and highly emotional issues attendant to medical malpractice litigation;
2. the present litigation process has served to break down the doctor/patient relationship, making every patient encounter a potential adversarial prelude, which, in turn, has hatched a new cost prohibitive phenomenon, "defensive medicine";
3. jury awards are too frequently disproportionate to the injuries;
4. the judicial system is not tailored to account for the many instances of medical negligence which do not find their way into the court system because they would not be sufficiently lucrative to warrant plaintiffs' attorneys risking a contingency fee representation arrangement, and
5. the Association of Trial Lawyers of America (ATLA), comprised almost exclusively of plaintiffs' attorneys, and others vehemently defend citizens', vis-à-vis litigants', rights to a civil jury trial.

Legal reforms could take any of a number of directions across a wide range of alternatives. On one end of the spectrum is the present free-market approach, while on the other is a fully government-regulated compensation system that legislates away lawsuits for medical malpractice. Options within that spectrum would involve various blends of regulation and roles of the private and public sectors.[53] As a nonattorney, it is well beyond my expertise to comment on any particular line of reform, but the need for structural reform appears clear.

Among the legal reforms which have been proposed are alternative dispute resolution (ADR) mechanisms instead of direct access to the court system, requiring a certificate of merit, limiting noneconomic damages, limiting attorneys' fees, requiring the loser to pay for court costs and attorneys' fees, placing dollar caps on awards, and modifying rules of evidence (e.g., eliminating joint and several liability).[54] Other proposed alternatives include the use of more specific contracts between patients and physicians[55] and a "no-fault" approach.[56] While some of the states have adopted some of these reforms, the Congress (composed mostly of attorneys) has shied away from substantial legal reforms, although some of these have been brought up for debate.[54]

Governmental Initiatives at Federal and State Levels

Two initiatives at the federal level warrant comment. In 1986, Congress passed the Health Care Quality Improvement Act, which resulted in the creation of the National Practitioner Data Bank. The stated goal of the data bank was to improve health care by providing a central repository about providers for use of health care organizations and state licensing boards, especially by preventing some problem providers from escaping detection by licensing or credentialing bodies by relocating to another state and misrepresenting their previous records. Reporting to the data bank is required for all malpractice claim payments and adverse decisions on licensure, clinical privileges, and professional society membership. The data bank became operational on September 1, 1990, and by the end of 1995 had accumulated over 120,000 reports on malpractice payments, licensing actions, and clinical privileges as well as 6.9 million queries from health care organizations.[57] Since the data bank was established, there have been some instances when plaintiffs have agreed to dismiss a defendant physician, substituting a hospital or other corporate entity, to avoid the practitioner making a report to the data bank. There also has been pressure from some quarters to establish a minimal reporting requirement for a malpractice claim (e.g., an award or settlement of $50,000).

The most recent federal initiative, in Spring 2000, was the Clinton administration's call for a new Center of Quality Improvement and Patient Safety, to be housed within the Agency for Health Care Research and Quality (AHRQ, formerly AHCPR). At the same time, a new Medicare regulation requires that all hospitals participating in Medicare implement patient safety programs, and new efforts are now required of hospitals and the FDA to reduce medication errors. All this followed the landmark 1999 report of the Institute of Medicine (IOM), *To Err Is Human*, which, on the basis of earlier studies in Colorado and Utah hospitals, projected that medical errors result in between 44,000 and 98,000 deaths every year in U.S. hospitals.[6] Since that time, Troyen Brennan, a key investigator in both studies, has refuted the implication that all or most of these deaths were caused by medical error. Many were not preventable, and Brennan notes that physicians reviewing hospital records in those two states made no judgment that these were actual errors. Further, he points to *improving* rates of injury in three studies cited in the IOM report—4.6 percent rate of injury due to medical care in California in 1976, 3.7 percent in New York in 1984, and 2.9 percent in Colorado and Utah in 1992.[58–60] Moreover, Brennan gives us this warning:[61]

An interpretation of the IOM findings as 98,000 deaths due to blunders and a cycle of inaction could give impetus to legislation requiring greater public disclosure, which in turn would lead to more lawsuits.

Therein lies the key problem overlooked by the IOM report. Any effort to prevent injury due to medical care is complicated by the dead weight of a litigation system that induces secrecy and silence. No matter now much we might insist that physicians have an ethical duty to report injuries resulting from medical care or to work on their prevention, fear of malpractice litigation drags us back to the status quo. To address the problem of iatrogenic injuries seriously, we must reform the system of malpractice litigation. If the only legislative result of the IOM report is federally mandated reporting, we will have failed, and once the publicity dies down, the rates of injury due to medical care will remain unchanged.

At the state level, 30 states and the District of Columbia have enacted legislation affording external appeals to panels of outside physicians for patients who have unsatisfactorily exhausted the internal review procedures within their health plans. The hope is that this process will provide patients with an alternative for grievance short of lawsuits. External reviews so far deal mainly with definitions of medical necessity, but there already is concern that these determinations need to be based on evidence, not the experience and biases of individual panel members. The experience with external review in Maryland after one year is promising—the entire review process takes no more than 30 to 45 days (accelerated in emergencies), there is no filing fee for patients, many complaints are filed by physicians on their patients' behalf, and about one half of cases are resolved in favor of the patients.[62]

Another important reform initiative at the state level that warrants mention is the Medical Injury Compensation Reform Act (MICRA), enacted in California in the mid-1970s. MICRA provided for private contracts for binding arbitration with a cap of $250,000 on noneconomic damages of a medical malpractice action. Arbitration effectively reduced the cost of medical malpractice litigation and professional liability insurance.[53]

Actions by Health Insurers

Many health insurers and managed care organizations have well-organized programs in place for quality assurance and risk management. An excellent illustration of an effective program is that initiated by Copic Insurance Company, a physician-owned and -directed medical liability insurance company founded by the Colorado Medical Society in 1983. All medical liability claims managed by the company are analyzed, entered into a statewide database, and used to develop risk management policies and physician education programs. Insured physicians are expected to follow established general and specialty-specific practice guidelines or satisfactorily defend the circumstances when they are not followed in the case of an individual claim. They also are expected to attend regularly scheduled continuing medical education programs on risk management. Insured physicians have had the opportunity to minimize their insurance premiums by participating in an experience-rating system. They start at the lowest level of a four-tiered premium program; if they obtain at least 75 percent of expected points expected for their specialty, they can remain at that level of discounted premiums (Table 12-5).[63]

Medical Education Efforts

Increasingly, medical education at the predoctoral, graduate (residency), and continuing medical education levels is placing emphasis on evidence-based approaches to medical knowledge and its clinical applications. Also, increasing emphasis is being placed on quality improvement of the clinical environment as it is remodeled into more integrated systems. Two examples of these educational efforts deserve mention here—clinical practice guidelines and physician communication skills.

Clinical practice guidelines have the potential to improve clinical practice and patient outcomes if they are firmly grounded on evidence of high quality and if they are tailored by conscientious physicians to the circumstances of individual patients' needs and preferences. They are challenging to construct, requiring epidemiologic and clinical expertise guided by the process of evidence-based medicine. In these terms, some guidelines are excellent, others are not, and at best, they can apply to only a minority of clinical decisions made everyday in clinical practice. Physicians may choose not to follow practice guidelines for many reasons, including lack of trust in their quality, lack of confidence in guideline developers, lack of motivation or time, the threat they pose to clinical autonomy, or doubt that they apply to their practice situation.[64,65]

As would be anticipated, clinical guidelines can cut several ways in their medicolegal applications. Brennan, for example, surveyed 580 malpractice attorneys in 1997 about their uses of these guidelines. He found that 54 percent of the time, guidelines were used against physicians not following them, while 23 percent of the time they were used to exonerate physicians who followed them.[66] Still another potential variant would be claims against physicians who followed hospitals' guidelines for discharging patients too soon from the hospital.[66]

Problems in communication between physicians and patients often lead to patient dissatisfaction and an increased propensity by patients to file malpractice claims,[67-71] even when there is no injury or lapse in quality.[72] Accordingly, training in communications skills for physicians is an important educational goal, not only for the purposes of risk management but also to increase the quality of care and informed involvement of the patient through shared decision making.

CONCLUDING COMMENTS

The foregoing reveals the inexorable growth in extent and complexity of health-related litigation. This could be good if it led to improved quality of patient care, but unfortunately, this is not the case. We have seen huge costs to

Table 12-5 Experience Rating System Showing Assessment of Negative Points Based on Adverse Action

Subject	Problem	Negative Points	Description
Quality of medical practice	Outside of specialty	1–6	Based on percentage of same specialists who do procedure.
	Inadequate training	1–6	Based on level of training needed.
	No expert support	1–6	Based on difficulty of obtaining expert support.
	Technical error	1–3	Based on preventability.
	Failure to diagnose	1–6	Based on inadequacy of workup compared with seriousness of potential diagnosis.
	Error of judgment	1–6	Based on ease with which judgment should have been made compared with seriousness of problem.
Medical records	Altered	6	Must be with obvious intent to alter impression of record.
	Illegible	1–3	Based on importance of note.
	No allergy flag	3	
	Poor organization	2	
	Inadequate notes	1–3	
	Delayed documentation	1–3	Critical documents—for example, operative notes, progress notes—immediately to three days. History and physical—preoperatively or before serious therapy. Narrative summaries whenever the hospital demands.
	Inadequate follow-up instructions	1–6	
Hospital privileges	Restrictions	1–3	
	Loss	4–6	
	Failure to notify Copic of loss	6	

continues

Table 12-5   (continued)

Subject	Problem	Negative Points	Description
Board of Medical Examiners	Letter of admonition	0–2	Depends on seriousness.
	Stipulations	1–6	Depends on seriousness.
	Failure to notify Copic of stipulations	6	Must be serious stipulations.
System failures	Failure to follow	1–6	Depends on seriousness of need to follow.
	Missed lab, X ray, or other information	3–5	
	Wrong side surgery	6	
	Failure to instruct	1–4	Depends on the seriousness of the disease for which the instructions are given.
	Failure to get consult	1–3	
Drug Enforcement Agency	Loss	6	
	Restrictions	3–5	Based on peer review.
Hospital utilization review and quality assurance	Two or more adverse letters	1–3	Depends on seriousness.
	Sanctions	4–6	
	Failure to notify	6	If serious.
	Sexual contact with patient	3–6	
Unprofessional behavior	Collection techniques	1–3	Outrageous conduct, defamation, and so forth.

Note: A menu of available points is provided to each physician, who must obtain 75 percent of the points every two years to remain in the lowest premium category.

Source: Reprinted with permission from Thomasson GO. Participatory risk management: Promoting physician compliance with practice guidelines. *Jt Comm J Qual Improv.* 1994;20(6):325.

everyone involved except the attorneys. Much as we have heard about the military-industrial or medical-industrial complex, our society seems unconcerned about an unfettered legal-industrial complex, which seems more pervasive by the year and is enabled by legislatures at both federal and state levels.

This chapter describes some of the flaws of the existing medicolegal system, which is broken. Founded on the claimant's right to a civil jury trial and with plaintiff attorneys standing to gain even when negligence cannot be proven, the system is slow and expensive in both time and dollars. Juries are overtaxed, often beyond their ability to understand the clinical issues, and "runaway" jury awards are not uncommon. As a result, the present medicolegal system leads to further inflation of health care costs, negatively affecting both purchasers and consumers. Moreover, a therapeutic relationship of trust between clinician and patient often breaks down into an adversarial situation, with more fragmentation and discontinuity of care. As we have seen, even state legislatures get into the act by requiring such services as mandatory screening for scoliosis or insurance coverage for bone marrow transplantation after high-dose chemotherapy for metastatic breast cancer, neither of which has supporting scientific evidence.

Just as the health care system needs structural reform, so does the medicolegal system. In fact, both need to be accomplished in tandem. Clinicians should be held accountable for acts of negligence. However, some of the needed initiatives to reduce the risks of medical error and improve the quality of health care, for example, certainly will fail if they expose physicians to further risk of liability claims.

The wide gulf in understanding between medicine and the law needs to be bridged. At a recent roundtable workshop sponsored by the Agency for Health Care Research and Quality and the Institute of Medicine, John Eisenberg (director of AHRQ) observed, "Here we are, experts in medicine on the one hand and in law on the other, and we are divided, as are the British and Americans, by a common language."[73] Some small steps have already been taken on each side which could help to narrow the gap. Through outcomes research and evidence-based approaches, medicine is strengthening the scientific base of clinical practice. On the legal side, a Supreme Court decision in 1993 (*Daubert* v. *Merrill-Dow Pharmaceuticals*),[74] charged trial judges with the responsibility to ensure the relevance and scientific credibility of scientific expert testimony.[73]

There are major conflict areas between the two professions as they relate to health care. One big one, for example, is the overriding concern of the legal system for the individual plaintiff, whereas the population-based paradigm of health care values the best possible care of a population with some potential tradeoffs for individuals.[75,76] In view of the pressing need to adapt legal thinking and doctrine to the new health care environment, Clark Havighurst, professor of Law at Duke University, recently urged the IOM to create (already under consideration pending funding) a permanent, professionally staffed Forum on Legal Issues in Health Care. Such a private, nonprofit entity could take the broad perspective toward legal reform in the public interest without the political pressures commonly directed toward Congress, state governments, and the courts.[77]

As we have seen in earlier chapters, science and the strengths of biomedical technology have been oversold to the public, which has come to expect all of the heralded benefits without risk or harm. Just as the health care system needs to be redesigned to enhance patient safety, so must the medicolegal system be reformed in the public interest. At the same time, the public needs to be re-educated to more realistic expectations of care and to become more actively involved in shared clinical decision making with their physicians and other providers. Related issues are further discussed in later chapters, especially those dealing with quality of care (Chapter 18) and health care reform (Chapter 24). In an era of increasing resource limits, everyone (including patients) needs to accept limits in our collective quest for cost-effective, accessible, affordable health care of high quality.

REFERENCES

1. Maier B. Punitive damages added in smoking case verdict. *New York Times.* March 28, 2000:A12.
2. Geyelin M. Investors greet tobacco award calmly. *Wall Street Journal.* April 10, 2000:A3.
3. Olsen W. "The runaway jury" is no myth. *Wall Street Journal.* July 18, 2000:A22.
4. Research Department, Physician Insurers Association of America. *Data Sharing Reports.* Rockville, MD: Physician Insurers Association of America, 1999.
5. Hickson GB, Clayton EW, Entman SS, et al. Obstetricians' prior malpractice experience and patients' satisfaction with care. *JAMA.* 1994;272:1583–1587.
6. Kohn LT, Corrigan JM, Donaldson MS (eds). *To Err Is Human: Building a Safer Health System.* Washington, DC: National Academy Press, 1999.
7. Eddy DM. *Clinical Decision Making: From Theory to Practice.* Boston: Jones and Bartlett Publishers, 1996.
8. Robertson WO. Systematic study of human errors can lead to remedies. *WSMA* [Washington State Medical Association] *Reports.* October 1998:7.
9. Brennan TA, Sox CM, Burstin HR. Relation between negligent adverse events and the outcomes of medical-malpractice litigation. *N Engl J Med.* 1996;335:1963–1967.
10. Bodenheimer TS, Grumbach K. *Understanding Health Policy: A Clinical Approach.* Norwalk, CN: Appleton and Lange, 1995:167.
11. Localio AR, Lawthers AG, Brennan TA, et al. Relation between malpractice claims and adverse events due to negligence: Results of the Harvard Medical Practice Study III. *N Engl J Med.* 1991;325:245–251.
12. Weiler PC, Hiatt HH, Newhouse JP, Johnson WG, Brennan TA, Leape LL. *A Measure of Malpractice: Medical Injury, Malpractice Litigation, and Patient Compensation.* Cambridge, MA: Harvard University Press, 1993.
13. Danzon PM. *Medical Malpractice: Theory, Evidence, and Public Policy.* Cambridge, MA: Harvard University Press, 1985.
14. Sloan FA. *Suing for Medical Malpractice.* Chicago: University of Chicago Press, 1993.
15. Brennan TA, Berwick DM. *New Rules: Regulation, Markets, and the Quality of American Health Care.* San Francisco: Jossey-Bass, 1996.
16. Misocky M. The patients' bill of rights: Managed care under siege. *J Contemp Health Law Policy.* 1998;15(57):72.
17. Studdert DM, Brennan TA. The problems with punitive damages in lawsuits against managed care organizations. *N Engl J Med.* 2000;342:280–283.
18. Stadtmauer EA, O'Neill A, Goldstein LJ, et al. Conventional-dose chemotherapy compared with high-dose chemotherapy plus autologous hematopoietic stem-cell transplantation for metastatic breast cancer. *N Engl J Med.* 2000;342:1069–1076.
19. Lippman ME. High-dose chemotherapy plus autologous bone marrow transplantation for metastatic breast cancer. *N Engl J Med.* 2000;342:1119–1120.
20. Advocacy: Dangerous to patient's health? *Fam Pract Report.* 2000;6(3):6.
21. Lawyers go for the HMO jugular. *Fam Pract News.* January 1, 2000:38.
22. Editorial. The AMA's lawyers. *Wall Street Journal.* October 31, 2000:A26.
23. Epstein SB. Knowing the limits of health care law. *Managed Care.* October 2000:37–44.
24. Eisenberg DM, Kessler RC, Foster C, Norlock FE, Calkins DR, Delbanco TL. Unconventional medicine in the United States. Prevalence, costs, and patterns of use. *N Engl J Med.* 1993; 328:246–252.
25. Blecher MB. Alternative medicine on pins and needles no more: Acupuncturists and others get mainstream nod. *Crain's Chicago Business.* January 27, 1997:4.

26. Studdert DM, Eisenberg DM, Mitler FH, Curto DA, Kaptchuk TJ, Brennan TA. Medical malpractice implications of alternative medicine. *JAMA*. 1998;280:1611.

27. Goldman EL. Legal pitfalls in alternative medicine. *Fam Pract News*. April 15, 1999:75.

28. Hodge JG, Gostin LO, Jacobson PD. Legal issues concerning electronic health information: Privacy, quality and liability. *JAMA*. 1999;282:1466–1471.

29. Hunt DL, Haynes RB, Hanna SE, Smith K. Effects of computer-based clinical decision support systems on physician performance and patient outcomes: A systematic review. *JAMA*. 1998;280:1339–1346.

30. Raschloe RA, Gollihare B, Wunderlich TA, et al. A computer alert system to prevent injury from adverse drug events: Development and evaluation in a community teaching hospital. *JAMA*. 1998;280:1317–1320.

31. Gostin L, Lazzarini Z, Neslund V, Osterholm M. The public health information infrastructure. *JAMA*. 1996;275:1921–1927.

32. Flahaula A, Dias-Ferrao V, Chaberty P, Esteves K, Valleron AJ, Lavanchy D. FluNet as a tool for global monitoring of influenza on the Web. *JAMA*. 1998;280:1330–1332.

33. Fein EB. For many physicians, e-mail is the high-tech house call. *New York Times*. November 20, 1997:A1, A18.

34. Bashshur RL. On the definition and evaluation of telemedicine. *Telemed J*. 1995;1:19–30.

35. Spielberg AR. On call and online. *JAMA*. 1998;280:1353–1359.

36. Kuszler PC. Telemedicine and integrated health care delivery: Compounding malpractice liability. *Am J Law Med*. 1999;25(2–3):297–326.

37. Hirose TT. The influence of the Product Liability Act, governmental regulation, and medical economics, medical devices and their clinical applications. *Artif Organs*. December 1996; 20(12):1274–1277.

38. Kolff WJ. Letter. *Artif Organs*. September 1997;21(9):1052–1053.

39. Deyo RA, Cherkin DC, Locter JD, Bigos SJ, Ciol MA. Morbidity and mortality in association with operations on the lumbar spine: The influence of age, diagnosis, and procedure. *J Bone Joint Surg Am*. 1992;74:536–543.

40. Deyo RA, Ciol MA, Cherkin DC, Loeser JD, Bigos SJ. Lumbar spinal fusion: A cohort study of complications, reoperations, and resource use in the Medicare population. *Spine*. 1993;18:463–470.

41. Deyo RA, Psaty BM, Simon G, et al. The messenger under attack—Intimidation of researchers by special interest groups. *N Engl J Med*. 1997;336:1176–1180.

42. Simon GE, Daniell W, Stockbridge H, Claypoole K, Rosenstock L. Immunologic, psychological, and neuropsychological factors in multiple chemical sensitivity: A controlled study. *Ann Intern Med*. 1993;119:97–103.

43. Psaty BM, Heckbert SR, Koepsell TD, et al. The risk of incident myocardial infarction associated with anti-hypertensive drug therapies. *Circulation*. 1995;91:925.

44. Fischer PM, Schwartz MP, Richards JW Jr, Goldstein AO, Rojas TH. Brand logo recognition by children aged 3 to 6 years: Mickey Mouse and Old Joe the Camel. *JAMA*. 1991;266:3145–3148.

45. DiFranza JR, Richards JW, Paulman PM, et al. RJR Nabisco's cartoon camel promotes camel cigarettes to children. *JAMA*. 1991;266:3149–3153.

46. Fischer PM. Science and subpoenas: When do the courts become instruments of manipulation? *Law and Contemp Prob*. 1996;59(3):159–167.

47. Robertson WO. Researchers intimidated. Hardball tactics used to challenge "unacceptable" findings. *WSMA* [Washington State Medical Association] *Reports*. June–July 1997:7.

48. Wehrmacher WH. Escalating health care costs: Costs of litigation. *Compr Ther*. September 1998;24(9):455–459.

49. Bureau of National Affairs. *BNA's Health Law Reporter*. 1994;3:495.

50. Charles SC, Warnecke RB, Nelson BA, Pyskota CE. Appraisal of the event as a factor in coping with malpractice litigation. *Behav Med*. 1988;14:148–154.

51. Charles SC, Pyskota CE, Nelson A. Physicians on trial: Self-reported reactions to malpractice litigation. *West J Med*. 1988;148:358–360.

52. White WF. Alternative dispute resolution for medical malpractice actions: An efficient approach to the law and health care. *Leg Med*. 1995:227–239.

53. Roeca AF. Personal communication, November 6, 2000.

54. Kolodner DE, Pleiffer M. Medical malpractice reform as a part of health care reform. *Medsurg Nurs*. October 1994;3(5):417–419.

55. Epstein RA. *Medical Malpractice: The Case for Contract*. New York: Center for Libertarian Studies, 1976.

56. Weiler PC. *Medical Malpractice on Trial*. Cambridge, MA: Harvard University Press, 1991.
57. Physicians Insurance Exchange. How does the National Practitioner Data Bank serve the public? *Physicians Risk Management Update*. 1997;8(1):1.
58. Brennan TA, Leape LL, Laird NM, et al. Incidence of adverse events and negligence in hospitalized patients—Results of the Harvard Medical Practice Study I. *N Engl J Med*. 1991;324:370–376.
59. Thomas EJ, Studdert DM, Burstin HR, et al. Incidence and types of adverse events and negligent care in Utah and Colorado. *Med Care*. 2000;38:261–271.
60. California Medical Association, California Hospital Association. *Report on the Medical Insurance Feasibility Study*. San Francisco: California Medical Association, 1977.
61. Brennan TA. The Institute of Medicine report on medical errors—Could it do harm? *N Engl J Med*. 2000;342:1125.
62. Frieden J. Resolving health plan disputes: More states implementing external appeals laws. *Fam Pract News*. February 5, 2000:69.
63. Thomasson GO. Participatory risk management: Promoting physician compliance with practice guidelines. *Jt Comm J Qual Improv*. 1994;20(6):317–329.
64. Pinsky LE, Deyo RA. Clinical guidelines: A strategy for translating evidence into practice. In: Geyman JP, Deyo RA, Ramsey SD (eds). *Evidence-Based Clinical Practice: Concepts and Approaches*. Boston: Butterworth–Heinemann 2000:119–123.
65. Cabana MD, Rand CS, Powe NR. Why don't physicians follow clinical practice guidelines? A framework for improvement. *JAMA*. 1999;282:1458–1465.
66. Frieden J. Lawyers using practice guidelines against doctors. *Fam Pract News*. September 15, 1997:70.
67. Levinson W. Physician-patient communication: A key to malpractice prevention. *JAMA*. 1994; 272:1619–1620.
68. Entman SS, Glass CA, Hickson GB, Githens PB, Whetten-Goldstein KS. The relationship between malpractice claims history and subsequent obstetric care.
69. *JAMA*. 1994;272:1588–1591.
70. Hickson GB, Clayton EW, Entman SS, et al. Obstetricians' prior malpractice experience and patients' satisfaction with care. *JAMA*. 1994;272:1583–1587.
71. Beckman HB, Markakis KM, Suchman AL, Frankel RM. The doctor-patient relationship and malpractice: Lessons from plaintiff depositions. *Arch Intern Med*. 1994;154:1365–1370.
72. Avery JK. Lawyers tell what turns some patients litigious. *Med Malprac News*. 1985;2:35–37.
73. *Medical Malpractice Report*. DHEW publication OS 73-89. Washington, DC: U.S. Department of Health, Education and Welfare; 1973.
74. Marwick C. Will evidence-based medicine help span gulf between medicine and law? *JAMA*. 2000;283:2775–2776.
75. Court ruling on "junk science" gives judges more say about what expert witness testimony to allow. *JAMA*. 1993;270:423.
76. Robertson WO. Traditional ethics versus distributive ethics: Which must come first—Care of the individual or care of the group? *WSMA* [Washington State Medical Association] *Reports*. September 1998:6.
77. Havighurst CC. American health care and the law—We need to talk! *Health Aff (Millwood)*. 2000;19(4):84–106.

PART TWO

WHERE ARE WE NOW?

13
Primary Care as a Battleground

If people were ever industrial robots, they might need no more than techno-logical medicine. But actually they are not (and I reckon never will be); and even in the most highly developed parts of the world they still need personal medicine too.

It is because they are aware of this that older people look back wistfully to the horse and buggy doctor. I know that the horse has died; and the buggy has fallen to bits. But we still have the doctor. And adapted to modern con-ditions, he could often, if he wished, be the patient's own doctor—and much the more useful for that.

T. F. Fox, 1962[1]

Having traced 12 major trends affecting the health care system over the last 50 or more years, it is time to shift our focus to where we now are in U.S. health care. Beyond revisiting how effective, or ineffective, strategies have been to alleviate problems of access, cost, and quality of health care, in Part Two we examine several other overall components of the system, including its primary care base, the changing roles of the private and public sectors, the impact of new information technology, and previous attempts to reform the system.

As we saw in Chapter 4, increasing specialization and subspecialization, together with the rapid growth of biomedical technologies, were dominant themes in the United States throughout the 20th century. While this has brought many strengths to our health care system, it also created distortions in a system overweighted by 70 percent specialists. Negative impacts of specialization include decreased access to primary care, increasing costs of care, and variable quality of care as a result of overuse, underuse, and misuse of biomedical technology.

In this chapter, we look at the foundation of the U.S. health care system—its primary care base. The opening quotation was made about 40 years ago by T. F. Fox, a physician, concerning the ongoing need for a personal physician. Since then, we have seen many definitions of this need, which have come forward to this day under the umbrella of "primary care physician." Past and current defi-nitions of primary care were discussed in Chapter 4 (pages 50–51).

As the health care system changes amid chaotic pressures from all sides, primary care remains situated at the center of the crossfire. On the one hand, many specialists see little need for primary care and wonder what is the problem with the status quo of our specialist-based system. On the other hand, the number of health care professionals wanting to take on part or all of primary care services continues to increase. Contentious issues range from the scope of practice to licensure, reimbursement, and prescribing privileges, and the debate cuts to the heart of clinical practice. Beyond the matter of definition of primary care and who should provide it is the unresolved question of how health care should be organized. We saw in Chapter 10 how different paradigms would affect the delivery of health care services. For example, health care would be organized quite differently if population-based care or disease management substantially replaced the still dominant biomedical model. The battles to be described on the primary care turf can best be understood as stemming from our national failure to reach a consensus on how to organize our health care system.

In an effort to shed some light on primary care as it relates to the health care "system," the purpose of this chapter is to briefly describe (1) the content of primary care, (2) who provides it, (3) how primary care providers are educated, (4) five current contentious issues, and (5) some international comparisons.

WHAT IS PRIMARY CARE?

The current definition of primary care by the Institute of Medicine (IOM) captures its main elements, as listed on page 50.[2] The IOM definition is based on the following five assumptions:[3]

1. Primary care is the logical foundation of an effective health care system because primary care can address the great majority of the health problems present in the population.
2. Primary care is essential to achieving the objectives that together constitute value in health care: quality of care, including achievement of desired health outcomes, patient satisfaction, and efficient use of resources.
3. Personal interactions that include trust and partnership between patients and clinicians are central to primary care.
4. Primary care is an important instrument for achieving stronger emphasis on both ends of a spectrum of health care needs—health promotion and disease prevention—and care of the chronically ill with multiple problems, especially the elderly.
5. The trend toward integrated health care systems in a managed care environment will continue and will provide both opportunities and challenges for primary care.

The goal of primary care is to provide readily accessible care that is comprehensive, coordinated, and continuous in such a way as to offer a seamless process of care. It is based as well on a personal patient-clinician relationship, whether accomplished mainly through an individual primary care clinician or supplemented through a team approach. Primary care is unrestricted by presenting problem or organ system; includes physical, mental, emotional, and social concerns of patients; and ranges from prevention of disease to diagnosis, treatment, and follow-up of health problems.[3] As Barbara Starfield pointed out, primary care is best seen as an approach to providing care, measurable by how well this approach is implemented, not entirely defined as a range of services or by whom they are provided.[4] Fitzhugh Mullan's new book, *Big Doctoring: Primary Care in America*, provides an eloquent portrait of the importance and strengths of primary care as practiced by well-trained and dedicated primary care clinicians in diverse settings.[5]

WHO DOES PRIMARY CARE?

By any measure, those practicing the three generally recognized primary care specialties—family practice, general internal medicine, and general pediatrics—all fully qualify as primary care physicians by virtue of their clinical training, commitment, and values.[6] The major differences between the three is the broader scope of practice in family practice, unrestricted as it is by age of patient. Osteopathic physicians usually are generalists as well, with a clinical education more similar than different from their allopathic counterparts.

Beyond these disciplines, active controversy continues as to the role other clinical specialties play in primary care. A classic example of the debate involves obstetrics-gynecology. Although obstetrician-gynecologists provide some primary care services to women,[7] their practice is limited by gender and tends to be specialty specific to pregnancy, breast disease, gynecologic conditions, and only limited preventive care services.[8] This controversy has been fueled in recent years by inclusion of obstetrics-gynecology as a primary care discipline by the Clinton administration and the actions by 36 state legislatures in mandating patient access to obstetrician-gynecologists in managed care plans.[9]

There are many other examples of limited specialties putting themselves forward as active providers of primary care services, especially under circumstances where direct access by patients to their specialties is being threatened in a managed care environment. Therefore, dermatology make claims as to how many "primary care" visits they provide for skin conditions; neurologists remind us how many patients they see with headaches, dizziness, or back pain; while cardiologists lay claim to many patient visits for hypertension and coronary disease. As Edward O'Neill, internist at the University of California, San Francisco, observes, "There are 150,000 'born again' primary care providers out there" as the marketplace becomes increasingly competitive.[10] No end to this trend seems to be in sight, as managed care plans bend to public demand for point-of-service open access to specialists and state legislatures respond to public pressure. By 1997, for example, Georgia passed a law requiring managed care plans to offer direct access to dermatologists without referral, while Indiana had mandated direct access to anesthesiologists, dermatologists, mental health professionals, and others.[11]

There seems to be an assumption (misplaced as it is with an uninformed and denigrative perception of the content and requirements of primary care) among many specialists that primary care is "easy" and "anyone can do it." Mark Rivo and his colleagues focused on that question in terms of the spectrum of clinical competencies required to manage the most common problems presenting in everyday primary care practice. They compiled a list of training components necessary for generalist practice, after analysis of three kinds of information: (1) leading causes of mortality and morbidity that could be reduced by primary care, (2) the most common complaints and problems that generalists could be expected to manage, and (3) the recommendations of experts concerning generalist competencies. They then compared requirements for residency training for five specialties against this list of competencies. They concluded that family practice, general internal medicine, and general pediatrics are well qualified for primary care practice, but that obstetrics-gynecology and emergency medicine fall far short of the required breadth of clinical competency for primary care.[12]

Another important content study lends further support to the premise that the three clinical (allopathic) specialties have the kind of clinical breadth required of generalists in primary care practice. Roger Rosenblatt and his colleagues extracted the 15 most common clinical clusters, representing about 50 percent of all outpatient visits to U.S. office-based physicians, from data of the National Ambulatory Medical Care Survey (NAMCS). They then examined which specialties accounted for these visits. They found that two thirds of visits were managed by the preceding three primary care specialties, with general or family practice accounting for over half the visits. Although some specialties provide care for a small number of common problems (e.g., orthopedic surgery for 56 percent of visits for fractures and dislocations, dermatology for 28 percent of visits for dermatitis or eczema), their ranges of care are far too limited to meet the needs of patients with undifferentiated presenting complaints in primary care[13] (Figure 13-1).

The Medical Expenditure Panel Survey (MEPS), a national probability survey sponsored by the Agency for Healthcare Research and Quality (AHRQ), provides a useful snapshot of patterns of primary care. In 1996, for example, MEPS interviewers found that four of five Americans could identify a usual source of care for new health problems (97 percent), preventive care (96 percent), and referral for subspecialty services (96 percent). Of these respondents, 56 percent reported an individual clinician, rather than a facility, as their usual source of care. Of these providers, 62 percent were family physicians, 16 percent general internists, 15 percent pediatricians, and 8 percent other providers. More important, those respondents having a usual source of care fared much better than those without a usual source of care, going without needed services only half as often as those without such access to care.[14]

Another part of the primary care debate involves nonphysician clinicians, nurse practitioners and physicians' assistants, who play a growing role in the delivery of primary care services. Both groups are being trained in growing numbers. The number of nonphysician clinicians (NPC) doubled between 1992 and 1997.[15] By 2000, more than 70,000 nurse practitioners and 30,000 physician assistants were in the nation's NPC workforce; these numbers are expected to grow to 100,000 and 55,000, respectively, by the year 2005.[16] Despite more similarities than differences in their clinical roles, there also are important differences between the two groups. The physician assistant profession has consistently been based on task delegation within a physician supervisory

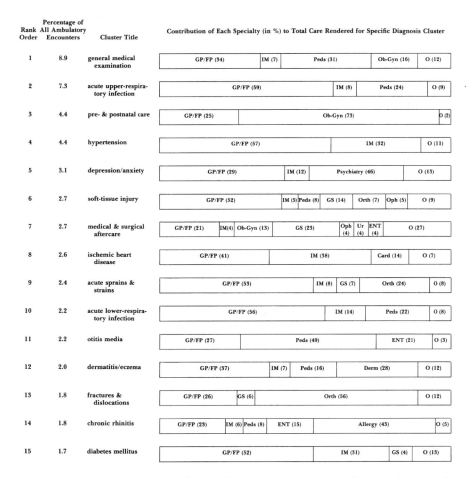

Figure 13-1 Most frequent ambulatory diagnoses in American medical practice according to physician specialty (National Ambulatory Medical Care Survey, 1977 and 1978). GP/FP, general practice and family practice; IM, internal medicine; Peds, general pediatrics; Ob-Gyn, obstetrics and gynecology; GS, general surgery; Orth, orthopedics; Oph, ophthalmology; Ur, urology; ENT, otrhinolaryngology; Card, cardiology; Derm, dermatology; and O, other. (Reprinted with permission from Rosenblatt RA, Cherkin DC, Schneeweiss R, Hart LG. The content of ambulatory care in the United States. *N Engl J Med.* 1983;309:892–897.)

relationship, as governed under states' Medical Practice Act provisions,[17] whereas the activities of nurse practitioners fall under states' Nurse Practice Acts. Nurse practitioners have pushed for independent practice or collaborative practice with physicians in a complementary, nondependent relationship. By 1998, 25 states and the District of Columbia had removed physician supervision and mandatory collaboration from their Nurse Practice Acts. Less than 15 percent of nurse practitioners are in independent practice, however, with most working in collaborative practice with physicians in various ambulatory settings.[18] About one quarter of physician assistants are hospital based, especially in surgical specialty practice, with about one half working with generalist physicians in ambulatory practice, most often with family physicians.[19]

EDUCATION FOR PRIMARY CARE

Returning to the work of Rivo and his colleagues, the 60 necessary training components for generalist practice of primary care are met by family practice (95 percent of components), internal medicine (91 percent), and pediatrics (91 percent). That measure of clinical breadth reveals that obstetrics-gynecology (47 percent) and emergency medicine (42 percent) lack the necessary breadth of training for a full spectrum of primary care. Rivo and colleagues recommend that residency programs training generalist physicians require training in at least 90 percent of these components, including at least 50 percent of the components in each of the seven categories and a continuity-of-care experience for a panel of patients during at least 10 percent of the entire period of residency training.[12]

Each of the three generalist allopathic specialties—family practice, general internal medicine, and general pediatrics—requires a three-year residency to become board eligible in their respective disciplines. These programs involve a mix between hospital-based rotations and outpatient training. Options for additional training also are available in certain areas, such as geriatrics, sports medicine, and obstetrics-gynecology.

Another variation among the generalist specialties are the "med/ped" programs, double-boarded programs in internal medicine and pediatrics of four years' duration. These programs comprise 24 months of medicine and 24 months of pediatrics and, by 1997, had graduated about 1,500 med/ped generalists.[20]

Although osteopathy was founded in 1864 on the basis of an alternative healing practice, spinal manipulation, over the years it has evolved much closer to allopathic medicine, to the point where it has lost much of its unique identity. Today's osteopathic schools are very similar to allopathic medical schools, with some students sharing classes, and osteopathic graduates more often than not enter allopathic residency programs. Although they represent only about 5 percent of U.S. physicians, osteopaths play a larger role in primary care—60 percent of osteopath graduates become generalists and 18 percent locate in rural areas.[21]

Although typical nurse practitioner programs involve about two years of didactic and clinical course work after nursing school, the minimal requirement for clinical training is only 500 hours.[22] This training is provided by nursing schools, leads to advanced nursing degrees, and usually is oriented to the care of specific populations (e.g., geriatric, pediatric, family nurse practitioners). The training emphasizes health promotion, preventive care, and lifestyle counseling, while claiming at the same time the capacity to manage 80 percent of primary care office visits.[16–18] Physician assistant programs also are about two years in duration, but the training usually is based in medical schools, with much of the teaching provided by physicians. The training generally involves 9 to 12 months of preclinical didactic course work followed by 9 to 15 months physician-supervised clinical education.[17]

SOME CONTENTIOUS ISSUES

There are a number of highly contentious issues in the primary care arena, involving not only diverse perceptions of primary care and competition among providers, but also stemming from conflicting paradigms of care. As we saw in Chapter 10, several competing paradigms are at work in today's confused health care "system." Concerning continuity of care, for example, there is every possibility that the more the disease management approach is carried out, the more fragmented primary care may become for chronically ill patients involved in those programs. Five major issues are considered here, which for the most part are interrelated.

Continuity of Care

Two approaches currently being implemented around the country are especially controversial in their impact on continuity of care for the patient and his or her primary care physician—the hospitalist movement and the disease management model. Proponents of the hospitalist model point to the increasing complexity and intensity of inpatient care, the growing difficulty of combined office and hospital practice among ever-busier primary care physicians, and the increased efficiency of care by hospitalists. In fact, there is a new National Association of Inpatient Physicians, a rapidly growing group. An accurate national count of hospitalists is not available, but current estimates range from 5,000 to 15,000.[23] Most hospitalists are recently trained internists, and some family physicians also gravitated to this role.[24] The hospitalist debate has generated intense controversy among the primary care disciplines themselves, with many concerned about loss of continuity of care by mandatory "hand-offs," loss of ethical protection for patients, erosion of inpatient skills, potential negative impacts on their continuing education, and decreased patient satisfaction.[25–28] Although more explicit separation of inpatient from outpatient care also may affect patient satisfaction, this factor still is unknown and not part of the equation.[28–30] As Faith Fitzgerald, an internist educator at the University of California Davis, observed:[31]

> lack of continuity of care may deny patients position in their own stories . . . physicians risk developing cynicism, burnout, and indifference in hospitalist systems that may or may not provide the best care for patients . . . efficiency does not equal excellence.

Chronic disease management poses another possible source of erosion of the physician-patient relationship. One example illustrates the potential problem. The Permanente Group in northern California established adult care management teams that include one nurse practitioner for every two primary care physicians. Patients with selected chronic illnesses therefore see the nurse practitioner for those targeted conditions, resulting in fewer physician visits.[10] Of course, that could work to the patient's benefit in some circumstances if communication between providers is effective, but the physician-patient relationship may be negatively affected, including the optimal coordination of care for patients with multiple medical problems.

Scope of Practice

If one assumes that optimal breadth and depth of primary care occurs when broadly trained physicians in the generalist specialties practice evidence-based medicine under the biopsychosocial model, including appropriate referral to consultants and teamwork with other health professionals, there still is room for controversy on the boundaries of that care. On the narrow end of a spectrum of primary care, referrals will be unnecessarily high, with increased costs and fragmentation of care. On the overly broad end of the spectrum, there is risk of reduced quality of care if the clinical competency of the clinicians is exceeded. The higher is the level of training of the clinician across the full breadth of primary care practice, the more effective primary care can be within an ongoing physician-patient relationship.

Boundary disputes are more common in areas where there is an overabundance of physicians, especially with a surplus of underemployed specialists. It is frequently difficult in such settings, for example, for a family physician planning on rural practice to acquire procedural skills in cesarean section or obstetric ultrasound. Disagreements over boundaries also are more common during the daytime than at night. It always has been a point of interest and amusement over my 40 years in medicine that a consulting specialist finds my skills greater at night than during the day.

Managed care brought some new issues to the fore concerning the scope of practice. The gatekeeper role placed a heavy burden on primary care physicians.[32] It has been largely discredited in recent years, as managed care organizations increasingly have bowed to public pressure to allow direct access to specialists by point-of-service provisions.[33,34] Some evidence suggests that the gatekeeping role overextended the scope of practice beyond primary care physicians' comfort level. A recent national study of over 12,000 primary care physicians and specialists by Robert St. Peter and his colleagues revealed that 30 percent of primary care physicians and 50 percent of specialists felt that the scope of primary care practice had increased over the preceding two years. About one quarter of primary care physicians reported that their scope had been overextended.[35] This situation led Grumbach to observe:[36]

The first sentence of Charles Dickens's *Tale of Two Cities* sums up the ambiguous state of primary care physicians in the United States: "It was the best of times, it was the worst of times . . ." For a primary care physician in the United States, the experience of managed care is just such a set of contradictions. Primary care physicians are loved, and they are defiled. They are the answer to the problem of too easy access to specialty care, and they are the cause of the problem of too difficult access to specialty care. They

Table 13-1 Duties of Health Plans in Supporting Generalist-Specialist Relationships

1. Health plans must provide adequate specialist care for the care of their membership by ensuring an adequate range, number, and availability of specialists.
2. Health plans should link generalists and specialists in systems that foster expeditious consultation and referral.
3. Health plans should adopt financial incentives that do not present a conflict of interest so intense as to dissuade generalists from seeking consultation or referral when needed.
4. Health plans should adopt financial incentives that do not present a significant barrier to the longitudinal care of patients by specialists when deemed medically appropriate.
5. Health plans should establish systems that favor the continuity of relationships between generalists and the specialists with whom they choose to consult.
6. Health plans should develop clinical guidelines with the active participation of generalists and specialists.
7. Health plans should develop criteria to be used for authorization of referral services with the active input of generalists and specialists. Upon adoption, these criteria should be shared openly with all physicians.
8. Health plans should share process and outcomes data regarding referral and associated care with generalists and specialists to aid their individual and joint improvement in the quality of care provided to patients.

Source: Reprinted with permission from Pearson SD. Principles of generalist-specialist relationships. *J Gen Intern Med.* 1999;14(suppl 1):S13–S17.

are empowered by their control of capitated budgets, and they are damned for controlling these budgets. They have been liberated from the corrupting temptations of fee-for-service medicine, and they have been seduced by the wickedness of financial incentives to limit care. They are expected to compensate for a seriously deficient system of health insurance financing, and they are victims of the grave limitations and discontinuities of the financing system. They are the type of physician everyone really needs, unless of course the person is actually ill, at which point a more qualified specialist should take over. We continue to await the unambiguous arrival of the golden age of primary care in the United States.

In response to these problems, replacement of the gatekeeper role with a coordinator role has been recommended for primary care physicians in managed care environments.[33] To implement the coordinator model, Bodenheimer, Lo, and Casalino recommend that managed care organizations take steps to facilitate communication and consultation between generalists and specialty consultants, upgrade the skills of primary care physicians, and reduce the number of specialists to appropriate levels.[33] Steven Pearson goes one step further in proposing duties for which health plans should be held accountable in reshaping generalist-specialist relationships[37] (see Table 13-1).

Outcomes, Quality, and Cost-Effectiveness

The issues of quality and cost-effectiveness of care provided by primary care physicians and specialists have generated ongoing debate within U.S. medicine, which in the absence of large numbers of outcome studies often led to more heat than light. Most studies of quality of care by generalists and specialists do not account for differences in the patient populations seen by the two groups. There are few randomized studies of this question, and many lack external validity.[38] Some studies show that specialists achieve somewhat better results when managing patients with problems within their specialty,[39] but they fare less well outside their domain of practice and refer less appropriately than generalists.[40] Martin Donahoe, an internist at Oregon Health Sciences University, conducted a MEDLINE search of all articles since 1966 comparing the knowledge base and quality of care of generalists and specialists in the United States. His 1998 report drew this conclusion:[41]

> Evidence is strongest that the knowledge base and quality of care provided by specialists exceeds those of generalists for certain conditions such as myocardial infarction, depression, and acquired immuno-deficiency syndrome. Differences in many other areas are multifactorial, and often a function of study design or patient selection. The differences, however, are not as striking or important to the health of the public at large as those deficiencies in disease management, preventive care, and health maintenance that are common to all physicians. Furthermore, overuse of diagnostic and therapeutic modalities by certain specialists leads to increased costs with either no benefit or added risks to patients. The quality and coordination of care provided by generalists and specialists may be improved through changes in education and training, via quality improvement methods of providing patient care, and by increasing visit length and optimizing use of referrals and strategies for generalist-specialist co-management. Further study of these areas is warranted and should concentrate on outcomes.

The controversy between generalists and specialists, and even within the involved specialty, is well illustrated by editorial debate between neurologists over the matter of primary care of patients with such common problems as headache and back pain. The Neurology Intersociety Liaison Group argues that most patients with chronic neurological problems should be managed by neurologists.[42] Another neurologist, Matthew Menken, contended that about half of a neurologist's time in office-based practice is spent treating headaches, backaches, and epilepsy, with an additional quarter of their time dealing with patients with ill-defined disorders and psychiatric problems, both well within the purview of primary care physicians. In the absence of evidence, he called into question three assumptions commonly made by neurologists: (1) that quality of care is necessarily better when provided by a specialist instead of by a generalist, (2) that generalists cannot keep up with the clinical knowledge needed to manage common problems, and (3) that specialists can assume primary care without training in primary care.[43]

The Council on Graduate Medical Education (COGME) concluded that generalist physicians provide more comprehensive and cost-effective care than other specialists or subspecialists.[12,44–46] Many studies have shown that primary care physicians are more sparing in their use of technology and have a higher threshold for admission to the hospital than specialists.[38] This was likewise true in the best comparative study of generalist and specialty practice, the Medical Outcomes Study, which adjusted for variation of severity of illness for patients with cardiac disease and diabetes mellitus.[45] Another interesting study sheds further light on the cost-effectiveness issue. Thomas Campbell and his colleagues examined claims data for 243,000 adult patients in an independent practice association (IPA) in Rochester, New York, finding that primary care physicians with higher proportions of recorded mental health diagnoses generated lower costs within their panel of patients and also had lower rates of hospitalization.[47] With more continuity of care and a more comprehensive approach, primary care physicians would appear to be much more likely to recognize psychosocial problems than their specialty colleagues.

Although the hospitalist model is taking root in many hospitals around the country, especially those large enough to support at least three full-time hospitalists, little is known about its impact on patient care, physician and patient satisfaction, and costs. A recent survey of members of the National Association of Inpatient Physicians revealed that the average number of inpatients cared for by hospitalists at any one time ranges from 11 to 15.[48] The largest study to date was performed by Kaiser Permanente in its 16 hospitals in northern California over a three-year period from 1994 to 1997. No significant changes were found in utilization or quality outcomes in hospitals that adopted a hospitalist model. Admission and readmission rates were the same, consultation requests decreased somewhat, and costs increased (by 13 percent in 1996 and 5 percent in 1997).[49] Another important study in a Medicare population provided evidence that continuity of care makes a difference in hospitalization rates. Weiss and Bluestein found lower rates of hospitalization and costs for patients who had been cared for by their primary care physicians for over five years.[50]

Fresh debate has been stirred up with the publication of a randomized trial comparing outcomes of patients treated by nurse practitioners and physicians. The trial was conducted in New York City between 1995 and 1997, comparing the care of 1,316 patients (77 percent female, 90 percent Hispanic, mean age 46 years). Patients were randomized to four primary care clinics (17 physicians) and one primary care clinic (7 nurse practitioners). Health status, physiologic test results, patient satisfaction, and service utilization were measured for both groups. Patients' outcomes were comparable, as were patient satisfaction and service utilization.[51] However, Harold Sox, an internist educator and consultant to another nurse practitioner practice, advises caution in interpreting these results. He observes that the trial lacks external validity, that the patient population was not broadly representative of primary care, that the clinician roles in inpatient care were not described, and that certain specific clinical tasks were not compared, such as making accurate diagnoses, evaluating emergency patients, managing sick inpatients, and caring for complex patients with multiple medical problems.[52]

Another recent study compared resource utilization of nurse practitioners and physicians in a primary care clinic at a Veterans Administration medical center over a one-year period. Resource utilization was higher for nurse practitioners for a majority of the 17 measures used in the study, with the largest differences involving the use of advanced imaging procedures (magnetic resonance imaging, computed tomography, and ultrasonography); there also was a 41 percent increased hospitalization rate for the nurse practitioner group.[53] Since the amount of clinical training of nurse practitioners is much less than physicians, there is room to question whether they can provide equivalent cost-effectiveness and outcomes of care across a full range of primary care practice. It is much easier to order additional studies, for example, than to decide against them, and additional clinical training and experience may be needed to reinforce one's clinical judgment.

Prescriptive Authority

The right of nonphysicians to prescribe medication is another issue causing considerable controversy. In recent years, advanced practice nurses and nurse practitioners have successfully acquired prescriptive authority, now holding such authority in all 50 states and the District of Columbia. In 17 of these states (and the District of Columbia), they can write prescriptions (even for controlled substances) with no physician involvement.[18] Physician assistants have prescriptive authority in 35 states (as well as the District of Columbia and Guam), but there is considerable variation from one state to another, ranging from protocol-based formulas for noncontrolled substances to prescribing controlled substances.[17]

Another field of growing controversy is the question of prescriptive authority for pharmacists. Pharmacy, as a profession, has been gradually moving away from a "dispensing model" toward a "pharmaceutical care model" since the 1970s. This trend accelerated in recent years, with the increasing application of disease management approaches to chronic illness, as well as the wider use of automated drug distribution systems. In Washington state, for example, pharmacists now can prescribe emergency contraceptive pills and prescribe and administer immunizations (mostly for influenza, pneumonia, and hepatitis for adults). Pharmacists likewise are seeking a larger role in monitoring drug therapy for such conditions as hypertension, diabetes mellitus, and anticoagulation therapy.[54]

Reimbursement

Reimbursement policies for nonphysician providers of primary care services have been controversial for years. Nurse practitioners have been the most successful of any of these groups in terms of reimbursement. The Balanced Budget Act of 1997 (BBA97), for example, extended direct reimbursement under Medicare (at 85 percent of the physician fee amount) to nurse practitioners in all nonhospital sites without the requirement of physician supervision.[16,52] Reimbursement for services provided by physician assistants is more complicated. BBA97 provided for direct payments to physician assistants (again, at 85 percent of physician fee levels) if state laws permit them to work as "independent contractors" with physicians.[16] Under the Medicare "incident-to" provision (i.e., services provided by the physician's staff that are integral, or incidental, to the physician's services), the services of nonphysician clinicians may be reimbursed at 100 percent of physician fee levels if seven conditions are met: "(1) the NPC must be employed by the physician; (2) physician must initially see the patient; (3) physician must be immediately available in the office to see/supervise the patient; (4) physician must actively participate in care of the patient; (5) services provided must be of the type provided by the physician and be covered; (6) services must be within the scope of the practice; and (7) services must be billed by the physician with the incident to modifier."[16] The "incident-to" provision is the most common approach used in practice, but state laws and reimbursement policies vary considerably from one state to another. Under Medicaid, for example, services provided by physician assistants are governed by the "incident-to" provision. Different states have various interpretations of this provision, especially as it relates to offsite practice locations with no direct physician supervision.[17]

The growing popularity of complementary and alternative medicine (CAM) also has led to reimbursement controversies, since some of these services compete with or have elements of mainstream primary care. Driven by public and political pressure more than science, 14 of 18 major managed care organizations and payers (including Aetna, Prudential, Kaiser Permanente, and Medicare) now offer at least 11 of 34 CAM therapies.[55] Medicaid reimburses chiropractic in 33 states, biofeedback in 10 states, acupuncture in 7 states, hypnotherapy in 6 states, naturopathy in 5 states, and lay midwifery and massage therapy in 2 states.[56] Blue Cross-Blue Shield now permits its HMO enrollees to choose chiropractors as their primary care providers, even though they lack prescriptive authorization.[55]

Naturopathy provides an interesting example of the Pandora's box of reimbursement. Naturopaths who completed a four-year program in one of the country's four naturopathic schools accredited by the Department of Education are eligible for licensure in 11 states. Leaders in the field of naturopathy are pushing for licensure in the other states, as well as more consistent standards of training, but the scientific basis and scope of practice of the field are still unclear to many. In Washington state, for example (one of the states where they are licensed and with its own naturopathic school), enabling legislation gives this definition of the field's scope of practice:[57]

> Naturopathic medicine or naturopathy is the practice by naturopaths of the art and science of the diagnosis, prevention, and treatment of disorders of the body by stimulation or support, or both, of the natural processes of the human body. A naturopath is responsible and accountable to the consumer for the quality of naturopathic care rendered.
>
> The practice of naturopathy includes manual manipulation (mechanotherapy), the prescription, administration, dispensing, and use, except for the treatment of malignancies or neoplastic disease, of nutrition and food science, physical modalities, homeopathy, certain medicines of mineral, animal, and botanical origin, hygiene and immunization, common diagnostic procedures, and suggestion.

The president of Bastyr University in Seattle, a naturopathic school, states that[58]

> naturopathic training overlaps orthodox medical education in basic sciences but emphasizes a holistic, multi-system view of pathogenesis and stresses natural treatments, including botanicals, nutrition, acupuncture, spinal manipulation, and psychosocial counseling.

Naturopaths have been approved to act as primary care providers by Washington state's Basic Health Plan, a state initiative serving a low-income population without health insurance.

SOME INTERNATIONAL COMPARISONS

Debate and tension between generalist physicians and specialists are common elsewhere around the world in Western industrialized nations. The more a country's health care system is founded on a strong primary care base, however, the better that country does in terms of control of health care costs, health status, patient satisfaction, and lower medication use. Barbara Starfield, a health services researcher at Johns Hopkins University School of Public Health, carried out a landmark study of the health care systems in 11 Western countries during the middle to late 1980s. Primary care orientation was measured and ranked according to 11 features of primary care:[59]

1. extent of universal financial access and extent to which access is guaranteed by a publicly accountable body
2. extent of explicit regulation to encourage equitable distribution of health-service resources
3. primary care assigned to one type of physician (vs. multiplicity of types)
4. earnings of primary care physicians compared to those of specialists
5. percentage of active physicians who do primary care
6. first-contact care (as assessed by extent to which access to specialist care is by referral from primary care)
7. longitudinality, as measured by responsibility to care for a defined panel of patients regardless of their health problems
8. comprehensiveness, as assessed by breadth and uniformity of benefits for preventive care
9. coordination, as assessed by extent of formal communication between primary care physicians and consultants
10. family centeredness, as reflected by extent of responsibility for care of families
11. community orientation, as assessed by the use of community or other epidemiological data in planning or evaluating services.

By these measures, the United States comes out dead last in terms of its primary care ranking and per capita health care expenditures and also performs poorly on public satisfaction, health indicators, and use of medication[60] (Table 13-2).

The countries with strong primary care tend to rely on general or family practice as the bulwark of primary care. The proportion of physicians in generalist practice is 70 percent in the United Kingdom and 50 percent in Canada.[60] In the Netherlands, the general practitioner serves a population of about 2,000 people, provides first-contact care for all patients, manages 94 percent of the presenting medical problems, and has a strong family orientation and a tradition of providing comprehensive care, including home visits.[61]

CONCLUDING COMMENTS

As is apparent from the foregoing, the United States has a relatively weak primary care base compared to many other industrialized countries. This is

Table 13-2   Ranks for Primary Care and "Outcome" Indicators

	Primary Care Ranking	*Outcome Indicators*				
		Satisfaction	*Expenditure per Head*	*Health Indicators**	*Medications per Head*	*Average Rank for "Outcomes"*
United States	11.0	8.0	11.0	8.0	7.0	8.5
Australia	8.0	5.0	6.0	5.0		5.3
Belgium	9.0		4.0	11.0	6.0	7.0
Germany (West)	10.0	3.0	8.0	9.5	9.0	7.4
Canada	6.5	1.0	10.0	3.0	8.0	5.5
Denmark	3.0		3.0	6.5	1.0	3.5
Finland	3.0		5.0	6.5		5.8
Netherlands	3.0	2.0	7.0	2.0	3.0	3.5
Spain	5.0	7.0	2.0	4.0	5.0	4.3
Sweden	6.5	4.0	9.0	1.0	2.0	4.0
United Kingdom	1.0	6.0	2.0	9.5	4.0	5.4

* Includes low-birthweight ratio; neonatal mortality; total infant mortality; life expectancy for males and females, separately, at ages 1, 20, 65, and 80; age-adjusted life expectancy; and years of potential life lost.
Source: Reprinted with permission from Starfield B. Is primary care essential? *Lancet.* 1994;344:1129–1133.

ironic, since the United States has such strengths in education for primary care as well as in biomedical technology. The nation has never come together to develop a consensus as to how primary care should be organized. Within our present loose system, patients frequently bypass primary care providers in seeking specialty care. This can lead to good clinical outcomes if their needs are well matched to specialist services but can easily result in omission of essential primary care services as well as potential harm from inappropriate services. Although the advent of "managed care" re-emphasized the importance of primary care, the increasing trend to point-of-service provisions in managed care organizations can decrease the effectiveness of primary care. Coherent financing and organizational structure are not yet in place to provide unequivocal support for the system's primary care base.

While today's primary care physicians are well trained to provide a comprehensive range of primary care services, pervasive disincentives to providers and patients often get in the way of these services being delivered. At a recent four-day meeting in Colorado Springs, Colorado, addressing the future of family practice and primary care, a sentiment freely expressed by attendees was, "It is hard to do the right thing in the wrong system."

The United States has all the necessary building blocks to restructure its health care system on a strong primary care foundation. The medical education establishment needs to build on its successful primary care programs, rebalance the mix between generalists and specialists, and encourage more collaboration among the primary care specialties. Other health professionals should become more involved with primary care education programs in an effort to model more effective interdisciplinary team practice. Health policy should be committed to providing an accessible generalist primary care physician for every American for a full range of comprehensive primary care through a personal and ongoing clinician-patient relationship that affords shared decision making and individualization of care. New dimensions of population-based care and chronic illness management need to be incorporated into primary care, as discussed in Chapter 10. Later chapters address other components of a strengthened primary care base, including incorporation of new information technology (Chapter 15) and redesign of clinical systems (Chapter 18).

REFERENCES

1. Fox TF. Personal medicine. *Bull NY Acad Med.* 1962;38:527–534.
2. Donaldson MS, Yordy KD, Vanselow NA (eds). *Primary Care: America's Health in a New Era.* Washington, DC: National Academy Press, 1996:155.
3. Donald MS, Vanselow NA. The nature of primary care. *J Fam Pract.* 1996;42:113–116.
4. Starfield BH. Is primary care essential? *Lancet.* 1994;344:1129–1133.
5. Mullan F. *Big Doctoring: Primary Care in America.* University of California Milbank Fund, 2001.
6. Rivo MI, Satcher D. Improving access to health care through physician workforce reform: Directions for the 21st century: Third report of the Council on Graduate Medical Education. *JAMA.* 1993;270:1074–1078.
7. Weiner JP, Starfield BH. Measurement of the primary care roles of office-based physicians. *Am J Public Health.* 1983;73:666–671.
8. Wall EM, Dennis LK. Will the real primary care provider please stand up? *J Am Board Fam Pract.* 1995;8:73–75.
9. Friedan J. Ob-gyns gain in direct access fight. *Fam Pract News.* November 15, 1998:53.
10. Terry K. Too many primary care doctors? It could happen. *Med Econ.* July 14, 1997:119–134.
11. Applelsy C. Open access plans: Will family physicians be left behind? *Fam Pract Manage.* March 1997:58–67.
12. Rivo ML, Saultz JW, Wartman SA, DeWitt TG. Defining the generalist physician's training. *JAMA.* 1994;271:1499–1504.
13. Rosenblatt RA, Cherkin DC, Schneeweiss R, Hart LG. The content of ambulatory care in the United States. *N Engl J Med.* 1983;309:892–897.
14. Center for Policy Studies in Family Practice and Primary Care. Policy center one-pager. The importance of having a usual source of care. *Am Fam Physician.* 2000;62(3):477.
15. Cooper RA. The growing independence of nonphysician clinicians in clinical practice. *JAMA.* 1997;277:1092–1093.
16. Wilson D, Pryor C. Adding mid-level practitioners to a group practice. *Group Pract J.* July–August 2000:47–49.
17. Jones PE, Cawley JF. Physician assistants and health system reform: Clinical capabilities, practice activities and potential roles. *JAMA.* 1994;271:1266–1272.
18. Flanagan L. Nurse practitioners: Growing competition for family physicians? *Fam Pract Manage.* October 1998:34–43.
19. Larson EH, Hart LG, Ballweg R. *National Estimates of Physician Assistant Productivity—WWAMI Center for Health Workforce Studies.* Seattle: University of Washington, January 2000:17.
20. Peck P. Med/ped specialists fight for FP-like status. *Fam Pract News.* September 15, 1997:64.
21. Howell JD. The paradox of osteopathy. *N Engl J Med.* 1999;341:1465–1467.
22. Personal communication, Larry Green, MD, November 30, 2000.
23. DeMott K. Hospitalists gain more support in primary care. *Fam Pract News.* October 1, 2000:34.
24. Wachter RM, Goldman J. The emerging role of "hospitalists" in the American health care system. *N Engl J Med.* 1996;335:514–517.
25. Weissler JC. The hospitalist movement: Caution lights flashing at the crossroads. *Am J Med.* 1999;107(5):409–413.

26. Schroeder SA, Schapiro R. The hospitalist: New boon for internal medicine or retreat from primary care? *Ann Intern Med.* 1999;130(4, Pt 2):382–387.
27. Goldman DR. The hospitalist movement in the United States: What does it mean for internists? *Ann Intern Med.* 1999;130(4, Pt 1):326–327.
28. Sox HC. The hospitalist model: Perspectives of the patient, the internist, and internal medicine. *Ann Intern Med.* 1999;130(4, Pt 2):368–372.
29. Pantilat SZ, Alpers A, Wachter RM. A new doctor in the house: Ethical issues in hospitalist systems. *JAMA.* 1999;282:171–174.
30. Chapman RW. The hospitalist: Implications for family practice. *Fam Med.* 1998;30(7):517–518.
31. Boschert S. Concerns temper enthusiasm for hospitalist systems. *Fam Pract News.* June 15, 1998:55.
32. Like RC. Primary care case management: A family physician's perspective. *Qual Review Bull.* 1988;14(6):177.
33. Bodenheimer T, Lo B, Casalino L. Primary care physicians should be coordinators, not gatekeepers. *JAMA.* 1999;281:2045–2049.
34. Holoweiko M. Bypassing primary care physicians. *Med Econ.* 1997;74(8):208–216.
35. St. Peter RF, Reed MC, Kemper P, Blumenthal D. Changes in the scope of care provided by primary care physicians. *N Engl J Med.* 1999;341:1980–1985.
36. Grumbach K. Primary care in the United States—The best of times, the worst of times. *N Engl J Med.* 1999;341:2008–2010.
37. Pearson SD. Principles of generalist-specialist relationships. *J Gen Intern Med.* 1999;14(suppl 1):S13–S17.
38. Bindman AB. Primary and managed care. Ingredients for health care reform. *West J Med.* 1994;161:78–82.
39. Rhee SO, Luke RD, Lyons TF, Payne BC. Domain of practice and the quality of physician performance. *Med Care.* 1981;19:14–23.
40. Robert ML, Rovner DR, Elstein AS, et al. Differences in medical referral decisions for obesity among family practitioners, general internists, and gynecologists. *Med Care.* 1984;22:42–55.
41. Donahoe MT. Comparing generalist and specialty care: Discrepancies, deficiencies, and excesses. *Arch Intern Med.* 1998;158:1596–1607.
42. Neurology Intersociety Liaison Group. Who provides neurologic care? *Health Aff (Millwood).* 1989;8(4):197–199.
43. Menken M. The role of the neurologist: The author responds. *Health Aff (Millwood).* 1989;8(4):199–200.
44. Franks P, Clancy CM, Nutting P. Gatekeeping revisited: Protecting patients from overtreatment. *N Engl J Med.* 1992;327:424–429.
45. Greenfield S, Nelson EC, Zubkoff M, et al. Variations in resource utilization among medical specialties and systems of care: Results from the Medical Outcomes Study. *JAMA.* 1992;267:1624–1630.
46. Rosenblatt RA. Specialists or generalists. On whom shall we base the American health care system? *JAMA.* 1992;267:1665–1666.
47. Campbell TL, Franks P, Fiscella K, et al. Do physicians who diagnose more mental health disorders generate lower health care costs? *J Fam Pract.* 2000;49:305–310.
48. Lurie JD, Miller DP, Lindenauer PK, Wachter RM, Sox HC. The potential size of the hospitalist workforce in the United States. *Am J Med.* 1999;106(4):441–445.
49. Craig DE, Hartka L, Likosky WH, Caplan WM, Litsky P, Smithey J. Implementation of a hospitalist system in a large health maintenance organization: The Kaiser Permanente experience. *Ann Intern Med.* 1999;130(4 Pt 2):355–359.
50. Weiss LJ, Bluestein J. Faithful patients: The effect of long-term physician-patient relationships on the costs and use of health care by older Americans. *Am J Public Health.* 1996;86(12):1742–1747.
51. Mundinger MO, Kane RL, Lenz ER, Totten AM, Tsai WY, et al. Primary care outcomes in patients treated by nurse practitioners or physicians: A randomized trial. *JAMA.* 2000;283:59–68.
52. Sox HC. Independent primary care practice by nurse practitioners. *JAMA.* 2000;283:106–108.
53. Hemani DA, Hill C, Al-Ibrahim M. A comparison of resource utilization in nurse practitioners and physicians. *Effective Clin Pract.* 2000;2(6):258–265.
54. Washington State Medical Association. Pharmacists want to shift from drug dispensing to managing drug therapy. *WSMA* [Washington State Medical Association] *Reports.* October 1999:1,3.
55. Jancin B. Rocky marriage: Payers and alternative medicine. *Fam Pract News.* January 1, 2000:38.
56. Brunk D. Some alternative treatments covered by Medicaid plans. *Fam Pract News.* January 1, 2000:44.

57. Washington State RCW 18:36A.040.
58. Goldman EL. Integrative care gains momentum. *Fam Pract News.* April 1999:6.
59. Starfield B. *Primary Care: Concept, Evaluation, and Policy.* New York: Oxford University Press, 1992.
60. Starfield B. Is primary care essential? *Lancet.* 1994;344:1129–1133.
61. Mullan F. The "Mona Lisa" of health policy: Primary care at home and abroad. *Health Aff (Millwood).* 1998;17(2):118–126.

14
Private versus Public Sectors and Public Health

In this country we are at a crossroads between Alistair Campbell's vision of health care as a shared value—something we all own and to which we all must have access—and the nightmare of a health care Third World in which a fat, bloated health care system lavishes its services on the insured rich while uninsured children and the excluded poor die of measles and polio. It seems to me that the choice is easy enough, especially in terms of what we want our legacy to be.

Emily Friedman[1]

Health care is a complex, personal service. The primary means for assuring quality of care and service should reside with health care professionals and health care organizations. However, the financing and delivery of health care is so connected with the public interest that there also must be public accountability. Government has a basic responsibility to ensure that health plans and providers are qualified and operate in the public interest.

Steve Zatkin[2]

The traditional perception of the U.S. health care system is that it is conducted predominantly in the private sector, with a relatively smaller public sector providing for those who cannot afford to pay for care. That perception no longer is true, if it ever was. Public expenditures for health care services now equal or exceed those in the private sector, and likely future trends point to a growing public sector as private health insurance becomes more expensive and less affordable. The shifting balance between private and public health care raises important questions, such as what are the goals, values, strengths, and limitations of each sector; what is the impact of the changing balance between them on access, cost, and quality of health care; and is the public interest being served by changing roles of each sector?

This chapter explores these questions by considering four dimensions of the subject: (1) the eroding insurance coverage and a declining private sector, (2) the growth of the public sector, (3) the roles of public health, and (4) whether the managed competition of health care serves the public interest.

ERODING INSURANCE COVERAGE AND THE DECLINING PRIVATE SECTOR

The foundation of the private sector in U.S. health care is provided by employer-based health insurance. This foundation was laid during the World War II years, with the confluence of three major forces—wage and price controls, worker shortages, and strong unions. There was a tendency for corporations to enter into a long-term social contract with their employees by providing them with health insurance.[3] This foundation has been falling apart in recent years. By 1996, only 64 percent of U.S. workers were covered by employer-based health insurance.[4]

The steady decline of employer-based health insurance is the single most important factor resulting in the growing number of Americans without health insurance. Fewer employers are offering health insurance, and when they do, more of the cost is shifted to employees. In addition, as the economy shifts from high-wage unionized manufacturing jobs with fringe benefits to lower-wage, nonunionized service jobs with fewer benefits, fewer employees can afford health insurance, even if offered. Moreover, an increasing proportion of the workforce works part time and is ineligible for health insurance.[5,6]

In their excellent analysis of the influence of large employers on the health care marketplace, Bodenheimer and Sullivan offer four reasons to seriously question whether health insurance should be dependent on the vicissitudes of the job market:[7]

1. Already, less than two-thirds of workers have employer-based insurance.
2. A large employer can force thousands of families to leave their personal physicians by switching from one HMO to another.
3. There is inequity in the quality of health insurance coverage because of varied income levels of workers.
4. Employers may not serve the best interests of their employees.

Based on these trends, Victor Fuchs concludes that health insurance should be disengaged from employment as an irrational framework for health insurance because of too many inequities and inefficiencies.[8]

Before the 1970s, "community rating," at least for large groups, was the predominant approach to health insurance, by which the source premium was charged to everyone in a geographical area. "Medical underwriting," by which higher premiums are charged to individuals or groups more likely to get sick, was considered unethical.[9] Today, however, the interests and perspectives of health plans often run counter to the welfare of patients through the widespread practice of "favorable risk selection." To an insurer, sick patients represent two kinds of risk—medical and financial.[10] It has been well documented that favorable risk selection has been pursued by some Medicare managed care plans since the 1980s.[10-18] Although in violation of Health Care Financing Administration regulations, a 1995 survey by the Office of the Inspector General of the Department of Health and Human Services found that 43 percent of Medicare beneficiaries were asked about their health status before enrollment.[19] A 1999 report by Arlene Bierman (Center for Outcomes and Effectiveness Research of the Agency for Health Care Research and Quality) and her colleagues demonstrated the strong influence of a single question in predicting the utilization and outcomes of health services. When asked the simple question, "In general, compared to other people your age, would you say your health is: excellent, very good, good, fair or poor?" enormous differences were later found for annual health care expenditures and hospitalization rates among 8,775 non-institutionalized Medicare beneficiaries. There was a fivefold difference in age- and sex-adjusted annual expenditures and hospitalizations between those rating their health as poor compared to those reporting their health as excellent.[10]

In his recent review of trends leading to declining health insurance coverage of all types, Robert Kuttner, a well-known health care analyst, identifies these nine trends:[20]

1. Rising premium costs, both for persons who have access to insurance through their employers and for those who buy insurance individually.
2. The trend toward temporary and part-time work, which seldom includes health care coverage.
3. A reduction in explicit coverage, most notably pharmaceutical benefits.
4. Greater de facto limitations on covered care, especially by health maintenance organizations (HMOs).
5. A broad shift from traditional HMOs requiring very low out-of-pocket payments to point-of-service plans and preferred-provider organizations (PPOs) requiring higher payments by patients.
6. Loss of Medicaid coverage due to welfare reform.
7. The rising cost of "Medigap" coverage for the elderly, which leads to substantial underinsurance.
8. The crackdown on illegal immigrants and the reduction in services to legal immigrants.
9. The trend away from community rating of individual insurance premiums, which results in rising costs and, hence, reduced rates of coverage for middle-aged persons.

These trends together have shifted the balance of health care coverage from the private to the public sector without providing a new foundation within a coherent health policy. An updated analysis of national health care expenditures confirms the extent of shift from private to public sectors. The Health Care Financing Administration (HCFA) placed the private share of payments at 55 percent in 1998. Daniel Fox of the Milbank Memorial Fund and Paul Fronstin of the Employee Benefit Research Institute challenged the HCFA methodology and estimated the private share at only 44 percent of 1998 health care spending.[21]

Comparisons of the mix between private and public sources of health care financing show that the United States is an outlier, compared with other industrialized Western countries. Public spending for health care ranges from two thirds in Australia to 71 percent in Canada and 84 percent in the United

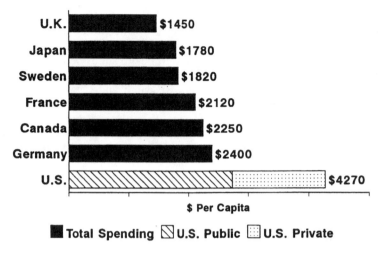

Figure 14-1 U.S. *public* spending per capita for health is greater than *total* spending in other nations, where public includes benefit costs for government employees and tax subsidy for private insurance. (Reprinted with permission from Woolhandler S, Himmelstein DU. *The National Health Program Slideshow Guide.* Cambridge, MA: The Center for National Health Program Studies, 2000; and Anderson GF, Hurst J, Hussey PS, Jee-Hughes M. Health spending and outcomes: Trends in OECD countries, 1960–1998. *Health Aff (Millwood).* 2000;9(3):150–157.)

Kingdom.[22] Nevertheless, when public expenditures for health insurance for government employees and tax subsidies for private health insurance are factored in, U.S. public per capita expenditures for health care exceed total health care spending in other countries (Figure 14-1).[23–25]

GROWING PUBLIC SECTOR

The shift from private to public financing of U.S. health care not only has been a continuing phenomenon since 1960 but is increasing in recent years. Public expenditures for health care grew at an annual rate of about 3 percent more than the private sector from 1960 to 1990, but the difference widened to 5 percent since 1990.[26] As more and more Americans found themselves without health insurance, government at the federal, state, and local levels has been called on to play a larger role in the financing, delivery, and regulation of health care services. Table 14-1 summarizes these roles. Several examples of expanded government initiatives in recent years include the Health Insurance Portability and Accountability Act (HIPAA), expansion of state Medicaid programs, and the $24 billion Children's Health Insurance Program enacted in 1997.[20] Federal intervention in health care repeatedly has been required to address the gaps left uncovered by the private sector, including loss of health insurance, decreasing access to care, supplier-induced demand, and biased risk selection.

Table 14-1 Summary of Governments' Major Health Care Roles

	Financing/Purchasing	*Delivery*	*Regulation*
Federal	Large role through Medicare and Medicaid; other categorical programs	Operates facilities for veterans and Native Americans	Sets standards for Medicare providers; determines what drugs and devices may be sold; sets standards for employee fringe benefits under ERISA
State	Funds Medicaid, mental health, medical education, and public health programs	Operates mental hospitals, health departments, and medical schools	Regulates insurance industry; licenses facilities and personnel; establishes health codes
Local	Subsidizes public hospitals; funds local health departments	Operates county and municipal hospitals; operates local health departments	Establishes local health codes

Source: Reprinted with permission from Brecker C. The government's role in health care. In: Kovner AR, Jonas S (eds). *Health Care Delivery in the United States.* New York: Springer Publishing Company, 1999:311.

Many providers, suppliers, insurers, consumers, and legislators still contend that the marketplace can resolve cost, access, and quality problems in health care delivery. There are some basic reasons why this does not hold true for health care, as it may in other sectors of the economy, however. In an efficient and competitive market, the consumer theoretically can avoid or discipline an opportunistic producer. That condition usually is unavailable to patients as they seek out health care services. Providers tend to set the terms, be they HMOs, hospitals, specialty services, or health professionals. Patients usually lack sufficient information to make fully informed choices and have to deal with the additional issues of time urgency and what is available within their community or area.

Consumer choices are restricted by policies of insurers and health plans, which often try to avoid community risk rating and coverage of sicker patients. Consumer options are further limited as the competitive marketplace goes through mergers and consolidation on the supply side. Meanwhile, of course, to the extent that providers are driven by profit and demand for their services, consumers are vulnerable to higher costs and lower value of purchased services.[9]

The health care marketplace is filled with entrepreneurial individuals and groups, for whom the main motive is profit. Figure 14-2, for example, shows the extent to which for-profit ownership still dominates HMOs, nursing homes, home care services, and dialysis centers.[25]

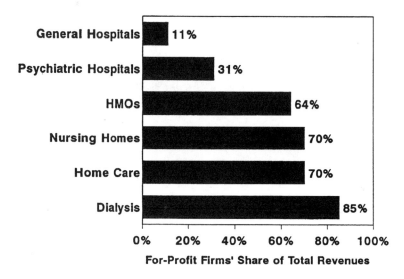

Figure 14-2 Extent of for-profit ownership, 1998. (Source: Data from Commerce and Interstudy. Reprinted with permission from Woolhandler S, Himmelstein DU. *The National Health Program Slideshow Guide*. Cambridge, MA: The Center for National Health Program Studies, 2000.)

If one wonders whether the shift from private to public sectors is merely a temporary phenomenon, which may revert back toward a predominantly private sector, that question is answered immediately by considering the impact of a growing and aging population on Medicare and Medicaid entitlements (Figure 14-3).

PUBLIC HEALTH

The goal of public health is "to secure health and promote wellness for both individuals and communities, by addressing the societal, environmental, and individual determinants of health."[26] With an increasing emphasis on health promotion and disease prevention in recent years, as well as an emerging paradigm of population-based care (Chapter 10), some observers have said that this should be a great time for public health. Yet, the field of public health remains misunderstood, underappreciated, and underfunded, accounting for only about 1 percent of national health expenditures in 1994.[27]

Arguably, many of the major improvements in the health of the American population have been accomplished more through public health approaches than by individual-based health care.[28] Indeed, a recent report from the Centers for Disease Control and Prevention list these 10 areas as the most important public

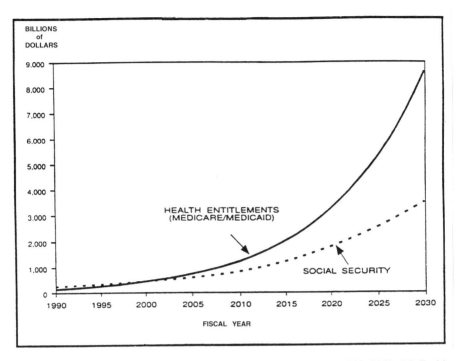

Figure 14-3 Projected social security and health entitlements for 1990–2030; Medicaid payments projection based on 1985–1990 compound annual growth rate of 12.7 percent per year. (Source: Data from Social Security Trust Fund, *Trustee's Report, 1990*, and Health Care Financing Administration, Office of the Actuary, December 1990.)

health achievements during the 1990s: (1) vaccination, (2) motor vehicle safety, (3) safer workplaces, (4) control of infectious diseases, (5) decline in deaths from coronary heart disease and stroke, (6) safer and healthier foods, (7) healthier mothers and babies, (8) family planning, (9) fluoridation of drinking water, and (10) recognition of tobacco use as a health hazard.[29]

Despite these important contributions, however, over the years, public health has had an uneasy relationship with the medical profession, characterized at times by suspicion but usually by disinterest. Table 14-2 reflects three historical stages in the relationships between public health and medicine in the United States.[26]

In its 1988 study of the future of public health, the Institute of Medicine identified three functional pillars of public health that the government should guarantee—assessment, policy development, and assurance[26] (Table 14-3). At the same time, the IOM described public health in America as being in disarray, a conclusion with which the American Public Health Association agreed.[21,26] David Satcher, as director of the Centers for Disease Control and Prevention, made this comment in 1994:[30]

Table 14-2   Stages of Relations Between Public Health and Medicine

Period	Public Health	Medicine
Pre 20th-century era of infectious disease: *Cooperation*	Focus on prevention: sanitary engineering, environmental hygiene, quarantine	Focus on treatment: direct patient care within comprehensive framework
Early 20-century era of bacteriology: *Professionalization*	Establishment of targeted disease control; Rockefeller Foundation report creates science-based schools of public health	Establishment of the biomedical model of disease, Flexner Report leading to standard science-based medical education
Post–World War II-era of biomedical paradigm: *Functional separation*	Focus on behavioral risk factors, development of publicly funded medical safety net (Medicaid/Medicare)	Pursuit of biological mechanisms of heart disease, cancer, and stroke, success with pharmacology, diagnostics, therapeutic procedures

Source: Data from Institute for the Future; Lasker R, Committee on Medicine and Public Health of the New Academy of Medicine. *Medicine and the Public Health: The Power of Collaboration.* New York: New York Academy of Medicine, 1997. Reprinted with permission from The Institute for the Future. *Health and Health Care 2010: The Forecast, the Challenge.* San Francisco: Jossey-Bass, 2000:140.

Table 14-3   The Three Pillars of Public Health

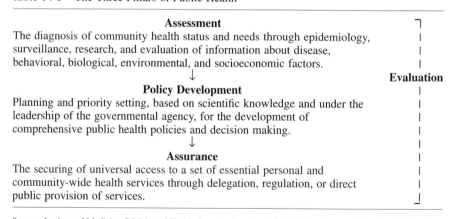

Source: Institute of Medicine, Division of Health Care Services, 1988. Reprinted with permission from The Institute for the Future. *Health and Health Care 2010: The Forecast, the Challenge.* San Francisco: Jossey-Bass, 2000:143.

Many agree that the present plight of public health is related, in great part, to the burden placed on public health at every level by the need to assure or provide access to health care for the underserved. As holes in the safety net of health care became larger, an increasing number of local and state health departments took on the responsibility for providing access to health care for the uninsured and other underserved. The energy and resources required to carry out this function have been devastating to our ability to promote the health of the public.

Public health today has an identity problem. It often is thought of simply as publicly funded health care for the poor.[26] It also confronts a dilemma. At a time when it should be entering its heyday, in terms of need and challenge, it mostly is taken for granted. It has done its original jobs well, such as protection of the water supply and control of epidemic diseases, but now is faced with new challenges for which there is inadequate funding—toxic substances in air, water, and food; drug abuse; teenage pregnancy; AIDS; and chronic diseases.[26]

MANAGED COMPETITION AND THE PUBLIC INTEREST

Since health care in the United States has been left to the forces of the competitive marketplace, many have asked whether the common good is being served by this collective policy decision (or nondecision, as it may be). Among these, Robert Fletcher, internist, educator, and former editor of the *Journal of General Internal Medicine*, notes that about 80 percent of health care in this country is now one or another form of managed care. He further notes, as have many others, that most managed care organizations do not commit enough resources to the common good and comments, "If the United States is to rely on market forces to deal with cost and quality, some other mechanisms must be put in place to make up for what has been left unattended."[31]

Managed care organizations can be categorized into socially-oriented and market-oriented forms of managed care along a spectrum of clear-cut differences of motivation and values. The socially-oriented end of the spectrum is exemplified by Group Health Cooperative of Puget Sound, established in 1948 and now including 660,000 enrollees in Washington state. HMOs of this type tend to share several characteristics: emphasis on prevention and patient education, pursuit of cost-effective care, physicians on salary, close monitoring of "best practice" with mechanisms to reduce unjustified outlier practices, and use of computers to facilitate these strategies, including use of clinical pathways and standard protocols. Market-oriented HMOs, at the other end of the spectrum, typically share some financial risk with physicians; pay them by capitation, with various additional bonus arrangements; place high-utilizing physicians at risk for "deselection" (firing); require primary care physicians to act as gatekeepers; attempt to enroll healthier enrollees and avoid sicker ones; and place more barriers to specialist referral and hospitalization. At this end of the spectrum, the emphasis is more on "managing costs" than "managing care."[32]

Of course, there are many gradations between the ends of this spectrum, but it still is a useful yardstick by which to measure the performance of managed care organizations. Both well-managed and poorly managed HMOs can be found at each end of the spectrum, but there is good evidence that more socially-oriented nonprofit HMOs serve the public interest better than most for-profit, market-driven HMOs. A 1997 study of all Medicare HMOs, for example, found that 9 of the 10 plans with the lowest disenrollment rates (averaging less than 6 percent) were nonprofit plans whereas 7 of the 10 plans with the highest disenrollment rates (about 50 percent) were for-profit plans.[33] In terms of patient satisfaction, a 1996 survey of HMO enrollees by the Consumers Union showed that the 11 top-ranked HMOs were nonprofit plans, while 12 of the lowest-ranked HMOs were for-profit plans.[34] Another survey, conducted by *U.S. News and World Report* in 1997, used data from the National Committee for Quality Assurance. This study assessed such factors as prevention, physician and patient turnover and satisfaction, access to care, and accreditation; of the 37 highest-ranked HMOs, 33 were nonprofit plans.[35]

Unfortunately, most HMOs fall on the market-oriented side of the spectrum rather than on the socially-oriented side.[1] Only one state—Minnesota—requires HMOs to be nonprofit, and some nonprofit HMOs start to resemble for-profit ones through the "vampire effect." The proportion of HMO enrollees in investor-owned health plans increased from 42 percent in 1987 to 62 percent in 1997.[36] There was a flurry of interest by Wall Street in health care organizations during the 1990s. As competition intensified and major payers (especially Medicare and Medicaid) made sharp budget cuts, however, many of these stocks underperformed the market. The result often was the sale of disappointing companies to other for-profit organizations, mergers, and consolidations. This rush to oligopoly actually reduced competition instead of increasing it.

The Minnesota experience with managed care provides an instructive case study in the dynamics and downside of managed competition. As a state with one of the highest rates of penetration of managed care in the country, it has been well documented that the trend toward consolidation of fewer, larger HMOs stifled competition among health plans, hospitals, and physicians. An in-depth report by Minnesota COACT (Citizens Organized Acting Together) in 1995 found that four health plan companies then enrolled about 80 percent of insured Minnesotans. However, lower costs and universal access never happened, and the number of uninsured increased in the state despite the state's public sector rolls increasing by 175,000 people between 1990 and 1994. Minnesota's health care costs were above the national average, there was anecdotal evidence of compromised quality of care, and the big health plan companies and hospital chains acquired strong political power and resisted public accountability.[37]

An excellent paper by Harry Cain illustrates the vastly different worldviews of private market versus public service approaches to health care. As one who has worked in both the public and private sectors, including as executive vice present of Blue Cross and Blue Shield Association in Chicago, Cain contrasts typical views of the "privatizer" (e.g., a market-oriented HMO) and the "publicizer" (e.g., a policy-oriented health planning person in government). Table 14-4 displays these marked differences, which go a long way in explaining today's problems in health care.[38]

The market ethos of the private sector does not serve the public interest. Consider these examples concerning comparisons of investor-owned health care facilities with nonprofit facilities:

- *Hospitals*—costs 3 to 11 percent higher, with higher overhead, fewer nurses, and death rates 6 to 7 percent higher.[39,40]

Table 14-4   A Comparison of Publicizer and Privatizer Views

Issue	Publicizer View	Privatizer View
Problem with current system	Public interests ill-served: Too many uninsured Costs too high Too much private profiteering	Market distorted by: Tax policy Risk selection in small-group, individual markets Excessive regulation
Highest values	Equity, predictability, security, control	Efficiency/effectiveness, flexibility, speed, change
Nature of beneficiary	Vulnerable, needs to be protected	Customer, needs to be satisfied
Price competition in health care	Cannot work	Is the only way
Favorite federal health program	Medicare	FEHBP
Successful health plan	Meets one goal: High-quality service at reasonable cost	Meets two goals: Attracts capital Attracts customers
Management focus	Cost and consistency Constituencies Motives and effort	Price and value Buyers and competitors Results
Managed care abuses	Make them illegal	Market will weed out
Providers and insurers	Suppliers or thieves (maybe both)	Partners or competitors (maybe both)
Who assures integrity of health plans?	Inspector general and audit army	Buyers/consumers with choices
Profit	Tolerable only at low level	Essential fuel; earn or die
Accounting statement	Every line	Bottom line
Conflict of interest	Should be a disqualifying condition	Get it on the table; take it into account
Insurance rating	Community rating; spread the risks	Large group experience; reward smart buyers
Insurance benefits	National standard benefit package, in splendid detail	Let markets decide; standardize only within accounts
Best allocator of resources	Public body backed by technically competent planning agency	The "invisible hand"
Approach to health care reform	Comprehensive; balance conflicting interests	Incremental; improve market dynamics

Note: FEHBP is Federal Employees Health Benefits Program.
Source: Reprinted with permission from Cain HP. Privatizing Medicare: A battle of values. *Health Aff (Millwood)*. 1997;16(2):185.

- *HMOs*—higher overhead (e.g., 25 to 33 percent for some of the largest HMOs).[41–43]
- *Dialysis centers*—death rates 30 percent higher, 26 percent less use of transplants;[44] 85 percent of U.S. dialysis centers are for-profit, and they are over $500/month/patient more expensive than Canadian dialysis centers, yet they have 47 percent higher death rates after controlling for age, sex, race, and comorbidities.[45]

- *Nursing homes*—more citations for poor quality, as illustrated by a 1998 study by the General Accounting Office of California nursing homes, most of which are for-profit; the GAO report found that 30 percent of the facilities had committed violations that "caused death or life-threatening harm" to patients.[46]
- *Mental health facilities*—in 1993, 84 percent of managed mental health firms were for-profit;[47] Arizona had to discontinue a Medicare contract for mental health care of 30,000 Medicare patients due to reports of thousands of patients losing services, staff layoffs, and imminent fiscal insolvency.[48]

In addition to these disturbing examples has been widespread fraud documented throughout the for-profit private sector of health care, some of which involves government contracts with the private sector for the care of Medicare and Medicaid patients. Here are some examples of actual criminal and civil fines/settlements involving corporate fraud in recent years:

- Beverly Enterprises settled for $175 million for Medicare fraud and must sell off the 10 nursing homes found to be worst offenders ($5 million criminal fine and $170 million civil fine, the largest ever for a nursing home company).[49]
- Knoll Pharmaceuticals settled for $135 million class action lawsuit for suppressing data that a cheaper generic was just as good as Synthroid.[50]
- Roche Holdings (Switzerland) and BASF (Germany) will pay $725 million in criminal fines for running a global cartel to fix prices on vitamins.[51]
- Medicare HMOs "routinely" mislead seniors about benefits according to a study of marketing materials.[52]
- HMOs are overcharging Medicare $1 billion to $2 billion a year for "highly inflated" administrative fees. In 1996, Medicare paid 31.7% of HMOs administrative costs but accounted for only 8.9% enrollment.[53]
- Medicare expelled 80 private for-profit mental health centers from the program after a Department of Health and Human Services investigation found that 91 percent of the claims were fraudulent. The problem began when Medicare started letting centers bill for intensive outpatient care as an "alternative" to hospitalization.[54]

Two veteran observers of managed competition provide these insightful perspectives on its negative impacts. According to Robert Kuttner,[43]

> For more than a decade, "market-driven health care" has been advertised as the salvation of the American health care system. In the early 1990s, entrepreneurs succeeded in obtaining the easily available cost savings, at great profit to themselves and their investors. By the late 1990s, however, pressure to protect profit margins had led to such dubious business strategies as the avoidance of sick patients, the excessive micromanagement of physicians, the worsening of staff-to-patient ratios, and the outright denial of care. In an industry driven by investor-owned companies, the original promise of managed care—greater efficiency in the use of available resources and greater integration of preventive and treatment services—has often degenerated into mere avoidance of cost.

Further, according to Claire M. Fagin, dean emeritus of the School of Nursing, University of Pennsylvania:[55]

Markets are amoral in general, that is sentimentally neutral, but in health care this general amorality has the potential to become immoral. The buyers, industry, and government want to reduce costs. The sellers, the managed care organizations, must reduce costs to remain competitive and provide profits to shareholders. Caregivers become implicit and explicit rationers of care who often benefit directly from rationing, a factor that is unique in the American system and exists nowhere else in the industrialized world. Thrown into the brew is ERISA (Employee Retirement Income Security Act), making managed care organizations legally unaccountable for shortcomings in the care they deliver. Put all this together and you have an ideal formula for immorality. I find it hard to come to grips with a system that profits by denying services, removes services from needy clients, blackmails or green-mails the subscriber and the federal government to pay more for these services, then returns profits to shareholders rather than devoting them to increasing access, innovation, and quality of care within the system.

As the consolidating market-driven private sector strangles competition throughout the health care system, even greater stress is placed on public hospitals and providers involved in medical education, indigent care, and public health initiatives. As we saw in Chapter 11, academic health centers (AHCs), faced with their threefold missions of patient care, teaching, and research, have found it difficult to compete with the deeply discounted terms of HMOs. Managed competition has had a devastating effect on AHCs, which generally are nonprofit and an essential part of safety net care. Intense cost containment through the various reimbursement arrangements of managed care also made it less possible for U.S. physicians to provide charity care. A national study of almost 11,000 physicians, for example, found that physicians who practice in areas with high managed care penetration provide considerably less charity care, although most of the surveyed physicians still provide at least 10 hours each week of charity care.[30]

CONCLUDING COMMENTS

The tensions and problems between the private and public sectors of U.S. health care expose the fragility and disjointed nature of our health care "system." As is apparent from the foregoing, the practices of the profit-driven corporate sector of health care place a higher value on return on investment than public service. Yet there still is little public outcry against the workings of the marketplace. Legislative agendas and proposals are still mostly for small ineffective incremental steps, based on the assumption that the marketplace can sort out system problems. As we have seen, however, markets in health care, especially with consolidation of smaller numbers of larger organizations, strangle competition while avoiding public accountability.

It is time to discard the concept of managed competition as ineffective therapy for the access, cost, and quality problems of U.S. health care. It has failed. Even Paul Ellwood came to this conclusion, a turnabout for the man who coined the term *HMO* in the 1970s, promoted HMOs as an alternative to national health insurance, and founded the influential pro-market Jackson Hole Group. In a 1999 talk at Harvard he surprised his audience by saying that[56]

> government intervention is needed to improve health care . . . Patients get atrocious care and can do very little about it . . . Market forces will never work to improve quality, nor will voluntary efforts by doctors and health plans.

Based on the nation's experience over the last 15 years, there can be little hope that the competitive marketplace of managed care will lead to a coherent health care system for the whole population. Major reform is needed, as will be revisited in Chapters 22 and 24.

REFERENCES

1. Friedman E. Prevention, public health, and managed care: Obstacles and opportunities. *Am J Prev Med.* April 1998:14 (3, suppl):102–105.
2. Zatkin S. A health plan's view of government regulation. *Health Aff (Millwood).* 1997;16(6):33–35.
3. Kuttner R. The American health care system: Employer-sponsored health coverage. *N Engl J Med.* 1999;340:248–252.
4. Fronstin P. *Sources of Health Insurance and Characteristics of the Uninsured.* Washington, DC: Employee Benefit Research Institute, December 1997.
5. Fronstin P, Snider SC. An examination of the decline in employment-based health insurance between 1988 and 1993. *Inquiry.* 1996–1997;33:317–325.
6. Cooper PF, Schone BS. More offers, fewer takers for employment-based health insurance: 1987 and 1996. *Health Aff (Millwood).* 1997;16(6):142–149.
7. Bodenheimer T, Sullivan K. How large employers are shaping the health care marketplace. *N Engl J Med.* 1998;338:1084–1087.
8. Fuchs VR. The Clinton plan: A researcher examines reform. *Health Aff (Millwood).* 1994;13(1):102–114.
9. Kuttner R. *Everything for Sale: The Virtues and Limits of Markets.* Chicago: University of Chicago Press, 1999.
10. Bierman AS, Bubolz TA, Fisher ES, Wasson JH. How well does a single question about health predict the financial health of Medicare managed care plans? *Eff Clin Pract.* 1999;2(2):56–62.
11. Riley F, Tudor C, Chiang YP, Ingber M. Health status of Medicare enrollees in HMOs and fee-for-service in 1994. *Health Care Financ Rev.* 1996;17(4):65–76.
12. Langwell KM, Hadley JP. Insights from the Medicare HMO demonstrations. *Health Aff (Millwood).* 1990;9:74–84.
13. Lichtenstein R, Thomas J, Adams-Watson J, Lepkowski J, Simone B. Selection bias in TEFRA at-risk HMOs. *Med Care.* 1991;29:318–331.
14. Riley G, Lubitz J, Rabey E. Enrollee health status under Medicare risk contracts: An analysis of mortality rates. *Health Serv Res.* 1991;26:137–163.
15. Porell FW, Turner WM. Biased selection under an experimental enrollment and marketing Medicare HMO broker. *Med Care.* 1990;28:604–615.
16. Brown RS, Clement DG, Hill JW, Retchin SM, Bergeron JW. Do health maintenance organizations work for Medicare? *Health Care Financ Rev.* 1993;15:7–23.
17. United States General Accounting Office. *Fewer and Lower Cost Beneficiaries Chronic Conditions Enroll in HMOs.* Washington, DC: GAO, 1997.
18. Neuman P, Maibach E, Dusenbury K, Kitchman M, Zupp P. Marketing HMOs to Medicare beneficiaries. *Health Aff (Millwood).* 1998;117:132–139.
19. Department of Health and Human Services, Office of the Inspector General. *Beneficiary Perspectives on Medicare Risk HMOs.* Washington, DC: DHHS, 1995.
20. Kuttner R. The American health care system: Health insurance coverage. *N Engl J Med.* 1999;340:163–168.

21. Fox DM, Fronstin P. Public spending for health care approaches 60 percent. *Health Aff (Millwood)*. 2000;19(2):271–274.
22. Rodwin VG. Comparative analysis of health systems: An international perspective. In: Kovner AR, Jonas S (eds). *Health Care Delivery in the United States*. New York: Springer Publishing Company, 1999:134.
23. Carrasquillo O, Himmelstein DU, Woolhandler S, Bor DH. A reappraisal of private employers' role in providing health insurance. *N Engl J Med*. 1999;340:109–114.
24. Anderson GF, Hurst J, Hussey PS, Jee-Hughes M. Health spending and outcomes: Trends in OECD countries, 1960–1998. *Health Aff (Millwood)*. 2000;9(3):150–157.
25. Woolhandler S, Himmelstein DU. *The National Health Program Slideshow Guide*. Cambridge, MA: The Center for National Health Program Studies, 2000.
26. The Institute for the Future. *Health and Health Care 2010: The Forecast, the Challenge*. San Francisco: Jossey-Bass, 2000.
27. O'Neil EH. The workforce for health. In: *2020 Vision: Health in the 21st century*. Institute of Medicine, Washington, DC: National Academy Press, 1996:93–101.
28. Institute of Medicine. *The Future of Public Health*. Washington, DC: National Academy Press, 1988:1–18.
29. Centers for Disease Control and Prevention. Ten great public health achievements—United States, 1900–1999. *MMWR Morb Mortal Wkly Rep*. 1999;48:241–243.
30. Satcher D. Public health and health care reform: Implications for family practice. *J Am Board Fam Pract*. 1994;7:511–515.
31. Fletcher RH. Who is responsible for the common good in a competitive market? *JAMA*. 1999;281:1127–1128.
32. Kuttner R. Must good HMOs go bad? First of two parts: The commercialism of prepaid group health care. *N Engl J Med*. 1998;338:1558–1563.
33. *Comparing Medicare HMOs: Do They Keep Their Members?* Washington, DC: Families USA, 1997.
34. When things go wrong. *Consumer Reports*. August 1996:39–42.
35. The HMO honor roll. *U.S. News & World Report*. October 23, 1997:62.
36. The Interstudy HMO Trend Report, 1987–1997. St. Paul, MN: Interstudy, August 1998.
37. Sullivan K. *Strangled Competition: A Critique of Minnesota's Experiment with Managed Competition*. St. Paul, MN: Minnesota COACT and COACT Education Foundation, 1995.
38. Cain HP. Privatizing Medicare: A battle of values. *Health Aff (Millwood)*. 1997;16(2):181–186.
39. Silverman EM, Skinner JS, Fisher ES. The association between for-profit hospital ownership and increased Medicare spending. *N Engl J Med*. 1999;341:420–426.
40. Woolhandler S, Himmelstein DU. When money is the mission—The high costs of investor-owned care. *N Engl J Med*. 1999;341:444–446.
41. *Best Week Life/Health Special Report*. April 12, 1999 (from SEC filings).
42. Himmelstein DU, Woolhandler S, Hellander I, Wolfe SM. Quality of care in investor-owned vs. not-for-profit HMOs. *JAMA*. 1999;282:159–163.
43. Kuttner R. The American health care system: Wall Street and health care. *N Engl J Med*. 1999; 340:664–668.
44. Garg PP, Frick KD, Diener-West M, Power NR. Effect of the ownership of dialysis facilities on patients' survival and referral for transplantation. *N Engl J Med*. 1999;341:1653–1660.
45. Hornberger JC, Garber AM, Jeffery JR. Mortality, hospital admissions, and medical costs of end-stage renal disease in the United States and Manitoba, Canada. *Med Care*. 1997;35(7):686–700.
46. *New York Times*. July 29, 1998.
47. Kihlstrom LC. Characteristics and growth of managed behavioral health care firms. *Health Aff (Millwood)*. 1997;16(4):127–130.
48. *Arizona Daily Star.* July 24, 1997, and August 29, 1997.
49. *Modern Healthcare*. February 7, 2000.
50. CBS. *60 Minutes*. December 19, 1999.
51. Ashraf H. UK government cuts disability. *Lancet*. 1999;353(9167):1863.
52. *New York Times*, April 13, 1999.
53. *New York Times*, August 11, 1998.
54. *New York Times*, September 30, 1998.
55. Fagin CM. Two American taboos: Criticizing the market and supporting universal health care. *Nursing Leadership Forum*. Winter 1999;4(2):50.
56. Ellwood P. *Boston Globe*, May 2, 1999.

15
Information Technology and Health Care

A 55-year-old Native American man returns for a regular office visit with his family physician at an Indian Health Service clinic in Phoenix, Arizona, for follow-up of his hypertension and diabetes. During the visit, a photograph of the retina is taken with a special camera (the procedure takes but a few seconds, a low-intensity flash is used, and no dilation of the eyes with drops is required). The image is transmitted instantly to the Joslin Diabetes Center's Beetham Eye Institute in Boston, where two independent readers promptly assess the image (an adjudicator is called in if they disagree). The patient is found to have retinal pathology consistent with chronic hypertension, which was not detected previously by office examinations. The physician is notified of this reading within the hour, and arrangements for ophthalmology consultation are made.

Sound futuristic? This vignette is but one example of advanced information technology *already available* and *operational* by telemedicine (termed *telehealth* in health policy circles). The Beetham Eye Institute established this facility for the remote screening of many patients who otherwise would not be likely to take the time and trouble (dilated eyes for half a day) to have a screening retinal examination. By Spring 2001, the institute expects to have the system operating from the East Coast to an air force base in Alaska as well as in many VA hospitals in between.[1]

As the example illustrates, the future already is here in some corners of the health care system, but these examples are much too infrequent and spotty to be considered anywhere close to mainstream health care. This chapter assesses the present applications of information technology from four points of view: (1) an overview of the adoption of these technologies within the health care industry; (2) information technology and clinical practice, with emphasis on the central role of the electronic medical record; (3) use of information technology by consumers; and (4) the changing relationships wrought by these technologies among providers, patients, and health plans.

INFORMATION TECHNOLOGY AND THE HEALTH CARE INDUSTRY

A revolution in communication and information technology (IT) has been in process in America for the last 15 years and already has transformed much of the business community in this country. The increasing power and reduced costs of microprocessors and lasers, together with resulting cost reductions in data processing and computer memory, have found wide application in finance, insurance, retail, distribution, and other industries.[2] At the same time, the Internet has become a common feature of everyday public life more rapidly than any other communication technology in history. By 1999, almost 100 million people (48 percent of adult Americans) were using the Internet to communicate or acquire information, products, and services.[3] The Internet acquired 50 million users in only five years, compared to 38 years for radio and 13 years for television to reach that number.

Health care services are not only knowledge intensive but extremely complex. There has been a widespread hope and expectation in recent years that the clinical enterprise can be rendered paperless and more efficient through new information technologies. A new industry developed, a commercial health information technology (HIT) industry, that attracted considerable interest and financing on Wall Street. The HIT industry sold $15 billion worth of products to providers and payers in 1997, ranging from medical business decision-support software to data warehousing, to clinical expert systems and electronic medical records (EMRs). Many of these products, however, met difficulty with adoption in real-world clinical practice, to the extent that the term *vaporware* was coined to describe products that are promising on paper and in sales presentations but not clinically useful.[4]

Despite some initial failures of new information technologies in clinical practice, it generally is recognized that IT will be one, if not the main, catalyst for change in the health care system over the next 10 years. The most important underlying technologies include microprocessors, data storage, software tools, networking and data compression, information appliances (including telephones and television sets), intelligent agents (for filtering and retrieving reliable information), security and encryption, Internet and the World Wide Web, three-dimensional computing for data visualization, databases, sensors (e.g., for blood pressure and blood sugar), and expert systems. The Institute for the Future forecasts that information technologies will have an impact on health care in four major areas:[2]

1. Process-management systems.
2. Clinical information interface.
3. Data analysis.
4. Telehealth and remote monitoring.

According to a 1997 Hospitals and Health Networks Leadership Survey, IT was ranked first among the top three strategic goals for managed care organizations and group practices. It also was listed first as the largest "strategic gap" for these two organizations, as well as hospitals.[5]

INFORMATION TECHNOLOGY AND CLINICAL PRACTICE

Use of Computers by Physicians

Until recently, except for practice management purposes, the enthusiasm for expanding computer use by physicians has been a mixed story. Many IT systems were imposed on physicians "from above," by hospitals, health systems, and health plans, with the result that some physicians may be distrustful of the systems' purposes. Some physicians may fear that information gained will be used to adversely profile their practices and utilization of resources, with the potential for disciplinary action or income reduction. On the other hand, a growing number of physicians are adopting a wider range of computer applications, particularly younger physicians, who are more facile with computers.[6] In just the last three years, the number of physicians using the Internet has risen rapidly. A Healtheon survey of 10,000 physicians showed that the proportion using the Internet doubled from 42 percent to 85 percent between 1997 and 1999.[7] Another study, reported in March 2000, revealed that 89 percent of surveyed physicians access the Internet either at the office or at home, for an average use of six hours per week.[8]

Handheld computers, portable electronic devices also known as *personal digital assistants* (PDAs), are the latest development in simple information technology seeing rapid adoption by practicing physicians. Compact and increasingly powerful, they have the big advantage of mobility as physicians move from one examination room to another, freeing them from their desktop computers. PDAs, ranging in cost from $149 to more than $1,000, share many features, including battery operation, an operating system, a display screen, ways to install information, a modem or capacity to accept one, an infrared transmitter, and a variety of software. Table 15-1 compares a wide spectrum of available PDAs in terms of features, capabilities, and costs.[9,10]

PDAs are being touted as an essential clinical tool, the "stethoscope of tomorrow." They can provide instant access to information on patients and consultants, practice guidelines, clinical textbooks, drug databases, and practice management information. All PDAs can be connected to desktop computers, while some allow connectivity to other PDAs, the Internet, and even other computer networks. Some also permit direct access to e-mail, without going through a desktop computer.[9]

Electronic prescribing by means of a PDA brings many advantages—rapid, legible prescriptions (as quickly as three seconds); information on dosage, patient instructions, and drug interactions; and even whether the drug to be prescribed is approved by the patient's health plan formulary. The patient's medication history can be downloaded from a desktop computer to a PDA, facilitating prescription refills without searching for a paper chart. Voice recognition capability is expected to become a common feature of PDAs in the near future.[11] Table 15-2 lists comparative ratings of leading medical software currently available for PDAs, as assessed recently by an 11-physician evaluation team, most based at the State University of New York Upstate Medical University in Syracuse.[10,12]

Table 15-1 Personal digital assistants at a glance

	Palm	Handspring	TRG	Handheld PCs	Pocket PCs
Distinguishing features	Palm is the trademark name of Palm PDAs—formerly called "PalmPilots." However "palm PDAs," "palm-sized PDAs," or "PDAs" with the Palm operating system" may also refer to Handspring and TRG PDAs	Handspring Visors were created by people who co-founded Palm. These devices run an enhanced version of the Palm OS and feature the ability to add modules for software, modems, MP3 players, etc.	TRG's TRGpro, which runs a version of the Palm OS, has a memory expansion slot	HPCs, which are too big for most pockets, include a built-in keyboard—which can range in size from fairly small to fairly large. They also feature a larger display than palm-size PDAs	The newest type of PDA, Pocket PCs run the latest version of the Windows CE OS. They're slightly larger than PDAs with the Palm OS, but they'll fit in your pocket
Operating system	Palm	Palm	Palm	Windows CE	Windows CE (Windows for Pocket PC)
Available models	Palm IIIc ($339) Palm IIIe ($149) Palm IIIxe ($249) Palm V ($325) Palm Vx ($399) Palm VII ($399) Palm VIIx ($449) Palm m100 ($149)	Visor Solo ($149) Visor ($179) Visor Deluxe ($249)	TRGpro ($329.99)	Hewlett Packard: HP Jornada 680 ($899), HP Jornada 690 ($999); NEC: MobilePro 780 ($899), MobilePro 880 ($1,099); Compaq: Aero 8000 ($899)	Compaq: IPAQ Pocket PC (about $499) and Aero 1550 ($499–549); Hewlett Packard: HP Jornada 540 series ($419–450); Casio: Cassiopeia E-115 ($599.95)

Memory	2 to 8MB	2 to 8MB	8MB	Up to 32MB	Up to 32MB
AC adapter included?	Yes	No	No, but you can add one	Yes	Yes
Grayscale or color display?	Grayscale except Palm IIIc, which offers color	Grayscale	Grayscale	Color	Color
Voice recorder included?	No, but you can add one	No	No	Yes	Yes
Wireless modem and wireless LAN card accepted?	Only Palm VII and VIIx have wireless modems built in. You can add one to the Palm V. Only Palm V and Vx accept wireless LAN cards	No	No	Yes	Only the Compaq IPAQ
Web site for more information	www.palm.com	www.handspring.com	www.trgpro.com	www.hp.com /jornada/products/ 680/overview.html www.neccomp.com /product_line.asp? prod_line_no = 4 www6.compaq.com /products/handhelds	www.microsoft.com /pocketpc
Notes	Memory (8MB) can be added only to some models	No Ethernet capability. Comes with connector to USB port		Includes conventional modem. No touch-screen keyboard. Cradle with some	USB port connector can be added to only some models

continues

Table 15-1 (continued)

Palm	Handspring	TRG	Handheld PCs	Pocket PCs
			models only. Some HPCs are pants- or lab-coat-pocket size. Others aren't pocket-size. Only NEC MobilePros come with character-recognition software. Full-sized keyboard can be added only to HP Jornadas. Connectors to USB port can be added to NEC	

Notes: All PDAs, except as indicated:
• Will fit into a shirt pocket.
• Are battery-operated.
• Have infrared capability.
• Come with connection to a PC's serial port. USB connection can be added.
• Include character-recognition software.
• Can be synchronized with a desktop PC.
• Can be augmented with separately available devices—such as more memory, a conventional modem, and a full-size keyboard, as well as separately available software—like a handwriting-recognition program.

Source: Reprinted with permission from Chesanow N. Know your needs, pick a device to fit. *Med Econ*. October 23, 2000:85.

Table 15-2 Comparing the leading medical software

Program Name	Device Used to Evaluate	Operating System(s) Tested	User-Friendliness (average score)	Program Performance (average score)	Clinical Value (average score)	Overall Score
Drug databases						
Apothecarium	Palm V	Palm	2.8	3.7	3.5	3.3
ePocrates qRx	Palm IIIe, Handspring Visor	Palm	3.3	3.3	4	3.5
Lexidrugs	HP Jornada 680, Palm V	WinCE, Palm	3.4	3.2	3.8	3.5
2000 PDR	Handspring Visor	Palm	3.5	2.8	2.8	3
Medical information databases						
Outlines in Clinical Medicine	HP Jornada 680	WinCE	3.7	2.5	3.3	3.2
5-Minute Clinical Consult 2000	HP Jornada 680, Palm V	WinCE, Palm	3.5	2.7	2.9	3.1
Pocket Clinician Library	HP Jornada 680, Palm IIIe	WinCE, Palm	3.3	2.6	2.5	2.8
Patient information management databases						
PatientKeeper	Palm IIIe	Palm	3.3	3.4	3	3.2
Patient Tracker	HP Jornada 680	WinCE	2.7	2.4	1	2
EBM						
InfoRetriever	HP Jornada 680, Compaq IPAQ Pocket PC	WinCE, Windows for Pocket PC	2.7	2.9	4	3.2

Notes: Ratings range from 1 (good) to 4 (excellent). When a program was evaluated by two or more physicians, the scores were averaged.
EBM = evidence-based medicine database; N/E = not evaluated; N/A = not applicable.
Source: Reprinted with permission from Chesanow N. Your ticket to fast, flawless prescribing. *Med Econ.* 2000;(October 23):93–122.

Electronic Medical Record

The electronic medical record (EMR), also known as the *computerized patient record* (CPR), represents the most important advance in medical record keeping since Larry Weed's development of the problem-oriented medical record in 1968.[13] The Institute of Medicine, in 1991, recommended that "health care professionals and organizations adopt the EMR, within the next decade, as the standard for medical and all other records related to health care."[14] The basic concept is that all medical information about a patient can be entered once, then stored electronically over the patient's lifetime, providing ready access quickly, in real time, to health professionals caring for the patient. Information about individual patients, as well as groups of patients, can be further supplemented by other relevant clinical information (e.g., practice guidelines, clinical reminders, clinical decision support systems), so that patient care can be rendered more efficient and of higher quality.

As all practicing physicians know all too well, the paper medical record has inherent problems in being cumbersome, challenging to sort through quickly, and often not available when a patient is being seen. Proponents and successful users of the EMR point to its many advantages, including ease of information entry and retrieval; readability, reliability, and durability; ease of sharing information; opportunity for improved quality of care; decreased variation in care; monitoring of health status of individuals and groups of patients; and facilitation of quality assurance and clinical research.[15] At the same time, many point equally vigorously to the potential problems of shifting to the EMR, including cost of hardware and software, data entry obstacles, lack of uniform standards, difficulty of transition from paper records, inexperienced vendors, provider resistance, and concerns about patient confidentiality and security of information.[16]

As with other desired outcomes as a result of implementation of information technology in health care, it is still premature to claim definitive improvements in quality of care, although that seems intuitively very likely if not inevitable in the long run. An example of the kind of outcome studies that need to be done is the recent evidence-based review of the effectiveness of the EMR as a tool for improving surrogate patient outcomes in the outpatient primary care setting (POEMs are the more important outcome, page 135, but are harder to come by). Seven prospective trials of complete EMRs were identified, together with nine prospective trials of hybrid EMRs. All but one trial reported positive results, particularly involving effectiveness of EMR-generated reminders on provider and patient compliance with health maintenance interventions.[17]

Only about 5 to 10 percent of U.S. physicians are estimated to be using the EMR,[18] but its use is increasing quite rapidly. A survey of 769 physicians reported in 2000 by Harris Interactive, a research firm, showed that 4.3 percent enter chart notes on a computer, 4.4 percent dictate into voice-recognition software, 0.2 percent use a handheld device (e.g., a Palm), and 57 percent expect to enter chart notes by voice-recognition software within five years.[19] Another recent study of all U.S. family practice residency programs (72 percent response rate) found that current use of EMRs was reported by only 17 percent of programs, but that 47 percent of programs planned to be using them within the next two years.[20]

Many larger health care organizations already have fully adopted EMRs and virtually eliminated the paper record, while creating effective systems for quality assurance and monitoring of clinical performance and productivity (e.g., Kaiser Permanente, Group Health Cooperative of Puget Sound, and the University of Washington Physicians Network).

Adoption of the EMR does not require the infrastructure of a large group practice or organization. Application service providers (ASPs) enable small offices with no EMR software to connect to their software systems via Internet connections. An increasing number of small primary care groups, even physicians in solo practice, have implemented EMR capability in their practices. William Davis is a family physician in a group practice of five providers in a small community in southeastern Minnesota with over 10 years' experience with EMRs (COSTAR, as developed at Massachusetts General Hospital and Harvard Medical School). He prints out a patient summary to accompany each patient visit, which includes disposition of previous visits or referrals, allergies, lifestyle indicators (e.g., smoking, alcohol, seat-belt use), major or chronic problems, minor problems, physical findings, laboratory and X-ray results, procedures, medications, special therapies, and ICD-9 and CPT codes. That group was able to search over 30,000 patient records for the immunization status of all children between two and three years of age in less than five minutes.[21] Another family physician, John Spicer, in rural solo practice, adopted another system (Physician Micro Systems, Inc.) to "find a way not to lose charts, to manage chaos," using his system for clinical purposes (e.g., assistance with disease prevention and health promotion) as well as practice management. He is unequivocal about not returning to paper records: "People who think they have the option of paper versus computerized charts—they don't understand. This is not an option anymore."[22]

According to Sheila Adams, an information systems manager for physicians' offices, an EMR system can be set up in an office practice over a period of six months to two years at a cost of $600 to $1,000 per workstation plus database server costs of at least $12,000. Basic system requirements include a database server, workstations, Internet access, modems and dedicated telephone lines, software that includes word processing and fax capability, backup for the database, interfaces for scheduling and billing, and network support. There is an initially steep learning curve for physicians and other staff members, and special attention must be directed to security and customizing to the particular practice.[23]

The EMR is at the heart of best medical practice in the 21st century, serving as the basic building block on which to redesign clinical practice for improved efficiency and quality of care. Other capabilities that are natural extensions of an EMR system include programs for continuous quality improvement; clinical decision support and reminder systems; electronic communication with patients, consultants, hospitals, and insurers; practice management; monitoring of health status for both individual patients and populations being served; and practice-based research.

Clinical Decision Support and Reminder Systems

Since the 1970s, many computer programs have been developed to assist the physician in the clinical decision-making process. Many of these, however, have not been widely adopted, either because they were focused on limited domains within medicine or because physicians lacked access to computerized workstations for such purposes.[24]

Today, there are an increasing number of successful applications of clinical decision support and reminder systems, particularly in managed care organizations and larger group practices. For example, Group Health Cooperative of Puget Sound, with over 900 staff physicians, has developed 30 evidence-based clinical practice guidelines. These are available to physicians at computerized workstations so that they can be used in everyday practice and also enable monitoring of patient outcome.[25–28] Computerized reminder systems have been demonstrated to reduce the incidence of serious adverse drug reactions.[29,30] A computer reminder system at Beth Israel Hospital in Boston provides physicians with prompts when they order prophylactic antibiotics to prevent *Pneumocystis* pneumonia in patients with low CD4 counts; requiring only one additional keystroke to order this medication, the average time between two CD4 counts less than 200 cells/mm^3 and the antibiotic prescription was reduced from 122 days for physicians not receiving reminders to 11 days for physicians receiving reminders.[31] Another good example of an effective computer reminder system is in everyday use at LDS Hospital in Salt Lake City as an aid in prescribing antibiotics. The system enables the physician to rapidly consider such factors as patient allergies, likely pathogens, local patterns of drug resistance, antibiotics on the formulary, hepatic and renal function, and results of cultures. Patients treated by this system were found to receive fewer doses of antibiotics and have fewer problems with drug therapy, shorter hospital stays, and lower costs of hospitalization.[32,33]

The most important advance for physicians in clinical decision making is the increasing availability of resources through the Internet and on CD-ROM, including bibliographic databases, reference texts, and clinical practice guidelines from credible organizations.[24] Resources are available on the World Wide Web to help direct physicians to the best available information on the Internet,[34] and other resources can assist physicians in designing their own clinical computing systems.[24,35,36]

Electronic Communication with Patients and Consultants

E-mail has become an increasingly common form of communication within society, estimated to be used by about half the U.S. population within the next year or so.[37] Again, after a slow start in health care, electronic communication between physicians and patients, as well as among physicians, is on the rise. A 1997 survey showed that nearly one half of the 40.6 million American adults who accessed the Internet within the past year did so to seek medical information,[38] while another 1996 study found that "information from my own doctor's office" ranked highest in terms of the kind of information which patients wanted to access on-line.[39]

The types of usage between physicians and patients varies considerably. Within an ongoing physician-patient relationship in one family physician's practice, it is being used for management and follow-up of minor illness, monitoring of chronic disease, sharing consultants' reports with patients (with the consultants' permission), and communication with consultants.[40] A 1993 study by Nelson and Stewart of over 4,000 e-mail users in 12 Department of Defense hospitals found that one third of respondents used e-mail for patient consultation and referrals, communication of test results, and patient follow-up. More than one quarter of the responding physicians used e-mail at least 10 to 15 times a day.[41] A recent study of over 1,300 U.S. physicians, reported in 2000, showed that about half these physicians use e-mail with their patients at least sometimes, with 10 percent using it at least weekly.[42] Based on the findings of a 1999 literature review of the use of e-mail between U.S. physicians and their patients, Cheryl Moyer and her colleagues drew the following conclusions:[43]

- Most patients still use the phone as the primary means of communicating with their physician's office; however, patients perceive e-mail communication to increase speed, convenience, and access to medical care.
- The majority of patients who use e-mail to communicate with their doctors are satisfied with this method of communication.
- Patients between the ages of 20 and 50 (the majority of subscribers to managed care organizations) are more likely to use e-mail to communicate with their doctors than are older patients.
- Medical center staff perceive e-mail to rival other forms of communication with regard to response rates, value, formality, cost effectiveness, communication style, and other factors.
- Reading and responding to patient e-mails does not appear to be overly time-consuming.
- E-mail is ideal for non-urgent problems such as refilling prescriptions, communicating laboratory results and making appointments; it is also well suited to patient follow-up, staff education and training, and patient care assignments.
- Consensus on how to handle unsolicited patient e-mails is lacking.

Despite its increasing use, e-mail communication between physicians and patients raises a number of concerns, still largely unresolved, such as privacy, confidentiality, reimbursement, and medicolegal issues.[37] Guidelines have been developed to address some of these as shown in Table 15-3.

Other Clinical Uses of Information Technology

Administration and Management

Information technologies have found earlier and wider applications in the administrative and financial aspects of health care than in clinical areas and by now mostly are automated. Figure 15-1, for example, displays the rapid growth in electronic health care claims over the last decade. New federal standards were announced in August 2000 intended to simplify processing of claims and reduce paperwork. All health plans will be required to accept these standard electronic claims, referral authorizations, and related transactions.[44]

High priorities for clinical applications of information technology by health care organizations include implementation of decision-support systems for cli-

Table 15-3   Recommendations of the American Medical Informatics Association

---

Communication guidelines
Establish turnaround time for messages
Do not use e-mail for urgent messages
Inform patients of privacy issues (who will see messages, will message be made part of
  the patient's medical record, etc.)
Establish types of transactions (prescription renewal, appointment scheduling) and
  sensitivity of subject matter (HIV, mental health) permitted over e-mail
Instruct patients to put category of transaction in subject line of message for filtering:
  prescription, appointment, medical advice, billing question
Request that patients put name and patient ID number in the body of the message
Configure auto reply to acknowledge receipt of messages
Print all messages with replies and place in patient's chart
Avoid anger, sarcasm, harsh criticism, and libelous references to third parties in messages

Medicolegal and administrative guidelines
Consider obtaining patient's informed consent for use of e-mail. Written forms should
  provide communication guidelines, give instructions for when and how to escalate to
  phone calls and office visits, describe security mechanisms in place, and indemnify the
  healthcare institution for information loss due to technical failures
Use password-protected screen savers for all desktop workstations in the office, hospital,
  and at home.
Never forward patient-identifiable information to a third party without the patient's
  expressed permission
Never use patients' e-mail addresses in marketing schemes
Use encryption for all messages when encryption technology becomes widely available,
  user-friendly, and practical
Do not use unencrypted wireless communication with patient-identifiable information
Commit policy decisions to writing and electronic form

Source: Reprinted with permission from Moyer CA, Stern DT, Katy SJ, Fendrick AM. "We got mail": Electronic communication between physicians and patients. *Am J Manage Care.* 1999;5(12):1519.

---

nicians, improved monitoring of patient outcomes, and increased connectivity through local and regional networks.[45]

Continuing Medical Education

Physicians increasingly are using computer-based technology to answer clinical questions and meet some needs for their own continuing medical education (CME).

Primary care physicians have been shown to generate an average of two questions for every three patients seen.[46] About one third of these questions concern treatment, another one quarter diagnosis, and 15 percent pharmacotherapeutics.[46-48] Many of these questions go unanswered or are partially answered, in some instances by the *Physicians Desk Reference* (PDR), hardly an evidence-based reference.[49]

Mark Ebell, a family physician educator at Michigan State University and codeveloper (with Henry Barry) of Info-Retriever software for accessing clin-

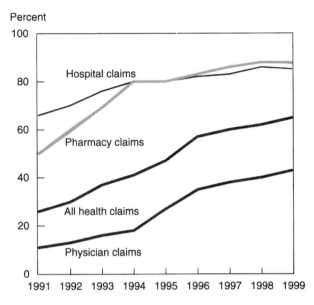

Figure 15-1 Electronic health care claims pick up the pace; percentage of electronic claims by source. (Reprinted with permission from Institute for the Future. *Health and Health Care 2010: The Forecast, the Challenge.* San Francisco: Jossey-Bass, 2000:113.)

ical databases,[49] classified medical information needs of physicians, as shown in Table 15-4. He and others have been working toward more rapid and effective ways of accessing relevant clinical information to answer clinical questions at the point of care.[49–52] MEDLINE searches can access the original research literature on a given subject, but they are time consuming and not usually helpful at the point of care when questions arise. Secondary sources, which have been filtered by peers for relevance and quality of evidence, are much more helpful and can be accessed quickly by new techniques. InfoRetriever, for example, includes the following resources, which can even be accessed by some handheld computers:[49]

1. Abstracts from the Cochrane Database of Systematic Reviews (more than 470; approximately 100 new each year).
2. *Journal of Family Practice* POEMs critical appraisals (more than 300; 100 new each year, desktop version only).
3. *Evidence-Based Practice*, newsletter, brief critical appraisals (600; 300 new each year).
4. Key evidence-based guidelines.
5. Detailed history, physical examination, and diagnostic test information integrated in a calculator for interpreting results.
6. Validated clinical prediction rules.
7. Drug information.

Table 15-4   Ways to Classify Medical Information Needs

Axis	Components	Example
Type of need	Unrecognized	Should have looked for drug interaction
	Recognized	Thought about drug interaction, but did not pursue
	Pursued	Looked for drug interaction information, but did not find it
	Satisfied	Found information about drug interaction
	Implemented	Does not prescribe a medication because of the interaction
Type of information	Etiology	Can *Mycoplasma pneumoniae* cause a sore throat?
	Differential diagnosis	What diagnosis should I consider in this patient with a sore throat?
	Clinical diagnosis	Is viral pharyngitis likely in a patient with exudate and adenopathy?
	Laboratory diagnosis	Is the rapid streptococcus screening test accurate enough to rule out streptococcal pharyngitis, if negative?
	Treatment	Is amoxicillin 500 mg bid × 6 d as effective as 250 mg tid × 10 d?
	Prognosis	If my patient is still symptomatic in 2 days, should I change therapy?
	Patient education	What should I tell my patient about communicability?
	Administrative	Does this patient's insurance pay the cost of antibiotics?
Organ-system	Cardiovascular	What is the appropriate starting dose for enalapril in an 80-year-old patient?
	Pulmonary	When should I start inhaled steroids in an asthmatic patient?
	Gastrointestinal	Is there a role for *Helicobacter pylori* eradication in nonulcer dyspepsia?
	Etc.	
Source of information	Colleague	Asked one of my partners
	Textbook	Consulted *Harrison's Textbook of Internal Medicine*
	Original research	Referred to a recent article in *Journal of the American Medical Association*
	Online database	Did a MEDLINE search
	Other	
Generalizability	Generalizable knowledge	What is the likelihood ratio for a CAGE alcohol screening score of 3?
	Patient-specific question	What is this patient's most recent serum creatinine level?

Note: CAGE—a mnemonic for trying to cut down on drinking, annoyance about criticism of drinking, guilt about drinking, and using alcohol as an eye-opener.

Source: Reprinted with permission from Ebell MH. Information at the point of care: Answering clinical questions. *J Am Board Fam Pract.* 1999;12:225–235.

Figure 15-2 graphically compares the search processes involved by the information mastery approach and traditional MEDLINE searches.

Web-based CME is challenging and increasingly replacing providers of traditional CME, such as courses and journals, which tend to be passive, noninteractive forms of learning. The Web has some advantages over traditional CME, including speed, timeliness, interactivity, the potential for tailoring content to individual needs, and cost savings in terms of both time and money. Providers of Web-based CME emphasize the "five C's" in their development of learning systems: convenience, customization, continuity, case based, and collaboration. A survey of CME professionals attending the 1999 Alliance for Continuing Medical Education (ACME) conference revealed that 87 percent of attendees agree that the Internet is an excellent medium to provide CME.[53]

Telemedicine (Telehealth)

Although the technology permitting telemedicine dates back to the 1960s, it still is early in its development in health care and well short of widespread use.

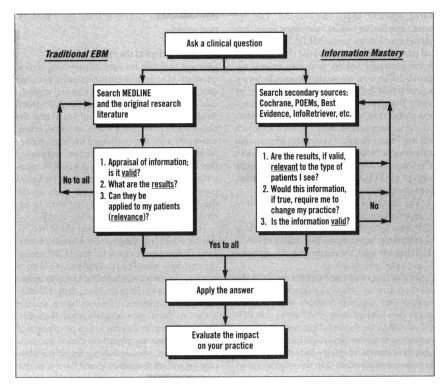

Figure 15-2 Information mastery versus traditional MEDLINE searches. (Reprinted with permission from Ebell MH. Information at the point of care: Answering clinical questions. *J Am Board Fam Pract.* 1999;12:225–235.)

Again, as with electronic communication between physicians and patients, its promise is enormous. Telemedicine applications include the following:[54,55]

- Initial urgent evaluation of patients, triage decisions, and pretransfer arrangements.
- Medical and surgical follow-up and medication checks.
- Supervision and consultation for primary care encounters in sites where a physician is not available.
- Routine consultations and second opinions based on history, physical examination findings, and available test data.
- Transmission of diagnostic images.
- Extended diagnostic work-ups or short term management of self-limited conditions.
- Management of chronic diseases and conditions requiring a specialist not available locally.
- Transmission of medical data.
- Public health, preventive medicine, and patient education.

Telemedicine is defined as the "delivery of health care and the sharing of medical knowledge over a distance using telecommunication systems" (e.g., interactive televideo; "store and forward" image and medical record transmission via personal computers, allowing receiving physicians to see static images at a later time; and remote monitoring).[56] Two technological advances in the 1990s have led to growing interest in telemedicine: (1) expanding use of high-speed, high-bandwidth telecommunication systems around the world and (2) the development of devices that can capture and transmit images in digital form.[57]

Figure 15-3 displays the rapid growth during the last several years of tele-consultation in the United States. A 1998 report of leading U.S. telemedicine programs revealed that some conducted over 4,000 interactive consultations per year. The four most active specialties involved were psychiatry (17.9 percent), cardiology (16.9 percent), ophthalmology (9.6 percent), and orthopedics (5.7 percent). A good example of the diversity of telemedicine applications is represented by the program at the University of Kansas, where telemedicine interactive consultations are established with 25 rural hospitals, 6 mental health facilities, 4 schools, a county jail, and various home health or hospice settings.[58]

Despite its increasing use, telemedicine raises many difficult issues that require some degree of resolution before its promise can be fully realized. Seven are briefly mentioned here:

1. *Cost.* Although the costs are declining each year, they still represent a significant barrier to widespread application of telemedicine services. Interactive video equipment costing over $100,000 in 1992 could be purchased for less than $20,000 by 1999.[55] Medical care of prisoners, however, is an area where the cost effectiveness of telecare clearly has been demonstrated, due to the otherwise high cost of transporting prisoners to outside physicians and facilities.[59,60]
2. *Licensing.* Most states require that physicians providing medical services across state lines hold unrestricted licenses in both states. A struggle now is taking place between states citing licensure restrictions and proponents of

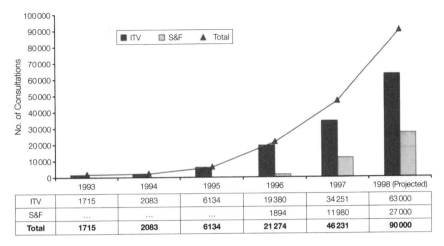

	1993	1994	1995	1996	1997	1998 (Projected)
ITV	1715	2083	6134	19380	34251	63000
S&F	...	...	...	1894	11980	27000
Total	**1715**	**2083**	**6134**	**21274**	**46231**	**90000**

Figure 15-3 U.S. teleconsultation trends: ITF indicates interactive television; S&F, store and forward. (Reprinted with permission from Allen A, Grigsby B. Fifth annual program survey, Part 2: Consultation activity in 35 specialties. *TeleMed Today.* 1998;6(5):18–19.)

telemedicine services. Many states permit consultation from out of state only if the consultant does not charge for services.[61]

3. *Reimbursement.* Some managed care organizations, private insurance companies, and state Medicaid programs provide reimbursement for telemedicine services, but payers remain cautious in their reimbursement policies. The Health Care Financing Administration (HCFA), for example, probably fearing new claims for reimbursement of telephone consultations as well as the potential for fraud and abuse, established four conditions for reimbursement of telemedicine services to Medicare beneficiaries: (1) the patient must live in an underserved rural area, (2) the referring clinician must be present, (3) store-and-forward consultations are not reimbursable (except for teleradiology), and (4) the consultant is required to remit one quarter of the payment to the referring clinician.[56]

4. *Security and Privacy.* Interactive video and store-and-forward exchange usually use telephone or cable lines, with decompression of the images at the receiving end. This is comparatively secure but involves some trade-off of cost and access. Two-way transmissions by satellite are not secure unless scrambling technology is used, which is expensive.[56,62]

5. *Medicolegal Liability.* Many questions concerning potential medicolegal liability for clinicians at both ends of telemedicine consultations remain unanswered. It will take years for questions such as these to sort themselves out:[55] Does a telemedicine consultation differ from any other type of consultation in the liability risk to the consultant or to the local practitioner? Should a videotape of a consultation serve as documentation? Should there be "sovereign immunity" for service to underserved areas?[55]

6. *Outcome Evaluation.* It still is too soon to have any solid studies on the impact of telemedicine services on access, cost, and quality of care. HCFA

started a Telemedicine Demonstration Project in 1993, for telemedicine services for Medicare patients.[63] Preliminary reports on patient satisfaction so far are encouraging.[55] Studies of the efficacy of teleradiology have demonstrated that on-screen interpretation is as reliable as hard copy interpretation as long as consultants are well trained and using proper equipment.[64]

7. *Lack of a "Health Information Policy."* An unanswered question concerns whether public policy should promote, retard, or remain neutral toward private innovation in health information technology development.[65]

INFORMATION TECHNOLOGY AND THE CONSUMER

The Information Revolution already has seen a majority of U.S. households computerized, with ready access to the Internet. Figure 15-4 shows this trend with a near doubling of computer ownership over the last decade. Patients often are frustrated by the difficulties in finding answers to their questions by telephone with their physicians or other health professionals, and increasingly turn to the Internet for help.[66] In 1999, 70 million Americans used the Internet to seek health information of one kind or another.[4] The most common types of information sought deal with complaints, diseases and syndromes, drugs, fitness, and nutrition.[67]

In past years, health sites on the Web provided mainly general reference materials, support groups, bulletin boards, and product promotions. Today, there are competing sites for consultation with physicians, online pharmacies, information about drug studies, storage of patient records, and chat sessions on disease-specific topics.[66] The menu of online offerings continues to expand and will

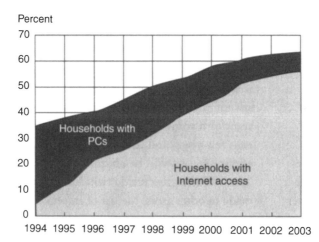

Figure 15-4 Internet and computer penetration of the household will continue to increase; percentage of U.S. households with PCs and Internet connections. (Reprinted with permission from Institute for the Future. *Health and Health Care 2010: The Forecast, the Challenge.* San Francisco: Jossey-Bass, 2000;119.)

include resources for shared decision making, self-care support tools, information about alternative medicine, and assistance with physician and provider assessment.[2] Referral services are readily available, such as Best Doctors (which for a $25 fee provides you with the names of two top specialists in your area).[68] Also, a growing number of Web-based companies offer discount information on physicians' fees. One example is HealthAllies.com, which lists 325,000 physicians and other health care providers (mostly PPO participants) and claims to have received 2.5 million hits in its first few months of operation.[69]

The quality of Web-based health sites varies widely. Some sites are done professionally and monitored carefully, providing excellent information to patients in a convenient and readily accessible manner. Other sites raise questions, sometimes serious ones, and presently insufficient quality control policies are in place for cyber medicine. Some sites offer personalized medical consultations, including review of the patient's medical history, laboratory test results, and treatment options, stopping just short of making diagnoses and prescribing medication. Other sites, such as CyberDocs, provide scheduled virtual appointments with panel physicians, including keyboard chats and video-conferencing with patients. This site (which carries its own malpractice liability insurance) offers diagnostic and treatment advice, including prescription of drug therapy. Some online "pharmacies" have prescribed Viagra and weight-loss drugs with no screening or physician consultation. Regulatory legislation is being considered in Congress, and the National Association of Boards of Pharmacy is planning to assess these sites for their seal of approval.[66]

CHANGING RELATIONSHIPS AMONG PROVIDERS, PATIENTS, AND HEALTH PLANS

The traditional relationships between physicians and patients, as well as between health plans and their enrollees, are changing considerably as patients increasingly empower themselves with health-related information on the Internet. More patients all the time are expecting access to their own electronic medical records, guarantees of confidentiality, and e-mail communication with their physicians for scheduling and rapid responses to their questions.[70] A recent survey even found that one third of online health seekers revealed they probably would switch physicians if they could not communicate with them by e-mail.[71]

Increasingly, consumers are bypassing their providers and even their health plans in seeking information they need to readjust their interaction with both systems. Patients can gain medical information on their health problems rapidly, acquire online second opinions from cyber physicians, and challenge the clinical judgment and recommendations of their own providers. On the positive side, this new environment can enable patients to participate more actively in their own care through an expanded process of shared decision making. On the potentially negative side, the physician-patient relationship may suffer in terms of continuity and trust; and some patients may find themselves adrift and anxious with too much unfiltered information.

Health plans increasingly provide more information online to their enrollees, ranging from clinical areas (e.g., disease management programs, patient education) to administrative information (e.g., locations, hours of operation, and professional qualifications at provider sites). Health plans also can be anticipated to interact more directly with patients, bypassing their physicians, with comparative information on quality and patient safety, and may even find that more direct medical advice may decrease costs by eliminating the need for some visits to physicians.[4]

In view of the rapid spread of information technology to consumers, the Institute for the Future, *Health and Health Care 2010: The Forecast, the Challenge*, predicts that many better-informed patients will reject their own providers and even their health plans as they become their own self-care managers. To the extent that this scenario takes place, physicians, other providers, pharmacists, hospitals, and health plans lose influence and consumers relate to them as undifferentiated suppliers.[2]

CONCLUDING COMMENTS

Business schools now are teaching their students that a second industrial revolution, propelled by information technology, is well underway. Recent decades have seen the advent of global information systems based on the marriage between computers and telecommunications. Considered futuristic only a few years ago, automatic banking, worldwide credit cards, airline reservations, and the World Weather Watch are routine parts of everyday life. Harlan Cleveland, after a long and distinguished career in academia, public administration, and the State Department, noted that IT accelerates decentralization of a "nobody-in-charge" society.[72]

The health care industry has been slower than many other industries to adopt IT but, as we have seen in this chapter, is starting to catch up. Further rapid development appears certain. There is no question that health care and medical practice will be transformed within the next 10 years, but it still is unclear what they will look like. On the one hand, health care applications of IT provide new opportunities to redesign clinical systems of care for improved efficiency, access, and quality of care. On the other hand, some downsides of these developments appear inevitable, including an accelerating "demand push" for more health care services, further inflation of health care costs, increased fragmentation of health care, and some erosion of the physician-patient relationship.

Many new organizational, political, ethical, and legal issues have been raised by IT, and it is not yet clear how most of these will play out in coming years. For example, although asynchronous electronic communication between physicians and patients offers time savings and convenience for all concerned, privacy, medicolegal, and reimbursement issues largely remain unresolved, lagging way behind the present technical capability to provide more health care services electronically. Fresh approaches will be required to address these issues, as physicians and other health care professionals develop a new partnership with patients who are more actively involved in their own care.

REFERENCES

1. Scherger JE. Primary care in 2010. *Hippocrates*. 2000;14:3.
2. Institute for the Future. *Health and Health Care 2010: The Forecast, the Challenge*. San Francisco: Jossey-Bass, 2000:109–122.
3. Americans seek health information online. *Reuters Health*. August 5, 1999.
4. Kleinke JD. Release 0.0: Clinical information technology in the real world. *Health Aff (Millwood)*. 1998;17(6):23–38.
5. *1998 Environmental Assessment: Setting Foundations for the Millennium*. Irving, TX: VHA Inc., 1998:129–152.
6. Goldsmith J. How will the Internet change our health system? *Health Aff (Millwood)*. 2000; 19(1):148–156.
7. Healtheon Corp. press release, May 6, 1999.
8. Harris interactive study reveals a lack of information technology use in medicine; increased use of computers by physicians could revolutionize the medical practice—But hasn't yet. *Business Wire*. March 28, 2000.
9. Chesanow N. Know your needs, pick a device to fit. *Med Econ*. October 23, 2000:81–104.
10. Chesanow N. Put a computer in your pocket. *Med Econ*. October 23, 2000:76–8.
11. Connaughton D. "Stethoscope of tomorrow" puts medical information at your fingertips. *Fam Pract Report*. October 2000:4.
12. Chesanow N. Your ticket to fast, flawless prescribing. *Med Econ*. October 23, 2000:93–122.
13. Weed LL. Medical records that guide and teach. *N Engl J Med*. 1968;12:593–600, 652–657.
14. Steen EB (ed). *Computer-Based Patient Record Institute (CPRI). Proc of the First Annual Nicholas E. Davies CPR Recognition Symposium*. Schaumberg, IL, 1995.
15. Wager KA, Ornstein SM, Jenkins RG. Perceived value of computer-based patient records among clinician users. *MD Comput*. 1997;14(5):334–336, 338, 340.
16. Wager KA, Lee FW, White AM, Ward DM, Ornstein SM. Impact of an electronic medical record system on community-based primary care practices. *J Am Board Fam Pract*. 2000;13:338–348.
17. Jerant AF, Hill DB. Does the use of electronic medical records improve surrogate patient outcomes in outpatient settings? *J Fam Pract*. 2000;49:349–357.
18. Ebell MH, Frame F. What can technology do to, and for, family practice? *Fam Med*. 2001;33(4):311–319.
19. Lowes R. Bits and bytes: How do you unload an obsolete computer? *Med Econ*. 2000; 77(15):35–36, 39–40.
20. Lenhart JG, Honess K, Covington D, Johnson KE. An analysis of trends, perceptions, and use patterns of electronic medical records among US family practice residency programs. *Fam Med*. 2000;32(2):109–114.
21. Davis W. Nine years of computerized patient records in a small family practice. *Fam Pract Manag*. March 1997:69–76.
22. Spicer J. Practicing without paper. *Fam Pract Manage*. 1999;6(3):40–43.
23. Brunk D. What to look for in an electronic records system. *Fam Pract News*. 2000;30(22):29.
24. Payne TH. Computer aids to clinical practice. In: Geyman JP, Deyo RA, Ramsey SD (eds). *Evidence-Based Clinical Practice: Concepts and Approaches*. Woburn, MA: Butterworth–Heinemann, 2000:145–152.
25. Braddick M, Stuart ME, Hrachovek J. The use of balance sheets in developing clinical guidelines. *J Am Board Fam Pract*. 1999;12:48–54.
26. Stuart ME, Macuiba JM, Heidrich F, Farrell RG, Braddick M, Etchison S. Successful implementation of an evidence-based clinical practice guideline: Acute dysuria/urgency in adult women. *HMO Pract*. 1997;11(4):150–157.
27. Handley MR, Stuart ME. An evidence-based approach to evaluation and improving clinical practice: Guideline development. *HMO Pract*. 1994;8:10–19.
28. Handley MR, Stuart ME. An evidence-based approach to evaluating and improving clinical practice: Implementing practice guidelines. *HMO Pract*. 1994;8(2):75–83.
29. Bates DW, Leape LL, Cullen DJ, et al. Effect of computerized physician order entry and a team intervention on prevention of serious medication errors. *JAMA*. 1998;280:1311–1316.
30. Raschke RA, Gollihare B, Wunderlich TA, et al. A computer alert system to prevent injury from adverse drug events: Development and evaluation in a community teaching hospital. *JAMA*. 1998;280:1317–1320.

31. Safran C, Rind DM, Davis RB, et al. Guidelines for management of HIV infection with computer-based patient's record. *Lancet.* 1995;346:341–346.
32. Pestotnik SL, Classen DC, Evans RS, Burke JP. Implementing antibiotic practice guidelines through computer-assisted decision support: Clinical and financial outcomes. *Ann Intern Med.* 1996;124:884–890.
33. Evans RS, Pestotnik SL, Classen DC, et al. A computer-assisted management program for antibiotics and other antiinfective agents. *N Engl J Med.* 1998;338:232–238.
34. Sikorski R, Peters R. Internet anatomy 101. Accessing information on the World Wide Web. *JAMA.* 1997;277:171–172.
35. Nielson C, Smith CS, Lee D, Wang M. Implementation of a relational patient record with integration of educational and reference information. *Proc Annual Symposium on Computer Applications to Medical Care.* 1994;125–129.
36. Tarczy-Hornoch P, Kwan-Gett TS, Fouche L, et al. Meeting clinician information needs by integrating access to the medical record and knowledge resources via the Web. *Proc AMIA Annual Fall Symposium.* 1997;809–813.
37. Sands DZ. Electronic patient-centered communication: Managing risks, managing opportunities, managing care. *Am J Manag Care.* 1999;5(12):1569–1571.
38. Brown M. *The HealthMed Retrievers: Profiles of Consumers Using Online Health and Medical Information.* New York: Cyber Dialogue; 1998.
39. Brown M. *Consumer Health and Medical Information on the Internet.* New York: FINDSVP Inc., 1996:46.
40. Scherger JE. E-mail enhanced relationships: Getting back to basics. *Hippocrates.* November 1999:7–8.
41. Nelson R, Stewart P. Use of electronic mail as a clinical tool. *Health Inf Manage.* 1994;8(3):33–36.
42. Vital signs. Physicians are beginning to use e-mail to reach patients. *Fam Pract News.* 2000;30(22):1.
43. Moyer CA, Stern DT, Katy SJ, Fendrick AM. "We got mail": Electronic communication between physicians and patients. *Am J Manage Care.* 1999;5(12):1513–1522.
44. Electronic standards streamline health care transactions. *AAFP* [American Academy of Family Physicians] *This Week.* 2000;1:28.
45. *1998 Environmental Assessment: Setting Foundations for the Millennium.* Irving, TX: VHA Inc., 1998:150.
46. Covell DG, Uman GC, Manning PR. Information needs in office practice: Are they being met? *Ann Intern Med.* 1985;103:596–599.
47. Smith R. What clinical information do doctors need? *BMJ.* 1996;313:1062–1068.
48. Woolf SH, Benson DA. The medical information needs of internists and pediatricians at an academic medical center. *Bull Med Libr Assoc.* 1989;77:372–380.
49. Ebell MH. Information at the point of care: Answering clinical questions. *J Am Board Fam Pract.* 1999;12:225–235.
50. Ebell MH, Barry HC. InfoRetriever: Rapid access to evidence-based information on a hand-held computer. *MD Comput.* 1998;5(5):289, 292–297.
51. Slawson DC, Shaughnessy AF, Bennett JH. Becoming a medical information master: Feeling good about not knowing everything. *J Fam Pract.* 1994;38:505–513.
52. Shaughnessy AF, Slawson DC, Bennett JH. Becoming an information master: A guidebook to the medical information jungle. *J Fam Pract.* 1994;39:489–499.
53. Lalonde J. The future of continuing medical education. *Group Pract J.* June 2000:26–28.
54. Grigsby J, Sanders JH. Telemedicine: Where is it and where it's going. *Ann Intern Med.* 1998;129(2):123–127.
55. Norris TE. Telemedicine: An update for family physicians. Presented at 27th Annual Advances in Family Practice and Primary Care. Seattle, University of Washington, September 1999.
56. Strode SW, Gustke S, Allen A. Technical and clinical progress in telemedicine. *JAMA.* 1999;281:1066–1068.
57. Thrall JH, Boland G. Telemedicine in practice. *Semin Nucl Med.* 1998;28(2):145–157.
58. Allen A, Wheeler T. The leaders: U.S. programs doing more than 500 interactive consults in 1997. *Telemed Today.* June 1998;6(3):36–37.
59. Kewsler D, Balch D. Development of a telemedicine and distance learning network in rural eastern North Carolina. *J Telemed Telecare.* 1995;1:179–182.
60. Murphy K. Telemedicine getting a test in efforts to cut costs of treating prisoners. *New York Times.* June 8, 1998:D5.
61. Childs N. Licensing still a barrier to interstate telemedicine. *Fam Pract News.* November 1, 1997:9.

62. Swartz D. Insuring the security of Internet-based telemedicine systems. *Telemed Today.* 1998;6(1):27–29, 36.
63. Health Care Financing Administration. Discussion of HCFA telemedicine demonstration. 1997. Available at: http://www.hcfa.gov/pubforms/telemed.htm. Accessed February 14, 1999.
64. Goldberg MA, Rosenthal DI, Chew FS, et al. New high-resolution teleradiology system: Prospective study of diagnostic accuracy in 685 transmitted clinical cases. *Radiology.* 1993; 186:429–434.
65. Moran DW. Health information policy: On preparing for the next war. *Health Aff (Millwood).* 1998;17(6):9–22.
66. Kalb C, Bransum D. Doctors go dot.com. *Newsweek.* August 19, 1999:65–66.
67. Miller TE, Reents S. The health care industry in transition: The online mandate to change, 1988. Available at: www.cyberdialogue.com/pdfs/wp/wp.cch.1999.transition. pdf. Accessed June 26, 2000.
68. Parker-Pope T. Six steps to help you start your own search for medical answers. *Wall Street Journal.* August 11, 2000:31.
69. Borzo G. Web companies offer discounts on doctors' fees. *Fam Pract News.* 2000;30(20):41.
70. Kassirer JP. Patients, physicians, and the Internet. *Health Aff (Millwood).* 2000;19(6):115–123.
71. Cyber Dialogue press releases. Cyberdialogue reports that doctors are missing internet health opportunity. October 12, 1999. Available at: www.cyberdialogue.com/press/releases/1999/10-12.cch.doctors.html. Online health information seekers growing twice as fast as online population. Available at: www.cyberdialogue.com/resource/press/releases/2000/05-23.cch.future.html. Accessed June 26, 2000.
72. Cleveland H. Coming soon: The nobody-in-charge society. *The Futurist.* September–October 2000:52–56.

16
Attempts to Control the Costs of Health Care

The key to the preservation of fee-for-service markets, as the Canadians seem to recognize, is not the micromanagement of the doctor-patient relationship but the management of capacity and budgets. The American problem is to find the will to set the supply thermostat somewhere within reason.

John Wennberg[1]

As we saw in Chapter 7, the escalating costs of health care services in the United States have been a persistent challenge to policy makers and payers for over 30 years. By now many strategies have been tried in an attempt to control these costs, starting especially in the public sector in the 1970s and spreading to the private sector by the 1980s. This chapter presents an overview of the effectiveness, or lack thereof, of these efforts, with five specific objectives: (1) outline the major strategies for cost containment in terms of supply and demand, (2) briefly summarize the experience with cost containment in the private and public sectors, (3) discuss the issue of soaring costs of prescription drugs as an illustrative example of the difficulties in controlling health care costs, (4) comment on the overall impact of cost containment on the health care system itself, and (5) summarize some important lessons from successful and failed approaches to cost containment.

BASIC APPROACHES TO CONTAINMENT OF HEALTH CARE COSTS

In earlier chapters, we noted the powerful impact on the health care system of technological innovation (Chapter 2), growth in numbers of increasingly specialized providers (Chapter 4), and excess hospital bed capacity (Chapter 11). These are all important drivers of increasing health care costs on the supply side, as is the matter of imperfect and asymmetric information of patients (i.e., the difficulty patients have in acquiring as much information concerning their health care decisions as they tend to have for purchasing decisions elsewhere in the economy).

On the demand side of the equation, we traced the expansion of health insurance coverage (Chapters 1 and 14), the growth of an aging population (Chapter 6), and increasing intensity of services, especially in the hospital (Chapter 11). These trends, together with aggressive marketing for the latest in technological innovation, also are strong drivers inflating both utilization and costs of health care services (Table 16-1).

Beyond the supply and demand of health care are two basic levels at which cost control measures can be applied: financing (insurance premiums or taxes levied by the government that support health plans or programs) and reimbursement (involving the flow of funds from insurance plans or government payers to physicians, hospitals, and other providers). Table 16-2 lists the major types of cost controls in each of these areas.

Regulatory cost controls have been utilized by the government at all levels, both in the financing and reimbursement arenas. Various competitive strategies

Table 16-1   Major Supply and Demand Factors which Increase Health Care Costs

Supply	*Demand*
Technological advances	Expansion of health insurance and coverage
Surplus of providers	Technological advances
Increased specialization	Increased intensity of care
Excess capacity of hospital beds	Population growth
Imperfect information of patients	Aging of population
Increased administrative overhead costs	Medicalization of health care
Defensive medicine	Marketing by suppliers

Table 16-2   Categories of Cost Controls

Financing controls
   Regulatory: limits on taxes or premiums
   Competitive: managed competition
Reimbursement controls
   Price controls
   Regulatory
   Competitive
Utilization (quantity) controls
   Aggregate units of payment: capitalization, DRGs, global
      budgets
   Patient cost sharing
   Utilization management
   Supply limits
Mixed controls

Source: Reprinted with permission from Bodenheimer TS, Grumbach K. *Understanding Health Policy: A Clinical Approach.* Norwalk, CT: Appleton and Lange, 1995;104.

also have been used for financing and reimbursement of health care services in both the public and private sectors. Economists have puzzled for years as to why the health care marketplace fails to behave as do competitive markets in other industries. Alain Enthoven, health economist at Stanford University and an early advocate of "managed competition" as a cost control strategy, argued that important differences unique to the health care market inhibit effective competition, especially when patients are insulated from the costs of insurance coverage (e.g., by employers paying the full premium) and when insurance companies compete on the basis of experience rating rather than on efficiency and quality of care (i.e., marketing to low-risk subscribers).[2] Another important difference in the health care market is the comparative lack of information concerning the price and quality of services being purchased.[3]

Since the early 1970s, cost containment efforts were led by public payers in four main directions: controls over hospital inputs (e.g., capital expenditures), hospital admissions, hospital rates, and development of more competitive delivery systems. As a result of the National Health Planning and Resources Development Act of 1974, local health systems agencies (HSAs) and state agencies for planning and development were created. Certificates of need (CON) were required for major expenditures, such as CT scanners. By the mid-1980s, however, these agencies were phased out as ineffective in containment of health care costs.[4,5]

Professional standards review organizations (PSROs) represented the first major national initiative in utilization review of health care services. The PSRO program was established in 1972 to promote effective, efficient, and economic care; prevent unnecessary care (especially hospital admissions); and assure a reasonable quality of care. Worthy as those goals were, however, PSROs had little effect on days of hospitalization and total costs of care, which generally were shifted to other payers. Whatever savings accrued to the Medicare program mostly were canceled out by administrative costs.[6] PSROs were replaced by peer review organizations (PRO) in 1984, which in 1989 extended their purview beyond hospital care to outpatient procedures and home health care. PRO contracts were awarded by competitive bids from the Health Care Financing Organization (HCFA), which in turn required explicit performance measures to be met (e.g., specific goals for reduction of unnecessary surgery or readmissions following substandard care). PRO was an expensive program, however, and of questionable effectiveness. In 1993, it took on a new strategy under the Health Care Quality Improvement Initiative. Its focus was changed to monitoring variation in processes and outcomes of care, then working with physicians and hospitals to improve these measures.[3]

Many states participated in programs to set hospital rates during the 1970s, but their effectiveness was limited and varied considerably from one state to another. Sloan found the cost growth per day and admission was 2 to 3 percent lower in states with rate-setting programs and estimated that hospital expenditures were decreased by 10 to 20 percent over the long run.[7]

By the mid-1980s, it was clear that more stringent cost containment measures were required, and private payers and employers joined public payers in a range of new cost control strategies, including what has become known as *managed care* (but frequently is more managed *costs* or *reimbursement* than care). Two of the most important approaches in the last 15 years have been the advent of prospective payment to hospitals by diagnosis-related groups (DRGs), as discussed in Chapter 11, and the increasing use of leverage by private payers in negotiating discounted reimbursement rates with providers.

With this background, it is of interest to see how effective these cost control efforts have been in the private and public sectors.

COST CONTAINMENT IN THE PRIVATE AND PUBLIC SECTORS

Private Sector

The dominant feature of the private sector since the 1980s has been the growth of preferred provider organizations (PPOs), health maintenance organizations (HMOs) of either the independent practice association (IPA) type or group and staff model type, and more recently, point-of-service (POS) programs. All these have been at the expense of traditional indemnity insurance programs. Recall from Chapter 1 (page 10) the dramatic enrollment shifts in health plans for covered employees from 1988 to 2000 in the United States showing erosion of indemnity plan enrollment from 73 percent to only 8 percent of enrollees over that 12-year period.[8]

PPOs take several approaches to cost control of health care services, price controls, utilization management, and cost sharing with enrollees. IPA HMOs also use price controls and utilization management and add gatekeeping, capitation, and selective contracting to the mix. Group and staff model HMOs rely on supply controls, simplified administration, and salaried providers within global budgets.[9] Utilization management typically takes many forms, including precertification of hospital admissions, required second opinions, individual case management, claims checking, and utilization reviews. HMO enrollment varies widely from one state to another, from a low of 3 percent in North Dakota to a high of 55 percent in California, according to an April 2000 survey by Medical Data International Inc. There is even greater variation in HMO penetration among metropolitan areas, with Sacramento, California, having the highest HMO enrollment in the country (82 percent).[10]

Most analysts credit managed competition in these various forms with some success in containment of health care costs, or at least slowing in the rapid escalation of costs seen in earlier years. National health expenditures for hospital care slowed during the early and mid-1990s as the nation's enrolled population in PPOs and HMOs increased.[11]

Despite limited success, cost containment of health care costs has been transitory and remains elusive. Consider these markers of the relentless pressures toward inflation of health care costs:

- Overall health care expenditures quadrupled from 1980 to 1995 (from about $250 billion to $1 trillion) in 1995 dollars.[12]
- The annual growth rate of HMO enrollment has slowed sharply from 16 percent in 1996 to a negative 0.5 percent in 2000 (Figure 16-1), marking the first time since 1973 that annual HMO enrollment has not increased.[13]

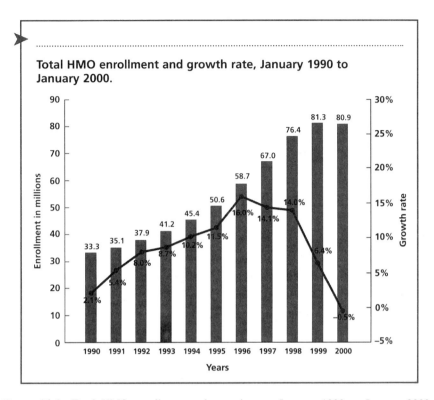

Figure 16-1 Total HMO enrollment and growth rate, January 1990 to January 2000. (Source: InterStudy Publications, September 21, 2000. Reprinted with permission from The InterStudy Competitive Edge HMO Directory 10.3, *Med Benefits.* 2000;17(20):8.)

- Shift of enrollment from one health plan to another has become common-place, often resulting in discontinuity of care; this is inflationary in itself, as demonstrated in a recent large study showing that continuity of care was associated with decreased resource utilization and lower pharmacy costs.[14]
- Cost containment efforts by managed care insurers and health plans have been relaxed over the last several years under heavy pressure from con-sumer backlash, tight labor markets, and federal and state legislation and litigation.[15]
- Employers are being hit by major health care cost increases for the third year in a row, including projected increases for 2001 of 12 percent for indemnity plans, 10 percent for PPOs and POS plans, and 13 percent for HMOs.[16]

As noted in Chapter 1, many HMOs have experienced heavy financial losses, and it appears that their initial profits were short lived. This is not surprising in view of the increasingly competitive nature of the health care marketplace, growing public disenchantment with managed care, and premium increases ini-tiated by many HMOs since the mid-1990s. As Jerome Kassirer and Marcia Angell observed:[17]

The fundamental problem is our fragmented, price competitive health care system. As long as one part of the system can improve its bottom line by shifting costs to another, there will always be creaming and dumping and other attempts to avoid caring for sick people. Managed-care businesses are now finding their prospects for large profits far less bright than in the past. More and more, they are being squeezed, as costs of care continue to rise and payers resist increases in premiums, while patients and doctors grow increasingly dissatisfied with cost-containment measures. Perhaps it will soon be possible to reconsider a more overarching reform that will eliminate both the incentive and the ability to shift costs. It makes no sense to have a health care system in which the name of the game is to avoid caring for sick people.

Public Sector

Medicare

As we saw in Chapter 7, the cost of hospital care makes up the single largest portion of overall health care expenditures (about one third). The DRG system was established in 1983 in an effort to contain those costs and, as shown in Figure 16-2, had their maximal effect on U.S. hospitals in 1990 to 1992, when aggregate inpatient margins fell into red ink. Of interest, however, is the rebound of these margins since 1994 to double digit margins in the black, to the extent that Congress froze the prospective payment update factor for 1998 and reduced increases for the following years.[18]

Medicare encouraged enrollment in capitated health plans for many years, but not until the early 1990s did significant enrollment occur. The enrollment rate in 1991 was 90,000 a month, and during the 1990s the proportion of the nation's elderly in Medicare managed care programs more than tripled to its present level of about 16 percent.[19] That number no longer is rising, however, as an increasing number of Medicare HMOs exit the market. Since the 1997 Balanced Budget Act (BBA97) was enacted, almost 1.5 million enrollees were disenrolled due to HMO departures,[20] and 50 percent of these returned to fee-for-service plans, hardly the intention of Congress.[19]

The Balanced Budget Act of 1997 mandated several major changes in Medicare, in an effort to apply further cost controls to the program. Beneficiaries were given more choice of health plans, including traditional fee-for-service care, high-deductible medical savings accounts, provider-sponsored organizations, and capitated plans. BBA97 also legislated prospective payment systems for hospital outpatient, home health care, and skilled nursing facility services. The most far-reaching (and controversial) provision of BBA97 was to establish a plan for risk adjustment of Medicare payments. Risk adjustment accounts for case mix or severity in adjusting payment on the basis of how sick one group of patients is compared to another group. Thus, the care of an uncomplicated diabetic patient would receive lower reimbursement than care of a patient with leukemia.[21] Previously, Medicare payments were adjusted for only four factors: age, sex, Medicaid eligibility, and nursing home status.[18]

Risk adjustment was started on January 1, 2000, for 10 percent of Medicare payments for providers of inpatient services. By 2003, 80 percent of these pay-

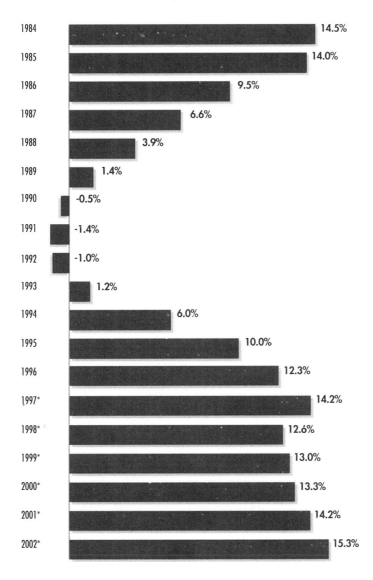

1984   14.5%
1985   14.0%
1986   9.5%
1987   6.6%
1988   3.9%
1989   1.4%
1990   -0.5%
1991   -1.4%
1992   -1.0%
1993   1.2%
1994   6.0%
1995   10.0%
1996   12.3%
1997*   14.2%
1998*   12.6%
1999*   13.0%
2000*   13.3%
2001*   14.2%
2002*   15.3%

* Estimated — 1998 and beyond include the effect of the Balanced Budget Act of 1997.

Figure 16-2 Aggregate prospective payment system inpatient margins: Prospective Payment Assessment Commission analysis of Medicare cost report data from the HFCA, updated by VHA. (Reprinted with permission from VHA. *1998 Environmental Assessment. Setting Foundations for the Millennium.* Irving, TX: VHA Inc., 1992:19.)

ments will be risk adjusted, and outpatient risk adjustment is scheduled to begin in 2004.[22] Despite the reasonable intent of policy makers to reduce the incentive for health plans to enroll relatively healthy people and to reimburse providers more equitably for the care of sick and disabled people, there are still some major problems in extending risk adjustment to ambulatory care, including the inadequacy of coding systems, difficulty in classifying many reasons for a visit, involvement of multiple providers for many patients' problems, and lack of availability of outpatient data in capitated plans.[22]

Faced with a large-scale exodus of Medicare HMOs from the market, the HCFA recently introduced a more flexible option on a pilot basis. A new Medicare + Choice plan, to be offered by Sterling Life Insurance, provides coverage for all Part A and Part B services as well as worldwide emergency care and more inpatient days. Enrollees pay a premium and additional out-of-pocket expenses but pay less for physicians' visits than under original fee-for-service Medicare. Physicians are paid on a fee-for-service basis with no requirement of utilization review.[23] It is too early to see how these initiatives by HCFA will play out, but clearly, policy makers are confronted by the need to balance cost containment with the need to assure patients of access to care.

Medicaid

The Medicaid program underwent an explosion in growth during the years 1988 to 1992, as a result of several factors: (1) a number of legislative mandates extending Medicaid coverage to children, pregnant women, the elderly, and the disabled; (2) medical price inflation; (3) increased utilization; (4) expansion of nursing home care; (5) disproportionate share payments (DSH) to hospitals (for uncompensated care of low-income persons); and (6) shifting of some services by the states to Medicaid coverage. As a result, Medicaid expenditures increased at an average rate of 22.4 percent a year in that period.[24]

The Medicaid program was seen as "out of control," and vigorous cost containment efforts were instituted in the early 1990s, including curtailment of reimbursement to providers, capping of DSH payments, case management, and encouragement of managed care programs. These steps quickly slowed the growth in both enrollment and spending within the Medicaid program, with expenditures decreasing to 9.5 percent growth per year between 1992 and 1995.[24] Compared to Medicare physician fees, Medicaid reimbursement fell by 14.3 percent between 1993 and 1998, to the point that access to care, and in some instances outcomes, were being threatened for patients on Medicaid in many parts of the country.[25–27]

A recent national survey of Medicaid managed care health plans revealed serious concerns about the increasingly fragile safety net health plans funded by Medicaid. About 60 percent of these plans were found to have lost money in 1997, and trends since then have not improved.[28] The pressure on safety net providers increased in recent years, as more employers require larger employee contributions for health insurance and as the number of working uninsured grows. Figure 16-3 shows the impact of these changes since 1992 in terms of federal DSH spending to safety-net providers for uncompensated care.

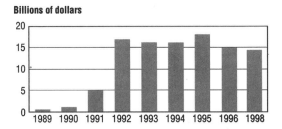

Figure 16-3 DSH spending explodes in the early 1990s. (Source: U.S. Government Accounting Office, The Urban Institute. Reprinted with permission from Institute for the Future. *Health and Health Care 2010: The Forecast, the Challenge.* San Francisco: Jossey-Bass, 2000:30.)

TWO OTHER COST CONTROL APPROACHES

While an encyclopedic discussion of cost containment of health care costs is beyond the scope of this chapter, two other approaches are of particular interest in reflecting other important dimensions of the overall problem.

The Oregon Health Plan

A pioneering initiative, the first of its kind, was launched in Oregon in 1987 in an effort to address two problems in health care: lack of insurance for low-income people and denial of life-saving treatment despite availability of coverage for less-effective treatment of less serious conditions. The idea that these problems should be addressed fairly and objectively on the basis of scientific evidence was launched by John Kitzhaber, an emergency room physician and president of the Oregon senate (later to become governor). The catalyst was the unfortunate case of a seven-year-old boy, Coby Howard, who died of acute lymphocytic leukemia after denial of a bone marrow transplant.[29] The Oregon legislature had discontinued Medicaid coverage for organ transplantation earlier that year.[30]

The essence of the Oregon Health Plan was the development of a priority list of diagnoses and treatments that would be covered in a Medicaid benefits package. The Oregon Health Services Commission was established in 1989 to create this list, and rankings were made based on the severity of illness and effectiveness of treatment or prevention. There was, and still is, widespread public input to this process through public meetings held around the state, promoting open debate of these issues. The commission gave consideration to life expectancy, quality of life, cost effectiveness, and number of people who could benefit from an intervention. Highest priority was given to treatment that prevents death and affords full recovery; lowest priority was assigned to treatment with minimal or no improvement in quality of life.[31] The first list was rejected by the federal government with the claim that the quality of life with disability was being undervalued, and the plan generated heated debate and controversy among health care professionals, bioethicists, policy analysts, and legislators. A new list was developed (with 85 percent of the first list's ranks remaining about the same), and the plan was approved and went into operation in 1994.[29] Table 16-3 shows the list as it was in 1995.

The Oregon Health Plan today is widely seen as an objective and fair approach to the painful need for rationing health care services at a policy level without succumbing to the "rule of rescue," which is the usual moral response to the plight of seriously ill individuals.[32] It also buffers physicians from the often conflicting responsibilities to advocate for the patient and at the same time conserve collective resources.[33] As Thomas Bodenheimer concludes "Oregon's list represents a new approach to the design of a benefits package, introducing a health policy issue that merits further discussion and debate."[29] However, the plan now faces an uncertain future as a result of several problems, including failure to obtain an ERISA waiver from the federal government and thereby achieve an employer mandate, shrinkage of the at-risk pool, inability to "move

Table 16-3   The Oregon Health Plan's Prioritized List of Health Services, 1995

The five top items

Line 1. Diagnosis: severe or moderate head injury, hematoma or edema with loss of consciousness. Treatment: medical and surgical treatment.

Line 2. Diagnosis: insulin dependent diabetes mellitus. Treatment: medical therapy.

Line 3. Diagnosis: peritonitis. Treatment: medical and surgical therapy.

Line 4. Diagnosis: acute glomerulonephritis, with lesion of rapidly progressing glomerulonephritis. Treatment: medical therapy, including dialysis.

Line 5. Diagnosis: pneumothorax and hemothorax. Treatment: tube thoracostomy or thoracotomy, medical therapy.

The five bottom items

Line 741. Diagnosis: mental disorders with no effective treatments. Treatment: evaluation.

Line 742. Diagnosis: tubal dysfunction and other causes of infertility. Treatment: in vitro fertilization, gamete intrafallopian transfer.

Line 743. Diagnosis: hepatorenal syndrome. Treatment: medical therapy.

Line 744. Diagnosis: spastic dysphonia. Treatment: medical therapy.

Line 745. Diagnosis: disorders of refraction and accommodation. Treatment: radial keratotomy.

Six items near the 1997 cutoff line

Line 576. Diagnosis: internal derangement of the knee and ligamentous disruption of the knee, grade III or IV. Treatment: repair, medical therapy.

Line 577. Diagnosis: keratoconjunctivitis sicca, not specified as Sjögren's syndrome. Treatment: punctal occlusion, tarsorrhaphy.

Line 578. Diagnosis: noncervical warts, including condyloma acuminatum and venereal warts. Treatment: medical therapy.

Line 579. Diagnosis: anal fistula. Treatment: fistulectomy.

Line 580. Diagnosis: relaxed anal sphincter. Treatment: medical and surgical treatment.

Line 581. Diagnosis: dental conditions (e.g., broken appliances). Treatment: repairs.

Note: Data were adapted from Oregon Health Plan Administrative Rules.

Source: Reprinted with permission from Bodenheimer T. The Oregon health plan—lessons for the nation. *N Engl J Med.* 1997;337:651–654.

the line" (of coverage) up as new services become covered, and decreasing trust and participation among health plans and providers.[34]

Fraud and Abuse

Fraud in the health care industry is by no means rare, and the government found it necessary to investigate and prosecute an increasing number of cases in recent years. Over $1.5 billion has been collected by the government in health care fraud settlements, mostly in the last several years. Two examples illustrate the kinds of fraudulent cases which have been found—a large dialysis service provider paid $375 million to settle allegations of false claims for laboratory tests and alleged kickbacks and a nursing home chain settled for $170 million dollars for allegations of overstating time spent by nurses with patients.[35] There is now even evidence that career criminals are involved in health care fraud activities, especially those who have been convicted of securities fraud, forgery, or narcotics trafficking. Recent investigations by the General Accounting Office uncovered seven cases of fraud involving Medicare, Medicaid, and private insurance with sham claims ranging from $795,000 to over $120 million.[36]

Another major concern is the extent to which some providers may "game the system" in reimbursement for services. This may be for their own self-interest, but in many instances appears to be an indirect and covert form of patient advocacy.[37,38] A recent national study of 1,124 practicing physicians (response rate 64 percent) revealed that such deception of third-party payers may be more widespread than previously thought. Of these physicians, 39 percent admitted to manipulating reimbursement rules "sometimes or more in the last year" so patients could receive care they felt was needed. Many believed that it often is necessary today to manipulate reimbursement rules to provide the best quality of patient care. Three tactics were used by some of these physicians—exaggerating the severity of patients' conditions, changing the billing diagnosis, and reporting false signs or symptoms to gain coverage for needed care.[39]

PRESCRIPTION DRUG COSTS: AN ILLUSTRATION OF THE COST CONTROL CHALLENGE

Since the cost of prescription drugs represents the single fastest growing part of health care expenditures, it is no accident that this was one of the hottest political issues in the 2000 election year. It therefore is useful and of special interest to consider this area as a brief case study of the cost containment problem.

Recall from Chapter 7 (page 90) that prescription drugs accounted for 8 percent of total U.S. health care expenditures in 1998, almost half of that for physician services (20 percent). During 1999, spending for prescription drugs soared by a staggering 17.4 percent, and projections for the next few years show no signs of slowing down (Figure 16-4). For people in their 70s, the average cost of a prescription rose 14 percent, with a 16.4 percent increase for those over 80 years of age.[40] Over the five-year period from 1994 to 1999, the prices

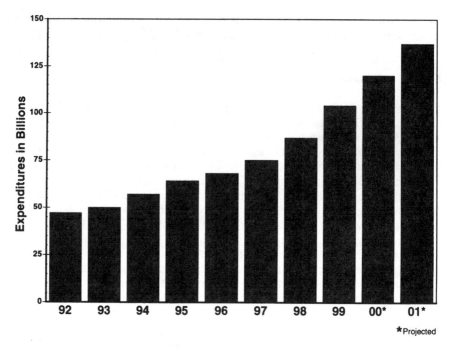

Figure 16-4   Total annual prescription-drug expenditures in the United States, in billions. (Source: HCFA, Blue Cross and Blue Shield Association, and Health Insurance Association of America. Reprinted with permission from McGinley L, Zimmerman R. High U.S. drug prices may give pharmaceutical makers a migraine. *Wall Street Journal.* July 21, 2000:B1, B4.)

of the 50 most commonly used prescription drugs used by older Americans grew twice as fast, on average, as the rate of inflation in 1998. Thirty-nine of these drugs were on the market over the entire period; of these, almost one half rose at more than twice the rate of inflation, while over one fourth rose at least three times the rate of inflation. Incredibly, the old standby Lanoxin, the most commonly prescribed drug for seniors, rose almost *seven* times the inflation rate.[41]

A recently reported study from Brandeis University, based on four years of prescription claims in an insured population of 1.4 million people, revealed even more worrisome findings over the years 1996 to 1999:[42]

- Prescription drug costs increased at an annual growth rate of 24.8 percent.
- Prescriptions per enrollee grew 14 percent per year.
- The number of prescriptions increased from an average of 16 to 23 per year for people over 65 years of age.
- One third of increased expenditures was accounted for by new drugs, approved after 1996.
- Cost of medication per day increased by 8 percent per year (mostly due to substitution of costlier for less costly ones).
- The proportion of people with drug expenditures over $2,000 per year quadrupled, from 1.3 percent to 5.3 percent.

The cost of prescription drugs in the free market of this country is much higher than north or south of our borders, as well as elsewhere around the world. Examples are striking. A month's supply of Zoloft, a popular antidepressant, costs a pharmacist $29.75 in Austria, $40.97 in Mexico, and $64.67 in the United States, while Clozaril, an antipsychotic, costs a pharmacist $51.94 in Spain and $317.03 in the United States.[43] A single tablet of Zocor, a cholesterol-lowering drug, sells for $1.82 in Canada and $3.82 in the United States.[44]

The impact of these changes is particularly serious for elderly Americans, one third of whom are without drug coverage. Elderly Americans without drug benefits pay an average retail price of $223.61 for an average prescription of Zoloft ($115.70 if insured) and $133.32 for Procardia XL, a cardiac drug ($70.00 if insured); these average retail prices went up by 25.5 percent and 20.4 percent, respectively, from 1994 to 2000.[45] By the year 2010, per person expenditures by the elderly for prescription drugs are projected to exceed $2,800 per year.[46]

Seniors covered by Medicare managed care plans also have been hit hard, as these plans increasingly impose more restrictions on drug benefits (benefits of only $500 per year in one third of the plans).[47] A recent national study of voluntary disenrollment among over 60,000 Medicare beneficiaries from four of these network model health plans found that 17 to 25 percent of them disenrolled after exhausting 1998 drug benefit caps.[48] About half of disenrollees return to traditional Medicare. Disenrollment may involve a change of drugs if a different formulary or new physician becomes involved and may result in increased costs if the patient needs further evaluation or monitoring as a result of changes in drug therapy.[47]

The pharmaceutical industry has been one of the most profitable of U.S. industries over the last five years, with double-digit earnings for each of those years (over 20 percent for some companies). According to Fortune 500 rankings for the period from 1995 to 1999, return on revenues for the pharmaceutical industry ranged from 14.4 percent to 18.6 percent compared to a median return of about 5 percent for Fortune 500 companies overall.[49] The industry pays less taxes than other U.S. industries (16.2 percent of total income for the 1990 to 1993 period compared to a 27.3 percent average for all U.S. industries).[49] The industry now faces a gathering storm of protest, from consumers, insurers, employers, health plans, government programs, policy makers, and legislators.[50]

Pharmaceutical companies are on the defensive even as they escalate their direct-to-consumer (DTC) marketing and promotion to physicians to record levels, as well as lobbying efforts to avoid price controls. Some of the DTC marketing presents a distorted case for treatment without clarifying potential harms of treatment, as illustrated by recent advertisements promoting use of tamoxifen for chemoprophylaxis of breast cancer.[51] The Federal Drug Administration found that some pharmaceutical companies repeatedly violate drug marketing laws in their DTC advertising (e.g., 11 times for Schering-Plough Corporation's antihistamine, Claritin, for misleading ads).[52] A recent report of the watchdog group Public Citizen found that the drug industry hired 297 lobbyists within the last three years (one for every two members of Congress) to lobby against any legislation that would regulate prices of pharmaceuticals and, at the same time, increased the industry's campaign contributions by 147 percent since 1994.[53]

The pharmaceutical industry's marketing practices to physicians frequently extend beyond ethical bounds in deliberately attempting to draw physicians into conflict-of-interest situations. Two examples make the point. Editors of medical journals often are approached by pharmaceutical companies to publish supplements on a specific clinical topic that will highlight one of their products as therapy for the condition. Some of these are legitimate, but many are disguised marketing papers. In many instances, the publisher stands to gain a generous "educational grant" in return for publishing the supplement. If rigorous peer review is made a requirement, the pharmaceutical company often withdraws its proposal, as occurred on a number of occasions in my editorial experience. A second example concerns the current widespread practice of physician profiling. A recent report in the *New York Times* exposed a little-known practice that does not stand the light of day. Many pharmaceutical companies buy information from the AMAs physicians' master file to develop physician prescriber profiles. (The AMA admits to $20 million in annual revenue from the sale of this information but denies ethical impropriety in doing so.) Pharmacies also may sell records of prescription drug sales to pharmaceutical companies (without patients' names), by which physicians' names can be identified. The companies then target physicians selectively by various means in an effort to influence their prescribing habits. One common way is to offer a meal or two plus an honorarium of up to $1,000 to attend (as "a consultant") an "educational workshop" on the drug being marketed.[54]

Although the pharmaceutical industry is quick to defend its prices as due to the high cost of research and development, as well as the public benefits from drug therapy, the industry's overall budget for marketing and administration is more than twice that of research and development. As Angell points out, "The large drug companies spend about 40 percent of their revenues on marketing, reap about 30 percent in profits, and spend a comparatively small 20 percent on research and development."[55]

The number of new drugs brought to market has been declining since 1996 (53 in that year, 30 to 35 in each of the years to follow). The industry is pressing forward with more "lifestyle" drugs, such as Merck's baldness drug and Bristol-Myer's drug for women to eliminate facial hair.[56] Since the patents of about 150 drugs with combined annual sales of $50 billion will expire within the next five years,[57] pharmaceutical companies are seeking FDA approval and new patents for "new drugs," which in many cases are repackaged older drugs, such as pairing two drugs into one. They also seek approval for more over-the-counter (OTC) drugs, in an effort to offset the impact of more of their products becoming generic within the next several years. At the same time, they are taking legal action against the attempts of generic drug makers to produce generic formulations of brand drugs, as illustrated by a recent case involving fluoxetine (Prozac).[58]

In a strong backlash to rising drug prices, concerted action is being taken in many directions in both the public and private sectors. It is currently estimated that 77 million Americans have either no coverage or inadequate insurance coverage for prescription drugs.[59] Congress is debating the addition of one or another form of prescription drug benefit to Medicare, but serious concerns about projected costs of such coverage are being raised. The Senate passed legislation permitting pharmacists and wholesalers to import cheaper drugs from other countries. Federal investigators are concerned that pharmaceutical companies have used deceptive practices in setting average wholesale prices for their products and are considering litigation against these companies.[60] At the state level, Maine passed a drug price-control law mandating that, by October 2000, all drugs sold there will cost no more than in Canada. This law is being challenged in federal court by the Pharmaceutical Research and Manufacturers of America (PhRMA) as an unconstitutional assault on interstate trade.[61] Employers increasingly are using three-tiered copayment schemes that favor use of generic drugs and are passing on more of prescription drug costs to their employees. For many employers, drug costs now equal or surpass costs of hospitals and physicians.[62]

The story for insurers is much the same. Blue Cross/Blue Shield of Michigan, with 4.7 million members, in 1997, became the first health plan in the country to have its pharmaceutical costs exceed its in-hospital costs. The company is expanding its efforts in control of drug costs by emphasizing generic substitution, increased education of patients and physicians, new information systems, drug utilization review, advocating against extension of patents for some brand drugs, and developing an Internet-based national purchasing network for 75 million members nationally.[63] The Blue Cross/Blue Shield Association also launched a new, nonprofit company, Rx Intelligence, governed by a board of 12, only 2 of whom represent health insurers. This group's mission is to conduct reviews and cost-benefit analyses of existing and new drugs in an effort to better inform physicians and patients.[63] Meanwhile, health plans and hospitals are expanding the role of pharmacy and therapeutics (P&T) committees to develop more "outcomes-based" formularies, incorporating consideration of pharmacoeconomics and quality of life issues.[64]

OVERALL IMPACT OF COST CONTROLS ON THE HEALTH CARE SYSTEM

Given the many cost-containment efforts at all levels within the health care system, especially over the past 20 years, the question remains as to how much difference they have made. From 1960 to 1990, when Medicare and Medicaid were introduced, annual public expenditures for health care grew by an average of 13.3 percent, about 3 percent more than the private sector. From 1991 to 1995, cost increases in the private sector slowed to less than 5 percent a year, compared to about 9 percent for the public sector. Part of the explanation for this difference is that the private sector was more aggressive in shifting to one or another form of managed reimbursement, but another part is that more costs were shifted from the private sector to the public sector. More stringent cost controls in the public sector were put in place by BBA97, which attempted to cap annual cost increases at 6 percent.[65]

As we saw earlier in this chapter, the promising progress in containment of health care costs in the private sector has been erased in the last several years, as health care inflation has returned to double digits.[16] The Institute for the Future forecasts the government's share of costs to increase to 52 percent by the year 2010 (compared to shares for consumers and employers of about 28

Percent of GDP

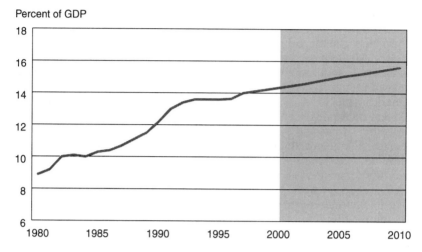

Figure 16-5 Projection of future health care spending, health care expenditures as a share of GDP. (Source: Institute for the Future. Reprinted with permission from Institute for the Future. *Health and Health Care 2010: The Forecast, the Challenge.* San Francisco: Jossey-Bass, 2000;30.)

and 20 percent, respectively.) Figure 16-5 provides an overall picture of continued increases in health care spending, reaching nearly 16 percent of GDP by 2010.

SOME LESSONS FROM THE U.S. COST CONTAINMENT EXPERIENCE

In my view, these conclusions can reasonably be drawn:

1. The inflationary trend of health care costs continues unabated despite limited success of some cost containment measures.

2. Cost shifting has taken place and is ongoing from the private sector to the public sector, with government now becoming the dominant payer of health care costs.

3. The area most refractory to cost controls, prescription drugs, is starting to pose even greater concerns than the cost of inpatient care.

4. Macro approaches probably are more effective than micromanagement of health care expenditures and will be required before health care inflation can be controlled. Luft and Grumbach made this point in 1994 when the Clinton health plan was being debated and rejected:[66]

> successful cost containment ultimately requires delineation of global spending limits and management of capacity within the health care system—In American staff- and group-model HMOs, the HMO obtains a global prepayment enrollment fee and then internally allocates budgets to provider units. For private insurance plans that lack the organizational

structures to manage internal provider budgets and capacity, the prospects for continued survival in the United States are bleak, whether the future lies with managed competition or single payer. Reliance on such cost containment methods as patient cost sharing at the point of service and utilization management from a distance is unlikely to achieve sustained control of expenditures.

5. Physicians and other providers can and often do "game the system" to increase reimbursement for health care services, often in response to patient demand and concern that what they consider necessary care be provided the patient.

6. The public appetite for more health care services, driven by aggressive marketing by suppliers and illustrated by the increased demand for prescription drugs, is unabated and shows no signs of public awareness of limited resources.

7. Politicians continue to shy away from dealing with the hard realities of limited resources, bending readily to public pressure for additional benefits while the nation's capacity to pay for relatively unlimited services becomes more strained.

CONCLUDING COMMENTS

Despite the much heralded promise of managed competition as a strategy for containment of rising health care costs, the last several years have shown the ineffectiveness of this approach to containment of health care costs. The marketplace thrives on growth and profit and does not operate with a mission to control costs. Early gains by HMOs evaporated as many HMOs either left the market or abandoned rigorous cost controls while passing these costs on to employers and consumers. The marketplace ethics of many for-profit HMOs have been shown to neglect the public interest, as graphically observed by Lawrence Hipshman of the Oregon Health Sciences University:[67]

> The managed care industry has offered ample evidence, however, that it requires externally derived controls and boundaries because the industry's prime objective is investor profits rather than service quality.
>
> Managed care industry executives earn millions. Industry mergers reap vast sums for the few while sapping capital from direct services. Industry methods impair the care provider/care seeker relationship. Millions are left without coverage. Premiums will rise to attract more investors (that is, make fatter profits). Is this what health care is about? Many Americans still believe that health care is a public resource that cannot, and should not, be left to unfettered market forces. If the industry wants to improve its image, it will need to respect and respond to that belief.

Beyond the for-profit managed care organizations, other parts of the for-profit private sector cast further doubt on the ability of the private sector to control health care costs in the public interest. The case study of the pharmaceutical industry, presented earlier, serves as a good example of the challenges in controlling the costs of prescription drugs. A fundamental question remains unanswered: What roles must the private and public sectors play to ultimately achieve more effective cost containment of health care, especially as these costs grow in response to vigorous marketing of health care services and products, with increasing "demand push" by consumers? That question is revisited in Part Three of this book. Meanwhile, in the next chapter, we turn our attention to the impact of escalating health care costs on access to care.

REFERENCES

1. Wennberg JE. Outcomes research, cost containment, and the fear of health care rationing. *N Engl J Med.* 1990;323:1202.
2. Enthoven AC. The history and principles of managed competition. *Health Aff (Millwood).* 1993;12(suppl):24.
3. Thorpe KE. Health care cost containment: Reflections and future directions. In: Kovner AR, Jones S (eds). *Health Care Delivery in the United States.* New York: Springer Publishing Company, 1999;439–473.
4. Joskow P. *Controlling Hospital Costs: The Role of Government Regulation.* Boston: MIT Press, 1981.
5. Sloan F, Valvona J, Becker E. Diffusion of surgical technology: An exploratory study. *J Health Econ.* 1986;5:31–40.
6. Congressional Budget Office. *The Impact of PSRO on Health Care Costs: An Update on the Congressional Budget Office's 1979 Evaluation.* Washington, DC: U.S. Government Printing Office, 1981.
7. Sloan F. Hospital rate review: A theory and empirical review. *J Health Econ.* 1984;3:83–86.
8. MB Stat. *Med Benefits.* 2000;17(20):11.
9. Bodenheimer TS, Grumbach K. *Understanding Health Policy: A Clinical Approach.* Norwalk, CT: Appleton and Lange, 1995:103–121.
10. Medical Data International Inc. California still dominant in HMO enrollment. *Med Benefits.* 2000;17(1):4.
11. Gaskin DJ, Kralewski J. The impact of HMOs on hospital use and cost. A matter of interpretation. *Am J Manage Care.* 1999;5(7):939–941.
12. Congressional Budget Office. *The Economic and Budget Outlook, 1998–2007.* Washington, DC: Government Printing Office, 1997:126.
13. The InterStudy Competitive Edge HMO Directory 10.3. *Med Benefits.* 2000;17(20):8.
14. Raddish M, Horn SD, Sharkey, PD. Continuity of care: Is it cost effective? *Am J Manage Care.* 1999;5:727–734.
15. Segal Company. 2001 Segal health plan cost trend survey. *Med Benefits.* 2000;17(22):6.
16. Hewitt Associates, LLC. Employers to face double-digit healthcare costs for third consecutive year. *Med Benefits.* 2000;17(22):5
17. Kassirer JP, Angell M. Risk adjustment or risk avoidance. *N Engl J Med.* 1998;339:1925–1926.
18. VHA. *1998 Environmental Assessment. Setting Foundations for the Millennium.* Irving, TX: VHA Inc., 1992.
19. Pretzer M. Medicare. The managed care program isn't working the way Congress intended. *Med Econ.* June 19, 2000:31.
20. Carrns A, Burton TM, Murray S. More HMOs to join retreat from Medicare. *Wall Street Journal.* July 3, 2000: A3-4.
21. Iezzoni LI, Aganian JZ, Bates DW, Burstin HR. Paying more fairly for Medicare capitated care. *N Engl J Med.* 1998;339:1933–1938.
22. Hagland M. Risk adjustment: Medicare's latest move to tinker with your income. *Med Econ.* June 19, 2000:45–52.
23. Rose JR. Reimbursement. Physicians may find these plans more to their liking. *Med Econ.* July 10, 2000:25.
24. Holahan J, Liska D. The slowdown in Medicaid spending growth: Will it continue? *Health Aff (Millwood).* 1997;16(2):157–163.

25. Norton S, Zuckerman S. Trends in Medicaid physician fees, 1993–1998. *Health Aff (Millwood).* 2000;19(4):222–232.
26. Fox M, Phua K. *Do Increases in Payments for Obstetrical Deliveries Affect Prenatal Care?* Public Health Rep 110, no. 3: 1995;319–326.
27. Cohen JW, Cunningham PJ. Medicaid physicians' fee levels and children's access to care. *Health Aff (Millwood).* Spring 1995:255–262.
28. Gray GH, Rowe C. Safety-net health plans: A status report. *Health Aff (Millwood).* 2000;19(1): 185–193.
29. Bodenheimer T. The Oregon health plan—Lessons for the nation. *N Engl J Med.* 1997;337: 651–654.
30. Welch HG, Larson EB. Dealing with limited resources: The Oregon decision to curtail funding for organ transplantation. *N Engl J Med.* 1988;319:171–173.
31. Tengs TO, Meyer G, Siegel JE, Pliskin JS, Graham JD, Weinstein MC. Oregon's Medicaid ranking and cost-effectiveness: Is there any relationship? *Med Decis Making.* 1996;16:99–107.
32. Jonsen A. Bentham in a box: Technology assessment and health care allocation. *Law, Med, Health Care.* 1986;14(3–4):172–174.
33. Loewy E. Society, physicians and ethics committees: Incorporating ideas of justice into patient care decisions. *Camb Q Healthc Ethics.* 1996;5:559–569.
34. Saultz J. Personal communication. October 13, 2000.
35. Health care fraud settlements. *Fam Pract News.* 2000;30(7):65.
36. Medicare fraud and the mob. *Fam Pract News.* December 15, 1999:33.
37. Morreim E. Gaming the system: Dodging the rules, ruling the dodgers. *Arch Intern Med.* 1991;151:443–447.
38. Lo B. Misrepresenting the patient's condition to gain benefits. In: *Resolving Ethical Dilemmas: A Guide for Clinicians.* Baltimore: Williams and Wilkins; 1995:223–229.
39. Wynia MK, Cummins DS, Van Geest JB, Wilson IB. Physician manipulation of reimbursement rules for patients: Between a rock and a hard place. *JAMA.* 2000;283:1858–1865.
40. Zimmerman R. Drug spending soared 17.4 percent during 1999. *Wall Street Journal.* June 27, 2000:A3,6.
41. Update. Prescription drugs. Hard to swallow: Rising drug prices for America's seniors. *Health Aff (Millwood).* 2000;19(1):254.
42. Prescription drug expenditures increase more than 24%. *Med Benefits.* 2000;17(3):5.
43. McGinley L, Zimmerman R. High U.S. drug prices may give pharmaceutical makers a migraine. *Wall Street Journal.* July 21, 2000:B1, B4.
44. McGinley L. Senate approves measure on import of cheap drugs. *Wall Street Journal.* July 20, 2000:A8.
45. Noonan D. The real drug war. *Med Benefits.* 2000;17(10):11.
46. Cost overdose. Growth in drug spending for the elderly, 1992–2010. *Med Benefits.* 2000;17(6):9–10.
47. Newhouse JP. Switching health plans to obtain drug coverage. *JAMA.* 2000;283:2161–2162.
48. Rector TS. Exhaustion of drug benefits and disenrollment of Medicare beneficiaries from managed care organizations. *JAMA.* 2000;283:2163–2167.
49. Woolhandler S, Himmelstein DU. *The National Health Program Slideshow Guide.* Cambridge, MA: The Center for National Health Program Studies, 2000.
50. Murray S, Lagnado L. Drug companies face assault on prices. *Wall Street Journal.* May 11, 2000:B1.
51. Press N, Burke W. If you care about women's health, perhaps you should ask about the risk of direct marketing of tamoxifen to consumers. *Effect Clin Pract.* 2000;3(2):98–104.
52. Adams C. FDA scrambles to police drug ads' truthfulness. *Wall Street Journal.* January 2, 2001:A24.
53. Murray S. Drug companies are spending record amounts on lobbying and campaign contributions. *Wall Street Journal.* July 7, 2000:A14.50.
54. High-tech stealth being used to sway doctor prescriptions. Available at: http://www.nytimes.com/2000/11/16/science/16PRES.html.
55. Angell M. The pharmaceutical industry—To whom is it accountable? Reply letter to editor. *N Engl J Med.* 2000;343:1417.
56. Harris G. New script. Drug firms, stymied in the lab, become marketing machines. *Wall Street Journal.* July 6, 2000:A1, A12.
57. McGinley L. Patent laws are questioned in drug study. *Wall Street Journal.* July 24, 2000:A3, A6.
58. Lilly sues drug maker in Prozac patent battle. *Wall Street Journal.* August 15, 2000:A16.

59. Merck-Medco. Your Rx plan prescription drug survey. *Med Benefits.* 2001;18(1):6.
60. McGinley L, Cloud D. Medicare to overhaul drug payments. *Wall Street Journal.* May 30, 2000:A3.
61. Heclinger J, Winslow R. Drug makers sue Maine to overturn new pricing law. *Wall Street Journal.* August 15, 2000:B8.
62. Borzo G. Practice trends. Insurer to give bonuses for curbing drug costs. *Fam Pract News.* July 1, 2000:34.
63. Winslow R. Blue Cross is launching entity to study drugs. *Wall Street Journal.* May 10, 2000:B2.
64. Solomon DK, Gourley DR, Brown JR, Gourley GA, Humma LM. Technology assessment and the drug use process. *Am J Manag Care.* February 1999;5(2):220–229.
65. Institute for the Future. *Health and Health Care 2010: The Forecast, the Challenge.* San Francisco: Jossey-Bass, 2000.
66. Luft HS, Grumbach K. Global budgets and the competitive market. In: Ginsberg E (ed). *Critical Issues in U.S. Health Reform.* Boulder, CO: Westview Press, 1994:319–320.
67. Hipshman L. Poor little rich men. *Health Aff (Millwood).* 2000;19(4):275–276.

17
Attempts to Improve Access to Health Care

> The plight of the uninsured is tolerated by Americans not because Americans are unusually callous toward the poor, but in part because the American health system has priced kindness out of the nation's soul.
>
> Uwe Reinhardt[1]

As we saw in Chapter 8, the United States has a persistent problem with access to health care by a large part of the population. We reviewed some of the complexities of the access problem, including the detrimental impact on the health status of those affected. We also touched on the two most important advances of the last 40 years in terms of increasing access to health care, the Medicare and Medicaid programs enacted in 1965, as well as the increasing fragility of the employer-based insurance system. This chapter builds on that background in an effort to (1) present a current portrait of the uninsured and underinsured population in the United States in 2000; (2) summarize the major efforts in the 1990s by federal and state governments, as well as the private sector, to increase access to health care; and (3) briefly consider projected trends for access to health care between now and 2010.

THE UNINSURED AND UNDERINSURED: A DIVERSE AND GROWING POPULATION

The picture is disturbing now and shows every sign of becoming more so. Despite the boom economy since the 1980s, together with low rates of unemployment, we have a three-tiered health care system solidly in place. Prevailing political rhetoric continues to espouse the ideal of a one-tiered system, but the reality is quite the opposite. Table 17-1 outlines three tiers of coverage within the U.S. population, including a disenfranchised group of over one quarter of the population and another one third who are insecurely franchised. The top tier comprises the affluent and the securely employed, who now have fewer

Table 17-1 The Tiers of Coverage

	Traditional Consumers	*New Consumers*
The securely enfranchised (roughly 38% of total U.S. population) Total U.S. population 1999 = 273,652,000	Age 18 to 64, no college education, high-income workers (and spouses) with no PCs but high job security, with private managed care plans or fee-for-service insurance (paid by employers or self)	Age 18 to 64, college-educated, high-income workers (and spouses) with high job security, with private managed care plans or fee-for-service insurance (paid by employers or by self)
	Age 65+, no college education, moderate to high savings/resources, no PCs, Medicare only or Medicare and private insurance	Age 55 to 64, early retirees, college-educated, high savings/resources, private managed care plans or fee-for-service insurance (paid by generous former employers or by self)
	Children securely insured	Age 65+, college-educated, moderate to high savings/ resources, with PCs, Medicare + private insurance Children securely insured
The insecurely enfranchised (roughly 34% of the total U.S. population)	Age 18 to 64, no college education, low-income workers (and spouses) with low job security, in managed care plans (paid by employers or military)	Age 18 to 64, college-educated, middle-income workers (and spouses) with PCs and low job security, in managed care plans (paid by employers, by military, or by self)
	Age 55 to 64, early retirees, no college education, low to moderate incomes, in managed care plans (paid by former employers who are not reassuring about keeping retiree benefits, or have already tried to reduce them)	Age 55 to 64, early retirees, college-educated, high incomes, in managed care plans (paid by former employers who are not reassuring about keeping retiree benefits, or have already tried to reduce them)
	Children securely insured	Age 18 to 54, no college education, high-income but low job security workers (and spouses), with PCs, in managed care plans (paid by employers) Children securely insured
The disenfranchised (roughly 28% of total U.S. population)	Age 18 to 64, no college education, unemployed and/or very poor, uninsured or on Medicaid	Age 18 to 34, temporarily uninsured, some college, with PCs. No full-time job yet or between early low income jobs.
	Children uninsured Children on Medicaid or other government assistance	

PC indicates ownership of a computer as a marker for some experience with information technology.

Source: Reprinted with permission from Institute for the Future. *Health and Health Care 2010: The Forecast, the Challenges.* San Francisco: Jossey-Bass, 2000:130.

restrictions on their care. The middle tier includes working Americans, whose benefits are threatened by job insecurity, low re-employability, benefit cuts by employers, or increasing difficulty in paying the larger insurance premiums being passed on by their employers. Age, race, education, and income level influence the insecurity of benefits.[2] The bottom tier is a growing group without access to mainstream health care who are either uninsured or on Medicaid and may or may not be served by an unreliable safety net.[2] The bottom tier includes an increasing number of people who have filed for bankruptcy, one quarter of whom were forced into bankruptcy by illness or injury.[3]

According to the U.S. Census Bureau, 42.6 million Americans were without health insurance for all of 1999 (15.5 percent of the population). This number decreased (from 16.3 percent in 1998) for the first time since 1987, when comparable figures first became available.[4] This decrease is accounted for mostly by expanded enrollment in Medicaid and CHIP.[5] There is wide variation by state in the proportion of the population without health insurance, ranging from a low of 6.9 percent in Rhode Island to a high of 25.8 percent in New Mexico.[4]

Having a job no longer correlates well with access to health care. As the Institute for the Future observed, the portion of the nation's workforce that is uninsured is growing, including workers who are self-employed, working part-time, multiple jobs, or are temporary workers (Figure 17-1).[2] The recently reported National Survey on the Uninsured, conducted by the Kaiser Family Foundation, revealed that 44 percent of almost 2,000 uninsured adults between 18 and 65 years of age are working full time, with an additional 17 percent working part time.[6] It has become a myth that lack of health insurance correlates exclusively with being poor. In California, as well as nationally, 40 percent of the uninsured have family incomes at least twice the federal poverty level,

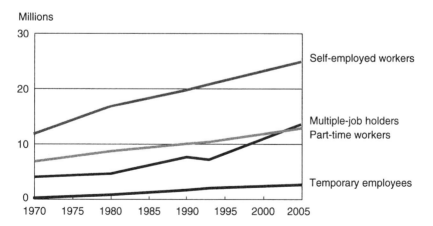

Figure 17-1 The flexible workforce is growing quickly. (Source: Institute for the Future; U.S. Bureau of Labor Statistics, Employment and Earnings. Reprinted with permission from Institute for the Future. *Health and Health Care 2010: The Forecast, the Challenges.* San Francisco: Jossey-Bass, 2000:123–137.)

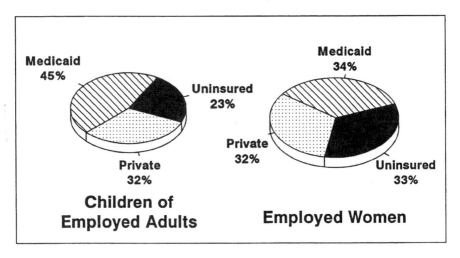

Figure 17-2 Former welfare recipients: Jobs may not bring coverage. (Source: Garrett B, Holahan J. Health insurance coverage after welfare. *Health Aff (Millwood)*. 2000;19(1):175. Reprinted with permission from Woolhandler S, Himmelstein DU. *The National Health Program Slideshow Guide*. Cambridge, MA: The Center for National Health Program Studies, 2000.)

while one quarter have family incomes of at least 300 percent of poverty levels.[7,8] The federal poverty level in 1998 was $17,000 for a single person and $33,000 for a family of four.[9]

Another recent study, conducted by Families USA, shows that many families lose health care coverage when returning to work as a result of "welfare reform." Almost a million low-income parents lost Medicaid coverage after moving from welfare to work. In many states, parents working full time for the minimum wage of $5.15 an hour could not qualify for Medicaid because of too much income but still couldn't afford private insurance.[10] Figure 17-2 shows the extent to which former welfare recipients lose health care insurance after joining the workforce.[11,12]

The consequences of a lack of insurance is well illustrated by the findings of the National Access to Care Survey, in which uninsured participants were asked whether they had experienced any of 15 highly serious or morbid symptoms; if so, whether they had received medical care; and if not, whether care was considered necessary. For those 15 presenting complaints, medical care was received by almost twice as many insured as uninsured (45.5 versus 24.3 percent). Care was considered necessary but not received for 13.6 percent of symptoms of the insured compared to 30.1 percent for the uninsured. Almost two thirds of uninsured not receiving care stated that not receiving care affected their health, with 57 percent feeling that they had personal, household, or work problems as a result.[13]

On the other side of the ledger, even those with health insurance increasingly find that some health care services no longer are covered, if they once were, as employers cut benefits and pass along more costs of care to their employees. In addition, for many years, some health care services, such as mental health care, have fallen far short of parity or equity with general medical care.[14] A recent study by the Kaiser Family Foundation found that one half of insured adults under age 65 reported some kind of problem with their health plan over the last year.[15]

SOME RECENT APPROACHES TO THE "ACCESS PROBLEM"

As the uninsured population continues to grow unabated and as other population groups experience or perceive access problems despite having various forms of insurance coverage, the government at the federal and state levels, as well as the private sector, have initiated various pragmatic responses to these problems. At best, some of these efforts had moderate success, others made no difference, and still others had unintended consequences. A brief review of the highlights of some of these efforts shows that more fundamental changes are required.

The Public Sector

Recent Federal Legislation

Health Insurance Portability and Accountability Act of 1996
The Health Insurance Portability and Accountability Act of 1996 (HIPAA), also known as the Kassebaum-Kennedy act, for their sponsors in the Senate, has been hailed as the most significant effort of the 1990s. The bill[16]

creates the first national standards for the availability and portability of group and individual health insurance coverage, relies on the states as well as the federal government to enforce these standards, begins the development of federal policy for the electronic transfer of medical information, provides tax incentives to purchase long-term care insurance, increases the tax deductibility of health insurance premiums paid by self-employed persons, permits terminally and chronically ill persons to receive life insurance benefits tax-free, and strengthens federal authority to regulate health care fraud and abuse.

HIPPA was passed by Congress with bipartisan support after much debate on some of its provisions. It set standards for health insurance coverage in five areas, to be regulated and enforced by both the federal government and the states. The highlights of the major provisions are presented here in abbreviated form:[16]

1. *Preexisting conditions.* Group health insurers (including HMOs and self-insured employers) may not limit or deny coverage for preexisting conditions for more than 12 months; after that waiting period, full coverage is "portable" if the employee changes jobs or the employer changes health plans.

2. *Availability of coverage for small employers.* Insurance carriers and health plans cannot refuse to offer small-group products to employers with 2 to 50 employees.
3. *Availability of coverage for individuals.* Insurers and health plans must offer coverage to persons who have had group health insurance for at least 18 months, who have exhausted coverage under the Consolidated Omnibus Budget Reconciliation Act of 1985 (COBRA), and who are ineligible for coverage under any other employment-based health plan.
4. *Discrimination based on health status.* Employers who offer health coverage may not exclude, or drop, an employee or dependent from coverage, or charge an employee higher premiums because of the history or health status of that employee or dependent.
5. *Renewability.* As long as premiums are paid, insurers may not drop coverage to employers, except in instances of fraud or misrepresentation by an employer.

Four years after its passage, the results of HIPAA are a mixed story. Without delving into the many complexities of this experience, several overall conclusions clearly can be drawn. On the plus side, HIPAA provides broad guarantees for group coverage, including standards for pre-existing condition exclusions that are uniform for insured and self-funded plans throughout the country. Before the passage of HIPAA, the federal government had largely deferred to the states for regulation of private health insurance, with the exception of the Employee Retirement Income Security Act of 1974 (ERISA), by which self-funded employer health plans were exempted from state regulation. With HIPAA, some minimum protections were established to cover the 48 million Americans previously exempted by ERISA, as well as consumers in other federally and state-regulated health plans. Group coverage was defined down to groups as small as two in many cases, and over 120 million people with private employer coverage became less likely to lose insurance coverage after a change of health status. A major goal of the legislation was to alleviate "job lock" (i.e., the hesitancy of employees to leave or change jobs because of fear over loss of coverage due to a new presenting condition exclusion period). Table 17-2 shows the number of states that have adopted various provisions of HIPAA.

On the negative side of the ledger, however, HIPAA has been disappointing in some respects. It has not been very effective in the individual market, especially since Congress had avoided (intentionally) any regulation of rating practices. For example, insurance is not really accessible to an individual if the insurer increases the rates by 2,000 percent after a change in health status, as was documented in one state. In addition, some states do not trust or welcome federal involvement in their regulatory responsibilities, and Congress did not appropriate funds for oversight, enforcement, and public education.[17]

Mental Health Parity Act of 1996

Insurance coverage for mental health care has been difficult to obtain for many years and, when available, typically had more limitations placed on it than for general medical coverage. Various historical factors have perpetuated this problem, including fear by insurers of experiencing escalating demand for ser-

Table 17-2   Selected State Small-Group Market Reforms, 1996

Provision	Number of States
States with some small-group market reforms	49
Small-group definition	
Includes groups of 2	33
Includes groups of 50	27
Guaranteed issue of all products	14
Guaranteed renewability	48
Limits on pre-existing condition exclusion periods	
Maximum exclusion period of 12 months or less	46
Maximum look back of 6 months or less	31
HIPAA-like definition of pre-existing condition	13
Creditable coverage defined similarly to HIPAA	19
Small-group rating limits (some or all products)	
Community rating or modified community rating	15
Rating bands	34

Note: Prior to passage of the Health Insurance Portability and Accountability Act (HIPPA) of 1996.

Source: Institute for Health Policy Solutions; and Georgetown University. Reprinted with permission from Pollitz K, Tapay N, Hadley E, Specht J. Early experience with "new federalism" in health insurance regulation. *Health Aff (Millwood).* 2000;19(4):11.

vices, adverse selection, and the existence of a long-standing safety net system for mental health care in the public sector.[18] In an effort to alleviate this disparity, the Mental Health Parity Act was passed in 1996 as the Domenici-Wellstone amendment to an appropriations bill. The bill took effect in January 1998, prohibiting larger, employer-based health plans (those covering more than 50 employees) from imposing lifetime caps and annual reimbursement ceilings for mental health services that are different from caps for other medical and surgical services. The scope of this bill was somewhat limited, however, since health plans that provided mental health coverage still could drop that coverage altogether and place annual day and visit limitations on covered services.[18] Although this legislation was not expected to fully redress long-standing inequities in coverage for mental health disorders, its passage was an important milestone in mental health care.

It is much too early to assess the impact of the Domenici-Wellstone bill, but there is good evidence that disparities and inequities remain for mental health services. Definitions of *parity* have been controversial. A 1997 study showed that at least three quarters of employer-sponsored health plans impose more restrictions on mental health coverage than on general medical coverage. Typical annual restrictions were 30 days for inpatient care and 24 days for outpatient visits. For those plans setting dollar limits, typical lifetime limits were $25,000 for both inpatient and outpatient care.[19] Another recent study found that the percentage of health plans placing day limits on inpatient psychiatric care increased from 38 percent in 1988 to 57 percent in 1997; for limits on outpatient visits, the corresponding increase was from 26 to 48 percent over that period.[20]

State Children's Health Insurance Program

Another important federal initiative was enacted in 1997 to assist in providing care to children without health insurance. The State Children's Health Insurance Program (CHIP) was passed as part of the Balanced Budget Act (BBA97). CHIP appropriated $20.3 billion in federal matching funds as block grants to states for the years 1997 to 2002, with another $20 billion planned for another five-year period beyond 2002. CHIP targets uninsured children in families with family incomes below 200 percent of poverty level. States have flexibility in implementing CHIP, including expansion of Medicaid, establishing a new program, or combining the two.[21] Despite federal efforts started in the late 1980s to expand Medicaid, it is estimated that about 10 million children in the United States still were uninsured in 1996.[22] It is not yet clear how many of these will receive coverage under CHIP, but there already are concerns that only a small fraction of these will become insured.[21] CHIP will be tracked to see how effective this block grant program can be in extending health care coverage to an uninsured population by this flexible approach, including whether or not it results in "crowding out" private insurance coverage. Barbara Starfield cautioned that evaluation of the program needs to go beyond mere coverage to assess the extent to which covered children actually receive high-quality primary care, with appropriate referral as needed.[23]

A Core Safety Net

Although fragile and loosely woven, a core safety net in the United States serves a wide range of vulnerable populations (Table 17-3). The safety net includes a patchwork system of federal, state, and local programs, including community health centers, public hospitals (and their emergency rooms and outpatient clinics), local health departments, not-for-profit community hospitals, and urban teaching hospitals. Other federally sponsored safety net health services are provided by the National Health Service Corps (NHSC), the Indian Health Service (IHS), the Veterans Health Administration, and school-based health centers. In addition, the number of state scholarship, loan forgiveness, and related programs doubled between 1990 and 1996. By 1996, these state programs had grown to over 1,300 physicians and 370 medical practitioners practicing in underserved areas as part of the core safety net.[24]

Financing mechanisms vary considerably among these safety net programs. Funding often is a tenuous mix of federal, state, and local funding sources. Managed care delivery systems play an increasing role in many safety net programs, including a growing number of community health centers.[25]

Medicaid and Related State Programs

Since its enactment in the mid-1960s, the Medicaid program has taken a turbulent, variable, and often controversial course and remains a fragile work in progress today. Nevertheless, it provides last-resort health care coverage for about one in eight Americans, and is the mainstay of whatever safety net exists around the country.[26] A snapshot of this program in the 1990s is essential to any assessment of the access problem today.

Table 17-3 The Core Safety Net Serves a Wide Range
of Vulnerable Populations

Uninsured and underinsured
  Working poor whose employers do not offer insurance
  Non-Medicaid-covered unemployed poor
  Children who are not included in parents' coverage
  Adults who cannot afford employer-sponsored coverage
Medicaid beneficiaries
Chronically ill individuals
People with disabilities
Mentally ill individuals
People with communicable diseases (e.g., HIV infection/
  AIDS or tuberculosis)
Legal and undocumented immigrants
Minorities
Native Americans
Veterans
Homeless people
Substance abusers
Prisoners

Source: Reprinted from Altman S, Reinhardt U, Shields A (eds). *The Future
of the U.S. Healthcare System: Who Will Care for the Poor and Uninsured?*
Chicago: Health Administration Press, 1998.

Although many perceive the Medicaid program as mostly involved with acute care services of adults and children, this has not been the case for years. Medicaid has become the largest payer of nursing home costs, accounting for 50 percent of these payments in 1995.[27] In addition to long-term care coverage, Medicaid covers large numbers of low-income elderly, blind, and disabled people. Among the 36.3 million enrollees in Medicaid in 1995, blind and disabled beneficiaries accounted for one third of Medicaid expenditures, while elderly beneficiaries received one quarter of expenditures in that year.[26]

Although public and policy attention has focused more on children than adults in recent years (e.g., the CHIP program), three quarters of the uninsured are nonelderly adults.[28] Federal matching funds to the states range from 50 to 77 percent. Eligibility for nonelderly adults is limited to single parents, pregnant women, couples with an unemployed primary earner, and the disabled.[29]

A major goal of Medicaid is to address coverage gaps within the states—that percentage of the state's population without coverage by private insurance, Medicare, or military-related coverage. Table 17-4 shows the extent to which Medicaid dealt with coverage gaps in 13 states in 1996. Only one in five uninsured Americans was covered by Medicaid or other state programs in 1996. In addition, there were wide differences among the states in extent of coverage, ranging from Texas on the low side to Minnesota on the high side.[29]

Expansion of the Medicaid program can be credited with slowing the rising rate of loss of employer-sponsored health insurance during the late 1980s and

Table 17-4   Role of Medicaid and State Programs in Filling the Coverage Gap, 1996

State Group	Coverage Gap[a]	Percent Covered by Medicaid or State Programs	Percent of Coverage Gap Filled
U.S. total	21.3%	4.3%	20.2%
Limited (mean)	26.4	3.5	13.3
TX	30.4[b]	3.5	11.5
FL	24.5	3.3	13.6
MS	25.9	5.6[b]	21.8[b]
AL	21.7[b]	3.8	17.5
CO	18.6[b]	2.4[b]	13.0
Moderate (mean)	22.4[c]	5.0[c]	22.2[c]
CA	27.6[b]	6.0[b]	21.6
NJ	16.4[b]	3.3[b]	20.0
MI	15.7[b]	4.6	29.2[b]
WI	12.2[b]	2.4[b]	19.3
Comprehensive (mean)	20.2[d]	6.1[d]	30.2[d]
NY	23.4[b]	7.0[b]	30.2
WA	19.8	5.6	28.5
MA	15.5[b]	4.0[b]	25.7
MN	14.5[b]	5.7	39.3[b]

[a] Percent of the nonelderly population not covered by private insurance, Medicare, or military-related coverage.

[b] State value is statistically different from group mean at the .05 level.

[c] Statistically different from group mean for limited states at the .05 level.

[d] Statistically different from group mean for both limited and moderate states at the .05 level.

Source: Tabulations from the 1997 National Survey of American Families. Reprinted with permission from Spillman BC. Adults without health insurance: Do state policies matter? *Health Aff (Millwood).* 2000;19(4):182.

early 1990s, but those gains were short lived. Despite a strong economy, the uninsurance rate has continued to grow. This has been due to several recent trends, including declines of Medicaid enrollment (by 3.3 million between 1994 and 1998, probably related to welfare reform) as well as decreasing private non-group coverage. Table 17-5 gives a national overview of the extent of health insurance coverage by source and income levels for 1994 and 1998, with uninsurance rates increasing in each income category.[30]

The connection of Medicaid to safety net plans varies greatly from one state to another. Medicaid experimented with many managed care plans around the country, but many of the Medicaid HMOs entering the market in the early 1990s have left as a result of financial losses. These departures raised major concerns about the commitment of commercial HMOs to care of Medicaid enrollees.[31] A 1998 national survey of 80 operational Medicaid managed care plans found that 60 percent of these safety net plans lost money in 1997, so the future viability of them is in doubt.[32]

With regard to the CHIP program, although about 2 million children had been enrolled by mid-2000, the number of uninsured children was not declining. This is due mainly to erosion of private sector coverage for low-income families, who cannot afford increasing employee shares of employer-based coverage

Table 17-5 Health Insurance Coverage Among Children and Adults, by Income Category, 1994–1998

	Children			Adults		
	Coverage Distribution within Income Category		Change in Millions of Persons	Coverage Distribution within Income Category		Change in Millions of Persons
Coverage Source	1994	1998	1994–98	1994	1998	1994–98
All incomes	73.9[a]	76.0[a]	2.1	165.8[a]	162.6[a]	6.8
Employer	60.50%	63.2%[b]	3.3[c]	66.0%	67.0%[b]	6.1[c]
Medicaid	18.1	15.2[b]	−1.9[c]	6.2	5.2[b]	−1.2[c]
Other public	2.4	2.0[b]	−0.2[c]	2.9	2.6[b]	−0.3[c]
Private nongroup	4.5	4.0[b]	−0.3[c]	6.3	5.5[b]	−0.8[c]
Uninsured	14.5	15.6[b]	1.2[c]	18.6	19.7[b]	3.0[c]
Less than 200% of poverty	34.6[a]	33.0[a]	−1.7	53.0[a]	49.5[a]	−3.5
Employer	32.4%	34.6%[b]	0.2	32.4%	32.1%	−1.3[c]
Medicaid	37.1	33.0	−2.0[c]	17.0	15.5[b]	−1.3[c]
Other public	2.7	2.3	−0.2[c]	5.0	4.9	−0.2
Private nongroup	4.3	3.6	−0.3[c]	8.5	7.5[b]	−0.8[c]
Uninsured	23.4	25.6[b]	0.6[c]	37.2	40.1[b]	0.2
200–399% of poverty	22.9[a]	23.2[a]	0.2	48.6[a]	49.1[a]	0.5
Employer	81.8%	81.2%	0.0	76.8%	74.8%[b]	−0.6
Medicaid	1.9	2.4	0.1	1.1	1.3	0.1
Other public	2.7	2.3	−0.1	2.4	2.1	−0.1
Private nongroup	4.9	4.6	−0.1	6.0	5.6	−0.2
Uninsured	8.6	9.7[b]	0.3[c]	13.8	16.2[b]	1.3[c]
400% or more of poverty	16.4[a]	19.9[a]	3.5	54.2[a]	64.0[a]	9.8
Employer	90.3%	89.8%	3.1[c]	89.1%	88.1%[b]	8.1[c]
Medicaid	0.8	0.6	0.0	0.3	0.2	0.0
Other public	1.0	1.2	0.1	1.3	1.1	0.0
Private nongroup	4.4	3.9	0.1	4.4	4.0[b]	0.1
Uninsured	3.7	4.5[b]	0.3[c]	4.9	6.6[b]	1.5[c]

Note: Excludes persons aged 65 and older and those in the armed forces.

[a] Millions of persons.

[b] Difference in percentages between 1994 and 1998 is statistically significant at the .10 level.

[c] Change in numbers of persons between 1994 and 1998 is statistically at the .10 level.

Source: Urban Institute, 1999, based on data from March Current Population Surveys, 1995–1999. Reprinted with permission from Holahan J, Kim J. Why does the number of uninsured Americans continue to grow? *Health Aff (Millwood).* 2000;19(4):192.

(often in the 30 to 40 percent range). It is estimated that as many as 21 million children in the United States (of a 74 million total) are experiencing significant access problems.[33]

Although Medicaid has served the country as the ultimate safety net for more than 30 years, the program is plagued by problems, including widely variable commitment and policies among states, difficulty in coordinating 150 related programs, provider resistance, and tension between federal and state governments.[26] Medicaid coverage still does not assure access to care. A 1994 national study, for example, found that acceptance of Medicaid patients ranged from 70 percent in Boston, Massachusetts, to 22 percent in Sacramento, California.[34]

The Private Sector

Many physicians and other health care professionals provide uncompensated care on a charitable basis to individual patients without the financial resources to pay for needed care. A national study by the Center for Studying Health System Change, for example, found that over one third of uninsured respondents reported having a physician's office as their usual source of care.[24] The AMA's Socioeconomic Monitoring System showed that, in 1994, physicians provided at least as much uncompensated care as U.S. hospitals.[35]

Larger and more organized approaches to the access problem in the private sector, however, are scarce. A notable exception is Reach Out, a $12 million national program established by the Robert Wood Johnson Foundation in 1993. The goal of this program is to complement publicly funded safety net providers by expanding the capacity of the private sector to provide care for the underserved. By mid-1999, 37 Reach Out projects were operational, involving almost 200,000 enrolled patients. The two most common models were free clinics and referral networks. The projects depend largely on voluntary service by physicians and other health professionals. Pharmacy assistance programs have been developed in some of these projects, and in some instances, statewide formularies have been established for project enrollees. It appears that two thirds of the Reach Out projects will be self-sustaining beyond grant support, with a transition to funding by local foundations and public agencies. While this kind of program cannot solve the larger national access problem, it has demonstrated the remarkable potential of the private sector to contribute to the public need on a local and regional basis.[36]

FUTURE PROJECTIONS

The Robert Wood Johnson Foundation, with its long concern for the problems of restricted access to health care in the United States, on the occasion of the foundation's 25th anniversary, asked the Institute for the Future to forecast its best estimate for the landscape of the health care system in 2010. Its forecast is represented in Figure 17-3, again in terms of three tiers of insurance, including a smaller carriage trade sector (fee-for-service and PPO), a larger tier of sequels of today's HMOs, and a stable lower tier of about 20 percent of Americans of the uninsured and Medicaid enrollees. The institute readily acknowledges, however, that the following six "wild cards" easily could alter its projections:[2]

1997 2007

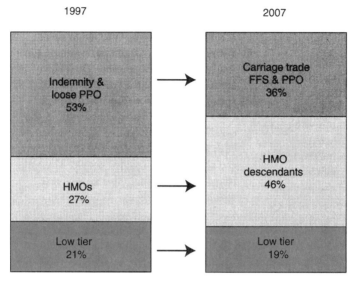

Figure 17-3 Tiers 'R' us . . . and will be. (Source: Institute for the Future. Reprinted with permission from Institute for the Future. *Health and Health Care 2010: The Forecast, the Challenges.* San Francisco: Jossey-Bass, 2000;123–137.)

1. A severe, protracted recession increases the number of uninsured and Medicaid eligibles by 75 percent each.
2. Universal health insurance legislation is enacted, reducing the number of uninsured to nearly zero.
3. Health insurance premiums become a taxable benefit; employers stop providing coverage and abandon the market as purchasers.
4. Medical savings accounts (MSAs), vouchers for Medicare, and other individual-based buying become significant forces, changing the group nature of the insurance market.
5. HMO enrollment growth in either Medicare or the commercial market slows substantially or even declines due to legislative, market, or other pressures.
6. A national health insurance system is adopted; private-sector insurance is eliminated.

The question of universal access warrants further comment. Although neither of the two major political parties took on this issue during campaign 2000, momentum is gathering in some quarters for bringing this goal to the front burner of the American health care agenda. Some states are developing ballot initiatives for universal coverage. There also is steadily increasing support within medicine for a national system of universal coverage. The Physicians for a National Health Program (PNHP) was founded in 1987, published its classic proposal for a national health program in 1989,[37] and has since grown to a membership of almost 9,000 U.S. physicians. More recently, a Physicians' Work Group on Universal Coverage (PWGUC) was formed. It now includes seven national medical organizations (including the AMA) and lobbied for universal health care coverage to take the No. 1 priority in the 2000 presidential campaign.[38] A recent survey has shown that 57 percent of medical school deans, department chairs, residency directors, physician faculty, residents, and medical students favor a single-payer system over both managed care and fee-for-service options.[39]

CONCLUDING COMMENTS

Although this chapter deals in large part with the problems of the uninsured and underinsured, adequate access to health care requires more than insurance coverage from either a private or public source. In an excellent recent paper, John Eisenberg and Elaine Power draw the analogy between health care access and an electrical system in which current passes through resistance, with voltage drops along the way. They correctly point out that access may be blocked, even for the insured, by "voltage drops" at these five points (Figure 17-4):[40]

1. Enrollment in available insurance plans.
2. Access to covered services, clinicians, and health care institutions.
3. Choice of plans, providers, and institutions.
4. Access to a consistent source of primary care.
5. Access to referral services.

We have seen, for example, the negative impact on access of geographic and specialty maldistribution of physicians (Chapter 4) as well as a comparatively weak primary care base compared to other industrialized nations with better performing health care systems. (Chapter 13).

This chapter provides abundant evidence that the U.S. health care "system" is failing badly in terms of access to care, just as the preceding chapter demonstrated for cost containment. Fundamental reform to assure universal access is

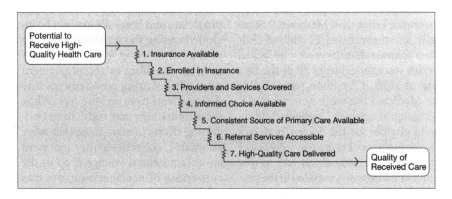

Figure 17-4   The cascade of voltage drops from insurance to quality health care. (Reprinted with permission from Eisenberg JM, Power EJ. Transforming insurance coverage into quality health care: Voltage drops from potential to delivered quality. *JAMA.* 2000;284:2100–2107.)

needed urgently for our ailing health care system with its leaky access sieve, as is revisited in Chapters 22 and 24. In the meantime, whatever can be done to strengthen the core safety net is worth doing. A good example of an important interim initiative is the recently established Community Access Program, a new federal program intended to strengthen the safety net through such means as improved information systems and language access programs.[41]

The next chapter deals with the third key component of the "iron triangle"—quality—and again we find major problems.

REFERENCES

1. Reinhardt UE. Publications and Reports. The future U.S. health care system: Who will care for the poor and uninsured? *Health Aff (Millwood)*. 1998;17(1):258.
2. Institute for the Future. *Health and Health Care 2010: The Forecast, the Challenges*. San Francisco: Jossey-Bass, 2000:123–137.
3. Medical problems and bankruptcy filings. *Med Benefits*. 2000;17(4):8.
4. Mills RJ. Health insurance coverage 1999, U.S. Census Bureau. *Med Benefits*. 2000;17(20):9–10.
5. Policy and practice. Medicaid enrollment rises. *Fam Pract News*. 2000;30(22):27.
6. The News Hour with Jim Lehrer and Kaiser Family Foundation, April 2000. *Med Benefits*. 2000;17(12):5–6.
7. Chollet D. Consumers, insurers, and market behavior. *J Health Polit Policy Law*. February 2000:30.
8. Brown ER, Wyn R, Levan R. *The Uninsured in California: Causes, Consequences, and Solutions*. Oakland: California Health Care Foundation, 1997:6.
9. Yegian JM, Pockell DG, Smith MD, Murray EK. The nonpoor uninsured in California, 1998. *Health Aff (Millwood)*. 2000;19(4):171–177.
10. Bowean L. Medicaid study says many parents lose coverage moving from welfare to work. *Wall Street Journal*. June 20, 2000:A4.
11. Garrett B, Holahan J. Health insurance coverage after welfare. *Health Aff (Millwood)*. 2000; 19(1):175–184.
12. Woolhandler S, Himmelstein DU. *The National Health Program Slideshow Guide*. Cambridge, MA: The Center for National Health Program Studies, 2000.
13. Baker DW, Shapiro MF, Schur CL. Health insurance and access to care for symptomatic conditions. *Arch Intern Med*. 2000;160:1269–1274.
14. Burnam MA, Escarce JJ. Equity in managed care for mental disorders. *Health Aff (Millwood)*. 1999;18(5):22–31.
15. National survey of consumer experiences with health plans. *Med Benefits*. 2000;17(13):1.
16. Atchinson BK, Fox DM. The politics of the Health Insurance Portability and Accountability Act. *Health Aff (Millwood)*. 1997;16(3):146–150.
17. Pollitz K, Tapay N, Hadley E, Specht J. Early experience with "new federalism" in health insurance regulation. *Health Aff (Millwood)*. 2000;19(4):7–22.
18. Frank RG, Koyanagi C, McGuire TG. The politics and economics of mental health "parity" laws. *Health Aff (Millwood)*. 1997;16(4):108–119.
19. Buck JA, Teich JL, Umland B, Stein M. Behavioral health benefits in employer-sponsored health plans, 1997. *Health Aff (Millwood)*. 1999;18(2):67–78.
20. *Health Care Plan Design and Cost Trends—1998 Through 1997*. Washington, DC: Hay Group, May 1998.
21. Halfon N, Inkeles M, DuPlessis H, Newacheck PW. Challenges in securing access to care for children. *Health Aff (Millwood)*. 1999;18(2):48–63.
22. Rosenbaum S, Johnson K, Sonosky C, Markus A, DeGraw C. The children's hour: The State Children's Health Insurance Program. *Health Aff (Millwood)*. 1998;17(1):75–89.
23. Starfield B. Evaluating the State Children's Health Insurance Program: Critical considerations. *Annu Rev Public Health*. 2000;21:569–585.
24. Institute of Medicine In: Lewin ME, Altman S (eds). *America's Health Care Safety Net: Intact but Endangered*. Washington, DC: National Academy Press, 2000:47–80.

25. Stacy NL. The experience and performance of community health centers under managed care. *Am J Manage Care.* 2000;6(11):1229–1239.
26. Friedman E. The little engine that could: Medicaid at the millennium. *Front Health Serv Manage.* Summer 1998;14(4):3–24.
27. Schneider A. *Overview of Medicaid Provisions in the Balanced Budget Act of 1997, P.L. 105–33.* Washington, DC: Center on Budget and Policy Priorities, 1997.
28. Vistnes JP, Monheit AC. *Health Insurance Status of the U.S. Civilian Non-institutionalized Population.* MEPS Research Findings no. 1. Publication no. 97 0030. Rockville, MD: Agency for Health Care Policy and Research, 1997.
29. Spillman BC. Adults without health insurance: Do state policies matter? *Health Aff (Millwood).* 2000;19(4):178–187.
30. Holahan J, Kim J. Why does the number of uninsured Americans continue to grow? *Health Aff (Millwood).* 2000;19(4):188–196.
31. McCue MJ, Hurley RE, Draper DA, Jurgensen M. Reversal of fortune: Commercial HMOs in the Medicaid market. *Health Aff (Millwood).* 1999;18(1):223–230.
32. Gray BH, Rowe C. Safety-net health plans: A status report. *Health Aff (Millwood).* 2000;19(1):185–193.
33. Friedrich MJ. Medically underserved children need more than insurance card. *JAMA.* 2000; 283:3056–3057.
34. Medicaid Access Study Group. Access of Medicaid recipients to outpatient care. *N Engl J Med.* 1994;330:1426–1430.
35. Cunningham PJ, Tu HT. A changing picture of uncompensated care. *Health Aff (Millwood).* 1997;16(4):167–175.
36. Scott HD, Bell J, Geller S, Thomas M. Physicians helping the underserved: The Reach Out program. *JAMA.* 2000;283:99–104.
37. Himmelstein DU, Woolhandler S, and the Writing Committee of the Working Group on Program Design. A national health program for the United States: A physician's proposal. *N Engl J Med.* 1989;320:102–108.
38. Finger AL. Caring for the uninsured: Will the problem ever be solved? *Med Econ.* December 20, 1999:132–141.
39. Simon SR, Pan RJ, Sullivan AM, et al. Views of managed care: A survey of students, residents, faculty and deans at medical schools in the U.S. *N Engl J Med.* 1999;340:928–936.
40. Eisenberg JM, Power EJ. Transforming insurance coverage into quality health care: Voltage drops from potential to delivered quality. *JAMA.* 2000;284:2100–2107.
41. Lurie N. Strengthening the U.S. health care safety net. *JAMA.* 2000;284:2112–2114.

18

The Quality of Health Care:
Myths, Reality, and Approaches
to Improvement

> The health care backpack is full of useless assumptions so old and so often repeated that they become facts from the mouth of Hippocrates and to question them risks one's relationships with co-professionals, but we are going to have to question them.
>
> Don Berwick, president and CEO, Institute for Health Care[1]

Concerns about quality have become central to the U.S. health care debate in recent years, at times to the point of overshadowing discussion of costs and access. Report cards on health plans, hospitals, medical groups, and sometimes even individual physicians are circulated widely.[2] Why this sea change, and why now?

Many interrelated factors have come together in bringing about the new emphasis on quality. The traditional perception that American health care is the best in the world no longer is defensible, as reports accumulate of its serious deficits compared to many other countries. As cost containment efforts proceed, health care purchasers seek more value for their money. Consumers, whether health plans, employers, or patients, demand more evidence of quality, and recent advances in quality assessment, outcomes research, and information technology can provide some needed benchmarks of quality.[2-5]

Prevailing worries about the quality of U.S. health care are paradoxical in view of the nation's remarkable technical and scientific strengths and potential to provide excellent care to some people, but the health care system does not fare well in terms of making such care widely available to the population.

To portray the current quality of U.S. health care, this chapter takes on five goals: (1) to examine the myths versus realities of its quality, (2) to discuss how *quality* is being defined, (3) to outline briefly some methods of measuring quality, (4) to review the major directions being taken in the private and public sectors to improve quality, and (5) to consider the lessons learned from these efforts.

QUALITY OF AMERICAN HEALTH CARE: MYTHS VERSUS REALITY

Largely because of the scientific prowess and expertise concentrated in highly specialized U.S. hospitals, for many years there has been a tendency for Americans to perceive their health care to be of the highest quality. This perception no longer holds up to rigorous scrutiny, if it ever did. Mark Schuster, E. A. McGlynn, and R. H. Brook, at RAND and the University of California, Los Angeles, recently did a thorough review of the quality-of-care literature for preventive, acute, and chronic care. Averaging out the results of many studies, they found that about 50 percent of people received recommended preventive care, while 70 percent received recommended acute care, and 60 percent received recommended chronic care. Contraindicated care was received by 30 percent of patients for acute care and 20 percent of patients for chronic care. They also found wide variations in quality of care among hospitals, cities, and states, as well as a large amount of inappropriate, nonbeneficial, and potentially harmful care.[6]

As discussed in Chapter 2 (pages 21–23), there are several common mechanisms that can make health care harmful (e.g., labeling of pseudodisease, lowered treatment thresholds).[7] Also, the quality of care can suffer in a wide spectrum of ways, as reflected by this observation by Gordon Schiff, A. B. Bindman, and T. A. Brennan:[8]

> Quality problems in the current system include denial of care, discrimination,[9] disparities geographic maldistribution,[10] lack of continuity, lack of primary care,[11] inadequate or lack of prenatal care,[12] failure to provide beneficial prevention,[13] substandard/incompetent providers,[14] declining patient satisfaction and impersonal care,[15,16] iatrogenesis (negligent adverse events),[17] diagnosis errors,[18] unnecessary procedures/surgery,[19] suboptimal medication prescribing usage,[20] and neglect of quality-of-life/psychosocial issues.[21]

Recent studies raise serious concern about the quality of health care in this country. Jason Lazarou, B. H. Pomeranz, and P. N. Corey, for example, on the basis of a meta-analysis of 39 prospective studies from U.S. hospitals, estimated that 2,216,000 of patients had serious adverse drug reactions in 1994, with 106,000 patients dying as a result.[22] Of further concern is the increasing trend for fatal medication errors and related causes over the 10-year period from 1983 to 1993 (Figure 18-1).

Although its estimates have been called into question by some on the basis of methodological concerns,[23] the recently published report of the Institute of Medicine, *To Err Is Human*, estimated that between 44,000 and 98,000 Americans die each year as a result of preventable medical errors.[24] Although useful in generating broader interest in quality improvement of health care, however, the IOM report lacked solid substantiating data for some of its extrapolations. Critics have pointed out that medical errors need to be defined and viewed in terms of their impact on adverse outcomes of care. As Timothy Hofer, E. A. Kerr, and R. A. Hayward note, there is a big difference between these two situations:[25]

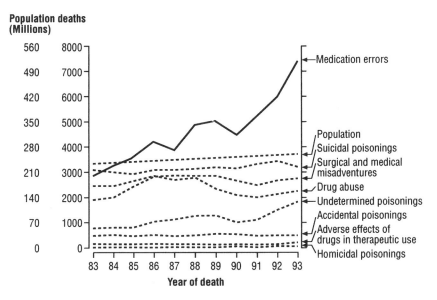

Figure 18-1 Trends in U.S. deaths from medication errors and from related causes, 1983–1993. (Reprinted with permission from Phillips D, Christenfeld N, Glynn LM. Increase in US medication-error deaths between 1983 and 1993. *Lancet.* 1998;351:643–644.)

• A patient scheduled for an amputation of the right leg has the left leg removed.
• While waiting for correction of coagulopathy, a patient with overwhelming infection, multiorgan failure, and pleural effusion dies before having thoracentesis to check for empyema.

In their analysis of a classic study of adverse events (AEs) in 1,133 patients within a random sample of 30,195 hospitalized patients in New York State in 1984, Lucien Leape and his colleagues categorized errors that result in medical injury as diagnostic, treatment, preventive, and other. They considered more than two thirds of AEs to be preventable, but the proportions of AEs due to negligence varied widely, based on the type of AE. Thus, although technical treatment errors were the most common, only one in five was deemed due to negligence. By contrast, one half of preventive errors was considered negligent, most commonly preventable falls. Table 18-1 presents their categorization of AEs together with their findings as to frequency of preventable errors.[26]

Medical errors, estimated to result in about 1 million preventable injuries each year in the United States,[27] can range across a wide spectrum of harmful events, including transfusion errors, adverse drug events, surgery on the wrong side, hospital-acquired infections, restraint-related injuries, falls, burns and pressure ulcers, and mistaken identity.[24] Mark Chassin, Robert Galvin, and other members of the National Roundtable on Health Care Quality have further characterized quality problems in health care in terms of[28]

Table 18-1   Frequency of Preventable Errors

Type of Error	No.	Frequency (%)	% of Errors Due to Negligence (%)
Diagnostic			
1. Error in diagnosis	11,731	17.1	71.1
2. Failure to use indicated tests	782	1.1	91.4
3. Use of outmoded tests	944	1.4	56.4
4. Failure to act on results of tests	1,579	2.3	55.2
Treatment			
5. Technical error	30,373	44.4	19.8
6. Error in administering treatment	776	1.1	9.1
7. Error in use of a drug	6,988	10.2	37.1
8. Delay in treatment	3,154	4.6	69.4
9. Inappropriate management	141	0.2	0
Preventive			
10. Failure to prevent injury	7,943	11.6	50.3
11. Inadequate monitoring	3,172	4.6	36.9
Other			
12. Failure in communication	244	0.4	52.6
13. Equipment failure	422	0.6	77.2
14. Other systems failure	136	0.2	0
15. Unclassified	260	—	—
Totals	68,645	100.0	39.7

Source: Reprinted with permission from Leape L, Lawthers AG, Brennan TA, Johnson WG. Preventing medical injury. *QRB Qual Rev Bull.* 1993;19(5):146.

- *Overuse.* Provision of a service when the potential harm exceeds potential benefit (e.g., unnecessary surgery or antibiotic prescription for a viral respiratory infection).
- *Underuse.* Omission of a service of proven benefit leading to loss of opportunity to improve health or function (e.g., failure to detect or treat hypertension or depression).
- *Misuse.* An appropriate service is provided, but a preventable complication occurs (e.g., a patient with known allergy to penicillin is given penicillin for streptococcal infection, thereby experiencing an allergic reaction).

Iatrogenic injuries and deaths may result from medical errors as well as adverse events from medical care with no recognizable medical error.[29] The combined effect from both causes have been estimated by Starfield to total about 225,000 deaths each year, including[19,22,30]

- 12,000 deaths from unnecessary surgery.
- 7,000 deaths from medication errors in hospitals.
- 20,000 deaths from other errors in hospitals.
- 80,000 deaths from infections acquired in hospitals.
- 106,000 deaths from nonerror, adverse effects of medications.

Starfield further notes that these numbers underestimate the problem for three reasons:[29]

(1) most of these projections are based on studies of hospitalized patients and much less is known about iatrogenic injuries in ambulatory care, (2) these estimates are for deaths only and do not include adverse events associated with disability or discomfort, and (3) the estimates for mortality are lower than those in the Institute of Medicine report.

If one still has any illusions about the quality of U.S. health care in view of this kind of evidence, they evaporate quickly in the face of international comparisons. Consider these rankings of the United States among 13 countries from a comparative study by Starfield, published in 1998:[31]

- 13th (last) for low-birth-weight percentages
- 13th for neonatal mortality and infant mortality overall
- 13th for years of potential life lost (excluding external causes)
- 11th for postneonatal mortality
- 11th for life expectancy at 1 year for females, 12th for males
- 10th for age-adjusted mortality
- 10th for life expectancy at 15 years for females, 12th for males
- 10th for life expectancy at 40 years for females, 9th for males
- 7th for life expectancy at 65 years for females, 7th for males
- 3rd for life expectancy at 80 years for females, 3rd for males

The average rank for 16 health indicators of the United States was 12th (second from the bottom), with the leading five countries being Japan, followed by Sweden, Canada, France, and Australia.[31] Figure 18-2 compares six industrial-

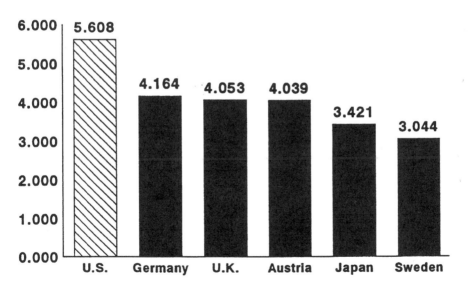

Figure 18-2 Potential years of life lost per 100,000 people for all causes, 1996–1997. (Source: OECD, 1999. Reprinted with permission from Woolhandler S, Himmelstein DU. *The National Health Program Slideshow Guide.* Cambridge, MA: Center for National Health Program Studies, 2000.)

ized countries in terms of potential years of life lost per 100,000 people from all causes.

Another study, reported in 2000 by the World Health Organization, used different indicators, including disability-adjusted life expectancy, child survival to five years of age, experiences in the health care system, social disparities of care, and family out-of-pocket expenditures for health care. Poor performance of the American health care system again was confirmed, with the average rank of the United States being 15th out of 25 industrialized countries.[32]

The increasing trend toward public reporting on quality of health care forces us to face the continuing and pervasive myth about quality of U.S. health care. Many people confuse technological sophistication with quality and still more believe that our own individual care meets acceptable quality.[33] When confronted by the superior quality rankings of our neighbor to the north (with its system of universal access to boot), even the U.S. media are quick to discount Canada's success by focusing on its negatives, such as overcrowding of emergency rooms and lengthy waits for elective surgery.[34]

QUALITY OF CARE: WHAT IS IT?

Until recent years, the definition of *quality* in health care has been global, not well understood, and difficult to measure. Although quality of care remains complex and multidimensional, major advances have been made, especially in the last 20 years, in achieving useful consensus around its definition and measurement. An overall mainstream definition of *quality*, as adopted by the Institute of Medicine (IOM) and the National Roundtable on Health Care Quality (which the IOM convened in 1996), defines the term as "the degree to which health services for individuals and populations increase the likelihood of desired health outcomes and are consistent with current professional knowledge."[35] Although a good start, this definition needs considerable elaboration in order to clarify and flesh out its dimensions. As Schuster and his colleagues add, "Good quality means providing patients with appropriate services in a technically competent manner, with good communication, shared decision making, and cultural sensitivity."[6]

There are many subtleties beyond these definitions. For example, technically competent care can be of poor quality if inappropriate. Further, the term *health services* includes much more than care of acute or chronic disease, such as disease prevention, health promotion, rehabilitative and palliative care, and also occurs in all settings of care. Moreover, quality of care requires access to care and leads to beneficial health outcomes for populations as well as individual patients.[35] *Health outcomes* likewise are more complex than may first appear. As we saw in Chapter 10, intermediate outcomes (e.g., improved laboratory tests) often are used in measuring the effectiveness of health services but may have little to do with outcomes that matter to patients (e.g., mortality, morbidity, or quality of life). In addition, consumer perspectives need to be incorporated into any definition of *quality of care*, including such aspects as amenities of the clinical setting, whether patients are treated in a timely manner and with respect, and the like.[4,36] Scott Ramsey, from his base at the Center for Cost and

Outcome Research at the University of Washington, defines *quality of health care* in terms of five dimensions beyond the technical quality of clinical interventions themselves: (1) insurance coverage, (2) access to care, (3) choice of provider, (4) service, and (5) information about health plans.[37]

HOW IS QUALITY OF CARE MEASURED?

The criteria for measurement of quality of care generally fall into one or another of three categories: (1) *structure* (e.g., characteristics of physicians or hospitals), (2) *process* (i.e., involving encounters between providers and their patients), and (3) *outcomes* (relating to the patient's subsequent health status). To be useful, it must be demonstrated that variations of one of these criteria are directly related to the others. For example, credible process criteria should lead to improved outcomes, and conversely, for outcomes criteria to be credible, they should result from processes of care that can be controlled by providers.[38]

Ideally, outcomes that matter to patients would be the most desirable criteria on which to base quality assurance programs, but in many instances, such outcomes are either too difficult or impractical to obtain (e.g., the long delay in some outcomes, such as the development of retinopathy in patients with diabetes). Process criteria therefore are used most commonly, but here again, process indicators must be carefully selected to be valid. Process criteria for controlling hypertension clearly are useful, since many studies show that mortality and strokes can be reduced by adequate control of blood pressure. On the other hand, the proportion of patients with inoperable lung cancer who develop metastases within six months of diagnosis is not a valid measure of quality, since the best available care cannot influence that outcome.[39]

Although methods to measure quality of care have advanced considerably in recent years, to the point where there is now general consensus that it can be credibly measured, its measurement remains an elusive challenge. As Bodenheimer observes:[2]

> Each intervention requires its own particular measurements of quality; some elucidate the processes of care, and some focus on outcomes. For patients with diabetes, the relevant measures might include the percentage of patients who undergo an annual retinal examination (a measure of process) and the percentage with normal glycohemoglobin levels (a measure of outcome). For patients with coronary heart disease, measures might include the percentage receiving aspirin and beta-blockers (process) and the percentage who have myocardial infarction or sudden death from cardiac causes (outcomes). Even when considering only one health care intervention—for example, coronary-artery bypass surgery—it is treacherous to compare the outcomes of one surgical team with those of another without adjusting for the age of the patients and the severity of their illness.

Additional problems are involved in the measurement of quality of health care. Many of the quality assurance measures in common use today, especially those used by health plans and managed care organizations, are process measures dealing with health of populations and not care of sick individuals. It is especially challenging to develop credible measures of outcomes of treatment for complex illnesses that are sensitive enough to account for individual variations. Since the "consumers" of information gathered by quality of care measurements often are health plans and not patients, there is an opportunity for such plans to "cream skim" low-risk populations and avoid the care of sick patients.[3]

Profiling of the clinical performance of individual physicians, although in common use, has generated particular controversy in recent years. In their landmark article, Hofer and his colleagues raised serious questions about the reliability of "report cards" for individual physicians. They conducted a cohort study of 3,642 patients with type 2 diabetes receiving care at three geographically and organizationally diverse sites (a large staff-model HMO, an urban university teaching clinic, and an urban private practice group). They found that only 4 percent or less of overall variance of hospitalization rates, visit rates, laboratory utilization rates, or glycemic control could be attributed to differences in physician practice. They further noted that high outlier physicians easily could "game the system" by pruning a few of their sickest patients from their practice—transferring only one to three such patients from their panel to other physicians would bring their profiles within the bounds of acceptable quality while even detailed case mix adjustment could not prevent such gaming.[39]

The development of quality of care measures that are easy to implement, robust, affordable, and applicable in many clinical settings remains a challenging but important goal. This is particularly true in ambulatory care, where clinical encounters are brief and often involve multiple conditions that are difficult to categorize.[40]

APPROACHES TO QUALITY ASSURANCE

Many initiatives have been taken in both the public and private sectors over the years in an effort to improve the quality of care. A review of some of the highlights of these initiatives provides a sense of promising directions and blind alleys, as well as the rationale for major changes in direction now underway. Of particular interest is the increasing awareness that defensive approaches to the prevention of medical errors usually are ineffective and that more fundamental redesign of practice patterns is required.

Private Sector

Accrediting Organizations

Organized efforts toward assuring quality of health care have a long history in the United States. The first such effort dates back to 1914 in Boston with the work of E. A. Codman in advocacy of systematic recording of surgical outcomes and analysis to improve practice.[41] A case report was published in 1918, with the first five years' results of that analysis at Massachusetts General Hospital.[42] Considered a radical by many at the time, Codman later moved to the American College of Surgeons, which published the "Minimal Standard for Hospitals" in 1917.[43]

In the second half of the 20th century, five major national organizations were established as accrediting bodies, with the goal to set national standards for clinical practice while reducing variations in practice and medically inappropriate care. Table 18-2 lists these organizations in terms of their respective target areas for accreditation and types of standards applied.

The Joint Commission on Accreditation of Healthcare Organizations (JCAHO) is the nation's oldest and largest accrediting body. It was founded in 1951 as the Joint Commission on Accreditation of Hospitals (JCAH) through the joint sponsorship of the American Hospital Association, the American Medical Association, the Canadian Medical Association (which withdrew in 1959), the American College of Surgeons, and the American College of Physicians. In later years, the American Dental Association and the American Nursing Association joined the group of sponsors. The organization was reconstituted as the present JCAHO in 1987, and it later extended its accreditation

Table 18-2 Overview of Accrediting Organizations

Accrediting Body	Target Areas for Accreditation	Types of Standards
Joint Commission on Accreditation of Healthcare Organizations (JCAHO)	Hospitals, home health, long-term care, behavioral health care, clinical laboratories, ambulatory care, health networks	Structural, organizational, patient focused
National Committee for Quality Assurance (NCQA)	Managed care plans	Clinical, administrative
American Medical Accreditation Program (AMAP)	Physician credentials and office practices	Environment of care, credentials, patient outcomes, clinical process
American Accreditation HealthCare Commission/ Utilization Review Accreditation Commission (AAHC/URAC)	Managed care organizations (emphasis on preferred provider organizations and workers' compensation programs)	Credentials verification, organization standards, workers' compensation, case management, health network, health utilization
Accreditation Association for Ambulatory HealthCare (AAAHC)	Ambulatory surgery, birthing centers, urgent care, community health centers, medical groups	Patient rights, governance, quality of care, environment, professional records

Source: Reprinted with permission from Viswanathan HN, Bpharm MS, Salmon JW. Accrediting organizations and quality improvement. *Am J Manage Care*. 2000;6(10):1118.

responsibilities beyond hospitals to include home health agencies (1988), managed care organizations (1989, but later discontinued), and health care networks (1994). As an independent, not-for-profit agency, the JCAHO evaluates and accredits almost 20,000 health care organizations and programs, including hospitals, home health agencies, integrated delivery networks, and long-term care, ambulatory care, and clinical laboratory facilities. In 1997, the JCAHO initiated ORYX, which incorporates performance measures into the accreditation process.[43]

The National Committee for Quality Assurance (NCQA) was established in 1979 by managed care organizations with the hope to avoid federal monitoring of health plans. The representation and mission of the NCQA were broadened in 1990 through a coalition with some large employers.[2] The NCQA has two major roles: (1) to accredit HMOs and (2) to publish performance measures in the Health Plan Employer and Information Set (HEDIS). In both instances, these activities are voluntary. By October 1998, about one half of the nation's 650 HMOs had requested accreditation surveys (96 percent received some level of accreditation). Although 30 large employers will not contract with unaccredited health plans, most employers do not require accreditation in their contracts. Public reporting of HEDIS data also is voluntary; less than one half of HMOs provided public reports of HEDIS 1997 data.[2] Today, more than 400 of the country's health plans use HEDIS measures, which include measures for heart disease, cancer, pneumonia, asthma, diabetes, chlamydia, mental health, smoking, and various preventive services.[44,45]

The American Medical Accreditation Program (AMAP) was developed by the AMA in collaboration with specialty, state, and local medical societies. AMAP is a voluntary, comprehensive accreditation program by which physicians can be evaluated against national standards, including standards for clinical process and patient outcomes. AMAP's activities include credentials verification, office reviews, self-assessment, and assessment of clinical performance and patient satisfaction. A 15-member Performance Measurements Coordinating Council has been established to coordinate performance assessment by the JCAHO, NCQA, and AMAP across the entire health care system.[43]

The American Accreditation Health Care Commission (AAHC) initially was formed as the Utilization Review Accreditation Commission in 1990. As a nonprofit organization, it is involved in promotion of continuous quality improvement for managed care organizations.[43]

The Accreditation Association for Ambulatory Health Care (AAAHC) is a private, nonprofit organization founded in 1979. Over 1,000 organizations are accredited by the AAAHC, including ambulatory clinics, HMOs, ambulatory surgery centers, birthing centers, urgent care centers, and community health centers.[43]

Other Organizations Involved in Quality Assurance

The Institute for Healthcare Improvement (IHI), founded 10 years ago by Donald Berwick, organized an annual National Forum on Quality Improvement in Health Care as well as a Breakthrough Series, which convenes leaders involved in the improvement of health care. Other important organizational approaches to quality improvement include[2]

- The Foundation for Accountability, established in 1995 in Portland, Oregon, on the initiative of Paul Elwood, with the goals to develop performance measures and educate consumers in their use.
- The National Roundtable on Health Care Quality, established by the Institute of Medicine in 1995, convening representatives from academic, provider, business, consumer, government, and publishing organizations.
- The National Patient Safety Foundation, established by the AMA in its Chicago offices in 1997, to change the attitudes of health professionals and the public regarding medical error.[46]
- The Consumer Coalition for Quality Health Care, based in Washington, D.C., and formed in 1993 by the American Association of Retired Persons and other consumer groups; it represents labor, the elderly, and advocacy organizations in bringing consumer perspectives to legislative and private sector initiatives in quality improvement.
- The National Coalition on Health Care, a nonprofit, nonpartisan organization based in Washington, D.C., concerned about the quality and cost of health care, and including representation from business, labor, consumer, religious, and provider groups.[47]
- The Institute for Safe Medication Practices (ISMP), a nonprofit organization providing education about adverse drug events through the ISMP Medication Safety Alert and related programs.[47]
- The Leapfrog Group was established in January 2000 as an initiative of the Business Roundtable, a nonprofit group that represents the Fortune 500 companies. This group is involved in promoting patient safety in hospitals, as illustrated by its evidence-based hospital referral (EHR) initiative, by "leapfrogging," to a new generation of innovation and strengthening consumers' ability to recognize and select safer and higher-value health care.[48]

Public Sector

The public sector also has placed increasing emphasis on quality improvement in recent years. As we saw in Chapter 16, peer review organizations (PROs), under contract from the Health Care Financing Administration (HCFA), since 1983 have been involved in monitoring variations in processes and outcomes of care. When complaints from patients are received, PROs review those cases and can deny payment for unnecessary services. The Quality Improvement System for Managed Care (QISMC) was established by HCFA in 1996 to set quality standards for Medicare and Medicaid managed care plans. HCFA is authorized to release performance data on health plans participating in these programs. Although it has not yet done so, HCFA eventually may require all hospitals providing care to Medicare beneficiaries to make public its performance measures so that consumers can better compare hospitals; a similar approach is under consideration for IPAs and group practices.[2] The Veterans Administration is piloting the use of HEDIS measures in some locations.

The Agency for Healthcare Research and Quality (AHRQ) is the lead federal agency involved in quality-of-care research. In its various activities, the AHRQ is working to promote evidence-based medicine, reduce medical errors, and expand research on the cost and utilization of health care services. Through its support of the Consumer Assessment of Health Plans (CAHPS) project, AHRQ is promoting the use of health-related quality of life measures both before and after treatment.[36]

In the aftermath of the landmark IOM report, *To Err Is Human*,[24] national attention at many levels has focused on the reporting of medical errors. The issue of mandatory reporting of medical errors has become a firestorm of controversy. The IOM report recommends a nonpunitive approach, including system responses to identified errors to decrease the chances of their recurrence. The IOM also recommended a Center for Patient Safety to be set up within AHRQ, together with a mandatory system for uniform reporting of serious medical errors at the state level. Assurance would be provided for confidentiality of these reports, free from legal discovery, although patients still could sue physicians with evidence collected from other sources. A survey by the National Academy for State Health Policy, in April 2000, revealed that 15 states required mandatory reporting of adverse events from general and acute-care hospitals, and 13 of these states required such reporting from free-standing ambulatory care settings. States varied in their protection of reports from legal discovery; only five states protected data in the case of a request under the Freedom of Information Act.[49] Various bills are being considered in Congress but have not yet been passed.

Meanwhile, other initiatives at the state level warrant mention. Some states have monitored and published survival rates for surgical procedures, which when adjusted for patient risk, have become accepted as valid measures of hospital and surgeon performance. New York state's analysis of mortality rates for patients having coronary artery bypass graft (CABC) procedures in its hospitals has been viewed by many as a model program, and some have argued that this led to decreased surgical mortality for this procedure.[50-52] On the disciplinary side of the ledger, state medical boards have increased their actions against physicians, from a total of 3,140 physicians in 1991 to 4,569 physicians in 1999.[53]

The federal government just released its new goals and priorities for Healthy People 2010, including 21 key objectives in 28 focus areas. Table 18-3 displays current performance rates for 10 leading health indicators, as well as target rates for 2010. Based on data through 1998, over 60 percent of the 319 objectives of Healthy People 2000 had been met or were expected to be met by the end of 1999.[54]

Some Current Approaches Toward Quality Improvement

Institutional Improvement

HEDIS presently is the major tool for measuring, managing, and improving health care in institutions within the private sector and is being applied progressively in the public sector as well. HEDIS has been used by health plans serving Medicare and Medicaid enrollees since 1996.[55] The HCFA mandated

Table 18-3 Healthy People 2010: Leading Health Indicators

Leading Health Indicator	Related Objectives	Current Rate*	2010 Target
Physical activity	Increase the proportion of adolescents who engage in vigorous physical activity that promotes cardiorespiratory fitness 3 or more days/week for 20 min/occasion (grades 9–12).	64%	85%
	Increase the proportion of adults who engage regularly, preferably daily, in moderate physical activity for at least 30 min/day.	15%	30%
Overweight and obesity	Reduce the proportion of children and adolescents who are overweight or obese (aged 6–19 years).	11%	5%
	Reduce the proportion of adults who are obese.	23%	15%
Tobacco use	Reduce cigarette smoking by adolescents (grade 9–12).	36%	16%
	Reduce cigarette smoking by adults.	24%	12%
Substance abuse	Increase the proportion of adolescents not using alcohol or any illicit drugs during the past 30 days (aged 12–17 years).	77%	89%
	Reduce the proportion of adults using any illicit drug during the past 30 days.	6%	3%
	Reduce the proportion of adults engaging in binge drinking of alcoholic beverages during the past month.	16%	6%
Responsible sexual behavior	Increase the proportion of adolescents who abstain from sexual intercourse or use condoms if currently sexually active (grades 9–12).	85%	95%
	Increase the proportion of adults who, if sexually active, use condoms.	23%	50%
Mental health	Increase the proportion of adults with recognized depression who receive treatment.	23%	50%

continues

Table 18-3   (continued)

Leading Health Indicator	Related Objectives	Current Rate*	2010 Target
Immunization	Increase the proportion of young children who receive all vaccines that have been recommended for universal administration for at least 5 years (aged 19–35 months).	73%	80%
	Increase the proportion of noninstitutionalized elderly adults who are vaccinated annually against influenza	63% (influenza)	90%
	and who have ever been vaccinated against pneumococcal disease (aged 65 years and older).	43% (pneumococcal)	90%
Injury and violence	Reduce deaths caused by motor vehicle crashes (all ages).	15.8/100,000	9.0/100,000
	Reduce homicides (all ages).	7.2/100,000	3.2/100,000
Environmental quality	Reduce the proportion of persons exposed to air that does not meet the U.S. Environmental Protection Agency's health-based standards for ozone (all ages).	43%	0%
	Reduce the proportion of nonsmokers exposed to environmental tobacco smoke (aged 4 years and older).	65%	45%
Access to health care	Increase the proportion of persons with health insurance (all ages).	86%	100%
	Increase the proportion of persons who have a specific source of ongoing care (all ages).	86%	96%
	Increase the proportion of pregnant women who begin prenatal care in the first trimester of pregnancy (all ages).	83%	90%

* Based on most recent data available.

Source: Reprinted with permission from Imperio WA. Healthy People 2010. Nation's health agenda for decade announced. *Fam Pract News.* 2000;30(5):9.

Table 18-4 Examples of Key Change Concepts (Human Factors Principles)

Reduce reliance on memory
Simplify
Standardize
Use constraints[a] and forcing functions[b]
Use protocols and checklists wisely
Improve information access
Decrease reliance on vigilance
Reduce hand-offs
Increase feedback
Decrease multiple entry and look-alikes
Automate carefully

[a] Constraint: Design of equipment or a process so that it is difficult to use it incorrectly; for example, preparation of medication in a single-use vial.

[b] Forcing function: Design of equipment or a process so that it is impossible to use it incorrectly; for example, smaller gas tank filler tubes for unleaded gasoline.

Source: Reprinted with permission from Leape LL, Kabcenell AI, Gandhi TK, et al. Reducing adverse drug events: Lessons from a breakthrough series collaborative. *Jt Comm J Qual Improv.* 2000;26(6):323.

reporting of selected HEDIS measures in 1998, and they were made available to the public on its website in 1999.[56] Many states adopted public reporting of HEDIS findings for their Medicaid programs. In addition, HEDIS is being extended well beyond its initial applications in managed care settings and increasingly is being applied to hospitals, PPOs, and medical groups.[54]

ORYX, as the outcomes-based accreditation system developed over the last several years by the JCAHQ, includes 60 selected measurement sets. Examples of ORYX indicators are percutaneous transluminal coronary angioplasty (PTCA) mortality, number of days from CABG surgery to discharge, and whether a digoxin level is measured or its level is above a specified limit.

The Breakthrough Series developed by the Institute for Healthcare Improvement represents an especially dynamic approach to institutional quality improvement today. This is a series of collaborative efforts involving teams from selected hospitals working with content and process experts to develop and implement "best practices" that will improve quality of care in the participating hospitals. A good example of this effort is the recent report of a collaborative program to reduce adverse drug events (defined as injuries related to the use or nonuse of medications). Over a 15-month period since 1996, medication processes were redesigned and applied in 38 hospitals, incorporating human factors principles demonstrated to be effective in reducing the chance of errors (Table 18-4). Series of changes developed toward a single aim were categorized as a *ramp*. A typical ramp for reducing errors for insulin use might include these:[57]

- Institute bedside blood glucose monitoring;
- Change the time that insulin is given related to breakfast;

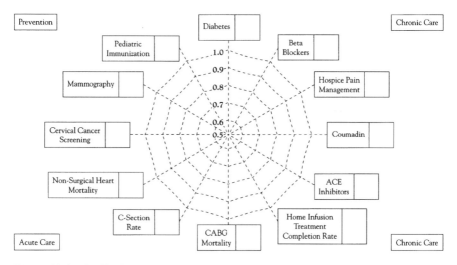

Figure 18-3 Quality indicators scorecard, Henry Ford Health System. (Reprinted with permission from Shortell SM, Gillies RR, Anderson DA, et al. *Remaking Health Care in America: The Evolution of Organized Delivery Systems.* San Francisco: Jossey-Bass, 2000:209.)

- Have some patients administer their own insulin; and
- Screen all patients for glucose levels <70.

A good example of a comprehensive scorecard to track system performance was developed by the Henry Ford Health System. Figure 18-3 displays such a scorecard, which includes quality measures ranging from prevention to acute and chronic care.[58]

Another example of a recent national effort to improve the safety of drug administration in hospitals is the self-assessment tool developed by the Institute for Safe Medication Practices. This 30-page assessment tool is available to all hospitals without charge through partnership of the ISMP and the American Hospital Association.[59]

Despite these promising developments toward improving institutional quality of care, continuous quality improvement (CQI) still is the dominant approach, and its record to date has been mixed at best. After conducting a systematic review of the recent literature on the impact of CQI on clinical practice, Stephen Shortell, C. L. Bennett, and G. R. Byck concluded that "no evidence has yet emerged of an organization-wide impact on quality."[60] Indeed, Berwick has moved beyond CQI as a model in favor of a systems approach to quality assurance.[61]

Improving Practice by Health Professionals
Although, over the last 30 years, peer review has been the basis for many attempts to monitor and improve the quality of care by physicians, it usually has been quite ineffective for several reasons. Interrater reliability has been a

persistent problem, as well as the often punitive approach taken in efforts to discipline physicians for identified discrepancies of practice. The fear of potential lawsuits, which could even involve peer reviewers, may permeate the peer-review process, and in some instances, physicians have been found to hide quality problems because of this fear.[62]

Quality assurance experts have sought other ways to measure quality of care so that best practices can be promoted more effectively. Chart abstraction has been well validated in the inpatient setting but has been much less useful in ambulatory care settings, for reasons including cost, time constraints of office visits, recording bias, and difficulty to account for case-mix variation.[63] A recent study compared chart abstraction with the use of standardized patients and patient vignettes as quality measures in outpatient practice. Vignettes or written case simulations were found to have advantages over the other two methods for their low cost and ease of application in many kinds of clinical practices. An example of a vignette for coronary artery disease would be this:[63]

A 65-year-old man, a new patient, comes to the clinic for follow-up of a myocardial infarction (MI) he had 3 months ago. In taking the history, the physician should ascertain that the patient is now free of pain and has no difficulty performing routine activities but continues to smoke although he has normal blood pressure. After the physician records what he or she intends to do in the physical examination, the findings are revealed by the vignettes or by the patient in response to physician questioning, and the physician then is asked what laboratory tests should be ordered (an electrocardiogram and cholesterol test), what the diagnosis is (uncomplicated MI), and how treatment should proceed. The physician should recognize that the MI is recent and associated with reversible risk factors and that the patient needs to be taking aspirin and a β-blocker.

Vignettes appear to be an inexpensive and effective way to measure the competence and practices of groups of providers, but they are less helpful if there are other reasons for poor quality of care.[59]

Clinical practice guidelines have become widely used in recent years in an effort to improve the quality of clinical practice, but their effectiveness has been underwhelming in most instances. Most studies of clinical guidelines for chronic illness, for example, found that they were not followed for a majority of patients and that unsatisfactory progress was made toward improving patient outcomes.[64] The experience of the emergency department at Children's Hospital of Philadelphia in applying an evidence-based risk assessment protocol for the care of febrile infants casts a bright light on the difficulties of quality assurance in the ambulatory setting. A conservative sample of 422 febrile infants was efficiently divided by the protocol into low- and high-risk groups, but beyond that, the protocol was not followed in about 7 percent of cases, both on the overtreatment side (hospitalization and septic workup for low-risk infants) and the under-treatment side (outpatient follow-up for high-risk infants); in addition, 7 percent of the infants who developed serious bacterial infections were not treated with antibiotics.[65] This problem led to the following important comments by James Glauber and his colleagues:[66]

This observation argues against the outlier assumption of quality assurance, namely that a few bad apples can be identified as the principal source of errors. Instead, the implication is that the 7% failure rate is a function of the system of care, not of individual vigilance or motivation.

It is doubtful that quality assurance initiatives will prevent recurrences. Continued quality assurance initiatives are a component of the system that performs at a 7% failure rate. Is this the level of quality that we wish to assure?—

The potential for the Philadelphia protocol, or any other evidence-based guidelines, to improve the lives of patients rests on the capability of the health care system to deliver the care as intended. The gap between intended care and received care will not be bridged solely through focused, dedicated individual effort, but will also require different methods that focus on systems. We must recognize that error is an expected product of any human process, identify the predictable sources of error, and then strive to design systems robust enough to interpret and prevent error. Error-proofing is far more powerful than exhortation.

System Redesign

Perhaps the most important and exciting development in quality assurance of health care in recent years is the new emphasis on system redesign of the process of patient care. Promulgated by the Institute for Healthcare Improvement and increasingly supported by other health care organizations, the continuing need for more structured re-engineering of the clinical enterprise is well illustrated by this scenario:[67]

'Ladies and gentlemen, welcome aboard Sterling Airline's Flight Number 743, bound for Edinburgh. This is your captain speaking. Our flight time will be two hours, and I am pleased to report both that you have a 97% chance of reaching your destination without being significantly injured during the flight and that our chances of making a serious error during the flight, whether you are injured or not, is only 6.7%. Please fasten your seat belts, and enjoy the flight. The weather in Edinburgh is sunny.'

As its authors (Berwick and Leape) comment, most people would not stay aboard that flight, yet this is a common problem in everyday clinical care, as demonstrated by the aforementioned experience in pediatric care in an excellent children's hospital as well as more widely in the quality-of-care literature.

A growing number of quality-improvement experts are looking to other industries for guidance on how to reconstruct processes of patient care into safer systems that proactively anticipate and prevent errors.[5,24,68-70] Health care admittedly is complex but so are other high-risk activities. In naval carrier operations, for example, 100 to 200 flight crew personnel fuel, load munitions, and maintain aircraft that take off and land at 48- to 60-second intervals, yet are able to experience only 1 "crunch" (when two aircraft touch, even without damage) in 8,000 moves.[71]

The Institute of Medicine recommends that safe clinical systems should anticipate and avert, if possible, three kinds of errors, as first proposed by J. Rasmussen[72] and later elaborated by J. Reason:[73] (1) skill-based slips and lapses,

Table 18-5 Principles for Design of Safe Health Care Systems

Principle 1. Provide Leadership
Make patient safety a priority corporate objective.
Make patient safety everyone's responsibility.
Make clear assignments for and expectation of safety oversight.
Provide resources, human and financial, for error analysis and systems redesign.
Develop effective mechanisms for identifying and dealing with unsafe practitioners.

Principle 2. Respect Human Limits in Process Design
Design jobs for safety.
Avoid reliance on memory.
Use constraints and forcing functions.
Avoid reliance on vigilance.
Simplify key processes.
Standardize work processes.

Principle 3. Promote Effective Team Functioning
Train in teams those who are expected to work in teams.
Include the patient in safety design and the process of care.

Principle 4. Anticipate the Unexpected
Adopt a proactive approach: examine new technologies and processes of care for threats to safety and redesign them before accidents occur.
Design for recovery.
Improve access to accurate, timely information.
Adopt a proactive approach: examine processes of care for threats to safety and redesign them before accidents occur.

Principle 5. Create a Learning Environment
Use simulations whenever possible.
Encourage reporting of errors and hazardous conditions.
Ensure no reprisals for reporting of errors.
Develop a working culture in which communication flows freely regardless of authority gradient; improve auditory communication.
Implement mechanisms of feedback and learning from error.

Source: Reprinted with permission from Kohn LT, Corrigan JM, Donaldson MS (eds). *To Err is Human: Building a Safer Health System*. Washington, DC: National Academy Press, 1999:143–154.

(2) rule-based errors, and (3) knowledge-based mistakes. Leape further subdivides the "pathophysiology of error" into cognitive mechanisms (often well handled rapidly without much effort unless interrupted, distracted, tired, etc.) and problem-solving processes (slower, sequential mental tasks, requiring more attention and more subject to error). Design approaches to the first group avoid reliance on memory, whereas the second group is best addressed by simplification of tasks, training that simulates problems, and practice in recovery from these problems.[24] The IOM lays out five principles for the design of safe systems in health care organizations (Table 18-5).[24] The Institute for Healthcare Improvement puts these principles into action through its collaborative demonstration projects in its Breakthrough Series.[61]

In the most recent report, the IOM proposes the following agenda for redesigning the 21st-century health care system:[74]

- That all health care constituencies, including policy-makers, purchasers, regulators, health professionals, health care trustees and management, and consumers, commit to a national statement of purpose for the health care system as a whole and to a shared agenda of six aims for improvement that can raise the quality of care to unprecedented levels.
- That clinicians and patients, and the health care organizations that support care delivery, adopt a new set of principles to guide the redesign of care processes.
- That the U.S. Department of Health and Human Services (HHS) identify a set of priority conditions upon which to focus initial efforts, provide resources to stimulate innovation, and initiate the change process.
- That health care organizations design and implement more effective organizational support processes to make change in the delivery of care possible.
- That purchasers, regulators, health professions, educational institutions, and HHS create an environment that fosters and rewards improvement by (1) creating an infrastructure to support evidence-based practice, (2) facilitating the use of information technology, (3) aligning payment incentives, and (4) preparing the work force to better serve patients in a world of expanding knowledge and rapid change.

LESSONS FROM QUALITY IMPROVEMENT EFFORTS

Based on the last two decades of quality improvement initiatives in health care, some important lessons have been learned. Eight lessons sort out, in my view, as especially noteworthy:

1. *Access to primary care of good quality is an essential requirement for overall quality of care.* Many studies have demonstrated a strong link between primary care and improved health status.[31,75–79] A recent national ecologic study, for example, showed that primary care exerted a strong influence on stroke and postneonatal mortality and that it also may alleviate the adverse effects of income inequalities on health.[80] Moreover, the international comparisons reported by Starfield of health status in 11 industrialized nations (pages 200–201) are compelling, since nations with better health outcomes tend to have stronger systems for primary care than the United States.[29]
2. *There are persistent and marked differences in quality of care based on geographic and facility variations.* The National Roundtable on Health Care Quality, in a 1998 report, concluded that too few health plans, hospitals, and integrated delivery systems had made impressive efforts to improve the quality of their care.[28] Even for those reporting their HEDIS measures, wide variations in clinical measures were found (e.g., a range from 11 percent to 77 percent in the proportion of patients with diabetes who had a retinal examination within the previous year).[81]
3. *Investor-owned HMOs have lower quality of care than not-for-profit HMOs.* A national study published in 1999 revealed that, compared to nonprofit plans, investor-owned HMOs scored worse on all 14 quality indicators reported to the National Committee for Quality Assurance (e.g., a 27 percent

lower rate of eye examinations for patients with diabetes and a 16 percent lower rate of appropriate drug treatment for patients after myocardial infarction).[82] These findings prompted this observation by Ida Hellander, executive director of Physicians for a National Health Program (PNHP) and coauthor of the study:[83]

> Our decade-old experiment with market medicine is a failure. Investor-owned plans have worse quality than non-profits, and non-profits are increasingly forced to mimic the for-profits. It's time to end our race to the bottom in health care and implement nationwide quality improvement and universal coverage through single-payer national health insurance.

4. *Regionalization to higher-volume hospitals would improve patient outcomes for some conditions.* Since the classic study by Harold Luft, J. P. Bunker, and A. C. Enthoven in 1979 found significantly lower inpatient mortality rates for some surgical procedures in higher-volume hospitals,[84] many studies and much debate have focused on the relation between volume and outcome. Critics of regionalization usually point to methodologic concerns about these studies, especially the need to adjust for severity and case mix. More sophisticated studies in recent years provide solid evidence that regionalization of care would provide better outcomes for many conditions. For example, a 1997 study in California hospitals showed that mortality was significantly lower in high-volume hospitals for elective abdominal aortic aneurysm repair, carotid endarterectomy, lower extremity arterial bypass surgery, coronary artery bypass surgery, coronary angioplasty, heart transplantation, pediatric cardiac surgery, pancreatic cancer surgery, esophageal cancer surgery, cerebral aneurysm surgery, and treatment of human immunodeficiency virus (HIV)/acquired immunodeficiency syndrome (AIDS).[85] The Leapfrog Group set EHR standards for a number of major procedures (e.g., at least 500 CABG procedures per year).[48] Although volume by no means is the single determinant of quality, consensus is growing that the care of many higher-risk conditions should be regionalized to higher-volume facilities.[86,87] At the same time, the volume-outcome relationship found for more complex procedures has been found not to hold for many less complex procedures, such as those commonly performed in small rural hospitals.[88] For example, comparable quality of care for low-risk obstetrics has been demonstrated in many small rural hospitals, while some studies also show lower cesarean section rates, fewer instrumental deliveries, lower use of epidurals, and lower rates of induction in these hospitals, while preserving comparable outcomes.[89–91]

5. *Although more advanced, clinical performance measurement has real limitations.* Despite their wide use, a growing number of recent studies call into question the effectiveness of clinical performance measures in improving the quality of care.[2,48] These are some of the problems:
   • Patients rank quality information far behind convenience, coverage, access, and cost in choosing health plans and providers.[92,93]
   • Consumers value information on health care choices much more from friends, family, and personal physicians than from government sources.[94]
   • Published performance data may not lead to an apparent impact on patient choices (e.g., CABG surgery in Pennsylvania).[95]

- Many health plans do not use performance data to select high-performance centers (e.g., CABG surgery in New York state).[96]
- If performance "report cards" did shift patients to higher-quality plans, these plans could be negatively affected by an adverse selection of sicker patients and "punished" in a competitive marketplace.[2]
- Almost half of employees in large companies and 80 percent in small firms have no choice among health plans.[97]
- Only 11 percent of employers in a 1998 report relied on quality data in selecting health plans; cost usually was the driving factor.[98]
- Since HEDIS measures address only a limited range of health care activities, their scores may rise without improvement in overall quality of care.[99]
- Since performance measures of individual physicians' practices correlate so poorly with process outcomes of care,[39] there still is no reliable method to measure performance at that level.
- Performance measurement is costly in terms of data collection, assessment, and dissemination; these costs are just passed on to purchasers and consumers, and lead to overall cost increases for health care services.[2]

6. *Quality assurance efforts may lead to negative, unintended consequences.* Aside from the time and effort required of health professionals and administrators to comply with reporting requirements for performance data, which can distract them from direct provision of care, other potential unintended consequences may adversely affect patient care. Two examples illustrate the point. We saw earlier how physician profiling may cause some physicians to "deselect" sicker patients from their practice to improve their profile. Another example is the likely result that, confronted by a steadily increasing burden of performance objectives, plans and clinicians may put disproportionate efforts into improving less important aspects of care while their performance of other, more important aspects of care decreases.[100]

7. *There is a clear and urgent need to redesign clinical practice on a systems basis.* Earlier in this chapter, we allude to a developing new emphasis on "systems change" of health care, led particularly by the Institute of Medicine and the Institute for Healthcare Improvement. The IHI's Idealized Design of Clinical Office Practices represents the scope of structural change of health care envisioned as the ultimate goal. IHI is working with 38 prototype sites toward creation of new practice designs, which will be disseminated more widely beyond 2001. Table 18-6 compares traditional practice with idealized practice as presently conceived.[101]

8. *A new culture of quality is needed within the health care industry.* Drawing from quality standards and experience in other industries, Mark Chassin, cochair of the IOM's National Roundtable on Health Care Quality, recently challenged the medical profession to work toward "six sigma quality" (i.e., tolerance of 3.4 errors per 1 million events).[102] By comparison, the frequency of deaths during anesthesia has been reduced to 5.4 per million (mostly as a result of improved monitoring techniques), but 580,000 per million patients with depression are incorrectly diagnosed or inadequately treated, while 790,000 per million patients surviving myocardial infarction do not receive beta-blockers.[102]

Table 18-6 Traditional Practice versus the Ideal

Traditional Practice	Idealized Practice
Patients wait days or weeks for an appointment; work is delayed into the future.	Patients are seen on the same day that they call for an appointment; practices do today's work today.
Patients are "on their own" after they leave the physician's office.	Patients can access information from their physician via e-mail or the practice's interactive Web site.
Patients play a passive role; physicians make decisions about what is best for patients.	Patients play an active role and take part in making decisions about their health care.
Medical records are designed for compliance, are chronological, and belong to the practice.	Medical records are designed to be useable, are problem-oriented and belong to the patient.
Clinical care is based on individual training and habit.	Clinical care is based on continually updated scientific evidence.
Patients are treated reactively and one at a time.	Entire populations of patients are managed proactively through patient registries.
Staff members develop new skills when it is imperative, job descriptions are fixed.	Staff members are encouraged to broaden their skills and develop cross-functionality.

Source: Reprinted with permission from Kilo CM, Endsley S. As good as it *could* get: Remaking the medical practice. *Fam Pract Manage.* 2000;7(5):49.

CONCLUDING COMMENTS

It is healthy, ironically enough, that the flaws of the U.S. health care system are becoming more widely recognized. For too long, many Americans have complacently assumed that the technical achievements of U.S. medicine must produce the best health care system in the world. It no longer is possible to believe that without an excessive dose of denial. Adding the system's quality problems to those of access and cost, as discussed in the last two chapters, one has to conclude that the system indeed is very sick.

There is room for optimism that some of the present trends will lead to systemwide improvement of health care. The increasing emphasis on outcome measures applied to the effectiveness of clinical interventions, together with the energetic efforts now taking place in both the private and public sectors to redesign systems of clinical practice, lead in that direction. These developments are propelled by a growing coalition of interests concerned with measures of quality and value of health care services, including more-knowledgeable consumers, purchasers, and payers.

While broader recognition of quality problems in health care and new efforts to improve its quality are welcome and necessary, there is room for concern that, once again, as with the wonders of medical technology, the risks of health care, as well as initiatives to alleviate them, are being oversold to the public. The IOM report on medical errors received immediate and widespread coverage by the media, but most of the reporting was not critical enough to move past the blame game to a better understanding of medical errors as system problems.[103] Moreover, it must be appreciated that many health care services carry inherent risk and promoting zero-risk expectations of health care would be a disservice to patients and the public.[104]

Several lessons from earlier chapters necessarily play a large role in determining the results of quality improvement efforts. First, for the many millions of uninsured and underinsured, quality of care is a cruel abstraction until universal access is assured (Chapters 8 and 17). Second, as the population ages and the burden of chronic disease further outweighs acute disease, the system needs to move beyond the biomedical model to also embrace disease management and population-based approaches (Chapter 10). Third, a solid primary care base is required to achieve optimal outcomes of care for populations, so that strategies to strengthen the primary care sector must underpin system improvement (Chapter 13). Fourth, nonpunitive attempts to improve quality of health care through self-reporting of adverse events will not be effective until a culture of system improvement becomes dominant, with protections from legal discovery (Chapter 12). And fifth, in view of the increasing complexity of health care and the remarkable advances in information technology, the electronic medical record will be the key building block on which to construct improved systems of care for both individual patients and populations being served (Chapter 15).

One other area deserves special emphasis—the deep and unresolved conflict of interest between the investor-owned, for-profit health care sector and the public interest. As we saw in Chapter 14 (pages 214–216), in many instances, the for-profit sector has been found to have worse patient outcomes than the not-for-profit sector. Although the for-profit business ethic is the American way, it undermines value in health care and works against the public interest. This particular issue must be confronted if any long-term system reforms are to become possible for the entire population, as will be revisited in Chapters 22 and 24.

REFERENCES

1. Berwick D. Excerpts from plenary address at Quality Improvement in Health Care. *Fam Pract Manage.* July–August 2000:26.
2. Bodenheimer T. The American health care system: The movement for improved quality in health care. *N Engl J Med.* 1999;340:488–492.
3. Angell M, Kassirer JP. Quality and the medical marketplace—Following elephants. *N Engl J Med.* 1996;335:883–885.
4. Kenagy JW, Berwick DM, Shore MF. Service quality in health care. *JAMA.* 1999;281:661–665.
5. Blumenthal D. Quality of health care. Part 4: The origins of the quality-of-care debate. *N Engl J Med.* 1996;335:1146–1149.
6. Schuster M, McGlynn EA, Brook RH. How good is the quality of health care in the United States? *Milbank Q.* 1998;76(4):517–563.
7. Fisher ES, Welch HG. Avoiding the unintended consequences of growth in medical care: How might more be worse? *JAMA.* 1999;281:446–453.

8. Schiff GD, Bindman AB, Brennan TA. A better-quality alternative. Single-payer national health system reform. *JAMA.* 1994;272:803–808.

9. Ansell DA, Schiff RL. Patient dumping. Status, implications, and policy recommendations. *JAMA.* 1987;257:1500–1502.

10. Hafner-Eaton C. Physician utilization disparities between the uninsured and insured. Comparisons of the chronically ill, acutely ill, and well non-elderly populations. *JAMA.* 1993; 269:787–792.

11. Starfield B. Primary care and health. A cross-national comparison. *JAMA.* 1991;266:2268–2271.

12. Braveman J, Bennett T, Lewis C, Egerter S, Showstack J. Access to prenatal care following major Medicaid eligibility expansions. *JAMA.* 1993;269:1285–1289.

13. Burack RC, Gimotty PA, Stengle W, Warbasse L, Moncrease A. Patterns of use of mammography among inner-city Detroit women: Contrasts between a health department, HMO, and private hospital. *Med Care.* 1993;31(4):322–334.

14. Kusserow RP, Handley EA, Yessian MR. An overview of state medical discipline. *JAMA.* 1987;257:820–824.

15. Blendon RJ, Hyams TS, Benson JM. Bridging the gap between expert and public views on health care reform. *JAMA.* 1993;269:2573–2578.

16. Rubin HR, Gandek B, Rogers WH, Kosinski M, McHorney CA, Ware JE Jr. Patients' ratings of outpatient visits in different practice settings: Results from the Medical Outcomes Study. *JAMA.* 1993;270:835–840.

17. Weiler PC, Hiatt HH, Newhouse JP, Johnson WG, Brennan TA, Leape LL. *A Measure of Malpractice.* Cambridge, MA: Harvard University Press, 1993.

18. Williamson JW, Walters K, Cordes DL. Primary care, quality improvement and health systems change. *Am J Med Qual.* 1993;82:37–44.

19. Leape LL. Unnecessary surgery. *Annu Rev Public Health.* 1992;13:363–383.

20. Manasse HR. Medication use in an imperfect world: Drug misadventuring as an issue of public policy, Parts 1 and 2. *Am J Hosp Pharm.* 1989;46:929–924, 1141–1152.

21. Carpenter WT Jr., Buchanan RW. Schizophrenia. *N Engl J Med.* 1994;330:681–690.

22. Lazarou J, Pomeranz BH, Corey PN. Incidence of adverse drug reactions in hospitalized patients: A meta-analysis of prospective studies. *JAMA.* 1998;279:1200–1205.

23. Sox HC, Woloshin S. How many deaths are due to medical error? Getting the number right. *Effective Clin Pract.* 2000;3(6):277–283.

24. Kohn LT, Corrigan JM, Donaldson MS (eds). *To Err Is Human: Building a Safer Health System. Institute of Medicine.* Washington, DC: National Academy Press, 1999.

25. Hofer TP, Kerr EA, Hayward RA. What is an error? *Effective Clin Pract.* 2000;3(6):261–269.

26. Leape L, Lawthers AG, Brennan TA, Johnson WG. Preventing medical injury. *QRB Qual Rev Bull.* 1993;19(5):144–149.

27. Weinbart SN, Wilson RM, Gibberd RW, Harrison B. Epidemiology of medical error. *BMJ.* 2000;320:774–777.

28. Chassin MR, Galvin RW. The urgent need to improve health care quality. Institute of Medicine National Roundtable on Health Care Quality. *JAMA.* 1998;280:1000–1005.

29. Starfield B. Is US health really the best in the world? *JAMA.* 2000;284:483–485.

30. Phillips D, Christenfeld N, Glynn LM. Increase in US medication-error deaths between 1983 and 1993. *Lancet.* 1998;351:643–644.

31. Starfield B. *Primary Care. Balancing Health Needs, Services, and Technology.* New York: Oxford University Press, 1998.

32. World Health Report 2000. Available at: http://www.who.int/whr/2000en/report.htm.

33. Epstein AM. Public release of performance data: A progress report from the front. *JAMA.* 2000;283:1884–1886.

34. Marmor T, Sullivan K. Canada's burning! Media myths about universal health coverage. *The Washington Monthly.* July–August 2000:15–20.

35. Lohr KN (ed). *Medicare: A strategy for Quality Assurance.* Washington, DC: National Academy Press, 1990.

36. Cleary PD, Edgman-Levitan S. Health care quality. Incorporating consumer perspectives. *JAMA.* 1997;278:1608–1612.

37. Ramsey SD. Personal communication, March 15, 2000.

38. Brook RH, McGlynn EA, Cleary PD. Part 2: Measuring quality of care. *N Engl J Med.* 1996;335:966–970.

39. Hofer TP, Hayward RA, Greenfield S, Wagner EH, Kaplan SH, Manning WG. The unreliability

of individual physician "report cards" for assessing the costs and quality of care of a chronic disease. *JAMA.* 1999;281:2098–2105.

40. Fihn SD. The quest to quantify quality. *JAMA.* 2000;283:1740–1742.
41. Codman EA. The product of a hospital. *Surg Obstet Gynecol.* 1914;18:491–496.
42. Codman EA. *A Study in Hospital Efficiency, as Demonstrated by the Case Report of the First Five Years of a Private Hospital.* Boston: T. H. Todd, 1918.
43. Viswanathan HN, Bpharm MS, Salmon JW. Accrediting organizations and quality improvement. *Am J Manage Care.* 2000;6(10):1117–1130.
44. National Committee for Quality Assurance releases HEDIS 2001 draft. *Am Fam Physician.* 2000;61(5):1240.
45. HEDIS measures within a Veterans Affairs medical center. *Am J Manage Care.* 2000;6(6):661–668.
46. Leape LL, Woods DD, Hatlie MJ, Kizer KW, Schroeder SA, Lundberg GD. Promoting patient safety by preventing medical error. *JAMA.* 1998;280:1444–1447.
47. Miller JE. Improving patient care: The family physician's role in reducing medical errors. *Fam Pract Manage.* February 2000:45–46.
48. Milstein A, Galvin RS, DelBanco SF, et al. Improving the safety of health care: The leapfrog initiative. *Effective Clin Pract.* 2000;3(6):313–316.
49. National Academy for State Health Policy. State reporting of medical errors and adverse events: Results of a 50-state survey. *Med Benefits.* 2000;17(11):10–11.
50. Jencks SF. Clinical performance measurement—A hard sell. *JAMA.* 2000;283:2015–2016.
51. Hannan EL, Kilburn H Jr, Racz ME, Shields E, Chassin ME. Improving the outcomes of coronary artery bypass surgery in New York state. *JAMA.* 1994;271:761–766.
52. Hannan EL, Siu AL, Kumar D, et al. The decline in coronary artery bypass graft surgery mortality in New York state. The role of surgeon volume. *JAMA.* 1995;273:209–213.
53. Practice Beat, Disciplinary actions—State medical boards step up the pace. *Med Econ.* June 19, 2000:2.
54. Imperio WA. Healthy People 2010. Nation's health agenda for decade announced. *Fam Pract News.* 2000;30(5):9.
55. O'Kane ME. HEDIS measurement moves outside the managed care box. *Am J Manage Care.* 2000;6(6):702–703.
56. New reporting requirements for Medicare health plans in 1997: HEDIS 3.0 measures and the Medicare Beneficiary Satisfaction Survey. Operational Policy Letter #47.U.S. Department of Health and Human Services, Health Care Financing Administration, 1997.
57. Leape LL, Kabcenell AI, Gandhi TK, et al. Reducing adverse drug events: Lessons from a breakthrough series collaborative. *Jt Comm J Qual Improv.* 2000;26(6):321–331.
58. Shortell SM, Gillies RR, Anderson DA, et al. *Remaking Health Care in America: The Evolution of Organized Delivery Systems.* San Francisco: Jossey-Bass, 2000:209.
59. Sweeney R, Lapp T. US hospitals receive medication safety assessment tool. *Am Fam Physician.* 2000;62(1):31.
60. Shortell SM, Bennett CL, Byck GR. Assessing the impact of continuous quality improvement on clinical practice: What it will take to accelerate progress. *Milbank Q.* 1998;76(4):593–624.
61. Berwick DM. The status quo must go! *Manage Care.* 1999;8(6): 32, 34–35, 39–42.
62. Prosser RL. Alteration of medical records submitted for medicolegal review. *JAMA.* 1992;267:2630.
63. Peabody JW, Luck J, Glassman P, et al. Comparison of vignettes, standardized patients, and chart abstraction: A prospective study of three methods for measuring quality. *JAMA.* 2000;283:1715–1722.
64. Ornstein SM, Jenkins RG. Quality of care for chronic illness in primary care: Opportunity for improvement in process and outcome measures. *Am J Manage Care.* 2000;5(5):621–627.
65. Baker MD, Bell LM, Avner JR. The efficacy of routine outpatient management without antibiotics of fever in selected infants. *Pediatrics.* 1999;103:627–631.
66. Glauber J, Goldmann DA, Homer CJ, Berwick DM. Reducing medical error through systems improvement: The management of febrile infants. *Pediatrics.* 2000;105(6):1330–1332.
67. Berwick DM, Leape LL. Reducing errors in medicine. *BMJ.* 1999;319:136–137.
68. Leape LL, Berwick DM. Safe health care: Are we up to it? *BMJ.* 2000;320:725–726.
69. Berkowitz KS. Improving health care by looking outside the industry. *Health Aff (Millwood).* 2000;19(4):276–277.
70. Lawrence DM. Managed care is not the problem. *Fam Pract News.* January 1, 2000:9.

71. Weick KE, Roberts KH. Collective mind in organizations: Heedful interrelating on flight decks. *Adm Sci Q.* 38:357–81.
72. Rasmussen J. Skills, rules, knowledge: signals, signs, and symbols and other distinctions in human performance models. *IEEE Transactions on Systems, Man and Cybernetics.* 1983;SMC-13:257–267.
73. Reason J. *Human Error.* New York: Cambridge University, 1990.
74. Institute of Medicine. Crossing the quality chasm: A new health system for the 21st century. *Medical Benefits.* 2001;18(6):5–6.
75. Shi L. The relation between primary care and life chances. *J Health Care Poor Underserved.* 1992;3(2):321–335.
76. Shi L. Primary care, specialty care, and life chances. *Int J Health Serv.* 1994;24(3):431–458.
77. Starfield B. *Primary Care: Concept, Evaluation, and Policy.* New York: Oxford University Press, 1992.
78. Bindman A, Grumbach K, Osmond D, Vranizan K, Stewart A. Primary care and receipt of preventive services. *J Gen Intern Med.* 1996;11:269–276.
79. Bodenheimer T, Lo B, Casalino L. Primary care physicians should be coordinators, not gatekeepers. *JAMA.* 1999;281:2045–2049.
80. Shi L, Starfield B. Income inequality, primary care, and health indicators. *J Fam Pract.* 1999;48:275–284.
81. Thompson JW, Bost J, Ahmed F, et al. The NCQAs' quality compass: Evaluating managed care in the United States. *Health Aff (Millwood).* 1998;17(1):152–158.
82. Himmelstein DU, Woolhandler S, Hellander I, Wolfe SM. Quality of care in investor-owned vs not-for-profit HMOs. *JAMA.* 1999;282(2):159–163.
83. Hellander I. Quality of care lower in for-profit HMOs than in non-profits. PHNP news release, July 12, 1999.
84. Luft HS, Bunker JP, Enthoven AC. Should operations be regionalized? The empirical relation between surgical volume and mortality. *N Engl J Med.* 1979;301:1364–1369.
85. Dudley RA, Johansen KL, Brand R, et al. Selective referral to high-volume hospitals: estimating potentially avoidable deaths. *JAMA.* 2000;283:1159–1166.
86. Hannan EL. The relation between volume and outcome in health care. *N Engl J Med.* 1999; 340:1677–1679.
87. Birkmeyer JD. High-risk surgery—Follow the crowd. *JAMA.* 2000;283:1191–1193.
88. Schlenker RE, Hittle DF, Hrincevich CA, Kaehny MM. Volume/outcome relationships in small, rural hospitals. *J Rural Health.* 1996;12(5):395.
89. Larson EH, Hart LG, Rosenblatt RA. Rural residence and poor birth outcome in Washington state. *J Rural Health.* 1992;8(3):162–170.
90. Hart LG, Dobie SA, Baldwin LM, et al. Rural and urban differences in physician resource use for low-risk obstetrics. *Health Serv Res.* 1996;31(4):429–452.
91. Rosenblatt RA, Saunders GR, Tressler CJ, et al. The diffusion of obstetric technology into rural U.S. hospitals. *Int J Technol Assess Health Care.* 1994;10(3):479–489.
92. Booske BC, Sainfort F, Hundt AS. Eliciting consumer preferences for health plans. *Health Serv Res.* 1999;34:839–854.
93. Lubalin JS, Harris-Kojetin LD. What do consumers want and need to know in making health care choices? *Med Care Res Rev.* 1999;56(suppl 1):67–102.
94. Robinson S, Brodie M. Understanding the quality challenge for consumers: The Kaiser AHCPR Survey. *Jt Comm J Qual Improv.* 1997;23(5):239–234.
95. Erickson LC, Torchiana DR, Schneider EC, Newburger JW, Hannan EL. The relationship between managed care insurance and use of lower-mortality hospitals for CABG surgery. *JAMA.* 2000;283:1976–1982.
96. Schneider EC, Epstein AM. Use of public performance reports: A survey of patients undergoing cardiac surgery. *JAMA.* 1998;279:1638–1642.
97. Gabel JR, Ginsburg PB, Hunt KA. Small employers and their health benefits, 1998–1996: An awkward adolescence. *Health Aff (Millwood).* 1997;16(5):103–110.
98. Prager LO. Top accreditor ties accountability to higher HMO quality. *Am Med News.* October 19, 1998:10,13.
99. Brook RH, Kamberg CJ, McGlynn EA. Health system reform and quality. *JAMA.* 1996;276:476–480.
100. Berman HS. Performance measures: The destination or the journey? *Effective Clin Pract.* 1999;2(6):284–288.

101. Kilo CM, Endsley S. As good as it *could* get: Remaking the medical practice. *Fam Pract Manage.* 2000;7(5):48–52.
102. Chassin MR. Is health care ready for six sigma quality? *Milbank Q.* 1998;76(4):565–591.
103. Dentzer S. Media mistakes in coverage of the Institute of Medicine's error report. *Effective Clin Pract.* 2000;3(6):305–308.
104. Larson EB, Newcomer LN, Brennan TA, et al. First do no harm—To err is human. *Effective Clin Pract.* 2000;3(6):294–296.

19
Previous Attempts to Reform the System

Having touched on the high points of major trends and current problems of U.S. health care over the past 100 years in the preceding 18 chapters, now we consider the effectiveness, or ineffectiveness, of the principal efforts to reform the health care system since 1900. The persistent problems leading to these reform initiatives were the lack of access to health care or its high cost, although as we saw in the last chapter, the issue of quality has arisen in the 1990s as another key problem stirring forces for change. Since the United States stands as the only industrialized Western nation without some kind of national health insurance program guaranteeing universal access and the problem of access is such a strong driver of reform initiatives, this chapter focuses on efforts to establish national health insurance (NHI).

Between 1912 and 1994, there were five major reform initiatives to create such a system, all unsuccessful. With a view to better understanding the reasons for the continued failure of major reform proposals, this chapter has three goals: (1) to briefly discuss the concept of representational communities as they relate to political change; (2) to examine the major reform initiatives in terms of their content, countervailing forces, and political outcomes; and (3) to derive what lessons can be taken from these experiences.

REPRESENTATIVE COMMUNITIES
AND POLITICAL CHANGE

Mark Peterson, a leading policy analyst and scholar in government affairs, offers a useful way to better understand the political process and outcomes of reform initiatives: the concept of representational communities (i.e., the organized interests in a particular policy domain). Competing interests are seen in terms of "stakeholders" (interests that benefit from the status quo) and "stake challengers" (interests that challenge the status quo because they either do not benefit or are harmed by it).[1]

As this concept applies to U.S. health care, Peterson makes the case that the representational community from 1890 to the 1950s was a homogenous block type. During these years, the major stakeholders (e.g., American Medical Association, American Hospital Association, specialty organizations, the health insurance industry, and after World War II, business) were not confronted by serious stake challengers. After the 1950s, he argued, a polarized *dyad* community was formed as an increasing number of stake challengers (e.g., consumer, civil rights, environmental, and women's groups) gained power and influence. These new stake challengers joined established stake challengers in creating a broader-based coalition for reform. By the 1990s, the "iron triangle" of closely allied stakeholders (the medical profession, insurance industry, and business) was facing stronger pressures from a gathering coalition of stake challengers, to the point that their traditional alliance was breaking down into competition among themselves.[1]

Today, even the AMA realizes that the status quo is not sustainable and has begun to support limited changes. The interests of hospitals and physicians no longer necessarily are unified. The interests of small business are not well represented by large employers, while the insurance industry has been fragmented by increasing competition.[1]

A 1985 survey by Jack Walker, based at the Institute for Public Policy at the University of Michigan, sheds light on evolving collective views about public policy for health care. Walker compared the perspectives of national voluntary associations by sector and year of founding with reference to their level of interest in federal expenditure, service, and regulation for health care. The years were selected on the basis of the politics of each period: 1945, when President Truman was beginning to promote compulsory social health insurance; 1970, just before President Nixon's call for NHI; and 1985, the year of the study and before reform initiatives of the 1990s. Table 19-1 displays the level of group support by sector for each of these years. Some fascinating observations can be derived from these numbers. For example, collectively all groups were almost evenly split over the need for greater federal involvement in health care. Nearly two thirds of citizens groups, regardless of the year of founding, favored a stronger federal role in health care. Groups founded in 1985 in the mixed profit/nonprofit and nonprofit sectors were much more likely to favor a larger federal role, whereas groups in the profit sector showed little interest in such a role.[2]

FIVE MAJOR ATTEMPTS TO ESTABLISH NHI

With that introductory background, it is interesting to observe and compare the political dynamics of each of the major attempts to establish a national health insurance program in the United States during the 20th century.

First Attempt: 1912–1917

National health insurance was first brought into public debate in the United States when the Progressive Party, under Theodore Roosevelt, made it a plat-

Table 19-1   Group Support for the Expansion of Federal Expenditures/Services and
Regulation in Health and Other Human Services, by Sector and Founding Date

Sector Represented	Year by Which Group Was Founded	N	Percentage Favoring "Much More" Federal Expenditure or Service	N	Percentage Favoring "Much More or More" Federal Regulation
All	1945	106	40	100	43
	1970	189	51	171	43
	1985	260	53	229	45
Profit	1945	28	21	30	10
	1970	44	30	44	11
	1985	54	26	56	14
Mixed profit/ nonprofit	1945	2	0	2	50
	1970	6	33	6	66
	1985	13	54	12	50
Nonprofit	1945	40	38	35	43
	1970	80	59	70	39
	1985	101	59	82	38
Citizen	1945	22	64	19	63
	1970	45	62	37	70
	1985	77	64	64	72

Source: Reprinted with permission from Peterson MA. Political influence in the 1990s: From iron triangles to policy networks. *J Health Polit Policy Law.* 1993;18(2):416.

form plank in 1912.[3] The trend over the preceding 30 years had been to establish such programs in many European countries, usually as sickness insurance (Germany was the first in 1883).[4] Congress held hearings in 1916 on a federal plan providing disability and sickness benefits, and several states introduced health insurance bills during those years, including New York, Massachusetts, and California.[3] Momentum seemed to be a gathering toward some sort of national plan, with even the AMA adopting the following resolution in 1917, as recommended by its social insurance committee:[5]

> the time is present when the profession should study earnestly to solve the questions of medical care that will arise under various forms of social insurance. Blind opposition, indignant repudiation, bitter denunciation of these laws is worse than useless; it leads nowhere and it leaves the profession in a position of helplessness as the rising tide of social development sweeps over it.

There is prophetic irony in this 1917 AMA position, since it would soon be overruled by strong resistance within the medical profession and the AMA would later resist all subsequent attempts to establish NHI.[3,6]

Between 1912 and 1917, despite energetic efforts by various reform groups, including a strong American Association for Labor Legislation (AALL), an alliance between employers and medicine developed that successfully defeated Progressive proposals for a national system of health insurance. As Paul Starr points out in his classic book, *The Social Transformation of American Medicine*, the strongest interest groups often had uncertain and conflicting positions as the public debate evolved. For example, the AMA initially showed support for NHI, then reversed itself, while organized labor ended up siding more with business than the reformers of the time.[4,7] By 1917, the collective opposition of state medical associations, together with the sudden change in national priorities with America's entry into World War I, for the time killed the movement toward a national insurance program.[4]

In his analysis comparing the failure of NHI in America in 1917 with successes in western European countries, Starr concluded that ideology, historical experience, and the overall political context played the most important roles in how interest groups formulated their positions. Compulsory health insurance was accepted more readily in Europe. In the United States, it was strongly opposed by organized medicine and many also felt that American values of individual initiative and self-reliance could be undermined by such a program. In addition, the authority of an American president was far less than a Bismarck or Lloyd George in pushing through a national program against political opposition.[4]

Second Attempt: 1932–1938

The increasing costs of medical care in the 1920s, especially of hospitalization, generated an increasing national concern about the costs of health care. In the later 1920s, an influential group was formed, the Committee on the Costs of Medical Care (CCMC). This was an independent commission with private funding and included economists, physicians, and public health professionals. The CCMC led the charge toward reconsideration of a national program of health insurance. As the Great Depression enveloped the country, a "new approach to health insurance was needed because the costs of medical care now involve larger sums of money and affect more people than does wage-loss due to sickness."[8] For a growing number of families, bills for medical care grew to a third or even half their annual income.[4]

In the landmark report of the Committee on Economic Security (which led to the Social Security Act of 1935), the principle of national health insurance was endorsed. However, largely due to the consolidated professional power within medicine, President Franklin D. Roosevelt decided not to confront the AMA's opposition at that time, and the Social Security Act became law with no provision for NHI. A newly founded, private health insurance company (Blue Cross) was being promoted as an alternative to compulsory health insurance.[9] Blue Cross leaders argued that Blue Cross coverage would[10]

> eliminate the demand for compulsory health insurance and stop the reintroduction of vicious sociological bills into the state legislature year after year— Blue Cross Plans are a distinctly American institution, a unique combination of individual initiative and social responsibility. They perform a public service without public compulsion.

The later 1930s saw a new push for some form of NHI, led especially by reform interests within the federal government but also supported, interestingly enough, by a small group of liberal academic physicians. By 1937, the Committee of Physicians for the Improvement of Medicine had over 400 members, and called for a national health policy which would include expansion of preventive care, public health and care for the "medically indigent."[4]

In 1937 a Technical Committee on Medical Care was established within the federal government, with the mission to formulate a national health program. Its final report proposed, among other things, increased assistance for those unable to pay for medical care and "consideration of a general medical care program supported by taxes, insurance, or both."[11] A National Health Conference was called for the summer of 1938 to discuss the technical committee's report. Very concerned about public support for compulsory health insurance, the AMA called an emergency session of its House of Delegates and endorsed, for the first time, cash indemnity insurance as well as expansion of public health services and federal assistance for care of the medically indigent. AMA's support for indemnity insurance was made contingent on the approval of county and state medical societies, while federal efforts on behalf of the medically indigent were to remain under local control.[12] The AMA, however, remained firmly opposed to national health insurance,[13] lobbied hard against it, then won the day as FDR decided to postpone NHI until a later campaign.[4]

Third Attempt: 1945–1950

Although President Roosevelt had earlier postponed NHI as a major issue, he did not abandon it, and in his 1944 State of the Union message returned the issue to the legislative agenda. He asked Congress for an "economic bill of rights," to include a plan for adequate medical care.[3] Roosevelt died before he could pursue the concept, but President Harry Truman proposed a comprehensive NHI program in 1946. The plan was to be administered through the Social Security system, and its basic provisions became incorporated into the Wagner-Murray-Dingell bill in Congress.[14] Intense public debate ensued, battle lines drawn between opposing forces, with the AMA and American Hospital Association (AHA) allied against it and the Committee on the Nation's Health, an ad hoc group of liberals and union leaders, leading the proponents.[3] Truman assured critics that "people would get medical and hospital services just as they do now," and that this program would not be "socialized medicine."[14] However, opposing interests again defeated NHI by lobbying a Republican-controlled Congress against the bill and playing to the public's neo-Cold War fears of "socialism."[15] The only solace to supporters of NHI was the passage in 1950 of amendments to the Social Security Act whereby federal "vendor payments" could be made to the states as matching funds for medical care of welfare recipients, thus providing the basis for future federal-state public assistance programs.[3,4]

This third battle over NHI had been especially bitter. The AMA claimed that Truman's plan would turn physicians into "slaves" and proposed instead an expansion of voluntary health insurance and indigent care services.[4,16] Initial public attitudes toward the NHI plan were favorable among 58 percent of respondents to national surveys in 1945[17] but eroded in later surveys, which showed a majority of people favoring voluntary insurance.[18] The AMA, which committed large amounts of campaign spending to the effort, had successfully led the opposition through alliances with the AHA, community organizations, large corporations, and public opinion.[19] Voluntary insurance also was supported by such groups as the American Bar Association, the Chamber of Commerce, and most of the country's press. As Starr observed, the rejection of NHI after World War II stands out as an exception to the postwar pattern of rising social welfare expenditures in the United States and other advanced Western societies.[4] Peterson noted that the major stakeholders in U.S. health care until the 1950s (e.g., the AMA, specialty organizations, and the AHA) held similar views of optimal governmental policy—"the government should protect their interests, including favorable tax policy but not intervene in the delivery and financing of health care."[1,4]

Fourth Attempt: 1973–1974

While the 1950s and 1960s were quiet on the NHI front, major shifts were taking place in the balance of power between stakeholders and stake challengers. A broader-based coalition for reform, together with increasing polarity with stakeholders, grew out of the battles over Medicare in the 1960s.[1] Health insurance for the elderly was a major issue during the presidential elections of 1960 and 1964. As a result, Medicare was passed in 1965 as the first compulsory national health insurance program, covering 10 percent of the population.[3]

After enactment of Medicare and Medicaid legislation in 1965, the next few years saw a broader movement toward some kind of national health insurance coverage. The battle lines between stakeholders and stake challengers again were drawn. Many agreed that health care was in crisis, and some held the medical profession responsible for the problems of health care. Many advocates of reform shared the view of one writer in *Fortune* in 1970: "The doctors created the system. They run it and they are the most formidable obstacle to its improvement."[20] Peterson paints the political landscape in those years in these interesting terms:[1]

> From different directions, the efficiency-oriented and the rights-oriented critics had arrived at many of the same reform proposals. Liberals had long supported prepaid group practice, expanded use of a health team including nurse practitioners and physicians' assistants, auditing of professional performance, and health planning as ways to improve medical care. In the early seventies, conservatives began to appropriate many of these ideas as ways to cut costs. Liberals also thought there would be savings from reform but hoped to use the savings to make health insurance universal and comprehensive. Yet even without consensus about the ends of reform, there was agreement about many of the means.

Perhaps the most fundamental issue being debated on this landscape was how the United States should interpret and apply the right to health care. Liberals argued that everyone should have "full and unencumbered access to all available medical services based on the medical needs of the individual."[21] Conservatives countered that the right to health care is a "qualified right granted patients but modified by the available resources within the health care system and the rights of physicians to control the practice of their professions."[21] The Supreme Court recognized "an acknowledged right to health derived from a constitutionally guaranteed right to life and happiness."[21,22]

Confronted by an increasingly powerful wave of reform sentiment, the AMA, in a reversion to its 1917 position, brought forward its Medicredit proposal as an alternative to NHI. Medicredit would provide tax credits for buying private insurance; as a limited subsidy, there were no built-in cost controls.[4] The AMA's proposal was soon challenged by other proposals, including the Health Security Program, introduced by Senator Edward Kennedy in 1970 (with the backing of the AFL-CIO and the Committee for National Health Insurance) and the National Healthcare Act (the private health insurance industry's proposal put forward in 1971).[3]

In 1970, the Nixon administration found itself dealing with numerous liberal initiatives from a Democrat-controlled Congress in a predominantly liberal political climate. Health care again was a pressing issue, and President Nixon put forward his own "Play-or-Pay" health care proposal as an alternative to Kennedy's single-payer plan. Play or Pay required employers to either offer acceptable coverage to their employees or pay a tax that would finance their coverage from an insurance pool that also would cover the unemployed.[23] The Nixon plan also promoted the widespread adoption of HMOs, with the hope to so cover 90 percent of the population by 1980.[24] His plan would have required employers to provide a minimum package of health insurance benefits under a National Health Insurance Standards Act, and a federally administered Family Health Insurance Program would be established to provide a basic benefit package for low-income families. The competing health care proposals generated intense debate, with opponents to the administration's plan labeling it a "windfall" to the private insurance industry while still not providing access to care for the entire population (20 to 40 million people still would not have health care coverage).[4]

President Nixon was besieged by Vietnam and the Watergate scandal, and it soon became impossible to forge bipartisan support for any health care proposal. A compromise proposal, put together by Senator Kennedy and Representative Wilbur Mills, would have required copayments of 25 percent and assured that no individual or family would pay more than $1,000 for health care in any year.[25] The Kennedy-Mills plan was rejected, however, by organized labor and other liberal organizations; and although most of the opposition to NHI had "melted away," there were insufficient votes in Congress to enact any of the proposals.[26–28]

The fourth attempt to establish NHI came quite close to passage. As Starr noted, "If the name on the Administration's plan had not been Nixon and had the time not been the year of Watergate, the United States might have had national health insurance in 1974."[4] Nixon had recast liberal ideas and moved far beyond a traditional conservative agenda. Unfortunately, however, the opportunity for structural reform of U.S. health care again was lost. A severe economic recession in 1974 and 1975, together with rising inflation, and a worldwide energy crisis, led to a backlash against the liberal agenda and the end of the post-World War II growth of social entitlements.[4] As Starr observed, the "politics of health care in the second half of the 1970s mirrored a general political stalemate in the society."[4] National concerns shifted to cost containment of rising health care costs in a market-driven marketplace.

Fifth Attempt: 1993–1994

As we saw in earlier chapters, the 1980s and early 1990s were marked by increasing competition and consolidation in a rapidly changing medical marketplace. Managed care (reimbursement) was taking center stage. Insurance carriers were shifting to managed care plans, with even the Blues converting to for-profit status and announcing their intent to provide 90 percent of their benefits through managed care contracts by the year 2000. Physicians became assimilated into the new world of independent practice associations, HMOs, and physician-hospital organizations, while pharmaceutical manufacturers began to develop drug distribution systems. Competition was the byword as increasing costs, decreasing access, and unpredictable quality threatened the fast-changing health care "system."[29]

The corporatization of U.S. health care spread rapidly during the 1980s and 1990s in a growing market increasingly filled by for-profit health plans and organizations. The nation's more than 1,200 insurers competed aggressively for the business of employers whose employees were young and well paid while avoiding groups with older employees more likely to need medical care.[30]

Health care reform was promised in the 1992 presidential campaign as part of the Democratic platform. The two years after President Clinton's election in 1992 were filled with a new flurry of legislative activity and intense debate in the administration and both houses of Congress. Table 19-2 outlines the main features of the five major proposals as they were debated in 1993 and 1994.[31] Four of the proposals represented variants of managed competition, conceived as competition among health plans, whereby each theoretically would offer a package of services and prices and all would have an incentive to contain rather than inflate costs.[23] The single-payer proposal was based on the Canadian system.

The single payer proposal (HR1200) put forward by Representative Jim McDermott (D-Wash), offered the most fundamental structural system reform of any of the options. Ironically, as the only proposal with grassroots support, it attracted the largest number of supporters in Congress of any of the competing proposals and was the only one to pass out of committee. But it soon was lost in the shuffle, as lobbyists and the media focused the debate on the Clinton Health Plan. The major media marginalized and even ridiculed the single-payer alternative as "extreme" or "utopian" and never fairly covered the Canadian system as a model for reform.[32] As Navarro pointed out, there are close ties between the media and the stakeholders through financial contributions as well as editorially (e.g., the editorial board of the *New York Times* includes CEOs of several insurance companies).[33] There was only one mention of the single-payer proposal in all of 1993 on ABC's "World News Tonight." Some TV station managers even admitted that they didn't want to antagonize the insurance industry (which was strongly opposed to a single-payer system) by running ads favoring a single-payer plan.[34]

Table 19-2   Key Features of NHI Proposals, 1993–1994

American Health Security Act (Clinton Health Plan)	The Clinton plan would require all Americans to purchase a government-specified standard benefit package through a government regulated alliance. Requires employers to pay at least 80 percent of the cost of their employees' premiums. Provides subsidies to small business with less than 50 employees and individuals/families below 150 percent of the federal poverty level. Limits annual spending growth to consumer price index (CPI) by regulating growth in premiums and imposing fee schedules without balance billing on providers. Tax deductibility only for approved benefits.
Single Payer (H. R. 1200)	Sponsored by liberal Democrats, it is modeled after the Canadian system. Federally mandated benefits administered by the states. Federal government finances 86 percent of cost through new payroll tax. Provider payments set through annually negotiated budgets. Annual expenditure growth limited to increases in gross domestic product (GDP).
Managed Competition (H. R. 3222)	It is the only plan with bipartisan support, which includes moderate House Democrats and Republicans. Modeled after the concepts espoused by Alain Entoven and the Jackson Hole Health Care Reform Group, it would require employers of less than 100 employees to join a health plan purchasing cooperative (HPPC), which would be a state-chartered non-profit cooperative, but the plan would not require employers to pay for their employees' coverage. Specifies a standard benefit package which must be offered by cooperatives, but others also may be offered. Medicaid would be abolished. The unemployed and employed below 200 percent of federal poverty level would receive subsidized coverage. Tax deductibility by businesses and individuals limited to the value of the lowest cost standard benefits plan offered by a cooperative.
Affordable Health Care (H. R. 3080)	This plan is sponsored by the House GOP leadership. Employers obligated to offer plans to workers. Insurers required to offer small employers standard and catastrophic plans, ignore pre-existing conditions and guarantee job change coverage. Extends Medicaid coverage to 200 percent of poverty. Relies on voluntary establishment of purchasing cooperatives with elimination of state barriers to managed care and mandated benefits. No specific cost containment provisions.
Health Equity and Access Reform Today (HEART)	Sponsored by Senate GOP leadership. All citizens required to purchase coverage or be penalized by Internal Revenue Service (IRS) 20 percent of the cost of the average regional plan. Employers must offer plans, but not pay for them. Vouchers provided for low-income families up to 240 percent of federal poverty level. Limits tax deductibility of benefits. Relies on voluntary regional purchasing alliances, consumer information, tort reform, and administrative simplification to contain costs.

Source: Reprinted with permission from Teach RL. Health care reform: Changes and challenges. Reform teleconference draws 4,000. *Medical Group Management Update.* November 1993:4.

The process involved in the Clinton Health Plan (CHP) is interesting, inasmuch as it foretold its political outcome. Hillary Rodham Clinton's Health Care Task Force was carefully selected to represent the key groups and players most involved in the medical/industrial complex and themselves responsible for the health care system's pervasive problems. The task was to develop a plan that could be approved by these players, which was dictated largely by the concept of managed competition as conceived earlier by the Jackson Hole Group. The insurance industry and business were the major players represented on the task force, but even they held deep divisions and separate agendas. Insurers were divided by size—the "Gang of Five" (oligarchs including Prudential, Metropolitan Life, Aetna, CIGNA, and John Hancock) versus many hundreds of small insurers with its own trade organization, the Health Insurance Association of America (HIAA). As different as were the interests and objectives of insurers by size, the same situation prevailed for employers. Big Business could support employer mandates, which became the anathema for small employers.

In an attempt to please divided factions within the Task Force, the CHP became such a tangle of compromises and contradictions that support among the represented groups soon began to fall away. Colin Gordon, who teaches American history at the University of Iowa and has a long interest in the politics of health care, described the political minefield as follows:[35]

> The CHP's fatal flaw, at least in these terms, lay in its attempt to combine employer mandates (which attracted health interests and repelled many employers) and cost control (which attracted employers and repelled health interests). This pairing made for a slow dance to the right, as reaction set in from all quarters against employer mandates, against spending controls, against any increased federal presence in health care. This reaction showed up, in turn, in the whining of Congressional conservatives, the CHP's drastic revision by Congressional Democrats, the various (misnamed) "mainstream" or "moderate" alternatives, and the final admission by Congressional leaders that they had nothing left to pass.

The CHP ended up as a 1,342 page bill (1,340 pages longer than the Canada Health Act). Even early supporters had become critics. Support in Congress became so diluted that the bill never actually got out of committee to a vote on the floor of the House.[35]

The fight over the CHP was fought among competing stakeholders to such a point of compromise that the proposal was dead on arrival in Congress. As Charles Andrews observed in *Profit Fever: The Drive to Corporatize Health Care and How to Stop It*:[36]

> Every special interest in the health industry—big insurance companies and middle-sized ones, the managed care industry, employers who provide health benefits and those who do not, big corporations and small business, hospitals, and physicians—rolled into Washington, D.C., with fat bankrolls and slick lobbyists.

The battle was particularly intense within the insurance industry itself. In the interests of smaller insurers, HIAA spent $14 million on a national television advertising campaign, "Harry and Louise," who sat at their kitchen table debating the CHP. They concluded that that plan could never work, that there must be a better way (never explained). They were really fighting the insurance oligarchy, the Gang of Five, who were pushing to drive small insurers out of business through their well-capitalized domination of the managed care market.[35] In the end, and in the absence of any leader concerned with the general welfare or even the broadest interest of the business class as a whole, the result nearly a year later was nothing.[36] Along the way, as a result of a political sellout to the insurance industry, the battle-scarred bill was dubbed by cynics as the "Health Insurance Industry Preservation Act."[35]

The failure of the CHP became a political debacle for the Clinton administration, at least partly responsible for heavy Democratic losses to the Republicans in the mid-year 1994 elections. After its demise, there was no shortage of analyses of its failure. It was widely criticized as too lengthy (1,342 pages), too complex, too expensive, and poorly conceived. Its complexity is well illustrated by its structure (Figure 19-1). Joseph Califano, who had served as President Carter's Secretary of Health, Education, and Welfare, was scathing in his comments: "Clinton's plan rests on the belief that an army of policy works can predict what would happen under a program that would change one-seventh of the economy, which 30 years of experience tells us we can't do."[37] Many felt that the length and complexity of the proposal gave ammunition to its critics. Small employers were especially vocal in opposing it. Walter McNerney offered

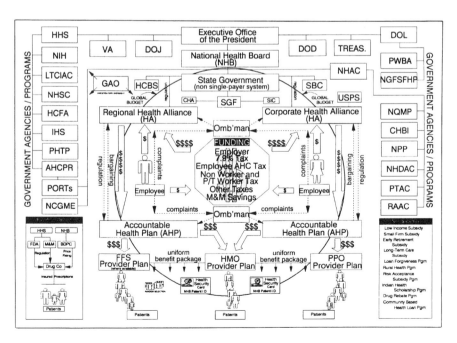

Figure 19-1 Flowchart of the proposed Clinton health plan. Courtesy of Representative Dick Armey, chairman of the House Republican Conference. (Reprinted with permission from Fischer P. The emperor's new clothes. *J Fam Pract.* 1993;37:543–544.)

several important factors in its defeat: growing antigovernment resentment, lack of support within the working middle class, public concern about increased taxes, and distrust of centralized top-down bureaucracies.[29] Quinton Young, an internist and national coordinator for Physicians for a National Health Program, summed up the political situation as follows:[35]

> The might of the anti-reform power-brokers literally blocked definitive consideration of the single-payer proposal. This was possible only because President Clinton, from the outset, acknowledged the superiority of this alternative while signaling his conviction that it was infeasible. That is, he lacked the political will to confront the powerful opponents and the political honesty to admit that his "mandated premiums" were as much of a tax as the progressive tax base of single payer. In the end, it was the fatally flawed CHP that was so infeasible it could not even get out of Committee! Let us speculate about a scenario that never emerged. Instead of his 1,340 page monstrosity, imagine if the President supported the McDermott-Conyers-Wellstone single-payer bill. With perhaps 150 votes in the House and, maybe, a dozen in the Senate, he could have faced the voters on November 8 as the champion of a People's health care plan. Is it not possible that the reactionary triumph could have been avoided? Remember, exit polls found the voters still designating health reform number one among their concerns. More importantly, would not some portion of the 61% of the electorate who didn't vote be finally moved to participate?

The most common explanation given in the mainstream media and academic press for the failure of the CHP was that the public was not ready and was confused and ambivalent. From his base on health policy at Johns Hopkins University, Vincente Navarro strongly disagreed with this assessment. He offered a compelling and well-documented case that class-based power brokers determined the outcome of the health care debate. The corporate class (including large employers, large and small insurers, and the medical industries) and the upper middle class (including small employers and professionals) were well financed and effective in exerting powerful lobbying influence upon both major political parties.[38] Navarro observed:[33]

> The United States is the only country where the welfare state is, for the most part, privatized. Consequently, when workers lose their jobs, health care benefits for themselves and their families are also lost. In no other country does this occur. This is why the corporate class and its instruments in the United States oppose establishing government-guaranteed universal entitlements: They strengthen the working class and weaken the capitalist class. The staggering power of the capitalist class and enormous weakness of the working class explains why health care reform failed again. The United States, the only major capitalist country without government-guaranteed universal health care coverage, is also the only nation without a social-democratic or labor party that serves as the political instrument of the working class and other popular classes. These two facts are related. In most advanced countries, the establishment of universal entitlement programs has been based on the political alliances of the working class with the middle classes, through the election of social-democratic governments or through their pressure on non-social-democratic governments.[38]

LESSONS FROM REFORM FAILURES

We reviewed five attempts to reform the U.S. health care system since 1912. All failed. What can be learned from this experience? Six overall lessons emerge from these repeated failures:

1. *Although representing only a small segment of society, the concentration of power and money in the hands of a few dominant stakeholders presents enormous obstacles to NHI.* So far they have felt sufficiently threatened to effectively prevent enactment of NHI and are sufficiently financed and organized to "buy off" both major political parties in defense of their self-interest. The stakeholders spent $300 million in defeating the Clinton Health Plan in 1993 and 1994 and stifled consideration of a single-payer alternative by promoting disinformation and marginal coverage of the Canadian system by the press.[32] Both major political parties are seduced by campaign finance contributions by these special interest groups, as concluded by William Greider in *Who Will Tell the People?* In his analysis of the power of money, the milk of U.S. politics, he observed: "Anomalous as it may seem, Wall Street is a major source of financing for the party of working people" (i.e., the Democratic Party).[39]

2. *Successful reform efforts need to be based on solid principles that are basic enough to be readily understood and supported by a broad spectrum of societal interests.* Two examples make this point. The failed Clinton Health Plan, designed by stakeholders committed to their own interests, was too complex and compromised to achieve grassroots support. The Canadian Health Plan, as we see in Chapter 23, was solidly based on only five principles, which were sustained throughout a heated political debate to eventual passage in 1984.

3. *Broad support of the middle class will be* **required** *before any major proposal for NHI is likely to be enacted.*[9,15,40] Such broad support will not be generated by a top-down approach, whereby lobbyists from national organizations of stakeholders work with their representatives in Congress to design the legislative agenda. That approach is bound to fail, as it did in 1993 and 1994, and doesn't lead to a groundswell of popular support for reform.

4. *Strong bipartisan support in Congress will be needed before any national health insurance plan can be passed.* With regard to the debate over the Clinton proposal in 1994, for example, the Democrats were divided, with conservative Democrats seeing no political gain in supporting universal coverage and preferring either the status quo or expansion of coverage through employer mandates.[41]

5. *Despite the increasing problems of access, cost, and quality of health care in the United States, the country remains on a path of incremental changes, thus far largely ineffective in dealing with these problems.* NHI was returned to the closet after the failure of health care reform in 1994 as the operative words within the marketplace continued to be *competition, consolidation, consumer choice,* and *return on investment.*

6. *While the problems of U.S. health care get worse and national reform efforts fail for lack of consensus, the states are likely to develop and test reform plans earlier than the federal government.* As shown in the last three

chapters, some states already are taking the lead in developing health care programs that improve access and quality of care while containing its costs. Hawaii represents an excellent case example; while providing nearly universal coverage, its total health care expenditures in 1993 were only 8 percent compared to 12 percent in the rest of the country, and it had better health outcomes in terms of longevity and fewer preventable deaths.[42] The states strongly support federally financed NHI but naturally want to retain their authority to set policy, regulate quality, and administer programs.[43]

CONCLUDING COMMENTS

This chapter has been discouraging to the extent that five well-motivated, serious attempts to reform U.S. health care over the last 90 years ended in failure, while its basic problems persist and worsen. The need for major reform has not gone away, however, just delayed until the sixth major attempt to enact NHI takes shape. An economic downturn will hasten the arrival of that time. Ideally, the lessons learned from previous reform failures will be recalled by policy makers and leaders of that effort. In view of the well-practiced, self-protective behavior of the stakeholders resisting change, campaign finance reform probably will be required before major reform can taken place. We revisit political developments since 1994 in the next chapter as they relate to the prospects for future reform efforts, to be considered in Chapters 22 and 24.

REFERENCES

1. Peterson MA. Political influence in the 1990s: From iron triangles to policy networks. *J Health Polit Policy Law.* 1993;18(2):395–438.
2. Walker JL. *Activities and Maintenance Strategies of Interest Groups in the United States, 1980 and 1985.* Ann Arbor: University of Michigan, Institute of Public Policy Studies, 1985, and Inter-University Consortium for Political and Social Research, 1991.
3. Somers AR, Somers HM. *Health and Health Care: Policies In Perspective.* Germantown, MD: Aspen Systems Corp, 1977:179–180.
4. Starr P. *The Social Transformation of American Medicine.* New York: Basic Books 1982.
5. Burrow JG. *AMA: Voice of American Medicine.* Baltimore: Johns Hopkins Press, 1963:144.
6. Compulsory health insurance. *JAMA.* 1920;74(18):1276.
7. Karson M. *American Labor Unions and Politics, 1900–1918.* Carbondale, IL: Southern Illinois University Press, 1958.
8. Davis MM. The American approach to health insurance. Milbank Q. July 12, 1934:214–215.
9. Rothman DJ. A century of failure: Health care reform in America. *J Health Polit Policy Law.* 1993;18(2):271–286.
10. Rothman DJ. The public presentation of Blue Cross, 1935–1965. *J Health Polit Policy Law.* 1991;16(4):671–693.
11. A National Health Program: Report of the Technical Committee on Medical Care. In: *Interdepartmental Committee to Coordinate Health and Welfare Activities, Proceedings of the National Health Conference, July 18–20, 1938.* Washington DC: U.S. Government Printing Office, 1938:29–63.
12. Proceedings of the special session. Minutes to the special session of the House of Delegates of the American Medical Association. *JAMA.* 1938;111(13):1191–1217.
13. Fishbein M. American medicine and the National Health Program. *N Engl J Med.* 1939; 220(12):495–504.

14. A National Health Program: Message from the president. *Soc Secur Bulletin.* 1945;8(12).
15. Thai KV, Qiao Y, McManus SM. National health care reform failure: The political economy perspective. *J Health Hum Serv Adm.* Fall 1998; 21(2):236–259.
16. Poen M. *Harry S. Truman versus the Medical Lobby: The Genesis of Medicare.* Columbia: University of Missouri Press, 1979:85–86.
17. Schiltz ME. *Public Attitudes Toward Social Security, 1935–1965.* Research report no. 33. Washington DC: Social Security Administration, Office of Research and Statistics, 1970:134.
18. Foote, Cone, and Belding. *Survey of Public Relations of the California Medical Profession.* Foote, Cone, and Belding, 1944:4–5.
19. Foote, Cone, and Belding. Survey of Public Relations. In: Schiltz ME. *Public Attitudes Toward Social Security, 1935–1965.* Research report no. 33. Washington DC: Social Security Administration, Office of Research and Statistics, 1970:136–139.
20. Cordtz D. Change begins in the doctor's office. *Fortune* January 1970;81(1):84.
21. Kaufmann CL. The right to health care: Some cross-national comparisons and U.S. trends in policy. Soc Sci Med. 1981;15(4):157–162.
22. Michelman F. Forward: On protecting the poor through the Fourteenth Amendment. The Supreme Court, 1968 term. *Harv L Rev.* 1969;83:7.
23. Kuttner R. *Everything for Sale. The Virtues and Limits of Markets.* Chicago: University of Chicago Press, 1997:114.
24. *New York Times,* February 19, 1971.
25. Insuring the nation's health. *Newsweek,* June 3, 1974:73–74.
26. Rivlin AM. Agreed: Here comes national health insurance. *New York Times.* July 21, 1974.
27. Iglehart JK. Consensus forms for national insurance plan, proposals vary widely in scope. *National Journal Reports* December 12, 1973;5:1855–1863.
28. Iglehart JK. Compromise seems unlikely on three major insurance plans. *National Journal Reports.* May 11, 1974;6:700–707.
29. McNerney WJ. C Rufus Rorem Award Lecture. Big question for the Blues: Where to go from here? *Inquiry.* 1996;33(2):110–117.
30. Consumers Union. *How to Resolve the Health Care Crisis: Affordable Protection for All Americans.* Consumer Reports Books, 1992:67.
31. Teach RL. Health care reform: Changes and challenges. Reform teleconference draws 4,000. *Medical Group Management Update.* 1993;(November):1, 4.
32. Brundin J. How the U.S. press covers the Canadian health care system. *Int J Health Serv.* 1993;23(2):275–277.
33. Navarro V. Why Congress did not enact health care reform. *J Health Polit Policy Law.* 1995; 20:196–199.
34. Health care notes. *The Texas Observer.* December 24, 1993:22.
35. Gordon C. *The Clinton Health Care Plan: Dead on Arrival.* Westfield, NJ: Open Magazine Pamphlet Series, 1995.
36. Andrews C. *Profit Fever: The Drive to Corporatize Health Care and How to Stop It.* Monroe, MN: Common Courage Press, 1995:49–58.
37. Will GF. Coming next, Clinton's year one. *Newsweek.* January 24, 1994;123(4).
38. Navarro V. Why some countries have national health insurance, others have national health services, and the U.S. has neither? *Int J Health Serv.* 1989;19(3):383–404.
39. Greider W. *Who Will Tell the People?* New York: Basic Books, 1993.
40. Blendon J, Brodie M, Benson J. What happened to Americans' support for the Clinton health plan? *Health Aff (Millwood).* 1995;14(2):7–23.
41. Brodie DW, Buckley KM. Health care reform in the 103rd Congress: A predictable failure. *J Health Polit Policy Law.* 1995;20(2):447–454.
42. Gilbert FI Jr. Health care in the United States: The need for a new paradigm. *Hawaii Med J.* 1993;52(1):8–10, 12–13.
43. Sparer MS. States and the health care crisis. *J Health Polit Policy Law.* 1993;18(2):503–513.

PART THREE

WHERE CAN WE GO FROM HERE?

20
Current Politics and Health Care Reform

With this chapter, we turn the corner and start into the last part of this book, which will focus on what can be done to address the various problems elucidated for the U.S. health care system as it exists in the year 2001. Recall that we have four major alternative approaches to reform of the present system: (1) incrementalism, the current policy choice; (2) building further on the employer-based health insurance system, with public sector coverage of the unemployed; (3) expanding coverage options within a consumer-choice model without involvement of employers; and (4) developing a single-payer system as a vehicle for universal coverage.

Since policy options depend so heavily on the political climate in which they are raised, this chapter describes today's politics concerning health care with four more specific objectives in mind: (1) to trace the major political developments concerning health care since defeat of the Clinton Health Security Plan in 1994, (2) to outline current competing perspectives and agendas regarding further changes in health care, (3) to describe some activities of the major stakeholders in the present system to resist reform and preserve the present pro-market approach to health care, and (4) to consider whether or not the public interest will be served within the present environment and trends.

POLITICAL DEVELOPMENTS SINCE 1994

Changing Public Opinion Concerning Health Care

The demise of the Clinton Health Plan was a watershed event that returned the health care debate to one of incrementalism, at most. The extent of this impact is illustrated by Blumenthal's observation:[1]

> One indication of how this defeat has changed public discourse on health care is that in the 1996 presidential election, for the first time since World War II, the Democratic candidate did not advocate universal health insurance coverage. By eliminating government as a credible source of solutions to problems

in health care, the defeat of the Clinton proposal for reform sparked our ongoing experiment with private health care markets, which is likely to prove the most enduring health care legacy of the tumultuous Clinton presidency. In effect, the burden is on the critics to prove that markets have failed before comprehensive health care reform will be taken seriously again.

The current health care debate is focused on circumscribed concerns, such as patients' bills of rights, prescription drug coverage for the elderly, containment of the increasing costs of prescription drugs, protection of consumers from abuse of managed care organizations, and extent of privatization of Medicare. No longer are the goals of universal access and comprehensive health care reform very high on the nation's legislative priority list.[2,3] There is growing evidence, however, that the public is becoming increasingly dissatisfied with the health care system and that another opportunity for major system reform will surface again in the not too distant future. Here are some findings of national Harris polls over the last few years (each including about 1,000 adult respondents):

- January 1996: Only 16 percent of Americans agree that "on the whole the health care system works pretty well and only minor changes are needed"; 59 percent think that "fundamental changes" are needed.[4]
- August 1996: 83 percent of Americans believe that ensuring universal coverage should be a national goal.[4]
- September 1997: 50 percent of respondents think the health care system is getting worse, while 54 percent believe managed care harms the quality of care.[5]
- September 1999: 82 percent of both the public and physicians now support "fundamental change or complete rebuilding of the entire health care system"; from 1994 to 1999, these figures increased from 79 percent for the public and from 57 percent for physicians.[6]
- July 2000: Public hostility to HMOs increased for the fifth consecutive year; 59 percent believed that HMOs compromise the quality of care, compared to 39 percent in 1995.[7]

Other national polls report results in the same directions, even including support for a larger role for government. A 1998 Pew survey found that 80 percent of Americans think that the government is doing a "poor" or "fair" job of ensuring that health care is affordable, while 58 percent believe that the government should assure access to care. Zogby, a Republican polling organization, in a 1998 survey, found that 51 percent of Americans would favor a "government-run health care plan that covered everyone in the same way, like that in Canada. It would cover all necessary medical costs and be paid for through taxes"; despite those potentially negative descriptors, only 38 percent were opposed.[7,8] Another national survey by the National Coalition on Health Care revealed that four out of five respondents believe that "medical care has become a big business that puts profits ahead of people" and that the federal government should play an active role in assuring access to care (Tables 20-1 and 20-2).[9,10]

A 1998 issue of the *Wall Street Journal*'s American Opinion feature focused on health care as "the issue of the decade" and put a spotlight on consumer per-

Table 20-1 Confidence in the Health Care System

	% Agree Completely	% Agree Somewhat	% Disagree Somewhat	% Disagree Completely
Medical care has become a big business that puts profits ahead of people.	52	30	11	4
The high cost of medical care is due in part to greed of the insurance companies.	43	31	14	8
Health insurance companies put the needs of customers ahead of profits.	10	14	31	43
I am not very optimistic about the future of health care.	32	26	27	13
There is not much care left in health care these days.	30	23	29	13
I or a family member have had a bad experience with medical treatment or care.	30	14	25	30
Health insurance companies really care about their customers.	9	23	32	33
Quality treatment is the most important thing to a health insurance company.	29	20	25	24
I do not have much confidence in the health care system to take care of me.	20	24	33	20
I feel I can trust my health insurance company to do the right thing for me.	20	29	26	33

Source: Reprinted with permission from ICR poll for the National Coalition on Healthcare, January 1997, and National Coalition on Healthcare. A Report of a National Survey. *J Health Care Finance.* 1997;23:12–20.

spectives. Concerning employer-based health insurance, a *Wall Street Journal*/NBC News poll of 2,006 Americans showed that a majority of respondents felt that employers, regardless of size, should be required to provide health insurance coverage for their employees. About half the respondents believed that the federal government should guarantee access to health care for all Americans, even if it meant an extra annual tax of $2,000.[11] With regard to the impact of HMOs, 86 percent of respondents to the 1998 *Wall Street Journal*/NBC News poll felt that HMOs and other managed care plans are more concerned with cost containment than providing good care. While crediting managed care with holding down costs and providing preventive care services, at the same time they blamed HMOs for limiting access to specialists and interference with the physician-patient relationship. As a result there is now widespread public support, even in the conservative South, for government regulation of HMOs.[12]

Table 20-2   The Role of Government

	% Agree Completely	% Agree Somewhat	% Disagree Somewhat	% Disagree Completely
The federal government can play an important role in making health care more affordable.	50	22	10	16
The federal government can play an important role in making health care better.	43	26	11	18
Government should stay out of health care altogether.	28	12	28	29

Source: Reprinted with permission from ICR poll for the National Coalition on Healthcare, January 1997, and National Coalition on Healthcare. A Report of a National Survey. *J Health Care Finance.* 1997;23:12–20.

There is increasing evidence that a sea change is occurring in public attitudes toward the role of government and that this change is crossing party lines. A 2000 poll commissioned by the Kennedy School, the Kaiser Family Foundation, and National Public Radio found that 88 percent of registered Democrats, as well as 53 percent of Republicans, want government to become more involved in assuring access to affordable health care. David Brooks, of the conservative *The Weekly Standard*, recently observed:[13]

> today, most people don't seem to see government as a major threat to their well-being. Instead, it's the vast impersonal forces of technological change, economic globalization, and a careening culture that appear most threatening. It seems that many voters are looking for an effective government that will be on their side as they try to shape their lives amidst these forces.

Continuing Corporatization of Health Care under Managed Competition

These changing public opinion polls are responding to the downside of the continuing corporatization and consolidation of U.S. health care under the umbrella of managed competition. For-profit HMOs now constitute two thirds of the nation's HMOs.[14] HMO premium revenues and profits are on the rise, and their average administrative costs are over 16 percent.[7,15,16] Inappropriate denial of emergency room services has been widely documented, (e.g., 43 percent rejection rate by CIGNA was discovered by the Pennsylvania Department of Health).[4,17] Widespread marketing abuses also have been reported, such as offering "free" health screenings to screen out sick or pregnant patients,[4,18] as well as disenrollment of patients (e.g., 1 in 10 Medicare HMO enrollees).[6,19]

Other segments of the medical marketplace are running after profits just as fast as for-profit HMOs, with little concern for the public interest or the public purse. For-profit home health agencies, for example, have been found by the federal Department of Health and Human Services to bill for more services than nonprofit providers. Although their patients were not older or sicker, their annual home health Medicare expenditures were over 25 percent higher in 1994.[4,20,21] In the mental health area, administrative costs and profits of for-profit behavioral health firms typically exceed 45 to 50 percent of billings.[4,22] Meanwhile, many hospitals are discharging patients prematurely, as they follow guidelines for hospital stays developed by such actuarial and consulting firms as Milliman and Robertson (M&R). M&R guidelines (e.g., three to four day stays for aortic valve repair, CABC, and partial colectomy) admittedly are not based on scientific evidence or patient outcomes but promulgated with the goal of increased efficiency.[6,23] M&R guidelines for pediatric hospital stays call for stays of three days for complicated appendectomy and one day for asthma, which have been called unreasonable and dangerous by many physicians (usual length of stay for these problems are 5.3 and 2.2 days, respectively, according to a national database of 2,400 hospitals).[24]

A group of Wall Street analysts convened by the Center for Studying Health System Change noted these several trends during the fall of 2000: (1) capitation as another failed experiment, (2) hospitals divesting themselves of money-losing physician practices, (3) physicians with declining negotiating power with stronger health plans and consolidating managed care organizations, and (4) employers accepting rapidly inflating insurance premiums because of the resistance of employees, in a time of low unemployment, to restrictions on health care choices.[25]

As we saw in earlier chapters, the managed competition marketplace has been an outright failure in controlling health care costs or ensuring access and quality of care. Health care inflation, as measured against past U.S. performance or that of other countries, *accelerated* over the last 20 years it has taken to capture two thirds of the employer-paid health insurance market. Much of the cost savings achieved under managed care was achieved by shifting costs to workers and patients.[26] As Robert Kuttner observed:[27]

> In America, the over-reliance on market logic and market institutions is ruining the health-care system. Market enthusiasts fail to tabulate all the costs of relying on market forces to allocate health care—the fragmentation, opportunism, asset rearranging, overhead, under-investment in public health, and the assault on norms of service and altruism. They assume either a degree of self-regulation that the health markets cannot generate, or farsighted public supervision that contradicts the rest of their world view. Health care now consumes fully one-seventh of our entire national income. There is no realm of our mixed economy where markets yield more perverse results.

Legislative and Campaign Politics

Intense partisanship and lack of bipartisan consensus have been the hallmarks of the political climate in recent years. With the exception of some mostly ineffectual federal legislation, Congress has avoided discussion or action on major health care reform proposals. We have seen seven years of "creeping progress" since the collapse of the Clinton Health Plan in 1994, but the major ills of the health care system remain untreated and are getting worse. Later in this chapter, a case is made that this is not accidental. As we just saw, strong and growing public sentiment believes that more needs to be done by government to reform the health care system, yet little real action is being taken. There is, however, a disconnection between public opinion and legislative action as powerful special interests benefiting from the status quo invest heavily in both major political parties.

Three examples of recent federal legislation are mentioned as illustrations of well-intended nonsolutions. The Balanced Budget Act of 1997 (BBA97) created Medicare + Choice plans in an effort to expand options for Medicare beneficiaries and control costs. Three years later, more than 1.6 million beneficiaries have had to switch plans or opt for the fee-for-service (FFS) program, as many such plans fled the market. In addition to discontinuity of care for such patients, the General Accounting Office found that Medicare spent 13.2 percent more on Medicare + Choice enrollees than would have been spent in the FFS program.[28] The Health Insurance Portability and Accountability Act of 1996 (HIPAA), as described in Chapter 17 (pages 269–270), made some marginal improvements, but has been difficult to implement in many markets and patients are not protected from large premium increases. The State Children's Health Insurance Program (CHIP) has not made much difference in coverage between 1997 and 1999, as shown in Table 20-3.

The National Bipartisan Commission on the Future of Medicare, established in 1997 by BBA97, illustrates the near political gridlock so common today in Washington. With 17 members under the cochairmanship of Senator John Breaux (D-La) and Representative Bill Thomas (R-Calif), the commission developed a package of proposals, only to fall one vote short of the number required to adopt them for its report. Even within this small body (which was seen by some as a stacked deck committed to privatizing Medicare), it was not possible to agree on the problems of Medicare and their relative priority.[29]

Table 20-3   Health Insurance Coverage of Children, by Income, 1997 and 1999

	Employer-Sponsored		Medicaid/State/SCHIP		Other		Uninsured	
	1997	*1999*	*1997*	*1999*	*1997*	*1999*	*1997*	*1999*
Below 100% of poverty level	19.3%	21.7%	55.6%	52.2%	3.5%	3.0%	21.7%	23.2%
Below 100%–199% of poverty level	54.7	51.8	17.8	21.9	5.2	4.4	22.3	21.8
Below 200%–299% of poverty level	82.3	76.7	5.3	7.7	3.5	4.5	8.9	11.2
Below 300% of poverty level	91.0	89.4	1.5	2.0	4.5	5.1	3.0	3.5
All incomes	66.8	66.7	16.8	16.4	4.2	4.5	12.2	12.5

Source: Reprinted with permission from Wigton A, et al. 1999 snapshots of America's families II. Urban Institute. *Med Benefits.* 2000;17(23):10.

The 2000 presidential campaign reflected another problem with the current health care debate: its narrow spectrum of differences among alternatives. Only Ralph Nader and the Green Party advocated major structural reform of the health care system through a single-payer program but received only 3 percent of the popular vote. Much heat and little light was generated in the health care political debate between the candidates of the two major parties. Table 20-4 lists the candidates' positions across a range of health care issues, with only minor differences in many cases.

In the aftermath of the 2000 presidential campaign and as the new Republican administration took office, health care again became more important on the legislative agenda. The four most pressing issues are (1) to provide prescription drug coverage for seniors, (2) enact a patients' bill of rights in managed care organizations, (3) help the uninsured get health insurance, and (4) make Medicare fiscally sound. President Bush's program is expected to follow a pro market approach, including a defined benefit/consumer choice option for Medicare beneficiaries, a $48 billion payment to the states to help low-income seniors buy prescription drugs, and refundable tax credits of $1,000 for individuals and $2,000 for families to help with purchase of health insurance.[30]

After one of the closest presidential elections in American history, the body politic and Congress is split almost down the middle. As the 107th Congress starts work in the new millennium, compromise and bipartisanship are required more than ever to avoid political gridlock. As Paul Gigot editorialized in the *Wall Street Journal* after the election: "the only consensus to these results is that there is no consensus."[31]

CONFLICTING PERSPECTIVES AND AGENDAS

Much as politicians and the public share no consensus about how to deal with the increasing ills of the health care system, so too wide differences of opinion lie among the many organizations and interests involved more directly in the health care delivery system. As seen in earlier chapters, managed care (or more accurately managed *reimbursement*) has been the target of the most intense reactions among health care providers the last 10 to 15 years. A recent survey of medical students, residents, faculty, and deans in U.S. medical schools (with over 2,100 respondents and a response rate of 80 percent) showed that 57 percent of the entire group preferred a single-payer health care system as the best one for the most people for a fixed amount of money. Only 21 percent preferred managed care, with 18 percent favoring a FFS system. The survey revealed widespread negative feelings in all groups toward managed care, while expressing broad agreement on the advantages of FFS care in terms of access, a supportive physician-patient relationship, and minimizing ethical conflict between patients and providers.[32]

The AMA and American Medical Student Association (AMSA) have taken very different positions on NHI. The AMSA has come out strongly for a national health program, held a rally in Washington, D.C., in Spring 2000, and lobbied members of Congress toward that goal. The AMA, meanwhile, continues to

Table 20-4   Comparison of Republican and Democratic Health Plans, 2000 Presidential Election

Issue	Governor Bush	Vice President Gore
Overall health care summary	Advocates reducing the number of uninsured citizens by subsidizing their purchase of private health insurance. Also supports limited patients' rights. Advocates additional private-sector health plan choices for Medicare beneficiaries, including options for prescription drug coverage (especially low-income seniors).	Supports incremental movement toward reducing the number of uninsured citizens, first by expanding coverage using existing programs. Also supports broad patients' rights legislation, including the right to sue a health plan for denied services. Defends the rights of the elderly to remain in traditional fee-for-service health insurance plans if they so desire. Advocates a prescription drug benefit that applies to all Medicare beneficiaries.
Tax credits	Would give people who don't have employer-sponsored health insurance an annual tax credit of up to $1,000 per individual and $2,000 per family to cover up to 90 percent of the cost of health insurance.	Advocates the use of tax credits as a way to make insurance more affordable for the uninsured. The tax credit would be the equivalent of 25 percent of a person's health insurance costs.
Children's Health Insurance Program (CHIP)	Wants to give states more flexibility in administering CHIP, a federal block grant, and allow them to expand CHIP to other eligible people, including some parents.	Supports enrolling more children and some parents in state CHIP and in Medicaid. Would expand eligibility to include children living at up to 250 percent of the federal poverty level (currently, a family of four earning $41,000) and make some states responsible for enrolling eligible children.
Medical savings accounts (MSAs)	Wants to make existing MSA pilot program permanent and to lift the federal cap of 750,000 in the number of accounts. Would allow all employers to offer MSAs, and would lower the minimum deductible to accompanying catastrophic health plans to $1,000 for an individual and $2,000 for families.	Opposes the widespread use of MSAs, which he argues would attract mostly healthy people and pull them out of the regular insurance market, ultimately boosting costs for others.

continues

Table 20-4   (continued)

Issue	Governor Bush	Vice President Gore
Patients' bill of rights	Supports giving patients in federally governed health plans a limited ability to sue their health plans for denied medical services.	Wants a broad patients' bill of rights that allows people who are denied medical services to sue their health plans.
Long-term care	Would make the cost of long-term care insurance fully deductible and establish a personal tax exemption for home caregivers.	Wants a $3,000 tax credit for home caregivers. Has not proposed a tax break for the purchase of long-term care insurance because he wants to see quality improvements in that market.
Group purchasing	Would allow small businesses to band together across state lines and form association health plans, in order to buy health insurance through bona fide trade associations.	Would give tax credits to small-business employees who join health care purchasing cooperatives, which could be run by nonprofit organizations or other groups. Opposes association health plans.
Medicare reform	Wants to build on the work of the National Bipartisan Commission on the Future of Medicare; its leaders recommend opening up Medicare to more health plans as a way to give the elderly more choices while lowering costs.	Advocates rooting out waste, fraud, and abuse and giving Medicare more competitive tools, so long as beneficiaries are protected from premium inflation.
Prescription drugs	Supports offering a prescription drug benefit to Medicare recipients through a greater choice of plans. Also supports giving financial assistance to low-income elderly people to help them pay for the plans.	Would create a prescription drug benefit that would cover half the cost of medicines up to $5,000 with no deductibles and catastrophic protections after $4,000 in out-of-pocket payments. Elderly people with annual incomes below $11,000 would pay no premiums or co-payments.
Medicare lockbox	Has not taken a position on Gore's proposal to put Medicare in an off-budget lockbox.	Wants to put Medicare in an off-budget lockbox, so that savings from Medicare cannot be spent on other programs.
Medicare trust fund	Proposes a unified trust fund for Medicare Part A, which covers hospitalization, and Medicare Part B, which covers doctor visits. Also supports doubling federal funding for	Advocates using $75 billion of budget surplus money over 10 years to extend the life of Medicare's hospital insurance trust fund until at least 2030.

continues

Table 20-4   (continued)

Issue	Governor Bush	Vice President Gore
	Medicare over 10 years, but has not said where the extra money would come from.	
Provider givebacks	Has not taken a position on a bill to restore funding to hospitals and other health care providers that was lost as a result of the Balanced Budget Act of 1997. Supported the first legislation to restore funding, proposed in 1999, and has said the issue is another reason to revamp Medicare.	Would use $40 Million in budget surplus money to restore funding to hospitals and other health care providers that was lost as a result of the Balanced Budget Act of 1997.

Source: Reprinted with permission from Hill J. Election 2000: A comparison of the Bush and Gore health plans. *Group Pract J.* 2000;(October):10–12.

firmly oppose NHI, calling instead for a mix of private and public approaches to coverage, with emphasis on consumer choice and the private sector.[33,34]

The backlash of the public against managed care has been joined by many providers as well. Many physicians in numerous specialties refuse participation in managed care plans. A more extreme reaction has occurred in Connecticut, where a group of psychotherapists severed ties with most insurance companies in 1995 and formed their own guild as an alliance of independent practitioners. Similar guilds have been formed elsewhere around the country, which usually negotiate their own fees and terms directly with patients without the bureaucratic constraints of health plans.[35]

Employers are being buffeted by rising health insurance premiums and are very concerned that patients' rights legislation could make them vulnerable if patients gain the right to sue their health plans. Although they are constrained by a tight labor market in a relatively strong economy and not yet seeking alternatives to the present system of employer-based health insurance, there is active discussion among employers of potential alternatives should a recession occur or if they become further stressed by health care inflation. Among potential alternatives is the controversial concept of "defined benefits." By this approach, employers would give their employees a fixed amount each year (e.g., $5,000); employees then would purchase their own health insurance, either individually or from a menu of group plans. Employees would be responsible for their own coverage and could not complain to their employers, who would be out of the loop for any complaints. Although potentially attractive to employers, especially as an option in the event of an economic downturn, the defined benefits approach has yet to be implemented. Critics argue that one major problem with defined benefits is that employees likely would be splintered into many potentially uninsurable segments while paying more for their insurance coverage.[36]

An interesting study of divergent views and common concerns of leaders involved in U.S. health care was reported by Janet Corrigan and Paul Ginsberg of the Center for Studying Health System Change in Washington. They interviewed 15 leaders of national organizations and trade associations, including organizations in medicine, other health professions, the hospital industry, health care management, the insurance industry, national business organizations, and the National Governors' Association. Almost all these leaders saw both positive and negative aspects of the rapid, nearly chaotic changes in the health care system. Most thought that "fat is being cut out of the system," but many felt that current changes may exacerbate system problems, particularly concerning growing numbers of uninsured and underinsured, erosion of confidence in the health care system, and have a negative impact on the physician-patient relationship and professional collegiality. Despite these concerns, however, the general feeling, in 1997, was still to let market forces run their course,[37] not surprising since they mostly represent the stakeholders in the present system.

A June 2000 survey by the Center for Studying Health System Change revealed that consumers feel that insurance companies now have too much say in clinical decisions and still largely credit their physicians with putting their patients' medical needs first.[38] Another national poll, this time by the Gallup Organization, showed that U.S. physicians still rank high among professions in "honesty and ethical standards" (fourth out of 28 professions, behind pharmacists, the clergy, and college professors); in the same poll, physicians' ratings for "very high" or "high" code of conduct increased from 47 percent in 1994 to 57 percent in 1998.[39]

PRO-MARKET STAKEHOLDERS' ACTIVITIES TO PRESERVE THE STATUS QUO

An enormously powerful and influential ongoing effort is being made to preserve the pro-market status quo by the major stakeholders in the present flawed health care system, which operates in their own self-interest. Two kinds of activities are cited here to illustrate the extent of these efforts, which otherwise largely are invisible behind the scenes.

Campaign Contributions and Lobbying Efforts

Since the health care industry accounts for one seventh of the U.S. economy, it is not surprising that it is filled with active lobbies representing many interests. The AMA established its political action committee (PAC), as the first such national trade or business PAC, in 1961. Since then, PACs have been formed by many interest groups and play a major role in political campaigns at both the federal and state levels. Table 20-5 lists PAC contributions from health-related interest groups to federal candidates in both major parties during the 1997/1998 and 1999/2000 election cycles. Although business and insurance lobbies line up predominantly with the Republicans, many groups hedge their

Table 20-5   PAC Contributions to Federal Candidates

	1999–2000			1997–1998		
Organization	Election Cycle	% to Democrats	% to GOP	Election Cycle	% to Democrats	% to GOP
American Medical Association	$1,942,623	47	52	$2,323,781	28	72
Blue Cross and Blue Shield Association	298,494	27	73	347,114	32	68
American Association of Health Plans	45,390	14	86	43,075	24	76
Health Insurance Association of America	143,128	20	79	114,862	24	76
National Federation of Independent Business	1,013,887	3	96	1,209,836	7	93
Association of Trial Lawyers of America	2,661,000	86	13	2,409,300	87	13

Source: The Center for Responsive Politics, compiled from data released by Federal Election Commission, July 1, 2001. Reprinted with permission from Pretzer M. What have medical lobbyists done for you lately? *Med Econ.* September 18, 2000:47–60.

bets on both sides of the aisle. It is noteworthy that not one group lobbies for single-payer reform of the health care system.

For the last three years, *Fortune* magazine conducted an annual survey of congressional representatives, their staffers, senior White House aides, hired lobbyists, and lobbying organization executives in an effort to assess which lobbyists wield the most power. By *Fortune*'s rankings in 1999, AARP ranked number one, while the National Federation of Independent Business tied for second with the National Rifle Association. Managed care lobbyists have been climbing in these rankings over the last several years, especially HIAA. Table 20-6 lists the expenditures of some of the major health industry lobbying groups during 1998 and 1999.

Although it is an open and murky question how influential all of this lobbying is in terms of actual votes, it is a good bet that it is very influential to many politicians, as they seek to build their campaign war chests for their next election. Some lawmakers acknowledge the persuasive power of money. Cecil Heftel, a five-term congressional representative from Hawaii who left the House in 1986 and works actively for campaign finance reform, has this to say about the influence of lobbyists:[40]

> Interest groups funnel money to political incumbents who have jurisdiction over issues that affect them most. In return for that money, which pays for the glossy, high-profile campaigns that win votes, members of Congress promote and pass legislation that benefits their big donors instead of their constituents.

Table 20-6 Power Ranking and Lobbying Expenditures by Health Care Organizations

Organization	Fortune Magazine 1999 Power Rank	1999 Lobbying Expenditures	1998 Lobbying Expenditures
American Medical Association	13	$18,010,000	$16,600,000
American Hospital Association	31	10,940,000	9,340,000
Blue Cross and Blue Shield Association	29	7,724,480	7,140,000
Pharmaceutical Research and Manufacturers of America	28	5,020,000	3,120,000
Health Insurance Association of America	25	4,760,000	4,900,000
American Association of Health Plans	48	2,480,000	2,040,000
Association of Trial Lawyers of America	6	2,360,000	2,184,929
National Federation of Independent Business	2	2,280,000	4,249,403
American College of Physicians—American Society of Internal Medicine	NR	2,120,000	1,968,142
American Academy of Family Physicians	NR	1,500,000	936,993
American Medical Group Association	NR	480,000	520,000
Medical Group Management Association	NR	240,000	200,000

Source: Expenditures from reports with the secretary of the Senate in compliance with the Lobbying Disclosure Act of 1995; power ranking from annual survey of Washington insiders published in *Fortune* magazine, December 6, 1999. NR: not ranked. Reprinted with permission from Pretzer M. What have medical lobbyists done for you lately? *Med Econ.* September 18, 2000:59.

Here are some examples of carefully targeted campaign contributions and lobbying activities by health industry special interest groups in recent years, as collated by serial newsletters of Physicians for a National Health Program:

- The AMA gave $4.1 million to candidates in the 1996 election, with most of the money going to pro-tobacco congressmen. The AMA contributed an average of $5,382 per pro-tobacco representative, and $2,103 to anti-tobacco members. Pro-tobacco candidates almost always endorse malpractice caps, hence attracting more AMA donations (Sharfstein, *Amer J Public Health*, August 1998).[41]
- Insurance companies and their allies opposed to the Patients' Bill of Rights spent $60 million on lobbying on all issues in the first six months of 1998, an average of $112,000 per lawmaker. The figure does not include $11 million in advertisements against managed care regulation nor millions in campaign contributions made in November's congressional campaigns (AP, *Chicago Tribune*, November 28, 1998).[42]

- The insurance industry spent $77.2 million on lobbying in 1998, even more than the tobacco industry, which spent $67.4 million opposing regulation (according to the Center for Responsive Politics, July 1999).[43]
- Between 1997 and 1999, the drug industry spent $235.7 million to lobby Congress, not including advertising, direct mail, and telemarketing. They spent an additional $38 million on ads through their front group, Citizens for Better Medicare.[44]
- Drug companies contributed $38.3 million to congressional campaigns in the last decade, with an increasing share (about two thirds) going to Republicans. Sen. Orrin Hatch (R-Utah) received $169,000 from drug companies in 2000 (more than any other senator), including a $14,000 donation and the use of a company airplane from Schering-Plough. The giant drug manufacturer is seeking patent extension for its allergy drug, Claritin. Two other senators favoring patent extension—John Ashcroft (R-Mo) and Robert Torricelli (D-NJ)—received $50,000 donations from Schering-Plough (according to the Center for Responsive Politics, June 2000).[7]
- Drug companies spent an all-time high of $83.6 million on lobbying in 1999, employing 297 lobbyists, or "one for every two members of Congress." In 1997 and 1998 their lobbying exceeded $70 million each year (see Prescription Drugs, available at: http://www.opensecrets.org, Center for Responsive Politics).[7]
- For-profit HMOs spent $34 million in a successful effort to defeat (barely) a statewide single-payer plan in Massachusetts during the November 2000 campaign.[44]
- The best example yet of money as the "milk of politics" is the comprehensive lobbying effort by the drug industry during the 2000 election campaign to keep the Democrats from regaining control of Congress. The pharmaceutical companies hope that the Republicans are more sympathetic to their fear of a Medicare prescription drug benefit that will lead to government price controls. They spent $80 million in that effort, the largest corporate campaign in U.S. political history.[45] They supported candidates who would favor prescription assistance for seniors with a moderate cap on out-of-pocket expenses instead of a Medicare prescription drug benefit. Of the 22 candidates backed by the drug industry, 18 won their elections.[46]

Biased and Misleading Media Campaigns

Along the same line, but this time through targeted media campaigns tantamount to thinly disguised marketing of their self interests, here are some examples of biased and misleading information promulgated by pro-market stakeholders in recent years:

- In 1993/1994, Proposition 186 in California, a single-payer initiative that collected more than 1 million signatures within 100 days, was defeated by a massive media campaign launched by Taxpayers Against the Government Takeover. This group included the Association of California Life Insurance Companies, a hospital association, the National Federation of Independent Businesses, and the state Chamber of Commerce; insurance companies paid 78 percent of the $6.9 million spent on television, radio, and direct mailing in a successful disinformation campaign.[47]

- Six of the nation's largest for-profit HMOs launched a multimillion-dollar campaign in 1996 aimed at gaining rosier media coverage of for-profit HMOs. The big six (U.S. Healthcare, United HealthCare, Health Net, Humana, FHP, and Pacificare) started the ad hoc Coordinated Care Coalition to conduct the campaign.[48]
- The trade association for HMOs, the American Association of Health Plans (AAHP, formerly the Group Health Association of America), hired the Sacramento-based consulting firm Goddard Claussen/First Tuesday in 1996 to carry out its own image-building campaign, including ads, meeting with reporters, and editorial board meetings. They planned to spend $250,000 on "planning and research" alone for their campaign and to air the ads 10,000 times in 20 major markets. Goddard Claussen was the firm that designed the "Harry and Louise" ads and the opposition to California's single-payer ballot initiative in 1994 (according to Modern Healthcare, *Washington Post*, February 12, 1996, and the *Managed Healthcare Market Report*, June 30, 1996).[48]
- Between 1992 and 1996, drug, medical device, biotechnology, and tobacco companies gave over $3.5 million to eight conservative think tanks working to limit the regulatory powers of the FDA (see "A Million for Your Thoughts: The Industry-Funded Campaign by Conservative Think Tanks Against the FDA," *Public Citizen Report*, July 1996).[4]
- One of the strategies used by the insurance industry to defeat the Clinton plan in 1993/1994 was the creation of "coalitions" to serve as front groups for the campaign. The Patients' Bill of Rights legislative fight has spawned a similar crop of new coalitions. For example, there is the Health Benefits Coalition (giant insurance companies and the National Federation of Independent Business, whose members refer to themselves as *employers*) (*Washington Times*, April 25, 1998), the Small Business Survival Committee, the Healthcare Leadership Council, and the HMO Group (25 HMOs that agree to accept partial regulation in order to defeat legislation that would allow patients greater protection, such as the right to sue HMOs for denials of care). The Small Business Survival Committee is funding an advertising campaign to oppose the HMO bill of rights. The Healthcare Leadership Council (HLC), a group of for-profit health care providers, launched a campaign to "correct the impression" that the health care system is failing to deliver adequate care to patients. The HLC distributes its book, *Medical Miracles: Saving Lives Every Day*, and sends daily faxes to Congress with "success stories." The Coalition for Patient Choice, another group fighting patient protection, actually is a lobbying group for medical savings accounts, funded primarily by the Golden Rule Insurance Company of Indianapolis, which sells MSAs (according to *New York Times*, July 21, 1998).[41]
- The nation's largest insurance company, Aetna-US Healthcare, teamed up with three conservative business groups, the U.S. Chamber of Commerce, the National Federation of Independent Business, and the National Association of Wholesalers-Distributors, to lobby for tax subsidies and credits for the purchase of insurance and to market new bare bones health

plans. Aetna also runs an expensive media campaign (including prime time television ads and full-page ads in the *New York Times*). Aetna claims its new "Affordable HealthChoices" plans "would cost as little as $46 a month for a single worker and $156 a month for a family" (according to *Los Angeles Times*, May 5, 1999). However, the new plans don't meet state mandates for coverage and come with a warning that they are "supplemental indemnity coverage" and "not a substitute for hospital or medical expense insurance or major medical expense insurance." For example, one of the new plans would pay only for up to six doctor visits a year and just $500 a day for the first three days in the hospital, less for subsequent days (see "Barebones Insurance Would Do Little to Help Uninsured Working Families," *Families USA*, May 17, 1999, and *New York Times* advertisement, May 11, 1999).[43]

• Drug companies launched a $30 million advertising campaign against Medicare coverage for prescription drugs in 1998. The ads feature the character "Flo" and are sponsored by the industry's "coalition" Citizens for Better Medicare. The Pharmaceutical Research and Manufacturers Association recruited Vice President Al Gore in their effort to block the government of South Africa from purchasing or manufacturing generic AIDS drugs for their 3.2 million HIV-positive citizens (see *Fortune*, April 26, 1999, and "Al Gore, AIDS Drugs, and Pharmaceutical Money," *Public Campaign*, June 16, 1999).[43]

All these media messages are carefully designed, as expected, to promote the sponsoring special interests, often cloaked under labels that sound too patriotic to disregard (e.g., Coalition for Patient Choice, Citizens for Better Medicare).

CAN THE PUBLIC INTEREST BE SERVED BY CURRENT APPROACHES?

Given the powerful political influence of pro-market special interests, which tend to perpetuate the increasing problems of the present health care system, the fundamental question becomes whether the public interest can ever be served in this political environment. Many examples of failed reform efforts are presented in the last chapter. Since the defeat of the Clinton Health Plan in 1994, the problems of the health care system have become worse. Public dissatisfaction with the system has increased, together with growing support for a larger role of government in health care. How can meaningful reform take place the next time around?

Two basic approaches appear to be necessary to move past ineffectual incrementalism to structural reform of the health care system. First, as is obvious from the foregoing, is an urgent need for campaign finance reform. Growing grassroots support for major reform of health care is being seen in many states around the country as well as in various national public opinion surveys. The lack of connection between the public will and the self-interest of corporate special interests must be broken through a more transparent political process. It is beyond my expertise to discuss how to implement campaign finance reform, but it is readily apparent that this needs to happen.

The second essential requirement for health care reform is some degree of resolution of the basic conflict between individual and societal perspectives. The underlying issues, of course, come down to who will pay, how much, and for whom.

Eddy framed individual versus societal perspectives in a useful way. The societal or public health perspective seeks to allocate a given health care resource across as many patients as possible, preferably an entire target population, with optimal efficiency. The individual perspective, by contrast, whether taken by an individual provider or patient, seeks to optimize that patient's care. The conflict occurs when total resources are limited, as they are, and when individuals use a disproportionate amount of health care resources without paying for it. The conflict is further exacerbated when individuals get sick. When they are well ("first position") they may be comfortable with a broader, societal perspective; but when they get sick ("second position"), they naturally are most concerned with receiving whatever services they want, regardless of who else has to pay for them.[49]

All of the country's health care financing mechanisms depend on the pooling of resources across segments of the population. Individuals pay into private insurance pools by premiums and into public pools (e.g., Medicare and Medicaid) by taxes. Conflicts arise when individuals draw more than their "fair share" from the pool, forcing others to replenish the pool or result in diminished services to others. There is less disagreement over services considered essential; as the benefits of services decrease and their costs increase, the conflicts become greater.[49]

Within our present health care system, the current clash between societal and individual perspectives perpetuates and accentuates conflict. Can the societal versus individual conflict be resolved within our political culture? The track record to date would make that open to serious question; there are solutions, although difficult. Eddy proposed a five-step approach, the logic of which is compelling:[49]

1. Recognize the problem (i.e., individuals given or receiving disproportionate services at society's expense harm the health and finances of other people like themselves).
2. Learn more about the benefit, harm, and cost of two to three dozen services for the most important health problems, then ask people whether the benefit and harm warrant the costs.[50]
3. Estimate the health outcome and cost of health care services suspected, on the grounds of clinical judgment or common sense, to be either overused or underused, then ask people whether they are worth the cost.
4. Incorporate findings of steps 2 and 3 into clinical practice policies.
5. Adhere to these clinical practice guidelines.

CONCLUDING COMMENTS

It is easy to become discouraged by the lack of real progress toward structural reform of our ailing health care system after at least 20 years' failure of the competitive marketplace approach. How much more time should be given to this experiment, and what real signs are there that it could yet work? The answers, in my view, are none and none. The stakeholders in the present system persist in their optimistic claims that the private sector marketplace will sort out the system's problems, but all the evidence is to the contrary. We have a multi-tiered health care system that is not sustainable. It is filled with inequities and waste and falls far short of what is possible and needed for the nation. Corporatization of health care now dominates the health care landscape and has become the problem rather than a solution.

The stakeholders of today's health care system are caught in a conflict of interest that works against the needs of consumers. Employers have a strong incentive to keep the costs of employer-based health insurance as low as possible, rather than serve as good proxies for their employees. Investor-owned managed care organizations have a strong incentive to maximize profits and return on investment for shareholders rather than serve as good proxies for physicians or patients.[51]

Although the United States has enjoyed the longest economic boom in its history, many indications suggest an economic downturn is on the horizon, perhaps sooner rather than later. It is not a matter of if, just when, such a downturn will lead to wider appreciation that the country's resources for health care in fact are limited. The politicians may be aware of these growing limits, but so far have seen it as political suicide to lead their constituents toward realistic, longer-term reforms. Still off-limits is the "R word" (rationing) but that is what we have to consider in the next chapter before we can assess organizational options and principles of health care reform in the final chapters.

REFERENCES

1. Blumenthal D. Health care reform at the close of the 20th century. *N Engl J Med.* 1999;340: 1916–1920.
2. DeBakey M. RX for the health care system. *Wall Street Journal.* October 8, 1998:A18.
3. Healthcare for the poor and uninsured: An uncertain future. In: Altman SH, Reinhardt UE, Shields AE (eds). *The Future U.S. Health Care System: Who Will Care for the Poor and Uninsured?* Chicago: Health Administration Press, 1998:1–22.
4. Data Update. *PNHP Newsletter.* November 1996.
5. Data Update. *PNHP Newsletter.* July 1997.
6. Data Update. *PNHP Newsletter.* March 2000.
7. Data Update. *PNHP Newsletter.* September 2000.
8. Fairness and accuracy in reporting, February 17, 2000.
9. ICR poll for the National Coalition on Healthcare, January 1997.
10. National Coalition on Healthcare. A report of a national survey. *J Health Care Finance.* 1997;23: 12–20.
11. Hunt AR. Public is split on how to pay for access. *Wall Street Journal.* June 25, 1998:A10.
12. Duff C. Americans tell government to stay out—Except in case of health care. *Wall Street Journal.* June 25, 1998:A9, A14.
13. Brooks D. The era of small government is over. *The Weekly Standard.* October 2, 2000:13–14.
14. Woolhandler S, Himmelstein DU. *The National Health Program Slideshow Guide.* Cambridge, MA: The Center for National Health Program Studies, 2000.
15. HMO Industry Report 10.2. *Med Benefits.* 2000;17(23):4.
16. *American Medical News.* February 21, 2000.
17. *Business and Health.* June 1996.

18. *Public Sector Contracting Report.* November 1995.
19. *New York Times.* July 2, 1999 and July 16, 1999.
20. *Modern Health Care.* August 4, 1996.
21. *New York Times.* July 27, 1997.
22. Magellan SEC form 10-K. Audit findings reported to the Congressional Budget Office, James Wrich, Inc.
23. *Wall Street Journal.* July 1, 1998.
24. Martinez B. Care guidelines used by insurers face scrutiny. *Wall Street Journal.* September 14, 2000:B1, B4.
25. Borzo G. Policy and practice. Health plans in the catbird seat. *Fam Pract News.* August 1, 2000:34.
26. Gordon C. *The Clinton Health Care Plan: Dead on Arrival.* Westfield, NJ: Open Magazine Pamphlet Series, 1995.
27. Kuttner R. *Everything for Sale: The Virtues and Limits of Markets.* Chicago: University of Chicago Press, 1999:140.
28. Levin-Epstein M. Washington watch. Quick fix may be in store for M + C, but meaningful change likely to wait. *Managed Care.* October 2000:16–17.
29. Vladeck BC. Plenty of nothing—A report from the Medicare Commission. *N Engl J Med.* 1999; 340:1503–1506.
30. Appleby J. Healthcare: changes are possible—and debate is certain—for Medicare, patients' rights. *USA Today.* December 14, 2000;3B.
31. Gigot PA. Two countries, one system. *Wall Street Journal.* November 9, 2000.
32. Simon SR, Pan RJ, Sullivan AM, et al. A survey of medical students, residents, faculty and deans at medical schools in the United States. *N Engl J Med.* 1999;340:928–936.
33. Frieden J. Policy and practice. Medical students want national health. *Fam Pract News.* April 15, 2000:58.
34. Dickey NW. The real future of medicine lies in patients' hands. *Med Econ.* June 9, 1997;74:188–98.
35. Murray S. With a "guild" therapists flew managed care. *Wall Street Journal.* November 22, 1999: B1, B4.
36. Jacob J. Multiple choice: managed care: What's next? *American Medical News.* May 1, 2000: 16–17.
37. Corrigan JM, Ginsberg PB. Association leaders speak out on health system change. *Health Aff (Millwood).* 1997;16(1):150–157.
38. *Medical Benefits.* 2000;17(14):11.
39. Pretzer M. What you'll miss most—and least—about the 20th century. *Medical Econ.* December 20, 1999:80–90.
40. Pretzer M. What have medical lobbyists done for you lately? *Med Econ.* September 18, 2000: 47–60.
41. Data Update. *PNHP Newsletter.* September 1998.
42. Data Update. *PNHP Newsletter.* March 1999.
43. Data Update. *PNHP Newsletter.* October 1999.
44. Data Update. *PNHP Newsletter.* May 2001.
45. Hamburger T, McGinley L. Drug lobby wins big with massive spending against Medicare plan. *Wall Street Journal.* November 9, 2000:B1, B4.
46. Health care issues. *Family Practice Report.* 2000;6(12):3.
47. Andrews C. *Profit Fever: The Drive to Corporatize Health Care and How to Stop It.* Monroe, MN: Common Courage Press, 1995:110–119.
48. Data Update. *PNHP Newsletter.* February 1996.
49. Eddy DM. Clinical decision making: From theory to practice. The individual vs. society. Resolving the conflict. *JAMA.* 1991;265:2399–2401, 2405–2406.
50. Eddy DM. Clinical decision making: From theory to practice. Connecting value and costs. Whom do we ask, what do we ask them? *JAMA.* 1990;264:1737–1739.
51. Angell M. Patients' rights bills and other futile gestures. *N Engl J Med.* 2000;342:1663–1664.

21
Rationing in a "Free Market" Society: Myths and Reality

As seen from earlier chapters, the intersection of access, cost, and quality of health care services results in some tradeoffs, no matter how affluent a society may be. As costs continue to rise, together with decreasing access and heightened concern about quality of health care, these tradeoffs in the United States become more apparent and controversial. To a large degree, these tradeoffs are imposed by a profit-driven marketplace. The needs of patients increasingly are at odds with the profit mission of for-profit HMOs, and any attempts to regulate HMOs are seen as "socialism."

Although health professionals, insurers, and legislators scrupulously avoid the word *rationing*, it is a fact of life in any health care system, as it has been in America from the start. Despite the appearance of many books on the subject over the last 25 years,[1-7] the American public and other interests involved in the delivery of health care prefer to substitute more euphemistic language for the dreaded "R word." The word becomes more emotionally charged as rationing becomes more explicit; in the past, it was more implicit and easier to overcome, since hospitals and physicians were able to provide more charity care in the pre-managed care era. Today, however, rationing of U.S. health care within the largely unregulated marketplace is an everyday occurrence, mostly on the basis of income, but also on the basis of age, race, class, health status, and other factors.

The health care debate now centers around various words other than *rationing*, including *medical necessity, appropriateness of care, benefits of treatment*, and *cost-effectiveness of care*. All these are approaches to policy and clinical decisions about allocation of health care resources, whether for the individual patient or population being served.

The word *rationing* conjures up various perceptions and reactions, depending on the individual's perspective and interests. During World War II, the word was accepted patriotically as the needed sharing and mutual sacrifice required of the American war effort, but today the word is used as a scare tactic by those invested in one or another part of the health care industry to oppose threatening change.[8] Therefore, although health care is actually rationed every day in one way or another, the word has a negative connotation in most quarters.

The term *rationing* is subject to various definitions.[9] To economists, the word means the process of allocating scarce goods in a fair manner. In health care, the term usually describes distributions based on cost, especially involving health care services considered too expensive for society to afford.[10] Others contend that *rationing* applies mostly to explicit decisions made at a system-wide level to limit services to some groups of people.[11] Still others argue that *rationing* means cost-based restraints on "necessary" services instead of limi-tations on beneficial services that, although effective and desired, are consid-ered beyond the category of "basic needs."[12]

Henry Aaron and William Schwartz, in the groundbreaking book *The Painful Prescription: Rationing Hospital Care*, use the term *rationing* in two distinct ways.[2] First, free market economies regularly deny goods and services to those who cannot pay for them. Price rationing of this kind has long been a barrier to the uninsured and many lower-income people. It is also becoming a barrier for many people with health insurance, as reflected by the frequency of medical bankruptcies among the insured. Second, a common and quite different sense of *rationing* applies to services denied to people who can pay for them.[13] This interpretation is particularly contentious today, as the health care debate plays out between patients versus corporate stakeholders, since about 80 percent of the population is affected by policy decisions of this type.

With this introduction to the matter of rationing, this chapter addresses five goals: (1) to discuss some myths concerning rationing of health care services in the United States, (2) to examine the issue of medical necessity and appropri-ateness of care and how these decisions are made within the for-profit managed care industry, (3) to summarize how cost-effectiveness adds to the equation, (4) to briefly discuss some ethical and legal issues involved in rationing of services, and (5) to examine how rationing is carried out through the process of "setting priorities" in other industrialized Western nations.

SOME MYTHS CONCERNING RATIONING OF HEALTH CARE

The most pervasive and corrosive myth concerning U.S. health care is that the marketplace can resolve the cost, access, and quality problems in health care delivery. That view is promulgated as the "American way" by the power-ful stakeholders in the pro-market status quo. We discussed some of the ways in which the free marketplace doesn't serve the public interest in health care in Chapter 14 (pages 213–218). Robert Evans, of the University of British Columbia, is quite clear on this point, in this scathing commentary:[14]

> There is in health care no "private, competitive market" of the form described in the economics textbooks, anywhere in the world. There never has been, and inherent characteristics of health and health care make it impossible that there ever could be. Public and private action have always been interwoven . . . Current interest in market approaches represents the resurgence of ideas and arguments that have been promoted with varying intensity throughout

this century. (In practice, advocates have never wanted a truly competitive market, but rather one managed by and for particular private interests.) Yet international experience over the last 40 years has demonstrated that greater reliance on the market is associated with inferior system performance— inequity, inefficiency, high cost, and public dissatisfaction. The United States is the leading example. So why is this issue back again? Because market mechanisms yield distributional advantages for particular influential groups.

1. A more costly health care system yields higher prices and incomes for suppliers—physicians, drug companies, and private insurers.
2. Private payment distributes overall system costs according to use (or expected use) of services, costing wealthier and healthier people less than finance from (income-related) taxation.
3. Wealthy and unhealthy people can purchase (real or perceived) better access or quality for themselves, without having to support a similar standard for others. Thus there is, and always has been, a natural alliance of economic interest between service providers and upper-income citizens to support shifting health financing from public to private sources. Analytic arguments for the potential superiority of hypothetical competitive markets are simply one of the rhetorical forms through which this permanent conflict of economic interest is expressed in political debate.

Another pervasive myth is that we don't ration health care in this country, as do countries with restrictive global budgets for health care, such as Canada, the United Kingdom, and European countries. While this myth continues to flourish, denial is still the main mechanism to overlook the ways in which health care is actively rationed on a daily basis in the real world. Consider these examples:

- Sick HMO patients have about twice the problem in gaining access to needed care compared to healthy patients in HMOs, PPOs, or point-of-service programs either by self referral or with a gatekeeper.[15]
- The sick poor are about seven times more likely to have worse health status after four years if receiving care in an HMO setting versus fee for service.[16]
- Managed mental health programs often have dangerously restrictive admission policies for detoxification (e.g., requiring delirium tremens prior to hospital admission).[17]
- Investor-owned HMOs provide one third fewer diabetic eye examinations than not-for-profit HMOs.[18]
- An HCFA study reported in 1996 found that immunization rates for poor Medicare beneficiaries were 26 percent lower among whites and 39 percent lower among African-Americans than all Medicare enrollees.[19]
- Although the rates of preventable hospitalizations vary considerably from one city to another, comparative differences between those in affluent and poor zip codes are much higher in U.S. cities than in Canadian cities (e.g., more than twice as prevalent in Buffalo, San Francisco, and New York than in Ottawa or Toronto).[20]

Another common myth concerns the extent of consumer demand for health care services in the United States compared to other industrialized Western countries. While surely there is a "demand push" for health care, especially for advances in medical technology, here as elsewhere, much of that is driven by aggressive marketing practices by suppliers further aided by the media. In actual fact, international comparisons reveal that Americans receive less health care than citizens in many other countries. These examples suggest the magnitude of these differences:

- Average per capita physician visits in the United States are 6 per year compared to 6.5 in Germany and France, 6.8 in Canada, and 16 in Japan.[21]
- In 1997, Americans accounted for 1.1 hospital inpatient days per capita compared to 2.5 in France, Australia, and Germany and 4 in Japan.[21]
- Many countries have higher annual rates for allogenic bone marrow transplantation; while the U.S. carries out 8.1 transplants per million people per year, that number is exceeded by the United Kingdom (8.2), Australia (8.8), Canada (8.9), Sweden (9.0), and France (13.4).[22]
- In 1990, Canada exceeded the United States in heart-lung transplants as well as liver transplants per 100,000 population.[23,24]

Additional evidence that belies insatiable consumer demand for health care in the United States compared to other countries is the wide geographic differences in physician practice patterns from one area to another, which indicate the powerful influence of *physician*-induced demand more than differences in consumer demand. Indeed, some investigators have argued that there may be no need to ration those clinical interventions of undoubted efficacy.[25,26]

WHAT CARE IS NECESSARY AND APPROPRIATE?

For many years in the past, insurers depended on treating physicians to define what health care services were necessary and appropriate. With the increasing costs of health care and expansion of public and private insurance coverage since the 1960s, however, these medical necessity decisions increasingly have been reviewed by Medicare, Medicaid, commercial insurers, and in more recent years, the managed care industry.[27] Today, care prescribed by treating physicians often is overruled by insurance reviewers, sparking an intense and ongoing debate about who should make these decisions. At the polar ends of this debate are the interests of physicians in defending their professional autonomy in making clinical decisions and serving as the patient's advocate versus the collective views of health plans and insurers, many of which have a fiduciary duty to maximize profits for investors.

There still is no consensus in the United States on how to make medical necessity decisions. Many rules for approving or denying coverage are in everyday use. Unfortunately, many of these rules are intended solely to reduce costs, with little to do with clinical efficacy or quality of care. Many of these rules are more actuarial than clinical, as illustrated by Milliman and Roberts (M&R) guidelines discussed in the last chapter. A rules-based approach in a managed care setting typically involves an initial review level (often a nurse, usually authorized to make approvals but often not denials of coverage) and a higher review level for appeals to medical directors of the HMO or health plan. Medical directors typically are charged to maintain target denial rates and under strong incentives to exceed these rates. The roles of treating and reviewing physicians are diametrically opposed to each other. The treating physician regards a denial decision as arbitrary, poor-quality care, intrusive to the physician-patient relationship, and a concern for malpractice liability. The medical director, on the other hand, sees his or her role as meeting the corporate mission of the organization, in many cases maximizing profits while limiting costs. The director's job is on the line if denial rates fall below target levels.

Another common approach to medical necessity decisions is through a process of internal review by a physician-owned or at-risk medical group. A typical review process in this setting involves most necessity determinations being made by the group's medical director, with an appeal process available to a multidisciplinary managed care review council. By this process, two basic questions are addressed, both raised by Aaron in the mid-1980s:[28] (1) In this instance, is the therapy beneficial and (2) are beneficial therapies worth the cost? The second question, of course, is the more difficult to deal with in most situations. How many resources can be taken from the collective pool to manage one patient's medical problems, for what benefit, and at what cost to the covered population? The cost question is especially challenging in the open-ended U.S. health care system, which operates with no global budget and at least 25 percent of health spending consumed by administrative overhead and profits. There is no reason to believe that resources denied one individual patient will go to other clinical services with larger benefits to the population.[28,29] Benjamin, Cohen, and Grochowski regard this as irrational allocation rather than rationing.[30]

In addition to basing coverage decisions on medical necessity, the "appropriateness" of services needs to be considered as well. Outcomes research is being looked to for guidance on benefits of treatment and clinical outcomes for patients. This is a positive development to the extent that rigorous peer-reviewed science informs medical decisions. In most instances, however, actuarial guidelines are used, based on unpublished proprietary data with no scientific foundation.[15] We saw examples in the last chapter whereby overly restrictive M&R guidelines are being promulgated on an efficiency and cost-saving basis to limit length of hospital stays with no supportive clinical reasons or evidence (page 331). Another example of this problem is the denial by insurers of coverage for growth hormone therapy for children in the face of a 96 percent treatment-approval rate among surveyed pediatric endocrinologists.[31]

An insider's view of the medical director's role in an investor-owned HMO reveals how morally and clinically bankrupt the system is regarding decisions of medical necessity. After nine years of clinical practice as an internist, Linda Peeno served in various administrative and executive roles for several managed care organizations. After four years in such roles, although well compensated, she left the managed care world for a new career in medical ethics and has been actively involved in teaching and consultation in that area. Her accounts of her experiences show how far corporate health care has strayed from the best interests of patients and their physicians. Beyond accountability to licensure boards, medical societies, or codes of medical ethics, the medical director, in effect, practices medicine without seeing the patient—often across state lines without a license in the patient's state—with just a telephone, a pen, and a rubber stamp. These medical necessity decisions are even beyond the reach of attorneys, since

HMOs are protected by ERISA, as we saw in an earlier chapter. Dr. Peeno describes her initial orientation to her "medical consultant" job with an HMO in these words from an accountant with the organization: "We take in a premium; we use about 10–15% to run the business, and we try to keep as much as possible of the rest. Your job is to help us do that."[32]

As a physician and consultant for the company, she had available to her many strategies to achieve that goal, including revising contract benefits, medical underwriting to avoid high-risk groups and individuals, and development of procedural barriers to approval of requests. Physicians in these roles typically are expected to deny at least 10 percent of approval requests, and their incomes are increased substantially by bonuses if they can exceed that rate.[32–36]

At best, insurance company decisions about medical necessity are arbitrary, often capricious, and made under a veil of secrecy. For example, Humana sub-contracts decisions about the need for hysterectomy to a separate for-profit company whose motivation is to deny as many requests as possible.[37] Medical necessity decisions often are made in urgent or emergency situations, such as for operative repair of a leaking abdominal aortic aneurysm.[38] Moreover, they often consume a large amount of time and expense on the part of treating physi-cians, raise frustrations for clinicians, and reveal the extent of control of the medical procession and even legislators by corporate special interests in an ongoing effort to preserve the market status quo.

Despite all the finger-pointing about the abuses of cost containment in managed care, there probably is a middle ground between polar opposite views on the impact of cost containment policies so far. On one extreme, profit-driven HMOs pursue their corporate interests, not the best interests of their enrollees, as we saw in Chapter 14 (pages 214–216) and Chapter 18 (pages 300–301) with the finding that investor-owned HMOs score worse on quality of care indica-tors than nonprofit plans.[39] Moreover, for-profit HMOs have come to dominate the marketplace through consolidation and mergers. On the other end of the spectrum, some of the few nonprofit HMOs able to survive have demonstrated better quality of care than the fee-for-service sector as a result of their system improvements (e.g., Group Health Cooperative in Seattle with its population-based care of diabetics[40] and Kaiser's Cooperative Health Care Clinic in Denver for the care of chronically ill elderly patients).[41]

COST-EFFECTIVENESS AND RATIONING

While potentially as important to the development of a rational health care policy as medical necessity, cost-effectiveness is even more difficult to assess and apply. Cost-effectiveness analysis (CEA) is a promising but still incom-pletely developed, poorly understood, and controversial approach to measuring the relative cost-effectiveness of clinical interventions. In an effort to improve the methodology and value of CEA for health policy uses, the U.S. Public Health Service, in 1993, convened an expert panel of nongovernment scientists and scholars to assess the state of the art of CEA and make recommendations for its further development. The report of the Panel on Cost-Effectiveness in Health and Medicine was published in 1996[42] and has been instrumental in the more recent improvements of CEA as a method to evaluate the outcomes and costs of clinical interventions. While CEA, by itself, cannot make clinical policy decisions for allocation of health care resources, when taken from a societal perspective, it can help to inform these decisions in a useful way. One example of the value of CEAs in health care policy is the decision by Congress to adopt the pneumococcal vaccine as the first preventive service to be covered by Medicare, based on a CEA conducted by the Congressional Office of Technology Assessment.[43]

The term *cost-effectiveness* often is misused and confusing to many. As Deyo has pointed out, a "low-tech" service may not be cost-effective (e.g., stool guaiac cards cost only $1 each and are very cost-effective if two cards are used for annual screening for occult blood, but if one uses a sixth card after five normal cards, the cost-effectiveness becomes extremely low—$47 million dollars, in 1975 dollars, for each additional case of cancer detected).[44,45] On the other hand, a "high-tech" intervention may be very cost-effective, such as a cardiac bypass graft procedure for left main disease with a cost-effectiveness ratio of about $2,300 to $5,600 per year of life saved.[46] CEA obviously is of no use if an intervention has not been demonstrated to be effective, nor is it needed if a new test or treatment is both less expensive and equally or more effective than an older intervention in common usage. CEAs are most useful to assess new tests or treatments that are both more expensive and more effective than standard interventions.[44] Figure 21-1 illustrates the cost-effectiveness of several interventions for cardiovascular disease, ranging from very cost-effective interventions (e.g., $1,000 to $17,000 for beta-blockers after myocardial infarction) to interventions with no cost-effectiveness (e.g., use of statin drugs for women

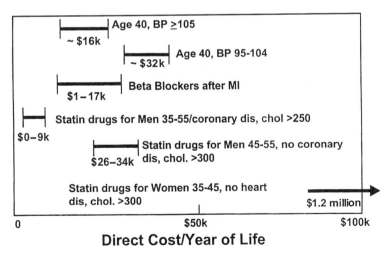

Direct Cost/Year of Life

Figure 21-1   Direct cost/year of life. Published values for the cost-effectiveness of treating hypertension and providing beta blockers post-myocardial infarction: BP = blood pressure. (Reprinted with permission from Deyo RA. Cost-effectiveness of primary care. In: Geyman JP, Deyo RA, Ramsey SD (eds). *Evidence-Based Clinical Practice: Concepts and Approaches*. Boston: Butterworth–Heinemann 2000:115.)

between 35 and 45 years of age with serum cholesterol values over 300 mg/dl but no heart disease).[44]

CEAs are often reported out in terms of quality-adjusted life years (QALY). This measure accepts that some outcomes are worse than death and that people usually are willing to take some risk of a bad outcome to gain a better outcome (i.e., to accept a potentially shorter life with higher quality and less morbidity).[47] As rough approximations, it has been shown that interventions with QALYs of less than $50,000 usually are readily adopted into clinical practice, while those over $120,000 per QALY are challenged; intermediate QALYs are subjected to some scrutiny and may or may not be adopted.[48]

As we saw in Chapter 16 (pages 253–255), the Oregon Health Plan for its state Medicaid population has drawn national attention and controversy since 1987, when the Oregon Legislature decided to stop paying for transplants. At that time, the state was faced with $48 million in social program needs but only $21 million in its budget. The policy decision was framed as in favor of basic health care for 5,700 women and children instead of high-cost transplants for about 30 individuals.[6] This problem represents a classic example of the conflict between individuals and the collective group or society. Such choices are made everyday and throughout the country but usually are not as obvious.

The Oregon Health Plan raised important questions within the ongoing national debate on the cost, access, and quality of health care. Leaders in Oregon used explicit outcomes based and preference-based methods to set priorities. Public views and preferences were sought through dozens of town-hall and statewide meetings, formal interviews with representatives of various groups, a telephone poll of 1,001 randomly selected people, and legislative votes.[6] However, this well-intentioned approach can be called into question as focusing on rationing care to the poor before reducing waste in the rest of the system. It maintained a fragmented system with high overhead and still failed to reduce the number of uninsured below 10 percent.

Theoretically, health care can be improved for all from cost savings if ineffective interventions are pruned out. Eddy offers a useful way to think about these issues.[6]

1. "Drawing lines between quality and cost."
   a. Frequency of treatments (e.g., Pap smears annually versus every 3 years? mammograms every 1 or 2 years?).
   b. Severity (e.g., what level of intraocular pressure warrants treatment to prevent glaucoma?).
2. "Sibling treatments" (i.e., when two treatments for the same problem are similar in benefit but have big cost differences, such as should a 1 percent decrease in mortality from the use of tissue-type plasminogen activator (t-PA) in acute myocardial infarction warrant its use instead of streptokinase, which costs about $1,500 less per patient?).
3. "It's not much, but it's all we've got" (e.g., "last hope" cancer treatments: What potential five-year, disease-free survival rate justifies high-dose chemotherapy and autologous bone marrow transplantation for women with metastatic breast cancer? 8 percent? If so, how about 2 percent?).
4. "It's all we've got, and it's a lot" (e.g., enzyme replacement therapy for Gaucher's disease, a rare genetic lysosomal storage disease, at an annual cost of between $200,000 and $400,000, which might be required for life).

5. "Futile care" (e.g., many interventions, known not to result in satisfactory quality of life, are used everyday at a cost of tens of billions of dollars in response to families' desires to "do everything possible" or physicians' inability to provide appropriate end-of-life care).

ETHICS, RATIONING, AND THE LAW

Many advocate, as seems the most fair to me, that a utilitarian approach to health care ethics should underpin our health care system (i.e., do the greatest good for the largest number of people). By that measure, however, the present system is unjust in many ways, as illustrated by the several examples cited at the opening of this chapter involving unconscionable rationing of health care services by such factors as income, race, health status, or class.

Emily Friedman, health policy analyst and health care ethicist cited in earlier chapters, frames ethical issues involved in health care in four main categories:[49]

1. *Access to care.* Since the best health care system in the world is of no help to people with no access to that system, this issue involves practices of insurers, providers, and managed care organizations, as well as access to technology and therapy.
2. *Conflicts of interest.* This group of issues involves potential conflicts of interest about the role of providers, case managers, and risk managers in managed care organizations, including the influence of financial incentives, the potential for conflicting and divided loyalties, and the goals of investor-owned organizations.
3. *Professionalism.* This category includes the maintenance of confidentiality and privacy of patient information, the health professional's own malpractice or witnessing of abuses in other areas, and human subject protections in clinical experiments.
4. *Public policy.* Issues here include inequities in access to care, patient protections, health care financing, quality standards, confidentiality, and monitoring or disciplinary actions for problems of professional practice.

Friedman, who teaches a course in rationing at Boston University, has this to say about the morality of rationing:[49]

There is a lot of unnecessary and useless care in this country, from using antibiotics to treat viral infections to unnecessary surgery. It not only wastes money; it also hurts patients. So confining ourselves to care that is known to work is a form of rationing that I consider moral. However, there's a difference between moral rationing and an HMO that gets the contract for a group of helpless, poor Medicaid patients; assigns them to a primary care provider who has no intention of ever seeing them; takes its 30% cut; and then takes the phone off the hook.

A group of physicians in Massachusetts, under the auspices of the Ad Hoc Committee to Defend Health Care, in 1997 drafted a call to action against the abuses of corporate health care, which treats patients as profit centers. The following excerpts from their paper should be heeded as essential guideposts to ethically based health care reform:[50]

The shift to profit-driven care is at a gallop. For nurses and physicians, the space for good work in a bad system rapidly narrows. For the public, who are mostly healthy and use little care, awareness of the degradation of medicine builds slowly; it is mainly those who are expensively ill who encounter the dark side of market-driven health care.

We criticize market medicine not to obscure or excuse the failings of the past, but to warn that the changes afoot push nursing and medicine farther from caring, fairness, and efficiency. We differ on many aspects of reform, but on the following we find common ground:

1. Medicine and nursing must not be diverted from their primary tasks: the relief of suffering, the prevention and treatment of illness, and the promotion of health. The efficient deployment of resources is critical, but must not detract from these goals.
2. Pursuit of corporate profit and personal fortune have no place in caregiving.
3. Potent financial incentives that reward overcare or undercare weaken patient-physician and patient-nurse bonds and should be prohibited. Similarly, business arrangements that allow corporations and employers to control the care of patients should be proscribed.
4. A patient's right to a physician of choice must not be curtailed.
5. Access to health care must be the right of all.

Discussions about ethical issues in health care often become confused and distorted by economic issues in the U.S. market-based system. A particular case in point is the heated debate about the "gatekeeper" role of primary care physicians in managed care settings. Specifically, is the role of the primary care gatekeeper to coordinate care and improve quality or to reduce costs? Howard Brody, a family physician–ethicist who heads the Center for Ethics and Humanities in the Life Sciences at Michigan State University, identified five common fallacies that may put meaningful debate of such ethical issues off track:[51]

1. "The more is better fallacy." Physicians and the public often view technological interventions as better than nonuse, even when benefits of treatment are limited or inappropriate. Fee-for-service care typically places no limits on such interventions, while managed care generally places restraints in their use. An implicit assumption that "more is better" frequently clouds ethical discussions of these interventions.[52]
2. "The good old days fallacy." This fallacy assumes that fee-for-service practice represents an infallible "moral yardstick" compared to assumed conflict of interest in managed care gatekeeping, which could not have been the case within FFS physician-patient relationships.[50] In other words, customary and familiar financial arrangements between physicians and patients in FFS practice cannot be assumed to be ethically superior to new arrangements in managed care.[53]
3. "The Marcus Welby fallacy." Dr. Marcus Welby, as the media's heroic patient advocate with just one patient at a time, encouraged an unrealistic image of patient advocacy. As Brody and others point out, invisible patients are put at increased risk if an individual patient uses up limited

resources so that a physician's advocacy duty must be simultaneously for the individual and the population being served.[54–57]

4. "The buck-stops-somewhere else fallacy." This assumes that rationing of health care services can be avoided by physicians, absolving them of any guilt.[52,58,59] Instead, however, since the physician's time is a limited resource, just like money, this fallacy denies the necessary judgments made by physicians during any practice day to spend more time with patients with more serious, worrisome, or puzzling problems.[54,60]

5. "The rose-is-a-rose fallacy." This fallacy assumes that all managed care organizations and plans are about the same. As we have seen, this is far from true, with major differences in goals, values, operations, and quality often observed among them, particularly between well-established not-for-profit staff HMOs and for-profit HMOs. A frequently mentioned but ironic illustration of this attitude is the condemning of resource allocation decisions made by a primary care physician caring for the patient face-to-face versus similar kinds of decisions rendered by a faceless administrative case manager who provides no care.

Turning to legal considerations of these issues, U.S. courts recognize the need for cost-consciousness in health care, but have held both insurers and providers responsible "when medically inappropriate decisions result from defects in the design or implementation of cost containment mechanisms . . ."[13,61] Today, the power of insurers is limited by law in two ways. The courts often counter insurers' attempts to deviate from clinically derived professional standards of care as the basis for determinations of coverage and medical necessity. Moreover, when patients have appealed insurers' decisions under ERISA, the courts consistently overturned decisions that were found to be "arbitrary and capricious and that represented an abuse of the trust between the insurer and the insured."[27] The courts have been very concerned that insurers have a conflict of interest, since they stand to gain as a result of denying coverage, and awarded large settlements to patients judged to be harmed by arbitrary HMO practices.[27,62]

SETTING PRIORITIES IN OTHER COUNTRIES

Other industrialized Western countries with better performing health care systems have been able to provide more care, with better patient outcomes, for much less money, all within a fixed global budget. How do they do it? Although the details vary from one country to another, they ration by setting national priorities and generally have been able to make reasonable choices (e.g., coverage of bone marrow transplants for leukemia but no coverage for Rogaine for hair growth).

Several common features to the priority setting process are found in those countries that effectively balance the health care needs of their populations with the costs of health care:[14]

1. Allocation of resources is consistent with overriding social and ethical values of equity.
2. Collective global budgets for health care are employed.

3. Public and private approaches are interwoven in the public interest, with varying degrees of regulation.
4. The government exercises general oversight and political responsibility for its health care system.

As Evans pointed out in a 1995 International Conference on Governments and Health Systems, these social objectives generally are accepted by such countries as guidelines for health policy:[14]

a. Effective health care, efficiently provided and equitably distributed across the population according to need;
b. Fair but not excessive reimbursement of providers; and
c. Equitable distribution of the burden of contributions according to ability to pay; within
d. An overall expenditure envelope that is consistent with the carrying capacity of the general economy, or rather of its members' collective willingness to pay.

A brief case example illustrates how priorities are set in England. Oxfordshire Health Authority is responsible for the health care of its population of about 600,000 people. It is a largely rural county with two urban centers. The Priorities Forum was established as a subcommittee of the Health Authority. It considers a wide range of issues, ranging from introduction of new drugs and treatments to exceptional needs of individual patients and reports its decisions in public meetings. Clinicians are actively involved in this process and asked to consider these three questions:[63]

1. If you want something outside your current fixed envelope of resource, can it be done by substituting a treatment of less value?
2. If demand for your service is increasing, what criteria are you using to agree on the threshold of treatment?
3. If you do not believe that it is possible either to draw thresholds of care or to substitute treatment then which service might you give a smaller resource to in order for you to enlarge yours?

Priorities are set by the Oxfordshire Health Authority within an ethical framework emphasizing

1. Evidence of effectiveness (including value, impact, and efficiency).
2. Equity (maximizing the welfare of patients within the available budget as well as giving priority to those most in need).
3. Patient choice (respecting patient choice and enabling their control over their own health care).

The Priorities Forum takes an evidence-based approach to its work. A recent example of its decisions is a policy statement that concluded, on the basis of limited efficacy so far, that donepezil will not be included in general practice or hospital budgets. No regulation prevents physicians from using the drug, but they are not encouraged to do so. As with other policies, they may be reviewed again in response to physician or patient requests as further evidence becomes available.[63]

Regardless of how any given country addresses the task of setting priorities for its health care system, the process is challenging and ongoing. The job is never done, is not easy, but is essential. However, as Evans observes concerning the United States: "In the one country where a coalition of private interests has prevented government from taking up this responsibility, the results have been spectacularly unsatisfactory."[14]

CONCLUDING COMMENTS

There is no free market in U.S. health care, and its increasing utilization and costs are driven more by for-profit special interests on the supply side than by excessive consumer demand. The paradox is that widespread rationing is taking place in the marketplace on the basis of income, class, health status, race, and other factors that is harmful to the most vulnerable parts of the population. Yet, the stakeholders in the present pro-market system contend that we provide the best of care and that rationing is to be avoided. It serves the interests of these mostly corporate stakeholders to denigrate the concept of a global budget for health care, to deny the existence or need for rationing as un-American, and to oppose the larger role of government in the health care marketplace.

While the U.S. health care system has become "fat and mean,"[64] its abuses and harms have not yet created enough public outrage to correct its inequities. Larry Churchill, in *Rationing Health Care in America: Perceptions and Principles of Justice*, says it well:[4]

> The well insured and the wealthy have not personally felt the effects of our current rationing scheme, which keeps it remote from their experience and safely associated with the British or other socialist or welfare health systems. For most of us who enjoy very good, and frequently more-than-necessary care, we fail to discern that our good fortune is bought, literally, at the price of maintaining a tacit system of allocation in which money (or its equivalent, insurance) guarantees access while lack of it guarantees sporadic, inferior, or no care. Bringing this forcefully to our attention is probably the most powerful argument that some form of health care allocation is necessary in all societies. The urgent question is which form.

And further, Paul Hoffman, with a long experience in health care management and biomedical ethics brings this perspective:[65]

> The largest obstacle to the institution of organized health care rationing to replace the random rationing we have presently is the absence of political will. Even raising the issue is considered politically unhealthy, primarily because there is a denial of the need to ration by society at large. This denial is grounded in the naïve assumption that savings achieved by reducing excessive administrative costs, unnecessary surgery, defensive medicine, inappropriate variations (geographic and otherwise) in medical practice patterns, and unhealthy behavior will be more than adequate to cover the cost of providing comprehensive medical services to everyone.

As earlier chapters demonstrated only too clearly, the U.S. health care system is sick, with serious performance problems across the board concerning access, cost, and quality of care. The core issues required to build a better health care system are now more visible on top of the table. Basic system reform is urgently needed, which leads us, in the next chapter, to consider what organizational options are available and preferable.

REFERENCES

1. Fuchs VR. *Who Shall Live: Health, Economics and Social Choice*. New York: Basic Books, 1974.
2. Aaron HJ, Schwartz WB. *The Painful Prescription: Rationing Hospital Care*. Washington, DC: The Brookings Institution, 1984.
3. Callahan D. *Setting Limits: Medical Goals in an Aging Society*. New York: Simon and Schuster, 1987.
4. Churchill LR. *Rationing Health Care in America: Perceptions and Principles of Justice*. Notre Dame, IN: University of Notre Dame Press, 1987.
5. Fein R. *Medical Care, Medical Costs: the Search for a Health Insurance Policy*. Cambridge, MA: Harvard University Press, 1986.
6. Eddy DM. *Clinical Decision Making: From Theory to Practice: A Collection of Essays from JAMA*. Boston: Jones and Bartlett Publishers, 1996.
7. Schwartz WB. *Life Without Disease: The Pursuit of Medical Utopia*. Berkeley: University of California Press, 1998.
8. Friedman E. Rationing: The specter of necessity. *Trustee*. 1995;48(3):12–15.
9. Ubel PA, Goold S. Recognizing bedside rationing: Clear cases and tough calls. *Ann Intern Med*. 1997;126:74–80.
10. Asch DA, Ubel PA. Rationing by any other name. *N Engl J Med*. 1997;336:1668–1671.
11. Relman AS. Is rationing inevitable? *N Engl J Med*. 1990;322:1809–1810.
12. Hadorn DC, Brook RH. The health care resource allocation debate. Defining our terms. *JAMA*. 1991;266:3328–3331.
13. Aaron H, Schwartz WB. Rationing health care: The choice before us. *Science*. 1990;247:418–422.
14. Evans RG. Going for the gold: The redistributive agenda behind market-based health care reform. *J Health Polit Policy Law*. 1997;22(2):427–465.
15. Is an HMO for you? (based on survey of 52,000 readers) *Consumer Reports* 2000;65(7):38.
16. Managed care. *JAMA*. 1996;276:1039–1086.
17. Wrich J. Audit findings submitted to Congressional Budget Office. March 1998.
18. Himmelstein DU, Woolhandler S, Hellander I, Wolfe SM. Quality of care in investor-owned vs. not-for-profit HMOs. *JAMA*. 1999;282:159–163.
19. Gornick ME, Eggers PW, Reilly TW, et al. Effects of race and income on mortality and use of services among Medicare beneficiaries. *N Engl J Med*. 1996;335:791–799.
20. Billings J, Anderson GM, Newman LS. Recent findings on preventable hospitalizations. *Health Aff (Millwood)*. 1996;15(3):23–49.
21. OECD, 1999 data for 1997 or most recent year.
22. GAO/PEMD 94-10. Comparisons of availability and appropriateness of BMT. March 1994:250–252.
23. OECD, 1995.
24. Bortin MM, Horowitz MM, Rimm AA. Increasing utilization of allogenic bone marrow transplantation. *Ann Intern Med*. 1992;116:505–512.
25. Frankel S. Health needs, health-care requirements, and the myth of infinite demand. *Lancet*. June 29, 1991:53–54.
26. Brook RH, Lohr KN. Will we need to ration effective health care? Issues Sci Technol. 1986;III:68–77.
27. Rosenbaum S, Frankford DM, Moore B, Borzi P. Who should determine when health care is medically necessary? *N Engl J Med*. 1999;340:229–232.
28. Aaron HJ. Questioning the cost of biomedical research. *Health Aff (Millwood)*. 1986;5(2):96–99.

29. Braithwaite SS. Distributive justice: Must we say yes when society says no? In: Monagle JF, Thomasma DC (eds). *Health Care Ethics: Critical Issues.* Gaithersburg, MD: Aspen Publishers, 1994:295–304.
30. Benjamin M, Cohen C, Grochowski E. What transplantation can teach us about health care reform. The Ethics and Social Impact Committee. *N Engl J Med.* 1994;330:858–860.
31. Finkelstein BS, Silvers JB, Marrero U, Neuhauser D, Cuttler L. Insurance coverage, physician recommendations, and access to emerging treatments: Growth hormone therapy for childhood short stature. *JAMA.* 1998;279:663–668.
32. Peeno L. A physician answers questions about denial of care in managed care corporations. (Citizen Action, 1996).
33. Peeno L. "The Letter I Should Have Written My 'Patients.'" Lecture given to the Illinois Campaign for Better Health Care, October 1998.
34. Peeno L. "One Physician's Confession: An Interview with Linda Peeno, MD." Excerpted from a Canadian Broadcast Company *Sunday Morning* segment, broadcast January 12, 1997.
35. Peeno L. "A Day in the Life of a Company Doctor." Excerpted from a talk before the Ad Hoc Committee to Defend Health Care, Boston, December 2, 1997.
36. Peeno L. "Approved or Denied—How HMOs Decide What Care You Need." *U.S. News and World Report.* March 9, 1998.
37. Hellander I. Personal communication, January 19, 2001.
38. Velanovich V, Creaghe SB, Smith RL. Managed care clinical corner: Abdominal aortic aneurism. *Am J Manag Care.* 1997;3(4):643–646.
39. Himmelstein DU, Woolhandler S, Hellander I, Wolfe SM. Quality of care in investor-owned vs. not-for-profit HMOs. *JAMA.* 1999;282:159–163.
40. McCulloch DK, Price MJ, Hindmarsh M, Wagner EH. A population-based approach to diabetes management in a primary care setting: Early results and lessons learned. *Eff Clin Pract.* 1998;1(1): 12–22.
41. Beck A, Scott J, Williams P, et al. A randomized trial of group outpatient visits for chronically ill older HMO members: The Cooperative Health Care Clinic. *J Am Geriatr Soc.* 1997;45:543–549.
42. Gold MR, Siegel JE, Russell LB, Weinstein MC (eds). *Cost-Effectiveness in Health and Medicine.* New York: Oxford University Press, 1996.
43. Office of Technology Assessment, U.S. Congress. *Review of Selected Federal Vaccine and Immunization Policies Based on Case Studies of Pneumococcal Vaccine.* Washington, DC: U.S. Government Printing Office, 1979.
44. Deyo RA. Cost-effectiveness of primary care. In: Geyman JP, Deyo RA, Ramsey SD (eds). *Evidence-Based Clinical Practice: Concepts and Approaches.* Boston: Butterworth–Heinemann, 2000:111–118.
45. Neuhauser D, Lweicki AM. What do we gain from the sixth stool guaiac? *N Engl J Med.* 1975; 293:226–228.
46. Tengs TO, Adams ME, Pliskin JS, et al. Five hundred life-saving interventions and their cost-effectiveness. *Risk Anal.* 1995;15(3):369–390.
47. Petitti DB. *Meta-Analysis, Decision Analysis, and Cost-Effectiveness Analysis: Methods for Quantitative Synthesis in Medicine.* New York: Oxford University Press, 1994.
48. Laupacis A, Feeny D, Detsky AS, Tugwell PX. How attractive does a new technology have to be to warrant adoption and utilization? Tentative guidelines for using clinical and economic evaluations. *CMAJ.* 1992;146:473–481.
49. Friedman E. Ethics, policy, and practice: Interview with Emily Friedman. *Image J Nurs Sch.* 1999; 31(3):259–262.
50. Ad Hoc Committee to Defend Health Care. For our patients, not for profit: A call to action. *JAMA.* 1997;278:1733.
51. Brody H. Common fallacies that stall discussions about ethical issues in managed care. *Fam Med.* 1996;28(9):657–659.
52. Sulmasy DP. Physicians, cost control, and ethics. *Ann Intern Med.* 1992;116:920–926.
53. May WE. On ethics and advocacy. *JAMA.* 1986;256:1786–1787.
54. Brody H. *The Healer's Power.* New Haven, CN: Yale University Press, 1992:190–202.
55. Eddy DM. Clinical decision making: from theory to practice. Rationing resources while improving quality. How to get more for less. *JAMA.* 1994;272:817–824.
56. LaPuma J. Anticipated changes in the doctor-patient relationship in the managed care and managed competition of the Health Security Act of 1993. *Arch Fam Med.* 1994;3:665–671.
57. Sabin JE. A credo for ethical managed care in mental health practice. *Hosp Community Psychiatry.* 1994;45:859–860.

58. Pellegrino ED. Rationing health care: The ethics of medical gatekeeping. *J Contemp Health Law Policy.* 1986;2:23–45.
59. Ethical issues in managed care. Council on Ethical and Judicial Affairs. American Medical Association. *JAMA.* 1995;273:330–335.
60. Clancy CM, Brody H. Managed care: Jekyll or Hyde? *JAMA.* 1995;273:338–339.
61. Blum JD. Cost containment measures: A physician's peril (*Wickline* v. *State of California*). *Legal Aspects of Medical Practice.* 1987;15(10):6.
62. Wagner J. Firestone v. Bruch sweeps clean, aftermath varies (*Firestone Tire & Rubber Co.* v. *Bruch*—489 U.S. 101 [1989]). *Benefits Law Journal.* March 1991(1):41–59.
63. Griffiths S, Reynolds J, Hope T. Priority setting in practice. In: Coulter A, Ham C. *The Global Challenge of Health Care Rationing.* Buckingham, MK: Open University Press, 2000:203–213.
64. Himmelstein DU. Testimony before the Managed Care Consumer Protection Forum, July 25, 1996.
65. Hoffman PB. Ethics in health care delivery. In: Kovner AR, Jonas S (eds). *Jonas and Kovner's Health Care Delivery in the United States.* New York: Springer Publishing Company, 1999:490.

22
Organizational Options for a Failing Health Care "System"

As seen only too clearly in preceding chapters, U.S. health care is in a chaotic state. Seven years after the demise of the overly complex Clinton Health Plan and continued pursuit of incremental "reforms" under managed competition, the number of uninsured is up by 10 million and the health care crisis is worse. Although many culprits are obvious (corporate HMOs, insurance industry greed, drug company profiteering, etc), the country is no closer to any resolution of this chaos. Marcia Angell, editor of *The New England Journal of Medicine*, sums up the current situation in these terms:[1]

> The American health care system is at once the most expensive and the most inadequate system in the developed world, and it is uniquely complicated. In 1997 we spent about $4,000 per person on health care, as compared with the next more expensive country, Switzerland, which spent some $2,500. Yet 16 percent of our population has no health insurance at all, and many of the rest have only very limited coverage. The hallmark of the system is its reliance on the private market to deliver and, to a lesser extent, to fund health care. Accordingly, health care is treated as a commodity provided by a huge number of competing organizations. The surest way for these organizations to thrive is to shift costs to one another by devising stratagems to avoid the most expensive patients—either those who are chronically ill, if payment is capitated, or those who are not insured for the services they need, if payment is on a fee-for-service basis. Other developed countries provide universal health care, considering it a social service, not a commodity.

In their excellent book *The Crisis in Health Care: Costs, Choices, and Strategies*, Dean Coddington and his colleagues made the following predictions in 1990 for outcomes under a market-based system:[2]

- No solution to the uninsured problem (expect more than 40 million uninsured).
- Double-digit health plan rate increases.
- Smaller employers dropping health plans or cutting coverage.

- Continued gaps in safety net coverage.
- Shift toward managed care and away from indemnity coverage.
- Large rate increases for private insurers in shrinking market.
- Increased copayments and deductibles for employees.
- Numerous failures of HMOs and withdrawal from market by larger insurance companies.
- Overall continued inflation of health care costs.
- Continued cost shifting in an increasingly fragmented market.

Eleven years later, all of these outcomes have taken place, exactly as predicted. As we saw in Chapter 17 (page 266), we now have a three-tier nonsystem with serious access, cost, and quality problems. Almost one in six Americans is without health insurance, and many millions are underinsured.[3] By the mid-1990s, national opinion polls showed that 75 percent of Americans believed that fundamental change of the health care system was required, with 84 percent perceiving a crisis in health care.[4,5] Public trust in the health care system is declining,[6] and health care is re-emerging as an important issue in electoral politics.[7]

Based on the foregoing, it is time to ask what organizational options are available to restructure the largest service industry in the world. Again, these basic policy options are (1) incremental changes to present system; (2) building further on the employer-based health insurance system, with public sector coverage of the unemployed; (3) abandoning the employer-based insurance system in favor of a consumer choice model without involvement of employers; and (4) adopting a single-payer system as a vehicle for universal coverage. This chapter has four objectives: (1) to briefly describe the paradox of the present situation that incrementalism has produced, (2) to review the failed strategies in recent years under incrementalism and the market-based system, (3) to outline three major alternatives for reform of health care, and (4) to revisit the political climate as it relates to alternative scenarios.

PARADOX OF THE PRESENT SYSTEM

In 1978, Paul Starr described the essential paradox of modern medicine in America in this way, equally true today:[8]

> American medicine today contains a paradox. Outwardly, its institutions, prosperous and authoritative, show imposing strength, yet their social and economic structure is fundamentally unstable, and long-standing assumptions that have governed their operation are in danger of breaking down.

Indeed, even though the United States pours much more money into its health care system than any other country in the world, its health care system ranks 37th in the world by WHO criteria when the outputs of its health care system are weighed against its inputs.[9] In an aging country with a growing burden of chronic illness, it is a system designed more for acute care of individuals by application of the biomedical model. Moreover, its flaws would have been more apparent and politically unacceptable sooner were it not for its affluence and the good fortune of the longest-running economic boom in its history.

Table 22-1 lists some leading examples, based on documented evidence, of the health care system's major problems in terms of access, cost, quality, and organization. Taken together, the weaknesses of the present system become only too obvious, and it is lamentable that a more effective movement for reform has not yet occurred.

As we saw in Chapter 20, about four of five Americans now believe that major reform of the health care system is urgently needed. The lack of a major public revolt so far is largely explained by the strength of special interests resisting change in the status quo.

It is ironic that, much as today's new emphasis on quality improvement in health care is needed and long overdue, this approach alone cannot solve the health care system's more fundamental weaknesses in terms of access, costs, and organizational structure. In fact, reform of the health care system is a prerequisite for a major improvement in quality of care.

FAILURE OF INCREMENTALISM AND MANAGED COMPETITION

As an ongoing patchwork system of private and public health care coverage, the landscape of U.S. health care has become progressively more fragmented. Changes that began in the private insurance market are now taking place in the public sector as well. As we saw in earlier chapters, HMOs, PPOs, and POS plans now dominate the marketplace, while indemnity plans continue to shrink and even some well-established staff-model HMOs are failing. Figure 22-1 compares the theoretical goals for managed competition versus the real-world picture of the present environment. Almost all HMOs today limit choice of provider and pay physicians through varied forms of discounted fee-for-service and capitation.[10] The failings of this patchwork, largely profit-driven marketplace is highlighted in Chapters 14 and 20. All have been perpetuated by promarket policies of incrementalism.

In response to public opposition to for-profit managed care (i.e., "mangled care") as practiced in a chaotic marketplace, legislators and policy makers have been busy trying to balance constituent anger with shoring up the HMO industry. Figure 22-2, for example, shows the number and percentage of states that adopted modest strategies between 1990 and 1995 to partially reform state health insurance practices. All of these policy instruments, however, exact a cost in undesirable tradeoffs, especially in raising costs and decreasing access to care (Table 22-2).

In an incisive paper, exploring how the commodification of health care distorts ethics and threatens equity, Larry Churchill makes this cogent observation:[11]

> Market forces in health care do not solve the access problem. They aggravate it. They create still further fragmentation between the insured and

Table 22-1   Problems with the U.S. Health Care System

Problem and Illustrative Examples	Discussion (by Chapter and Reference)
Decreasing access to health care	
42.6 million uninsured Americans	17[4]
40 percent of the uninsured have annual incomes at least twice the federal poverty level (which was $33,000 for a family of four in 1998)	17[7,8]
Only two thirds of U.S. employers offer health insurance	8[3]
20 percent of the uninsured cannot afford health insurance when offered by employers	8[4]
One quarter of all nonelderly Americans is uninsured for at least one month every year	8[26]
In many states parents working full time for the minimum wage of $5.15 an hour neither qualify for Medicaid nor can afford health insurance	17[10]
Compared to the insured, the uninsured are sicker and have less preventive care, higher rates of preventable hospitalizations, and higher mortality rates	8[17–22]
A severe protracted recession will increase the number of uninsured and those on Medicaid by 75 percent each by 2007	17[2]
Increasing cost of care	
Overall health expenditures quadrupled from 1980 to 1995 ($250 billion to $1 trillion) despite all cost containment efforts	16[12]
Fourfold increase in per capita health care spending from 1988 to 1998, now over $4,000 per year	7[3]
Average annual increase of costs of prescription drugs was 24.8 percent from 1996 to 1999	16[43]
12-fold increase in spending for home health care from 1980 to 1998	7[2]
Overall medical care costs projected to increase by 12.2 percent in 2001 for active employees and 13.3 percent for Medicare retirees	7[12]
About 26 percent of the nation's total health care expenditures are taken up by administrative costs	24[13]
Annual per capita costs of hospital billing and administration are more than five times higher in the United States than Canada ($372 vs. $65)	7[6]
Inconsistent, often poor quality of care	
Quality of care problems result from many factors, including denial of services, geographical variations, lack of primary care and continuity, iatrogenesis, unnecessary care, and neglect of quality-of-life or psychosocial issues	18[8,9,11,17,19,21]
A recent study by RAND showed that	18[6]
50 percent of people receive recommended preventive care	
60 percent receive recommended chronic care	
70 percent receive recommended acute care	
30 percent receive contraindicated acute care	
20 percent receive contraindicated chronic care	

continues

Table 22-1 (continued)

Problem and Illustrative Examples	Discussion (by Chapter and Reference)
The Institute of Medicine has estimated that 44,000 to 98,000 Americans die each year as a result of preventable medical errors	18[26]
Among 13 industrialized countries, the United States ranks last for low-birth-weight percentage, neonatal and infant mortality overall, and years of potential life lost	18[31]
A recent report by the World Health Organization ranks the United States 15th out of 25 industrialized countries for overall performance of the health care system	18[32]
Nonsustainable, overly complex, inefficient health care system with poor performance	
A weak primary care base ranks the United States last of 11 industrialized nations by 11 criteria	13[59]
Overly specialized physician workforce	4[16]
A major reason for poor outcome performance of the health care system	18[31]
Health care system based more on acute care and the biomedical model than chronic care model	10[13,15,33,34]
Market-driven private sector often is in conflict with the public interest: Investor-owned HMOs score worse on all 14 quality-of-care indicators than nonprofit plans (1999 study)	18[81]
Over 1,200 insurers and increasing burden of bureaucracy and paperwork	22[30]
Health administrative costs account for about 26 percent of total health care spending	24[13]
Steady decline in employer-based health insurance (only 64 percent of U.S. workers covered in 1996)	14[4]
Increasing need for public sector "safety net" U.S. public sector spending per capita exceeds *total* health care spending of any other industrialized country	14[25]
Public sector increasingly fragile: Two thirds of public hospitals lost money in 1997	11[46]
60 percent of 80 operational Medicaid managed care safety-net plans lost money in 1997	17[32]

uninsured, the employed and the unemployed, the sick and the well. But to be fair, markets were never designed to achieve equity in access. As David Manning, vice-president of Columbia/HCA put it, markets are designed to create winners.[12] What must be recognized is that in a largely unregulated competitive environment, winners will achieve their victory by the most direct route, rather than the most socially beneficial one, and they will treat the losers as someone else's problem.

Beyond his moral objections to actuarial practices of risk rating, Churchill presents a compelling argument that a community-rating system should be used

Managed Competition: How It Was Supposed to Be

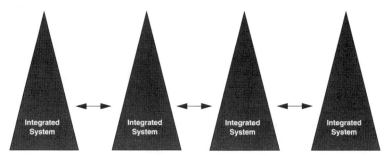

World of:
- competition between vertically integrated systems
- exclusive relationships
- empowered consumers

How It Really Is

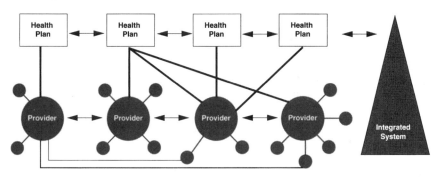

World of:
- horizontally integrated delivery systems
- nonexclusive relationships
- competition among plans and providers
- confused consumers

Figure 22-1   Managed competition. (Reprinted with permission from The Institute for the Future. *Health and Health Care 2010: The Forecast, the Challenge.* San Francisco: Jossey-Bass, 2000:49.)

in the interests of equity as well as cost containment. Drawing from the analysis of Donald Light,[13] he comments further:[11]

> Risk-rating adds substantially to the total administrative costs, since it requires managers and actuaries to separately rate policies for individuals who are themselves subject to changes in their health status and must therefore be *re*rated. There is also the cost of comparison shopping for the best rates by consumers, in a system in which there is no publicly or professionally agreed upon rationale for assessing and assigning risks in the first place. Finally, even those (now healthy and presumably low risk) persons who

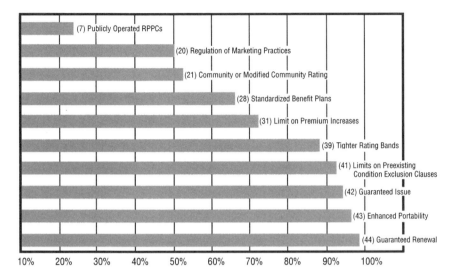

Figure 22-2 The prevalence of specific policy instruments in state health insurance reforms, 1990–1995: Number and percent of states adopting specific instruments, among states enacting small-group market reforms. (Reprinted with permission from Oliver TR. The dilemmas of incrementalism: Logical and political constraints in the design of health insurance reforms. *J Policy Anal Manage.* 1999;18(4):652–683.)

might negotiate a low rate for themselves are not immune to the other forces that lead to cost-shifting, so that the presumed advantages of risk-rating for the healthy diminish in a system as fragmented and volatile as the present one. And, of course, any remaining advantage for the patient-consumer from risk-rating vanishes with age or serious illness. After all is said and done, the only beneficiaries of risk-rating seem to be insurers.

MAJOR ORGANIZATIONAL OPTIONS

Before focusing on the major organizational alternatives for the structured change of today's health care system, it is useful to take a broad macro view of evolving health care systems in industrialized countries. The work of Victor Rodwin provides an interesting comparison of five major types of health care systems as they have evolved over the last 100 years (Table 22-3). The United States falls into a type 2 pluralistic category.[14]

Returning again to the analysis by Coddington and his colleagues, three basic alternative reform scenarios are available to the United States, beyond the present failing policy of market-based incrementalism now in place. Only the third option would guarantee universal access. The first two options would continue as a pluralistic hybrid private/public mix. The first option retains an employer-based insurance system, the second abandons that system in favor of

Table 22-2   Policy Goals, Instruments, and Key Tradeoffs

Policy Goals and Instruments	Intended Policy Results	Policy Tradeoffs
Improved access		
Guaranteed renewal	Prevents insurers from cancelling insurance due to poor health or high medical expenses.	Higher premiums as poorer risks are retained in group's risk pool. Increased difficulty in obtaining initial insurance coverage.
Guaranteed issue	Guarantees that health insurance is available regardless of health status or past medical expenses.	Higher premiums as poorer risks are retained in group's risk pool. Higher premiums may drive the "better" health risks from insurance market.
Limits on preexisting condition exclusion clauses	Enhances portability of insurance, since coverage of a condition cannot be denied if previously insured and reduces waiting period for coverage if previously uninsured.	Creates a disincentive to purchase health insurance before it is needed.
Social solidarity in rating and underwriting		
Limits on variation in premium	Narrows the variation in premium between and within groups due to real or perceived health risks (reducing premiums for poorer risks) and broadens the pool across which such risk is spread.	Higher premiums for better risks, perhaps driving them from the insurance market. Potentially reduces incentives for healthier lifestyles.
Limits on use of group characteristics in rating and underwriting	Reduces the ability of insurers to use selected groups' characteristics as a basis for issuing and pricing insurance.	Higher premiums for better risks, perhaps driving them from the insurance market.
Community and modified community rating	Broadens the pool across which risk is spread and restricts characteristics for rating purposes. Improves access and reduces cost for highest risk groups.	Higher premiums for better risks, perhaps driving them from the insurance market.
Fair and efficient market competition		
Standardized benefit plans	Increased competition from product comparison on cost. Expected to create downward pressure on premiums.	No ability to design plans to meet specific needs of group. Potential for adverse selection when not mandated for entire market.

continues

Table 22-2   (continued)

Policy Goals and Instruments	Intended Policy Results	Policy Tradeoffs
Fair marketing rules	Eliminates the most egregious strategies for risk selection and discloses insurer rating practices.	Inserts government into operation of market.
Limits on premium increases	Maintains affordability and increases retention of insurance coverage.	Impedes the free operation of market forces.
Health plan purchasing cooperative (HPPC)	Can reduce administrative and commission costs, especially for smallest groups.	Potential for adverse selection when market rules are not uniform inside and outside the HPPC.

Source: Reprinted with permission from Oliver TR. The dilemmas of incrementalism: Logical and political constraints in the design of health insurance reforms. *J Policy Anal Manage.* 1999;18(4):652–683.

a consumer-choice model, and the third adopts a unified or single-payer system managed by either the states or the federal government. Table 22-4 lists the main features of each of these alternatives. While it is not the intent here to discuss all of the currently debated strategies being considered within each option, these three basic alternatives provide a useful framework to examine some typical approaches within each option.[2] Options 1 and 2 can overlap, of course, such as for Medicare reform, which could take place under either option.

Option 1. Employer-Based Insurance plus Universal Coverage

As we saw in Chapter 8 (pages 106–107), the voluntary employer-based insurance system increasingly is tenuous and now covers only 64 percent of the nonelderly workforce. Although more than 152 million workers receive at least partial health benefits through a private or public employer,[15] and this number represents 93 percent of all privately insured Americans, the employer-based insurance system is an "accidental system," hastily put together during the wartime economy of World War II. At a time of serious labor shortages, federal officials and the Internal Revenue Service ruled that employers' contributions for health insurance for their employees should be tax-exempt for workers and tax-deductible for employers. Enrollment in private health insurance through employers then grew from 1.4 million before the war to 60 million in 1951.[15,16]

There still are strong proponents for building the U.S. health care system on a voluntary base of employer-based insurance.[17] That course clearly is in the self-interest of a $300 billion private insurance industry, as well as businesses that don't want to pay for health benefits. However, doubts concerning the future of employer-based insurance have increased during the 1990s, as the

Table 22-3   The Evolution of Health Systems

Health System	Type 1: Private	Type 2: Pluralistic	Type 3: National Health Insurance	Type 4: National Health Service	Type 5: Socialized Health Service
General definition	Health care as item of personal consumption	Health care as predominantly a consumer good or service	Health care as an insured, guaranteed consumer good or service	Health care as a state-supported consumer good or service	Health care as a state-provided public service
Position of the physician	Solo entrepreneur	Solo entrepreneur and member of variety of groups, organizations	Solo entrepreneur and member of medical organizations	Solo entrepreneur and member of medical organizations	State employee and member of medical organizations
Role of professional associations	Powerful	Very strong	Strong	Fairly strong	Weak or nonexistent
Ownership of facilities	Private	Private and public	Private and public	Mostly public	Entirely public
Economic transfers	Direct	Direct and indirect	Mostly indirect	Indirect	Entirely indirect
Prototypes	U.S., Western Europe, Russia in the 19th century	U.S. in 20th century	Sweden, France, Canada, Japan in 20th century	Great Britain in 20th century	Soviet Union in 20th century

Source: Rodwin VG. *The Health Care Planning Predicament: France, Quebec, England, and the United States.* Berkley: University of California Press, 1984:245. Adapted from Field, MG. *Comparative Health Systems: Differences and Convergence,* final report under Grant N. HS-00272. Rockville, MD: National Center for Health Services Research, 1978. Reprinted with permission from Rodwin VG. Comparative analysis of health systems: An international perspective. In: Kovner AR, Jonas S (eds). *Health Care Delivery in the United States.* New York: Springer Publishing Company, 1999:122.

system shrank while total employment expanded. As a political economist, Uwe Reinhardt sees the balance sheet for employer-based health insurance in these terms:[18]

Pros
- Status-quo; difficulty in eliminating its tax preference.
- Risk pooling.
- Innovation through decentralization.
- Consumers' preferences.

Cons
- "Uninsurance" if a worker is not qualified or loses the job.
- Job lock.

Table 22-4 Alternative Scenarios

Scenario 1—Universal Access/Shakeout in Managed Care
Universal access to health care for Americans
Number of managed care companies reduced by half or more
More market power among payers
Continuation of employer-based health plans
Medicare reimbursement stabilized

Scenario 2—Consumer-Choice
Universal access to health care for Americans
Consumers purchase health care directly from insurers or managed care firms
Incentives for consumers to become cost-effective users of health care system
Medicare participants will use vouchers to purchase their own health plans
Employers may assist employees in purchasing health care, but are out of the payment
  system

Scenario 3—Single-Payer System
Either state or federal government will be the single payer
Universal access to health care for Americans
Likely to be modeled after the Canadian system
Reduction of competition among hospitals and physicians
Health plan and insurance industries will cease to exist; no need for Medicare

---

Source: Reprinted with permission from Coddington DC, Keen DJ, Moore KD, et al. *The Crisis in Health Care: Costs, Choices, and Strategies.* San Francisco: Jossey-Bass, 1990:189–190.

- Inequity.
- Lack of choice.
- Lack of privacy.
- Administrative complexity.
- Lack of transparency.

On balance, Reinhardt concludes that the cons outweigh the pros, suggesting the need at least for a parallel insurance system not linked to the workplace.[18]

Reform of the employer-based insurance system could include a variety of government regulations mandating coverage and benefits. A typical example of this approach is the Pay-or-Play plan proposed by President Nixon in the early 1970s, whereby employers would either provide coverage or pay into a special fund to cover health care costs for those outside the employer-based system. Such regulations naturally would be resisted by many employers (especially those with small businesses). Premium costs would escalate, since no provisions would be made for cost containment. Although this option requires the least amount of change from the present system, it builds on an already-fragile employer-based insurance system and almost certainly would involve enough pain to business, labor, providers, and consumers that its reforms, even if enacted, would still be insufficient. And, of course, this approach would require the public sector to provide access for the uninsured and there would still be gaps in coverage for those in part-time jobs or leaving the workforce.

Option 2. "Consumer Choice" ("Individual Mandate") and Universal Coverage

Option 2 is gaining popularity among advocates for pro-market solutions to health insurance coverage. It would shift the responsibility from employers to consumers in terms of the purchase of health insurance and payment for health services. It would reduce the health care market to its most basic unit: the consumer. The consumer-choice model is based on the assumptions that a free market can occur in health care, that consumers can be informed about an adequate number of options, and that they will spend their own money more prudently than other people's money.[19] Theoretically, consumers would be provided enough information on costs and the value of their options to be able to make informed choices.[2]

Reform proposals now being debated for Medicare provide examples of moving in the direction of a consumer-choice model. For-profit HMOs have lobbied strongly for privatizing Medicare. Theoretically, HMOs compete in the market based on cost, value, and patient satisfaction.[20] In fact, however, many HMOs enroll the healthy and avoid the sick. Senators John Breaux (D-La) and Bill Frist (R-Tenn), who cochaired the former National Bipartisan Commission on the Future of Medicare and remain key players in the continuing health care debate, have advocated a "premium support" plan whereby beneficiaries would receive a limited amount from the government to purchase a health plan providing defined benefits. The amount of premium support would vary according to the beneficiary's age, sex, geographic area, health risk status, income and assets, and use of services.[21] Critics point out that there would be no assurance that premium support would be enough to pay for a good health care policy.

Another proposal for Medicare reform would replace guaranteed benefits with vouchers whereby seniors could purchase their own health insurance. Still another proposal, this time for Medicaid, would provide tax credits as a means to purchase health insurance.[22] This concept has received some bipartisan support as a way of moving people away from employer-based insurance and government programs like Medicaid but hasn't yet developed much momentum.

Still another approach intended to facilitate the consumer-choice model is the concept of medical savings accounts (MSAs). This approach was enacted as a demonstration program as part of the Health Insurance Portability and Accountability Act of 1996. By February 2000, however, only 54,000 Americans among 750,000 eligible U.S. workers in small businesses had availed themselves of this approach.[23]

The Bush administration proposes a package of health care measures solidly based on the consumer-choice model, including tax credits, MSAs, and flexible savings accounts (whereby $500 can be carried over from one year to the next). The administration's proposal for Medicare reform is based on the Federal Employees Health Benefits Program (FEHBP). As a new plan, MediCARxES (Medicare Choice and Access to Prescription Drugs for Every Senior) would fully cover premium costs for all seniors with incomes at or below 135 percent of the poverty level, while 25 percent of premium costs for prescription drug coverage would be provided for seniors above 175 percent of the poverty level. In addition, the administration will propose the Immediate

Helping Hand Program, which would allocate $48 billion of direct support to states for four years to cover prescription drug costs for seniors with annual incomes below 135 percent of poverty levels.[24]

These approaches toward a consumer-choice model have generated strong counterarguments. Kuttner disputes the assumptions underlying the consumer-choice model with this warning about the false premises of this kind of pro-market "reform":[25]

> First, it assumes that competing health plans will take a high road of offering better service, rather than a low road of risk selections and secret financial incentives to participating doctors. Second, it assumes consumers will have a free choice among competing plans. Third, it assumes that good plans will drive out the bad ones, rather than vice versa. Fourth, it assumes that plans will not acquire a degree of monopoly power. And it presumes that consumers will be adequately informed about competing plans.

Based on their study and analysis of these proposals, the Physicians for a National Health Program (PNHP) raise these further objections:[26]

To tax subsidies and vouchers,
- Taxes go to wasteful private insurers, with overhead of 13 to 30 percent.
- Amounts paid are too low for good coverage, especially for the sick.
- High costs are charged for little coverage, much of the subsidy replaces employer-paid coverage.
- These plans encourage a shift from employer-based to individual policies with overhead of 35 percent or more.
- Costs would continue to rise (e.g., FEHBP).
- Most participants are unable to purchase wisely (e.g., frail elders, severely ill, policies too complicated, poor literacy).

To medical savings accounts,
- Sickest 10 percent of Americans use 72 percent of care; MSAs cannot lower these catastrophic costs.
- The 15 percent of people who get no care would get premium "refunds," removing their cross-subsidy for the sick but not lowering use or cost.
- Discourages prevention.
- Complex to administer, insurers have to keep track of all out-of-pocket payments.
- Congressional Budget Office projects that MSAs would increase Medicare costs by $2 billion.

Option 3. Single-Payer System

Since its classic paper proposing a national health program in 1989,[27] Physicians for a National Health Program has gained strength in numbers and influence as its concept becomes a more attractive alternative to the present disarray in the U.S. health care system. As we have seen, the current system is failing in its three basic elements—access, cost, and quality—and all incremental band-aid solutions provide no significant or lasting improvements. Advocates of a single-payer system see it as the only alternative among available policy options that can resolve the twin crises of rising health care costs and inadequate coverage. As the initiating sponsor of a single-payer plan in Congress, Representative Jim McDermott (D-Wash) describes this system as follows:[28]

> Single-payer health system reform severs the link between employment and health insurance. A single-payer system is essentially a financing mechanism that preserves the primary foundation of the American health care delivery system—the physician-patient relationship. The single payer—the government—provides the insurance for health care for all Americans, and the states negotiate the fees of health care providers. The health care delivery system remains primarily in private hands with free choice of provider. The government manages the rate of growth of price increases. This is the system that exists in varying forms in every society in the Western world, one that has brought health standards that are superior or equal to ours by most morbidity and mortality measurements, and one that has left its physicians and patients content.
>
> In single-payer systems throughout the world, patients choose their own practitioners, and physicians do not have to justify individual treatment decisions to insurance companies or their government or seek permission in advance to perform procedures. This is the system that has been proven to actually work to control costs, guarantee access, assure quality, and command loyalty by both patients and physicians.

Figure 22-3 summarizes PNHPs proposal as collated by Thomas Bodenheimer.

Among the many questions which have been raised about a single-payer system, these two are the most common. Answers by Gordon Schiff and David Himmelstein, as presented in Windsor, Ontario, in 1996, are illuminating and persuasive:[29]

> *Question: Isn't National Health Insurance (NHI) socialized medicine? And wouldn't it require doctors to give up control? Isn't competition more efficient?*
>
> *Answer:* NHI is not socialized medicine, but socialized insurance. And there are other essential services we've "socialized," such as retirement income support (Social Security), police protection, fire departments, the military, etc.
>
> In medicine, substantial evidence suggests that competition increases administrative waste, increases the subservience of physicians and patients to outside control, and often increases costs and decreases efficiency. NHI can liberate physicians and patients. Doctors in every other industrialized country experience less interference in their practices than we do. Corporations are dictating whom we can see, what we can do, where we can refer patients, even what we can say to them.
>
> Corporations are making medical decisions behind closed doors, as well as decisions on physicians' fees and working conditions. In Canada, physicians negotiate their fees with the government, and the sparks fly, but the doctors have a seat at the table. And there is virtually no interference in clinical practice.
>
> Market incentives often waste money and worsen quality. For example, hundreds of millions of dollars are being spent developing medical infor-

Physicians for a National Health Program
Proposed National Health Program Summary

PNHP's proposal would remove all financial barriers to medical care. Every American would be covered for necessary medical care by a public insurance plan administered by state and regional boards. PNHP envisages a program that would be federally mandated and ultimately funded by the federal government but administered largely at the state and local level. The plan borrows many features from the Canadian national health program and adapts them to the unique circumstances of the United States.

Coverage. Coverage would include standard medical care as well as care for mental health, long-term illness, dental services, occupational health services, and prescription drugs and equipment.

Payment. Patients would receive a National Health Program (NHP) card entitling them to care at any hospital or doctor's office. Patients would not be billed for approved medical care. They would not pay any deductibles, co-payments, or out-of-pocket costs. All approved costs would be payed by the NHP.

Hospitals. Most hospitals and nursing homes would remain privately owned and operated and would receive an annual "global lump sum" from the NHP to cover all operating costs. Global operating budgets would be negotiated with the NHP board. Funds for capital expansion would be distributed separately by regional NHP boards on the basis of health planning goals.

Physicians. Private doctors would continue to practice on a fee-for-service basis, with fee levels set by the NHP board, and would submit bills to the NHP. Physicians could bill patients only for services not covered by the plan. HMOs would receive a yearly lump sum from the NHP for each patient. Neighborhood health centers, clinics, and home care agencies employing salaried doctors and other health providers would be funded directly from the NHP on the basis of a global budget.

Prescription drugs and medical equipment. The NHP would pay pharmacists' wholesale costs plus a reasonable dispensing fee for prescription drugs. Medical equipment would be covered in a similar fashion.

Insurance. Private insurance that duplicates NHP coverage would be eliminated, saving an estimated $44 billion* a year in industry profits and overhead, simplifying paperwork for doctors and hospitals, and generating additional billions of dollars of savings on providers' billing and administrative costs.

Cost containment. Costs would be constrained through streamlining of billing and bureaucracy, improved health planning, and the NHP's ability to set and enforce overall spending limits.

Funding. Funds for the national health program could be raised through a variety of mechanisms. In the long run, funding based on an income tax or other progressive tax might be the fairest and most efficient solution. During the transition period, the national health program could be financed from federal funds allocated to Medicare or Medicaid; state and local funds for health care; a payroll tax on employers that takes the place of employer payments to private insurance companies; and taxes on individuals equivalent to the amount now spent on out-of-pocket payments.

* Estimated savings of $100 to $150 billion in 2001.

Adapted by Bodenheimer from PNHP handouts and "A National Health Program for the United States: A Physician's Proposal," by David U. Himmelstein, Steffie Woolhandler, and the Writing Committee of the Working Group on Program Design, New England Journal of Medicine, January 12, 1989:320, pp.102–108. For further information, contact Physicians for a National Health Program, 332 S. Michigan, Ste. 500, Chicago, IL 60604, (312) 554-0382.

Figure 22-3 Physicians for a National Health Program proposed national health program summary. (Reprinted with permission from Bodenheimer T. Single-payer—Fifty payers? Alternative payers for universal health insurance. *Health/PAC Bulletin.* Fall 1992:24–28; and updated concerning estimated savings of a National Health Program in 2000 from Kirschenbaum CB, Woolhandler S. Why single payer? Why now? *J Am Med Womens Assoc.* Winter 2000;55(1):37–38, 46.)

mation systems. The public is paying, but efforts are being squandered on hundreds of incompatible systems, mostly designed for billing. Resources that could go into developing truly useful automated medical records are being wasted.

The first principle of continuous quality improvement is that job security is essential, so that everyone can get involved in the process without fear. But when the big accounting firms and for-profit health care companies (e.g., Columbia/HCA has their contract with Ernst and Young) get together to "re-engineer" hospitals, the first thing they do is lay off workers.

As Bodenheimer and Grumbach noted,[30] there are two basic approaches to controlling costs: "reins" or "fences." Do you control the amount of land cattle can graze by putting reins and a keeper on every cow, or do you fence the pasture? Do you control physicians by reviewing each service and referral or do you put a financial fence, a global budget, around physicians as a whole, leave them broad latitude in clinical decision making, while minimizing financial incentives that interfere with clinical judgment?

Question: If someone wants to pay a little more to get their MRI right away, why shouldn't they be able to?

Answer: If you let the wealthy bypass queues by paying an extra fee, you release the pressure to keep funding adequate for the system as a whole. This is apparent in the British system, and in our Medicaid.

Supplemental insurance to cover the extras, like a private room or TV set, is okay. But private insurance that duplicates the public system will destroy it. Private insurers would work hard to undermine the public system, since only poor public coverage—or deceptive marketing— would induce people to pay for private policies. That's why Congress didn't allow insurers to sell policies duplicating Medicare benefits.

Physicians who want to opt out of the system entirely and see only private paying patients could do so. But taking both public and private payment for covered services should be outlawed to assure that physicians don't skimp on the public patients in order to make more time to care for lucrative private patients, or pressure patients into the private sector by creating public sector queues, as occurs in the U.K.

Up to 30 cents of every health care dollar now go to corporate profits, bureaucracy, and 1,200 different insurers. On the basis of a U.S. Government Accounting Office (GAO) study in 1991,[31] PNHP projects that the $100 billion saved each year from those costs could readily pay for a single-payer national health program by redirecting those funds more directly to patient care and away from administrative costs. The difference in administrative overhead costs of the private and public sectors is striking—only 1 percent for Canada's single-payer system and 2 percent for the U.S. Medicare program.

As Bodenheimer observed, the United States may see different versions of single-payer systems demonstrated in different states before a national health program is enacted.[32] Hawaii is the closest to a single-payer system already in successful operation.[33] Other states hope to move in that direction.

THE POLITICAL DEBATE: THREE KEY ISSUES

Three key issues underlie much of the ongoing political debate concerning how to proceed in addressing the obvious major problems of the current health care system. To a considerable degree, these overlap and all three remain unresolved:

1. How much competition versus regulation?
2. For universal coverage, who pays?
3. Should health insurance and health care be provided on a profit or nonprofit basis?

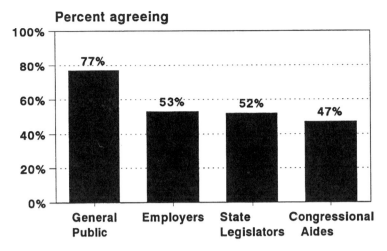

Figure 22-4 Harris poll: "Government should provide quality medical coverage to all adults. . . ." (Source: USA Today/Harris poll, November 23, 1998. Reprinted with permission from Woolhandler S, Himmelstein DU. *The National Health Program Slideshow Guide.* Cambridge, MA: Center for National Health Program Studies, 2000.)

The public debate quickly becomes distorted as market forces collide with the public interest. The debate plays out in a culture that values corporations above collectivism and government. Based on a 1999 Harris poll, there is strong public interest for a system of universal coverage, which also is favored by over half the employers and state legislators (Figure 22-4). Despite that level of public support for universal coverage, however, political gridlock persists as the special interests give money to and lobby Democrats and Republicans almost equally.

The 2000 presidential campaign provided a good example of political paralysis. Republicans tended to emphasize a market-based system, using tax credits, vouchers, or MSAs for more "consumer choice" of health plans. Democrats also favored tax credits and expanded consumer choice, as well as adding a prescription drug benefit for Medicare beneficiaries. Neither party took a bold approach to restructuring the health care system.[34] Only Ralph Nader's Green Party was a clear advocate for rebuilding the system based on a single-payer model.

In his interesting book on globalization, *The Lexus and the Olive Tree*, Thomas Friedman designed a matrix to illustrate the four basic political identities that people can choose concerning globalization.[35] Such a framework is helpful to display a spectrum of perspectives from market pluralism to single-payer on the horizontal axis and from for-profit health care and insurance to universal coverage by the public sector on the vertical axis. (Figure 22-5). Concerning the health care debate, for example, market pluralism and for-profit health care and health insurance have vested interests in the private sector, the

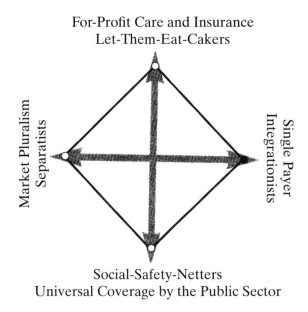

Figure 22-5 Political identities and health care policy. (Adapted with permission from Friedman TL. *The Lexus and the Olive Tree*. New York: Farrar, Straus and Giroux, 1999:353.)

insurance industry, and many health professionals, while single-payer advocates are vested more in the public interest and universal access than their own pocketbooks.

Unfortunately, the public debate so far has been more dollar driven than value driven. Consider this powerful indictment by Woolhandler and Himmelstein:[36]

> Our main objection to investor-owned care is not that it wastes taxpayers' money, not even that it causes modest decrements in quality. The most serious problem with such care is that it embodies a new value system that severs the communal roots and samaritan traditions of hospitals, makes doctors and nurses the instruments of investors, and views patients as commodities. In nonprofit settings, avarice vies with beneficence for the soul of medicine; investor ownership marks the triumph of greed. A fiscal conundrum constrains altruism on the part of nonprofit hospitals: No money, no mission. With for-profit hospitals, the money is the mission; form follows profit.
>
> In our society, some aspects of life are off-limits to commerce. We prohibit the selling of children and the buying of wives, juries, and kidneys. Tainted blood is an inevitable consequence of paying blood donors; even sophisticated laboratory tests cannot compensate for blood that is sold rather than given as a gift. Like blood, health care is too precious, intimate, and corruptible to entrust to the market.

As we saw in Chapter 20, about four of five Americans now believe that universal coverage for health care should be established in this country. Also, a growing majority of the public supports a larger role for government in health care. But, as we also saw in Chapter 20, the corporate special interests have effectively blocked all efforts toward NHI. Good examples include the pharmaceutical industry lobbying against potential price controls (Chapters 16 and 20) and the insurance industry lobbying against media coverage of a single-payer program through major advertising support to the media (Chapter 20).[37]

CONCLUDING COMMENTS

In my view, based on the best evidence available as highlighted in the first 22 chapters of this book, the U.S. health care system is sicker than many realize. Incrementalism already has failed, but powerful stakeholders are committed to maintain, if not the status quo, at least pro-market changes that continue to serve their interests. An increasing gap lies between the interests of corporate health care organizations and consumers, as well as a growing number of physicians and other health professionals, and the public interest continues to get lost as the battle for control of the system wages on between the stakeholders and stake challengers.

Based on the course and experience of health care politics in recent years (Chapter 20), as well as the already enunciated health care policies of the Bush administration, it appears likely that option 2 will receive the most interest by legislators over the next several years. But, as we have seen, there is no reason to believe that either option 1 or 2 will provide lasting system reform to assure universal access for affordable health care.

The single-payer option is the only policy alternative that can sufficiently reform our failing system and simultaneously address the problems of access, costs, and quality of health care. There is strong public support for it. It would provide universal access while achieving sufficient cost savings to finance a simplified and more efficient system. Physicians and other health professionals would be liberated from much of the regulatory and billing bureaucracy of the present system. Provider and patient satisfaction likely would increase. A more efficient system could focus more effectively on monitoring and improving the quality of care.

Attractive as the single-payer option is, however, it remains an open question as to when the political environment for health care will change enough to enact a single-payer system. As an experienced observer of this changing environment, Eli Ginzberg made this observation in 1999:[38]

Since managed-care plans will not be in a position to constrain rising health care costs in the face of consumers' demands for more choices and reduced interference in the patient-physician relationship, and since future health care costs must be controlled, at least as far as government expenditures are concerned, the best alternative is for government to provide essential coverage to the entire population and then let persons who want more and better care to cover the additional costs out of their own pockets, through privately purchased insurance, or through employer benefits.

We revisit approaches and prospects for health care reform in the last chapter, but first let's see what can be learned in the next chapter about the experience of some other industrialized Western nations with far better-performing health care systems than our own.

REFERENCES

1. Angell M. The American health care system revisited—A new series. *N Engl J Med.* 1999;340:48.
2. Coddington DC, Keen DJ, Moore KD, et al. *The Crisis in Health Care: Costs, Choices, and Strategies.* San Francisco: Jossey-Bass, 1990.
3. Mills RJ. Health insurance coverage 1999. U.S. Census Bureau 2000 (September 28). *Med Benefits.* 2000;17(2):9–10.
4. Princeton Survey Research Associates. *Newsweek Poll.* Storrs, CN: Roper Center for Public Opinion Research, June 17, 1994.
5. *Gallup/CNN/USA Today Poll.* Storrs, CN: Roper Center for Public Opinion Research, January 24, 1994.
6. Gray BH. Trust and trustworthy care in the managed care era. *Health Aff (Millwood).* 1997;16(1):34–49.
7. Vital signs. *Fam Pract News.* 2000;30(9):1.
8. Starr P. Medicine and the waning of professional sovereignty. *Daedalus.* 1978;107(1):176.
9. U.S. health system ranks 37th in the world. *PNHP Newsletter.* September 2000:1.
10. The Institute for the Future. *Health and Health Care 2010: The Forecast, the Challenge.* San Francisco: Jossey-Bass, 2000:45–50.
11. Churchill LR. The United States health care system under managed care. How the commodification of health care distorts ethics and threatens equity. *Health Care Anal.* 1999;7(4):393–411.
12. Manning D. Speech given at the Appalachian Health Care Conference, Johnson City, Tennessee, October 12, 1995.
13. Light DW. The practice and ethics of risk-rated health insurance. *JAMA.* 1992;267:2503–2508.
14. Rodwin VG. Comparative analysis of health systems: An international perspective. In: Kovner AR, Jonas S (eds). *Health Care Delivery in the United States.* New York: Springer Publishing Company, 1999:116–151.
15. Law S. Blue Cross: What Went Wrong? New Haven, CN: Yale University Press, 1974:11–13.
16. Gabel JR. Job-based health insurance; 1977–1998: The accidental system under scrutiny. *Health Aff (Millwood).* 18(6):62–74.
17. Custer WS, Kahn CN, Wildsmith TF. Why we should keep the employment-based health insurance system. *Health Aff (Millwood).* 1999;18(6):115–123.
18. Reinhardt UE. Employer-based health insurance: A balance sheet. *Health Aff (Millwood).* 1999;18(6):124–132.
19. DiPiero A, Kilo CM. Will payment innovations benefit your practice? *Hippocrates.* 2000;14(12):32–37.
20. Cain HP. Privatizing Medicare: a battle over values. *Health Aff (Millwood).* 1997;16(2):181–186.
21. Inglehart JK. The American health system—Medicare. *N Engl J Med.* 1999;340:327–332.
22. Goldberg RM. A surprisingly good health care plan. *The Weekly Standard.* January 3, 2000(10):20–21.
23. Frieden J. Practice Trends. Demonstration project off to slow start. Deductibility, complexity slow growth of MSAs. *Fam Pract News.* February 1, 2000:53.
24. Bush GW. The Republican and Democratic candidates speak on health care. *N Engl J Med.* 2000;343:1184–1186.
25. Kuttner R. *Everything for Sale: The Virtues and Limits of Markets.* Chicago: University of Chicago Press, 1999;130.
26. Woolhandler S, Himmelstein DU. *The National Health Program Slideshow Guide.* Cambridge, MA: The Center for National Health Program Studies, 2000.
27. Himmelstein DU, Woolhandler S, and the Writing Committee of the Working Group on Program Design. A national health program for the United States. A physician's proposal. *N Engl J Med.* 1989;320:102–108.

28. McDermott J. Evaluating health system reform. The case for a single-payer approach. *JAMA.* 1994;27:782–784.

29. Schiff G, Himmelstein DU. Questions and answers about single-payer national health insurance. Speech presented at Windsor, Ontario, May 19, 1996.

30. Grumbach K, Bodenheimer T. Reins or fences: A physician's view of cost containment. *Health Aff (Millwood).* 1990;9(4):120–126.

31. U.S. General Accounting Office. Canadian health care: Lessons for the U.S., 1991.

32. Bodenheimer T. Single-payer—fifty players? Alternative payers for universal health insurance. *Health/PAC Bulletin.* Fall 1992:24–28.

33. Gilbert FI Jr., Nordyke RA. The case for restructuring health care in the United States: The Hawaii paradigm. *J Med Syst.* 1993;17(3–4):283–288.

34. Scott JS. Universal health care revisited. *Healthc Financ Manage.* 1999;53(6):32–33.

35. Friedman TL. *The Lexus and the Olive Tree.* New York: Farrar, Straus and Giroux, 1999:353.

36. Woolhandler S, Himmelstein DU. When money is the mission—The high costs of investor-owned care. *N Engl J Med.* 1999;341:444–446.

37. Hale MM. Dealing with the conflict of interests in health care reform. *J Health Hum Serv Adm.* Fall 1998;21(2):162–180.

38. Ginzberg E. The uncertain future of managed care. *N Engl J Med.* 1999;340:144–146.

23
Lessons from Other Countries

As we saw in earlier chapters, the United States compares poorly with most other industrialized Western nations in terms of the three basic elements of health care: access, cost, and quality. However, even though the other industrialized nations provide universal access, they still struggle with common issues of cost containment, quality, and for many, the right balance between public and private sectors. Nothing is static about any of these health care systems. All are struggling to achieve the best combination of access, cost, and quality.

Rodwin's formulation of evolving health systems (Table 22-3) provides a useful backdrop for this chapter. Emerging countries in the developing world, as well as many Western nations during the 19th century, tend to have the least organized or equitable care systems, all private and entrepreneurial. The United States matured somewhat beyond that to a type 2, pluralistic system, but most more successful health care systems have progressed farther by providing one or another form of universal access. The big question facing the United States now is whether and how it can change as a type 2 system or evolve further to a type 3 system, in either case affording expanded access while improving quality and becoming more cost effective.

This chapter addresses three goals: (1) to present cross-national comparisons in terms of strengths and problems of health systems in six other industrialized Western countries; (2) to examine more closely the experience of the Canadian system, with lessons we can draw from that; and (3) to briefly discuss lessons and themes among industrialized nations as they struggle to stabilize and improve their respective systems.

SOME CROSS-NATIONAL COMPARISONS

Before making further comparisons between the U.S. health care system and systems in other industrialized Western nations, let's review comparisons already made:

- Rankings for primary care in 11 countries (Table 13-2).
- Potential years of life lost per 100,000 people in six countries (Figure 18-2).
- Public spending per capita for health care in seven countries (Figure 14-1).
- Health care spending in six countries (Table 7-5).
- Health spending for the elderly in eight countries (Table 6-2).
- Hospital billing and administrative costs, United States and Canada (Figure 7-3).
- Physicians' billing and office expenses, United States and Canada (Figure 7-4).

In all of these instances, the United States ranked well behind comparison countries. Now we need to fill in the picture by adding other comparisons and brief descriptions of six countries with much more successful health care systems.

Table 23-1 compares consumers' reports on access and cost in five countries in 1998. The United Kingdom is a classic example of a national health service (NHS) while Canada illustrates a more recent variant of a national health insurance (NHI) model operating in a national/provincial framework with more parallels to the United States.[1] The United States ranked somewhat higher concerning times when needed care was not obtained, but access to specialists was quite comparable across the board. Waiting times for elective surgery tended to be shorter in the United States, with the longest waits experienced in the United Kingdom. Out-of-pocket expenditures for health care were highest in the United States.[2]

Table 23-2 displays consumers' views on the quality of care in the same five countries in 1998. Here, the ratings are remarkably similar in most respects. One particular difference, however, is the pattern of longer physician office visits in the United States compared to some other countries, especially the United Kingdom. Visit times were quite similar in the United States and Canada.[2]

As we saw in Chapter 18, in 1998, Barbara Starfield reported a comparative ranking of health outcomes by 16 indicators among 13 industrialized Western nations.[3] The United States fared poorly in these rankings, as shown in Table 23-3. The countries that perform best on these indicators have predominantly public sector health care systems assuring universal access to care.

In terms of the relative effectiveness of cost containment of health care costs in eight countries, Figure 23-1 shows that most other countries experienced some growth in per capita health spending between 1990 and 1998, but the United States was less successful than any other country in holding down spending. The most difficulty in cost containment was seen in the United States, Germany, and Japan, but both Germany and Japan expanded their systems to include long-term care.

To get some sense of what lies behind these numbers, a brief profile of each nation's health care system is illuminating. Six countries are selected here to illustrate different variants from which some useful lessons can be drawn.

United Kingdom

Britain's National Health Service recently celebrated its 50th anniversary. It was founded shortly after World War II, at a time when the health care environment

Table 23-1 Consumers' Reports on Access to and Cost of Care, in Australia, Canada, New Zealand, the United Kingdom, and the United States, 1998

	AUS	CAN	NZ	UK	US
Access: Percent who reported					
That there was a time in the past 12 months when they needed medical care but did not get it	8%	10%	12%	10%	14%
Difficulties seeing specialists and consultants when they needed to					
Extremely difficult	5	6	7	3	9
Very difficult	9	10	10	7	6
Somewhat difficult	21	30	18	19	24
Not too difficult	25	22	26	30	24
Not at all difficult	29	25	30	25	32
Waiting times for nonemergency surgery for themselves or a family member					
None	5	16	25	7	10
Less than 1 month	46	28	26	23	60
1–3.9 months	32	43	28	36	28
4 months or more	17	12	22	33	1
Cost: Percent who reported					
Having problems paying medical bills in past year	10	5	15	3	18
That they or a family member have not filled a prescription because they could not afford it	12	7	15	3	18
Having bills for medical services that were not covered by insurance and for which they paid out of pocket					
None	7	27	12	44	8
$750 or less	65	54	66	36	54
$751–$2,000	15	7	7	1	21
More than $2,000	4	2	3	0	8

Note: Monetary units are converted to and shown in U.S. dollars.

Source: Commonwealth Fund 1998 International Health Policy Survey. Reprinted with permission from Donelan K, Blandon RJ, Schoen C, et al. The cost of health system change: Public discontent in five nations. *Health Aff (Millwood).* 1999;18(3):210.

was quite similar to problems in the United States today—a patchwork mixture of private and public coverage, serious gaps in care and coverage, many hospitals in financial trouble, geographic maldistribution of providers and services, and poor coordination among various parts of the "system."[4] To resolve these major problems, the National Health Service was established as a national commitment to provide medical care to the whole population regardless of ability to pay. Despite its problems over the years, it has been widely recognized for its success in cost containment while providing universal access to medical care

Table 23-2   Consumers' Views on Their Care, in Australia, Canada, New Zealand, the United Kingdom, and the United States, 1998

	AUS	CAN	NZ	UK	US
Overall medical care: Percent who said that The medical care that they and their family received in the past 12 months was					
Excellent	19%	24%	20%	15%	19%
Very good	35	30	34	35	30
Good	31	30	29	31	33
Fair	11	11	9	12	12
Poor	2	2	2	2	3
Physician care: Percent who said that Care received at last doctor visit was					
Excellent	36	37	34	19	29
Very good	32	30	36	37	30
Good	21	22	20	25	24
Fair	9	6	7	10	12
Poor	2	4	3	4	4
The length of the most recent doctor visit was					
5 minutes or fewer	17	12	14	31	11
6–10 minutes	26	21	30	34	19
11–15 minutes	29	25	25	13	19
16–20 minutes	15	19	14	7	18
More than 20 minutes	12	20	15	5	30
The time their doctor spent with them was					
About right	84	82	84	78	74
Too short	13	15	14	14	23
Too long	2	2	1	2	1
Hospital care: percent who said that Their overall hospital experience was					
Excellent	27	28	24	28	26
Very good	30	26	31	34	28
Good	22	18	23	20	28
Fair	10	17	12	8	7
Poor	11	10	9	10	11
The length of their hospital stay was					
About right	73	72	65	77	78
Too short	17	19	22	11	12
Too long	9	8	11	12	10

Source: Commonwealth Fund 1998 International Health Policy Survey. Reprinted with permission from Donelan K, Blandon RJ, Schoen C, et al. The cost of health system change: Public discontent in five nations. *Health Aff (Millwood).* 1999;18(3):212.

Table 23-3   Cross-National Comparisons of Health Care Systems by Health Outcome
Indicators

Health Indicator	U.S. Ranking Among 13 Countries	Average Ranking for 16 Indicators (1 best, 13 worst)
1. Low-birth-weight percentage	13	Japan #1
2. Neonatal mortality	13	Sweden #2
3. Overall infant mortality	13	
4. Post-neonatal mortality	11	Canada #3
5. Potential life lost (excluding external causes)	13	
6. Life expectancy at 1 year (females)	11	France #4
7. Life expectancy at 1 year (males)	12	Australia #5
8. Life expectancy at 15 years (females)	10	Spain #6
9. Life expectancy at 15 years (males)	12	Finland #7
10. Life expectancy at 40 years (females)	10	The Netherlands #8
11. Life expectancy at 40 years (males)	9	United Kingdom #9
12. Life expectancy at 65 years (females)	7	
13. Life expectancy at 65 years (males)	7	Denmark #10
14. Life expectancy at 80 years (females)	3	Belgium #11
15. Life expectancy at 80 years (males)	3	United States #12
16. Age-adjusted mortality	10	Germany #13

Source: Starfield B. Is US health really the best in the world? *JAMA*. 2000;284:483–485.

with comparable or superior health care outcomes compared to other leading
health systems.

Consider these impressive achievements of the British experience over the
last 50 years:[4,5]

- Primary care is ranked number one in the world (about 70 percent of all
  physicians are in general practice).[6]
- A management decision was made to set lifetime earnings of general practitioners (GPs) at about the same level as specialists (although merit awards
  and private practice do favor the specialists over and above their salaries).
- No payment required at the point of service.
- The NHS annual budget held below 6 percent of GDP.
- Public satisfaction and support for the NHS is higher than any other
  country.

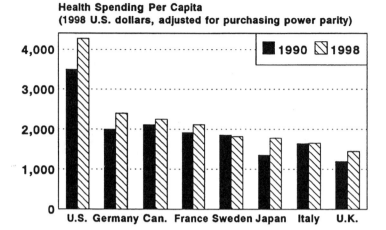

**Health Spending Per Capita
(1998 U.S. dollars, adjusted for purchasing power parity)**

Figure 23-1   Health spending, 1990 and 1998: U.S. costs rose more than other nations'. (Source: *Health Aff (Milwood).* 2000;19(3):150. Reprinted with permission from Woolhandler S, Himmelstein DU. *The National Health Program Slideshow Guide.* Cambridge, MA: Center for National Health Program Studies, 2000.)

General practitioners have an independent contract with the government, based largely on capitation payments. Since 1990, a system of additional bonuses has been in place for specific services or successful outcomes of care (e.g., care of patients over 75 years of age, prenatal and postnatal care, achieving goals for immunization of registered children). In essence, the NHS is a managed care structure based on a general practice foundation, with GPs on capitated contracts and specialists on salary at hospitals and clinics owned by the system. The UK has a tax-financed system, like other European countries (Norway, Sweden, Denmark, Finland, Ireland, and Iceland). There is a relatively small private sector, with only 9 percent of the population covered by private insurance, although 22 percent of the professional and managerial classes have such coverage and seek private care.[5] Interestingly, the NHS experimented with competition between GPs on global budgets during the 1990s but abandoned that approach after six years, due to increasing administrative costs and inequities throughout the system.[4]

Despite this impressive track record, the United Kingdom faces many of the same kinds of problems encountered by other nations, including:[5]

- Rising demand for health care services.
- Increased public expectations with less forbearance of limits.
- Potential feelings of disenfranchisement to an autocratic bureaucracy.
- Lack of a clinical information system that can track patient care over time.
- Discontinuity between hospital and ambulatory care.
- Excessive workload of many providers, especially in primary care, with increasing stress, recruitment, and retention problems; large exodus from the nursing profession and many physicians are from overseas.[7]

Denmark

Denmark has had a single-payer national health system since 1961. It is predominantly a public sector system, with 85 percent of health care costs financed through taxes. Its population of 5.3 million people corresponds to the population of Mississippi. About one quarter of the population has private health insurance, which is used mostly for pharmaceutical costs and dentistry. Most health professionals are salaried employees in public institutions. Hospitals are run by 14 counties and the city of Copenhagen. Over 98 percent of Danish hospital care is provided in public hospitals.[8] The Danish Council of Ethics was established in 1988, and serves an advisory function to health authorities concerning such matters as ethical issues on the use of new treatments and medical technology, as well as setting priorities.[9]

There is a strong primary care base in Denmark. Of the active physicians in 1997, about 3,700 were general practitioners and 900 were specialists. The country's Health Care Reimbursement Scheme subsidizes care for people through one of two ways:

- Group 1 patients must register with a GP, with a free choice of physicians, who coordinates their care and makes referrals to specialists when needed; no payment is made for visits to the GP or his or her substitute.
- Group 2 patients may, but are not required to, choose a GP; they may seek specialist care directly but receive only partial subsidy for the costs of care by either GPs or specialists.

Children under the age of 16 years are covered under their parents' group plan. When children reach 16 years of age, they are asked to choose their own coverage, and 97.6 percent choose Group 1.[9]

GPs are reimbursed on a capitation basis (40 percent) and fee for service (60 percent). The average panel size for GPs is 1,600 patients. Specialists are paid mostly on a fee-for-service basis. There are no copayments for physician (under Group 1) or for hospital care, but patients do pay between 25 and 50 percent of drug costs.[9]

The strengths of Denmark's health care system include:

- A strong primary care base, ranked third among 11 countries by Starfield.[6]
- Ranked first among 11 countries for lowest number of medications per patient.[6]
- Effective cost containment, with health care accounting for 6 percent of GDP in 1997.
- Relatively stable, well-organized decentralized system with universal coverage and good health outcomes for its population.

As is true of any country's health care system, however, there are some problems on the other side of the ledger. These include:[8]

- Discontinuity between ambulatory and hospital care.
- Long waiting times for elective procedures (e.g., over 3 months for one third of patients).
- Allocation decisions concerning use of medical technologies often are distorted by media coverage, leading to irrational coverage decisions.

Germany

National health care in Germany has a long history, dating back to 1845 in Prussia, even before Germany was unified. The Sickness Fund (Kranken-Kassen) was established by the first chancellor of Germany, Otto von Bismarck, in 1884. Since then, these public funds have been the main financing mechanism for German health care. Today over 600 sickness funds provide coverage for 88 percent of the population; private insurance covers 8 percent, while 4 percent are uninsured. Enrollment in a sickness fund is mandatory for workers earning less than deutsche mark (DM) 35,000 per year. Employers share the costs of coverage equally with employees, who spend an average of 12 percent of their annual income for this coverage.[10]

Near universal access to health care is provided to the population through a public/private mix (78 percent public/22 percent private). Physicians are paid on a voucher system, with each physician submitting all vouchers for each month to the Sickness Fund for payment.[10]

Germany has a strong primary care base, although the number of GPs has declined from 50 percent of office-based physicians to less than 40 percent over the past 20 years. Since the 1980s, the Bundestag (Parliament) has attempted various reforms to strengthen the primary care base, but specialty-dominated physicians' organizations and the sickness funds so far have resisted them.[11]

Although universal access to health care has been a long-standing strength of the German system, there are problems in some areas:[6]

- A two-tiered system based on ability to pay, with some people who can afford private care bypassing and weakening the public system.
- Friction between private practice physicians and salaried hospital-based specialists.
- Discontinuity between outpatient and hospital care.
- Relatively low public reimbursement to physicians, resulting in high volume practice with short patient visits.
- An average hospital stay of two weeks (in 1993).
- High administrative costs.
- Increasing surplus of physicians leading to increased utilization of services and costs.

Japan

There are many similarities between the health systems in Germany and Japan, not surprising since the Japanese system modeled itself after Germany in the late 1800s. Both systems provide almost universal coverage, freedom of choice of physicians, fee-for-service practice, segregation between hospital and outpatient physicians, and quasi-governmental roles for professional organizations. An employer mandate for health insurance coverage for employees in the marine industry was enacted in 1922. Other industries were covered by such plans in later years, and universal coverage was completed in 1958 by extension of coverage to the elderly and the unemployed through the community-based health insurance plan.[10]

The Japanese system operates on a "point-fee" structure, with each service worth a specific number of points. In effect, it is a simpler form of the U.S. relative value system. Each consumer has a card, which is presented to the provider at the time of each visit. Providers bill the insurer each month. The Japanese system is quite complex, involving more than 5,000 insuring entities. All insurers require individual contributions and cap out-of-pocket expenditures. The system is financed through premium contributions divided equally between employers and employees.[10]

Cost sharing for elderly patients was instituted in 1982 and has remained controversial, since it limits access to care for this vulnerable population (Japanese citizens over 70 years of age and bedridden persons over age 65).[12]

Japan's health system has some impressive strengths, including its universal coverage (60 percent employee insurance, 40 percent community-based NHI) and its quality of primary care rankings—first among 13 industrialized countries in Starfield's 1998 report and first among six industrialized countries in terms of potential years of life lost per 100,000 people from all causes.[3] However, the system also faces some problems:[10]

- Relatively low reimbursement of physicians' office visits has led to overutilization of care and high volume practice (13 percent of physicians see over 100 patients a day, with an average of 66 a day).
- Preventive care and counseling are limited by short visits.
- Overuse of technology (e.g., more CT scanners per capita in Japan than in United States; many of these are owned by physicians).[10,13]
- Friction between hospital and clinic physicians.
- Excessive use of medication, partly as a result of Japanese physicians dispensing as well as prescribing drugs.

Australia

On the surface, Australia and the United States have much in common—a shared heritage, similar medical practice, parallel public and private sectors, and a common nomenclature. Australia even has an AMA—the Australian Medical Association. However, as John Peabody, S. R. Bickel, and J. S. Lawson point out in a report on their health care system, George Bernard Shaw's classic comment applies—"two countries separated by a common language."[14]

Australia's health care system is a mixed public (67 percent) and private (33 percent) system based on a blend of structured and financing arrangements that shape the practice of medicine.[15] Costs are regulated by a combination of global hospital budgets, fee schedules, and constraints on the use of technology. Australia had voluntary health insurance partly subsidized by the government after World War II. Compulsory health insurance was enacted in 1975. After 1975, many controversial attempts were made to modify the system, including returning to voluntary health insurance and making private insurance a pretax benefit. These attempts failed because 10 to 16 percent of the population had no hospital coverage and could not afford private insurance, even with government subsidies.[16] In 1984, Medicare was introduced to provide universal coverage for both inpatient and outpatient care. Medicare is financed by a 1.4

percent federal income tax (the Medicare levy) covering about 15 percent of the total costs of physicians and hospital services, with the rest financed by state and federal taxes, as well as fees paid by patients.[17]

An ongoing debate in Australia concerns the relative roles of the publicly funded Medicare program and private health insurance. In 1996, private health insurance accounted for only 11 percent of health expenditures, and out-of-pocket payments by individuals accounted for another 16 percent of expenditures. Despite some growth in private insurance coverage in recent years, especially for hospital care (e.g., 30 percent of the population with such coverage in 1998), there is no broad support for private insurance due to its high premium costs and large, often unpredictable, out-of-pocket expenses.[15] In an effort to promote a larger role for private health insurance in recent years, the government spent $1.5 billion in various tax incentives but raised the level of private insurance coverage by only 2.7 percent.[18]

Physicians working in outpatient clinics of public hospitals are either paid on a per-session basis or as salaried employees of the hospital. Physicians in private practice are paid on a fee-for-service basis under Medicare fee schedules. Physicians may set their own fees, but private insurance cannot cover any gap above Medicare's fee schedule for inpatient medical services.[14] About 80 percent of the GPs accept assignment (i.e., accept Medicare fees as full payment), but many specialists do not, leading to increased out-of-pocket expenditures by patients. The average physician's salary in Australia is 2.2 times the average Australian salary, in contrast to a 5.4 multiple in the United States.[19]

There are some major strengths of the Australian health system:

- Relatively stable public/private system with universal access and successful cost containment (annual per capita expenditures about half those of the United States).[19]
- Relatively strong primary care, based on general practice (42 percent of the country's physicians).
- Free choice of GPs, who maintain community-based health care programs and act as gatekeepers for specialist referrals.
- High levels of public support for Medicare and the public sector.
- More effective constraints on technology diffusion than in the United States (e.g., cosmetic surgery is not covered by Medicare unless for medical indications).

On the other hand, Australia faces these problems in its health system:[14]

- Increasing utilization of services, with high rates of physician visits and hospitalizations.
- Waits for elective procedures.
- Tension between public and private sectors.
- Trend toward increased use of expensive technologies in private hospitals.

Canada

Since Canada shares a border with the United States, as well as many similarities of history, economics, and culture, its profile is presented in more detail than those for the preceding countries. Canada started moving toward its present health care system in 1957, when the national government established a set of principles encouraging the provinces to create their own health plans. Federal payments were made to provinces, which agreed to administer and partly finance a universal plan, initially for hospital care and later for medical insurance as well.[20,21] By 1971, all 10 provinces had established hospital and medical insurance programs that met federal requirements for 50 percent matching funds.[22] Five basic principles—*public administration, comprehensiveness, universality, portability,* and *accessibility*—finally led to the unanimous passage by Parliament of the Canada Health Act in 1984. A fascinating account of the political dynamics leading to Canada's single-payer system is presented in detail in the 1998 book *Universal Health Care: What the United States Can Learn from the Canadian Experience.*[23]

The Canada Health Act requires the provinces to prohibit "extra billing" by physicians (i.e., above the provincial fee schedule). Failure to do so would forfeit federal matching funds. Although vigorously opposed by organized medicine, the national commitment to universal access regardless of ability to pay was upheld. It is illegal for Canadian physicians or hospitals to "extra bill" patients for services covered by the Medicare program. All general hospitals are operated on a nonprofit basis and funded mainly through global provincial budgets. Patients have free choice of physicians, who must practice within the public system or see private patients who must pay directly out of pocket.[20] Patients may see a specialist without referral from their family physician, but this is the exception and specialists are reimbursed at lower rates in those instances.[11] Physicians are reimbursed at considerably lower rates than in the United States. That comparison, however, needs to account for other differences between the two countries: In Canada, for example, medical education is free, malpractice insurance is paid by the government, office overhead is lower, and physician salaries are comparable to other professionals in the country.[11] Table 23-4 shows how the range of services covered under the Canadian system are financed and delivered.

Faced with increasing costs, the Canadian federal government started reducing its contributions to provincial health insurance plans more than 20 years ago.[20] By the mid-1990s, the differing perspectives of government payers, physicians, and the public are reflected by this summary by Reg Perkin of the College of Family Physicians of Canada:[24]

> The government payer, particularly during this time of economic recession, is obsessed with cutting costs and is targeting physicians to take cuts in income and to justify the need for and cost-effectiveness of the services being provided. The payer is imposing caps on physician income, dropping from coverage some nonessential services, and restricting billing numbers to new physicians.
>
> The physician provider, working largely in a fee-for-service system, is caught between a hard cap on gross income and the rising costs of running a practice. Physicians are also under stress from increasing bureaucratic interference with the practice of medicine and increasing demands from patients who have no direct financial accountability for the services that they request.
>
> The Canadian public, as consumers of medical care, do not wish to lose the first dollar coverage, freedom of choice, and unimpeded access to the

Table 23-4   Financing and Delivery Service, Canada, 1994

Service Type	Financing	Delivery
Hospital services	100 percent public for medically necessary services (no user charges permitted); private payment for upgraded accommodation or non–medically necessary services provided in hospitals.	Mixed public/private. Varies across provinces. Government generally exerts a strong regulatory presence.
Physician services	100 percent public for medically necessary services (no extra-billing permitted); private payment for non–medically necessary services.	Private—physicians are independent and self-regulating; some models of primary care delivery (e.g., CLSCs or community clinics in Quebec) are more akin to government agencies.
Services provided in private clinics	Privately funded for services not defined as medically necessary. Some clinics charge a facility fee to patients for medically necessary services over and above the funding provided by the provincial health insurance plan.	Privately owned and operated— limited regulation.
Dental and optometry care	Mostly private (insurance or out of pocket); some provincial plans provide coverage for children and seniors.	Private and self-regulating—e.g., dentists and optometrists.
Prescription drugs	Mixed public/private; provincial plans pay for approximately 40 percent of all prescription drugs dispensed outside hospitals. Coverage is typically limited to seniors and welfare recipients. Drugs dispensed in hospitals are covered in hospital budgets. Balance is funded by a combination of private insurance plans and out of pocket payments.	Private—delivery includes prescription by physician and dispensing by pharmacist or hospital.
Nonprescription drugs	Mostly private (out of pocket).	Private—over-the-counter.
Services of other professionals	Mostly private (insurance or out of pocket).	Private (e.g., psychologists, physiotherapists, chiropractors, midwives, private duty nurses).

continues

Table 23-4   (continued)

Service Type	Financing	Delivery
Alternative medicines	Mostly private—some limited coverage provided by provincial plans; remainder is paid for through private insurance plans and/or out of pocket.	Private—e.g., naturopaths, homeopaths, practitioners of oriental medicine, traditional Aboriginal healers.
Long-term care (residential)	Mixed public/private; public portion covers insured health care services; private portion covers room and board.	Mixed public/private.
Home care	Partial public coverage provided in most jurisdictions; informal caregivers play an important role.	Mixed public/private.
Ambulance services	Partial public coverage in some provinces; special programs for residents of remote areas.	Mostly private operators.
Public health programs	Public.	Public.
Services to Aboriginal peoples	Public.	Mixed public/private (federal government employees deliver some services directly).

Source: Canada, National Forum on Health. The Public and Private Financing of Canada's Health System. Ottawa: National Forum on Health, September 1995:6–7. Reprinted with permission from Armstrong P, Armstrong H. *Universal Health Care. What the United States Can Learn from the Canadian Experience.* New York: The New Press, 1998:6–32.

health care services that they need or perceive that they need. Patients feel threatened when economic constraints cause delays in accessing diagnostic or therapeutic services both in and out of the hospital. Canadians regard their health care system as a basic right and a cornerstone of the country's social structure.

Table 23-5 provides a snapshot of the distribution of public and private spending for health care services in 1996. In terms of overall cost containment of health care costs, Canada has been much more effective than the United States, as shown in Figure 23-2.

The Canadian system has a number of impressive strengths:

- Strong primary care based on family practice (50 percent of the nation's physicians).

Table 23-5   Public and Private Sector Health Expenditures,
by Category, Canada, 1996

Category	Distribution of Public Spending	Distribution of Private Spending
Hospitals	43%	14%
Physicians	21%	1%
Other institutions	10%	11%
Other expenditures	8%	17%
Drugs	7%	31%
Public heath	7%	0%
Capital	3%	2%
Other professionals	2%	25%

Source: Health Canada. *National Health Expenditures in Canada
1975–1996: Fact Sheets.* Ottawa: Minister of Public Works and Government
Services, 1997. Reprinted with permission from Armstrong P, Armstrong H.
Universal Health Care. What the United States Can Learn from the Canadian
Experience. New York: The New Press, 1998:103.

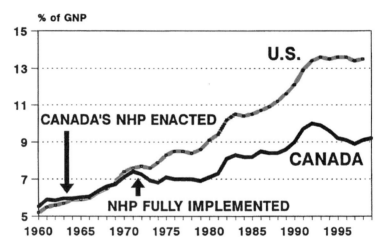

Figure 23-2   Health costs as percent of GNP: Unitcd States and Canada, 1960–1999.
(Source: Statistics Canada, Canadian Institute for Health Information, and NCHS/Commerce
Department. Reprinted with permission from Woolhandler S, Himmelstein DU. *The National
Health Program Slideshow Guide.* Cambridge, MA: Center for National Health Program
Studies, 2000.)

- Ranked third among 13 industrialized Western nations by 16 outcome measures for quality of care.[3]
- Cost-effective provision of universal access care.
- Very low administrative costs within single-payer program.
- Effective regulation of private insurance as protection of public system.
- High level of public support for the NHI system.

Again, however, like any other health care system, there are some major problems in Canada:[20]

- Overcrowding of hospitals and emergency rooms in some cities.
- Long waiting lists for some elective services.
- Increasing pressure (mainly from the insurance industry, specialist physicians, and business interests)[25] to lift the ban on private insurance coverage and privatize the system.
- Dissatisfaction and low morale among many health professionals.
- Disparities between generalist and specialist physician incomes.
- Fee-for-service reimbursement, with low fees encouraging high-volume practice with disincentives to health promotion and counseling.[24]
- Increasing controversy over determinations of medical necessity.[7]
- Concern about a physician shortage aggravated by a 10 percent cut of medical school enrollment in 1993, attrition of physicians by retirement, and other factors.[26]

WHAT CAN BE LEARNED FROM THE CANADIAN SYSTEM

Some Lessons

After extended study of the Canadian health care system, Pat and Hugh Armstrong, both involved in teaching and research at Carleton University in Ottawa, together with Claudia Fegan, recently president of the medical staff at Michael Reese Hospital in Chicago, offer these 12 lessons which the United States can (and should) learn from the Canadian experience:[23]

1. It is possible to develop a universal health system that covers everyone for necessary care.
2. A public system can remove financial barriers to health care.
3. A public insurance scheme does not necessarily mean that governments provide the services or control the institutions directly.
4. With public insurance, hospitals can secure stable financing. (Many hospital administrators would say today that they are underfunded.)[7]
5. Doctors can retain their right to diagnose and treat on the basis of the needs of patients rather than cost.
6. Doctors need not suffer financially, either. Indeed, their security, income, and conditions of work may improve.
7. A public plan can be based on simple legislation that establishes principles without demanding uniformity.
8. A federal scheme can still allow local choices.

9. Opposition can be organized, powerful and recurring, but it can also be countered.
10. Public support grows through experience with a plan that works.
11. The task of providing a universal scheme for accessible, high-quality, cost-effective health care is never completed, but rather must be seen as a process evolving in response to new needs and possibilities.
12. A public scheme is cheaper.

To that list, two more can reasonably be added, based on well-documented experience over the years:

13. The Canadian policy of controlling positions in residency training programs by specialty has effectively assured a strong base of generalist physicians on which to base its health care system.[11,24]
14. Coverage for long-term care can be added within a universal access system without bankrupting the system.[27]

Some Myths

Despite the evidence documenting the considerable success of the Canadian health care system, in this and preceding chapters, and even its superiority over the U.S. system on many counts, there are pervasive myths south of our common border about the Canadian system. Three common myths are cited here, as answered by the Canadian Medical Association in 1993 and equally relevant today.[28]

Myth 1. The Canadian system is "overregulated" because patients are not free to choose their physician.

Canadians are in fact "free to choose" their own primary care physician. Physicians are also free to choose their patients in non-emergency situations (i.e., not take on new patients).

In terms of referrals, governments do try to encourage patients to go to a primary care physician first by fee differentials (i.e., specialist gets paid at GP rate for unreferred consultation).

More generally, governments in Canada have been loath to intervene directly in the patient-physician relationship. So, if the patient wishes to change physicians or to have different family members see different physicians, the patient is free to do so.

Myth 2. The Canadian system is often described in terms of its "sole-source funding" advantages. Are Canadian physicians not state employees as civil servants and does this not have an adverse affect on the quality of care Canadians receive?

It is wrong to talk of socialized medicine. Canada's system is really "socialized health insurance." Physicians are, in most cases, paid on a fee-for-service basis or otherwise contract to provide services on a capitation or other basis.

Physicians in Canada have considerably more clinical autonomy than the growing number of physicians in the U.S. subject to so-called managed care systems.

The medical profession in Canada is largely self-policing—power of "self-regulation." Questions regarding over-utilization are subject to joint peer-review.

Myth 3. Canada does not have as much "technology" as the United States. Is it fair to say that the quality of medical care in Canada is inferior to that in the United States?

Technology is not always the only or best way to address dominate health problems. Many of the comparisons (Canada/U.S.) are exaggerated—most ignore the key question of whether and under what circumstances a particular technology has proven its relative efficacy or effectiveness (e.g., mobile lithotripsy as it applies to gallstones).

Canadians by any standard measure of relative health status, rank well ahead of their U.S. neighbors—infant mortality, life expectancy, etc. Physician population ratios are comparable—with Canadians having far superior access to primary care (50 : 50 GP to specialist ratio in Canada vs. 20 : 80 ratio in U.S.). The same *acute* care bed to population ratio as U.S. We rank far ahead of the U.S. in infant and maternal mortality—a fact related to our universal health insurance system which allows for appropriate and timely prenatal care.

Canadian physicians are at least as well trained as their American colleagues (licensure/certification requirements shared). Since all medical training in Canada is associated with accredited teaching facilities, the curriculum may be more responsive to changing health needs.

Other issues frequently raised about the Canadian health care system generate considerable discussion, often based on misinformation. It is true, for example, that many Canadians cross the border to have some surgical procedures (e.g., coronary artery bypass graft) done in the United States, but these numbers are often exaggerated. Waiting times for elective surgery are longer than in the United States, but emergency cases have priority access and get these procedures done when they are needed.[29] Concerning migration of physicians across the border, many Canadian physicians have been attracted to the United States by higher salaries and lower taxes. However, some of these physicians end up returning to Canada, and a 1993 report by American investigators revealed stronger support for the Canadian system among physicians with experience in both countries.[30] According to the Canadian Institute for Health Information, the number of Canadian physicians moving abroad hit a five-year low in 1999. In that year, 585 physicians left the country, while 343 physicians moved back to Canada, and 243 doctors moved to Canada from the United States and other countries, for a net gain of one physician.[31]

The issue of rationing often is raised about the Canadian system, as if that does not occur in the United States. The difference is that rationing of health services in Canada is done on the basis of global restrictions on health budgets and professional judgments of relative medical necessity,[28] while in the United

States, health care is rationed by ability to pay. Still another issue raised between the two countries is the difference in their respective tax burdens. Here again, the differences are not as extreme as is assumed by many. Taxes levied at all levels of government in Canada totaled 36.8 percent of GNP in 1996 while the comparable figure in the United States was 28.5 percent, one of the lowest among industrialized countries.[20] With regard to administrative efficiency, Canada's health care system functions with an overhead of only about 1 percent, far lower than the 15 to 30 percent level that applies within the U.S. private insurance industry.[32]

Despite some frustration by consumers and providers within the Canadian health care system, public support remains exceptionally strong. Consider these findings from a November 2000 national poll of over 2,500 Canadians by *HealthInsider*, a survey conducted periodically for corporate, nonprofit, and government organizations:[33]

- Support for the five principles of the system remains extremely high: universality, 98.7 percent; accessibility, 98.4 percent; portability, 98.6 percent; comprehensiveness, 97.9 percent; public administration, 83.8 percent.
- Only 9 percent of respondents who had been patients in the last year were "somewhat" or "very dissatisfied" with their care, while 93 percent of women and 83 percent of men were "very" or "somewhat satisfied" with their care.
- Regional variations by province ranged from a high of 94 percent (Atlantic Canadians) to a low of 85 percent (Albertans) in overall satisfaction with the public health care system.
- Although 34 percent of Canadians believe that major changes are required to make the system work better, 44 percent feel that the system works well and that only minor changes should be considered.

Special Interests and the Media

It is not surprising that the preceding kinds of myths and misinformation can persist when one considers how the media can distort issues by noncoverage, lack of research or critical inquiry, or biased reporting. In an important recent article, Theodore Marmor (professor at Yale University and author of *The Politics of Medicare*) and Kip Sullivan (an attorney and health care analyst) make a persuasive case that the U.S. media have neglected coverage of the Canadian health care system and, when covered, failed to rigorously examine it. Worse, the case is made that the media easily do the beckoning of special interests with everything to lose if that system moves south of the 49th parallel. They note that anti-Canadian system stories reported at intervals over the last 15 years have been fueled by special interest groups aligned against the Canadian system. They observe that a *New York Times* reporter who wrote about Canada's overwhelmed emergency rooms during a flu epidemic (as also occurs in the United States), as a generalist, knew little about the Canadian system itself and had recently covered a wide range of unrelated subjects (e.g., gun control, the history of Montreal, immigrants from Kosovo). They further exposed a March 2000 example of intentionally slanted coverage, a multimedia campaign sponsored by a pharmaceutical industry front group (Citizens for

Better Medicare) urging American seniors to reject the Canadian approach to drug coverage and pricing, with the implication that lower prices won't be possible in the United States without onerous government controls. These biased reports can perpetuate inaccurate myths if not rebutted by more objective reporting, as is seldom the case.[32]

A cross-border perspective that Americans need to hear but tend to tune out or deny is this observation by Robert Evans (University of British Columbia) and Noralou Roos (University of Manitoba):[34]

> Different health care systems are not the whole, or even the principal, explanation for Canadians' better health. The American environment is more brutal for the less successful. In simple economic terms, for example, everyone knows that Americans enjoy higher incomes, on average, than do Canadians. Little known, and rarely reported in either country, is the fact that in the United States a much larger—and growing—proportion of total income goes to those at the very top of the income distribution. Thus, although the rich in America are much richer, the poor are much poorer than their Canadian counterparts. In 1995, although the top 20 percent of U.S. families were substantially better off than their Canadian counterparts, most of the rest—roughly half of all families—were absolutely worse off than the corresponding socioeconomic groups in Canada. The difference is largely attributable to Canada's structure of tax-financed social programs.
>
> Why is this important? There is strong evidence of a link between income distribution and overall health status: inegalitarian societies, as exemplified by the United States, which concentrate wealth in the hands of a few, tend to be unhealthy.

SOME CROSS-NATIONAL THEMES AND LESSONS

Based on the health care experience of other industrialized Western nations, what common themes and lessons emerge for the United States? In my view, the following sort out from these national profiles:

1. It is a big political challenge to establish a national health care system that provides universal access to care. Strong political leadership is required to face down powerful interests opposing such a plan. However, other countries faced with the same challenges now being experienced in the United States (e.g., runaway health care costs, large uninsured and underinsured populations) resolved these problems through strong value-based national policies (e.g., the United Kingdom in 1948, Australia in 1975, Canada in 1984).

2. Consensus around basic principles, including concepts of social justice and service of the collective good, preceded and determined the shape of whatever system of universal access was established in any particular country (e.g., Canada in 1957).

3. Tension between the public and private sectors continues within any national system of universal access, but the public sector must be dominant. Among the six countries profiled here, the public sector represents at least

two thirds to three fourths the overall system, with the United Kingdom having the largest public sector (85 percent). Successful systems provide sufficient resources to the public sector for it to be the standard setter for health care (e.g., public hospitals as the major teaching hospitals and centers of excellence, as in the United Kingdom and Australia).

4. Underfunding of the public sector can undermine the quality of care. For example, when national fee schedules are set too low for physician services, physicians typically respond by developing high-volume practices with very short visits.

5. The private practice of medicine can be preserved within a national system of compulsory health insurance. For example, there is less government or health insurer intrusion into the daily clinical practice of medicine in the United Kingdom, Australia, or Canada than in the present market-based U.S. system.

6. Free choice of physician can be retained with national systems of compulsory health insurance, again as exemplified in the United Kingdom, Australia, and Canada. This can be in contrast to many circumstances today in the United States, where choice of physician is limited to a panel determined by a third-party payer.

7. A successful NHI program requires a strong workforce of primary care physicians. Generalist physicians account for 70, 50, and 42 percent of all physicians, respectively, in the United Kingdom, Canada, and Australia, in each case serving in a community-based coordinator and gatekeeping role. Although direct access to specialists is permitted in some countries (e.g., Australia), financial disincentives are built in to discourage that practice.

8. In countries that allow some private insurance in addition to a public system of national health insurance, effective regulation of private coverage and practice is required to preserve the integrity of the public system. To that end, for example, Australia restricts the allocation of private beds within public hospitals.[14]

9. The need for ongoing cost containment of health care services is a problem in all industrialized Western countries, regardless of their organizational or financing structures. Increasing utilization of health care services driven by marketing by suppliers and practice patterns of physicians crosses all borders. However, all other countries contain these costs more effectively than the United States (Figure 23-1).

10. Some system of rational constraints on the supply of technology is necessary to contain costs and achieve a sustainable health care system. The United Kingdom for many years has been in the forefront of demonstrating effective ways to do this without compromising health status and patient outcomes, but other countries (e.g., Australia and Canada) likewise put in place effective constraints against unbridled application of new technology.

11. High quality of care can coexist with national systems affording universal access to health care, as demonstrated by Starfield's studies[35] and, more recently, by an extensive WHO report.[36]

12. Administrative simplicity is an important feature of single-payer national systems of universal access. Low overhead costs and high efficiency can be achieved within NHI systems, as exemplified by Canada, with its 1 percent overhead in its program.[34]

CONCLUDING COMMENTS

Many Americans tend to view our system as "the best in the world." As we have seen in this and earlier chapters, this perception is completely unfounded, with much evidence to the contrary, and is at best naïve and at worst arrogant, with a strong dose of denial in-between.

How can we regard what seem to be relevant lessons from other countries? In my view, while the details may vary, the problems faced by other countries, as well as their experience in dealing with them, have some strong generic similarities. For example, the self-serving behavior of the private insurance industry, the pharmaceutical industry, and even in some instances the medical profession are much more similar than different from one country to another. Our problems aren't all that exceptional, and structural reforms of our sick system may require some of the approaches taken by other countries.

There is no perfect health care system and tradeoffs are unavoidable to achieve the best compromise in the public interest among competing interests. However, compared to many other health care systems, ours is much more imperfect. We have a system with unaffordable costs, inadequate access, and often poor quality, which provides unacceptable value in return for increasing public and private expenditures. Our "system" is too complex, administratively top heavy, and has too little accountability within it. In view of the 43 million uninsured people in the United States, together with uncontrolled health care costs and mediocre quality of care, a universal access system seems to be *required* to achieve high quality of care and contain costs. The United States is at a crossroads in terms of health care reform, but that is the subject of the next and last chapter.

REFERENCES

1. Rodwin VG. Comparative analysis of health systems: An international perspective. In: Kovner AR, Jonas R (eds). *Health Care Delivery in the United States*. New York: Springer Publishing Company, 1999:134.
2. Donelan K, Blandon RJ, Schoen C, et al. The cost of health system change: Public discontent in five nations. *Health Aff (Millwood)*. 1999;18(3):210.
3. Starfield B. Is US health really the best in the world? *JAMA*. 2000;284:483–485.
4. Light DW. The 1998 APHA annual lecture. What the UK can teach the US about health care. *J R Soc Health*. 1999;119(4):261–263.
5. Light DW. Future challenges for hospitals and health care: An international perspective on the NHS 50th anniversary. *World Hosp Health Serv*. 1999;35(1):2–11.
6. Starfield B. Is primary care essential? *Lancet*. 1994;344:1129–1133.
7. Personal communication, Professor Ian McWhinney, December 6, 2000.
8. Jorgensen T, Huenegaard A, Kristensen FB. Health technology assessment in Denmark. *Int J Technol Assess Health Care*. 2000;16(2):347–381.
9. Ministry of Health. *Health Care in Denmark*. Copenhagen: March 1997.
10. Schlitt M. Health care systems in Japan and Germany provide facts, not theories. *J Med Assoc Ga*. 1993;82(12):651–655.
11. Mullan F. The Mona Lisa of health policy: Primary care at home and abroad. *Health Aff (Millwood)*. 1998;18(2):118–126.
12. Steslicke WE. Health care and the Japanese state. In: Field MG (ed). *Success and Crisis in National Health Systems: A Cross-National Approach*. New York: Routledge, 1989:101–127.

13. Personal communication. Ida Hellander MD, executive director of Physicians for a National Health Program, January 15, 2001.
14. Peabody JW, Bickel SR, Lawson JS. The Australian health care system. Are the incentives down under right side up? *JAMA*. 1996;276:1944–1950.
15. Hall J. Incremental change in the Australian health care system. *Health Aff (Millwood)*. 1999;18(3):95–103.
16. Organization for Economic Cooperation and Development (OECD). *The Reform of Health Care Systems: A Review of Seventeen OECD Countries*. Paris: Organization for Economic Cooperation and Development, 1994:55–80.
17. Collopy BT. Audit activities in Australia. *BMJ*. 1991;303:1523–1525.
18. Health as a premium. *Sydney Morning Herald*. December 5, 1998.
19. Altman S, Jackson T. Health care in Australia: Lessons from down under. *Health Aff (Millwood)*. 1991;10(3):129–146.
20. Iglehart JK. Revisiting the Canadian health care system. *N Engl J Med*. 2000;342:2007–2012.
21. Taylor MG. *Health Insurance and Canadian Public Policy: The Seven Decisions That Created the Canadian Health Insurance System*. Montreal: McGill—Queen's University Press, 1978.
22. Naylor CD. *Private Practice, Public Payment: Canadian Medicine and the Politics of Health Insurance, 1911–1966*. Kingston, Ontario: McGill—Queen's University Press, 1986.
23. Armstrong P, Armstrong H. *Universal Health Care. What the United States Can Learn from the Canadian Experience*. New York: The New Press, 1998;6–32.
24. Perkin RL. Family general practice models in Canada. *J Am Board Fam Pract*. 1994;7:526–529.
25. Personal communication. Walter Rosser MD, University of Toronto, January 26, 2001.
26. Personal communication. James Rourke MD, University of Western Ontario, January 22, 2001.
27. Kane RL. Lessons in long-term care: The benefits of a northern exposure. *Health Econ*. 1992;1(2):105–114.
28. Schiff G, Himmelstein DU. Informing the U.S. debate on the Canadian health care system: "Top ten myths." Canadian Medical Association, handout, 1993.
29. Naylor CD. A different view of queues in Ontario. *Health Aff (Millwood)*. 1991;10(3):110–128.
30. Hayes G, Hayes SC, Dykstra T. Physicians who have practiced in both the United States and Canada compare the systems. *Am J Public Health*. 1993;83(11):1544–1548.
31. Data Update. *PNHP Newsletter*. May 2001.
32. Marmor T, Sullivan K. Canada's burning! Media myths about universal health coverage. *Washington Monthly* July–August 2000:15–20.
33. Picard A. Health care not so bad: Survey. *The Globe and Mail* [Toronto] November 27, 2000.
34. Evans R, Roos NP. What is right about the Canadian health care system? *Milbank Q*. 1999;77(3):393–399, 276.
35. Starfield B. Is US health really the best in the world? *JAMA*. 2000;284:483–485.
36. World Health Report 2000. Available at http://www.who.int/whr/2000en/report.htm.

24
Principles and Some Basic Pathways for Health Care Reform

Among the lessons that ought to have been learned during the last 30 years is that the "natural" evolution of change is not necessarily in the public interest; that the bête noir of change is not necessarily "socialized medicine" as the AMA tirelessly warned us for decades—compared to the draconian intrusions of industrialized medicine on free choice and privacy; and that organized medicine, hospitals, and medical schools are not dependable fountains of wisdom and leadership in the midst of change. Our "expert" institutions and organizations have exposed themselves as bastions of resistance, self-interest, and exploiters of the public purse. More than anything else they resemble the medieval clergy in maintaining their death-grip on privilege, power, and self-aggrandizement.

G. Gayle Stephens[1]

As we saw in Chapter 22, the current U.S. health care system indeed is sick. It has advanced chronic multisystem disease, and its problem list is extensive. Structural reform has been eluding all efforts of incrementalism to treat its ills. Sick as it is, powerful interests are blocking major reform, which boils down to money. In 1980 Arnold Relman described the medical-industrial complex and warned of its corrosive effects on medicine and health care.[2] Consider these examples as to where managed competition and market forces have brought U.S. health care at the start of the 21st century:

- About one quarter of the population is disenfranchised and another one third insecurely franchised to health care coverage[3] (Chapter 17, page 266).
- Only about two thirds of patients receive recommended acute and chronic care, while contraindicated care is received by 30 percent (acute care) and 20 percent (chronic care)[4] (Chapter 18, page 282).
- Adverse events in medical care are common, and two thirds are preventable in some studies[5] (Chapter 18, page 283).
- Poor quality of care results not only from misuse of technology or services but also from overuse and underuse[6] (Chapter 18, page 284).

- For 15 serious presenting complaints, medical care is received by almost twice as many insured as uninsured people[7] (Chapter 17, page 268).
- Although the United States spends nearly twice as much on health care each year per capita than Canada,[8] its overall quality of care compares poorly in terms of patient care outcomes (e.g., 12th among 13 industrialized Western countries versus Canada's third place rank)[9] (Chapter 18, page 285).
- In 1998, 70 percent of nursing homes and home care services were for-profit, as well as two thirds of HMOs[8] (Chapter 14, page 210).
- The pharmaceutical industry is one of the most profitable U.S. industries (14.4 to 18.6 percent return on investment in last five years),[8] while the costs of prescription drugs are increasing faster than any other part of health care expenditures (annual growth rate of 24.8 percent from 1996 to 1999).[10]
- Although direct-to-consumer (DTC) drug advertising has been shown to be misleading, at times with exaggerated claims,[11] DTC drug advertising has grown rapidly in recent years since FDA regulations were relaxed; drug companies now spend 33 times the amount spent on mass media ads in 1991 (including $1.1 billion on television ads) and sales of the 25 most advertised drugs recently increased by 43 percent in a single year.[12]
- About 26 percent of the nation's total health care expenditures are taken up by administrative costs.[13]
- With both the public and private sectors increasingly fragile, the U.S. health care system ranks 15th out of 25 industrialized Western nations in overall performance[14] (Chapter 18, page 286).
- All efforts to structurally reform the U.S. health care system by introducing universal access through a national health care program (five attempts since 1912) have been strongly and successfully resisted by special interest groups defending the status quo (Chapter 19).[15,16]

These illustrations of one or another aspect of U.S. health care are appalling and unacceptable in the most affluent nation on earth. There is harm, not just absence of benefits, within this huge industry, despite its size and imposing technological strengths.

In a fascinating and provocative presentation at a recent conference in Colorado Springs exploring future directions of family practice within a changing health care system, Stephens compared the present U.S. health care system to the Chimera of ancient Greek mythology. Although many versions and interpretations of this myth have come down to us through history over the last 3,000 years, most involve a fearful creature, a female monster that breathed fire, was strong and swift-footed, and with three heads (usually including a lion, a goat, and sometimes a dragon or serpent). The Chimera terrorized parts of ancient Greece. Bellerophon, a young hero from Corinth, was commissioned by a king to slay the monster, considered by many to be an impossible task. With the help of his winged horse, Pegasus, however, Bellerophon was able to fly over the Chimera and slay it from above.[17] Figure 24-1 represents one such Chimera. The medical analogy can be completed in various graphic ways; for example, the lion's head could be the for-profit HMO industry, the goat's head could be the enormous insurance or pharmaceutical industry, with the third head as other powerful special interest groups resisting structural system reform.

Figure 24-1 Chimera and Bellerophon. (Reprinted with permission from Stephens GG. How are family doctors agents of political and social change? Speech presented at Keystone III Conference, Colorado Springs, CO, October 4, 2000.)

In any event, evidence reviewed in this book with respect to incremental efforts to improve this country's health care system, within a largely unregulated private sector with marketplace values, exposes the ineffectiveness of this approach after 20 to 30 years. As Stephens reminds us at the beginning of this chapter, not all change is in the public interest.[1]

The system's present problems need major reform, not minor course changes—big change, not fine-tuning. A new framework is needed, not just adding on or remodeling the system's weak foundation. In more graphic terms, the swamp needs to be drained before the alligator problem can be controlled. This last chapter outlines some useful principles and basic pathways for long overdue system reform.

PRINCIPLES OF HEALTH CARE REFORM

We saw in the last chapter an excellent example of major health care reform being developed on the basis of social values and a small number of essential guiding principles. Canada's five key principles—public administration, comprehensiveness, universality, portability, and accessibility—achieved national consensus over a period of years and formed the organizational framework for the successful Canadian health care system.[18] Other successful health care systems have been shaped by value-driven principles, so that form *can* follow values.

The United States would do well to proceed in a similar manner. The Clinton Health Plan of 1994 was defeated by a well-funded Health Insurance Association of America (HIAA) public relations campaign ("Harry and Louise") and the coordinated efforts of other special interests vested in the pro-market system. The public never really understood "managed competition," while it supported the goal of expanded coverage. The proposal became an easy target for its critics and opponents, who labeled it too complex and bureaucratic.

What values should the United States embrace as it confronts the medical Chimera? Canada's general principles have much to recommend them and would lead to important reforms south of our common border as well. For the sake of discussion, however, other thoughtful analysts have made some excellent suggestions for such basic principles.

Several years ago, an international working group from four countries—the United States, the United Kingdom, Mexico, and South Africa—convened in London to draft ethical principles that could (should) underlie any health care system. Now known as the Tavistock Group, it included physicians, nurses, academicians, ethicists, health care executives, a jurist, an economist, and a philosopher. This group recommended that the following ethical principles should govern any health care system:[19]

1. Health care is a human right.
2. The care of individuals is at the center of health care delivery but must be viewed and practiced within the overall context of continuing work to generate the greatest possible health gains for groups and populations.
3. The responsibilities of the health care delivery system include the prevention of illness and the alleviation of disability.
4. Cooperation with each other and those served is imperative for those working within the health care delivery system.
5. All individuals and groups involved in health care, whether they provide access or services, have the continuing responsibility to help improve its quality.

Another useful set of health care principles, this time focusing on quality of care, was formulated by Gordon Schiff and his colleagues in a paper proposing single-payer national health system reform. They offered these 10 important principles:[20]

1. There is a profound and inseparable relationship between access and quality: universal insurance coverage is a prerequisite for quality care.
2. The best guarantor of universal high-quality care is a unified system that does not treat patients differently based on employment, financial status, or source of payment.
3. Continuity of primary care is needed to overcome fragmentation and overspecialization among health care practitioners and institutions.
4. A standardized confidential electronic medical record and resulting database are key to supporting clinical practice and creating the information infrastructure needed to improve care overall.
5. Health care delivery must be guided by the precepts of continuous quality improvement (CQI).
6. New forums for enhanced public accountability are needed to improve clinical quality, to address and prevent malpractice, and to engage practitioners in partnerships with their peers and patients to guide and evaluate care.
7. Financial neutrality of medical decision making is essential to reconcile distorting influences of physician payment mechanisms with ubiquitous uncertainties in clinical medicine.
8. Emphasis should shift from micromanagement of providers' practices to macroallocation decisions. Public control over expenditures can improve quality by promoting regionalization, coordination, and prevention.
9. Quality requires prevention. Prevention means looking beyond medical treatment of sick individuals to community-based public health efforts to prevent disease, improve functioning and well-being, and reduce health disparities.
10. Affordability is a quality issue. Effective cost control is needed to ensure availability of quality health care both to individuals and the nation.

Many of the preceding principles overlap, but the major themes fall under a smaller group of principles, such as universal access, affordability, continuity of care, comprehensiveness, quality assurance, public accountability, and a population perspective. Most of that was subsumed, in fewer words, and acted on in Canada more than 20 years ago.

Whatever principles are adopted to underpin a health care system, their selection represents ethical statements of the society. Some important consequences of libertarian views (private systems) and egalitarian views (public systems), as conceptualized by Alan Williams, an English health economist, sort out as they relate to health care (Table 24-1).[21] As Williams readily admits, however, private and public systems usually fall short of these ideals in actual practice. The extent of that shortfall depends on three main factors: the particular role of physicians within the system, market deficiencies on the supply side, and problems with information on the demand side.[21]

Given the challenge of developing a health care system that provides accessible and affordable health care of reasonable quality to an entire population, it is very doubtful that the for-profit sector has much to contribute to that goal. Many experienced observers have argued that excesses of the private for-profit

Table 24-1 Essential Characteristics of Idealized Health Care Systems Based on Libertarian Views (Private Systems) and Egalitarian Views (Public Systems)

System Element	Private System	Public System
Demand	Individuals are the best judges of their own welfare.	When ill, individuals are frequently imperfect judges of their own welfare.
	Priorities are determined by people's own willingness and ability to pay. The erratic and potentially catastrophic nature of demand is mediated by private insurance.	Priorities are determined by social judgments about need. The erratic and potentially catastrophic nature of demand is made irrelevant by the provision of free services.
	Matters of equity are dealt with elsewhere (e.g., in the tax and social security systems).	Since the distribution of income and wealth is unlikely to be equitable in relation to the need for health care, the system must be insulated from its influence.
Supply	Profit is the proper and most effective way to motivate suppliers to respond to the needs of demanders.	Professional ethics and dedication to public service are the appropriate motivation of suppliers, who should focus on success in curing and caring.
	Priorities are determined by people's willingness and ability to pay and by the costs of meeting their wishes at the margin.	Priorities are determined by identifying the greatest improvements in caring or curing that can be effected at the margin.
	Suppliers have a strong incentive to adopt least-cost methods of service provision.	Predetermined limits on available resources create a strong incentive for suppliers to adopt least-cost methods of service provision.
Adjustment mechanism(s)	Many competing suppliers ensure that prices are kept low and reflect costs.	Central review of activities generates efficiency audits of service provision; management pressures keep the system cost-effective.
	Well-informed consumers are able to seek out the most cost-effective form of treatment for themselves.	Well-informed clinicians are able to prescribe the most cost-effective form of treatment for each patient.
	If medical practice is profitable at the price that prevails in the market, more people will go into medicine; hence, supply will be demand responsive. If, conversely, medical practice is unrenumerative, people will	If there is demand pressure on some facilities or specialties, resources will be directed toward extending them. Facilities or specialties on which demand pressure is slack will be slimmed down to release resources for other uses.

continues

Table 24-1 (continued)

System Element	Private System	Public System
	leave it, or stop entering it, until the system returns to equilibrium.	
Success criteria	Consumers will judge the system by their ability to get someone to do what they demand, when, where, and how they want it done.	The electorate judges the system by the extent to which it improves the health status of the population at large in relation to resources allocated to it.
	Producers will judge the system by how substantial a living they can make through it.	Producers judge the system by its ability to enable them to provide the treatment they believe to be cost-effective.

Source: Reprinted with permission from Williams A. Priority setting in a needs-based system. In: Committee on Technological Innovation in Medicine, Institute of Medicine, Gelijns AC (ed). *Technology and Health Care in an Era of Limits.* Washington DC: National Academy Press, 1992:90–91.

sector so distort the system that universal coverage with public standards and accountability never can be achieved. Earlier chapters of this book provide ample evidence that such is the case in the United States over the past 30 years.

SOME BASIC PATHWAYS TOWARD HEALTH CARE REFORM

The United States has a tradition and history of letting form follow the marketplace. Such is the case with the present unsustainable health care system with its well-documented problems of access, cost, and quality. Incrementalism has been tried and consistently failed to remedy these problems over the last 20-plus years. In view of the failure of incrementalism and the near certainty, in my view, that pro-market "reforms" will be no more successful, I propose the following basic pathways as a guide to new directions that will lead toward real and sustainable improvement in access, cost, and quality of health care in the United States.

Develop a Single-Payer National Health Program

As we saw in Chapter 22, three major options are left, after failure of incrementalism of managed competition, to expand access within the U.S. health care system: (1) build around the present employer-based health insurance system, (2) shift to a consumer-choice (individual mandate) model, or (3) adopt a single-payer system. Although options 1 or 2 likely would be more attractive to politicians, each has major downsides in terms of cost, complexity, and inefficiencies. Both would continue the patchwork mix of private and public sectors and leave many millions uninsured and underinsured. In each case, the for-profit motivation of the private sector would continue to work against the public interest in ways already well documented (e.g., Chapter 14, pages 213–217).

As shown in Figure 22-3, a single-payer unified national health program along the lines proposed by Physicians for a National Health Program (PNHP) would provide universal coverage in the most direct and simplified way by eliminating the huge bureaucracy of 1,200 plus insurers and health plans, which now stand between physicians and patients while accounting for up to 30 percent of health care expenditures. Of course, many administrative details would have to be worked out through a bipartisan process, but the general concept of a unified, tax-based foundation with comprehensive benefits, in the judgment of many as well as the experience of comparable nations, would go further than any other approach to structurally reform our health care system in terms of access, cost containment, and improved system performance.

The Canadian approach to political acceptance could serve us well on this side of the border. As we saw in the last chapter, the Canadian federal government established the principles for its national health program, which then became requirements for the provinces to receive matching funds for provincial health care. Over the course of a few years, all 10 provinces adopted the Canadian single-payer system, albeit with retention of provincial responsibilities for governnance.[22]

Adopt Campaign Finance Reform

As was described in Chapter 19, special interests have defeated all previous major attempts to reform the U.S. health care system. The most recent example is the massive advertising campaign mounted by health insurance industry lobbyists against the Clinton Health Plan in 1994. In the same way as the AMA defeated Truman's health care plan in 1948, by labeling it "socialized medicine," the insurance industry in 1994 distorted the debate by appealing to antigovernment sentiment and railing against "government-run health care." The "Harry and Louise" television ad campaign conducted by the HIAA effectively confused the public and raised fear that people would lose the ability to choose their physicians. For major health care reform to be adopted, stakeholders defending the status quo have to be defeated by a massive public movement, including strong grassroots and middle-class support as well as bipartisan support in Congress. For that to become possible, many activists believe that campaign finance reform is a necessary precursor.

Expand the Public Sector

In the last chapter, our cross-national profiles of health care systems in comparable industrialized Western nations showed that the public sector must be the dominant sector for any system of national health insurance to succeed. In fact, most countries have public sectors representing at least 75 or 80 percent of their health care systems. Further likelihood of success for an NHI system is achieved where the public sector is adequately financed, supports medical education and research, and is active in setting high standards for quality of care. Australia, Canada, and the United Kingdom are examples where that is the case. An underfunded public sector, on the other hand, works in the other direction, by encouraging excesses of high-volume practice (e.g., Japan and Medicaid in the United States).

Academic health centers and medical schools are facing serious financial difficulties all around the country as they pursue their triple mission of teaching, clinical research, and patient care. They face a hostile environment in which teaching largely is unfunded and patient care typically is an underfunded public sector, safety-net responsibility. While some redistribution by specialty may be needed in graduate medical education, federal and state financing of essential medical education functions must be built into a reformed and improved health care system. Indeed, implementation of a single-payer national health program would eliminate the present controversial system of Medicare payments for medical education (both direct and indirect payments) and provide direct federal financing of future medical education.

Build Coalitions

Coalition building obviously will be important to achieve sufficient national consensus and political will to implement significant health care reforms. As noted by Thai, Qiao, and McManus, this will become most likely and politically feasible when both the benefits and costs of proposed reforms are distributed widely (majoritarian politics).[15] Some large groups, such as employers, are divided in their interests (e.g., the interests of large employers do not necessarily coincide with those of small employers). Stakeholders in the past have been able to ignite divisions between groups to their advantage. When the interests of the major segments of society merge for fundamental health care reform in their interest as well as the public interest, the present political logjam can be broken. The most important groups to make that happen would appear to be business, employees (including organized labor), consumers, and health care professionals. They must mobilize to convince legislators to back serious system reform.

Implement Tort Reform

As we saw in Chapter 12 (pages 174–175), there are major problems in the current medicolegal system, including shortcomings of lay juries and negative impact on the physician-patient relationship, on the one hand, and its failure to deal with many instances of medical negligence, on the other.[23] Additional negative impact will hamper quality improvement efforts to report medical errors unless such reports are freed from legal discovery.

The joint efforts of the Agency for Health Care Research and Quality (AHRQ) and the Institute of Medicine (IOM), in seeking new understanding between the legal and medical professions, are in the right direction. A wide gulf in perspective lies between the two professions, as illustrated by the paradigm differences of population-based medicine (with some potential tradeoffs for individuals) and the overriding concern of the legal system for the individual plaintiff. This gap must be narrowed, and the defensive resistance by the Association of Trial Lawyers of America (ATLA) must be recognized more widely for what it is—an often invisible but enormously powerful self-interest group of its own.

It should be noted that a single-payer system would help to eliminate some of the costs now associated with medicolegal disputes by obviating the need for those one third of lawsuits filed for future medical expenses.

Increase Public Education

A more responsible role of the media will be required to objectively cover health care issues in the public interest. Media that are beholden to stakeholders defending the status quo need to be exposed and discredited as unreliable sources of reliable information. Campaign finance reform also is needed to expose such relationships with legislators. That there is a long way to go in this regard is shown by the media's slanted and inadequate coverage of the Canadian health care system (Chapter 23, pages 402–403) and their conflict of interest in receiving major advertising support from special interests threatened by a single-payer system.

Admittedly, the preceding six directions are short on specifics but nevertheless would result in needed course changes in the right direction. More specific strategies could evolve by remaining true to underlying principles and values, with the long-term public interest as the overall goal. These directions likely will seem overly simplistic to some, but in their defense, the forest often is more difficult to see than the trees, especially for those involved in the current health care morass. A good example of the obvious being slow to be recognized is the problem-oriented medical record (POMR). Physicians for generations struggled with, but accepted as inevitable, a totally disorganized medical record until Larry Weed came along in 1970 with his logical solution, the POMR.[24] The concept became widely adopted, albeit with minor modifications, by the entire medical profession, but its logic was not recognized for all too long before that occurred.

If these six basic pathways are seriously pursued in the United States, the result would be a sustainable health care system that best meets the public interest. Inevitable political tradeoffs will be needed to achieve the best compromise between universal access and the needs of the entire population and the interests of specific interest groups. If this country can expand its public sector as the foundation of best medical practice while reining in the abuses of the private sector, the country will be well served. As already demonstrated in other industrialized Western countries, a single-payer system can reduce the overwhelming administrative burden in health care with less interference in the physician-patient relationship than that which now plagues physicians and patients in the United States.

MEDICINE CAN CONTRIBUTE TO HEALTH CARE REFORM

The medical profession's involvement and leadership necessarily play a key role toward long-term health care reform, but some reassessment and shift of perspective will be required before that can be as effective as it needs to be. As pointed out in earlier chapters, organized medicine more often has resisted change than advocated for it (e.g., the AMA's battle against Medicare and Medicaid in the 1960s). Since that battle was lost, the AMA has steadily lost membership (now only about one third of American physicians, down from one half 10 years ago). It also suffered in moral credibility (e.g., its need to renounce an exclusive endorsement of Sunbeam products in response to vocal critics charging conflict of interest).[25]

Today, the medical profession has been splintered into many specialty and subspecialty groups, and for many its public image is tarnished. As power and influence shifted over the last 20 years from the professional to the corporate sector, health care has become a commodity and the service ethic has been eroded by marketplace ethics. Many physicians have been unavoidably caught up in the pressures of a chaotic marketplace controlled by managers and corporate interests. As managed care (reimbursement) gained sway, participating physicians felt an uncomfortable conflict of interest under systems of capitation reimbursement. A 1997 report illustrates the extent to which physicians feel that capitation is unethical[26,27] (Figure 24-2).

George Lundberg, for many years editor of the *Journal of the American Medical Association*, described the long-standing tensions between business

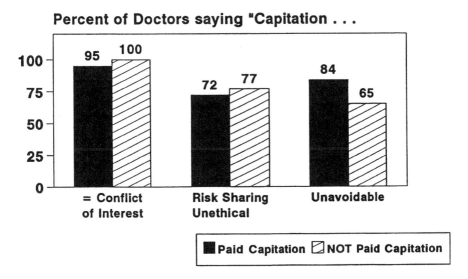

Figure 24-2 Most physicians believe capitation is unethical, including those paid capitation. (Reprinted with permission from Wynia MK, Picken HA, Selkers HP. Physicians' views on capitated payment for medical care: Does familiarity foster acceptance? *Am J Manage Care.* 1997;3(10):1497.)

and professionalism in medicine as medicine's rocking horse (Figure 24-3), with a shifting balance between economic and altruistic goals. He calls for a pendulum shift back to the professional and altruistic pole by renewal of an overriding service ethic in medicine.[28,29]

It is time for professional renewal in medicine.[30–32] Within a new professionalism in American medicine, many pressing areas call for active physicians' involvement and leadership. In my view, these are some of the most obvious areas:

- Recommit to a service ethic as the raison d'être of medicine.
- Embrace evidence-based and population-based medicine while preserving a personal partnership with individual patients.
- Re-examine professional roles in an effort to avoid fiduciary or other conflicts of interest that work against the needs of patients or populations being served.
- Take the lead in determining necessary care and delivering appropriate care of the best possible quality within available resources; Don Berwick suggests this as a covenant: "We will promise to deliver, reliably and without error, all the care that will help and only the care that will help."[33]
- Redesign practice systems based on evidence-based practice guidelines with the goal to increase efficiencies and cost-effectiveness of health care services.
- Advocate for major structural reform of the health care system (i.e., a single-payer NHI system) that serves the public interest exclusively, not the interests of special groups.

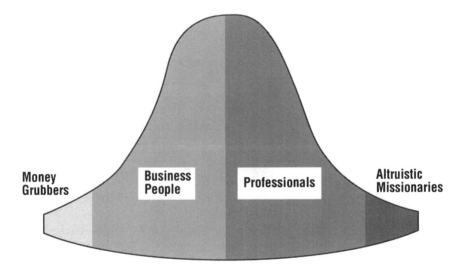

Figure 24-3 Medicine's rocking horse. The natural tensions that have always been between the business and professionalism of medicine. (Reprinted with permission from Lundberg GD. The failure of organized health system reform—Now what? Caveat anger—Let the patient beware. *JAMA.* 1995;273:1539–1541.)

- Become educated on the advantages and disadvantages of organizational options for health system reform.
- Push medical and specialty organizations to look outward toward system reform rather than inward at their own interests.
- Work across specialty organizational boundaries toward increased professional alliances within medicine and a stronger voice in health care reform. (Imagine the influence, for example, if 100,000 plus physicians were to become active members of PNHP.)
- Increase public awareness of the everyday problems in today's failing health care "system."

WHAT NEXT?

As the keynote speaker at a recent Conversation About the Future Forum held at the University of Washington, Glen Hiemstra, a futurist, observed that we are in the middle of a technoeconomic revolution with at least as much change as occurred during the first 30 to 40 years of the 20th century, which saw the emergence of the automobile, the movie camera, X rays, the airplane, the atomic age, and the replacement of gas illumination by electricity. He predicts that the next 20 to 25 years will be driven by digital technology, biotechnology, and nanotechnology.[34]

In *Health and Health Care 2010: The Forecast, the Challenges*, the Institute of the Future forecasts three possible scenarios for U.S. health care over the next 10 years, all assuming a continuation of incrementalism with no major system reform. Its possible scenarios range from stormy (scenario 1, with inflation of health care costs to 19 percent of GDP, radical tiering of access and care, 65 million uninsured, and overwhelmed state Medicaid budgets) to sunny (scenario 3, with health care spending at 15 percent of GDP and 30 million uninsured) (Figure 24-4). Most would agree that it is not sunny when 30 million people are uninsured. Moreover, economic downturns are more likely than not over these next 10 years and will make the worse scenarios more likely.[3]

Hiemstra advises us to imagine the future and ask what is probable, what is possible, and what is preferred.[34] That exercise leads me to reject all of the Institute of the Future's scenarios as undesirable, to be avoided if at all possible. On the other hand, these are the most probable outcomes based on present trends of incrementalism and patchwork pro-market measures being considered under either option 1 (building on employer-based health insurance) or option 2 (expanding consumer choice). A better future—both preferred and possible— would be a single-payer national health program, if the basic pathways discussed earlier are seriously pursued and sufficient public awareness and support can be developed toward more effective reform of a failing health care "system." Don McCanne and Steffie Woolhandler, activist physicians committed to a National Health Program, are eloquent and clear on what needs to be done:[35]

We have the wealth. We have the resources. We have the capacity. We have the most technologically advanced health care system. . . . We need to make

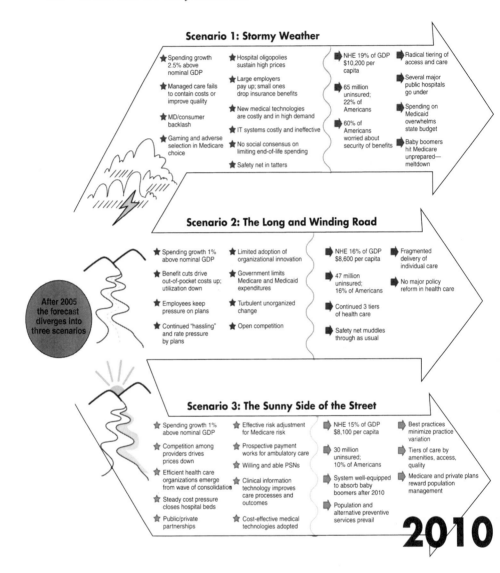

Scenario 1: Stormy Weather

★ Spending growth 2.5% above nominal GDP

★ Managed care fails to contain costs or improve quality

★ MD/consumer backlash

★ Gaming and adverse selection in Medicare choice

★ Hospital oligopolies sustain high prices

★ Large employers pay up; small ones drop insurance benefits

★ New medical technologies are costly and in high demand

★ IT systems costly and ineffective

★ No social consensus on limiting end-of-life spending

★ Safety net in tatters

➡ NHE 19% of GDP $10,200 per capita

➡ 65 million uninsured; 22% of Americans

➡ 60% of Americans worried about security of benefits

➡ Radical tiering of access and care

➡ Several major public hospitals go under

➡ Spending on Medicaid overwhelms state budget

➡ Baby boomers hit Medicare unprepared— meltdown

Scenario 2: The Long and Winding Road

After 2005 the forecast diverges into three scenarios

★ Spending growth 1% above nominal GDP

★ Benefit cuts drive out-of-pocket costs up; utilization down

★ Employees keep pressure on plans

★ Continued "hassling" and rate pressure by plans

★ Limited adoption of organizational innovation

★ Government limits Medicare and Medicaid expenditures

★ Turbulent unorganized change

★ Open competition

➡ NHE 16% of GDP $8,600 per capita

➡ 47 million uninsured; 16% of Americans

➡ Continued 3 tiers of health care

➡ Safety net muddles through as usual

➡ Fragmented delivery of individual care

➡ No major policy reform in health care

Scenario 3: The Sunny Side of the Street

★ Spending growth 1% above nominal GDP

★ Competition among providers drives prices down

★ Efficient health care organizations emerge from wave of consolidation

★ Steady cost pressure closes hospital beds

★ Public/private partnerships

★ Effective risk adjustment for Medicare risk

★ Prospective payment works for ambulatory care

★ Willing and able PSNs

★ Clinical information technology improves care processes and outcomes

★ Cost-effective medical technologies adopted

➡ NHE 15% of GDP $8,100 per capita

➡ 30 million uninsured; 10% of Americans

➡ System well-equipped to absorb baby boomers after 2010

➡ Population and alternative preventive services prevail

➡ Best practices minimize practice variation

➡ Tiers of care by amenities, access, quality

➡ Medicare and private plans reward population management

2010

Figure 24-4   Scenario 1, stormy weather; scenario 2, the long and winding road; scenario 3, the sunny side of the street. (Reprinted with permission from Institute for the Future. *Health and Health Care 2010: The Forecast, the Challenges.* San Francisco: Jossey-Bass, 2000:Appendix.)

only one basic change. We need to discard the antiquated, cruel, wasteful, ineffective, corporate model health plans and replace them with an efficient, publicly administered, universal risk pool. To those who tell us that the political will to implement it doesn't exist, we can only reply that creating this political will must be the highest priority of all who hope to achieve a decent healthcare system in this country.

In late May 2001, a physicians' working group for single-payer national health insurance presented its proposal for health care reform at a hearing sponsored by the Congressional Black Caucus, the Congressional Progressive Caucus, and the Congressional Hispanic Caucus. Together, the three caucuses represent about 120 Democratic members of Congress. The working group's members include the presidents of the National Medical Association, the American Medical Women's Association, and the American Medical Student Association, as well as past presidents of the American Academy of Pediatrics and the American College of Physicians—American Society of Internal Medicine. Following is a partial summary of their testimony:[36]

> We endorse a fundamental change in America's health care—the creation of a comprehensive National Health Insurance (NHI) program. Such a program—which in essence would be an expanded and improved version of Medicare—would cover every American for all necessary medical care. Most hospitals and clinics would remain privately owned and operated, receiving a budget from the NHI to cover all operating costs. Investor-owned facilities would be converted to not-for-profit status, and their former owners compensated for past investments. Physicians could continue to practice on a fee-for-service basis, or receive salaries from group practices, hospitals, or clinics.
>
> A National Health Insurance program would save at least $150 billion annually by eliminating the high overhead and profits of the private, investor-owned insurance industry and reducing spending for marketing and other satellite services. Doctors and hospitals would be freed from the concomitant burdens and expenses of paperwork created by having to deal with multiple insurers with different rules—often rules designed to avoid payment. During the transition to an NHI, the savings on administration and profits would fully offset the costs of expanded and improved coverage. NHI would make it possible to set and enforce overall spending limits for the health care system, slowing cost growth over the long run.
>
> A National Health Insurance program is the only affordable option for universal, comprehensive coverage. Under the current system, expanding access to health care inevitably means increasing costs, and reducing costs inevitably means limiting access. But an NHI could both expand access and reduce costs. It would squeeze out bureaucratic waste and eliminate the perverse incentives that threaten the quality of care and the ethical foundations of medicine.

CONCLUSION

This book has been my best effort to bring to bear the most credible evidence available to focus on the major trends affecting the U.S. health care system, an assessment of its present strengths and weaknesses, and options for system reform and improvement. The health care "system" is extremely complex and a moving target, but the evidence supports the view that the system indeed is seriously ill and in urgent need of structural reform. Both near-term and long-term scenarios are unhealthy unless incrementalism is abandoned as ineffective and a national effort launched toward systemic reform. Some oxen in the commons oppose that level of reform and need to be gored (even if a sacred cow) if they stand in the way of the reform required to assure universal access to cost-effective care of the best quality achievable within available resources.

The future of American health care is far from clear. Its near-term scenarios differ widely. The stakes are high, and a continued incremental approach to patchwork "solutions" appears certain to fail in the long term. Large and escalating expenditures are returning too little value to the public, and too many Americans receive little or no health care.

Can this sick health care "system" be fixed? Yes, and some therapeutic approaches have been offered, but effective reforms must be major and will be painful to some in a transitional period. A case can be made for both optimism and pessimism that effective reform will be accomplished.

On the positive side, these are reasons to be optimistic:

- The process of health care is changing rapidly and the old system mostly has broken down, so that creative restructuring of health care is more possible than in earlier years.
- All the building blocks for an excellent health care system are available if they are put together in a new way.
- Although the United States is in political gridlock, it by no means is in organizational or technological gridlock.
- The growing disenchantment with health care across many groups in society may lead to a groundswell of public support for its reform.
- There already is increasing public concern about problems of access, cost, and quality of health care.
- Many young health professionals entering the workforce do not carry the baggage of past attitudes and expectations and tend to be more supportive of major reform.
- Ironically, any economic downturn (certain to happen, the only questions are when and for how long) will bring the problems of health care to the front burner of public concern and generate more support for major reform.

On the other side of the ledger, there is room for pessimism about near-term serious system reform, for two major reasons:

- Powerful for-profit special interests control the legislative process, have successfully defeated health care reform on many occasions in the past, and certainly will pose formidable opposition to future reforms that threaten the status quo.
- Our political system is more suited to incrementalism and avoidance of controversial major changes unless circumstances arise that become national emergencies.

What will happen? That is an entirely open question. It remains to be seen. As Winston Churchill said more than 50 years ago, "You can count on Americans to do the right thing, but only after they have tried everything else."[18 (p. xiii)] Let's hope we already have exhausted most of the undesirable alternatives.

REFERENCES

1. Stephens GG. Family practice and social and political change. *Fam Med.* 2001;33(4):250.
2. Relman AS. The new medical-industrial complex. *N Engl J Med.* 1980;303:963–970.
3. Institute for the Future. *Health and Health Care 2010: The Forecast, the Challenges.* San Francisco: Jossey-Bass Publishers, 2000:123–137.
4. Schuster M, McGlynn EA, Brook RH. How good is the quality of health care in the United States? *Milbank Q.* 1998;76(4):517–563.
5. Leape L, Lawthers AG, Brennan TA, Johnson WG. Preventing medical injury. *QRB Qual Rev Bull.* 1993;19(5):144–149.
6. Chassin MR, Galvin RW. The urgent need to improve health care quality. Institute of Medicine National Roundtable on Health Care Quality. *JAMA.* 1998;280:1000–1005.
7. Baker DW, Shapiro MF, Schur CL. Health insurance and access to care for symptomatic conditions. *Arch Intern Med.* 2000;160:1269–1274.
8. Woolhandler S, Himmelstein DU. *The National Health Program Slideshow Guide.* Cambridge, MA: The Center for National Health Program Studies, 2000.
9. Starfield B. *Primary Care. Balancing Health Needs, Services, and Technology.* New York: Oxford University Press, 1998.
10. Prescription drug expenditures increase more than 24%. *Med Benefits.* 2000;17(3):5.
11. Bell RA, Kravitz RL, Wilkes MS. Direct-to-consumer prescription drug advertising: 1989–1998. *J Fam Pract.* 2000;49;329–335.
12. Findley S. Research brief. National Institute for Health Care Management Research and Educational Foundation (September 2000). *Med Benefits.* 2000;17(20):5–6.
13. Kirschenbaum CB, Woolhandler S. Why single payer? Why now? *J Am Womens Assoc.* Winter 2000;55(1):37–38, 46.
14. World Health Report 2000. Available at: http://www.who.int/whr/2000en/report.htm.
15. Thai KV, Qiao Y, McManus SM. National health care reform failure: The political economy perspective. *J Health Hum Serve Adm.* Fall 1998;21(2):236–259.
16. Goldsmith AA. *Business, Government, Society: The Global Political Economy.* Chicago: Richard D. Irwin, 1996.
17. Bardi U. Chimera: a site dedicated to the ancient myth of the Chimera. Available at: http://www.unifi.it/unifi/surfchem/solid/bardi/chimera/.
18. Armstrong P, Armstrong H. *Universal Health Care. What the United States Can Learn from the Canadian Experience.* New York: The New Press, 1998:6–32.
19. The Tavistock Group. A shared statement of ethical principles for those who shape and give health care: a working draft. *Effective Clin Pract.* 1999;2(3):143–145.
20. Schiff GD, Bindman AB, Brennan TA, et al. A better quality alternative: Single-payer national health system reform. *JAMA.* 1994;272:803–808.
21. Williams A. Priority setting in a needs-based system. In: Committee on Technological Innovation in Medicine, Institute of Medicine, Gelijns AC (ed). *Technology and Health Care in an Era of Limits.* Washington DC: National Academy Press, 1992:79–95.
22. Perkin RL. Family general practice models in Canada. *J Am Board Fam Pract.* 1994;7:526–529.
23. White WF. Alternative dispute resolution for medical malpractice actions: An efficient approach to the law and health care. *Leg Med.* 1995:227–239.
24. Weed LL. *Medical Records, Medical Education, and Patient Care.* Cleveland: Case Western Reserve University Press, 1970:13.
25. Kassirer JP, Angell M. The high price of product endorsement. *N Engl J Med.* 1997;337:700.
26. Wynia MK, Picken HA, Selkers HP. Physicians' views on capitated payment for medical care: Does familiarity foster acceptance. *Am J Manage Care.* 1997;3(10):1497–1502.
27. Woolhandler S, Himmelstein DU. *The National Health Program Slideshow Guide.* Cambridge, MA: Center for National Health Program Studies, 2000.
28. Lundberg GD. The failure of organized health system reform—Now what? Caveat anger—Let the patient beware. *JAMA.* 1995;273:1539–1541.
29. Lundberg GD. Countdown to millennium—Balancing the professionalism and business of medicine: Medicine's rocking horse. *JAMA.* 1990;263:86–87.
30. Pellegrino ED. Medical professionalism: Can it, should it survive? *J Am Board Fam Pract.* 2000;13:147–149.
31. Bulger RJ. The quest for a therapeutic organization. *JAMA.* 2000;283:2431–2432.

32. Mechanic D. Managed care and the imperative for a new professional ethic. *Health Aff (Millwood).* 2000;19(5):100–111.
33. Berwick DM. Plenary address at the Institute for Healthcare Improvement's 11th annual Forum on Quality Improvement in Healthcare. New Orleans, December 9, 1999.
34. Hill S. Futurist says change will accelerate in 21st century. *University Week* [Seattle, University of Washington]. 2000;17(21):4.
35. McCanne D, Woolhandler S. The corporate model has failed: We need to create a publicly administered universal risk pool. Press release. Chicago: PNHP, January 5, 2001.
36. Physicians for a National Health Program. Press release, Chicago, May 23, 2001.

Author Index

A
Aaron, H. J., 351
Adams, Sheila, 229
Andrews, Charles, 318
Angell, Marcia, 249–250, 363
Annas, George, 82
Armstrong, Hugh, 399
Armstrong, Pat, 399
Austin, B. T., 138

B
Barondess, Jeremiah, 47
Barsky, Arthur, 31–32, 67
Benjamin, Walter, 57
Bennett, J. H., 135
Berwick, Don, 281
Bierman, Arlene, 207
Bindman, A. B., 282
Binney, Elizabeth, 33–34
Blendon, Robert, 65, 106
Blumenthal, D., 327–328
Bodenheimer, T., 206, 287, 376, 378
Boult, Chad, 80–81
Brandeis University, 256
Brennan, T. A., 282
Brennan, Troyen, 165, 175–176
Brody, Howard, 356
Brook, R. H., 282
Brooks, David, 330
Bunker, J. P., 153, 301

C
Cain, Harry, 214
Califano, Joseph, 319

Campbell, Thomas, 197
Center for Studying Health System
  Change, 102, 276
Chambers, Christopher, 79
Chassin, Mark, 283–284, 302
Chen, Lincoln, 29–30
Churchill, Larry, 63, 359, 365–369
Cleveland, Harlan, 240
Coddington, Dean, 363–364
Cohen, Jordan, 126
Consumers Union, 99
Corrigan, Janet, 337
Coye, Molly, 150

D
Deyo, Richard, 21, 171
Donahoe, Martin, 196

E
Ebell, Mark, 232–233
Eddy, David, 18, 113, 343, 354–355
Eisenberg, David, 167
Eisenberg, John, 180, 278
Ellwood, Paul, 217–218
Engel, George, 131
Enthoven, A. C., 153, 247, 301
Epstein, Steven, 126–127, 166–167
Estes, Carroll, 33–34
Evans, Robert, 348–349, 403

F
Fagin, Claire M., 216–217
Fegan, Claudia, 399
Fischer, Paul, 172–173

425

Fisher, Elliott, 19, 20, 145
Fitzgerald, Faith, 193
Fletcher, Robert, 213
Fox, Daniel, 207
Fox, T. F., 187
Friedman, Emily, 114, 130, 205
Friedman, Thomas, 379–380
Fuchs, Victor, 18, 116, 206

G
Gabel, Jon, 106–107
Galvin, Robert, 283–284
Gambliel, Sandy, 48
Gary, B. H., 122
Gilbert, Fred, 131
Ginsberg, Paul, 337
Ginzberg, Eli, 61, 146, 381
Glauber, James, 297–298
Goldsmith, Jeff, 9–10
Golenski, John, 130, 143
Goodman, Lenn, 29
Goodman, Madeleine, 29
Goodwin, James, 34
Gordon, Colin, 318
Greider, William, 321
Grumbach, Kevin, 66, 194–195, 260–261, 378

H
Harvard School of Public Health, 64–65
Havighurst, Clark, 180
Hayward, R. A., 282–283
Heftel, Cecil, 338
Hellander, Ida, 301
Herodotus, 44
Hiemstra, Glen, 419
Himmelstein, David, 376–377, 380
Hipshman, Lawrence, 261
Hofer, Timothy, 282–283
Hoffman, Paul, 359
Hollis, Steven, 150, 151

I
Ignani, Karen, 166
Illich, Ivan, 29
Inglehart, John, 70
Institute for the Future, 240
Institute of Medicine, 54, 84

J
Johnson, Donald, 70

K
Kassirer, Jerome, 69, 249–250
Kerr, E. A., 282–283

Kindig, David, 46
Knouss, Robert, 43
Kolff, Willem, 170
Kuhn, Thomas, 129
Kuttner, Robert, 207, 216, 331, 375

L
Leape, Lucien, 283
Light, Donald, 368
Luft, Harold, 153, 260–261, 301
Lundberg, George, 417–418
Lynn, Joanne, 76–77

M
Manning, David, 367
Marsh, Lawrence, 119
Mattox, Kenneth, 136
McCanne, Don, 419–420
McDermott, Jim, 376
McGivney, William, 18
McGlynn, E. A., 282
McKinlay, Jeff, 33–34
McNerney, Walter, 18
Menke, W. G., 45–46
Menken, Matthew, 131, 134, 196
Moser, Dennis, 129
Moyer, Cheryl, 231
Mullan, Fitzhugh, 189

N
National Coalition on Health Care, 104–105
National Survey of America's Families, 106
Navarro, Vincent, 320
Neff, Kent, 129

O
O'Neil, Eugene, 54
O'Neill, Edward, 189

P
Pacala, James, 80–81
Pardes, Herbert, 155–156
Pawlinson, Gregory, 139
Peeno, Linda, 351–352
Pellegrino, Edmund, 12–13, 57
Perkin, Reg, 395, 397
Perreira, K. M., 122
Peterson, Mark, 309, 314
Power, Elaine, 278
Princeton Survey Research Associates, 65–66
Psaty, Bruce, 172

Q
Quill, Timothy, 82–83

R
Radovsky, S. S., 119
Ramsey, Scott, 286–287
Reinhardt, Uwe, 266, 372–373
Relman, Arnold, 31, 407
Risse, Guenther, 145–146
Rivo, Marc, 46, 192
Rivo, Mark, 190
Robert Wood Johnson Foundation, 107, 109, 123–125
Robertson, William, 164, 173
Rodwin, Victor, 369
Roemer, Ruth, 63
Roos, Noralou, 403
Rosenblatt, Roger, 51–52, 190
Rosser, Walter, 52

S
Sackett, David, 135
Satcher, David, 211–213
Scherger, Joseph, 137–138
Schiff, Gordon, 282, 376
Schlesinger, Mark, 122
Schroeder, Stephen, 50–53, 51
Schultz, Donald, 117
Schuster, Mark, 282
Schwartz, William, 61
Shaughnessy, A. F., 135
Simon, Gregory, 171–172
Slawson, David, 135
Sox, Harold, 197
Spicer, John, 229
St. Peter, Robert, 194

Starfield, Barbara, 189, 284–285, 386
Starr, Paul, 311–312, 314, 315–316, 364
Stephens, G. Gayle, 407
Stevens, Rosemary, 56
Suchman, A. L., 115–116
Sullivan, K., 206

T
Tarlov, Alvin, 9, 129–130
Thomas, Lewis, 17

W
Wagner, Edward, 138
Walker, Jack, 310
Wanzer, S. H., 82
Watson Wyatt Worldwide, 96
Weed, Larry, 228–229, 416
Wehrmacher, William, 173–174
Welch, Gilbert, 19, 20
Wennberg, Jack, 135
Wennberg, John, 245
Whitcomb, Michael, 47–48
White, William, 174
Wilkinson, Anne, 76–77
Williams, Alan, 411
Woolhandler, S, 380, 419–420
World Health Organization, 286

Y
Yankelovich Partners, 62
Young, Quinton, 320

Z
Zatkin, Steve, 205
Zola, Irving, 29
Zuckerman, Howard, 116–117

Subject Index

A

AARP, 338
abortion, 68
academic health centers, 154–156, 217
access, 101–112
  consequences of inadequate, 268–269
  demographics of the uninsured,
    105–107
  efforts to improve, 266–280
  ethical issues in, 355–357
  future of, 276–278
  health care as right and, 62–63
  impact of decreased, 107–109
  indicators to monitor, 109
  managed care and, 109–111
  quality of care and, 300
  size of problem in, 101–105
  universal, 276–277
accreditation, 288–290
Accreditation Association for Ambulatory
  Health Care, 290
activity limitations, 75–76
acupuncture, 167, 168
acute care
  in the biomedical model, 131, 134
  integrating with long-term care, 81
Ad Hoc Committee to Defend Health
  Care, 355–356
administrative costs, 90, 92, 404, 408
administrative information technology,
  231–232
administrators, power shift toward, 114
advance directives, 79
advertising, 17–18, 257–258, 342, 408

against NHI plans, 318–319
Advisory Commission on Consumer
  Protection and Quality in the Health
  Care Industry, 69–70
Aetna-US Healthcare, 341–342
Agency for Health Care Policy and
  Research, 171
Agency for Healthcare Research and
  Quality, 190, 292
Allegheny Health System, 125
Alliance for Continuing Medical
  Education, 235
alternative dispute resolution, 174–175
alternative health care, 39
  litigation over, 167–168
  reimbursement for, 199
ambulatory services, 151–152, 290
American Accreditation Health Care
  Commission, 290
American Association for Labor
  Legislation, 311
American Association of Health Plans,
  68–69, 341
American College of Physicians, 44
American College of Surgeons, 44
American Health Security Act, 317
American Hospital Association, 68–70
American Medical Accreditation Program,
  290
American Medical Association (AMA)
  Council on Medical Education, 4
  Division of Graduate Medical
    Education, 47
  lobbying by, 7, 337, 339

American Medical Association (cont.)
  on NHI, 333, 336
  NHI attempts and, 312, 313–314
  pharmaceutical companies and, 258
  Socioeconomic Monitoring System, 276
American Medical Student Association,
    333, 336
appeals processes, 176
applications service providers, 229
Approaching Death, 84
appropriateness of care
  determining, 350–352
  litigation over, 165–167
arrhythmia suppression, 135
artificial nutrition and hydration, 83–84
Ashcroft, John, 340
Association of Trial Lawyers of America,
    71, 161, 174
Australia, health care system in, 393–394
autologous bone marrow transplantation,
    18, 165–166
autonomy, 121–125

B
Baby Boom, aging of, 73–75
Balanced Budget Act (1997), 13
  CHIP, 272
  cost controls in, 259
  medical education funding under, 155
  Medicare HMOs and, 250
  nonphysician reimbursement under,
    198–199
  outpatient services under, 152
  residency positions under, 47
  rollbacks in, 89
BASF, 216
Beetham Eye Institute, 221
Beth Israel Hospital, Boston, 230
Beverly Enterprises, 216
Big Doctoring: Primary Care in America
    (Mullan), 189
Bill of Patients' Rights, 69–70
biomedical model, 129–134, 142
  problems with, 131, 134
biopsychosocial model, 131
Blue Cross and Blue Shield, 5, 199
  managed care, 8
  on NHI, 312
  pharmaceutical costs of, 259
Breakthrough Series, 295–296
breast feeding, 33, 39
Breaux, John, 332, 374
burden of disease, 76
Bush, George W., 333, 374

C
Camel cigarettes, 172–173
campaign financing, 331–333, 337–340,
    342, 414
Campbell, Tom, 125–126
Canada, health care system in, 386,
    394–403
  cost and outcomes in, 98
  elderly care in, 85
  lessons from, 399–403
  political acceptance of, 414
case management, 115
Center for Patient Safety, 292
Center for Studying Health System
    Change, 102, 337
Center of Quality Improvement and
    Patient Safety, 175
Centers for Disease Control and
    Prevention, 75, 210–211
certificates of need, 247
cesarean sections, 35
chart abstraction, 297
children, access to insurance for, 109
Children's Health Insurance Program, 208
Children's Hospital, Philadelphia, 297–298
chiropractors, 167–168, 199
choice, 404
  in patient satisfaction, 65–68
  payer influence in, 119, 121
  universal coverage plus, 374–375
cholecystectomy, 153–154
chronic illness
  aging population and, 75–77
  death from, 82
  focus on, 77
  management of, 81, 138–140
  physician-patient relationship and,
    193–194
  system redesign and, 304
class action lawsuits, 166
*Clinical Decision Making: From Theory to
    Practice* (Eddy), 113
clinical gaze, 33–34
clinical performance measurement,
    301–302
Clinton, Bill
  Bill of Patients' Rights and, 69–70
  health plan of, 318–320, 327–328, 341,
    410
Clinton, Hillary Rodman, 318
coalition building, 415
Codman, E. A., 288–289
collective bargaining, 125–127
Committee on Economic Security, 312

Committee on the Costs of Medical Care, 5, 312
Commonwealth Fund, 103–104
communication, 177
e-mail, 168, 230–231, 239
Community Access Program, 279
community-oriented primary care, 137
community rating, 206–207
competition vs. regulation, 378–381
computerized patient records, 228–229
conflicts of interest, 344
ethical issues in, 355–357
litigation and, 171–173
consensus, 403
consent, informed, 68
Consolidated Omnibus Budget Reconciliation Act (COBRA) (1985), 270
consolidation, 7–12
hospital, 149–151
impact of on competition, 214
Consumer Assessment of Health Plans, 292
Consumer Coalition for Quality Health Care, 291
consumer-protection, 11
continuity of care, 193–194
hospitalization and, 197
continuity-of-care laws, 119, 120–121
continuous quality improvement, 296, 377
control issues, 113–128
physician responses to, 125–127
physician satisfaction and, 121–125
power shifts, 114–118
regulation, 118–121, 125–127
coronary artery bypass grafts, 154
corporatization, 330–331
cost containment, 245–264, 404
approaches to, 245–248, 378
backlash against, 249
conclusions on, 260–261
fraud and, 255
in hospitals, 147–148
impact of, 259–260
by managed care, 11
Oregon approach to, 253–255
prescription drugs and, 255–259
private sector, 248–250
public sector, 250–253
specialization and, 50–53
by Washington Business Group on Health, 141
cost-effectiveness
definition of, 353–354

in primary care, 195–198
rationing and, 352–355
of technology, 20–21
cost-effectiveness analysis, 352–355
costs, 89–100
administrative, 90, 92
aging and, 78–80, 210, 211
appropriate care and, 351
division of, 95
international comparisons of, 85, 97–98
medical as percentage of GDP, 89
patient bills of rights and, 69–70
patient expectations and, 61–62
of private health insurance, 95–97
projected future, 98–99
of telemedicine, 236–237
U.S, 89–95
of U.S. health care, 363
Council on Graduate Medical Education (COGME), 46, 48, 196–197
credibility, 62
Crisis in Health Care, The: Costs, Choices, and Strategies (Coddington), 363–364
CyberDocs, 239

D
Daubert v. Merrill-Dow Pharmaceuticals, 180
Davis, William, 229
death
end-of-life care and, 81–84
from medical errors, 284–285
medicalization of, 34
surgical volume and, 153–154
decentralization, 240
decision making
in rationing, 354–355
support systems for, 231–232
technology support for, 229–230
defensive medicine, 173
defined benefits, 336–337
demand management, 115, 349–350
dementia, 76, 83–84
Democratic party, 379
Denmark, health care in, 391
Denver Health, 157
deselection of patients, 302
diabetes mellitus, 35–37
diagnoses
improved in medicalization processes, 35
most common, 5–6
in the Oregon Health Plan, 253–255

diagnosis-related groups (DRGs), 149,
    248, 250
diagnostic testing, 23
DiFranza, Joseph, 172–173
Digital Equipment Company, 142
Dingell, John, 69
direct access laws, 118
direct-to-consumer (DTC) advertising,
    17–18, 257–258, 342, 408
disease
    burden of, 76
    changing definitions of existing, 35–37
    definitions of new, 37–38
    epidemiological transition of, 29–30
    management, 115
disease management model, 193, 304
disproportionate share payments, 252, 253
Domenici-Wellstone amendment, 270–
    271
Dowling, William, 8–9
drugs, prescription
    administration safety improvement, 296
    costs of, 89, 90, 97, 255–259
    international cost comparisons of, 257
    prescriptive authority and, 198
    projected costs of, 98–99
    reminder systems for, 230
    resistance of to cost controls, 260

E
education, public, 416
egalitarian views, 412–413
elderly patients, 73–88
    content of care and, 75–77
    costs of care and, 78–80
    demographics of aging and, 73–75
    drug costs for, 257
    health care expenditures by, 95
    international comparisons of care for,
        84–85
    medicalization of aging and, 33–34
    organizational aspects for care of,
        80–81
    palliative and end-of-life care for, 81–84
electronic medical records, 228–229
electronic prescribing, 223–227
e-mail, 168, 230–231, 239
emergency medicine, 192
    denials of, 330
eminence-based medicine, 135
Employee Benefit Research Institute,
    64–65
employer-based insurance, 65
    choice in, 65–68

cost of, 95–97, 249
    erosion of, 206–208
    expansion of Medicaid and, 273–274
    lack of access in, 106–107
    patients' rights and, 336–337
    public opinion on, 329
    redesigning, 140–142
    uninsured/underinsured in, 267–268
    universal coverage plus, 371–373
encainide, 21
end-of-life care, 81–84
England, Mary Jane, 142
enrollment shifts, 249
ERISA (Employee Retirement Income
    Security Act), 118, 217, 270, 357
    Oregon Health Plan and, 254
errors, medical, 282–283, 292. *See also*
    quality assurance; quality of care
    system redesign and, 298–300
ethics
    continuity of care and, 193
    of end-of-life care, 82, 83–84
    fallacies in, 356–357
    in health care reform, 410–413
    of HMOs, 351–352
    HMOs and, 365–369
    pharmaceuticals companies and,
        257–258
    population-based care and, 136–138
    of rationing, 355–357
evidence-based medicine, 115, 134–136
    definition of, 135
    hospital referrals, 291
    in litigation, 165–166
    in medical education, 177
extrapolation, excessive, 26

F
Families USA, 98–99
Family Health Insurance Program, 315
family practice, 189
family support, 74–75
Federal Employees Health Benefits
    Program, 374
federal involvement
    in access improvement, 269–272
    cost controls and, 259–260
    in generalist physician training, 47
    in health care funding, 89–90
    in legal reform, 175–176
    medical education funding, 155
    NIH attempts by, 310–320
    public health and, 208–213
    public opinion on, 330

regulation, 170
in regulation, 118
in research funding, 17
fee-for-service programs, 332
fetal monitoring, 35
financial integration, 115–116
financing, 246–247
Flexner, Abraham, 4–5
Flexner Report, 4–5, 44
Food and Drug Administration, 25
Forum on Legal Issues in Health Care, 180
Foundation for Accountability, 291
fragmentation, 43
fraud, 216, 255
Freedom of Information Act, 292
Frist, Bill, 374

G
gag rules, 11, 68, 165
gaming the system, 255, 261, 288. *See also* fraud
Gang of Five, 318
gastrostomy tubes, 83–84
general/family practice
decline of, 44–45
ideal specialization ratio with, 46–50, 56–57
knowledge and quality of care in, 196–198
power shift toward, 114
as specialization, 45
general internal medicine, 189
geriatric medicine, 77. *See also* elderly patients
Germany, health care system in, 386, 392
Global Burden of Disease Study, 76
globalization, 379–380
Goodrich case, 165–166
Great Britain, 358
National Health Service, 386–390
technology adoption in, 19
Great Society program, 7
Group Health Cooperative of Puget Sound, 137, 213, 230

H
Harvard Medical Practice Study, 164
Harvard University, 4
Hatch, Orrin, 340
health
determinants of, 31
lifestyle choices and, 75–76, 77
HealthAllies.com, 239
Health and Health Care 2010, 240

health care
aligning physicians with, 116–117
boundaries of, 29–33
client-oriented vs. finance-oriented, 80–81
fragmentation of, 43
future of, 419–421
goals of, 29–30
history of U.S., 3–4
impact of medicalization on, 38–39
locus of control in, 113–128
medicalization of, 29–41
myths about U.S., 282–286
paradigms of, 129–144
patient priorities in, 64–65
profit vs. nonprofit, 378–381
public opinion of, 327–330
as a right, 62–64, 314–315
safety net in, 272–276
supply and demand in, 245–246
system evolution, 372
system redesign, 298–300
three-tier system of, 266–267
Health Care Financing Administration, 89, 207, 291
Healthy Aging Project, 79–80
telemedicine and, 237
Health Care Quality Improvement Act, 175
Health Care Quality Improvement Initiative, 247
Health Care Reimbursement Scheme, 391
Health Equity and Access Reform Today (HEART), 317
Health Industry Manufacturers Association, 170
health information policies, 238
Health Insurance Association of America, 318, 410
Health Insurance Portability and Accountability Act, 70, 208, 269–270, 332
health maintenance organizations (HMOs)
accreditation of, 290
competitive environment of, 249–250
consolidation of, 12
enrollment in, 12
ethics of, 351–352
for-profit, 330–331
hospital interactions with, 146–147
media campaigns by, 341
patient satisfaction with, 214
penetration rates of, 248
physician satisfaction and, 121–125

health maintenance organizations (cont.)
political contributions by, 340
political support for, 365–367
population-based care in, 136–138
public opinion on, 329
quality of care by ownership type,
300–301
referrals rates in, 110
right to sue, 11–12, 71, 166–167
rise of, 7–12
Health Plan Employer and Information Set
(HEDIS), 290, 291, 292, 295–296
health technology assessment (HTA),
24–25
Healthy Aging Project, 79–80
Healthy People 2010, 292, 293–294
heart disease, 76
HEDIS. *See* Health Plan Employer and
Information Set (HEDIS)
Helping Hand Program, 375
Henry Ford Health System, 296
Henry J. Kaiser Family Foundation, 64–65
*Hidden from View: The Growing Burden
of Health Care*, 99
high-dose chemotherapy, 18
Hill-Burton Act, 146
Hippocrates, 136
HMO Act (1973), 68
hospice, 34, 39, 84
hospital-based networks, 125
hospitalists, 152–153, 193, 197
hospitals, 145–160
administrative costs in, 92
birthing rooms, 39
capacity of, 149
cost containment in, 147–148, 247
costs of, 90, 92–95
discharge procedures, 19–20
end-of-life care and, 82
history of, 5, 145–147
hospitalist model and, 152–153
lack of insurance and, 107, 109
medicalization of childbirth and, 33–34
mergers and consolidation of, 149–151
ownership of, 150
physician-hospital organizations, 8
premature discharge from, 331
public, 156–157
regionalization of, 153–154
rural, 157–158
service shifts in, 151–152
teaching, 44, 154–156
trends in, 147–154
utilization of, 148–149

Howard, Coby, 253
hypercholesterolemia, 35–37
hypertension, 35–37
hypoglycemia, 37–38

I
iatrogenic injuries, 284–285
"incident-to" provisions, 198–199
independent practice associations (IPAs),
7–8, 248
Indian Health Service, 272
individual vs. societal perspective, 343,
354
Info-Retriever, 232–233, 235
information, shared, 115
information needs, classification of, 233,
234
information technology, 221–243
in clinical practice, 223–238
consumers and, 238–239
decision support and reminder systems,
229–230
electronic medical records, 228–229
impact of on relationships, 239–240
Institute for Healthcare Improvement, 84,
290–291, 295–296, 298
Institute for Safe Medication Practices,
291, 296
Institute for the Future, 259–260, 267,
276–277
Institute of Medicine (IOM)
definition of quality by, 286
on electronic records, 228
To Err Is Human, 175–176
primary care definition, 188
primary care physician definition, 50, 51
on system redesign, 298–300
Institute of Medicine, 211, 212
Institute of the Future, 76
insurance
community rating system, 206–207
cost of private, 95–97
costs of, 89, 101–102
eroding coverage of, 206–208
fraud, 255
health care expenditures by, 95
hospice coverage in, 84
impact of technology on, 21
lobbying by, 339
medical necessity decisions by, 352
patient expectations and, 61
power shift toward, 114
profit vs. nonprofit, 378–381
public opinion on, 337

quality assurance prorams, 176–177
rise of, 5
sources and income levels, 274, 275
trends in, 207
voluntary, 6
vs. access, 104
integration, 7–12
hospital, 150–151
infrastructure for, 115–116
intensive care units, 158
internal medicine, 192
internal review processes, 351
international comparisons, 364–365,
385–406
drug costs, 257
of health care costs, 97–98
of health care financing, 207–208
of health care quality, 285–286
of primary care, 200
of rationing, 357–359
technology adoption and, 19
International Conference on Governments
and Health Systems, 358
International Covenant on Economic,
Social and Cultural Rights, 62
Internet, 62
consumer use of, 238–239
continuing medical education on, 233,
235
decision making resources on, 230
litigation and, 168–169
physician use of, 223
irritable colon, 37–38

J
Japan, health care system in, 386, 392–393
job security, 377
Johns Hopkins University, 4
Johnson, Lyndon, 7
Joint Commission on Accreditation of
Healthcare Organizations (JCAHO),
289–290

K
Kahn, Charles, 69
Kaiser Permanente, 137
Kennedy, Edward, 315
Kitzhaber, John, 253
Knoll Pharmaceuticals, 216

L
Lanoxin, 99
Leapfrog Group, 291, 301
legal issues, 357, 415–416

Lexus and the Olive Tree, The (Friedman),
379–380
libertarian views, 412–413
licensing issues, 236–237
lifestyle, 75–76, 77
*Life Without Disease: The Pursuit of
Medical Utopia* (Schwartz), 61
litigation
alternative medicine, 167–168
electronic health information/services,
168–169
impact of, 173–174
managed care, 165–167
medical devices, 169–170
medical malpractice, 162–165
reforms and, 174–177
special interests and, 171–173
litigation, impact of, 161–183
longevity, 4, 73–75
Medicare and, 78–79
lumbar spinal fusion, 171

M
macromanagement, 260–261
Maine, drug price-control law, 259
malpractice
claim triggers, 163–164
insurance premiums, 173
litigation, 162–165
managed care
access and, 109–111
backlash against, 11–12, 336
biomedical model and, 130–131, 132,
134
choice in, 65–68
competency areas for, 54–56
corporatization under, 330–331
as cost control, 247–248
definition of, 8–9
elderly care in, 80–81
ERISA and, 118
evolutionary stages in, 9–10
features of, 9
litigation over, 165–167
NHI attempts and, 316, 318–320
patient opinions of, 65–68
power shift toward, 114
the public interest and, 213–217
public opinion on, 329
rise of, 7–12
scope of practice and, 194–195
socially oriented vs. market-oriented, 213
specialization and, 53–55
teaching hospitals under, 155–156

managed competition, 248, 317
  failure of, 247, 331, 365–369
management information technology,
  231–232
market mechanisms
  failure of, 247, 348–349
  the public interest and, 214–217
market pluralism, 379–380
Marmor, Theodore, 402
massage therapy, 167, 168
McDermott, Jim, 316
media
  biased/misleading campaigns in,
    340–342
  myths about Canadian system and,
    402–403
  on NHI attempts, 316
  technology hype by, 18
Medicaid, 7
  access through, 63
  aging population and, 210, 211
  cost containment in, 252
  creation of, 314
  fraud, 216, 255
  health care expenditures by, 95
  "incident-to" provisions, 198–199
  lack of access to, 106
  preventive care in, 104
  public hospitals and, 157
  as safety net, 272–276
  welfare reform and, 101–102, 106, 207,
    268
medical devices, litigation over, 169–170
Medical Devices Improvement Act (1975),
  169
medical education
  continuing, 232–235
  on end-of-life care, 84
  evidence-based approaches in, 177
  Flexner Report and, 4–5, 44
  for generalists, 47, 190
  health insurers and, 176–177
  history of U.S., 3–4
  payer financing of, 156
  for primary care, 192–193, 201–202
  U.S. system of, 154–155
Medical Expenditure Panel Survey, 190
Medical Injury Compensation Reform Act
  (MICRA), 176
medicalization, 29–41
  backlash against, 39
  definition of, 29
  disease definition changes in, 35–38
  impact of, 38–39

  origins of, 31–33
  sociomedical-cultural, 33–34
  technology in, 35
  types of, 33–38
Medical Outcomes Study, 51, 196–197
Medical Practice Act, 191
medical savings accounts, 334–336, 374
Medicare, 7, 207
  access through, 63
  aging population and, 210, 211
  in Australia, 393–394
  Balanced Budget Act impact on, 13
  + Choice plan, 252
  cost containment in, 250–252
  creation of, 314
  drug benefit, 98–99, 342, 374–375
  drug costs in, 257
  fraud, 216, 255
  HMOs, 13, 80, 250
  hospice coverage in, 84
  hospitals and, 147–148
  increasing longevity and, 78–79
  medical education funding under, 155
  privatization of, 374
  public hospitals and, 157
  reform of, 374–375
  residency programs under, 47
Medicare Balanced Budged Refinement
  Act (1999), 47
MediCARxES, 374–375
Medicredit, 315
Medigap coverage, 207
MEDLINE, 233, 235
MedPartners, 125
mental health care, 269
Mental Health Parity Act (1996),
  270–271
micromanagement, 260–261
middle classes, 321
military antishock trousers, 135–136
Mill, John Stuart, 136
Milliman and Robertson guidelines, 331,
  350
Mills, Wilbur, 315
Minnesota, managed care in, 214
minorities, 74–75
misruse errors, 284
mitral valve prolapse, 37–38
model of disease, 26
monasteries, 145–146
Montana Medical Assostance Facility, 158
multidisciplinary teams, 80, 137
multiple chemical sensitivity, 171–172
myocardial infarction, 172

N
Nader, Ralph, 333, 379
National Academy for State Health Policy, 292
National Access to Care Survey, 102–103
National Ambulatory Medical Care Survey, 110, 190
National Association of Inpatient Physicians, 193, 197
National Bipartisan Commission on the Future of Medicare, 332, 374
National Center for Complementary and Alternative Medicine, 39
National Center for Health Care Technology, 24
National Coalition on Health Care, 291
National Committee for Quality Assurance, 290
National Federation of Independent Business, 101–102, 338
National Healthcare Act, 315
National Health Expenditures Projection Team, 98
national health insurance
    conflicting agendas for, 333–337
    Democratic and Republican plans compared, 334–336
    key features of proposed, 317
    lessons from, 321–322
    past attempts at U.S., 309–323
    in the U.K., 386–390
National Health Insurance Standards Act, 315
National Health Planning and Resources Development Act (1974), 153, 247
National Health Services Corps, 272
National Institutes of Health, 25
National Labor Relations Board, 126
National Patient Safety Foundation, 291
National Practitioner Data Bank, 175
National Resident Matching Program, 47
National Rifle Association, 338
National Roundtable on Health Care Quality, 291, 300
naturopathic medicine, 199
necessary and appropriate care, 350–352
network adequacy laws, 119
neurology, 196
New Deal, 5
New York Times, 161
Nixon, Richard, 310, 315, 373
nonphysician clinicians, 190–192, 198–199
Norwood, Charles, 69

Nurse Practice Acts, 191
nurse practioners, 197–198
    primary care provision by, 190–192
    reimbursement for, 198–199
    training of, 192
nursing, 6, 114
nursing home costs, 273, 408

O
obesity, 35–37
obstetrics-gynecology
    medicalization of childbirth and, 33–34, 35, 39
    as primary care providers, 189
Office of Technology Assessment, 24
Oregon Health Plan, 10, 253–255, 354
organizational structures, 363–383
    consumer choice plus universal coverage, 374–375
    employer-based plus universal coverage, 371–373
    incrementalism and managed competition, 365–369
    issues in, 378–381
    problems in current, 364–365
    single-payer system, 375–378
Organization for Economic Cooperation and Development (OECD), 97
ORYX, 295
Osler, William, 4–5
osteopathy, 192
outcomes. *See also* evidence-based medicine
    cost-effectiveness of, 18
    definition of, 286
    health care spending and, 97–98
    impact of lack of access on, 107–109
    impact of specialization on, 51
    as malpractice claim triggers, 163–164
    monitoring, 231–232
    in primary care, 195–198
    reducing negative, 25–26
    surrogate, 21, 22
    technology and negative, 21–23
    telemedicine and, 237–238
overlap syndromes, 37–38
overuse errors, 284
Oxfordshire Health Authority, 358

P
PACE (Program of All-Inclusive Care of the Elderly), 81
palliative care, 81–84

Panel on Cost Effectiveness in Health and
    Medicine, 352, 354
paradigms of health care, 129–144
    biomedical model, 129–134, 142
    chronic disease management, 138–140
    conflict between, 142
    definition of, 129
    employee care systems, 140–142
    evidence-based care, 134–136
    population-based care, 136–138
patient expectations, 52, 61–72, 261
    health care as a right and, 62–64
    patients' rights and, 68–70
    priorities in, 64–65
patient-oriented evidence that matters
    (POEMS), 135–136
patient-physician relationship, 173–174,
    177
    chronic illness management and,
        193–194
    Web-based health and, 239
patient satisfaction, 13, 327–330, 364
    access and, 103–104
    in Canada, 402
    choice and, 65–68
    with HMOs, 214
    international comparisons of, 386, 387,
        388–389
    specialization and, 50–53
Patients' Bill of Rights, 11
    coalitions against, 341
    insurance lobbying against, 339
patients' rights, 62–64, 68–70
    employer-based insurance and, 336–
        337
    health care as, 62–64
pediatrics, 192
    expansion of, 32
    as primary care providers, 189–192
peer review organizations, 247, 291,
    296–298
Pegram v. Herdrich, 166–167
personal digital assistants, 223–227
pharmaceutical industry, 257–258
    advertising campaigns by, 17–18,
        257–258, 342, 408
    cost of drugs and, 89
    lobbying by, 340
    marketing by, 17–18
Pharmaceutical Research and
    Manufacturers of America, 259
pharmacists, 198
physician-hospital organizations (PHOs), 8

Physician Insurers Association of America,
    162–163
physician organization arrangements
    (POAs), 116–117
Physician Payment Review Commission,
    25
physicians
    aligning with care systems, 116–117
    autonomy of, 121–125
    collective bargaining by, 125–127
    control of costs by, 21
    costs of services by, 90
    demand role of, 349–350
    generation of services by, 24
    nurse practitioner outcomes compared
        with, 197–198
    participation of in reform, 417–419
    payer influence over, 119, 121
    performance profiling of, 288
    profiling and incentivization, 116
    public opinion on, 337
    relationship with patients, 173–174
    shortage of, 45
    supply of, 7, 46–47
    technology acceptance by, 24
    treating vs. reviewing, 351
physicians' assistants, 190–192
    reimbursement for, 198–199
    training of, 192–193
physician satisfaction, 50–53, 121–125
Physicians Desk Reference, 232
Physicians for a National Health Program,
    277, 375–376
Physicians for Responsible Negotiation,
    126
Physicians' Work Group on Universal
    Coverage, 277–278
Play-or-Pay health care, 315, 373
point-fee structure, 392–393
point-of-service laws, 118
point-of-service (POS) programs, 11, 248
political activity
    biased/misleading campaigns in,
        340–342
    health care reform and, 327–345
    legislative and campaign, 331–333
    reform initiatives and, 309–310
    by special interests, 7
population-based care, 114–115, 136–138,
    304
    vs. individual patient care, 142
practice guidelines, 115, 177, 297–298
preceptorship system, 3–4

preexisting conditions, 269
preferred provider organizations, 248
premenstrual syndrome, 37–38
prenatal care, 109
prescriptions, electronic, 223–227
prescriptive authority, 198
President's Advisory Commission on
    Consumer Protection and Quality in
    the Health Care Industry, 68
primary care, 187–204
    as base of health care, 304
    continuity of care in, 193–194
    definition of, 188–189
    education for, 192–193
    goal of, 188–189
    international comparisons of, 200
    issues in, 193–199
    in NHI systems, 404
    prescriptive authority in, 198
    quality and cost-effectiveness in,
        196–198
    reimbursement and, 198–199
    reorientation of system toward, 56–57
    scope of practice in, 194–195
    who provides, 189–192
*Primary Care: America's Health in a New
    Era,* 50, 51
primary care physicians
    community-oriented, 137
    definitions of, 50–51
    gatekeeper role of, 356
    as gatekeepers or coordinators, 195
    patient choice of, 66
    relationships with specialists, 195
    specialists as, 51–52
"Principles for Consumer Protection," 69
privacy, right to, 68, 237
private/public sector, 205–219
    access efforts and, 269–276
    cost containment in, 248–253
    erosion of private, 206–208
    expansion of public, 414–415
    growth of public, 208–210
    public health and, 210–213
    the public interest in, 213–217
    tensions between, 403–404
problem-oriented medical records, 416
process criteria, 287–288
product liability, 169–170
professionalism, 355–357, 417–419
*Profit Fever: The Drive to Corporatize
    Health Care and How to Stop It,* 318
profit vs. nonprofit, 304, 378–381

Progressive Party, 310–311
Proposition 186 (California), 340–341
provider contracts, 115
Public Citizen, 257–258
public health, 205–219, 210–213
public policy, 355–357
"Putting Patients First," 68–69

Q
quality-adjusted life years, 354
quality assurance, 175–177
    approaches to, 288–300
    unintended results in, 302
Quality Health Care Coalition Act,
    125–126
Quality Improvement System for Managed
    Care, 291
quality of care, 281–308
    definition of, 286–287
    improvement efforts, 292–300
    international comparisons of, 285–286
    lessons from improvement efforts in,
        300–303
    measuring, 287–288
    myths about American health care,
        282–286
    specialization and, 50–53
    at teaching hospitals, 155, 156
    technology and, 21–23

R
R. J. Reynolds Tobacco Company,
    172–173
ramps, 295–296
*Rationing Health Care in America:
    Perceptions and Principles of Justice*
    (Churchill), 63
rationing of health care, 347–362
    appropriate and necessary care in,
        350–352
    Canadian system and, 401–402
    cost-effectiveness and, 352–355
    definition of, 348
    ethics and, 355–357
    international comparisons of, 357–359
    law and, 355–357
    myths about, 348–350
Reach Out, 276
referrals, 110
    evidence-based, 291
    Internet, 239
    self-, 110, 111
    standing referral laws, 119

reform principles, 407–424
regionalization, 153–154, 301
regulation vs. competition, 378–381
regulatory costs, 246–247
reimbursement. *See also* managed care
    Canadian, 395
    cost controls in, 246–247
    median by specialty, 91
    telemedicine and, 237
reminder systems, 229–230
renewability, 270
Republican Party, 379
research funding, 17
restructuring, 54, 56
risk adjustment, 250, 252, 367–368
Robert Wood Johnson Foundation, 276
Roche Holdings, 216
Roe v. Wade, 68
Roosevelt, Franklin D., 5, 312
Roosevelt, Theodore, 310–311
Roper Center for Public Opinion
    Research, 64–65
Rx Intelligence, 259

S
scoliosis, 32–33
scope of practice, 194–195
self-employed, 267
self-help groups, 39
self-referrals, 110, 111
single-payer proposals, 316, 333, 375–378,
    413–414
    Canadian, 395
    Denmark system, 391
Siskiyou County Medical Society, 92, 94
six sigma quality, 302
Social Security Act (1935), 5, 74, 313
*Social Transformation of American
    Medicine, The* (Starr), 311–312
somatization of complaints, 37–38
special interests, 337–340
    AMA as, 7
    litigation and, 171–173
    myths about Canadian system and,
        402–403
    NHI attempts and, 311–312, 318–320
    patient bills of rights and, 71
    pharmaceuticals, 257–258
specialization, 6, 43–59, 187
    access to, 110
    in elderly care, 80–81
    fragmentation of care from, 43
    generalist/specialist mix in, 46–50,
        56–57

history of, 44–46
knowledge and quality of care in,
    196–198
managed care and, 53–55
negative effects of, 50–53
power shift from, 114
primary care by, 189–192
pros and cons of, 45–46
relationships with generalists and, 195
standing referral laws, 119
State Children's Health Insurance Program
    (CHIP), 272, 274–275, 332
state governments
    cost controls by, 247
    in legal reform, 175–176
    legislation by, 118–119, 120
    in medicalization, 32–33
    reform plans by, 321–322
    as safety net, 272–276
Sterling Life Insurance, 252
structured discharge procedures, 19–20
Study to Understand Prognoses and
        Preferences for Outcomes and Risks
        of Treatment (SUPPORT), 79
Sullivan, Kip, 402
surrogate outcomes, 21, 22
system redesign, 298–300, 302, 352
    past attempts at, 309–323

T
Tavistock Group, 410
Taxpayers Against the Government
    Takeover, 340–341
teaching hospitals, 154–156, 217
    specialization and, 44
Technical Committee on Medical Care,
    313
technological imperative, 18
    public demand for, 142
technology, 15–28, 404
    adoption process for, 24
    assessment of, 24–25
    in Canada, 401
    change drivers, 17–18
    chronology of, 16
    costs of, 20–21
    definition of, 15, 17
    information, 221–243
    levels of, 17
    managing, 23–26
    negative outcomes of, 21–23
    pros and cons of, 19–20
    public demand for, 17–18, 180–181
    quality of care and, 21–23

telehealth. *See* telemedicine
telemedicine, 168–169, 221–243
    applications in, 236
    issues in, 236–237
Temporary Assistance for Needy Families
    (TANF), 95
Thomas, Bill, 332
tobacco companies, 161, 172–173, 339
To Err Is Human, 175–176, 282, 292
Torricelli, Robert, 340
tort reform, 415–416
treatment
    cost-effectiveness of, 18
    deleting ineffective, 354–355
    negative outcomes from, 21–23
Truman, Harry S, 310, 313
*2020 Vision: Health Care in the 21st
    Century*, 54

U
underuse errors, 284
uninsured patients. *See also* access
    demographics of, 105–107, 266–269
    income and, 267–268
    perceptions about, 65
    public hospitals and, 156–157
    reasons for lack of access by, 101–105
United Hospital Fund, 103

Universal Declaration of Human Rights,
    62
*Universal Health Care: What the United
    States Can Learn from the Canadian
    Experience*, 395
U.S. News and World Report, 214
U.S. Preventive Services Task Force, 32
utilization management, 248
utilization of hospitals, 148–149
utilization reviews, 122–123, 247

V
Veterans Health Administration, 272,
    291
violence, as health care issue, 30–31
Von Korff, M., 138

W
Wagner-Murray-Dingell bill, 313
Washington Business Group on Health,
    96, 140–142
wild assumed guesses (WAGs), 136
women
    in medicine, impact of, 49–50
    uninsured, 107, 108
workforce changes, access and, 267–268
World Health Organization, 62, 76
World War II, 6